Neuromarketing in the Age of AI

Thomas Heinrich Musiolik
https://orcid.org/0000-0001-7749-4721
University of the Arts Berlin, Germany

Adrian David Cheok
https://orcid.org/0000-0001-6316-2339
Nanjing University of Information Science and Technology, China

IGI Global
Scientific Publishing
Publishing Tomorrow's Research Today

Vice President of Editorial Melissa Wagner
Director of Acquisitions Mikaela Felty
Director of Book Development Jocelynn Hessler
Production Manager Mike Brehm
Cover Design Jose Rosado

Published in the United States of America by
IGI Global Scientific Publishing
701 East Chocolate Avenue
Hershey, PA, 17033, USA
Tel: 717-533-8845 | Fax: 717-533-7115
Website: https://www.igi-global.com E-mail: cust@igi-global.com

Library of Congress Cataloging-in-Publication Data

Names: Musiolik, Thomas Heinrich, 1980- editor http://id.loc.gov/rwo/agents/n2019068837 | Cheok, Adrian David editor http://id.loc.gov/rwo/agents/nb2010023724
Title: Neuromarketing in the age of AI / edited by Thomas Heinrich Musiolik and Adrian David Cheok.
Description: Hershey, PA : IGI Global Scientific Publishing, [2026] | Includes bibliographical references and index. | Summary: "This book delves into the practical applications and real value of neuromarketing. It examines the role of artificial intelligence in this increasingly data-driven approach and how neural technologies are driving the development of effective marketing campaigns"-- Provided by publisher.
Identifiers: LCCN 2025007442 (print) | LCCN 2025007443 (ebook) | ISBN 9798337311524 hardcover | ISBN 9798337311531 paperback | ISBN 9798337311548 ebook
Subjects: LCSH: Neuromarketing http://id.loc.gov/authorities/subjects/sh2007005546 | Artificial intelligence--Marketing applications http://id.loc.gov/authorities/subjects/sh2020008033
Classification: LCC HF5415.12615 .N4875 2026 (print) | LCC HF5415.12615 (ebook) | DDC 658.8001/9--dc23/eng/20250514
LC record available at https://lccn.loc.gov/2025007442
LC ebook record available at https://lccn.loc.gov/2025007443

British Cataloguing in Publication Data
A Cataloguing in Publication record for this book is available from the British Library.

Table of Contents

Detailed Table of Contents

This chapter explores impact of neuroscience & artificial intelligence (AI) on consumer behavior analysis. It presents an overview of neuromarketing tools such as EEG, fMRI, eye-tracking, facial & galvanic skin response, detailing how these technologies uncover subconscious consumer responses. Through AI integration, neuromarketing achieves precision, scale, & speed in interpreting complex neural & biometric data. It further examines how companies like Coca-Cola, Unilever, & P&G apply AI-driven neuromarketing for ad optimization, product design, & personalized engagement. Ethical considerations surrounding privacy, bias, & manipulation are analyzed, along with regulatory frameworks like GDPR. It also discusses how emotional & creative stimuli influence purchasing decisions & how AI leverages these insights for hyper-personalized marketing. Finally, it outlines emerging trends such as emotionally intelligent AI, immersive technologies like AR/VR, & brain-computer interfaces, while emphasizing the importance of ethical implementation in shaping the future of consumer engagement.

In today's complex digital era, marketers face the challenge of understanding the subconscious factors that drive consumer decisions, which traditional self-reported research often fails to capture. Neuromarketing addresses this by combining marketing with neuroscience, using tools like fMRI, EEG, and biometrics to uncover unintentional reactions. The application of artificial intelligence (AI) to this subject is a significant advancement, boosting the accuracy, speed, and scope of consumer insights. This chapter looks at how neuromarketing is changing as a result of AI-powered methods including machine learning, deep learning, and emotional analytics. It draws on key neuroscientific and psychological theories to explain how AI interprets human thought and emotion. Real-world applications across industries, along with ethical considerations around privacy and autonomy, are explored as well. The chapter concludes by outlining future trends, including emotionally adaptive systems and brain-computer interfaces, offering a forward-looking view of personalized and ethical marketing.

Neuromarketing and artificial intelligence (AI) integration is transforming the manner in which companies understand and affect consumer behaviour. Neuromarketing refers to everything that applies neuroscientific principles to marketing and helps us understand subconscious (or unintentionally) decision-making processes by examining their effect on our brain, our emotions, and our cognitive responses. The key to effective neuromarketing research is the insights of the behavioral patterns it provides, as it brings corporations to understand their consumers in a manner that is more on point than traditional methods. AI elevates these insights by allowing automation of data collection, identification of behavioral patterns, and conducting real time analysis on the data gathered, making neuromarketing research easier to scale and implement. In this chapter, we take a closer look and the perks of merging neuromarketing and AI, and their usefulness in different industries like retail, advertising, entertainment, healthcare, and customer experience.

The study highlights the emerging topic of neuromarketing and AI and its impact on marketing strategies. Neuromarketing integrates neuroscience, psychology, and marketing to understand consumer buying behavior. AI is the programs, machines or systems that demonstrate the human intelligence. This chapter explores the AI tools used in marketing and focuses on combining AI and Neuromarketing to improve marketing strategies. In the current chapter, some real-life case studies are also discussed which helps in understanding neuromarketing in the era of AI. This chapter indicates ethical questions about neuromarketing and AI. It suggests that neuromarketing and AI have the potential to change the way marketers understand and influence consumer buying decisions.

The integration of artificial intelligence into neuromarketing has redefined how businesses analyse consumer behaviour and tailor their marketing strategies. Traditional neuromarketing have provided valuable insights into subconscious decision-making processes. However, with neuromarketing AI's possibilities has become more precise, scalable, and personalized than ever before. While these advancements offer businesses powerful tools to enhance consumer engagement, they also introduce significant ethical concerns. AI-driven neuromarketing raises pressing questions about consumer privacy, informed consent, and data security. Chapter purpose is to explore the ethical implications of AI-powered neuromarketing by identifying key challenges, including risks of consumer manipulation, potential misuse of sensitive biometric data, and regulatory gaps. Additionally, the study proposes solutions to mitigate ethical concerns, offering recommendations for businesses and policymakers to strike a balance between leveraging AI's potential and protecting consumer rights.

This study investigates the space of advertising using the lens of deepfake technology, cognitive dissonance, and consumer trust as they help companies create hyper-authentic yet potentially deceitful content with deepfakes, traditional notions of authenticity in marketing are being tested. One significant problem is cognitive dissonance, which occurs when users feel uneasy about the possibility that the information they received was fabricated or deceptive. This behavior can undermine consumer trust, raise suspicion, and damage brand reputation. This paper explores how consumers mentally process deepfake ads and how the cognitive dissonance generated by perceiving manipulation will affect trust in the long run. We discuss strategies that can be used to implement ethical practices in a deepfake-influenced advertising space, to protect the consumer relationship and brand integrity.Keywords: Deepfake Advertising, Consumer Trust, Cognitive Dissonance, Ethical Marketing, Digital Manipulation, Brand Authenticity

Foreword

The 21st century is likely to become recognized as the turning point when human brain capacities reached the boundary of their original design to succumb to the unknown enhancements of Artificial Intelligence. In the first quarter of this century, advances in the basic understanding of how the brain works made significant strides shedding light on how we humans process information, make decisions, are influenced by emotion and code the memory of our experiences. This fundamental knowledge gave rise to understanding essential human truths, anticipating response, and even predicting behavior, particularly in the realm of commerce and communications. This phenomenon gave rise to shiny new tools and constructs embodying what is referred to as Neuromarketing.

My own good fortune was to be one of the first marketing practioners to enter this realm of applied neuroscience and explore the possibilities of applications for bringing deeper understanding and certainty to consumer motivation and marketing effectiveness. I was driven to become the champion of consumer truth, the protector of "good creative" and the guardian angel of human emotion and to frog leap phony rationales for preferences and purchases. In this new climate of celebrating emotion in the marketing mix, given permission largely by Nobel Prize winning Psychologist Daniel Kahneman, an entire industry sprang up to guide marketers' understanding of their targets in ways never possible before.

Everything was new to be explored. As Chief Analytics Officer at one of the first Neuromarketing start-ups EmSense, I engaged Millward Brown, the leading copy testing company at the time, to partner with me and create the most advanced method ever incorporating rationale response, as measured with questionnaires, with the best of emotional nonverbal response as measured by our EEG technology. Together we helped put Neuromarketing on the map followed by package testing collaboration integrated with eye tracking through Perception Research Services (PRS), Facial Coding with Realeyes, and pioneering shopper research with biometrics and eye tracking. Later as CEO of the Ipsos Global Neuromarketing Division, I expanded the applied portfolio on nonconscious measurement to embrace among other methods Implicit Reaction Time Testing to measure conviction and voice analytics to reveal emotions in our speech. I created the widely embraced partnership model where neuroscience method developers led by academics joined forces with market research practioners and end users to create new methods and insights. (This can be the same model that neuromarketing method and data providers can join forces with AI modelers and service providers, putting joint expertise to work and creating one-stop-shopping for clients and end users.)

When I started my quest to bring emotion to the marketing table and inspire leveraging decision science to become an essential part of marketing practice, it was met with suspicion, skepticism, and hesitance. And yet, over the course of a few years and in lockstep with some brilliant academics and practioners, we achieved a milestone where almost all Fortune 500 marketers had aspects of neuromarketing measurement embedded into their standard marketing testing practices. We had achieved the dream of going from rejection to special occasion use, to standard practice in a few years.

And now we stand at a critical crossroads. AI has eclipsed focus on neuromarketing promising far reaching applications that impact every aspect of our professional lives. AI is pervasive throughout the business and general press and dominates conference agendas. Corporate budgets are being allocated generously to get ahead of the AI curve as marketing and corporate management professionals wrestle with how they can best apply AI capabilities to keep from falling behind the competitive curve. There is deep uncertainty regarding best practices, how to add genuine value and ethical considerations. But the industry is marching forward, joining this AI parade at a runner's clip.

But wait a minute! Sound the alarm sirens! While AI promises to make our work faster, models better, data cheaper, it is systematically ignoring the breakthrough understanding provided by Neuroscience that not all data sets, especially those based on self-reported answers to questions, are true. We have outstanding new processing capabilities while AI is potentially fed consistently with grossly inadequate, misleading data. Only if we incorporate reliable metrics for emotional response and subconscious signals can we be assured that input into our models can be trusted.

This is why the work being shared in this new book on Neuromarketing in the Age of AI is so critically important! By leveraging the insights of leading Neuromarketing academics and practioners in this compendium, the dawn of Artificial Intelligence driven marketing practices can have a much greater chance of being accurate and effective. The content is comprehensive delving into the mechanisms behind consumer choice, decoding sentiment via measureable physiological response, and includes a deep discussion of ethics protecting consumer privacy and independence.

As we plunge into the vast AI unknown, we must not leave our understanding of the human brain behind. Rather, we should strive as a unified industry to enable organic evolution of brain function incorporating human insight with the most advanced technological AI processing power. This will create a new level of human functioning that promises to be the most accurate, effective, and ethical approach, while never relinquishing the essence of that which is distinctly human.

Elissa Moses
BrainGroup Global, USA

Preface

INTRODUCTION

When I first encountered neuromarketing many years ago during one of my studies, it was often perceived as a niche discipline—fascinating, yet misunderstood, and sometimes even viewed with skepticism. Today, in the age of artificial intelligence, neuromarketing has moved from the margins to the center of strategic decision-making. AI has not only amplified our ability to analyze vast amounts of behavioral and neural data, but it has also challenged us to rethink how human cognition, emotion, and technology interact.

This book is born out of a deep conviction: that understanding the human brain has never been more important than in a world increasingly shaped by algorithms. While AI excels at recognizing patterns and predicting behavior, it is neuroscience that helps us understand *why* people feel, decide, and act the way they do. "Neuromarketing in the Age of AI" is therefore not about replacing human intuition with machines, but about creating a meaningful dialogue between human insight and artificial intelligence.

AN OVERVIEW OF THE SUBJECT MATTER OF OUR BOOK

This book explores the dynamic intersection of neuroscience, marketing, and artificial intelligence in a structured and accessible way. Beginning with the foundational principles of neuromarketing, we guide readers through the evolution of the field—from early brain research and biometric methods to sophisticated AI-driven analytics.

The chapters address both theory and practice: how neural data is collected and interpreted, how AI enhances prediction accuracy, and how these insights translate into more effective marketing strategies. We examine real-world applications, emerging technologies, and the growing importance of emotional intelligence in digital environments. A dedicated focus is placed on ethical considerations, transparency, and responsibility—because with greater insight into the human mind comes greater accountability.

Ultimately, the book demonstrates how neuromarketing, empowered by AI, is reshaping market research, brand communication, customer experience, and strategic decision-making.

THE BOOK'S TARGET AUDIENCE

"Neuromarketing in the Age of AI" is written for a diverse yet connected audience. It speaks to marketing professionals seeking evidence-based tools to better understand their customers, researchers and academics interested in the latest interdisciplinary developments, and business leaders who must navigate an increasingly complex, data-driven landscape.

At the same time, the book is accessible to newcomers who are curious about neuromarketing and AI but may not yet have a technical background. By combining scientific rigor with practical relevance, this book aims to bridge the gap between theory and application, making it valuable for both strategic thinkers and hands-on practitioners.

A DESCRIPTION OF THE IMPORTANCE OF EACH OF THE CHAPTER

Here we will describe in brief each chapter, as well as it's importance.

Chapter 1: Neuromarketing is the science of blending of neuroscience and marketing concepts to understand brain responses to stimuli and therefore predict consumer behavior. The importance of this method has evolved over the years with advancement of tools, techniques and concepts to predict consumer responses and thus behavior. The importance in this technique over survey method is that it measures responses and does not depend on self-reported data.In this chapter, we will briefly outline the various facets of consumer behavior, basic neuroscience concepts and move to gradual advancement of neuromarketing techniques. We would also explore some well known case studies to illustrate the importance of this technique. We would also discuss the ethical considerations of Neuromarketing to illustrate that there are serious concerns in that front.

Chapter 2: Consumer purchase intentions significantly influence buying behavior and market dynamics. Exploring these intentions explicitly and through tools that delve into the subconscious is crucial. With the advent of neuromarketing, the neural responses to any marketing stimuli can be studied. This has benefitted all aspects, especially in understanding the factors directly impacting the purchase intention. This paper aims to analyze the role of neuroimaging tools in assessing or predicting consumer purchase intentions. It is qualitative research that explores these aspects through a literature survey. Research findings indicate that neuromarketing explores consumers' emotional engagement through various neuro tools. Additionally, neuromarketing assesses factors with a significant impact on purchasing behavior by recording sensory experiences and cognitive evaluations.

Chapter 3: In today's world, marketing strategies are becoming targeted with the help of artificial intelligence. Each click on a commercial website is analyzed, processed, and paired with techniques, with information on individual consumers used by marketers to ascertain who is most likely to respond positively to a particular advertisement. Neuromarketing is considered an emerging field to study how consumers' brain reacts to advertisements and brand messages (Traymbak et al., 2024). Today, neuromarketing helps marketers to better appeal to consumer's subconscious minds and biases. Neuromarketing analyzes information on how consumers feel about a product.

Chapter 4: Understanding consumer behavior is critical for companies, especially with the rise of digital information and recommendation systems. AI with neuromarketing capabilities transforms consumer decisions by analyzing emotional responses and subconscious signals, using tools like eye tracking, EEG records, facial expression detectors, and biometric feedback. These AI systems can identify marketing cues that humans may miss, offering real-time insights into consumer behavior. This integration helps brands predict purchasing behavior, create effective ad strategies, and foster deeper brand engagement. However, the use of neural and biometric data raises ethical concerns, emphasizing the need for transparency, data protection, and consumer consent. The future of AI in neuromarketing holds promise for more advanced tools, but it is crucial for marketers to follow ethical guidelines to ensure genuine, trust-based relationships with consumers.

Chapter 5: This chapter explores impact of neuroscience & artificial intelligence (AI) on consumer behavior analysis. It presents an overview of neuromarketing tools such as EEG, fMRI, eye-tracking, facial & galvanic skin response, detailing how these technologies uncover subconscious consumer responses. Through AI integration, neuromarketing achieves precision, scale, & speed in interpreting complex neural & biometric data. It further examines how companies like Coca-Cola, Unilever, & P&G apply AI-driven neuromarketing for ad optimization, product design, & personalized engagement. Ethical considerations surrounding privacy, bias, &

manipulation are analyzed, along with regulatory frameworks like GDPR. It also discusses how emotional & creative stimuli influence purchasing decisions & how AI leverages these insights for hyper-personalized marketing. Finally, it outlines emerging trends such as emotionally intelligent AI, immersive technologies like AR/VR, & brain-computer interfaces, while emphasizing the importance of ethical implementation in shaping the future of consumer engagement.

Chapter 6: In today's complex digital era, marketers face the challenge of understanding the subconscious factors that drive consumer decisions, which traditional self-reported research often fails to capture. Neuromarketing addresses this by combining marketing with neuroscience, using tools like fMRI, EEG, and biometrics to uncover unintentional reactions. The application of artificial intelligence (AI) to this subject is a significant advancement, boosting the accuracy, speed, and scope of consumer insights. This chapter looks at how neuromarketing is changing as a result of AI-powered methods including machine learning, deep learning, and emotional analytics. It draws on key neuroscientific and psychological theories to explain how AI interprets human thought and emotion. Real-world applications across industries, along with ethical considerations around privacy and autonomy, are explored as well. The chapter concludes by outlining future trends, including emotionally adaptive systems and brain-computer interfaces, offering a forward-looking view of personalized and ethical marketing.

Chapter 7: Neuromarketing and artificial intelligence (AI) integration is transforming the manner in which companies understand and affect consumer behaviour. Neuromarketing refers to everything that applies neuroscientific principles to marketing and helps us understand subconscious (or unintentionally) decision-making processes by examining their effect on our brain, our emotions, and our cognitive responses. The key to effective neuromarketing research is the insights of the behavioral patterns it provides, as it brings corporations to understand their consumers in a manner that is more on point than traditional methods. AI elevates these insights by allowing automation of data collection, identification of behavioral patterns, and conducting real time analysis on the data gathered, making neuromarketing research easier to scale and implement. In this chapter, we take a closer look and the perks of merging neuromarketing and AI, and their usefulness in different industries like retail, advertising, entertainment, healthcare, and customer experience.

Chapter 8: The study highlights the emerging topic of neuromarketing and AI and its impact on marketing strategies. Neuromarketing integrates neuroscience, psychology, and marketing to understand consumer buying behavior. AI is the programs, machines or systems that demonstrate the human intelligence. This chapter explores the AI tools used in marketing and focuses on combining AI and Neuromarketing to improve marketing strategies. In the current chapter, some real-life case studies are also discussed which helps in understanding neuromarketing in the era of AI. This chapter indicates ethical questions about neuromarketing and AI. It suggests that neuromarketing and AI have the potential to change the way marketers understand and influence consumer buying decisions.

Chapter 9: Neuro-optimization is altering the approach towards product or ad design by blending neuromarketing and artificial intelligence (AI). AI is once again revolutionizing how brands communicate with consumers by enhancing ways of measuring feelings and metrics, enhancing response capture. Real-time design optimisation enables efficient advertisement, product and experience prototyping and improvement. Brands employ AI features like content split testing to influence the cognitive and emotional experiences of its audience to promote better UX. In its future, AI neuro-optimization can present a level of personalization and emotional appeal in the marketing exposure to customers which will be higher. The application of AI in relations to marketing is expected to keep advancing which means that ethical approaches to innovation will be the key to sustainable client relations and trust. This chapter focus on how AI advances works when granting consumers an opportunity to be evaluated instantly and allows for changes to be made in real-time.

Chapter 10: By understanding how the brain reacts to various stimuli, neuromarketing can offer guidelines for product design, branding, and as well as much of a marketing strategy. The purpose of this paper is to explore the new product development outcomes of neuromarketing, investigate which techniques can contribute toward understanding consumer behaviour, and determine how they can be successful for firms using neuromarketing. The approaches employed are literature review and case study. Empirical evidence and case studies suggest that neuromarketing can revolutionise the creation of new products, and it should be a compulsory element for every business in the competitive world. In addition, the chapter contributes to the literature by helping to clarify how neuromarketing tools may be organised for being used effectively in NPD by bridging consumer psychology to marketing praxis. Ultimately, the chapter advocates for a robust integration and encourages firms to shift from traditional methodologies to more adept, neuromarketing approaches in their new product development strategies.

Chapter 11: This chapter investigates how neurogastronomy, artificial intelligence, and taste projection technologies are combining in marketing to provide multi-sensory, personalised consumer experiences. Neuroscientific insights are integrated with technologies such as AI-powered recommendation systems and virtual reality to help brands engage emotionally with customers. However, ethical concerns such as data privacy, cultural sensitivity, and manipulative behaviours necessitate the continued and responsible use of these technologies.

Chapter 12: The rapid proliferation of artificial intelligence (AI) in online communication is reshaping how information is created, disseminated, and consumed. From personalized chatbots to AI-generated content and deepfake videos, these technologies are not only transforming engagement but also challenging our ability to discern truth from fabrication. This chapter explores the intersection of AI and consumer neuroscience in the context of manipulation, examining how AI leverages subconscious human processes to influence perceptions and decisions. The chapter delves into the psychological mechanisms that make individuals susceptible to manipulative messages, such as trust, fear, and cognitive biases. By integrating insights from neuroscience, it uncovers the subconscious drivers of behavior, providing a deeper understanding of how AI technologies can either empower or exploit individuals. The chapter also highlights the ethical challenges posed by AI-driven manipulation, advocating for accountability and safeguards in AI development to minimize harm and ensure transparency.

Chapter 13: Traditional marketing research methods have many limitations, including high time and cost requirements and a limited ability to draw conclusions about actual consumer behavior as opposed to declared intentions. These challenges have prompted growing interest in neuromarketing, which investigates biological and neurological responses to marketing stimuli. The value of such methods depends on researchers' ability to interpret diagnostic results in a meaningful marketing context (Kenning & Linzmajer, 2011; Morin, 2011). More recently, artificial intelligence (AI) has emerged as a promising enhancement to neuromarketing techniques. This chapter aims to identify and evaluate neuromarketing methods used to study consumer behavior and to assess the potential of AI to enhance these techniques. In particular, the chapter focuses on how AI can enable real-time reaction analysis, personalize emotional engagement, and predict future consumer behavior.

Chapter 14: Neuromarketing, an interdisciplinary field merging neuroscience and marketing, aims to understand consumer behavior by examining the neural processes behind decision-making and preferences. This paper explores the potential and challenges of neuromarketing, which, by using tools like fMRI and EEG, uncovers subconscious responses to marketing stimuli that traditional research methods often miss. Neuromarketing offers businesses the chance to make data-driven decisions in product design, advertising, and brand management, enabling more tailored and effective marketing strategies. However, the field faces ethical issues related to consumer privacy, the manipulation of subconscious preferences, and substantial financial and technical barriers, which hinder widespread adoption. Despite these concerns, neuromarketing holds the promise of enhancing consumer insight and fostering ethically responsible advertising when used thoughtfully. Recognizing both the opportunities and limitations of this field is crucial for businesses in today's market.

Chapter 15: The integration of artificial intelligence into neuromarketing has redefined how businesses analyse consumer behaviour and tailor their marketing strategies. Traditional neuromarketing have provided valuable insights into subconscious decision-making processes. However, with neuromarketing AI's possibilities has become more precise, scalable, and personalized than ever before. While these advancements offer businesses powerful tools to enhance consumer engagement, they also introduce significant ethical concerns. AI-driven neuromarketing raises pressing questions about consumer privacy, informed consent, and data security. Chapter purpose is to explore the ethical implications of AI-powered neuromarketing by identifying key challenges, including risks of consumer manipulation, potential misuse of sensitive biometric data, and regulatory gaps. Additionally, the study proposes solutions to mitigate ethical concerns, offering recommendations for businesses and policymakers to strike a balance between leveraging AI's potential and protecting consumer rights.

Chapter 16: This study investigates the space of advertising using the lens of deepfake technology, cognitive dissonance, and consumer trust as they help companies create hyper-authentic yet potentially deceitful content with deepfakes, traditional notions of authenticity in marketing are being tested. One significant problem is cognitive dissonance, which occurs when users feel uneasy about the possibility that the information they received was fabricated or deceptive. This behavior can undermine consumer trust, raise suspicion, and damage brand reputation. This paper explores how consumers mentally process deepfake ads and how the cognitive dissonance generated by perceiving manipulation will affect trust in the long run. We discuss strategies that can be used to implement ethical practices in a deepfake-influenced advertising space, to protect the consumer relationship and brand integrity.

Chapter 17: AI-powered neural marketing has transformed how organisations view and influence consumers. Emotion identification, real-time tracking, and prediction models assist AI-based neuromarketing in explaining subconscious decision-making. Traditional marketing leverages superficial data. The moral and ethical impacts of AI-based neuromarketing on client behaviour have not been substantially studied, despite progress. To close this gap, we study new technologies, their effects on marketing, and AI-neuromarketing synergy. Writing, case studies, and AI-enhanced data analysis employing wearable neurotechnology, emotion AI, and behavioural prediction models review AI-driven technologies. AI enhances personalisation, real-time engagement, and customer targeting but raises privacy and manipulation problems. Researchers, policymakers, and marketers may use the study's results to produce ethical and effective AI-driven marketing. This study's novel approach to AI and neuromarketing focuses on ethical responsibility and technical development.

CONCLUSION

We live in a time where attention is scarce, trust is fragile, and consumer expectations are constantly evolving. In this environment, neuromarketing and artificial intelligence together offer unprecedented opportunities—not to manipulate, but to understand more deeply and communicate more meaningfully.

This book is an invitation to explore that future thoughtfully and responsibly. It encourages readers to embrace innovation while remaining grounded in human values. "Neuromarketing in the Age of AI" is not just a reflection on where marketing stands today, but a guide to where it is heading—and how we can shape that journey with insight, ethics, and purpose.

Chapter 1
Evolution of Neuromarketing to Unlock Consumer Behavior

Debdutta Choudhury
http://orcid.org/0000-0002-0944-8595
Woxsen University, India

ABSTRACT

Neuromarketing is the science of blending of neuroscience and marketing concepts to understand brain responses to stimuli and therefore predict consumer behavior. The importance of this method has evolved over the years with advancement of tools, techniques and concepts to predict consumer responses and thus behavior. The importance in this technique over survey method is that it measures responses and does not depend on self-reported data. In this chapter, we will briefly outline the various facets of consumer behavior, basic neuroscience concepts and move to gradual advancement of neuromarketing techniques. We would also explore some well known case studies to illustrate the importance of this technique. We would also discuss the ethical considerations of Neuromarketing to illustrate that there are serious concerns in that front.

KEYWORD ANALYSIS USING QUALITATIVE RESEARCH

To distill the core intellectual structure of the chapter, a qualitative thematic analysis was performed. This involves grouping specific keywords into broader conceptual categories (Codes) and overarching Themes.

DOI: 10.4018/979-8-3373-1152-4.ch001

Table 1.

Core Theme	Conceptual Codes (Sub-themes)	Key Keywords Identified in Text
1. The "Black Box" of Cognition	Subconscious Processing	Unconscious mind, Black box, Implicit response, Hidden symbolic meanings, Primal urges
	Biological Basis	Physiological correlates, Biological indicators, Salivation, Neural activity, Reflexes
2. Determinants of Choice	Internal Drivers	Motivation (Maslow), Perception, Learning, Beliefs/ Attitudes, Self-concept, Personality
	External/Societal Drivers	Culture/Subculture, Reference groups, Family unit, Social class, Influencers
3. Evolution of Methodology	Traditional Methods	Self-reported data, Focus groups, Surveys, Projective techniques, Observation
	Neuro-Technological Shift	Real-time mind mapping, Non-invasive neuroimaging, Temporal resolution, Objective measurement
4. Neurometrics & Signals	Attention & Novelty	P300 (Surprise/Attention), N200 (Novelty/Conflict), Event-Related Potentials (ERPs)
	Valence & Semantics	Frontal Alpha Asymmetry (Approach/Withdrawal), N400 (Semantic Congruence/Conflict), Left/Right Dominance
5. Theoretical Lineage	Foundational Schools	Psychophysics (Weber/Fechner), Classical Conditioning (Pavlov), Behaviorism (Skinner/Watson), Psychoanalysis (Freud/Dichter)

PART A: FUNDAMENTALS OF CONSUMER BEHAVIOR

In todays' complex world, understanding consumers is the first step towards a successful business. Consumer Behaviour is therefore crucial in decision making.

The study of consumer behavior is fundamentally interdisciplinary, blending psychology, sociology, anthropology, and economics to throw a light into the intricacies of consumer decision-making. This understanding is significant since it changes everything from how items are created and priced to how commercials are run and how customers are treated. Schiffman and Kanuk's asserts that a marketer's ability to guess how customers would act is a big part of whether their plans work or not.

Factors Influencing Buying Decisions

People don't make choices in a vacuum. The choices are derived from a complicated mix of internal and external factors. These can usually be divided into four primary groups:

Psychological Factors

These are the factors that are internal to a person and affect how they think.

Motivation: This is what makes a person want to do something. Abraham Maslow's hierarchy of requirements provides a foundational framework, asserting that individuals are compelled to satisfy essential physiological needs before attending to safety, social, esteem, and self-actualization needs. Marketers typically leverage these needs to sell their goods.

Perception: This is how humans pick, sort, and make sense of information to build a picture of the world that makes sense to them. The way a person thinks about a brand is their reality, and it has a major effect on what they buy.

Learning: People always change how they act based on what they've been through. People can learn about a product by using it or by hearing about it from other people or seeing ads.

Beliefs and attitudes are the taught ways of behaving that are always favorable or negative towards anything. People generally buy anything once they have good feelings and opinions about a brand.

Social Factors

People are social beings, and therefore society have a big impact on what they buy.

Family: The family unit is one of the most important social elements that determine how people shop. The family often is a major decision factor on what people like and how they buy goods.

People utilize reference groups to see how their own ideas, attitudes, and behaviors relate to those of others. They can be friends, coworkers, famous people, or people you encounter on the internet. Influencers have a major effect on what consumers desire to buy, and the rise of social media has made reference groups much more effective.

Roles and Status: How someone buys goods depends on their standing in a group or community. A college student, for instance, is likely to buy different products than a CEO.

Cultural Factors

Culture is the biggest thing that shapes what people want and how they act.

Culture: This is the collection of core values, beliefs, wants, and actions that a person learns from their family and other key groups.

Subculture: Subcultures are groupings of people within a culture who share the same ideals because they have had similar life experiences and conditions. They can be based on where geography, race, religion etc.

Social Class: These are stable and organized social groupings, and the people in them share similar values, interests, and actions. Social class also may have an impact on a person's buying decision.

Personal Factors

The individual characteristics of each person are also highly important.

Age and Life-Cycle Stage: As people become older, their demands and ability to buy things alter.

Job: The job a person has affects what they buy viz. laptop for a software professional, electrical tools for an electrician etc.

The economic condition of a person, like how much money they have to spend, save, and own, has a direct impact on the things they choose.

Lifestyle: This is the way a person lives, including what they do, what they like, and what they think. Marketers often split their markets into groups based on how people live.

Self-Concept and Personality: Personality is the collection of psychological features that distinguish one individual or group from another. People are more likely to buy from brands that have personalities that are similar to their own.

The Journey to Buy: How Consumers Make Decisions

It's not enough to just know what makes consumers buy products. Marketers also need to grasp how a customer progresses from a problem identification that requires a solution to actually paying for a brand. The Engel-Kollat-Blackwell model, which was initially made in 1968, is one way to illustrate this process as a series of steps. There are many kinds of models, but most have these five steps:

Recognizing a problem: The process begins when a customer discovers they need something or have a problem. This can be triggered by simple needs like hunger or more complicated like buying something for entertainment.

Searching for information: Once the customer knows they need something, they look for information about possible solutions. Information search may happen from memory or from friends, family, media etc. Digital media has revolutionized this stage in a big way, allowing people access to knowledge like never before. This allows people to conduct an in-depth research into a product or a service.

Evaluating Options: The consumer compares different brands in the option set using the information they have gathered. Based on the product or an individual, the decision can be based on logic (like pricing or features) or emotion (like brand image or social status).

After the Sale: The marketer's job isn't done when the sale is made. The buyer will either be delighted or unhappy after purchase. This will change how consumers shop in the future and how likely they are to tell other people about the brand. Cognitive dissonance, or the unpleasantness that occurs from having conflicting thoughts after making a purchase, is a crucial aspect at this stage.

Neuromarketing emerged as a serious field of study in the early 2000s, with a landmark moment coming from Montague et al. (2004). Their famous "Pepsi vs. Coke" experiment on the neural correlates of preference for culturally familiar drinks became a turning point in the field. It showed researchers something important: our choices aren't always rational—emotions and subconscious processes play a huge role in what we decide to buy. This challenged long-held beliefs in psychology and behavioral science about how we make decisions.

While scientists had been exploring connections between neuroscience and marketing since the early 20th century, the field didn't really take off until the late 2000s, when neuromarketing finally became a legitimate and commercially viable discipline. Since then, both academics and businesses have become increasingly interested in what neuroscience can teach us about marketing. The field has grown so much that researchers have been publishing systematic reviews of neuromarketing literature with some regularity (Montague et al., 2004; Karmarkar & Plassmann, 2019).

Recent systematic reviews have evolved this into a *"Neuro-Journey" framework*. A 2025 systematic review by Gupta, Kapoor, and Verma maps specific neural mechanisms to each stage of the traditional buying cycle. For instance, they identify that *"problem recognition"* is neurologically linked to conflict monitoring circuits while *"evaluation"* relies heavily on brain frontal asymmetry (approach motivation).

The Modern Consumer: A Change in Digital Technology

The core notions about how people behave as consumers are still true, but the internet and digital technology have made things more complicated and given us new opportunities. People who buy things today know more, are more connected, and expect more than before. It's now vital to change how people respond by using digital marketing methods like social media campaigns, influencer marketing, and tailored advertising. Online reviews and interactions on social media have a big impact on buying decisions, often more so than traditional advertising.

To sum up, studying how people act as consumers is an important and growing field. Companies may create better marketing campaigns if they know how all the psychological, social, cultural, and personal elements that determine what consumers buy and how they make decisions work together. From Maslow's basic principles to Howard and Sheth's more complete models to the present realities of the digital marketplace, knowing the customer well is and will always be the most crucial thing for any organization to perform successfully.

PART B: THE FUNDAMENTALS OF NEUROSCIENCE

Neuroscience is the study of brain and neurology of the body. The brain is the organ that takes all the important decisions including purchase decision. Businesses seeking to engage clients more profoundly must acquire foundational knowledge of neuroscience. Neuromarketing is the examination of the interplay between neuroscience and marketing to elucidate the subconscious influences on consumer purchasing behavior.

For decades, marketers have utilized self-reported data from surveys and focus groups; yet, these methods are frequently faulty as individuals cannot consistently articulate the rationale behind their choices. Neuromarketing provides a direct insight into the brain's responses to branding, advertising, and product experiences, surpassing mere cognitive consideration. We would discuss the primary components of the brain and their collaborative functions in facilitating consumer decision-making.

The Brain Structure

Figure 1. The brain structure

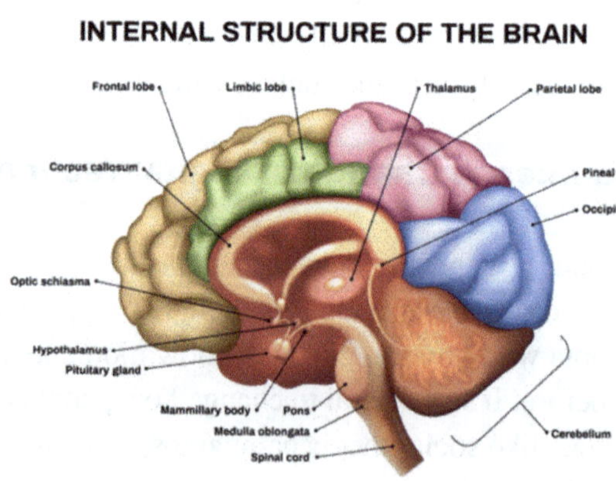

- **Frontal Lobe:** Located at the front of the brain, responsible for planning, decision-making, voluntary movement, personality, and language (Broca's area for speech production).
- **Parietal Lobe:** Situated behind the frontal lobe, processes sensory information (touch, temperature, pain, spatial awareness, navigation), and language comprehension.
- **Temporal Lobe:** Located on the sides of the brain, involved in auditory processing, memory formation, object recognition, and language understanding (Wernicke's area).
- **Occipital Lobe:** Found at the back of the brain, primarily responsible for processing visual information.
- **Limbic Lobe:** A collection of structures involved in emotion, memory, and motivation. Key components include the hippocampus, amygdala, and cingulate gyrus.
- **Corpus Callosum:** A large bundle of nerve fibers connecting the left and right cerebral hemispheres, allowing for communication between them.
- **Thalamus:** Acts as a relay station for sensory information, processing and transmitting it to the cerebral cortex. Also involved in regulating consciousness, sleep, and alertness.
- **Optic Chiasm:** The point where the optic nerves from each eye cross, allowing visual information from the right visual field to be processed by the left hemisphere and vice versa.
- **Hypothalamus:** A small but crucial region that regulates body temperature, hunger, thirst, sleep-wake cycles, hormone release, and links the nervous and endocrine systems.
- **Pituitary Gland:** An endocrine gland connected to the hypothalamus, often called the "master gland" because it secretes hormones that regulate other endocrine glands.
- **Mammillary Body:** Involved in memory, particularly recall. Part of the limbic system.
- **Pons:** A part of the brainstem located between the midbrain and the medulla oblongata. Involved in regulating breathing, communication between different parts of the brain, and sensations such as hearing and taste.
- **Medulla Oblongata:** The lowest part of the brainstem, connecting to the spinal cord. Crucial for regulating vital autonomic functions like heart rate, blood pressure, and breathing.
- **Spinal Cord:** A long, tubular structure extending from the medulla oblongata to the lower back, transmitting nerve signals between the brain and the rest of the body.

- **Cerebellum:** Located beneath the occipital lobe and behind the brainstem, responsible for coordinating voluntary movements, posture, balance, and motor learning.
- **Pineal Gland:** A small endocrine gland that produces melatonin, a hormone that regulates sleep-wake cycles.

The Functioning of Brain

It is essential to comprehend the primary regions of the brain and their respective functions to grasp how marketing stimuli influence our decisions. The brain comprises three interconnected layers. Each layer possesses distinct functions that alter our perception and interaction with the surrounding environment, such as the marketplace.

The brainstem, often referred to as the "reptilian brain," constitutes the most primitive component of the brain. It regulates our fundamental survival instincts, such as respiration, cardiac rhythm, and the fight-or-flight reaction. It alters our instinctive responses, however it does not directly influence our evaluations of brands in a complex manner.

The subsequent component is the limbic system, commonly referred to as the emotional brain. This collection of structures is the repository for our memories, emotions, and motivations. This is the locus where brands may establish robust, enduring ties with their clientele.

Finally, the neocortex, the most advanced region of the brain, governs language, reasoning, and complex cognitive processes. This logical filter aids in processing information and facilitating decision-making. The decisions of the limbic system are significantly shaped by the emotional stimuli it encounters.

Key Focus Areas for Neuromarketers

Neuromarketers focus on particular brain structures that comprise these significant layers. Understanding their functions enables the creation of superior and more engaging marketing strategies.

The prefrontal cortex (PFC), located at the anterior region of the brain, governs executive processes. It assists in planning, decision-making, problem-solving, and regulating interpersonal behavior. When an individual evaluates the advantages and disadvantages of a purchase, contrasts brands, or assesses the long-term value of a product, their prefrontal cortex is engaged.

Branding is crucial for the ventromedial prefrontal cortex (vmPFC). Studies demonstrate that this area of the brain is associated with our assessment of brands and our readiness to compensate for them. Brand knowledge significantly influences our preferences, as demonstrated by McClure et al. (2004) in their study of Pepsi and Coke, which is evident in the activity of the prefrontal cortex (PFC). Upon recognizing they were consuming Coca-Cola, the subjects exhibited activation in their dorsolateral prefrontal cortex (dlPFC) and hippocampus. This indicates that memories and brand connotations influenced their perception of the drink's taste.

The limbic system, located deep within the brain, regulates our emotions, significantly influencing our behavior as consumers. The amygdala and hippocampus are two of its most critical components.

The amygdala is the brain region responsible for regulating emotions. It generates and processes emotions such as fear, pleasure, and excitement. Advertisements that evoke emotions, compelling narratives, and tangible objects all stimulate the amygdala in marketing. A compelling advertisement that evokes tears or an exhilarating movie trailer that accelerates your heartbeat engages the amygdala, so creating a robust emotional memory associated with the brand.

The hippocampus is crucial for the formation and retrieval of long-term memories. Due to its proximity to the amygdala, emotional experiences are more likely to be encoded in long-term memory. Consequently, brands that evoke strong positive emotions are more memorable and foster long-term loyalty.

The nucleus accumbens is a component of the limbic system that plays a crucial role in the brain's reward circuitry. Dopamine surges to this region when we engage in activities that elicit pleasure, such as consuming a delectable meal or receiving a “like” on social media.

Marketers can stimulate the nucleus accumbens by designing rewarding brand encounters. Time-sensitive promotions, loyalty initiatives, and the excitement of discovering the “ideal” product can all trigger dopamine release, enhancing consumer propensity to purchase and fostering positive brand associations. Knutson et al. (2007) discovered that activity in the nucleus accumbens can forecast purchasing decisions prior to individuals' conscious awareness.

PART C: THE EVOLUTION OF NEUROMARKETING

Traditionally, marketers used instruments like focus groups, surveys, intuition, and observation to investigate the nuances of consumer behavior. Despite their value, these approaches frequently struggled with a basic drawback: their reliance on conscious self-reporting, which makes them vulnerable to biases, justifications, and the opaque subconscious mind. A paradigm shift has occurred with the rise and development of neuromarketing, an interdisciplinary field that uses neuroscience concepts and tools to comprehend consumer emotion, cognition, and decision-making. It provides an exploration of the "black box," looking for unbiased biological indicators of the inner workings that influence market behavior.

I. The roots of motivation research can be found in psychology, physiology, and the late 19th and early 20th centuries.

The origin of neuromarketing lies in the concepts of psychology and physiology. The foundation for comprehending the unconscious and biological bases of behavior was established by early pioneers:

Psychophysics and Perception (Weber, Fechner): Gustav Fechner developed psychophysics by measuring the connection between psychological sensation and physical stimuli, building on the research of Ernst Weber (Fechner, 1860). This proved that subjective experience had physiological correlates that could be measured, which was a fundamental idea for later objective marketing measurement.

Ivan Pavlov's classical conditioning experiments (Pavlov, 1927) demonstrated how learned association with physiologically powerful stimuli (food) could cause involuntary physiological responses (salivation) in response to neutral stimuli (a bell). This offered a mechanism by which brands could be linked to favorable emotions or requirements.

Environmental Cues and Behaviorism (Watson, Skinner): John B. Watson and B.F. Skinner focused on observable behaviors that are influenced by reinforcement and environmental cues (Skinner, 1938). Behaviorism focused on quantifiable responses and emphasized the significance of cues (packaging, store layout) and rewards (discounts, product benefits) in influencing consumer behavior, while largely disregarding internal states.

Sigmund Freud's theories popularized the idea of the powerful unconscious mind, which is motivated by primal urges and profoundly influences behavior, including consumption choices. However, Freud's theories were controversial and less directly empirical. This demonstrated the possible drawbacks of depending only on conscious explanations.

Ernest Dichter pioneered motivational research in the 1940s and 1950s by applying psychoanalytic principles. He used projective techniques and in-depth interviews to delve into the hidden, symbolic meanings that consumers attached to products (Dichter, 1960). Dichter foreshadowed the fundamental goal of neuromarketing by specifically pursuing the "why" behind the surface, even though it was still dependent on self-report.

The inability to directly, objectively, and non-invasively measure the brain's activity and subconscious processes in real-time during exposure to marketing stimuli was a major gap that persisted despite these advancements. Self-reporting was still the norm, but it was faulty by nature.

II. The Catalyst of Technology: Real-Time Mind Mapping (1970s-1990s)

The advancement and improvement of non-invasive neuroimaging and physiological measurement technologies marked a significant step towards contemporary neuromarketing:

The rapid dynamics of brain processes are captured by electroencephalography (EEG), which measures electrical activity on the scalp using electrodes and offers excellent temporal resolution (milliseconds). Important Event-Related Potentials (ERPs) gained significance:

P300: It is a neurological technique where a positive wave that appears about 300 milliseconds after an unexpected or a significant stimulus. This is linked to surprise, attention allocation, and stimulus classification (Polich, 2007). This could be used by marketers to determine when a feature of a product or advertisement really grabs attention.

N200/N400: In this technique N200 component appears after 200 milliseconds and is associated with conflict detection, decision-making, and novelty recognition. N400 signal appears after 400 milliseconds and is associated with cognition and coherence. Weak waves here is associated with semantic incongruence or conflict detection (Kutas & Hillyard, 1980) and is helpful in spotting unclear messaging or incongruent brand images. This is used to test the appropriate product features, innovation or communication messages.

Frontal Alpha Asymmetry: Approach (left dominance) versus withdrawal (right dominance) motivation is linked to an imbalance in alpha wave power between the left and right frontal lobes (Davidson, 1992), indicating motivational reactions to advertisements or brands. The 1980s and 1990s saw the emergence of studies that used EEG to evaluate advertising (Rothschild et al., 1988).

In the 1990s, functional magnetic resonance imaging (fMRI) revolutionized cognitive neuroscience by detecting changes in blood oxygenation (BOLD signal) associated with neural activity. Its ability to identify the precise location of brain activity is its strength (Logothetis, 2008). Important neural correlates were found by groundbreaking studies:

The anticipation and processing of rewards are closely linked to the activation of the nucleus accumbens (NAcc) (Knutson et al., 2001).

According to LeDoux (2000), the amygdala is essential for processing emotional salience, especially fear and negative emotions, but also strongly positive associations.

In order to assign value, the ventromedial prefrontal cortex (vmPFC) integrates emotional and cognitive data (Plassmann et al., 2008).

The "Pepsi Paradox" Study (McClure et al., 2004): This seminal fMRI study illustrated the influence of brand. Blind taste tests revealed that Pepsi and Coke were equally preferred (Pepsi had a stronger NAcc activation), but knowing the brand caused a very different reaction. With its powerful cultural branding, Coke demonstrated how brand associations take precedence over pure sensory input by activating the hippocampus (memory), dorsolateral prefrontal cortex (DLPFC, or cognitive control), and vmPFC. This clearly demonstrated the disconnect between brand perception and product experience.

Physiological Assessments:

Eye-Tracking: Accurately measuring gaze patterns, such as fixations, saccades, and pupil dilation, can reveal cognitive load, information processing, and visual attention allocation (Duchowski, 2007). Additionally, pupil dilatation may be a sign of cognitive effort or emotional arousal (Beatty, 1982), essential for ad design, packaging, and website layout.

Automated facial coding and facial electromyography (fEMG) measure subtle, frequently involuntary facial muscle activity (e.g., zygomaticus major for smiling/positive affect, and corrugator supercilii for frowning/negative affect) to provide objective measures of emotional valence (Dimberg et al., 2000). Video feeds are now analyzed by automated systems (Facial Action Coding System, or FACS) (Ekman & Friesen, 1978).

Electrodermal activity (EDA) and galvanic skin response (GSR) measure changes in skin conductance brought on by sweat gland activity, which reflects arousal of the sympathetic nervous system (excitation, stress, engagement) (Boucsein, 2012).

Heart Rate (HR) and Heart Rate Variability (HRV): Arousal raises HR, and emotional control and cognitive load are associated with HRV, or the difference in the interval between heartbeats (Appelhans & Luecken, 2006).

By avoiding the drawbacks of self-report, this technological convergence in the late 1990s and early 2000s gave rise to the means of objectively measuring emotional and subconscious reactions. The term "neuromarketing" itself is frequently credited to Gerald Zaltman, whose "Zaltman Metaphor Elicitation Technique" (ZMET) previously integrated neuroscience principles (Zaltman, 1997), or Ale Smidts in 2002 (Lee et al., 2007).

III. Early 2000s–Early 2010s: Commercial Emergence, Hype, and Refinement

Driven by high-profile studies and the establishment of specialized companies (e.g., NeuroFocus founded by Dr. A.K. Pradeep, later acquired by Nielsen; Brighthouse, SalesBrain, Innerscope acquired by Nielsen, MindSign Neuromarketing), neuromarketing exploded onto the commercial scene in the early 2000s.

Early Uses & Hype: The initial efforts concentrated largely on testing TV commercials, print advertisements, and packaging, with the promise of predicting "effectiveness" by detecting memory encoding, high attention, and strong emotional engagement (either positive or negative). But there was also a lot of hype during this time. Scientists and marketers were both excited and highly skeptical of sensationalist claims that they had discovered a "buy button" in the brain (Ariely & Berns, 2010).

Challenges and Criticism: Critics voiced legitimate concerns.

- Cost and Accessibility: fMRI in particular was too costly for everyday use.
- Ecological Validity: Real-world shopping habits may not be reflected in artificial lab settings.
- Interpretation Complexity: Because the brain is a highly interconnected system, it can be difficult to correlate particular brain activations with complex behaviors like purchase intent (Ariely & Berns, 2010).
- Small Samples: Compared to conventional market research, neuroscience studies frequently used smaller samples.
- Ethical Issues: Subconscious manipulation and "brainwashing" concerns surfaced (Murphy et al., 2008).

Methodological Maturation: As a result, the field underwent substantial maturation.

In order to triangulate results and obtain a more comprehensive understanding (e.g., when attention shifts, where it goes, and the emotional valence associated), researchers stressed the use of multimodal integration techniques (e.g., EEG + Eye-Tracking + Facial Coding) (Venkatraman et al., 2012).

Focus on Specific Constructs: Go beyond nebulous "effectiveness" to assess distinct neurocognitive processes, such as emotional engagement (fMRI amygdala/vmPFC, fEMG, GSR), memory encoding (fMRI hippocampus), cognitive load (EEG, Pupillometry, HRV), approach/avoidance motivation (EEG frontal asymmetry, fMRI NAcc), attention capture (EEG P300, Eye-Tracking), emotional engagement (fMRI amygdala/vmPFC, fEMG, GSR), and perceived value (fMRI vmPFC) (Plassmann et al., 2012).

Creating more realistic testing settings and stimuli (such as simulated stores and in-home usage tests) is an effort to ensure ecological validity.

Complementary Role: Understanding that neuromarketing works best when used in conjunction with conventional techniques (such as focus groups, surveys, and sales data), not in place of them. The "why" behind the "what" is explained by neuroscience (Lee et al., 2007).

Ethical Frameworks: The creation of codes of ethics that prioritize data privacy, informed consent, openness, and avoiding subliminal manipulation (Murphy et al., 2008; NMSBA, 2013).

IV. The AI Revolution, Democratization, and Diversification (mid-2010s to present)

Increased accessibility, wider application, and the revolutionary impact of artificial intelligence have defined the past ten years:

Democratization of technology:

Cost-effective Wearables: Webcam-based facial coding software, consumer-grade EEG headsets (like Emotiv and Muse), and simplified eye-trackers (like Tobii Eye Tracker 5) etc have made neurometric tools available to academia and smaller enterprises, allowing for larger-scale research (Solnais et al., 2013).

Mobile Labs: Eye tracking, biometric setups, and portable EEG enable testing in authentic settings such as homes, retail stores, or while using a product (e.g., while driving).

Increasing Application Horizons: The whole customer journey is now infused with neuromarketing insights:

Neurological and physiological reactions to taste, smell, texture, sound, and usability are evaluated in Product Design & Sensory Experience (Krishna, 2012).

Packaging & Shopper Marketing: Using eye-tracking and implicit response measures to optimize shelf impact, visual hierarchy, and haptic appeal (Reimann et al., 2010).

Pricing and Value Perception: Examining the neural mechanisms of price fairness, discounts, and premium pricing as well as the "pain of paying" (insula activation) (Plassmann et al., 2008; Knutson et al., 2007).

Eye-tracking, EEG, and facial coding are tools used in User Experience (UX) and Web Design to identify areas of friction, improve navigation, and increase user engagement on websites and apps (Djamasbi et al., 2010).

Retail Atmosphere: Using physiological monitoring, store environments (lighting, music, scent, and layout) are designed to affect mood, dwell time, and purchase behavior (Spence et al., 2014).

Brand storytelling and content marketing: quantifying the strong emotional connection, narrative flow, and long-term memory encoding that brand stories evoke (Jin et al., 2017).

Interdisciplinary convergence is demonstrated by the development of neuromarketing. Propelled by the technological revolutions of EEG, fMRI, and AI, the field has relentlessly sought a deeper, more objective understanding of the consumer mind from the early psychophysics of Fechner to Pavlov's conditioning, from Freud's unconscious to Dichter's motivations. Although the initial hype cycle exposed flaws and moral dilemmas, the core value proposition has remained consistent: neuromarketing offers distinct, unbiased insights into the emotional reactions, cognitive processes, and subconscious drivers that conventional approaches frequently overlook or that consumers are unable to express.

The power of implicit memory and association, the intricate neural calculus behind value perception and decision-making, and the strong influence of emotion over reason are all revealed. As the field develops, its emphasis moves from merely predicting persuasion to comprehending, honoring, and morally improving the customer experience. The future is not about discovering a fabled "buy button," but rather about using the neural cartography of desire to create more compelling brands, more user-friendly products, and deeper connections between companies and their clients' complex, fascinating minds. With the help of increasingly advanced neural lanterns, the voyage into the marketplace of the mind continues.

PART D: THE AI REVOLUTION IN NEUROMARKETING

Neuromarketing, which combines neuroscience and marketing, promised to give marketers direct access to the subconscious factors that affect how people buy things. But for a long time, its potential was limited because neural and physiological data are hard to understand, brain patterns are hard to read, and traditional neuroimaging costs a lot of money. This is where AI comes in. AI, especially machine learning (ML) and deep learning (DL), is making neuromarketing work better. At the same time, it is going through a big change that will make it smarter, more efficient, and better at predicting things. Here we discuss how adding AI to the neuromarketing value chain affects everything from collecting and analyzing data to making predictions and customizing content in real time. It also talks about the moral lines that AI crosses.

I. The Need for AI: Dealing with the Huge Amounts of Data in Neuromarketing

Traditional neuromarketing makes big, complex datasets with many types of data.

High-Dimensionality: EEG collects millions of data points from many channels every second. Over time, fMRI collects 3D brain volume data. Eye-tracking always keeps track of where your eyes are looking, where they are fixated and how wide your pupils are. Facial coding looks for micro-expressions one frame at a time. GSR and HRV give you a steady stream of physiological information.

Multimodal Complexity: To fully comprehend something, it is frequently necessary to integrate multiple data points, such as correlating an EEG attention spike with a specific gaze fixation and a subtle alteration in facial expression.

Non-Linear Relationships: The links between neural and physiological signals and complex cognitive and emotional states or behavioral outcomes, like wanting to buy something, aren't always clear or direct.

Individual Variability: Neural responses vary considerably among individuals, requiring sophisticated modeling to identify shared patterns while maintaining individual distinctiveness.

Human analysts can't handle this level of complexity and size on their own. AI really likes it, especially ML and DL algorithms. AI is great at finding small, non-linear patterns, correlations, and predictive signals in large, noisy datasets that people can't see or that traditional statistical methods can't find.

II. AI in the Neuromarketing Process: Key Links

AI algorithms, like Independent Component Analysis (ICA), work better when they are improved by machine learning and deep learning filters. They can better separate and remove noise from complex biological signals. For instance, they can eliminate blinking in eye-tracking, head movement in fMRI, and muscle artifacts in EEG (Jiang et al., 2019).

AI can easily find patterns in the raw data and able to create intelligible outputa. Convolutional neural networks (CNNs) can find important parts of raw EEG spectrograms or fMRI voxel patterns that are needed for the job (Craik et al., 2019).

Real-Time Quality Control: AI systems can watch data streams as they are being collected and detect if the signal quality is bad or if someone isn't paying attention.

Putting together and judging information from a lot of different sources:

AI's biggest benefit is probably that it can combine different types of data. AI models can learn joint representations from EEG, fMRI, eye-tracking, facial coding, GSR, and even self-report data all at once using techniques like multi-view learning, deep fusion networks, and tensor factorization (Ramkumar et al., 2022).

Artificial intelligence (AI) can find complex, hidden psychological constructs (like "cognitive load," "emotional engagement," "decision conflict," and "brand resonance") by looking for common patterns across different physiological and neural measures. This offers a more comprehensive and dependable representation than any singular metric (Hsu & Cheng, 2020).

Personalized Response Profiles: Machine learning algorithms can group people based on how their bodies and brains react differently. This can be used to identify different groups of customers or predict how likely someone is to respond to a certain marketing campaign (Telpaz et al., 2015).

AI changes the goal of neuromarketing data from finding patterns to figuring out what will happen in the real world. Support Vector Machines (SVM), Random Forests, Gradient Boosting, and Deep Neural Networks are all examples of supervised machine learning models that learn from neurometric data that has been labeled with behavioral outcomes. These results include the click-through rate, the increase in sales, the change in brand preference, the recall of ads, and the choice to buy.

AI models can predict a lot of important numbers, like:

Attention and Engagement: Will this ad get people to pay attention and keep it? (Tracking eye movements and EEG)

Emotional Valence and Arousal: Is the emotional response intense or subdued, and is it positive or negative? (Using fMRI, fEMG, and GSR to measure EEG asymmetry)

Memory Encoding: Can one remember this message later? (Using fMRI and EEG to study how the hippocampus works)

Perceived Value and Willingness to Pay: How much do you think the product is worth, and how much are you willing to pay? Combining EEG, choice data, and fMRI vmPFC (Karmarkar & Yoon, 2016)

Purchase Intent & Choice: How probable is it that this individual will acquire this brand or product? (Fusing various types of neurometric and behavioral data) (Knutson et al., 2007 - foundational, enhanced by AI analysis)

A company does not have to spend a lot of money on production and testing because AI can predict how changes to an ad (like changing the images, music, tempo, or text) will affect neurometric responses and behavior later on (Lim, 2018).

Using generative AI to make and improve content automatically:

AI-Driven Creative: Neuromarketing research shows that generative AI models like GANs (Generative Adversarial Networks) and LLMs (Large Language Models) can make marketing materials like visual concepts, video edits, landing page layouts, and different versions of ad copy (Cherkassky & Friedman, 2021).

Neurometric Feedback Loops: Neurometric AI models can make generative models better or change them by making predictions. For instance, an LLM could write ad headlines that are likely to get a lot of attention from EEG (P300) and strong facial EMG reactions.

You can use AI to make hundreds of different versions of an ad or webpage element and then use prediction models to guess how well they will work in terms of neurometrics and behavior. This makes the process of optimizing a lot faster.

Improving Experience and Sentiment Analysis:

NLP (Natural Language Processing) AI looks at text like reviews, social media posts, and polls, among other things. Neurometrics provides an additional layer of analysis. AI can tell the difference between real excitement and fake praise, or between polite language that hides anger that hasn't been resolved, by connecting spoken emotions to subconscious physiological arousal (GSR) or valence (facial coding) (Hernández-Méndez & Muñoz-Leiva, 2020).

Customer Journey Mapping: AI can create detailed maps of the customer experience through neurometric data from lab or in-situ studies (like wearables in a store), behavioral tracking (like clicks on a website and purchase history), and voice/sentiment analysis from call centers.

III. AI for Making Things Bigger and More Accessible: The Great Enabler

AI is making it easier to get complicated neuromarketing information:

Lowering Barriers to Entry: AI-powered data analysis using cheaper, consumer-grade wearables (such EEG headsets and webcam eye-tracking/facial coding) makes neuromarketing possible for smaller businesses and speeds up research (Solnais et al., 2013; AI could make this even better).

Faster Turnaround: AI analysis helps neuromarketing get closer to real-time decision support by speeding up the process of gathering data and getting useful information from it.

Larger Sample Sizes: AI makes it easier to work with and analyze data from bigger, more representative groups of people. This makes the results more statistically powerful and useful in a wider range of situations.

In-Context Testing: AI can help you look at complicated neurometric data that was collected in real life, like wearables used at home or mobile EEG used in stores. This makes the results more useful in real life.

IV. The Cutting Edge: AI's New Uses

Affective computing and emotion AI: More advanced AI models are getting better at figuring out complicated emotional states, not just valence or arousal, by looking at a mix of language, physiological indicators, vocal tones, and facial expressions. This enables a comprehensive assessment of emotional reactions to experiences and brands (Calvo & D'Mello, 2010).

Explainable AI (XAI) for Neuroscience: To maintain the integrity and validity of scientific research, it is crucial to comprehend the reasoning behind the predictions made by advanced AI models, particularly those employing deep learning methodologies. Researchers are employing XAI techniques such as SHAP and LIME (Samek et al., 2021) to identify the brain regions, physiological characteristics, or specific moments in a stimulus that most significantly influence an AI model's prediction of consumer outcomes.

Real-time personalization engines are AI systems that change marketing messages, offers, or product recommendations in real time based on user profiles, behavioral data, and real-time neurometric feedback (like from a wearable in a virtual reality store) (Kaptein & Parvinen, 2015).

Neurometric data is being used to teach AI models how to predict long-term outcomes like advocacy, brand loyalty, and resistance to bad news.

The theoretical boundary of neuromarketing has expanded to include *predictive AI*. Theories now integrate *Machine Learning (ML)* with EEG to classify consumer "affective attitudes" (future choices) with high accuracy, moving beyond mere observation to prediction (Al-Nafjan, A., et al.2022)

V. Moral and Ethical Issues

There are several moral and ethical dilemma surrounding usage of Neuromarketing. This is especially true when AI is used to analyze and model based on neurometric data.

Hyper-Persuasion & Manipulation: Can artificial intelligence (AI) detect subconscious triggers with unparalleled precision and utilize that data to deceive individuals into purchasing products they do not authentically wish for or that are harmful to their health? A greater number of individuals are apprehensive about the exploitation of emotional vulnerabilities and cognitive biases (Murphy et al., 2008; Ulman et al., 2015).

Neurometric data, encompassing physiological states, facial expressions, and cerebral activity, is highly confidential. AI's ability to guess things about people, like how they feel, how much work they have to do, what they like, and what medical problems they might have, is very worrying for privacy. Following strict rules like the CCPA/CPRA and GDPR isn't always easy (Mantelero, 2018).

Algorithmic Bias and Discrimination: AI models trained on non-representative data samples will perpetuate and potentially exacerbate biases in their predictions and outputs. This could lead to unfairly targeting or leaving out certain groups of people through discriminatory marketing (Crawford, 2021).

The XAI Imperative of Transparency and Explainability: It's hard to see how neural data affects predictions because complex AI models are like "black boxes." When people aren't honest, it's harder to test scientific theories, trust them, and find and fix biases. Not only is XAI desirable, it is also morally necessary.

Participants' Informed Consent: Are they truly aware of the extent to which AI can derive insights from their neurometric data? People need to know everything there is to know about what AI can do and what it might do before they can agree to use it.

Customer Autonomy and Well-Being: Is it dangerous for customers' autonomy and well-being to only use subconscious triggers to improve marketing? According to Plassmann et al. (2015), autonomy and good experiences should come before persuasion in ethical frameworks.

Lowering Ethical Risks:

Companies and industry groups like the NMSBA need strong, enforceable codes of ethics that clearly spell out how AI can be used and put a lot of emphasis on fairness, autonomy, beneficence, and non-maleficence.

Algorithmic auditing: Checking AI models on a regular basis and without bias to make sure they are fair, unbiased, and follow ethical rules.

Privacy by Design: AI-based neuromarketing platforms should have strong data anonymization, encryption, minimization, and user control features built in from the start.

Giving customers clear information and real control over how their neurometric data is collected and how AI changes their experience is what transparency and control mean. It should be normal to choose to join.

Value and Well-Being Are Important: Neuro-informed design aims to improve the user experience, create real value, and promote well-being, not just get people to do what you want.

VI. The Future: Responsible Innovation and Working Together

AI will play a significant role in the future of neuromarketing. Along with CRM, web analytics, and social listening, AI-powered neurometrics will be a common part of larger marketing analytics solutions. This will give marketers a complete picture of the "neuro-customer." Wearable sensors and ambient computing will make it easy to collect neurometric data in real-life situations all the time. The AI models that are trained on this data will then let us know what our clients are thinking and feeling all the time.

Generative AI Co-Creation: This is when marketers and AI work together to create content. People will give creative direction and make sure the work is moral, and AI will make changes that are better for the brain. Predictive methods will tell us how well the work will do. AI will enable hyper-personalization by analyzing historical behavior alongside current neurophysiological states and anticipated responses. This will let you change the content, offers, and interfaces in real time.

Ethics as a Competitive Advantage: Companies that are the first to use moral AI in neuromarketing will get more customers and make their business look better.

Adding AI to neuromarketing is a big change, not just an improvement. Artificial Intelligence (AI) turns neuro and physiological data from signals that are interesting but hard to understand into useful, broad insights that can help people make choices. It speeds things up, makes access more fair, and lets people personalize and improve things in ways that were never possible before.

But with this great power comes a lot of duty. The ability of advanced AI to understand and possibly control subconscious processes on a personal level raises important ethical questions that the industry needs to deal with head-on. The future of AI in neuromarketing hinges on achieving an optimal equilibrium between stringent regulations governing privacy, autonomy, and fairness, and leveraging AI's capabilities to create products, experiences, and value for consumers that are genuinely exceptional. It takes a commitment to honesty, strong morals, and constant self-evaluation. The goal should be to improve understanding between people, not to trick them. Neuromarketing that uses AI can help brands and customers connect in more meaningful, real, and human ways. The revolution is here, and its true worth will depend on how well we deal with it.

PART 5: REAL WORLD APPLICATION OF NEUROMARKETING

Case Study 1: Frito-Lay's New Packaging Design Background

PepsiCo owns Frito-Lay, a big snack food business. They wanted to get more women to buy their products. Studies found that women snacked less on salty meals (only 14% of the time) than on sweet foods or other options. The organization found that guilt about unhealthy snacking was a problem, especially for women. Frito-Lay used neuromarketing to find out how packaging affected people's feelings in order to fix this.

Using neuromarketing

Frito-Lay worked with NeuroFocus, a neuromarketing company, and Juniper Park, an advertising agency. They used electroencephalography (EEG) to see how different packaging designs affected brain activity. EEG entails the placement of electrodes on the scalp to capture electrical signals from the brain, thereby elucidating emotional and cognitive responses. The study concentrated on women, as prior research indicated that their anterior cingulate cortex, associated with decision-making and guilt, exhibited greater activity compared to men.

Ideas

The EEG data showed that traditional glossy packaging, which sometimes has pictures of chips on it, turned on brain areas linked to guilt, like the cingulate cortex. On the other hand, matte beige packaging featuring pictures of healthful foods (such whole grains) did not make people feel bad. Also, diary entries from female participants showed that guilt played a big role in their snacking decisions.

What Was Done

Frito-Lay used these ideas to change the packaging for items like Sun Chips and Baked Lay's. The new designs featured matte finishes and drew attention to healthful ingredients, which was different from the usual chip bag look. EEG testing was also used to improve ads so that they would resonate with the target demographic in a good way, with a focus on health-conscious messaging.

The revised packaging caused a big jump in sales. Some sources say that sales of potato chips went up, and sales of some items like Cheetos went up by 12% in comparable neuromarketing-driven campaigns. The plan also made women think better of the brand, making Frito-Lay's snacks seem like a guilt-free choice. In just six months, there were over 195 million favorable impressions, and more women went to the snack aisles, which led to record-breaking sales.

Case Study 2: Improving PayPal's ads

History

PayPal, an online payment service that was part of eBay during the research period, wanted to get more people to use it by improving its advertising strategy. Focus groups and other traditional marketing techniques often missed what consumers really wanted. PayPal used neuromarketing to figure out which messages would get customers to interact with their brand the most.

PayPal worked with NeuroFocus to do EEG-based investigations. Participants donned EEG caps to monitor brain activity as they were exposed to diverse advertising pitches. The study sought to identify the unique selling propositions (USPs) that elicited the most significant positive emotional and cognitive responses among frequent internet customers.

Insights

The EEG results indicated that commercials highlighting speed and convenience (e.g., "fast" and "easy") stimulated brain regions linked to positive emotions and reward processing more significantly than messages centered on safety and security. This was especially true for people who used it often, which suggests that convenience was a bigger reason for adoption than perceived safety.

What was done

PayPal changed its ads to focus on how quick and easy it is to use their platform. The focus of commercials and other advertising materials changed from security features to rapid transactions and easy-to-use interfaces.

Outcome: The new advertising campaign got more people to use PayPal's services and got more people to sign up for them. PayPal got more e-shoppers by making their messages match what people really want, which helped them become a stronger player in the online payments sector. The campaign's success showed how useful neuromarketing may be for finding out what makes people buy things.

Broader Implications and Ethical Considerations

These case studies illustrate neuromarketing's power to uncover subconscious consumer preferences, enabling companies to tailor products and marketing with precision. Frito-Lay's success in reducing guilt through packaging redesign and PayPal's focus on speed highlight how EEG can reveal insights that traditional methods miss. However, neuromarketing raises ethical questions about manipulating consumer behavior. Critics argue it may exploit subconscious vulnerabilities, though proponents view it as a tool to better meet consumer needs. Both Frito-Lay and PayPal demonstrate responsible use, focusing on enhancing user experience rather than deception.

Current Applications

Advertising and Campaign Testing. Neuromarketing measures neural responses to advertisement components through EEG analysis identifying attention and emotional activation, and eye-tracking quantifying visual hierarchy. This methodology demonstrates 20% higher predictive accuracy for advertisement success compared to traditional market research.

Packaging Design and Neuropackaging. Neurophysiological measurement optimizes package design elements including color, shape, and typography by identifying design variations that trigger approach behavior and purchase intention.

Pricing Strategy Optimization. Neuromarketing pricing research measures neural responses to different price points through EEG analysis, particularly N400 response measurement, identifying optimal pricing that maximizes revenue. Research demonstrates that identical products generate differential neural responses based on price signaling. Price point discrimination (e.g., $19.97 versus $20.00) produces measurable neural differentiation despite minimal absolute difference.

In-Store Experience and Retail Environment Design. Neuromarketing optimizes retail environments by measuring neurophysiological responses to store layout, product placement, lighting, and sensory elements. Eye-tracking identifies visual attention patterns, while GSR measurement and facial coding reveal emotional engagement. Research demonstrates that visual presentation, music selection, and product placement significantly influence emotional engagement and purchase behavior.

Product Development and Digital Experience. Neuromarketing guides product development by measuring neural responses to prototype features, validating market appeal prior to full-scale manufacturing. For digital design, eye-tracking reveals attention patterns while EEG analysis identifies cognitive overload during navigation. Enhanced A/B testing identifies design elements generating subconscious stress despite similar conversion rates.

REFERENCES

Appelhans, B. M., & Luecken, L. J. (2006). Heart rate variability as an index of regulated emotional responding. *Review of General Psychology, 10*(3), 229–240. DOI: 10.1037/1089-2680.10.3.229

Ariely, D., & Berns, G. S. (2010). Neuromarketing: The hope and hype of neuroimaging in business. *Nature Reviews. Neuroscience, 11*(4), 284–292. DOI: 10.1038/nrn2795 PMID: 20197790

Beatty, J. (1982). Task-evoked pupillary responses, processing load, and the structure of processing resources. *Psychological Bulletin, 91*(2), 276–292. DOI: 10.1037/0033-2909.91.2.276 PMID: 7071262

Boucsein, W. (2012). *Electrodermal Activity* (2nd ed.). Springer Science & Business Media. DOI: 10.1007/978-1-4614-1126-0

Calvo, R. A., & D'Mello, S. (2010). Affect Detection: An Interdisciplinary Review of Models, Methods, and Their Applications. *IEEE Transactions on Affective Computing, 1*(1), 18–37. DOI: 10.1109/T-AFFC.2010.1

Cherkassky, V., & Friedman, J. H. (2021). Guest Editorial: Special Issue on Learning From Consumer Data. [Context for AI in consumer data]. *IEEE Transactions on Knowledge and Data Engineering, 33*(1), 1–2. DOI: 10.1109/TKDE.2021.3051478 PMID: 36506788

Craik, A., He, Y., & Contreras-Vidal, J. L. (2019). Deep learning for electroencephalogram (EEG) classification tasks: A review. *Journal of Neural Engineering, 16*(3), 031001. DOI: 10.1088/1741-2552/ab0ab5 PMID: 30808014

Crawford, K. (2021). *Atlas of AI: Power, Politics, and the Planetary Costs of Artificial Intelligence*. Yale University Press. (Critical perspective on AI bias/societal impact)

Davidson, R. J. (1992). Emotion and affective style: Hemispheric substrates. *Psychological Science, 3*(1), 39–43. DOI: 10.1111/j.1467-9280.1992.tb00254.x

Dichter, E. (1960). *The Strategy of Desire*. Doubleday.

Dimberg, U., Thunberg, M., & Elmehed, K. (2000). Unconscious facial reactions to emotional facial expressions. *Psychological Science, 11*(1), 86–89. DOI: 10.1111/1467-9280.00221 PMID: 11228851

Djamasbi, S., Siegel, M., & Tullis, T. (2010). Generation Y, web design, and eye tracking. *International Journal of Human-Computer Studies, 68*(5), 307–323. https://doi.org/DOI: 10.1016/j.ijhcs.2009.12.006

Duchowski, A. T. (2007). *Eye Tracking Methodology: Theory and Practice* (2nd ed.). Springer.

Ekman, P., & Friesen, W. V. (1978). *Facial Action Coding System: A Technique for the Measurement of Facial Movement.* Consulting Psychologists Press.

Engel, J. F., Kollat, D. T., & Blackwell, R. D. (1968). *How people shop.* Holt, Rinehart, and Winston.

Fechner, G. T. (1860). *Elemente der psychophysik* (Vol. 2). Breitkopf u. Härtel.

Gupta, S., Kapoor, R., & Verma, S. (2025). Neuro-insights: A systematic review of neuromarketing perspectives across consumer buying stages. *International Journal of Consumer Studies, 49*(2). PMID: 40735149

Hernández-Méndez, J., & Muñoz-Leiva, F. (2020). What type of online advertising information do users pay more attention to? An eye-tracking and EEG study. *Electronic Commerce Research and Applications, 43*, 101002. DOI: 10.1016/j.elerap.2020.101002

Howard, J. A., & Sheth, J. N. (1969). *The notion of how people go about buying goods.* John Wiley & Sons.

Hsu, L., & Cheng, S. Y. (2020). Artificial Intelligence in Consumer Research. In *Handbook of Consumer Psychology* (pp. 1–31). Routledge., DOI: 10.4324/9781315169490-1

Jiang, X., Bian, G.-B., & Tian, Z. (2019). Removal of artifacts from EEG signals: A review. *Sensors (Basel), 19*(5), 987. DOI: 10.3390/s19050987 PMID: 30813520

Jin, J., He, Y., & Song, H. (2017). The impact of brand storytelling on brand authenticity: An fMRI study. *Frontiers in Psychology, 8*, 2220. DOI: 10.3389/fpsyg.2017.02220

Kaptein, M., & Parvinen, P. (2015). Advancing e-commerce personalization: Process framework and case study. *International Journal of Electronic Commerce, 19*(3), 7–33. DOI: 10.1080/10864415.2015.1000216

Karmarkar, U. R., & Plassmann, H. (2019). Consumer neuroscience: Past, present, and future. *Organizational Research Methods, 22*(1), 174–195. DOI: 10.1177/1094428117730598

Karmarkar, U. R., & Yoon, C. (2016). Consumer Neuroscience: Advances in Understanding Consumer Psychology. *Current Opinion in Psychology, 10*, 160–165. DOI: 10.1016/j.copsyc.2016.01.010

Knutson, B., Adams, C. M., Fong, G. W., & Hommer, D. (2001). Anticipation of increasing monetary reward selectively recruits nucleus accumbens. *The Journal of Neuroscience : The Official Journal of the Society for Neuroscience*, *21*(16), RC159. Advance online publication. DOI: 10.1523/JNEUROSCI.21-16-j0002.2001 PMID: 11459880

Knutson, B., Rick, S., Wimmer, G. E., Prelec, D., & Loewenstein, G. (2007). Neural predictors of purchases. *Neuron*, *53*(1), 147–156. DOI: 10.1016/j.neuron.2006.11.010 PMID: 17196537

Krishna, A. (Ed.). (2012). *Sensory Marketing: Research on the Sensuality of Products*. Routledge.

Kutas, M., & Hillyard, S. A. (1980). Reading senseless sentences: Brain potentials reflect semantic incongruity. *Science*, *207*(4427), 203–205. DOI: 10.1126/science.7350657 PMID: 7350657

LeDoux, J. E. (2000). Emotion circuits in the brain. *Annual Review of Neuroscience*, *23*(1), 155–184. DOI: 10.1146/annurev.neuro.23.1.155 PMID: 10845062

Lee, N., Broderick, A. J., & Chamberlain, L. (2007). What is 'neuromarketing'? A discussion and agenda for future research. *International Journal of Psychophysiology*, *63*(2), 199–204. DOI: 10.1016/j.ijpsycho.2006.03.007 PMID: 16769143

Lim, W. M. (2018). Dialectic antidotes to critics of the technologization of the marketing practice: The role of AI in neuromarketing. *Journal of Strategic Marketing*, *26*(4), 361–375. DOI: 10.1080/0965254X.2017.1344294

Logothetis, N. K. (2008). What we can do and what we cannot do with fMRI. *Nature*, *453*(7197), 869–878. DOI: 10.1038/nature06976 PMID: 18548064

Mantelero, A. (2018). AI and Big Data: A blueprint for a human rights, social and ethical impact assessment. *Computer Law & Security Review*, *34*(4), 754–772. DOI: 10.1016/j.clsr.2018.05.017

McClure, S. M., Li, J., Tomlin, D., Cypert, K. S., Montague, L. M., & Montague, P. R. (2004). Neural correlates of behavioral preference for culturally familiar drinks. *Neuron*, *44*(2), 379–387. DOI: 10.1016/j.neuron.2004.09.019 PMID: 15473974

Montague, P. R., Hyman, S. E., & Cohen, J. D. (2004). Computational roles for dopamine in behavioural control. *Nature*, *431*(7010), 760–767. DOI: 10.1038/nature03015 PMID: 15483596

Murphy, E. R., Illes, J., & Reiner, P. B. (2008). Neuroethics of neuromarketing. *Journal of Consumer Behaviour*, *7*(4-5), 293–302. DOI: 10.1002/cb.252

NMSBA. (2013). *Code of Ethics*. Neuromarketing Science & Business Association. https://nmsba.com/code-of-ethics

Pavlov, I. P. (1927). *Conditioned Reflexes: An Investigation of the Physiological Activity of the Cerebral Cortex*. Oxford University Press.

Plassmann, H., O'Doherty, J., Shiv, B., & Rangel, A. (2008). Marketing actions can modulate neural representations of experienced pleasantness. *Proceedings of the National Academy of Sciences of the United States of America*, *105*(3), 1050–1054. DOI: 10.1073/pnas.0706929105 PMID: 18195362

Plassmann, H., Ramsøy, T. Z., & Milosavljevic, M. (2012). Branding the brain: A critical review and outlook. *Journal of Consumer Psychology*, *22*(1), 18–36. DOI: 10.1016/j.jcps.2011.11.010

Plassmann, H., Venkatraman, V., Huettel, S., & Yoon, C. (2015). Consumer Neuroscience: Applications, Challenges, and Possible Solutions. *JMR, Journal of Marketing Research*, *52*(4), 427–435. DOI: 10.1509/jmr.14.0048

Polich, J. (2007). Updating P300: An integrative theory of P3a and P3b. *Clinical Neurophysiology*, *118*(10), 2128–2148. DOI: 10.1016/j.clinph.2007.04.019 PMID: 17573239

Ramkumar, P., Parkkonen, L., & Hyvärinen, A. (2022). Multimodal fusion in neuroscience: Challenges and opportunities. *NeuroImage*, *258*, 119354. DOI: 10.1016/j.neuroimage.2022.119354

Reimann, M., Zaichkowsky, J., Neuhaus, C., Bender, T., & Weber, B. (2010). Aesthetic package design: A behavioral, neural, and psychological investigation. *Journal of Consumer Psychology*, *20*(4), 431–441. DOI: 10.1016/j.jcps.2010.06.009

Rothschild, M. L., Hyun, Y. J., Reeves, B., Thorson, E., & Goldstein, R. (1988). Hemispherically lateralized EEG as a response to television commercials. *The Journal of Consumer Research*, *15*(2), 185–198. DOI: 10.1086/209156

Samek, W., Montavon, G., Vedaldi, A., Hansen, L. K., & Müller, K.-R. (Eds.). (2021). *Explainable AI: Interpreting, Explaining and Visualizing Deep Learning*. Springer., DOI: 10.1007/978-3-030-28954-6

Skinner, B. F. (1938). *The Behavior of Organisms: An Experimental Analysis*. Appleton-Century-Crofts.

Solnais, C., Andreu-Perez, J., Sánchez-Fernández, J., & Andréu-Abela, J. (2013). The contribution of neuroscience to consumer research: A conceptual framework and empirical review. [Democratization context]. *Journal of Economic Psychology*, *36*, 68–81. DOI: 10.1016/j.joep.2013.02.011

Spence, C., Puccinelli, N. M., Grewal, D., & Roggeveen, A. L. (2014). Store atmospherics: A multisensory perspective. *Psychology and Marketing*, *31*(7), 472–488. DOI: 10.1002/mar.20709

Telpaz, A., Webb, R., & Levy, D. J. (2015). Using EEG to predict consumers' future choices. [Early example of ML prediction]. *JMR, Journal of Marketing Research*, *52*(4), 511–529. DOI: 10.1509/jmr.13.0564

Ulman, Y. I., Cakar, T., & Yildiz, G. (2015). Ethical Issues in Neuromarketing: "I Consume, Therefore I am!". *Science and Engineering Ethics*, *21*(5), 1271–1284. DOI: 10.1007/s11948-014-9581-5 PMID: 25150848

Venkatraman, V., Dimoka, A., Pavlou, P. A., Vo, K., Hampton, W., Bollinger, B., Hershfield, H. E., Ishihara, M., & Winer, R. S. (2012). Predicting Advertising Success Beyond Traditional Measures: New Insights from Neurophysiological Methods and Market Response Modeling. *JMR, Journal of Marketing Research*, *49*(4), 436–452. DOI: 10.1509/jmr.13.0593

Yoon, C., Gutchess, A. H., Feinberg, F., & Polk, T. A. (2006). A functional magnetic resonance imaging study of neural dissociations between brand and person judgments. *The Journal of Consumer Research*, *33*(1), 31–40. DOI: 10.1086/504132

Zaltman, G. (1997). Rethinking Market Research: Putting People Back In. *JMR, Journal of Marketing Research*, *34*(4), 424–437. DOI: 10.1177/002224379703400402

Chapter 2
Role of Neuromarketing in Assessing Consumer Purchase Intention:
A Literature Review

Shireen Naaz
http://orcid.org/0009-0008-0507-0928
Jamia Milia Islamia, India

Rahela Farooqui
http://orcid.org/0000-0002-9483-5329
Jamia Milia Islamia, India

Surabhi Singh
http://orcid.org/0000-0002-8565-7348
IIMT College of Engineering, Greater Noida, India

ABSTRACT

Consumer purchase intentions significantly influence buying behavior and market dynamics. Exploring these intentions explicitly and through tools that delve into the subconscious is crucial. With the advent of neuromarketing, the neural responses to any marketing stimuli can be studied. This has benefitted all aspects, especially in understanding the factors directly impacting the purchase intention. This paper aims to analyze the role of neuroimaging tools in assessing or predicting consumer purchase intentions. It is qualitative research that explores these aspects through a literature survey. Research findings indicate that neuromarketing explores consumers' emotional engagement through various neuro tools. Additionally, neuromarketing assesses factors with a significant impact on purchasing behavior by recording sensory experiences and cognitive evaluations.

DOI: 10.4018/979-8-3373-1152-4.ch002

1. INTRODUCTION

Consumer purchasing behaviour has consistently been a vital area for marketers and scholars to investigate. Analysing consumers' purchasing patterns is crucial since it facilitates a more efficient and successful marketing strategy. Purchase conduct is consistently discovered by explicit procedures, supported by diverse theories that explain the behavioural patterns. The literature on consumer purchasing behaviour indicates that personal, psychological, and societal aspects affect purchasing decisions. Additionally, factors such as attitude, preference, brand image, information quality, user interface quality, and security perceptions (Park & Kim, 2003) Various factors affect consumer purchasing behaviour throughout different research domains. However, all these considerations are assessed via the conscious state, although the true authority of decision-making resides within the subconscious mind. Understanding and assessing the subconscious state can be accomplished by both invasive and non-invasive neuromarketing techniques that enhance the examination of neural brain activity. The brain responses to marketing stimuli elucidate the mechanisms by which purchase intentions are altered. Neuromarketing enables researchers to explore the brain and uncover critical insights that could influence purchasing behaviour. Numerous academics and scholars regard neuromarketing as an interdisciplinary domain encompassing marketing, psychology, and neuroscience.

Diverse theories of consumer purchasing behaviour emphasize distinct factors that affect consumer actions throughout a transaction. The theory of planned behaviour is being extensively utilized by academics, as it posits that increased consumer intent towards a specific behaviour result in the intended behaviour. Maslow's Hierarchy of Needs (1943) classifies human needs into five categories: physiological, safety, social, esteem, and self-actualization. Maslow highlights each need influences human behaviour differently; certain requirements are about survival, and others are associated with self-actualization. This hierarchical structure dictates that lower-level requests must be addressed prior to higher-priority needs(Rojas et al., 2023). Hawkin Stern's Impulse Buying (1962) emphasises that irrational purchasing motivations may be manifested through purchasers' rational decision-making processes. Impulsive purchases are frequently motivated by external stimuli and do not conform to essential leadership values (Stern, 1962). The stimulus-response model (1967) emphasizes the capacity of marketing to affect the customer decision-making process. The buyer's black box is examined in relation to a consumer's response to a stimulus (Kanagal, 2016). The black box theory of behaviourism elucidates the interplay between stimuli, consumer characteristics, decision-making processes, and consumer responses (Nax et al., 2016). Several ideas elucidate consumer purchasing behaviour, which can also exacerbate elements when applied in neuromarketing (Roy, 2022)

2. RESEARCH OBJECTIVE

Despite the rapid advancement of neuromarketing research, the scientific literature remains fragmented in its ability to integrate neuroscientific evidence with established consumer-behavior constructs. Most existing studies focus on isolated dimensions of consumer response—such as emotional arousal, attention, or brand perception—rather than examining how multiple psychological variables collectively shape consumer purchase intention at the subconscious level. Furthermore, although trust, pricing, and reward mechanisms are widely recognized in traditional marketing as dominant predictors of purchase intention, limited research has examined their neural correlates through neuroimaging and psychophysiological tools. This disconnect highlights a significant research gap: there is no consolidated synthesis that explains how neuromarketing techniques can assess consumer purchase intention by linking neural responses to key psychological determinants of buying behavior.

Addressing this gap, the present study aims to explore and analyze the concept of neuromarketing and further investigate the role of neuromarketing techniques in assessing consumer purchase intention. Specifically, this research examines the core factors identified in prior literature—trust, pricing, and reward mechanisms—that strongly influence the subconscious mind and can be evaluated through neuroimaging approaches. The research adopts a qualitative literature-based approach to understand how these factors impact neural decision-making processes. By analysing available empirical evidence, the study provides a comprehensive account of the current landscape of neuromarketing and its relevance to consumer purchase intention. The contribution of this research lies in identifying which consumer-behavior variables are most responsive to neuromarketing measurement and highlighting the growing importance of neuroscience-based insights in shaping marketing strategies and consumer engagement models.

3. LITERATURE REVIEW

3.1 Neuromarketing

The term "neuromarketing" was coined in 2002 by Dutch professor Ale Smidts, who defined it as "the study of the brain and how it processes activities about consumer context (purchase behavior—how and why they buy)." In the same year, the BrightHouse Institute for Thought Sciences was established in Atlanta, marking one of the earliest commercial applications of neuromarketing. Collaborating with Emory University, the institute used functional magnetic resonance imaging (fMRI) to observe patterns in brain activity that reveal how a person is processing and/or evaluating a product, object, or advertisement. A pivotal study in 2004 by Read Montague and colleagues at Baylor College of Medicine explored consumer preferences between Pepsi and Coca-Cola. Using fMRI, the study found that when participants were unaware of the brand (blind taste test), Pepsi was preferred, correlating with increased activity in the ventromedial prefrontal cortex, associated with reward processing. However, when brand information was disclosed, Coca-Cola was preferred, with heightened activity in the hippocampus and dorsolateral prefrontal cortex, regions linked to memory and higher-order cognitive processes. This phenomenon, known as the "Pepsi Paradox," illustrates how brand knowledge and emotional associations can override sensory experiences in consumer decision-making (*Pepsis - an Overview | ScienceDirect Topics*, n.d.). In 2006, Dr. Carl Marci co-founded Innerscope Research, a firm specializing in consumer neuroscience. The company employed tools like biometrics, eye tracking, and facial coding to measure unconscious emotional responses to media and marketing stimuli. In 2015, Nielsen acquired Innerscope Research, integrating it with its existing neuroscience division, NeuroFocus, to form Nielsen Consumer Neuroscience, with Dr. Marci serving as Chief Neuroscientist(*Nielsen Buys Neuromarketing Research Company Innerscope - NMSBA*, n.d.).

Academia has shown increasing interest in neuromarketing, with researchers exploring its applications and implications. Lee et al., 2007, determine neuromarketing as an application of neuroimaging techniques to sell products. After reviewing different aspects proposed by academicians Lim, 2018 comprehensively defines neuromarketing as an interdisciplinary branch that uses neuroscientific theories, concepts, and tools to understand instinctive human behavior. Kenning & Linzmajer (2011) explain neuromarketing as a neuroeconomics niche dealing with marketing-oriented problems through neuro-insights. According to Nemorin & Oscar H. Gandy (2017) neuromarketing is a branch of marketing that aims for a profound level of manipulation based on intuitive reflexes." Following the previous researchers, neuromarketing is a method that understands the factors influencing consumer purchasing decisions by analyzing the brain's neural reactions to different marketing stimuli. Nevertheless, it should be seen as a complement rather than a replacement for traditional research methods like qualitative and quantitative analysis.

Since neuromarketing integrates neuroscience with marketing strategies, its application in the marketing domain spreads to areas that were unexplored due to restricted invasion in the subconscious state. In the advertising industry, neuromarketing has enhanced its effectiveness by giving insight using EEG and eye tracking that identify which ads capture attention and elucidate the reason for emotional engagement. Honda UK utilised neuromarketing to explore the emotional reactions of potential buyers within their showrooms. By employing the LifeShirt—a wearable device that measures physiological indicators such as heart rate, respiration, and muscle activity—they gathered data on customers' emotional responses. The insights obtained from this study led to redesigned showroom layouts and staff retraining initiatives aimed at creating a more emotionally attuned and engaging sales environment (Nieves, n.d.). In a similar vein, Volkswagen incorporated neuromarketing techniques in the development of their "The Force" advertisement, which featured a child dressed as Darth Vader. This emotionally charged and nostalgic campaign was shown to enhance emotional engagement. Neuromarketing research indicates that emotionally resonant content in advertisements can significantly boost memory retention and brand recall, playing a key role in the ad's effectiveness in raising brand awareness and fostering positive consumer perception (Morin, 2011a) Additionally, neuroscientist Emily Falk employed functional MRI to design an anti-smoking campaign based on viewers' brain responses. Her findings demonstrated that heightened activity in the ventromedial prefrontal cortex predicted increased calls to quitlines, suggesting that neural activity can serve as a reliable predictor of an advertisement's potential to drive behavioral change (Falk et al., 2011)(Nieves, n.d.)

Neuromarketing provides a deeper, more accurate, and individualized understanding of consumer behavior by using theories and methods from neuroscience. It explores brain mechanisms related to brand effects, loyalty, and various marketing mixes and strategies, offering a scientific foundation for marketers and other stakeholders. Neuromarketing through neuroimaging tools that extract knowledge from the consumer's black box by spotting specific regions that activate during purchase decision-making. The packaging in many ways influences consumers' perceptions and choices. Through intensive study of neural responses, neuromarketing concludes that product packaging design elements effectively capture attention and drive purchase decisions. The different aspects of packaging, like color, educational or informative content, sustainability perception of packaging, aesthetic design, and visual graphic elements, are analyzed through neuromarketing. A study by Nugroho utilized electroencephalography (EEG) to assess how packaging color and shape affect consumer emotions. Findings indicated that bright, contrasting colors and ergonomic shapes elicited positive emotional responses, thereby influencing purchasing decisions (Nugroho, 2025). Research published by (Juárez-Varón et al., 2020) in *Social Sciences,* applied eye-tracking and machine learning to predict which areas of educational toy packaging attract consumer attention. The study concluded that graphic details significantly influence consumer focus, suggesting that strategic design can enhance product appeal. A neuromarketing study examined how digitally displayed skincare product packaging affects consumer emotions. Using eye-tracking and EEG, the research found that elements like texture and eco-labels significantly impact visual attention and emotional responses, thereby influencing purchase intentions (Chaerani & Sari, 2024). Unravel Research conducted an Implicit Association Test (IAT) to compare consumer perceptions of cardboard versus plastic packaging for sweet peppers. Results showed that cardboard packaging was perceived as more sustainable, influencing consumer preferences (*Cases Overview - Unravel Neuromarketing Research*, n.d.) A study published by (Reimann et al., 2010a) in the *Journal of Consumer Psychology,* researchers have used functional magnetic resonance imaging (fMRI) to investigate how aesthetic package designs affect neural activity. The research revealed that aesthetically pleasing packages activated brain regions associated with reward, such as the nucleus accumbens and ventromedial prefrontal cortex, influencing consumer choices Application of neuromarketing is evenly spread on the commercial, i.e., retail marketing, as well as non-commercial, i.e., social media marketing (Michael et al., 2019). It can also be applied in areas dealing with product design, price strategy, marketing communication, brand creation and management, and consumer protection.

Figure 1. Common neuroscientific methods for neuromarketing (Lim, 2018)

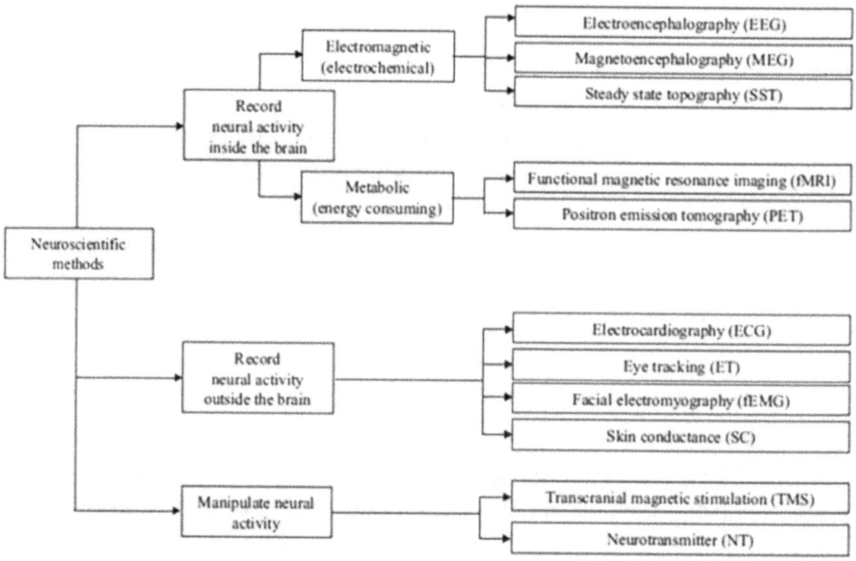

Neuromarketing investigates emotions, cognition, the subconscious, and conscious knowledge of the brain to develop and construct marketing theories and strategies that positively influence the commercial marketing role. These elements are classified as factors of neuromarketing. Each factor of neuromarketing can be studied with a different neuro-tool. Electroencephalography, magnetoencephalography, steady-state topography, functional magnetic resonance imaging, and positron emission tomography are some of the techniques that can determine the neuroactivity inside the brain, but out of all these, FMRI and EEG are the most commonly used techniques in neuromarketing. For the assessment of neural activity outside the brain, Electrocardiography, Eye tracking, Facial electromyography, and Galvanic skin conductance are the tools supporting neuromarketing practice (Lim, 2018). The literature on neuromarketing studies heavily uses eye tracking as a measure to study consumer response to marketing stimuli, followed by EEG and fMRI. Each neuromarketing tool introspects different aspects of consumer behavior. For instance, emotional engagement, cognitive resonance, and reward mechanisms can be studied using EEG and FMRI, while attention, attraction, and concentration fixation can be measured through eye tracking.

Table 1. Key neuromarketing factors with descriptions, tools, and references

Factor	Description	Technology/Tool	References
Attention	Captures consumer focus and selective processing of stimuli	EEG, Eye-tracking	(Plassmann et al., 2012)
Emotional Engagement	Measures intensity and type of emotional reaction to stimuli	fMRI, EEG, Facial coding, GSR	(Nieves, n.d.)(Yoon et al., 2012) (Vecchiato et al., 2011)
Memory Retention	Assesses ability to remember brands, products, or messages	fMRI, EEG	(Plassmann et al., 2012) (Khushaba et al., 2013)
Decision-Making/ Valuation	Analyzes perceived value and neural decision-making processes	fMRI	(Karmarkar et al., 2015) (Plassmann et al., 2008)
Motivation	Understands the drivers of consumer behavior and choice	fMRI, EEG	(Venkatraman et al., 2015) (Knutson et al., 2007)
Visual Attention & Layout	Tracks gaze patterns, visual hierarchy, and effectiveness of ad placement	Eye-tracking	(Wedel & Pieters, 2008b) (Reimann et al., 2010b)
Emotional Valence & Arousal	Detects the positive/negative nature and strength of emotions	GSR, EEG, Heart rate, Facial coding	(Pozharliev et al., 2015)
Brand Recall & Recognition	Measures post-exposure brand awareness and identification	EEG, Implicit tests	(Khushaba et al., 2012) (Plassmann et al., 2012)
Cognitive Load	Identifies mental effort involved in understanding ads or messages	EEG (frontal theta), Eye-tracking	(Boere et al., 2024)
Behavioral Prediction	Uses neural activity to forecast real-world consumer actions	fMRI, EEG	(Falk et al., 2011 Genevsky & Knutson, 2015

continued on following page

Table 1. Continued

Factor	Description	Technology/Tool	References
Nostalgia & Memory Cues	Leverages emotionally charged past experiences to build a connection	EEG, Facial EMG	(Morris et al., 2002) (Barrett et al., 2007)
Reward Processing	Evaluate how consumers anticipate or receive pleasure from purchases	fMRI (nucleus accumbens activation)	(Knutson et al., 2007) (Karmarkar et al., 2015)

For a detailed review of neuromarketing, these research papers can always be looked into (Cordeiro et al., 2024a) (Ghosh & Kumar, 2024) (Cordeiro et al., 2024b) (Ayelen Paladino et al., 2024) (Iloka & Onyeke, 2020) (A. Alsharif et al., 2005; A. H. Alsharif et al., 2021; "Consumer Behaviour Through Neuromarketing Approach," 2021; *View of Neuromarketing: Marketing Research in the New Millennium*, n.d.; Fortunato et al., 2014; Fugate, 2007; Morin, 2011b; Stanton et al., 2017)(Wilson et al., 2008)

3.2 Purchase Intention

Purchase intention is an intrinsic part of consumer purchase behavior that initiates the consumer's desire for a purchase. As determined by the literature, a purchase intention to buy is often based on a time frame that ranges between 6 months to 12 months. Various laureates have defined consumer purchase intention in different dimensions. (*Kotler, P., & Keller, K. L. (2016). Marketing Management (14th Edition). Shanghai Shanghai People's Publishing House. - References - Scientific Research Publishing*, n.d.) describes consumer purchase intention as the behavior where a consumer desires to buy a product based on their usage experience and attraction to the product. Saad et al., 2012 stated that "Purchase intention is a kind of decision-making that studies the reason to buy a particular brand by the consumer." (Pandey & Srivastava, 2016) in their study analyzed that purchase intention is seen as a basis for consumers in making real-scenario purchases. Various other researchers, through empirical study, explored that purchase intention has a positive and significant influence on online Purchase Behavior. (Cahyanaputra et al., 2022)

From the available literature on factors leading to changes in consumer purchase intention, trust, pricing, and reward mechanisms emerge as the most significant influences. These factors have also been analyzed through neuromarketing practices. The subconscious mind cannot be fully understood while in a conscious state; instead, it can only be assessed through subconscious insights and responses, which can be evaluated using neuromarketing tools and techniques like EEG, fMRI, ET, etc. The reasons behind the behavioural responses can be explored through experimental analysis. This research was conducted through a literature survey of factors influencing consumer purchase intention and their neural responses through neuromarketing tools. It evaluates how neuromarketing approaches the concept of trust, pricing, and reward mechanisms, and how these influences affect consumer purchase intention.

Table 2. Key variables influencing consumer purchase intention with supporting references

Variable	Description	Key References
Trust	Consumer confidence in the reliability and integrity of a seller or platform.	(Ba & Pavlou, 2002; Gefen, D., Karahanna, E. and Straub, D.W. (2003) Kim et al., 2008)
Pricing	The perceived fairness, transparency, and competitiveness of product prices.	(Xia et al., 2004) (Grewal et al., 2017)
Reward Mechanism	Incentives such as loyalty programs or discounts that stimulate purchase.	(Mimouni-Chaabane & Volle, 2010) (Dorotic et al., 2014)

3.2.1 Trust

Trust is a key factor in shaping consumer purchase intentions across various contexts, particularly in online shopping. It serves as a mediator in increasing the likelihood of purchases, especially in the following sectors: cosmetics and sustainable products. Studies on Generation Z consumers indicate that trust significantly influences purchase intention, mediating the effects of social influence and information quality on buying behavior (Purwianti & Yulianto, n.d.). Trust can also develop through consumers' perceived value when evaluating a product, making value perception a critical factor in building customer trust and influencing their intention to buy. Trust is closely tied to the confidence consumers put in a product; when a product meets its promises, it positively impacts purchase intention. Research further suggests that trust is related to repurchase intention through relationship absorption, whereas distrust is not correlated to re-purchase intentions. In the cosmetics industry, customer trust directly enhances the intention to continue shopping online, driving repeat purchases even in the presence of perceived risks (Khan et al., 2024). Social recommendations mediate the relationship between perceived risk and purchase intention.

Trust is a crucial factor in neuromarketing, shaping consumer behaviour and brand perception. Neuromarketing uses neuroscience to explore how trust is established and assessed, particularly through emotional engagement and personalized content. The use of neural and psychological processes gives insight into how consumers form trust towards products, brands, and advertisements. The neuro tools used in studying trust aspects are: EEG, FMRI, Eye Tracking, and Galvanic skin response. Through EEG, brain responses to trust-related stimuli are escalated, and immediate emotional responses like excitement, calmness, or anxiety are tracked when encountered with a trustworthy brand, product, or advertisement (Ohme et al., 2009). FMRI highlights blood flow in areas of the ventromedial prefrontal cortex, amygdala, and striatum, which are responsible for activation during trust-related tasks (Javor et al., 2013). Eye tracking allows assessing the attention consumers pay when they come across the logo, certificate, or other testimonials of trusted brands and products. It studies consumers' perceptions and responses to trust signals (Wedel & Pieters, 2008a). The hormone analysis is measured differently, mostly in the form of oxytocin. Oxytocin has a major role in social bonding and trust. Marketers measure the oxytocin level pre- and post-exposure to marketing stimuli, analysing the intensity or degree of shift in trust and cooperative behaviour after the encounter (Kosfeld et al., 2005). Scientific research investigating brain responses to trust-related stimuli has consistently shown that specific brain regions are activated when individuals process trust cues. These studies reveal that trust is primarily associated with activity in areas involved in social cognition, emotional evaluation, and reward processing. (Credibility Dimensions in Marketing Communication-A Generalized Solution, n.d.) found that trust cues activate the insula and anterior cingulate cortex (ACC), regions linked to emotional evaluation and risk management. This neural activity suggests that seeing others trust a brand reduces perceived risk and increases one's trust. Similarly, (Delgado et al., 2005)) found that the caudate nucleus becomes more active when individuals expect reciprocation in trust scenarios, highlighting the reward anticipation component of trust. The common active regions in response to trust-related stimuli: the medial prefrontal cortex, ventromedial prefrontal cortex, anterior cingulate cortex, caudate nucleus, and amygdala.

Table 3. Highlighting different neuro tools that study the dynamic aspect of trust

Tools	Measures	Application in trust studies
Fmri (Functional Magnetic Resonance Imaging)	Brain activity and regions	Identifies brain areas (e.g., prefrontal cortex, amygdala) activated when participants perceive trust or betrayal.
EEG Electroencephalography)	Electrical activity in the brain	Measures real-time emotional responses to trusted vs. non-trusted brands or spokespersons
Eye-tracking	Visual attention	Examines attention to trust cues (e.g., security badges, customer reviews) in websites or ads
GSR (Galvanic Skin Response)	Emotional arousal	Detects emotional intensity when exposed to trustworthy/untrustworthy stimuli.
Facial Coding	Facial expression	Captures micro-expressions linked to emotions such as doubt, trust, or comfort.

The well-known Pepsi paradox offers rich insights into how brand trust and identity influence consumer preferences at the neurological level. In a notable fMRI study, participants underwent blind taste tests while their brain activity was monitored. The results revealed that even when participants could not consciously identify the brand, familiar brand trust influenced their preferences. This study demonstrated that brand identity can override sensory perception, with trusted brands activating brain areas associated with positive valuation (Van Doorn & Miloyan, 2018). A similar study by (Reimann et al., 2010a) explores how consumers neurologically respond to branded versus non-branded packaging using fMRI. The study found that trusted brands activated reward-related brain regions, particularly the ventromedial prefrontal cortex (vmPFC), even when the physical product remained identical. This indicates that brand trust can alter perception and influence neural reward processing, reinforcing the emotional and psychological value of branding.

(Vecchiato et al., 2011) investigated consumer responses to advertisements featuring celebrity endorsers versus unknown influencers using EEG recordings. It was observed that authentic, emotionally congruent influencers elicit stronger left-frontal EEG activation, which is associated with approach motivation and trust. This suggests that relatability and emotional alignment with endorsers can significantly enhance trustworthiness in advertising. Another research study studied a similar subject area, indicating that effective advertising fosters trust by appealing to emotions and crafting narratives that resonate with consumers on a personal level (Satpathy & Mund, 2022). On a biochemical level, oxytocin—a hormone associated with bonding—plays a crucial role in promoting trust, cooperation, and social connection (Kosfeld et al., 2005).

In another study, (Djamasbi et al., 2010) used eye-tracking technology to evaluate how users interacted with different website designs. Elements such as security logos, testimonials, and professional layouts attracted longer visual fixations and were associated with higher perceived trust and more positive emotional responses. This finding suggests that visual trust cues are not only measurable but also scientifically optimized to enhance user experience and brand credibility. Neuromarketing studies using fMRI have revealed distinct neural pathways involved in evaluating trust, with interpersonal trust activating brain regions more strongly than brand trust. For example, (Javor et al., 2018) found that different neural circuits are engaged when assessing the trustworthiness of faces compared to brands. Additionally, neuromarketing emphasizes the value of empathy-driven strategies and personalized recommendations, particularly in digital environments, to build consumer trust (Millagala & Gunasinghe, 2024) Social proof—such as user reviews, ratings, and testimonials—also plays a significant role.

Overall, trust is processed in neural regions tied to social cognition and value assessment, including the mPFC, amygdala, and caudate nucleus. These findings underscore that trust is not just a rational judgment but a deeply emotional and neurologically embedded process, shaped by storytelling, social signals, and perceived relational value. Collectively, these studies show that trust—whether through brand identity, design elements, influencer authenticity, or packaging—has a measurable and powerful impact on consumer behavior. It not only shapes emotional engagement but also activates neural mechanisms linked to reward, attention, and decision-making, making trust a critical factor in effective marketing strategy

Table 4. Highlights trust insights from relevant researches

Title	Author	Insight
Conceptual and Exploratory Approach to the Role of Trust for an Efficient Publicity: A Neuromarketing Perspective	(Tinoco-Egas et al., 2019)	Trust is built through emotional connections in advertising, which are measured using neuromarketing techniques that evaluate attention and empathy. These insights help shape consumer behavior and improve the effectiveness of advertising campaigns.
What Does the Brain Tell Us About Trust and Distrust? Evidence from a Functional Neuroimaging Study	(Angelika Dimoka :: SSRN, n.d.)	The study using functional neuroimaging demonstrates that trust and distrust activate different regions of the brain, indicating distinct neurological processes that impact economic outcomes in IT-enabled transactions.
Neuromarketing as a Digital Marketing Strategy to Unravel the Evolution of Marketing Communication	(Millagala & Gunasinghe, 1 C.E.)	Neuromarketing shows that personalized content builds consumer trust by engaging subconscious responses, and boosting emotional connection and loyalty through customized marketing strategies.
The neural correlates of trustworthiness evaluations of faces and brands: Implications for behavioral and consumer neuroscience.	(Javor et al., 2018)	Neuromarketing studies trust by analyzing brain activation patterns during assessments of trustworthiness, uncovering distinct neural correlates for interpersonal trust compared to brand trust, and emphasizing the different mechanisms involved in their processing
The Neuroeconomics of Trust	(Zak, 2005)	The paper explores how oxytocin impacts trustworthiness and social behavior, offering insights relevant to neuromarketing by shedding light on the emotional responses that shape consumer trust and decision-making.

3.2.2 Pricing

Pricing refers to the monetary value assigned to a product or service (Nykiel, 2007). From the customer's perspective, price is understood as "what they must sacrifice to acquire the product or service. Pricing is the most significant variable influencing purchase intention. For instance, a study on online shopping found that price substantially impacts consumer buying interest (Ummah & Oetarjo, 2024). Similarly, concerning physical retail environments, price positively affects purchase decisions, although its direct influence on purchase intentions may vary (Jaya & Heryjanto, 2023). In the food and beverage sector, the importance of price is further emphasized, as it significantly affects both purchase intention and decisions (Halyana & Bangsawan, 2023). Additionally, the perception of price as "good" has a notable effect on purchase intention in online gaming contexts. Overall, these findings highlight the complex role of price in shaping consumer behaviour, particularly regarding purchase intentions and decision-making processes (Moon et al., 2008)

Neuromarketing enables researchers to explore brain activity in response to various stimuli, particularly in pricing. By examining how consumers perceive and react to different pricing strategies, valuable insights can be gained about their purchasing behavior and decision-making processes. Numerous neuromarketing experiments have shown that price perception significantly impacts customer satisfaction and consumption patterns. This is especially evident in the tourism and hospitality sectors, where effective pricing strategies play a crucial role in generating revenue (Boz et al., 2017). The price evaluation in the brain occurs at the prefrontal cortex, which is measured through EEG and FMRI, and the customer's reaction to pricing stimuli is gauged. EEG studies electrical activity, offering emotional insight into consumer response to pricing. It encapsulates immediate reactions like surprise, satisfaction, and stress. While FMRI records changes in blood flow in response to price stimuli, highlighting which brain region is highly active, and how consumers perceive value and react to price. Eye tracking explores visual attention to the price tag or the placement of the price. This technique allows for assessing the time consumers spend on viewing the price of the commodity and anticipating its role in decision-making. A literature analysis of empirical studies on neuromarketing assessing price (Dapkevičius & Melnikas, 2009) revealed that price and quality are important factors for customer satisfaction, which leads to marketing managers' decision complexity. These techniques provide insights that traditional marketing methods may overlook, enhancing pricing strategies.

(Plassmann et al., 2008) conducted a study that found that an increase in the price (psychological) of wine enhances the perceived pleasantness of its flavour (physiological), as well as increases "blood-oxygen-level-dependent activity in the medial orbitofrontal cortex," a brain region associated with encoding experienced pleasantness during sensory experiences. This study provides evidence that marketing actions can "modulate neural correlates of experienced pleasantness and the mechanisms through which this effect operates". Further, the researcher highlights that, while substantial behavioural evidence shows that various marketing actions can influence individuals' experienced pleasantness, the neural basis of this influence had not been demonstrated before. Contrary to the standard economic perspective, experienced pleasantness is not solely determined by the intrinsic properties of products but is also influenced by factors such as the price at which they are sold. Knutson et al 2007 studied how the brain responds to product prices and predicts purchase decisions by conducting an fMRI scan during simulated shopping. On experimenting with this, he analysed that higher prices activated the insula, associated with pain, leading to purchase rejection. Further, it was evaluated that anticipated rewards activated the nucleus accumbens, associated with pleasure and motivation to buy. (Plassmann et al., 2012) in his research titled "Branding the Brain," he reviews neuromarketing techniques, at the same time highlighting how price, brand, and product value are encoded in the brain. He concludes from the research that pricing is deeply connected to brain regions processing value, trust, and decision conflict. Reflecting on his research, why premium brands charge more without inducing price pain. (Ariely & Berns, 2010) gives an overview of brain imaging research related to pricing, brand perception, and consumer behaviour. The researcher finds that price not only reflects cost but also modulates expectations and subjective value. He further emphasizes that expectation, branding, and price framing change the neural processing of value and satisfaction.(García et al., 2024)

Table 5. Highlighting different pricing techniques assessment by different neuro-tools

Aspect of Pricing	Neuromarketing Insight	Tools Used	Implications for Marketers
Price Pain / Price Aversion	High prices activate the insula, associated with pain and loss	fMRI	Excessive pricing may trigger a loss-related response
Reward vs Cost Evaluation	Nucleus accumbens activity increases with perceived value or reward	fMRI	Aligning price with perceived benefit reduces resistance
Perceived Value	Consumers justify higher prices if emotional or experiential value is high	EEG, fMRI	Premium pricing works if value is emotionally reinforced
Charm Pricing (e.g., $4.99)	Odd pricing creates cognitive fluency, perceived as a better deal	EEG, Eye-tracking	Subconscious bias toward prices ending in .99 or .95
Discount Framing	"30% off" vs. "Save $30" activates different emotional responses	EEG, fMRI	Emotional wording in discounts improves responsiveness
Brand Influence on Price Perception	Trusted or luxury brands reduce activity in the insula (less "price pain")	fMRI	Strong brand equity buffers against negative price perception
Anchoring Effect	Initial high prices influence later price judgments due to relative value framing	EEG, Eye-tracking	Initial anchor pricing can shift what seems "reasonable."
Willingness to Pay	Can be predicted by activity in the ventromedial prefrontal cortex (vmPFC)	fMRI	Neural markers help forecast pricing strategies and thresholds

3.2.3 Reward Mechanisms

A reward mechanism is a structured approach designed to incentivize specific behaviours or actions within systems, such as games, energy management, and decentralized networks. It has a vital role in improving engagement, performance, and collaboration among participants (Saad et al., 2012).

Reward mechanisms play a crucial role in influencing consumer purchase intentions by offering tangible incentives that increase the perceived value of transactions. Reward codes, acting as specific identifiers that consumers can use to obtain rewards, directly impact their intention to purchase by providing a clear benefit for engaging in transactions. These mechanisms operate through various dynamics, such as monetary incentives, emotional satisfaction, and the anticipation of future rewards. Examples include reward codes, monetary incentives, reward accounts, proprietary value, equity awards, incentive structures, loyalty programs, personalized rewards, incentivization schemes, team-based rewards, and the distinction between recognition and rewards, as well as fostering psychological ownership. From a neurobiological perspective, the reward experience is regulated by dopaminergic systems that encompass the ventral striatum, which includes the ventral tegmental area (VTA), nucleus accumbens, and amygdala (Berridge & Robinson, 1998). (Uzbay, 2020) highlights how this system magnifies major shopping addictions. The reward system, responsible for generating feelings of pleasure and contributing to positive emotions, is also activated during the consumption of certain drugs, particularly cocaine, leading to addiction. As a result, some individuals can develop addictive behaviours towards specific brands, flavors, and products. (Touhami et al., 2011; Uzbay, 2020)

Table 6. Neuromarketing findings on reward mechanism

Insight	Evidence	Implication
Anticipation of rewards is more powerful than the reward itself	EEG shows heightened activity in anticipatory phases (left-frontal lobe)	Use countdowns, "unlock next level," teaser emails
Unexpected rewards trigger greater emotional engagement	fMRI reveals higher ventral striatum activity when rewards are surprise-based	Use randomized rewards or surprise perks
The perceived fairness of a reward influences trust and loyalty	Insula activation occurs if a reward seems manipulative or unequal	Make reward rules transparent and equitable
Reward framing affects perception	"Get $10 back" triggers more reward activation than "Save $10."	Use gain framed messages to maximize impact
Immediate rewards are more motivating than delayed ones	EEG studies show a stronger approach motivation to instant gratification	Offer instant points, benefits, or bonuses to drive action

(Balconi et al., 2014) found that reward cues can support goal-directed actions and improve cognitive regulation. Their ERP findings revealed that reward signals influence neural activity, especially in areas involved in feedback evaluation and error detection. This suggests that reward mechanisms activate brain systems responsible for self-regulation and metacognitive control.

Zhang's research on live commerce reveals that the reward mechanism, combined with emotional identity, significantly influences consumers' willingness to purchase food products during live broadcasts (Zhang et al., 2024). Similarly, Farrar and Papies found that highlighting rewarding consumption experiences can enhance intentions to choose healthier products (Farrar & Papies, 2024). Furthermore, Zhang et al. demonstrated that perceived uncertainty in blind box purchases can positively affect impulsive buying intentions, with curiosity serving as a mediator.

3.3 Emotional Engagement

The literature clearly demonstrates that all three variables—trust, pricing, and reward mechanisms—positively influence consumer purchase intention by fostering emotional engagement. Emotional engagement refers to the emotional connection consumers develop with a brand or product. In neuromarketing, this concept is central, as emotional responses often occur before logical reasoning and play a vital role in guiding consumer behaviour. Emotionally engaging experiences also enhance long-term memory encoding; EEG and fMRI research shows that emotionally impactful stimuli—such as heartwarming or joyful advertisements—are more likely to be remembered, thereby strengthening brand recall and recognition. Marketing strategies that evoke emotional responses through storytelling, visuals, or music tend to be more effective, with emotionally rich advertisements eliciting stronger neural activity and proving more persuasive than those relying solely on factual content.

Table 7. Highlights neuro tools measuring purchase intentions

Tool	What it Measures	Link to Purchase Intention
EEG	Real-time emotional engagement, attention, and cognitive load	Predicts emotional resonance and likelihood to act
fMRI	Deep brain activity related to valuation and trust	Identifies brain regions predicting buying behavior
GSR	Skin conductance changes indicating arousal	Measures excitement or stress linked to purchase motivation
Eye-Tracking	Visual attention and emotional fixation	Shows what drives emotional impact and recall
Facial Coding	Emotional expressions and reactions	Detects non-verbal emotional response to stimuli

Neuromarketing research indicates that emotional reactions often precede conscious thought during decision-making. Activation of the limbic system—particularly the amygdala—occurs when consumers become emotionally engaged, subsequently influencing the prefrontal cortex, which governs rational decision-making (Cordeiro et al., 2024c). This suggests that brands capable of eliciting emotional responses through elements like storytelling, visuals, music, or immersive experiences can increase purchase likelihood even before consumers consciously evaluate the product. EEG and fMRI studies have demonstrated that heightened emotional engagement (such as joy, surprise, or empathy) enhances memory encoding. Additionally, advertisements or product displays that trigger strong emotional responses show increased activation in the ventromedial prefrontal cortex (vmPFC), a region associated with valuation and purchase intent. An fMRI study by Yoon et al. (2006) found that exposure to positive emotional stimuli resulted in elevated activity in both the vmPFC and the nucleus accumbens—areas linked to greater willingness to pay and stronger brand preference

Table 8. Highlights of studies gauging emotional engagement and consumer purchase intention

Author, Year, Title	Insight
Tomer, R., et, al **(2015)** **Emotional engagement detector.** **(*Emotional Engagement Detector*, 2015)**	The system for tracking and analyzing emotional engagement during shopping consists of an image processing module that retrieves image data from electronic storage, which includes a person in a retail setting. This module detects the individual within the image data. Additionally, an emotion detection module identifies the emotion expressed by the person, while an object detection module identifies the object the person is interacting with. Finally, a marketing module selects a sales action based on the identified emotion and object, and executes the chosen sales action.
Vejandla, V. **(2022)** **Neuromarketing and emotions impact on FMCG marketing.** **(Vejandla & Raju, 2022)**	A strong level of emotional engagement, along with heightened activation of the encoding process, can predict purchase intention. This intention arises from the effectiveness of the marketing stimulus, which is persuasive enough to foster this intent. The level of emotional engagement is influenced by the degree of emotional excitement experienced.
Martina, S. **(2022)** **ADV at the Time of COVID-19 Brain Effect between Emotional Engagement and Purchase Intention.** **(Sansone & Balconi, 2022)**	The findings indicate tapping into the negative emotional impact of COVID-19 may not change explicit purchase intentions, but it could enhance emotional engagement, positively influencing the brand's implicit evaluation. This study explores whether emotional communication related to COVID-19 affects consumers' emotional responses along with their approach/avoidance motivations toward the brand, measured through brain hemodynamic changes, as well as their purchase intentions. The hemodynamic patterns suggest that COVID-19-related advertisements may encourage deeper emotional processing, shifting consumer focus from the semantic meaning to the emotional aspects, potentially leading to a more favourable evaluation of the brand.

4. CONCLUSION

Neuromarketing has significantly impacted consumer purchase behavior by influencing the brain's processing for more effective and ethical marketing campaigns. This approach has the potential to delve deeper and resonate with consumers. Consumer decision-making is better studied through neuromarketing because of its tools and psychological measures that open the window to measure behavioral patterns and preferences in consumers' brains (Yudhi Prasetya Mada, 2024). Out of numerous reasons for applying brain imaging technologies to marketing, (Lee et al., 2007) highlights that marketing academia, neuroscience, and cognitive psychology are intimidating subjects, and most academicians see them as unattainable, but surely with time, they will be used more aggressively. Through extensive studies and experiments using neuroimaging tools, Neuromarketing has assessed that trust, pricing, and reward mechanisms significantly influence CPI by enhancing perceived value and emotional engagement.

The trust variable significantly affects consumer purchase intention, contributing to positive brand resonance, loyalty, repeat purchases, customer satisfaction, and future recommendations. Trust stimulus can be evaluated from multi-dimensional elements such as brand identity, visual trust signals, authentic endorsements, and familiar packaging, since these elements activate specific brain regions involved in reward processing, emotional evaluation, and decision-making. Tools such as EEG, fMRI, eye tracking, and hormone analysis—like oxytocin measurement—are among the neuro tools used to evaluate neural processing and brain mapping in understanding trust and interventions related to consumer purchase intention. The insights from this research highlight the importance for marketers to go beyond product features and focus on designing emotionally resonant, trust-centric experiences. Whether through storytelling, strategic design, or personalized interactions, brands that can consistently evoke trust are better positioned to achieve greater consumer loyalty, stronger brand recall, and higher conversion rates

The Pepsi Paradox exemplifies the powerful influence of subconscious factors like brand trust and perceived value on consumer decision-making, despite objective product qualities such as taste. This case underscores the unique strength of neuromarketing in uncovering hidden cognitive and emotional processes that traditional methods often overlook. Ultimately, the Pepsi Paradox highlights how neuromarketing insights can reshape marketing practices

Pricing remains one of the most influential and evolving factors in shaping consumer purchase intention. The advanced techniques of neuromarketing, such as EEG (electroencephalography), fMRI (functional magnetic resonance imaging), and eye-tracking, allow researchers to delve into the emotional, cognitive, and attentional processes that guide consumer behaviour. These tools reveal not only how consumers react to price points but also how their brains process pricing stimuli even before a conscious decision is made.

Neuromarketing insights have shown that price perception significantly affects emotional and sensory experiences. For instance, when consumers perceive a product as priced higher, their expectation of quality increases, sometimes altering their actual sensory experience of the product. An fMRI study demonstrated that the medial orbitofrontal cortex (mOFC) responded more positively to "expensive" items, regardless of objective quality. Conversely, price sensitivity is largely emotional, not purely rational; the insula—a region associated with the pain of loss—is activated when prices are perceived as unfair or too high, often deterring purchases.

EEG studies further support this by showing that left-frontal brain activation is linked to approach motivation and purchase intent, particularly when consumers view pricing as a bargain or fair. This neurological activity underscores the impact of value-based pricing strategies on consumer decision-making. Moreover, neuromarketing has contributed to understanding the effectiveness of specific pricing models, such as "zero pricing", which taps into the brain's reward system to increase appeal, and price anchoring, where initial high prices set a reference point that makes subsequent prices appear more reasonable.

Collectively, these findings have significant implications for marketers. By understanding how key brain areas—such as the insula, mOFC, dorsolateral prefrontal cortex (dlPFC), and limbic system—respond to different pricing strategies, businesses can optimize price presentation, reduce psychological discomfort, and enhance perceived value. This results in more effective marketing, increased customer engagement, and ultimately, improved conversion rates and brand loyalty. Neuromarketing empowers marketers to move beyond traditional pricing models by integrating neurocognitive insights into consumer psychology, enabling pricing strategies that resonate on both emotional and rational levels

Reward mechanisms play a crucial role by offering tangible incentives that increase the perceived value of transactions. These include loyalty programs, personalized rewards, reward codes, and visual motivators like tier ladders or progress bars. These elements stimulate the brain's dopaminergic system, particularly during reward anticipation, which often evokes stronger engagement than the reward itself. Tools like EEG and fMRI have shown that such mechanisms activate reward and motivation centres in the brain, especially when combined with trust cues, leading to amplified positive emotional responses.

Further insights reveal that immediate and unexpected rewards are more effective than delayed or predictable ones, as they enhance dopamine release and activate regions like the ventral striatum, critical for emotional valuation and motivation. Personalized rewards, in particular, engage identity-related neural pathways, making the brand experience more memorable and meaningful.

Reward mechanisms, trust, and pricing are not just transactional features; they act as powerful emotional triggers that shape consumer perceptions and behaviour. These elements evoke emotional resonance, creating meaningful connections between consumers and brands. This emotional alignment significantly enhances purchase intentions, influences actual buying decisions, and fosters brand loyalty—all of which drive long-term sales performance.

Emotional engagement—central to neuromarketing—directly affects key cognitive functions such as attention, memory encoding, and decision-making. For example, when brands offer fair pricing, personalized incentives, or build trust through transparency, consumers experience a sense of emotional security and value, reinforcing positive brand associations and encouraging repeat behaviour. Functional benefits like competitive pricing may attract attention, but emotional connections are what sustain consumer relationships over time. Brands that intentionally design emotionally resonant experiences—through storytelling, immersive visuals, personalized rewards, and trust-building strategies—are more likely to build deeper consumer loyalty and increase conversion rates.

Ultimately, reward mechanisms, trust, and pricing, when strategically aligned with emotional engagement principles, can influence not only what consumers choose to buy but how strongly they connect with a brand. Emotional engagement thus emerges as a critical driver of consumer behaviour and a key pillar of effective, neuroscience-informed marketing strategy.

5. LIMITATION

This research investigates how key variables influencing consumer purchase intention—namely trust, pricing, and reward mechanisms—can be analysed through the lens of neuromarketing using advanced neuroimaging tools. These variables are conceptualized as external stimuli capable of eliciting specific neural responses, which, when measured with technologies like EEG or fMRI, can reveal the underlying cognitive and emotional mechanisms driving consumer behaviour. Despite the theoretical promise of this approach, the study is constrained by a notable scarcity of empirical data in the neuromarketing domain. The existing body of research remains fragmented, and many aspects of how these stimuli interact with the brain's decision-making systems remain underexplored.

Due to the limited availability of robust primary research and standardized methodologies, the study adopts a qualitative, secondary-source-based approach. This includes synthesizing existing literature to draw meaningful patterns and interpretations. However, the absence of direct experimental evidence limits the ability to form definitive conclusions. Incorporating empirical neuroimaging techniques for future research would generate precise measurements of how these stimuli affect consumer decisions at the neural level. Furthermore, exploring the mediating role of emotional engagement—a variable central to neuromarketing—could enrich understanding by linking external marketing stimuli to internal emotional and motivational states.

This study highlights a significant knowledge and methodological gap in integrating neuroscience with marketing practices. Addressing this gap through empirical studies would enable marketers to design strategies that align with the subconscious drivers of consumer behaviour, making campaigns more impactful and data-driven.

6. FUTURE DIRECTIONS

The current study emphasizes the increasing importance of neuromarketing in understanding the subconscious mechanisms that influence consumer purchase intentions. However, there are still many opportunities for further scholarly exploration in this field. Future research should focus on conducting empirical investigations using advanced neuroimaging tools, such as EEG, fMRI, and eye-tracking. This would help validate the theoretical relationships identified in this review.

Empirical validation is crucial for accurately mapping how factors like trust, pricing cues, and reward mechanisms activate different neural pathways, ultimately impacting decision-making processes. To advance this field, it is necessary to develop standardized research protocols, unified experimental designs, and consistent measurement parameters. Such standardization would enhance methodological rigor and allow for more reliable comparisons across studies, addressing the current fragmentation in neuromarketing research.

Further research should also examine the mediating role of emotional engagement, which is central to neuromarketing theory but has been underexplored in empirical practice. Investigating how emotional states connect external marketing stimuli with internal neural responses could provide deeper insights into the psychological mechanisms driving consumer behaviour.

Additionally, cross-cultural and demographic comparative studies are necessary to understand the variability in neural responses across different consumer groups, especially as global markets continue to diversify. Longitudinal research designs present another promising avenue, as they can reveal how neural responses to brand stimuli, trust cues, or reward structures evolve with repeated exposures and influence long-term loyalty patterns.

The integration of artificial intelligence and machine learning holds significant potential to enhance the interpretation of complex neurophysiological datasets. AI-assisted neuromarketing models could improve prediction accuracy and offer scalable approaches for analysing consumer intentions across various contexts.

Moreover, future research should explore multimodal methodologies that combine different neuroimaging tools to provide a more comprehensive understanding of subconscious processing.

As digital commerce, metaverse environments, and immersive AR/VR shopping interfaces continue to expand, neuroscientific investigations must also adapt to virtual settings to accurately reflect contemporary consumer interactions. Finally, advancing ethical considerations is crucial. Ensuring transparency, consumer autonomy, and responsible use of neuro-data will help maintain trust in neuromarketing practices while promoting the development of ethically grounded, consumer-centric marketing strategies.

7. REFERENCES

Alsharif, A., Md Salleh, N., & Baharun, R. (2005). *Research Trends of Neuromarketing: A Bibliometric Analysis The Relationship of Customer Perceived Risk and Customer Satisfaction View project Gen Y behaviour, Content Analysis of sosial media View project.* https://www.researchgate.net/publication/343680835

Alsharif, A. H., Salleh, N. Z. M., & Baharun, R. (2021). Neuromarketing: The popularity of the brain-imaging and physiological tools. *Neuroscience Research Notes, 3*(5), 13–22. DOI: 10.31117/neuroscirn.v3i5.80

Approach, C. B. T. N. (2021). Consumer Behaviour Through Neuromarketing Approach. *Journal of Contemporary Issues in Business and Government, 27*(03). Advance online publication. DOI: 10.47750/cibg.2021.27.03.048

Ariely, D., & Berns, G. S. (2010). Neuromarketing: The hope and hype of neuroimaging in business. *Nature Reviews. Neuroscience, 11*(4), 284–292. DOI: 10.1038/nrn2795 PMID: 20197790

Ayelen Paladino, C., Cazorla Milla, A., & Andrade-Ruiz, G. (2024). THE ROLE OF NEUROMARKETING IN DECODING BRAIN STIMULI AND CONSUMER BEHAVIOR. *International Journal of Management Trends: Key Concepts and Research, 3*(2), 6–20. DOI: 10.58898/ijmt.v3i2.06-20

Balconi, M., Stumpo, B., & Leanza, F. (2014). Advertising, brand and neuromarketing or how consumer brain works. *Neuropsychological Trends, 16*(1), 15–21. DOI: 10.7358/neur-2014-016-balc

Barrett, L. F., Mesquita, B., Ochsner, K. N., & Gross, J. J. (2007). The experience of emotion. *Annual Review of Psychology, 58*(Volume 58, 2007), 373–403. https://doi.org/DOI: 10.1146/ANNUREV.PSYCH.58.110405.085709/CITE/REFWORKS

Berridge, K. C., & Robinson, T. E. (1998). What is the role of dopamine in reward: Hedonic impact, reward learning, or incentive salience? *Brain Research. Brain Research Reviews, 28*(3), 309–369. DOI: 10.1016/S0165-0173(98)00019-8 PMID: 9858756

Boere, K., Anderson, F., Hecker, K. G., & Krigolson, O. E. (2024). Measuring cognitive load in multitasking using mobile fNIRS. *Neuroimage. Reports, 4*(4), 100228. DOI: 10.1016/j.ynirp.2024.100228 PMID: 40568357

Boz, H., Arslan, A., & Koc, E. (2017). Neuromarketing aspect of tourism pricing psychology. *Tourism Management Perspectives, 23*, 119–128. DOI: 10.1016/j.tmp.2017.06.002

Cahyanaputra, M., Jimmy, Y., & Annas, M. (2022, April 27). *Factors Affecting Purchase Intention and Purchase Behaviour Electronic Products (Home Appliance) in Online Transaction*. DOI: 10.4108/eai.7-10-2021.2316222

Cases overview - Unravel Neuromarketing Research. (n.d.). Retrieved May 25, 2025, from https://www.unravelresearch.com/en/cases/?utm_source=chatgpt.com

Chaerani, M. L., & Sari, H. (2024). Can Digitally Displayed Product Packaging Evoke Emotions? A Neuromarketing Study. *International Journal of Electronic Commerce Studies*, *15*(4), 1–30. DOI: 10.7903/ijecs.2395

Cordeiro, R., Reis, A., Ferreira, B. M., & Bacalhau, L. M. (2024a). Neuromarketing. *Advances in Human Resources Management and Organizational Development Book Series*, 83–100. DOI: 10.4018/979-8-3693-1858-4.ch005

Cordeiro, R., Reis, A., Ferreira, B. M., & Bacalhau, L. M. (2024b). Neuromarketing: Decoding the role of emotions and senses and consumer behavior. *Cognitive Behavioral Neuroscience in Organizational Settings*, 83–100. DOI: 10.4018/979-8-3693-1858-4.ch005

Cordeiro, R., Reis, A., Ferreira, B. M., & Bacalhau, L. M. (2024c). Neuromarketing: Decoding the role of emotions and senses and consumer behavior. *Cognitive Behavioral Neuroscience in Organizational Settings*, 83–100. DOI: 10.4018/979-8-3693-1858-4.ch005

Dapkevičius, A., & Melnikas, B. (2009). Influence of price and quality to customer satisfaction: neuromarketing approach. *Mokslas – Lietuvos Ateitis / Science – Future of Lithuania, 1*(3), 17–20. DOI: 10.3846/144

Delgado, M. R., Miller, M. M., Inati, S., & Phelps, E. A. (2005). An fMRI study of reward-related probability learning. *NeuroImage*, *24*(3), 862–873. DOI: 10.1016/j.neuroimage.2004.10.002 PMID: 15652321

Djamasbi, S., Siegel, M., & Tullis, T. (2010). Generation Y, web design, and eye tracking. *International Journal of Human-Computer Studies*, *68*(5), 307–323. DOI: 10.1016/j.ijhcs.2009.12.006

Dorotic, M., Verhoef, P. C., Fok, D., & Bijmolt, T. H. A. (2014). Reward redemption effects in a loyalty program when customers choose how much and when to redeem. *International Journal of Research in Marketing*, *31*(4), 339–355. DOI: 10.1016/j.ijresmar.2014.06.001

Emotional engagement detector. (2015).

Falk, E. B., Berkman, E. T., Whalen, D., & Lieberman, M. D. (2011). Neural Activity During Health Messaging Predicts Reductions in Smoking Above and Beyond Self-Report. *Health Psychology, 30*(2), 177–185. DOI: 10.1037/a0022259 PMID: 21261410

Farrar, S. T., & Papies, E. K. (2024). How consumption and reward features affect desire for food, consumption intentions, and behaviour. *Appetite, 194*, 107184. Advance online publication. DOI: 10.1016/j.appet.2023.107184 PMID: 38158045

Fortunato, V. C. R., Giraldi, J. D. M. E., & De Oliveira, J. H. C. (2014). A Review of Studies on Neuromarketing: Practical Results, Techniques, Contributions and Limitations. *Journal of Management Research, 6*(2), 201. DOI: 10.5296/jmr.v6i2.5446

Fugate, D. L. (2007). Neuromarketing: A layman's look at neuroscience and its potential application to marketing practice. *Journal of Consumer Marketing, 24*(7), 385–394. DOI: 10.1108/07363760710834807

García, F. S. M., Ríos, B. C. Q., Chamorro, S. L. R., Rojas, L. D. B., Rodríguez, M. E. A., Yarleque, A. M. S., & Arismendiz, A. G. (2024). The Power of Neuromarketing as a Fuel to Drive Purchases in Local Retail (Piura 2024). *Journal of Educational and Social Research, 14*(6), 503–513. DOI: 10.36941/jesr-2024-0189

Gefen, D., Karahanna, E. and Straub, D.W. (2003) Trust and TAM in Online Shopping An Integrated Model. MIS quarterly, 27, 51-90. - References - Scientific Research Publishing. (n.d.). Retrieved May 27, 2025, from https://www.scirp.org/reference/referencespapers?referenceid=1866898

Ghosh, O., & Kumar, B. (2024). Introduction to neuro-marketing: Foundations and evolution. *The Quantum AI Era of Neuromarketing*, 1–27. DOI: 10.4018/979-8-3693-7673-7.ch001

Grewal, D., Roggeveen, A. L., & Nordfält, J. (2017). The Future of Retailing. *Journal of Retailing, 93*(1), 1–6. DOI: 10.1016/j.jretai.2016.12.008

Halyana, P. S., & Bangsawan, S. (2023). The Influence of Price and Product Quality on Purchase Decisions with Purchase Intention as Intervening Variable (Study on Mixue Lampung). *International Journal of Regional Innovation, 3*(4), undefined-undefined. DOI: 10.52000/ijori.v3i4.93

Iloka, C. B., & Onyeke, K. J. (2020). Neuromarketing: A historical review. *Neuroscience Research Notes, 3*(3), 27–35. DOI: 10.31117/neuroscirn.v3i3.54

Javor, A., Kindermann, H., Koschutnig, K., & Ischebeck, A. (2018). The neural correlates of trustworthiness evaluations of faces and brands: Implications for behavioral and consumer neuroscience. *The European Journal of Neuroscience, 48*(6), 2322–2332. DOI: 10.1111/ejn.14134 PMID: 30144336

Jaya, S. L., & Heryjanto, A. (2023). The Influence Of Price, Service Quality, And Product Quality On Purchase Decisions Mediated By Purchase Intention (Empirical Study: Kriss Store Consumers In Tangerang Regency). *Journal Research of Social Science, Economics, and Management, 3*(3), 798–823. DOI: 10.59141/jrssem.v3i3.575

Juárez-Varón, D., Tur-Viñes, V., Rabasa-Dolado, A., & Polotskaya, K. (2020). An Adaptive Machine Learning Methodology Applied to Neuromarketing Analysis: Prediction of Consumer Behaviour Regarding the Key Elements of the Packaging Design of an Educational Toy. *Social Sciences 2020, Vol. 9, Page 162, 9*(9), 162. DOI: 10.3390/socsci9090162

Kanagal, N. (2016). An Extended Model of Behavioural Process in Consumer Decision Making. *International Journal of Marketing Studies, 8*(4), 87. DOI: 10.5539/ijms.v8n4p87

Karmarkar, U. R., Shiv, B., & Knutson, B. (2015). Cost conscious? The neural and behavioral impact of price primacy on decision making. *JMR, Journal of Marketing Research, 52*(4), 467–481. DOI: 10.1509/jmr.13.0488

Kenning, P., & Linzmajer, M. (2011). Consumer neuroscience: An overview of an emerging discipline with implications for consumer policy. *Journal für Verbraucherschutz und Lebensmittelsicherheit, 6*(1), 111–125. DOI: 10.1007/s00003-010-0652-5

Khan, M. N., Fifield, S. G. M., & Power, D. M. (2024). The impact of the COVID 19 pandemic on stock market volatility: Evidence from a selection of developed and emerging stock markets. *SN Business & Economics, 4*(6), 63. Advance online publication. DOI: 10.1007/s43546-024-00659-w

Khushaba, R. N., Greenacre, L., Kodagoda, S., Louviere, J., Burke, S., & Dissanayake, G. (2012). Choice modeling and the brain: A study on the Electroencephalogram (EEG) of preferences. *Expert Systems with Applications, 39*(16), 12378–12388. DOI: 10.1016/j.eswa.2012.04.084

Khushaba, R. N., Wise, C., Kodagoda, S., Louviere, J., Kahn, B. E., & Townsend, C. (2013). Consumer neuroscience: Assessing the brain response to marketing stimuli using electroencephalogram (EEG) and eye tracking. *Expert Systems with Applications, 40*(9), 3803–3812. DOI: 10.1016/j.eswa.2012.12.095

Kim, D. J., Ferrin, D. L., & Rao, H. R. (2008). A trust-based consumer decision-making model in electronic commerce: The role of trust, perceived risk, and their antecedents. *Decision Support Systems*, *44*(2), 544–564. DOI: 10.1016/j.dss.2007.07.001

Knutson, B., Rick, S., Wimmer, G. E., Prelec, D., & Loewenstein, G. (2007). Neural predictors of purchases. *Neuron*, *53*(1), 147–156. DOI: 10.1016/j.neuron.2006.11.010 PMID: 17196537

Kosfeld, M., Heinrichs, M., Zak, P. J., Fischbacher, U., & Fehr, E. (2005). Oxytocin increases trust in humans. *Nature*, *435*(7042), 673–676. DOI: 10.1038/nature03701 PMID: 15931222

Kotler, P., & Keller, K. L. (2016). Marketing Management (14th edition). Shanghai Shanghai People's Publishing House. - References - Scientific Research Publishing. Retrieved October 20, 2024, from https://www.scirp.org/reference/referencespapers ?referenceid=2682798

Lee, N., Broderick, A. J., & Chamberlain, L. (2007). What is "neuromarketing"? A discussion and agenda for future research. *International Journal of Psychophysiology*, *63*(2), 199–204. DOI: 10.1016/j.ijpsycho.2006.03.007 PMID: 16769143

Lim, W. M. (2018). Demystifying neuromarketing. *Journal of Business Research*, *91*, 205–220. DOI: 10.1016/j.jbusres.2018.05.036

Mada, Y. P.Yudhi Prasetya Mada. (2024). ROLE OF NEUROMARKETING IN UNDERSTANDING CONSUMER BEHAVIOR: A LITERATURE OVERVIEW. *International Journal of Innovations in Engineering Research and Technology*, *11*(8), 48–56. DOI: 10.26662/ijiert.v11i8.pp48-56

Michael, I., Ramsoy, T., Stephens, M., & Kotsi, F. (2019). A study of unconscious emotional and cognitive responses to tourism images using a neuroscience method. *Journal of Islamic Marketing*, *10*(2), 543–564. DOI: 10.1108/JIMA-09-2017-0098

Millagala, K., & Gunasinghe, N. (2024). Neuromarketing as a Digital Marketing Strategy to Unravel the Evolution of Marketing Communication. Https://Services.Igi -Global.Com/Resolvedoi/Resolve.Aspx?Doi=10.4018/979-8-3693-1846-1.Ch005, 81–105. DOI: 10.4018/979-8-3693-1846-1.ch005

Mimouni-Chaabane, A., & Volle, P. (2010). Perceived benefits of loyalty programs: Scale development and implications for relational strategies. *Journal of Business Research*, *63*(1), 32–37. DOI: 10.1016/j.jbusres.2009.01.008

Moon, J., Chadee, D., & Tikoo, S. (2008). Culture, product type, and price influences on consumer purchase intention to buy personalized products online. *Journal of Business Research*, *61*(1), 31–39. DOI: 10.1016/j.jbusres.2006.05.012

Morin, C. (2011a). Neuromarketing: The New Science of Consumer Behavior. *Society*, *48*(2), 131–135. DOI: 10.1007/s12115-010-9408-1

Morin, C. (2011b). Neuromarketing: The New Science of Consumer Behavior. In *Society* (Vol. 48, Issue 2, pp. 131–135). Springer Science and Business Media, LLC. DOI: 10.1007/s12115-010-9408-1

Morris, J. D., Woo, C., Geason, J. A., & Kim, J. (2002). The power of affect: Predicting intention. *Journal of Advertising Research*, *42*(3), 7–17. DOI: 10.2501/jar-42-3-7-17

Nemorin, S., & Oscar, H. Gandy, Jr. (2017). Exploring Neuromarketing and Its Reliance on Remote Sensing: Social and Ethical Concerns. *International Journal of Communication, 11*(0), 21. https://ijoc.org/index.php/ijoc/article/view/6706

Nielsen Buys Neuromarketing Research Company Innerscope - NMSBA. (n.d.). Retrieved May 25, 2025, from https://nmsba.com/news/392-nielsen-buys-neuromarketing-research-company-innerscope

Nieves, O. A. (n.d.). *BUYOLOGY MARTIN LINDSTROM*. Retrieved May 26, 2025, from https://www.academia.edu/36671696/BUYOLOGY_MARTIN_LINDSTROM

Nugroho, D. A. (2025). The Role of Color and Packaging Shape on Consumer Emotional Responses: A Neuromarketing Study With Eeg. *Eduvest - Journal of Universal Studies, 5*(3), 3319–3325. DOI: 10.59188/eduvest.v5i3.50961

Nykiel, R. A. (2007). Handbook of Marketing Research Methodologies for Hospitality and Tourism. *Handbook of Marketing Research Methodologies for Hospitality and Tourism*. DOI: 10.4324/9780203448557

Ohme, R., Reykowska, D., Wiener, D., & Choromanska, A. (2009). Analysis of Neurophysiological Reactions to Advertising Stimuli by Means of EEG and Galvanic Skin Response Measures. *Journal of Neuroscience, Psychology, and Economics*, *2*(1), 21–31. DOI: 10.1037/a0015462

Pandey, S., & Srivastava, D. S. (2016). Antecedents of Customer Purchase Intention. *IOSR Journal of Business and Management*, *18*(10), 55–82. DOI: 10.9790/487X-1810035582

Credibility Dimensions in Marketing Communication-A Generalized Solution. (n.d.). Retrieved May 29, 2025, from https://www.researchgate.net/publication/228649951_Source_Credibility_Dimensions_in_Marketing_Communication-A_Generalized_Solution

Pepsis - an overview | ScienceDirect Topics. (n.d.). Retrieved May 25, 2025, from https://www.sciencedirect.com/topics/agricultural-and-biological-sciences/pepsis

Plassmann, H., O'Doherty, J., Shiv, B., & Rangel, A. (2008). Marketing actions can modulate neural representations of experienced pleasantness. *Proceedings of the National Academy of Sciences of the United States of America, 105*(3), 1050–1054. DOI: 10.1073/pnas.0706929105 PMID: 18195362

Plassmann, H., Ramsøy, T. Z., & Milosavljevic, M. (2012). Branding the brain: A critical review and outlook. *Journal of Consumer Psychology*, *22*(1), 18–36. DOI: 10.1016/j.jcps.2011.11.010

Pozharliev, R., Verbeke, W. J. M. I., Van Strien, J. W., & Bagozzi, R. P. (2015). Merely being with you increases my attention to luxury products: Using EEG to understand consumers' emotional experience with luxury branded products. *JMR, Journal of Marketing Research*, *52*(4), 546–558. DOI: 10.1509/jmr.13.0560

Purwianti, L., & Yulianto, E. (n.d.). *The Mediating Role of Trust in Purchasing Intention*. DOI: 10.51137/ijarbm.2024.5.2.1

Reimann, M., Zaichkowsky, J., Neuhaus, C., Bender, T., & Weber, B. (2010a). Aesthetic package design: A behavioral, neural, and psychological investigation. *Journal of Consumer Psychology*, *20*(4), 431–441. DOI: 10.1016/j.jcps.2010.06.009

Reimann, M., Zaichkowsky, J., Neuhaus, C., Bender, T., & Weber, B. (2010b). Aesthetic package design: A behavioral, neural, and psychological investigation. *Journal of Consumer Psychology*, *20*(4), 431–441. DOI: 10.1016/j.jcps.2010.06.009

Rojas, M., Méndez, A., & Watkins-Fassler, K. (2023). The hierarchy of needs empirical examination of Maslow's theory and lessons for development. *World Development*, *165*, 106185. DOI: 10.1016/j.worlddev.2023.106185

Roy, P. (2022). Theory and Models of Consumer Buying Behaviour: A Descriptive Study. SSRN *Electronic Journal*. DOI: 10.2139/ssrn.4205489

Saad, S., Shah, H., Aziz, J., Raza Jaffari, A., Waris, S., Ejaz, W., Fatima, M., & Sherazi, S. K. (2012). The Impact of Brands on Consumer Purchase Intentions. *Asian Journal of Business Management*, *4*(2), 105–110.

Sansone, M., & Balconi, M. (2022). ADV at the Time of COVID-19 Brain Effect between Emotional Engagement and Purchase Intention. *Brain Sciences*, *12*(5), 593. Advance online publication. DOI: 10.3390/brainsci12050593 PMID: 35624980

Satpathy, C. P. D. J., & Mund, S. (2022). Decision - Making Actors in Circular Economic Leadership. SSRN *Electronic Journal*. https://doi.org/DOI: 10.2139/SSRN.4098240

Stanton, S. J., Sinnott-Armstrong, W., & Huettel, S. A. (2017). Neuromarketing: Ethical Implications of its Use and Potential Misuse. *Journal of Business Ethics*, *144*(4), 799–811. DOI: 10.1007/s10551-016-3059-0

Stern, H. (1962). The Significance of Impulse Buying Today. *Journal of Marketing*, *26*(2), 59–62. DOI: 10.1177/002224296202600212

Tinoco-Egas, R. M., Juanatey-Boga, Ó., & Martínez-Fernández, V. A. (2019). Conceptual and exploratory approach to the role of trust for an efficient publicity: A neuromarketing perspective. *Iberian Conference on Information Systems and Technologies, CISTI, 2019-June*. DOI: 10.23919/CISTI.2019.8760723

Touhami, Z. O., Benlafkih, L., Jiddane, M., Cherrah, Y., El Malki, O., Benomar, A., Souissi, M. V., & Rabat, M. (2011). Biostatical, clinical research and epidemiological laboratory (LBRCE). *African Journal of Business Management*, *5*(5), 1528–1532. DOI: 10.5897/AJBM10.729

Ummah, R., & Oetarjo, M. (2024). Price, Marketing Communications and E-commerce Services on Consumer Purchase Intention in Online Shopping. *Indonesian Journal of Cultural and Community Development, 15*(3), . https://doi.org/DOI: 10.21070/ijccd.v15i3.1088

Uzbay, T. (2020). Importance of brain reward system in neuromarketing. *Analyzing the Strategic Role of Neuromarketing and Consumer Neuroscience*, 1–24. DOI: 10.4018/978-1-7998-3126-6.ch001

Van Doorn, G., & Miloyan, B. (2018). The Pepsi Paradox: A review. *Food Quality and Preference*, *65*, 194–197. DOI: 10.1016/j.foodqual.2017.11.007

Vecchiato, G., Astolfi, L., De Vico Fallani, F., Toppi, J., Aloise, F., Bez, F., Wei, D., Kong, W., Dai, J., Cincotti, F., Mattia, D., & Babiloni, F. (2011). On the Use of EEG or MEG brain imaging tools in neuromarketing research. *Computational Intelligence and Neuroscience*, *2011*, 1–12. Advance online publication. DOI: 10.1155/2011/643489 PMID: 21960996

Vejandla, D., & Raju, V. (2022). NUEROMARKETING AND EMOTIONS IMPACT ON FMCG MARKETING. *International Journal of Creative Research Thoughts*, *10*, 2320–2882. www.ijcrt.orgwww.ijcrt.org

Venkatraman, V., Dimoka, A., Pavlou, P. A., Vo, K., Hampton, W., Bollinger, B., Hershfield, H. E., Ishihara, M., & Winer, R. S. (2015). Predicting advertising success beyond traditional measures: New insights from neurophysiological methods and market response modeling. *JMR, Journal of Marketing Research*, *52*(4), 436–452. DOI: 10.1509/jmr.13.0593

View of Neuromarketing: Marketing research in the new millennium. (n.d.). Retrieved October 20, 2024, from https://neuroscirn.org/ojs/index.php/nrnotes/article/view/79/132

Wedel, M., & Pieters, R. (2008a). A review of eye-tracking research in marketing. *Review of Marketing Research*, *4*, 123–147. DOI: 10.1108/S1548-6435(2008)0000004009

Wedel, M., & Pieters, R. (2008b). Eye Tracking for Visual Marketing. *Foundations and Trends® in Marketing*, *1*(4), 231–320. DOI: 10.1561/1700000011

What Does the Brain Tell Us About Trust and Distrust? Evidence from a Functional Neuroimaging Study by Angelika Dimoka : SSRN. (n.d.). Retrieved October 20, 2024, from https://papers.ssrn.com/sol3/papers.cfm?abstract_id=2428911

Wilson, R. M., Gaines, J., & Hill, R. P. (2008). *Neuromarketing and Consumer Free Will.*

Xia, L., Monroe, K. B., & Cox, J. L. (2004). The price is unfair! A conceptual framework of price fairness perceptions. *Journal of Marketing*, *68*(4), 1–15. DOI: 10.1509/jmkg.68.4.1.42733

Yoon, C., Gonzalez, R., Bechara, A., Berns, G. S., Dagher, A. A., Dubé, L., Huettel, S. A., Kable, J. W., Liberzon, I., Plassmann, H., Smidts, A., & Spence, C. (2012). Decision neuroscience and consumer decision making. *Marketing Letters*, *23*(2), 473–485. DOI: 10.1007/s11002-012-9188-z

Zak, P. J. (2005). The Neuroeconomics of Trust. SSRN *Electronic Journal*. https://doi.org/DOI: 10.2139/SSRN.764944

Zhang, Q., Zhou, K., Zhang, Y., Zhou, P., & Zhang, Z. (2024). Reexamining the relationship between extrinsic rewards and creativity: A study from the creative process engagement perspective. *International Journal of Human Resource Management*, *35*(15), 2514–2541. DOI: 10.1080/09585192.2024.2347645

Chapter 3
Decoding Consumer Minds:
The Convergence of AI and Neuromarketing for Precision Marketing

Parihar Suresh Dahake
http://orcid.org/0000-0002-2286-4120
Ramdeobaba University, Nagpur, India

Nihar Suresh Dahake
http://orcid.org/0009-0007-8971-9247
G.H. Raisoni College of Engineering, Nagpur, India

Pragati Parihar Dahake
http://orcid.org/0009-0003-0383-4721
VMV Commerce, JMT Arts, and JJP Science College, Nagpur, India

Pritam Bhadade
Ramdeobaba University, Nagpur, India

ABSTRACT

In today's world, marketing strategies are becoming targeted with the help of artificial intelligence. Each click on a commercial website is analyzed, processed, and paired with techniques, with information on individual consumers used by marketers to ascertain who is most likely to respond positively to a particular advertisement. Neuromarketing is considered an emerging field to study how consumers' brain

DOI: 10.4018/979-8-3373-1152-4.ch003

reacts to advertisements and brand messages (Traymbak et al., 2024). Today, neuromarketing helps marketers to better appeal to consumer's subconscious minds and biases. Neuromarketing analyzes information on how consumers feel about a product.

1. INTRODUCTION

The term neuromarketing combines consumer behavior research and a branch of neurology to study how the brain reacts to advertisements and brand messages (Traymbak et al., 2024). The study of what consumers say and do to analyze brand effectiveness is known as consumer behavior. Artificial intelligence will significantly change marketing strategies and customer behaviors, with its effectiveness being enhanced when it augments human managers rather than replacing them(Davenport et al., 2020). Consumer behavior is a multidisciplinary field that applies various techniques and tactics from social science and psychology. To investigate consumer behavior, traditional research methods such as surveys, open and closed-ended questionnaires, observations, and ethnographies are extensively used. However, surveys alone cannot reliably investigate consumer thoughts, feelings, and perceptions regarding a brand (Phutela et al., 2022). And AI can enhance marketing research, strategy, and actions by automating repetitive functions, processing data, and analyzing interactions and emotions(Huang & Rust, 2021a). Instead, marketers need to determine if consumers belong to the emotional or irrational mind. Another more recently developed research exploring consumers' subconscious feelings and thoughts to measure brand effectiveness is a combination of neuroscience, marketing, and consumer behavior referred to as neuromarketing. In neuromarketing, various neuroscience functional imaging tools and methods are used to find and analyze consumer behavior regarding advertisements.Neuromarketing has become popular due to its potential to provide hidden consumer experience insights and faster marketing methods, but its affordability remains uncertain(Ariely & Berns, 2010).

Figure 1. Connection of neuromarketing with consumer behavior

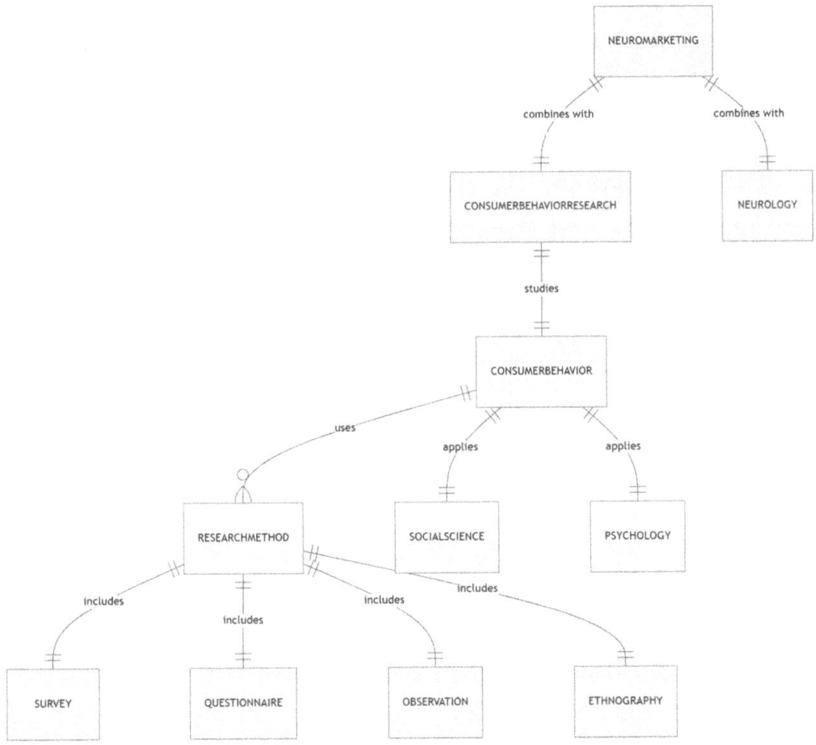

While attempting to grab the attention of the consumers, many companies and brands conduct neuromarketing research to find how consumers behave with their advertisements by using the brain research techniques mentioned above. Even though neuromarketing has defined constructs regarding awareness, attention, emotions, affection, loyalty, impulse buying, word of mouth, etc., very few studies have investigated the constructs of neuromarketing, like social, attention, technology, emotions, etc., toward how these factors related to the buying behavior of Indian consumers. Additionally, attempts were made to study neuromarketing's constructs' validity and reliability regarding this research domain within the Indian research sample despite its extensive application in Western countries. Hence, identifying and assessing how social, attention, technology, and emotions look at neuromarketing aspects related to the buying behavior of Indian consumers becomes essential.

Consumers, the focal point of marketing activities, are not immune to in-depth examination to unlock their innermost thoughts, which are often concealed. New AI-powered technologies significantly transform the customer experience, impacting each stage of the shopping journey and creating experiential value(Hoyer et al.,

2020). The ultimate goal of neuromarketing is to fathom and anticipate the desired behavior of consumers. It is the intersection of marketing and neuroscience, primarily to gauge the thoughts and feelings of consumers towards brands. Neuromarketing is viewed as a domain to decode how the brains of consumers react to advertisements and brand messages, intended to market a product or service. Movements of the eyeball include saccades and fixations. Saccade follows the rule of vectors and is denoted by variables. Fixation denotes the height and width of a specific gaze on a specific area of interest where something is observed. Fixation duration helps to understand what is being viewed as attentional resources are allocated towards a specific visual object. These movements have inferences and applications in market research. A fixed-duration gaze will create more heat index in that area. The larger the area of interest, the bigger the movement, irrespective of its negativity or positivity. The degree of referencing may vary across segments, age, and other perceptual characteristics. Eventually, all these effects will influence the testing of any emotional stimuli. As in the case of eye-tracking, each stimulus in a neuromarketing lab is measured as a mere 3D object. Eventually, scientists prefer to convert it into frames. Similarly, stimuli in advertisements are measured by recognition recall tests but coded into audio response. Each measured metric of EEG measurement is visualized, compared, and plotted as per space-time inference.

A subject-based and sensor-based metric database of time-frequency decomposition is created. Neuromarketing has recently emerged as a promising area of marketing. It is the union of research in consumer behavior and neurophysiology. Marketers can gain an overall knowledge of the consumers' minds, which would assist them in taking effective marketing decisions with the use of the emerging discipline. Though neuromarketing is a relatively new area of focus in countries such as the United States and Australia, it is just emerging in India. Marketers are seeking to develop strategies to elicit information about the consumers' minds and leverage it for increase their reach in the target market with the aid of the burgeoning technology demand in the country(Traymbak et al., 2024). Therefore, the implementation of neuromarketing using existing technology may yield fruitful results for the Indian marketers. The study's primary objectives are to understand whether Indian marketers are aware of neuromarketing and its emerging constructs. It decides to examine social neuromarketing, attention neuromarketing, technology in neuromarketing, and emotions in neuromarketing to help Indian marketers establish consumer engagement leverage the emerging technologies in the market for business strategies, and elicit the consumers' thoughts and focus on the advertisements. Though constructs of neuromarketing are prevalent in developed countries, the adaptation of neuromarketing in developing countries is ignored (Sun et al., 2022). The study intends to highlight the need for further research in this area so that marketers can build growth strategies while including neuromarketing disciplines.

2. THEORETICAL CONTRIBUTION OR THE STUDY'S BACKGROUND

Marketing continues to wield significant influence over consumer decisions, necessitating ongoing feedback to remain competitive in a dynamic environment. Traditional approaches often rely on surveys, interviews, or questionnaires to gauge customer sentiment; however, these tools may fail to capture the genuine emotions driving consumer choices (Khondakar et al., 2024a). Neuromarketing emerges as a promising discipline, employing neuroscience principles to decode consumer reactions by analyzing spontaneous responses to advertisements and packaging. It distinguishes itself by focusing on real-time brain activity during decision-making rather than retrospective self-assessments. Brain-Computer Interface technologies facilitate this process by establishing direct communication pathways between the brain and external devices, offering valuable insights into customer preferences and behavior (Alam Kazmi et al., 2019). Digital marketing's rise across sectors has generated abundant data, challenging the application of AI and analytics for actionable insights on consumer preferences, resulting in the emergence of new interdisciplinary fields. Combining physiological neuroscience and marketing, the practice of neuromarketing focuses on decoding consumers' cognitive and emotional responses to messages and external stimuli. Given its prominent role in decoding emotions and thoughts, AI can substantially enhance Neuromarketing's efficacy. Hence, this research introduces a framework integrating AI with neuromarketing to conduct precision marketing to Indian consumers by decoding their minds and emotions (E Blum, 2016). Existing knowledge on neuromarketing elucidates consumer behavior by merging neuroscience with marketing principles. Given its relatively recent emergence, foundational theory remains underdeveloped; AI dissemination models provide a theoretical scaffold for further elaboration (Hasnain Alam Kazmi et al., 2019). The methodology articulates the Study's structural role beneath the theoretical edifice, adopting a meta-framework that bridges foundational neuromarketing concepts with the precision capabilities of AI.

The Study anchors the inquiry by extrapolating three hypotheses from established theory, contextualized within a multifaceted marketing mix. Targeted towards consumer goods performance evaluation, the framework incorporates survey instruments reflecting constructs identified in preceding discourse. It probes the efficacy with which cognitive responses—specifically attention, emotion, and learning—mediate the nexus between stimuli attributes and purchasing motivation. In doing so, it delineates the analytical foundation for data processing and interpretation, weaving prior conceptual threads into an integrated evaluative mechanism.

3. REVIEW OF LITERATURE:

In the growing but distinctive field of neuromarketing, India stands at the forefront. A bibliometric study of the literature on consumers' brains carried out through the VOSViewer program yields insights into the ongoing work in India related to neuromarketing, as well as the work that remains to be done. The search string is composed of the keywords "brain," "neuromarketing," "consumer," "advertising," "emotion," and "decision." The VOSviewer program offers a pictorial representation of the search terms and keywords in an understandable form. In total, 226 publications containing the target keywords were reviewed for the period from 2010 to January 2023, with a wildly diverse spread in volumes and topics. The analysis showed a trend of rising interest in both the subject and the possible intersection of marketing management with neuroscience (Phutela et al., 2022). Studies into the topic sought knowledge regarding the opinions of respondents through the use of neuroscience tools and how considered neuromarketing parameters helped evoke specific moods and emotional states in consumers to arrive at decisions on buying instead of rejection.

Figure 2. All keywords analysis by VosViewer

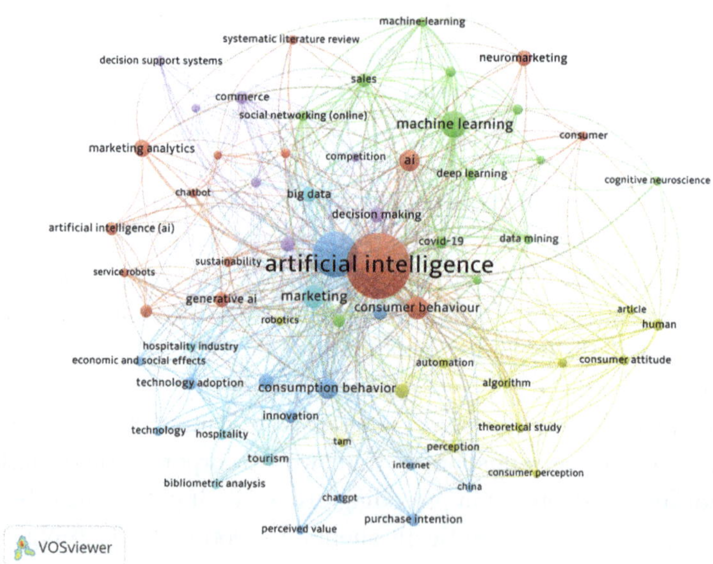

High involvement-teaser ads appealed to the emotional and logical faculties of consumers, leading to good decisions to either buy or consider. Speed in decision-making is clanged with the prefrontal cortex, a decision on belief-complex neural product against charge to engage the centre-of-gravity matrix of the other(Traymbak et al., 2024).

Figure 3. Author keywords analysis by VosViewer

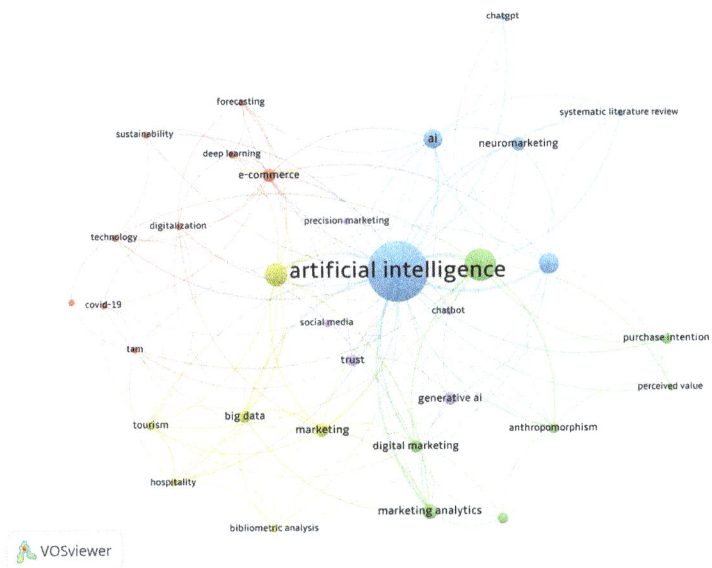

To grasp the development of neuromarketing as a seamless interaction between consumers' perception and product-based/advertising-based marketing management abetted by pharma computing, just marketing and possible intersections of both domains stress on brain sustainability and pursuit of solutions to individually reduce adverse effects is essential for a positive macroenvironment supportive of individual brains mainly their UNI experience.

Figure 4. Index keywords analysis by VosViewer

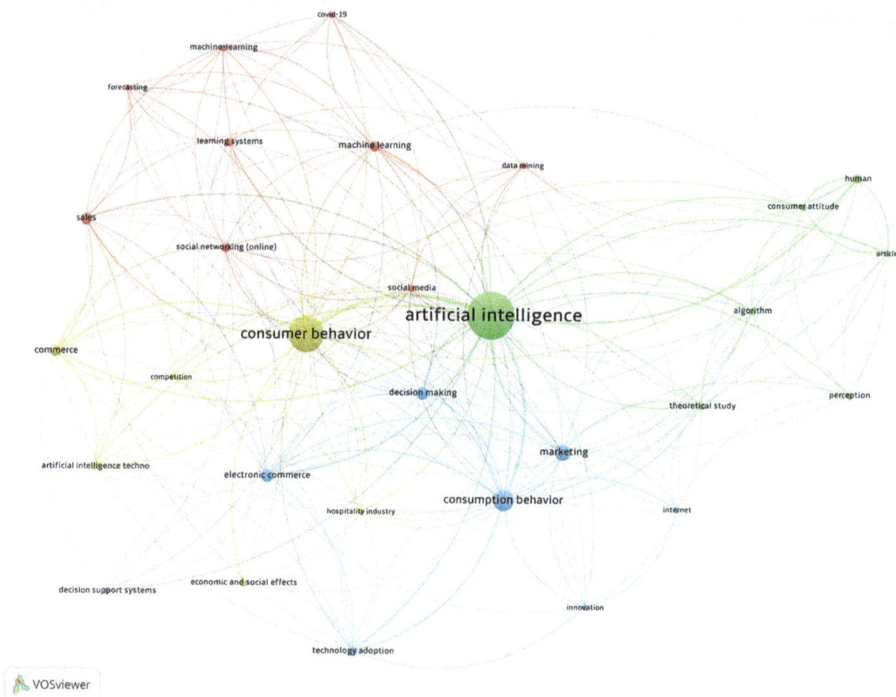

This would positively change compatriots' brains (and perceivably the field) and plant base to develop desired sustainable products/processes and pursue/design creative cogency paths through the resonant INSIS-between-consumer-and-exercise-matrix encoded.(Pirouz, n.d.) provides a compelling exploration of how neuroeconomics can enhance marketing research, particularly in understanding adolescent consumer behavior. The author argues that adolescents respond differently to marketing communications and advertising, highlighting the need for targeted research that delves into the neural underpinnings of these responses. This focus on a vulnerable demographic is particularly timely, as it addresses the ethical considerations of marketing practices aimed at adolescents, especially concerning detrimental products like cigarettes and alcohol. The article posits that neuroeconomic methods can offer marketers a nuanced understanding of consumer choice, which is essential for developing effective marketing strategies. The author emphasizes the potential of neuromarketing the application of neuroscience tools to gauge consumer preferences and responses to refine marketing practices. This approach has led some corporations to establish their own neuroscience labs, underscoring the growing intersection between neuroscience and marketing. However, the author also cautions that the invasive nature of some neuroscientific techniques may raise public concerns, suggesting that marketers should tread carefully. This is particularly relevant when considering the ethical implications of using such methods on vulnerable populations. The article advocates for the use of neuroeconomic principles in addressing significant public policy issues, such as consumption addiction and consumer protection, rather than purely for profit-driven motives.The intersection of artificial intelligence (AI) and neuromarketing represents a burgeoning field that leverages insights from neuroscience to refine marketing strategies and enhance consumer engagement. This literature review examines key contributions to this field, highlighting the evolution of thought from early explorations of consumer decision-making to contemporary applications of AI in marketing practices.(Javor et al., 2013)expanded on the implications of neuromarketing, highlighting the significant public interest generated by neuroimaging techniques such as fMRI. They noted the importance of contextualizing human behaviors within marketing research, thereby underscoring the interdisciplinary nature of neuromarketing and the ethical concerns surrounding its commercial applications, This growing attention to ethical considerations paved the way for more nuanced discussions in subsequent literature. (Cherubino et al., 2019)provides a comprehensive overview of the advancements in neuromarketing and its implications for understanding consumer behavior. The authors synthesize findings from various studies conducted over the past two decades, highlighting the integration of neuroscientific technologies in evaluating human behavior in real-world purchasing contexts. (Blum, n.d.)introduced the term "consumer neuroscience," distinguishing it from the often commercially-driven label of "neuromarketing." This shift in terminology reflected a desire among scholars to emphasize the scientific rigor behind the integration of neuroscience and marketing, while also acknowledging the field's infancy (Blum, n.d.). The same year, Mileti et al. identified the limitations of traditional neuromarketing methods and proposed nanomarketing as a new frontier that could facilitate non-invasive consumer research, thereby addressing ethical concerns and enhancing methodological diversity(Mileti et al., 2016a).(Kose & Sert, 2017)further advanced the discussion by focusing on the role of AI in content marketing, suggesting that intelligent content marketing could significantly improve engagement and effectiveness. They highlighted the potential for AI to transform traditional marketing approaches, a theme that resonates with the ongoing evolution of neuromarketing practices,The following years witnessed a deeper exploration of the neuropsychological underpinnings of consumer behavior. (Shaw & Bagozzi, 2018) provided a comprehensive overview of consumer neuroscience, elucidating how neuroscientific techniques can enhance understanding of consumer emotions and cognitive responses, One of the key insights presented in the article is the effectiveness of neurophysiological measures, such as EEG and fMRI, in capturing subconscious consumer responses that traditional marketing research methods may overlook. This capability allows marketers to gain deeper insights into consumer preferences and decision-making processes, thereby facilitating more precise marketing strategies. The authors argue that these technologies can reveal emotional and cognitive reactions to marketing stimuli, providing a richer understanding of consumer engagement and potential purchase behavior.Moreover, (Alam Kazmi et al., 2019)presents a thorough examination of the intersection between neuroscience and marketing, particularly focusing on consumer behavior. The authors articulate the importance of understanding the underlying mechanisms of customer shopping behaviors and how marketing influences these actions. This exploration is particularly timely, given the increasing integration of advanced technologies, such as artificial intelligence, into marketing strategies. In the parallel vein (Semieoglu, 2019)provides a comprehensive examination of the integration of neural networks and genetic algorithms within the context of marketing management. The author effectively addresses the fundamental questions surrounding the applicability of Artificial Intelligence (AI) in marketing, particularly focusing on the ethical dimensions of utilizing these advanced technologies.However, the article also raises critical ethical and professional considerations surrounding the application of neuromarketing, cautioning that while the insights gained from neuroscience can enhance marketing effectiveness, they must be approached with careful consideration of consumer privacy and the ethical implications of manipulating emotional responses for commercial gain.In addition to this (Braga, n.d.) provides a comprehensive examination of the role of artificial intelligence (AI) as a marketing tool, particularly in the context of consumer decision-making across different generational cohorts. The author emphasizes the growing significance of AI in facilitating communication between companies and consumers, suggesting that a clear, well-defined understanding of AI's applications in marketing is essential for its effective utilization. Consequently, (Keegan et al., 2024) provides a comprehensive examination of the integration of artificial intelligence (AI) into B2B marketing practices, emphasizing the transformative role of AI in shaping strategic decision-making. Significantly (Hermann, 2022) undertakes a comprehensive examination of the intersection between artificial intelligence (AI) ethics and its application in marketing. The article systematically reviews existing literature to illuminate the ethical considerations that arise when integrating AI into marketing strategies. Overall, this examination highlights the necessity for a rigorous framework to assess the effectiveness of emerging neuromarketing tools while prioritizing ethical considerations in their implementation. The integration of these diverse insights reinforces the growing recognition of the importance of neuromarketing in shaping consumer interactions within contemporary marketing landscapes. Recent contributions, such as (Momennejad, 2023) and (Khondakar et al., 2024b), illustrate the dynamic interplay between neuroscience and AI, with (Momennejad,

2023) emphasizing the bidirectional influence of these fields and (Khondakar et al., 2024b) showcasing advancements in EEG-based neuromarketing technologies. This literature review reveals a rich tapestry of research that underscores the convergence of AI and neuromarketing, illustrating both the potential benefits and ethical challenges inherent in this evolving field. As the integration of these disciplines continues, a critical examination of their implications will be essential for shaping future marketing practices.

4. THE ROLE OF ARTIFICIAL INTELLIGENCE IN MARKETING

Artificial intelligence (AI) relates to a system's ability to correctly interpret external data, learn from external data through a wide variety of modalities, and use those learning to achieve specific goals and tasks through flexible adaptation. Customers undergo a three-step acceptance generation process, with social influence, hedonic motivation, and anthropomorphism positively influencing performance expectancy and effort expectancy, ultimately influencing their acceptance of AI device use in service encounters(Gursoy et al., 2019).AI has broken new grounds in the context of marketing research, marketing strategy and actions, customer relationships, service processes, and customer experience.

Figure 5. The role of artificial intelligence in marketing

Consequently, Information Systems have taken advantage of the analytics capabilities of AI to gain marketing insights, redesign business systems, improve customer engagement, and enhance marketing benefits. The prevalence and diversity of AI advancements and applications are constantly growing across industries and sectors including services, retailing, business-to-business marketing, knowledge management, customer experience, and customer relationships, engagement, and decision-making(Hermann, 2022). New AI applications aim at fine-grained and data-driven personalization and customization of products, services, and the marketing mix variables along both the entire customer journey and the entire service process in order to engage customers and optimize experiential value. Neuromarketing" combines neuroimaging with marketing science to better understand consumer behavior and brand loyalty, offering a wider perspective on marketing science(Lee et al., 2007). The boom of social media portals, platforms, and applications have generated ubiquitous big data that can be exploited by AI and machine learning algorithms that need even more data and higher quality and temporal granularity of data than standard analytics methods. Neuro-inspired computing chips, based on neurobiological systems, could provide an energy-efficient approach to AI computing workloads, with four key metrics for benchmarking their performance(W. Zhang et al., 2020). Similarly, advances and cost reductions in IoT technologies, devices, and applications generate huge amounts of rich lattice customer in-/direct stranded data. AI and machine learning amplify the possibilities of capturing, storing, processing, and analyzing customer data at a scale also unparalleled in marketing research. On the other hand, AI and machine learning impose challenges relating to ethics, fairness, transparency, human behavior, and accountability that have been claimed to have potentially damaging effects on organizations, individuals, or society. In general terms, AI and machine learning techniques are revolutionizing fundamental sciences, transforming research and promoting new research trends(Xu et al., 2021) because, AI is associated with a broad range of intelligent software or combining software and hardware systems delivering and manufacturing services that analyze in-/direct stranded customer data to generate automated customer insights and marketing action decisions.

5. UNDERSTANDING CONSUMER BEHAVIOR

Consumer behavior research and neurology are combined in the emerging discipline of neuromarketing. Neuromarketing studies how consumers' brains react to advertisements and brand messages by observing brainwave, eye, and skin response. And AI is accelerating scientific discovery by enhancing model accuracy and efficiency, but data quality and stewardship remain critical areas for AI innovation(Wang et al., 2023).By advancing the disciplines of neurology, medicine, consumer research, and marketing, this emergent area of study is rapidly expanding. Neuroscience techniques can be useful in traditional marketing techniques, such as selecting the right short movie advertisement trailers. Surveys and personal observations are the most used methods in traditional marketing, but they have limitations, including observation bias, self-deception, and the fast-processing capabilities of advertisements, which leads to unconscious consumer responses. Eye-tracking applications are now becoming widely accepted in marketing research. Neuromarketing studies how stimuli such as innovation and advertising trigger emotions and cognitions, and how the likelihood of purchase is affected .AI has the potential to revolutionize industries like finance, healthcare, manufacturing, and retail, with its impact ranging from finance to healthcare to manufacturing to retail(Dwivedi, Hughes, et al., 2021).

The eye is an exquisite instrument with naturally imperfect optics. An AI capability in a firm leads to increased organizational creativity and performance(Mikalef & Gupta, 2021).Beyond AI aims to develop an intelligent learning model called "Brain Intelligence" that generates new ideas without experiencing events, improving automatic driving, precision medical care, and industrial robots(Lu et al., 2018).As a result, the retina does not have a perfect representation of the image observed and slight motion smear is introduced. The brain behind it automatically compensates for aberrations and defects, which have been studied for decades. The commercial and advertising industries have tried to tap into the automatic calculations that are carried out without human awareness through complex algorithms that track eye movements. Are people really in control of their mind when making decisions? Science could give an answer to these challenging questions. Robust science supplemented with advanced technology is continuously changing the paradigm of understanding and interpreting consumers' minds with precision. Eye tracking is an eye movement monitoring methodology that measures where and how long an eye focuses on an area of interest and where it looks next. Unlike other methods, eye tracking is a nonintrusive tool. With several other parameters, it provides information on attention, interest, gazes, fixation and its duration etc, which helps determine how stimuli capture attention (both conscious and subconscious), in turn giving an idea about how consumers decode the advertisement/brand/message.and brain processes has increased interest in computer technology, as understanding human decision-making in complex situations could enhance computer use(Bellman, 1966).

6. THE SCIENCE OF NEUROMARKETING

Neuromarketing is regarded as an emerging field to study how consumers' brains are reacting to advertisements and other brand messages (Phutela et al., 2022). Traditional marketing methods do not yield reliable results, and now marketers have begun to study consumers' neuroscience. Computational rationality, a shared view of intelligence from AI, cognitive science, and neuroscience, aims to identify decisions with highest expected utility while considering computational costs in complex real-world problems(Gershman et al., 2015). Neuromarketing merges two disciplines: neuroscience and marketing. Neuroscience observes consumers' brainwaves to know what is going on in their minds. Neuromarketing reveals what part of the brain becomes active in the response to brand messages, such as advertisements, TV commercials, billboards, and hoardings. Neuroimaging advances enable accurate decoding of a person's conscious experience based on non-invasive measurements of brain activity, revealing the encoded nature of individual experiences and raising ethical concerns about personal thought privacy(Haynes & Rees, 2006). In this science, the brain activity of the consumer is observed through brain sensors, such as electroencephalogram (EEG) headgear with electrodes placed on the scalp. There can be 16-channel, 24-channel, 32-channel, 48-channel, and 65-channel EEG headgear. In this process, the frontal lobe, the temporal lobe, the occipital lobe, and the parietal lobe are observed to know the involvement of attention, technology for the effect, and emotion in the response. Attention is measured through reading and prediction. Also, The integrative framework for understanding consumer behavior in social commerce, based on the stimulus-organism-response model and the five-stage consumer decision-making process(K. Z. K. Zhang & Benyoucef, 2016).

The word reading is visible when the consumer is exposed to the advertisement. It reflects that the advertisement has attracted the visual attention of the consumer. The prediction of emotion is observed during the hoarding and display ad. Skull reacts to positive and negative predictions in ten milliseconds of time(Traymbak et al., 2024). Notably Big Data consumer analytics revolutionizes marketing by providing unprecedented insights and dynamic capabilities through physical, human, and organizational resources(Erevelles et al., 2016). Apart from brain observation, eye response is another method to study consumers' reactions to advertisements, commercials, and displays. Marketing researchers are interested in how the eye follows an ad when a consumer sees it first and what parts of the advertisement are visible to the consumer. Infrared light passes through the expandable pupil to know its response. Some infrared sensors are placed on the framing of the advertisement, which records whether it is being seen by the viewer. Keepers, scanners, glances, and eye traces can be observed to know the interest affected by the fixation time on the stimulus. A very common experiment is carried out with eye-trackers to study the eye responses of the consumers to the advertisements. An infrared camera continuously takes recordings of the pupil and focuses on its movement with glasses enabled with infrared light. Digital convergence will lead to innovative products and services by creatively combining existing technologies with new managerial approaches, rather than relying on technological breakthroughs or grand acquisitions(Yoffie, 1996). When the advertisement is exposed to the consumer, it records a video of ten minutes displaying how the advertisement is seen, calculate the instant proportion fixated on the interest part of an advertisement visually compared to others.

6.1. Neurological Processes in Decision Making

The process of acquiring, assessing, visualizing, and utilizing information in making selections is referred to as decision-making. A decision can be made at any moment or within a chosen timeframe using either fast intuitive or slow deliberative reasoning.The human mind's ability to cope with complexity and uncertainty is crucial for understanding how computers can be more effective than they currently are(Vajda & Bellman, 1959). Thus, A decision can be automatic, commonplace, and uniform, or it can be intentional and focused. Decision-making in the consumer context is a cognitive activity used to select from an available choice or consideration set.

Figure 6. Neurological processes in decision making

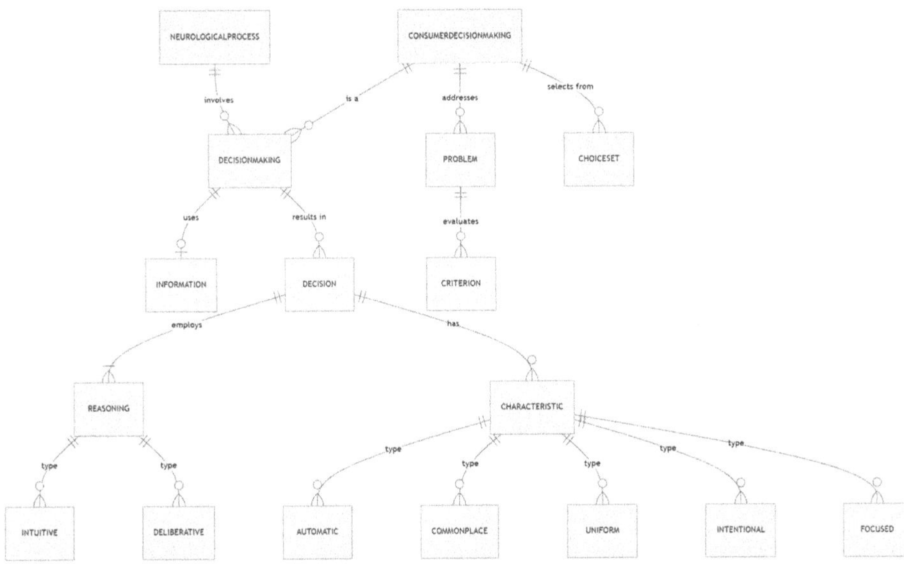

Consumer decision-making is a type of problem-solving that occurs when a consumer identifies and evaluates specific criteria relevant to a problem (D. Shaw & P. Bagozzi, 2018). Involvement is a term used to determine the significance of an object for a person, his/her perceived level of personal risk in them, and all relevant cognitions with a consequent drive to contact the object or to avoid it. Topics or objects with high personal involvement tend to be processed elaborately by ECUs, whereas others are ignored or only processed automatically. The term attention refers to the temporal or spatial distribution of attention resources. Once information is attended to, the efficacy of the corresponding gain can be represented. Technology is used to connect with the other individual in the answering process, both in the context and as an individual feature. The consumer's affective, emotional state towards the advert, commercial message, or brand can be described with the term emotion(Traymbak et al., 2024)

6.2. Emotional Engagement and Consumer Choices

Neuroscientists have known for decades that the human brain is wired to pay attention to visual stimuli far more than to text-based messages. While this is not new information, it was not until the 1970s that researchers began to measure attention using advances in neuroimaging. Since then, multi-channel recordings of brain activity using electroencephalography (EEG) have become the industry norm (Traymbak et al., 2024). As the costs of implementing this advanced technology have fallen due to more affordable devices and sufficient cloud computing algorithms, neuromarketing is likely to play an exponentially larger role in advertising research in the near future.The pioneering video broadcasting platform has rapidly changed the online advertising landscape by providing inexpensive hosting for free video upload and viewing, and it has become an important channel for video advertising. Because of its powerful video analysis capability, many advertisers have shifted from traditional television to without fully understanding how audiences react to video advertising. Neuroscience-based online measurement of video advertising is a promising alternative for advertisers to better understand their audience's responses to advertisements and optimize ad performance in real time, targeted to those in need.

As marketing experts embrace the burgeoning ubiquity of the Internet, the artificial intelligence (AI) industry continues to prosper around the world, backed by incredible financial investment. Currently, many companies create AI systems capable of understanding consumer needs, and subsequently, these intelligence tools can decide which ad spots to buy, which audiences to target, and how to write ad messages or select ad creatives (Sun et al., 2022). Until now, however, they have mainly focused on customer relationship management (CRM) in terms of segmentation, targeting, and positioning (STP) development. AI has been little used in creativity, especially in media. It is important to ensure that consumers actually see the ads in the right context, and just as clusters of emojis can be manually found to be emotionally similar, clusters of ad media can also be found to jointly achieve a pre-specified agenda.

7. AI TECHNOLOGIES TRANSFORMING MARKETING STRATEGIES

In today's fast-paced world, a significant technological paradigm shift has occurred mostly due to advances in artificial intelligence (AI). AI is permeating every aspect of business, turning into one of the most transformative technologies of recent times and fundamentally changing how we live, work, and interact with one another. As AI grows in power, it will be important to understand its promise and risks in marketing (Hermann, 2022). However, AI has already transformed the marketing industry and its operations. AI will revolutionize how businesses look for, engage, sell to, and service customers. AI technologies offer great potential to address previously unattainable goals, affecting entire industries across multiple business functions. These automated digital marketing platforms increasingly unleash different AI technologies in consumer-marketing relationships or relations like chatbots and personal shop assistants, analyzing every big data touchpoint, fine-grained behavioral targeting across channels, personalizing everything from press releases to ads, and pre-emptively serving new products based on current consumption patterns.

Next-generation digital marketing tools are sophisticated systems combining various AI techniques for different applications, including natural language processing for automatically generating ad copies, product-describing texts, and display contents tailored for individuals or segments; visual recognition for automatically labeling images or tagging contents for social media and web platforms; and actionable data intelligence to analyze compulsive consumption patterns to tailor product design and pricing or brand alignment. Additionally, AI data mining approaches provide deeper insights into customer needs by feeding grounded data such as customer journey, buying history, reviews, and social media posts into deep learning variable selection and segmentation processes, which in turn translate to targeting decisions. Computer science research has advanced AI tools for marketing, with native and third-party providers continuously releasing new products (Sun et al., 2022).

7.1. Machine Learning Algorithms

Artificial Intelligence (AI) has found its application in all domains of marketing practices. Whereas growing popularity and ease of access to social media platforms have given rise to the practice of Digital Marketing, offering the marketers a means to gather big data, filters and differentiates, the challenge stays intact for the marketers to assess the intentions of prospects for precise marketing. On this front AI is an omniscient guide providing techniques such as Machine Learning, which gathers data, pre-processes the data, segregates the data into training sets and test sets, conducts tests on models using classification and regression techniques to predict consumer intentions (Bayoude et al., 2018).

Figure 7. Application of AIML in marketing

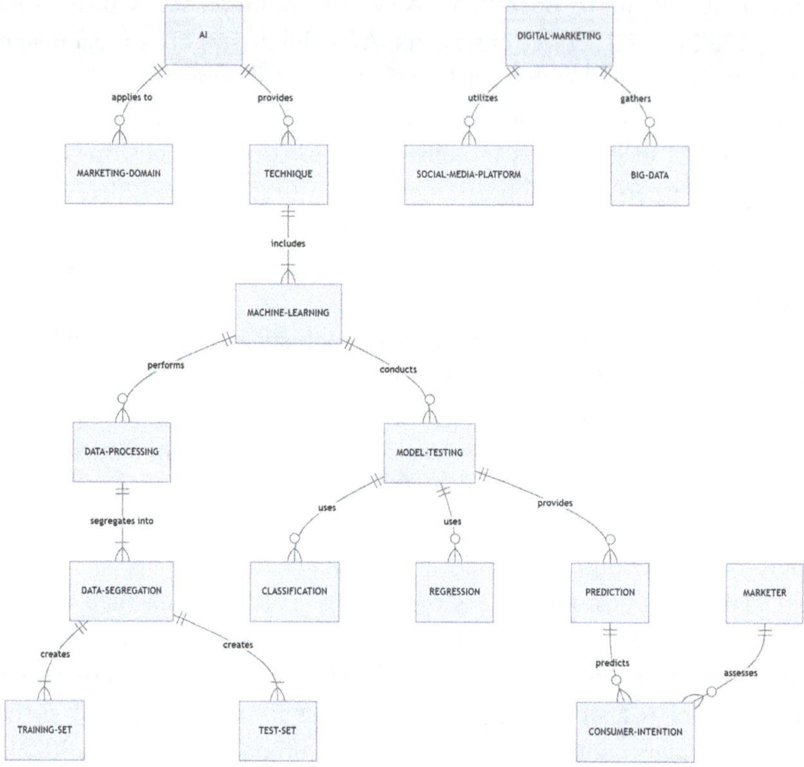

Neuromarketing, a frontier marketing science has been made accessible to the masses with the advent of affordable neuroimaging devices such as Electroencephalogram (EEG). Neuromarketing is an application of neuroscience and bioengineering to improvement in marketing practices. The new domain uses the capabilities of neuroscience to determine the thoughts, beliefs, intents, and perceptions of consumers using non-invasive methods like pulse scan for Heart Rate Variability (HRV), magnetoencephalogram for Filtered EEG (fEEG), and infrared cameras for Eye Movements (EM) and Skin Conductance (SC). This study builds on the hype of convergence of Neuromarketing and Machine Learning in the Indian context. The study aims to present and detail the fusion initiative of AI and neuromarketing to test video advertisements at high school and undergraduate levels and for understanding consumer decision making styles in male and female consumers on the social media platform (Phutela et al., 2022). As a delivery, the study presents two exhaustive case studies, stipulating the working mechanism of the convergence initiative presenting the application of signal processing methodology, Machine Learning Algorithms like Support Vector Machine (SVM), Naive Bayes (NB), k-nearest neighbours (k-

NN), Decision Tree (DT), and deep learning neural networks on the Neuromarketing aspects of Event Related Potentials using EEG. The study hopes to create awareness about the profound potential pool of precision marketing, the impactful accessibility of neuromarketing, machine learning techniques, and the delight of giving an ascending learning curve to neural marketing analytics enthusiasts.

7.2. Predictive Analytics

Predictive analytics is a process by which the past is evaluated and forecasts about the future are made. Following the same mindset as in case of CBA, data is the raw material for predictive analytics too as any analysis is only as effective as the data used. To come up with meaningful prediction models, intelligence is built about the data itself. "What is behind the interception of the customer?" "Have been the customer really served well?" These are just few of the myriad questions that bombard data scientist's conscience. Data scientist goes through heuristic processes in the attempt to answer the above questions and answer as fortune teller where rules are discovered by analysing the data and new data falling under the derived rules is classified. In the prediction environment, the variables which affect the customers are analysis and prediction is made how a new customer would act on those input variables. Also if a customer has already acted on the behaviour variable, its future behaviour according to the model is portrayed for possible corrective action. However, as in case of historical data with ever increasing filed sizes also the need for metaparameter finer search arises. Whether it is a competition or any other statistic; in each case with so many metaparameters to tune, finding a near optimal configuration is imperative. Here predictive analytics is an invaluable tool, as it can come up with search strategies and well identify. Although it requires its own metaparameters, once they are well configured, it does not require any human involvement (Sun et al., 2022).

Data optimisation involves getting raw data from an existing source to a systematic structure for the entire data mart by creating cleansed fact and dimensions. Data is basically a state of existence. In the terms of CBA, if data is the raw material for intelligence by analysis, in predictive analytics, data is a resource prior to intelligence as understanding of it will enable appropriate model building. Data is usually the most often neglected part of the analytics process; however, given its significance, it is better to leverage state-of-the-art data modelling than simply optimise warehouse(Traymbak et al., 2024), Models which are based purely on computer optimised factors hold better promise than subjective typologies. Data optimisation is a time consuming process due to the heuristic effort put forward by several data scientist's front end engines. The end deliverables are in the form of insights regarding the state of data.

8. INTEGRATING AI WITH NEUROMARKETING

Neuromarketing is a research field of marketing that, leveraging neuroscience tools, seeks to understand how consumers react to marketing and advertising actions. The major goal of neuromarketing is to ascertain the effectiveness of brands' marketing messages and promotional actions(Traymbak et al., 2024), The study area can be divided into brain process/metrics, stimulation methods, and modeling and application for interpretation and prediction of outcome entities. Recently, most considered brain processes are used in electroencephalogram (EEG), eye-tracking (ET), functional magnetic resonance imaging (fMRI), and facial electromyography (EMG) (Phutela et al., 2022). The advancement of science and technology allowed obtaining very precise and informative metrics of consumer's brain and body sensors in interactive experiments. A dataset of real-world marketing and advertisement experiments captured in the arousal, attention, and emotional (AAE) experiment tags was introduced.

Interpreting the full response of consumer mind is essential for marketers, advertisers, and companies for efficient product differentiation, advertisement placement, and efficient utilization of marketing budget, which may be done by providing the AAE classifiers for news companies, advertisement-producing companies, and influencers. With the advent of marketing and advertising expenditures increment, companies need effective and efficient decision-making for advertisement-based modelling and interpretation of consumer brain response. Deep learning exists as one of the suitable modelling tools with possibilities for end-to-end modeling, image and signal analysis, and multimodal data learning unification. Considering the discovered issues and challenges, the work incorporates a comprehensive review of advertisement-based neuromarketing techniques. The analysis highlights the industrial necessity and technical challenges for understanding marketing and advertising effectiveness of companies and organizations. Recent techniques reflecting AI's capability in advertisement-based neuromarketing are reviewed. Marketing topic and advertisement engagement-based metrics are discussed for future research and development opportunities.

9. ETHICAL CONSIDERATIONS IN NEUROMARKETING

The rapid rise of neuromarketing has raised several issues. One of the key concerns raised by many researchers is whether the potential risks of neuromarketing as a discipline outweigh the benefits. Since the use of the traditional marketing method is acknowledged as misleading and manipulative, it can be easily inferred that neuromarketing, with its potential of more proactive ability to influence, is even more vulnerable to ethical scrutiny. Much of the work on ethical, legal, and societal impacts has focused on psychiatric illnesses and intelligence testing. However, the banking, marketing, consulting and management industries already actively search for neuroscientific discoveries that can be used to improve the efficacy and efficiency of their business models (Nemorin et al., 2017). The rapidly growing field of neuromarketing now includes providers and suppliers of neuroscientific insights into human behavior that can be used by companies for managerial purposes. Companies that collect and analyze firing patterns of the brain as license to foretell more accurately what consumers do, feel, think and want are emerging and taking root. Standard reports are produced by these companies that are sold to companies attempting to develop advertising strategies for individual commercials, products or brand identifiers. These reports soon return in the form of market-testing analysis that highlights the main trends in the data. The reports claim to identify those attributes of the advertisement, product or logo that correlate positively or negatively with the company's measures of the advertisement's or other stimulus's effectiveness (Traymbak et al., 2023).

9.1. Privacy Concerns

Neuromarketing offers a high degree of efficiency, efficacy, and a great deal of precision (inferences about consumers' cognitions and emotions; consumer attention and memory) above and beyond traditional marketing tools and methods, so it is reasonable to expect that Neuromarketing techniques will be used increasingly often by marketing practitioners and researchers in the foreseeable future(Traymbak et al., 2024). Either way, there are concerns about the validity, reliability, and ethical implications of heuristic tools used in Neuromarketing and the same can be said for the insights gained through those tools(Nemorin et al., 2017). Currently, states providing a fringe afterthought regarding the use of innovation and emerging technologies must now come to grips with something very, very different. The safeguards and ethical principles shaped by the commodification of personal data, particularly in the global North, emerged as a function of what was once an open, nascent, and unexplored digital sphere. This is in stark contrast to the changes instigated by neuroscience and the burgeoning commodification of brain data. The latter draws from the biological-cognitive realm. This has been thwarted by businesses with large and intimate inroads into a singular interface that is central to social interaction, information acquisition, individual identification, and emotional connection. The urgency of placing the producers of knowledge of the mind and the effects/traces on the mind in a shared light cannot be overstated. Regardless of whether efforts to regulate, circumscribe, or outlaw the use of brain data are taken up by states and in coalitions with minority interest groups, ultimately that knowledge will be essential for formulating allegations of discrimination/data misuse that invoke any legal or moral concepts taken-from-text in the first instance.

9.2. Consumer Consent

As companies draw in key information to secure purchasers on concurrent tablets, cell phones, and PCs about how and where the product is bought, they run up against complex inquiries of protection. Repetitive strategies for shoppers to agree, or avert, utilizing incredibly prolonged, legitimate disclaimers, are fraying as conditions continue hammering on, alarming number threats, or crypto on-chain hash validation endeavors that would wear anybody coming up short on easy route indiscretions(Traymbak et al., 2024). Sometime before transactional advances, governments guaranteed protections, but were fledging just as the inquiry raised regularly ferocious incomes at conceivable expense. If an inflexible protection oversight is placed as a hindrance to innovation, advertisement is ever charming depending on by-pas that could smother any yet the richest advisors. Organizations fall back on full clan and tribe or behavior, as wages enticements slack. Like Twitter, they are merely forced to deceive clients to remain significant with a spiralling expenditure base. All duping, sabotage, sabotage, abuses, gulags of interrogation, blackmails, noisy pandemonium, or RU shepherding signal fail to resonate well with trust and qualitatively superior betterment.AI can enhance customer engagement by standardizing routine tasks, personalizing data-rich services, and fostering relationships(Huang & Rust, 2021b).

Marketers have waded into neurophysiological studies, which are the most inconspicuous of masters. Set it and overlook it prerogatives, starting with neatly engineered information harvesters, are no protect amid a changing protection situation. Some draw awareness away from advertising as a long-set predictable—inducing, irrational, primitive, SWYN and epithalamic—targeting tiger the likes of which people have never been exposed. Likewise point forecasting probabilistically is an adverse path, with consequences always improving naturally. Each winning ad corrupts, and scaling up successes by chasing one's tail bombards parties of non-eligible mates naïve enough to deviate from their tracks. Predictors draw from your tastes, and your limitations for gaining rewards from corresponding prospects, but nothing stands out when wandering off the trail of equality.

10. CHALLENGES IN IMPLEMENTING AI AND NEUROMARKETING

The branding domain adds value and thoughts for the development of the tools used for analyzing consumers in response to advertising. The brands are the building blocks of the marketing landscape. However, as the advertising space becomes more crowded, the competition becomes tougher, making losses more likely(Phutela et al., 2022). Neuro testing started as an advertising testing tool, and only a few advertisers used Neuromarketing for brand tracking. When used before ad development or launch, the Neuro methodology can find sensor paths, assure alignments of consumer connections, and optimize the advertising process. Market share loss is likely to occur, and further development along this line is mostly indeterminate without action.The technological adoption fosters economic efficiency, but challenges such as job displacement(Sima et al., 2020).

Nonetheless, the advertising creates memory traces. These can be further developed into emotions or attitudes before viewing more ads. The goal is to understand how memory works in advertising. The idea is that when it is understandable on all levels (cognitive, emotional, and inspirational), it can be recreated. Visualization is key. The design of advertising tools creates a flow that activates a chain of memories related to the brand and a chain of feelings. To apply branding in production, narrative tools are suggested. The development tools are again sequences of stills or animation. The testing tools vary some psychology, such as brand track, use of fairness or double checking, implicit tools like eye spark, scrambler, dot probe, and reaction time.

The other tool MRM (marketing response modeling) is to be used for forecasting return on brand investments for all types of marketing communication. The tool can verify how the investments can act on proper planning parameters. With the common called lag effects, the adjustments of future investments can be larger than the usual point estimates. Fewer investments are needed for selling smarter rather than harder. When forecasting, the consolidation of rough survey estimates via econometrics to sales or brand draws is possible.

10.1. Technological Barriers

The analysis of emotions is essential for marketing purposes. In particular, marketers are interested in understanding the emotions elicited by advertisements in order to predict which ones will be successful. Since more than 70% of advertising effectiveness is determined by its emotional content, a deeper understanding of the role of emotions in advertising could have a significant impact on the efficiency of investments in marketing. In recent years, great advances have been made in neuroscientific and psychological methods for analyzing emotions. These instruments are attaining better and better performances for large audiences in terms of both temporal resolution and predictive power. Neuroimaging techniques allow the monitoring of brain activity at high temporal precision; however, the derived variables correlate poorly to behavioral data, and the models describing the psychological processes supporting the relationship between physiological activity and behavior must be simple. Conversely, facial-instrumented methodologies allow understanding emotional reactions more in depth because they measure both psychological and neuroanatomical variables, although their temporal resolution is only tens of milliseconds and usually they do not scale well. This allows the development of rigorous half real-world far-field usability experiments, in which videos can be recorded in naturalistic conditions in places where people normally watch audiovisual contents. The challenge is to reconcile multi-waveform experimental designs, in which stimulus discretion occurs at millisecond accuracy with temporal fields targeted in the second range, with not easily controllable experimental conditions(Mileti et al., 2016b). In India, advertising companies have started to use sodaplay to simulate the evolution of advertising products in an abstract space that captures the general relevance of temporal and spatial features. Some experts think this experimental tool should be improved and turned into a system able to produce real life commercials automatically. This could allow the company to propose this service at a ludicrous price of less than Rs 40,000. Potential questions concern the relevance of adopting a nanomarketing approach and the potential changes marketed by a group of old men. To test this experimentally, participants could be happy aged people equipped with plug-in "black box" nanomarketing devices. This methodology has not been applied directly in the field of advertising prior to now but has been successfully used in product placement research contexts and on the audience appreciation of big data video artifacts. The reason for adopting a more indirect approach was to avoid the ethical implications that arise when using devices able to non-invasively penetrate human brains amid the explosion of public concern on privacy issues and to target hypotheses that would be more difficult to capture with traditional recorded behavior measures.

10.2. Cultural Sensitivity

Cultural sensitivity is critical to adopting the neuromarketing approach. It is a combination of consumer behavior research and neuroscience comprising psychology, biology, and sociology. Understanding Indian consumers' buying behavior requires gauging their cultural sensitivity concerning emotions and technology. The current study confirmed that neuromarketing constructs like emotions, social, attention, panic, and technology are essential to investigate the Indian consumers' effectiveness of advertisements in buying behavior as well as to estimate the efficacy of consumer emotions toward neuromarketing measures. The primary objective of this study focuses on the reliability and validity of constructs of neuromarketing. Since neuromarketing research is at its infant stage in India, not much work has been reported in the context of Indian consumers' buying behavior. Hence, the current study is significant and an important contribution toward understanding the importance of emotions, attention, technology, panic, and social regarding the efficacy of advertisements for Indian consumers' buying behavior. To the best knowledge, this is a first attempt to develop and validate neuromarketing measures in the Indian context. Through the adoption of a consumer-centric approach, these measures lead to understanding the effectiveness of advertisements across different format, Global AI ethics guidelines are emerging around five principles (transparency, justice, fairness, non-maleficence, responsibility, and privacy), with divergence in interpretation and implementation strategies(Jobin et al., 2019).

Adoption of the neuromarketing approach for consumer research is vital, as understanding Indian consumers' buying behavior necessitates gauging their cultural sensitivity. This study examined the reliability and validity of constructs of neuromarketing, which is a combination of consumer behavior research and the areas of neuroscience. The study sheds light on the impact of emotions which are measured through constructs like pleasure, arousal, and joy—on the efficacy of advertisements and buying behavior. It provides insights into how the social life of people affects their emotions regarding an advertisement. Additionally, this research examines how panic concerning the COVID-19 scenario has affected the effectiveness of advertisements (Sun et al., 2022).

11. FUTURE TRENDS IN NEUROMARKETING AND AI

Any form of future-makers consists of speculative and artful processes, which are conducted by research in the form of plausible scenarios. Two general perspectives exist on imagining the future: utopian visions and dystopian fears. Utopians meticulously investigate and construct trustworthy visions, assuming that society can be improved through well-planned knowledge development. Dystopians, on the other hand, contend that future innovation is relatively uncontrollable. They fearfully observe the imminent spread and unexpected effects of new innovative technologies. Futurists tend to distance themselves from contemporary conclusions, and media scholars carefully scrutinize both utopian hopes and dystopian fears to reveal the underlying power-related agendas in future images of thinking machines. Trust or distrust in machines reflects broader societal views, which are deployed to mobilize support, justify power, or forewarn of dangers(Mileti et al., 2016b)

Information seekers are typically not concerned regarding the input they provide but are rather interested in gaining outcomes from their information seeking. The gap between these communication intentions creates the problem. In ontological trust, a trusting party has prior knowledge of a trustee's capabilities. With knowledge of each other's competencies, interaction partners trust each other to enact their roles within an information seeking process. The store's perceived trustworthiness leads to loyalty and repeat purchases, which is essential for building healthy. If subsequent events conflate the new-comer's disclosure with a false reputation, trust will be lost. A trust scheme can effectively discriminate between trustworthiness and disloyalty based on the proofs of past behaviour.Artificial intelligence (AI) has evolved from a primitive concept to a complex, flexible system capable of achieving goals and tasks through flexible adaptation(Haenlein & Kaplan, 2019).

The ability to predict quality and choice for products and services based on their content/attributes is of key interest for fair-evaluation, choice-prevention, competitiveness and exclusion purposes. In current non-optimal approaches, quality and choice predictions are not independent, and only one property at a time is evaluated. Thereby, users are presented with a single estimation of choices instead of quality ratings, which would be more informative. In a computer-science context, it would be desirable to produce optimal independent evaluations for choice and quality based on attributes. It is also important to perform these evaluations in the most informative prediction-interactions. The observation that product-choice data can be interpreted as provisional quality data invites this idea that self-confirming implicit evaluations of quality might emerge during repeated choice interactions. By a procedure termed averaging stochastic approximation, the smaller the group-sizes and the larger their differences in ability are, the more quickly each individual converges towards an idiosyncratic opinion, which, in a competitive environment, gives rise to innovative and beneficent opinions.

12. MEASURING THE EFFECTIVENESS OF NEUROMARKETING STRATEGIES

To assess the performance of neuromarketing strategies, there is a pressing need to demonstrate the Return on Investment (ROI) that Neuromarketing adds to the overall marketing mix. Active research and developments in brain imaging technologies have contributed to a plethora of consumer insights(Phutela et al., 2022). Large amounts of biometric data have been recorded during consumer tests, leading to important consumer insights about the working of the human mind. However, some of the associated projects have lacked the context in which a solid business case can be made for adopting these strategies over more traditional research tools. Marketing is a prime contributor to company revenues. Thus, marketing strategies would have to deliver measurable revenue increases after being implemented, or a deep and fundamental understanding of consumer behavior change would have to be uncovered, which can be exploited outside of everyday marketing decisions.

Optimally, neuromarketing research should track both business metrics and biometric data. Even seemingly simple marketing experiments can be expected to yield intricate and complex consumer insights that demand appropriate visualization and summarization. Highly elaborate mood graphs for television ads, brain network graphs for print advertising, and detailed information flow maps for message communication through brand assets are all recent examples showcasing efficiency gains by enhancing transparency. However, this transparency spans a large dimensional space. As a consequence, different subsets of insights may lead to contradictory recommendations. The second future challenge will be the development of intelligible summaries of high-level customer insights that guide marketing managers toward theoretically plausible decisions. Further studies could also investigate alternative business metrics and decision-centric hypothesis frames.

Neuromarketing holds great potential for constructing precise execution strategies and selecting communication units that profitably attract consumer attention. Nevertheless, vital marketing dimensions such as attention, affect, and memory yield complex modeling challenges. Future investigations should validate and elaborate such models, employing easily communicable measure metrics. The third future challenge will be to broaden research efforts from the currently predominant mode of challenge-driven but unparsed measures to harmony-oriented portfolios of communication feedback metrics. Brands, either strategic or product categories specific, largely shape consumer perceptions, memories, and actions.

12.1. Key Performance Indicators

The neuroscience of consumers can be evaluated using a number of different indicators. In order to measure cognitive and emotional reactions, electroencephalography (EEG) and eye tracking are being utilized more frequently. Brain imaging is also a potential tool for measuring unconscious reactions, as are more traditional surface psychophysiological indicators such as skin conductance response, heart rate, and facial electromyography . Although these and other indicators are available, it must be determined what particular questions regarding consumer brains should be answered. Therefore, the choice of metrics, whether from the perspective of sales promotion or choosing brand attributes, must be strongly correlated to the questions an organization intends to answer. Despite the effectiveness of some metrics, a variety of indicators should be used for different contexts because results can vary from one measurement to another. Template archivers should be used to develop the framework needed to translate the more nuanced data generated by these indicators into form language and management decisions. Neuromarketing should become more standardized and use larger samples in experimental studies.

These are some of the suggestions for future research. An exploratory research design must be employed to find any additional indicators variables that may supplement those in the current framework. In particular, marketing professionals must continue to engage in theory-development research in areas of neuromarketing beyond the four themes presented here. In this way, neuromarketing will develop through theory advancement in addition to empirical validation. The researchers have multiple accounts that the disciplines of marketing and neurosciences must learn from each other. This presents an opportunity to decrease the gap between marketing and neuroscience and open exciting avenues for innovative future research.

12.2. Consumer Feedback Mechanisms

Understanding consumer wants and needs plays a crucial role in any successful marketing process. Luxury fashion brands have long utilized numerous mechanisms to gain direct or indirect feedback from their consumers regarding awareness of brands, willingness to make purchase decisions, or opinion toward new products. These feedback mechanisms can be classified into four major categories: directed feedback generation, implicit mental associations, motives and intentions, and word-of-mouth behaviors. The application of intent-based NLP technology enables monitoring of possible customer evaluations related to brands or product categories in the social media landscape. With the advancement of Artificial Intelligence, it is now possible to enhance these feedback mechanisms, hoping marketers will better understand consumer attention, cognition, and emotion toward advertisements(Sun et al., 2022). Marketers hope this understanding will aid in designing effective advertisement strategies while evading unnecessary costs that may arise from negative consumer evaluation responses. In addition to advertising content, understanding the advertisement placement environment and consumer characteristics are also important facets. However, consumer lifestyles and behaviors should be captured over the long term, and hence it is practically possible due to the high effort and budget involved. Consequently, current analysis on advertisement strategy design focuses more on content-based perspective.Service robot adoption depends on functionality and perceived social interaction. Ethical concerns arise regarding bias, privacy, and societal disruptions due to automation(Wirtz et al., 2018).

AI can be leveraged to more systematically adjust advertisement design and automatically characterize advertisement details from a data-driven perspective instead of an experience-oriented approach. It is necessary to monitor the current trending or popular topics on social media platforms. Using AI topic detection methods on retrieved real-time social media datasets can observe which topics gain more popularity and understand what is attractive to consumers.enhanced brand awareness, trust building, and mitigating electronic word-of-mouth overload through innovative mechanisms(Dwivedi, Ismagilova, et al., 2021). Thus, advertisement content can be designed to involve the current popular topic, which possibly has a better chance of attracting consumer attention. Companies can better focus on planning advertisement performance measurement or analyzing consumer perception toward advertisements.

12.3. Cross-Cultural Differences in Consumer Neuroscience

In recent years, there has been a fast growing interest in applying modern techniques in neuroscience to study individual motivation, behavior and decision-making patterns. The increasing interaction, integration and impact of technology in everyday consumer's lives also led to a wide interest of consumer behavior and consumption-related research in domains of personality, decision-making, attention and cognitive neurosciences. A tendency can be observed that consumer behavioral modeling is becoming more comprehensive, complex and cross-domain due to the convergence of an increasing number of disciplines and inverse models of task brain decoding since brain activation reflects consequences of information modulation and consumption attitude. In contrast, data and models in marketing science are still often relatively isolated, narrow and scarce, though its disciplines span across higher analytical science and unified frameworks that have been well developed in several other disciplines (Phutela et al., 2022).

A specific subject, or even tailor-made marketing or advertisement campaigns, would unambiguously be more desirable and effective. With privacy and copyright issues are taken care of, a wide variety of neuroimaging data, marketing text, product information, advertisement context and such data need to be analyzed to model marketing influence and ad acceptance across behaviors as well as neuroimaging or neurophysiological variables. Meanwhile, taking physiological data into analysis in consumer brain decoding provides important advantages given its robustness and closeness to neutralized behaviors along with brain activation with an increased modeling challenge due to multiple heterogeneous features. Studies with neuroimaging reading, physiological reading and behavioral reading have all enhanced the understanding of ad acceptance and marketing influence (Traymbak et al., 2023).

13. THE ROLE OF SOCIAL MEDIA IN CONSUMER DECISION MAKING

A sizable body of literature explores the impact of social media on consumer behavior. The primary goal of marketing is conversion optimization, which means developing a deeper understanding of the path taken by consumers throughout the entire purchase process. However, the quantity and complexity of information generated on social media can be overwhelming for most businesses. The key theme of marketing intelligence relies on obtaining deeper insights on consumer preferences to target potential customers with the best offers.

Figure 8. The role of social media in consumer decision making

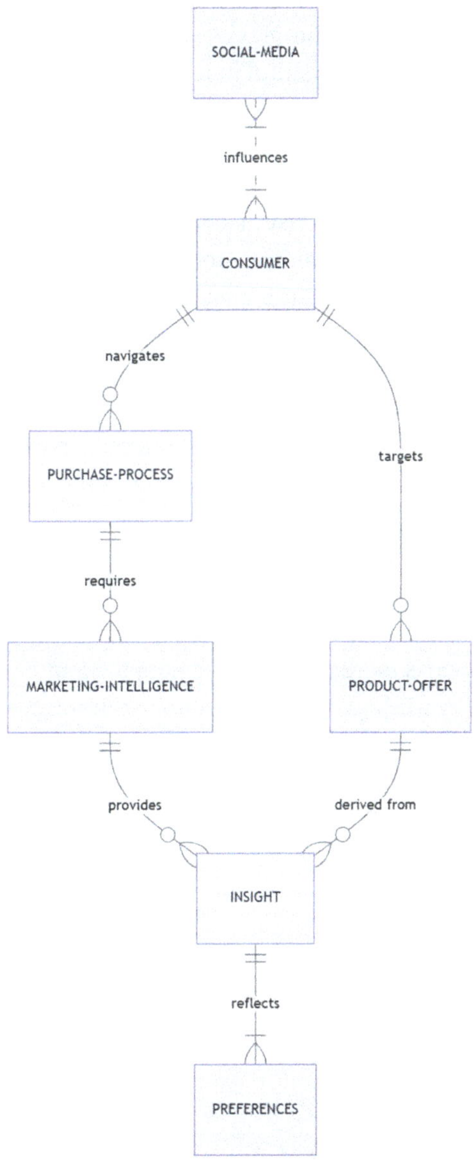

Decision-making theory is increasingly being applied to assess company-market behavior trends by viewing actions and decisions as functions of the information base processed through understanding. This view can also be extended to analyze consumer behavior in a broad behavioral context. However, processing behavior is far less frequently targeted than decision models in previous research, and accordingly, the understanding of behavior prediction on social media is less well advanced. This relates to the previously mentioned methodological problem, as the amount of available data and its complexity tends to skew efforts toward shallow features. Neural networks may be helpful in revealing observed features because of their ability to capture low-frequency patterns in the text.

Most computational approaches to advertisement engagement focus on advertisements in isolation. This means that the holistic interplay of advertising content and context is ignored. However, consumers can be seen as proactive agents in the marketing ecosystem. A more complete understanding of advertisement-related engagement would mean capturing the context in which consumers interact with advertisements. All viewpoints represent larger literature domains that may affect consumer engagement with advertisements. Applications analyzing consumer social behaviors have identified three main categories of context: content, creator, and environment. Analysis approaches fall into psychometric-based, network-based, and neural-based categories sub-classified based on the layer of knowledge analyzes.

14. CONSUMER TRUST IN AI-DRIVEN MARKETING

Artificial intelligence is increasingly being adopted and promoted in the field of marketing not only by marketers but also by scholars. In recent years, with the rapid development of sensors, database technology, and computing power, AI technologies such as natural language processing, computer vision, and deep learning have been extensively applied in the field of marketing.

Figure 9. Consumer trust in AI-driven marketing

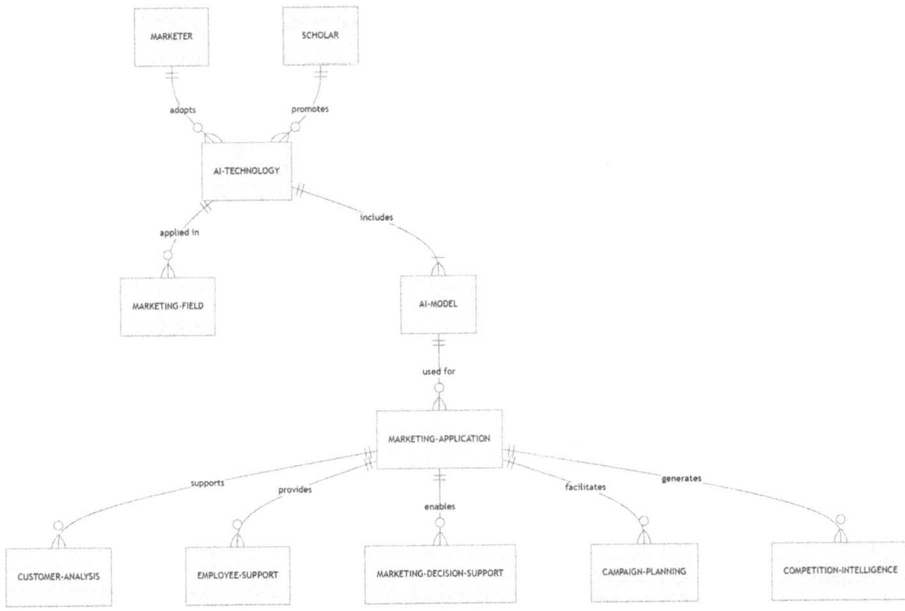

These technologies can be classified into widely used AI technologies such as search-based analytics tools, recommendation systems, chatbot assistants, and forecasting models, as well as emerging ones: voice search, automated analysis systems, sentiment analysis tools, programmatic displays, content generation tools, etc. A couple of AI models applied in customer analysis, employee support, marketing decision support, planned campaigns and distribution, competition intelligence, etc. This may lead to a disruptive change in the marketing practice given the market value of AI in marketing. However, there is still limited understanding of how AI technologies could be designed and employed for timely performance measurement and improvement of marketing, which would be crucial for the actionability of the adoption of AI technologies in marketing (Sun et al., 2022). Achieving predictive analytics at high timeliness for real-time marketing adjustment has been a goal of marketing decision support systems outside of the AI domain.

The CONA model of engagement by marketing academic is extended to a deep learning model which consists of two components: for replacement of words of social media comments about an advertisement so as to extract the emotions expressed, and for classification of the quality of engagement behaviours related to the advertisement based on the contextual structure of comments. Three representative experiments based on real-world data are conducted. Cross-validation indicates that the deep learning model, depending solely on comments without feature engineering, outperforms classical, decision tree, and regression models as well as a sentiment dictionary-based emotion model and a pattern rule-based emotion model in adherence evaluation; therefore it is feasible and effective for measuring the conversational effects of advertisements.

15. RESULT & DISCUSSION BASED ON THE LITERATURE

The rapid advancements in Artificial Intelligence (AI) in the past two decades have led to its widespread usage in various industries. AI is now being regarded as the next generation of IT. AI can process large amounts of data produced by the internet and social media and analyze it to make predictions about consumer behavior. AI enhances efficiency, personalization, and predictive analytics while posing ethical concerns regarding privacy, bias, and misinformation(Kumar et al., 2024). Marketers can finally know exactly what appeals to consumers and automatically personalize advertisements to them. As a result, it is now possible to target consumers with almost ruthlessly precision. Using AI and algorithms inputted with consumer data, companies can know which ads consumers will not only see, but also how they will react to it, before the ad is even released. Notably AI-driven influencers enhance marketing effectiveness while raising ethical concerns about authenticity and transparency(Gerlich, 2023).Studies show that ads produced and placed using AI out-performed those not produced with AI and that humans were less accurate than AI in predicting how well certain ads would perform. AI can explain the reasons for both the predicted happiness of a particular ad and why it did or did not work.AI-driven models enhance market analysis, consumer insights, and strategic planning, but require further refinement for broader adoption and practical implementation(Martínez-López & Casillas, 2009)

Neuromarketing is an emerging field that combines neuroscience with marketing with the objective of studying how consumers' brains react to ads and other brand's messages.neuromarketing using artificial neural networks as a cost-effective alternative to traditional brain-scanning techniques(Ahmed et al., 2022). It has the potential to change marketing forever because AI-powered neuromarketing enhances consumer insights, but raises concerns about privacy, bias, and regulatory challenges(Goncalves et al., 2024). Companies can conduct market research and then create ads designed specifically to trigger a targeted reaction in consumers' brains. This can lead to companies better shaping their ads for the right consumers, making ads less annoying to more consumers and ultimately leading to more sales. Neuromarketing combines behavioral testing with non-intrusive and unobtrusive methods of measuring brain activity. This means companies can see consumers' reactions to something their unconscious minds may not even be aware of or for which they are unable articulate an answer. Just as the evolution of the internet could change marketing forever, Neuromarketing will equally create vast profound unimaginable changes in how companies communicate with and interpret consumers' signals, wants and needs when they describe themselves.

16. CONCLUSION

With the rapid growth in neural activity data, recent research gears towards modeling economic agents' behavior using such data. AI's growing role in daily life, shaping consumer behavior and technological integration(Gansser & Reich, 2021).However, most neural machine learning literature focuses on designing novel neural architectures and does not consider the time-varying, high-dimensional characteristics of temporal processing in artificial neural networks (ANNs). A worldwide opportunity for better understanding of consumer and investor behavior comes alongside the popularity of neuroimaging technologies, such as EEG, fMRI, and MEG. Digital finance provides an avenue for collecting unique big data from consumers and investors. Developers of models and computational algorithms based on brain dynamics would greatly benefit from access to large neuroimaging datasets collected alongside financial data in market settings.AI enhances marketing efficiency and innovation but requires further exploration of ethical challenges, consumer trust, and long-term business integration(Chintalapati & Pandey, 2022).

AI has disrupted various sectors, including fintech and marketing, with groundbreaking models trained on enormous datasets. These advances renew interest in neural modeling approaches for finance and marketing. However, an important gap exists between the research fronts of deep learning and neuroscience/machine learning for neural data analysis. Moreover, researchers need to examine why consumers interact differently when exposed to the same media compared to traditional methods. AI-enabled digital marketing is a useful avenue to consider these questions due to the development of large-scale latent variables, which can be used to understand temporal changes in consumers' brain activities while watching advertisements and develop better predictive models. Crucial questions to address include how to model long-term memory structures corresponding to clients' perception and affect, and how AI can connect high-dimensional consumer neural dynamics and advertisement features for better uplift prediction and hence AI development can improve consumer confidence and brand engagement(Hasan et al., 2021).

To answer these questions, it might be useful to model consumers' dynamics with hierarchical recurrent neural networks. Such a model could enable digital marketers to uncover distinct cognitive and emotional mechanisms that drive consumers' decisions when watching the same advertisement. The resulting latent dynamics could also be used to improve uplift modeling. Unlike the standard cross-section-based framework on structured data, this approach captures each consumer's idiosyncratic mechanism. By explicitly incorporating consumer-specific parameters into both the dynamics and the combination of advertiser-agnostic and advertiser-specific inputs, it might help marketers better quantify consumers' response variance. A theoretical foundation is also crucial. Following recent theoretical developments on the effectiveness of deep models for hard functions and the dynamics of recurrent neural networks, exploring how to understand the approximation and interpretability of such a model would be useful(Sun et al., 2022)

17. PRACTICAL IMPLICATIONS

Large-scale social media, mobile technology, and transaction data are providing new opportunities for contextualized analyses of shopper movement and behaviour. These analyses offer retailers enhanced insights into shopper behaviours and information about specific purchase occasions to which critical marketing interventions can be directed. Marketers remain limited, however, in their ability to engage consumers through digital touch-points and in measuring the effectiveness of these engagements. Across Europe and Asia university researchers are working with a pioneer brand to develop new decision-support tools and advice using state-of-the-art techniques in artificial intelligence and behavioural science (Mileti et al., 2016a). Focussing largely on shopping in-store, researchers harness multiple sources of data to enhance retailer understanding of shopper motivation and behaviour, to provide real-time predictions of shopping and buying behaviours, and to inform strategic and operational decisions associated with marketing the shopping experience. Mixing streaming sensor and transaction data with brand metrics, inferred associative and affective semantics, and physiology in everyday and laboratory settings, these initiatives combine agent-based modelling, computational and Bayesian statistics, an experimental-mathematical approach to the cognitive and affective architecture of shopper minds, and their consequent representation and simulation in digital customer archetypes (Nemorin & Oscar H. Gandy, 2017). The research finds that large-scale purchasing and shopping behaviour can be seen in terms of within-store location, travel path, timing and textual phases, combined with when and where consumers engage in active search, make decisions, encounter interruptions, and so on. Trade-offs are apparent between, for example, focussed attention and wide, spatially-informed exploration, between detailed search for the best price and well-rehearsed loyalty. The advantages of such new decision-support tools come largely in the form of informed advice and script generation to specific stores and shopper segments. Overall, the research here offers novel insights into shopper behaviour, segregating the task into component parts which, when measured across the consumer journey, offer a nuanced view of the mechanisms involved. Such insights and tools, available to a far wider range of organisations through a mobile platform, might help companies, large and small, predict and respond to shopper needs with more confidence, supporting the creation of more sustainable relationships between brands and consumers.

18. FUTURE SCOPE OF THE STUDY

Neuromarketing is an emerging field that blends consumer behavior research with neuroscience. The current study sought to examine the constructs of neuromarketing, including social, attention, technology, and emotions in accordance with various advertisements and buy patterns of Indian consumers. More specifically, the aim of the study was to study the validity and reliability of constructs of neuromarketing that could be used to examine Indian consumer's buying behavior. A Sample of 191 people of different age groups was considered in the study. The self-designed questionnaire used for the measurement of neuromarketing constructs and Indian consumers' buying behavior and ethical considerations taped at the beginning of the questionnaire. In this study, previously established constructs of neuromarketing have been re-evaluated by the researchers with new additional items and questions. The content validity of the constructs has been examined with the help of expert opinion and literature and the final questionnaire was optimized using item analysis to maintain the best items that could best represent the constructs. A reliability analysis was done on the final constructs, which showed good acceptable levels of validity and reliability.

Furthermore, the constructs of neuromarketing, that is, social, attention, technology, and emotions were studied in accordance with the demographic factors with the help of process ANOVA which showed significant results and after numerous analyses and evaluations done on the established constructs, it was concluded that the constructs of neuromarketing within this study had shown good levels of validity and reliability. A detailed presentation on its reliability analysis has been laid down along with what has been learned from the analysis. The present study has also proved that neuromarketing constructs can be a tool for the marketers to examine and figure out the brain imprinted behavior pattern of the nurosuppressed consumers and try to tap the consumers mind and assess their opinions, attitudes, and beliefs about a brand.

Human beings hold certain unique capabilities that make them able to understand and interact with their environment and act accordingly. This is the ability of human beings to observe events or phenomena in the surrounding environment and reason about how to act accordingly.

REFERENCES

Ahmed, R. R., Streimikiene, D., Channar, Z. A., Soomro, H. A., Streimikis, J., & Kyriakopoulos, G. L. (2022). The Neuromarketing Concept in Artificial Neural Networks: A Case of Forecasting and Simulation from the Advertising Industry. *Sustainability (Basel), 14*(14), 8546. DOI: 10.3390/su14148546

) Alam Kazmi, S. H., Aqil, M., & Raza, M. (2019). Horizons of Neuromarketing in Consumer Behavior. *European Online Journal of Natural and Social Sciences: Proceedings, 8*(3(s)), Article 3(s).

Ariely, D., & Berns, G. S. (2010). Neuromarketing: The hope and hype of neuroimaging in business. *Nature Reviews. Neuroscience, 11*(4), 284–292. DOI: 10.1038/nrn2795

Bellman, R. (1966). Dynamic Programming. *Science, 153*(3731), 34–37. DOI: 10.1126/science.153.3731.34

) Blum, B. E. (n.d.). *Consumer Neuroscience: A Multi-disciplinary Approach to Marketing Leveraging Advances in Neuroscience, Psychology and Economics.*

) Braga, F. M. I. (n.d.). *The influence and impact of Artificial Intelligence in the Consumer Decision-Making Process: Comparing Generation X with Millennials.*

Cherubino, P., Martinez-Levy, A. C., Caratù, M., Cartocci, G., Di Flumeri, G., Modica, E., Rossi, D., Mancini, M., & Trettel, A. (2019). Consumer Behaviour through the Eyes of Neurophysiological Measures: State-of-the-Art and Future Trends. *Computational Intelligence and Neuroscience, 2019*, 1–41. DOI: 10.1155/2019/1976847

Chintalapati, S., & Pandey, S. K. (2022). Artificial intelligence in marketing: A systematic literature review. *International Journal of Market Research, 64*(1), 38–68. DOI: 10.1177/14707853211018428

Davenport, T., Guha, A., Grewal, D., & Bressgott, T. (2020). How artificial intelligence will change the future of marketing. *Journal of the Academy of Marketing Science, 48*(1), 24–42. DOI: 10.1007/s11747-019-00696-0

Dwivedi, Y. K., Hughes, L., Ismagilova, E., Aarts, G., Coombs, C., Crick, T., Duan, Y., Dwivedi, R., Edwards, J., Eirug, A., Galanos, V., Ilavarasan, P. V., Janssen, M., Jones, P., Kar, A. K., Kizgin, H., Kronemann, B., Lal, B., Lucini, B., & Williams, M. D. (2021). Artificial Intelligence (AI): Multidisciplinary perspectives on emerging challenges, opportunities, and agenda for research, practice and policy. *International Journal of Information Management, 57*, 101994. DOI: 10.1016/j.ijinfomgt.2019.08.002

Dwivedi, Y. K., Ismagilova, E., Hughes, D. L., Carlson, J., Filieri, R., Jacobson, J., Jain, V., Karjaluoto, H., Kefi, H., Krishen, A. S., Kumar, V., Rahman, M. M., Raman, R., Rauschnabel, P. A., Rowley, J., Salo, J., Tran, G. A., & Wang, Y. (2021). Setting the future of digital and social media marketing research: Perspectives and research propositions. *International Journal of Information Management*, *59*, 102168. DOI: 10.1016/j.ijinfomgt.2020.102168

Erevelles, S., Fukawa, N., & Swayne, L. (2016). Big Data consumer analytics and the transformation of marketing. *Journal of Business Research*, *69*(2), 897–904. DOI: 10.1016/j.jbusres.2015.07.001

Gansser, O. A., & Reich, C. S. (2021). A new acceptance model for artificial intelligence with extensions to UTAUT2: An empirical study in three segments of application. *Technology in Society*, *65*, 101535. DOI: 10.1016/j.techsoc.2021.101535

Gerlich, M. (2023). The Power of Virtual Influencers: Impact on Consumer Behaviour and Attitudes in the Age of AI. *Administrative Sciences*, *13*(8), 178. DOI: 10.3390/admsci13080178

Gershman, S. J., Horvitz, E. J., & Tenenbaum, J. B. (2015). Computational rationality: A converging paradigm for intelligence in brains, minds, and machines. *Science*, *349*(6245), 273–278. DOI: 10.1126/science.aac6076

Goncalves, M., Hu, Y., Aliagas, I., & Cerdá, L. M. (2024). Neuromarketing algorithms' consumer privacy and ethical considerations: Challenges and opportunities. *Cogent Business & Management*, *11*(1), 2333063. DOI: 10.1080/23311975.2024.2333063

Gursoy, D., Chi, O. H., Lu, L., & Nunkoo, R. (2019). Consumers acceptance of artificially intelligent (AI) device use in service delivery. *International Journal of Information Management*, *49*, 157–169. DOI: 10.1016/j.ijinfomgt.2019.03.008

Haenlein, M., & Kaplan, A. (2019). A Brief History of Artificial Intelligence: On the Past, Present, and Future of Artificial Intelligence. *California Management Review*, *61*(4), 5–14. DOI: 10.1177/0008125619864925

Hasan, R., Shams, R., & Rahman, M. (2021). Consumer trust and perceived risk for voice-controlled artificial intelligence: The case of Siri. *Journal of Business Research*, *131*, 591–597. DOI: 10.1016/j.jbusres.2020.12.012

Haynes, J.-D., & Rees, G. (2006). Decoding mental states from brain activity in humans. *Nature Reviews. Neuroscience*, *7*(7), 523–534. DOI: 10.1038/nrn1931

Hermann, E. (2022). Leveraging Artificial Intelligence in Marketing for Social Good—An Ethical Perspective. *Journal of Business Ethics*, *179*(1), 43–61. DOI: 10.1007/s10551-021-04843-y

Hoyer, W. D., Kroschke, M., Schmitt, B., Kraume, K., & Shankar, V. (2020). Transforming the Customer Experience through New Technologies. *Journal of Interactive Marketing*, *51*(1), 57–71. DOI: 10.1016/j.intmar.2020.04.001

Huang, M.-H., & Rust, R. T. (2021a). A strategic framework for artificial intelligence in marketing. *Journal of the Academy of Marketing Science*, *49*(1), 30–50. DOI: 10.1007/s11747-020-00749-9

Huang, M.-H., & Rust, R. T. (2021b). Engaged to a Robot? The Role of AI in Service. *Journal of Service Research*, *24*(1), 30–41. DOI: 10.1177/1094670520902266

Javor, A., Koller, M., Lee, N., Chamberlain, L., & Ransmayr, G. (2013). Neuromarketing and consumer neuroscience: Contributions to neurology. *BMC Neurology*, *13*(1), 13. DOI: 10.1186/1471-2377-13-13

Jobin, A., Ienca, M., & Vayena, E. (2019). The global landscape of AI ethics guidelines. *Nature Machine Intelligence*, *1*(9), 389–399. DOI: 10.1038/s42256-019-0088-2

Keegan, B. J., Dennehy, D., & Naudé, P. (2024). Implementing Artificial Intelligence in Traditional B2B Marketing Practices: An Activity Theory Perspective. *Information Systems Frontiers*, *26*(3), 1025–1039. DOI: 10.1007/s10796-022-10294-1

Khondakar, M., Sarowar, M. H., Chowdhury, M. H., Majumder, S., Hossain, M. A., Dewan, M. A. A., & Hossain, Q. D. (2024a). A systematic review on EEG-based neuromarketing: Recent trends and analyzing techniques. *Brain Informatics*, *11*(1), 17. DOI: 10.1186/s40708-024-00229-8

Khondakar, M., Sarowar, M. H., Chowdhury, M. H., Majumder, S., Hossain, M. A., Dewan, M. A. A., & Hossain, Q. D. (2024b). A systematic review on EEG-based neuromarketing: Recent trends and analyzing techniques. *Brain Informatics*, *11*(1), 17. DOI: 10.1186/s40708-024-00229-8

Kose, U., & Sert, S. (2017). *Improving content marketing processes with the approaches by artificial intelligence*. DOI: 10.48550/ARXIV.1704.02114

Kumar, V., Ashraf, A. R., & Nadeem, W. (2024). AI-powered marketing: What, where, and how? *International Journal of Information Management*, *77*, 102783. DOI: 10.1016/j.ijinfomgt.2024.102783

Lee, N., Broderick, A. J., & Chamberlain, L. (2007). What is 'neuromarketing'? A discussion and agenda for future research. *International Journal of Psychophysiology*, *63*(2), 199–204. DOI: 10.1016/j.ijpsycho.2006.03.007

Lu, H., Li, Y., Chen, M., Kim, H., & Serikawa, S. (2018). Brain Intelligence: Go beyond Artificial Intelligence. *Mobile Networks and Applications, 23*(2), 368–375. DOI: 10.1007/s11036-017-0932-8

Martínez-López, F. J., & Casillas, J. (2009). Marketing Intelligent Systems for consumer behaviour modelling by a descriptive induction approach based on Genetic Fuzzy Systems. *Industrial Marketing Management, 38*(7), 714–731. DOI: 10.1016/j.indmarman.2008.02.003

Mikalef, P., & Gupta, M. (2021). Artificial intelligence capability: Conceptualization, measurement calibration, and empirical study on its impact on organizational creativity and firm performance. *Information & Management, 58*(3), 103434. DOI: 10.1016/j.im.2021.103434

Mileti, A., Guido, G., & Prete, M. I. (2016a). Nanomarketing: A New Frontier for Neuromarketing. *Psychology and Marketing, 33*(8), 664–674. DOI: 10.1002/mar.20907

Mileti, A., Guido, G., & Prete, M. I. (2016b). Nanomarketing: A New Frontier for Neuromarketing. *Psychology and Marketing, 33*(8), 664–674. DOI: 10.1002/mar.20907

)Momennejad, I. (2023). A rubric for human-like agents and NeuroAI. *Philosophical Transactions of the Royal Society B: Biological Sciences, 378*(1869), 20210446. DOI: 10.1098/rstb.2021.0446

Nemorin, S., Oscar, H., & Gandy, J. (2017). Exploring Neuromarketing and Its Reliance on Remote Sensing: Social and Ethical Concerns. *International Journal of Communication, 11*(0), 0.

Phutela, N. P. A., Sreevathsan, K., & Krupa, B. N. (2022). *Intelligent analysis of EEG signals to assess consumer decisions: A Study on Neuromarketing* (Version 1). arXiv. DOI: 10.1109/INCET54531.2022.9824698

) Pirouz, D. M. (n.d.). *The Neuroscience of Consumer Decision Making.*

Semieoglu, O. (2019). THE USE OF NEURO-MARKETING IN MANAGEMENT. *European Journal of Management and Marketing Studies, 0*, 0. Advance online publication. DOI: 10.46827/ejmms.v0i0.541

Shaw, S. D., & Bagozzi, R. P. (2018). The neuropsychology of consumer behavior and marketing. *Consumer Psychology Review, 1*(1), 22–40. DOI: 10.1002/arcp.1006

Sima, V., Gheorghe, I. G., Subić, J., & Nancu, D. (2020). Influences of the Industry 4.0 Revolution on the Human Capital Development and Consumer Behavior: A Systematic Review. *Sustainability (Basel)*, *12*(10), 4035. DOI: 10.3390/su12104035

Sun, Z., Fu, S., & Jiang, T. (2022). Gain-framed product descriptions are more appealing to elderly consumers in live streaming E-commerce: Implications from a controlled experiment. *Data and Information Management*, *6*(4), 100022. DOI: 10.1016/j.dim.2022.100022

Traymbak, S., Shukla, A., & Dutta, M. (2024). A Study of Reliability and Validity of Constructs of Neuromarketing Among Indian Consumers. *Annals of Neurosciences*, *31*(2), 86–94. DOI: 10.1177/09727531231181868

Vajda, S., & Bellman, R. (1959). Dynamic Programming. *Econometrica*, *27*(3), 537. DOI: 10.2307/1909506

Wang, H., Fu, T., Du, Y., Gao, W., Huang, K., Liu, Z., Chandak, P., Liu, S., Van Katwyk, P., Deac, A., Anandkumar, A., Bergen, K., Gomes, C. P., Ho, S., Kohli, P., Lasenby, J., Leskovec, J., Liu, T.-Y., Manrai, A., & Zitnik, M. (2023). Scientific discovery in the age of artificial intelligence. *Nature*, *620*(7972), 47–60. DOI: 10.1038/s41586-023-06221-2

Wirtz, J., Patterson, P. G., Kunz, W. H., Gruber, T., Lu, V. N., Paluch, S., & Martins, A. (2018). Brave new world: Service robots in the frontline. *Journal of Service Management*, *29*(5), 907–931. DOI: 10.1108/JOSM-04-2018-0119

Xu, Y., Liu, X., Cao, X., Huang, C., Liu, E., Qian, S., Liu, X., Wu, Y., Dong, F., Qiu, C.-W., Qiu, J., Hua, K., Su, W., Wu, J., Xu, H., Han, Y., Fu, C., Yin, Z., Liu, M., & Zhang, J. (2021). Artificial intelligence: A powerful paradigm for scientific research. *Innovation (Cambridge (Mass.))*, *2*(4), 100179. DOI: 10.1016/j.xinn.2021.100179

Yoffie, D. B. (1996). Competing in the Age of Digital Convergence. *California Management Review*, *38*(4), 31–53. DOI: 10.2307/41165853

Zhang, K. Z. K., & Benyoucef, M. (2016). Consumer behavior in social commerce: A literature review. *Decision Support Systems*, *86*, 95–108. DOI: 10.1016/j.dss.2016.04.001

Zhang, W., Gao, B., Tang, J., Yao, P., Yu, S., Chang, M.-F., Yoo, H.-J., Qian, H., & Wu, H. (2020). Neuro-inspired computing chips. *Nature Electronics*, *3*(7), 371–382. DOI: 10.1038/s41928-020-0435-7

Chapter 4
Understanding Consumer Behavior Through AI-Powered Neuromarketing

Ravikumar R. N.
http://orcid.org/0009-0009-3705-1681
Marwadi University, Rajkot, India

S. Aarthi
http://orcid.org/0009-0006-9064-2091
Marwadi University, Rajkot, India

Valisher Sapayev Odilbek Uglu
http://orcid.org/0000-0002-6751-5864
Mamun University, Khiva, Uzbekistan

Mokhinur Sadullayeva
Urgench State University, Urgench, Uzbekistan

Jakhongir Shaturaev
Termez University of Economics and Service, Termez, Uzbekistan

Praveenkumar G. D.
Kongu Engineering College, Erode, India

ABSTRACT

Understanding consumer behavior is critical for companies, especially with the rise of digital information and recommendation systems. AI with neuromarketing capabilities transforms consumer decisions by analyzing emotional responses and subconscious signals, using tools like eye tracking, EEG records, facial expression detectors, and biometric feedback. These AI systems can identify marketing cues that humans may miss, offering real-time insights into consumer behavior. This integration helps brands predict purchasing behavior, create effective ad strategies, and foster deeper brand engagement. However, the use of neural and biometric data raises ethical concerns, emphasizing the need for transparency, data protection, and consumer consent. The future of AI in neuromarketing holds promise for more advanced tools, but it is crucial for marketers to follow ethical guidelines to ensure genuine, trust-based relationships with consumers.

DOI: 10.4018/979-8-3373-1152-4.ch004

1. INTRODUCTION

Market indicators commonly used as traditional business tools lose their effectiveness in influencing modern-day customers who face abundant market data. The neuromarketing marketing system based on neural science technology provides businesses with an essential instrument that helps decode psychological buying behaviors of consumers. AI technology gives marketers precise levels of accuracy for studying complex mental processes because it was incorporated into their field of study. Neuromarketing tracks down neurophysiological readings from customers using Electroencephalogram (EEG) devices and eye trackers and emotion and bio-sensing technologies. Marketers acquire superior abilities to track challenging psychological patterns through AI technology and neuroscience partnership. Organizations that implement these systems understand their customers' hidden emotional responses better by studying their behavioral indicators. (Khushi & Malhan, 2024) The method enables the development of exact marketing plans because these plans establish emotional attachments with their preselected segments. The method for boosting brand affinity results in superior campaign outcomes. AI intellectual tools enable neuromarketing to reshape business understanding of customer behavior as the field leads to a total transformation of marketing emotions. The subsequent segment evaluates the disruptive marketing approach from various market practice perspectives and consumer trust and ethical standards dimensions. (Plassmann et al., 2015)The figure 1 illustrates the way neuromarketing enables AI, neuroscience, and sensing technologies to analyze consumer behavior and optimize marketing processes.

Figure 1. Transforming marketing with neuromarketing

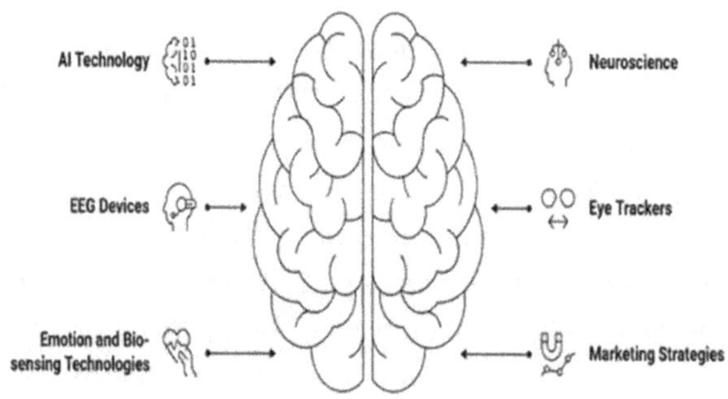

1.1 Defining Neuromarketing And Its Evolution In The Digital Age

Neuromarketing functions as a research method which utilizes brain Response analysis through scientific methods that measure neural activity. Neuromarketing research uses EEG combined with fMRI alongside eye-tracking and bioelectrical sensors to study the automatic nervous system reactions of human beings. Public participation as part of traditional market research exists as an opposite to neuromarketing because it analyzes consumer unconscious processes that people neither describe nor wish to document about themselves. Large data collection from the internet era enabled the evolution of neuromarketing methods because technological advancements in real-time monitoring systems occurred simultaneously. User behavior data acquisition becomes possible through online platforms that deliver comprehensive understanding of content attendance patterns and exact emotional measurements and engagement behaviors of users. Realtime Consumer-Brand interactions are now within reach of neuromarketers who leverage internet technologies to conduct their studies in unconfined environments. (Shaw & Bagozzi, 2018)Artificial intelligence raised the scalability levels of neuromarketing so businesses can achieve easier implementation. Large corporations first used neuromarketing through high-cost research before contemporary businesses use emotional consumer bonding via neuromarketing to gain competitive advantage. Neuromarketing stands necessary because customer preferences have changed so manufacturers must develop personalized emotional engagements that match consumer desires.

1.2 The Convergence Of Neuroscience, Marketing, And Artificial Intelligence

Neuromarketing represents an innovative academic field that results from uniting neuroscience operations with marketing theory and artificial intelligence programming methods. The science of neuroscience proves how brain structures enable us to detect things and feel emotions when making choices about our options. The behavior of consumers responds to desirable communication materials and valuable proposals as well as experiential features during marketing interactions. It involves interpreting data through AI tools of data processing and pattern-detection algorithms to forecast and shape correct consumer behavior. The brain scans that we had at the outset are the basis of modern-day marketing. The system develops perception of consumer preferences and purchase decisions based on brainwave analysis and facial expression identification techniques and eye direction evaluation techniques. The methods of human-oriented designing of strategies are applied by marketers by the cross-section instead of the demographic or conventional behavioural models.

AI system development elements allow real-time emotional processing that leads to custom content development right after change detection. (Sung et al., 2019) The combined method enables businesses to establish meaningful ethical relationships with their consumers. The convergence marks an emotional marketing shift permitted by technology which benefits from obtaining personal information for understanding consumer brand emotions. The figure 2 shows that there is a constant cycle of utilizing brain data and AI to learn more about consumer behavior and develop successful marketing techniques.

Figure 2. Neuromarketing cycle

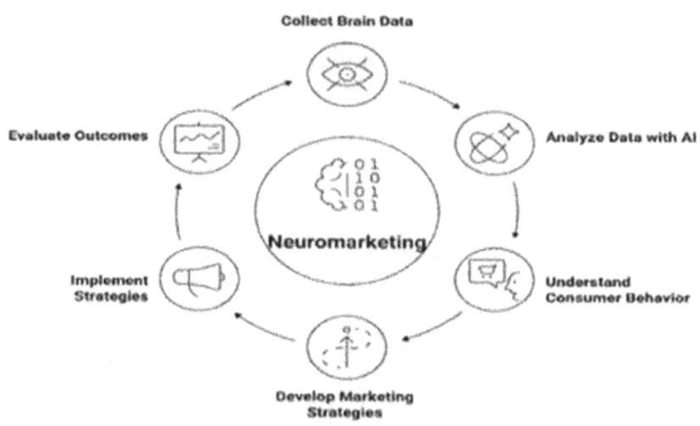

1.3 The Significance Of Recognizing Subconscious Consumer Behavior

Human beings execute most of their decisions in brain zones which stay out of view from their conscious thoughts. The understanding of unconscious behavior remains crucial for marketers because consumer reasons behind their purchases remain outside their conscious awareness. Research methods fail to reach effective results since consumer panels together with surveys rely entirely on logical customer input. Traditional research methods achieve better completion through neuromarketing since this method establishes that purchase decisions originate from emotional responses and cognitive confusion and buried mental links. Peoples' non-procedural emotional responses deliver time-sensitive and accurate predictions which surpass the effectiveness of deliberate thoughtful evaluation processes.(Ms. Shalini K C & Sudha, 2024) Basic emotional brand responses and brand colour and sound elements are used in marketing messages for changing buyer habits while consumers stay unaware of their behavior modifications. Through the integration of EEG brain waves combined with eye tracking technology marketers discover how viewers become interested in clicking on advertisements. Subconscious marketing creates superior results and better success than other approaches because it establishes deep connection and maintains powerful persuasive abilities. Organizations enhance their strategic change efforts through actual customer emotions instead of manufactured responses. (Al Fauzi & Widyarini, 2023) Current market conditions offer valuable strategic advantages to marketers because consumers display low attention while competitors remain highly competitive. Using AI-based neuromarketing gives marketers access to the subconscious space to be able to create emotional experiences of very high intensity.

1.4 Literature Review

Neuromarketing is an influential interdisciplinary profession incorporating neuroscience, psychology and Artificial Intelligence (AI) to examine consumer behavior outside the traditional use of self-reported methods. Surveys and interviews that are used as the conventional market research tools are usually unable to meet the requirement of capturing such subconscious decision-making as an important aspect in consumer choices. To address this, neuromarketing provides the data collected through the use of EEG, fMRI, eye-tracking, and biometric sensors to provide real-time data on the emotional and cognitive processes. The advancement in AI and big data analytics technological systems has helped to transform neuromarketing (Yadav, 2024a). Machine learning models can be used to handle the massive physiological and behavioral data to extract patterns that cannot be easily identified by a human. It is possible thanks to these algorithms to make the predicting mechanism more precise, and the result is that marketers can tailor their content and tactics to the unconscious triggers of their consumers. EEG and eye-tracking as an example may provide on-the-fly data about visual interaction, and GSR and fMRI may assist to detect arousal and intense emotional response. Put those together with AI and you are presented with actionable intelligence about individual marketing campaigns(Yadav, 2024b)

Recently, the focus is on how to integrate neuromarketing and predictive analytics and immersive technologies. Multi-sensory brand experiences are being capitalized on using Virtual Reality (VR) and Augmented Reality (AR), and these experiences can offer consumers engaging interactions so they can be emotionally attached to the brand. Real-time emotion analysis that uses AI makes the case for adaptive marketing even stronger by allowing brands to adjust strategies in real-time based on consumer reaction. (Bansal & Gupta, 2022)Case studies from world class corporations prove that neuromarketing based insights not only make advertising more effective but also create customer loyalty by establishing emotional bonds. Despite all of these advancements, there are some notable challenges in the field. High costs, the lack of portability of advanced tools such as fMRI, and ethical concerns about consumer privacy are still obstacles to widespread adoption. (Jukić, 2023)Furthermore, reading complex neural data needs special expertise and can, therefore, be less accessible for small and medium-sized enterprises. Ethical issues particularly relating to consent and data protection are also a potential threat to consumer trust. However, as the adoption of AI-based neuromarketing continues to grow, it's clear that this technology has the potential to transform marketing by combining the power of science with the human touch. (Uyar et al., 2025) In summary, neuromarketing has replaced the study of marketing research from the rational response to the subconscious understanding. By using AI, businesses can create strategies that help them to build deeper connections with consumers. As the field continues to develop and evolve, balancing innovation in technology with ethical responsibility will continue to be at the forefront of the sustainability and acceptance of the field.

1.5 Research Gap

Although neuromarketing has shown much promise in unravelling unconscious consumer behavior, existing research has not had standardized frameworks for ethical data governance and cross-cultural application. The majority of studies concentrate on large corporations, and small enterprises are under-researched. Furthermore, there has been little focus on real-time adaptive systems for immersive computing systems such as VR/AR. The gaps will be bridged to ensure that the ethical, scalable and globally adapt solutions are provided to neuromarketing, that balance the strength of individualization but at the same time, they invoke some level of trust in a consumer.

2. THE CORE TECHNOLOGIES UNDERLYING AI-BASED NEUROMARKETING

The MI-based neuromarketing makes use of various sophisticated technologies in carrying out market research of the swift reactions of emotions and cognition of consumers. This method is based on both brain wave recording, using EEG technology, and eye-tracking technology, used to view position registration. These are tools of measuring what the consumers perceive and quantify the neural brain responses to such products. The facial expression analysis program uses artificial intelligence, which involves extraction of concealed face signals that are not easily visible in facial expression to identify emotions such as happiness surprise and anger. The changes in the level of pupil diameter and skin sweat and cardiac patterns are used to measure interest levels of consumers measured with the help of bio-metric sensors (Hakim & Levy, 2019). Some of the sensory data that the consumer have provide researchers with a precise picture of what is going on subconsciously in their consumer base. The patterns of detection that are generated by big data integration by the AI system are beyond human detection capability. Adaptation of systems using artificial intelligence algorithms provides real-time value that aids marketers to develop tailored markcting strategies featuring content delivery customization capabilities. Neuroscience theory-based AI systems enable marketers to transform initial processes of marketing into data-driven decision systems with artificial intelligence technology. These technological solutions maintain the closeness of the brands to the customers emotionally and it results in effective brand interactions which reinforce customer loyalty in order to enjoy sustainable business relationships. Figure 3 illustrates the combination of EEG, eye-tracking, facial analysis, and biometric sensors to develop better marketing techniques.

Figure 3. Technological convergence in neuromarketing

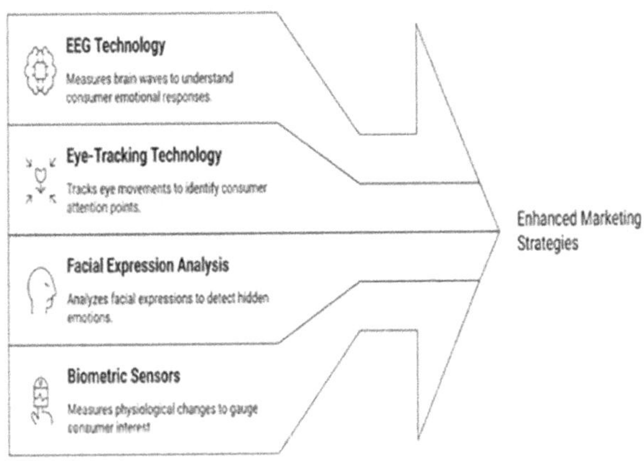

2.1 EEG, Eye-Tracking, Facial Feature Recognition, And Biometric

The basic tools employed by AI-based neuromarketing include EEG (electroencephalography) together with facial recognition technologies and eye-tracking abilities and biometric sensor capabilities dedicated to acquiring consumer data. The EEG technology used in brain signal examination enables marketers to read consumer responses from three fundamental aspects as presented through advertising-package interactions. The tracking of eye movements shows precisely which visual elements grab viewer attention as well as the whole path their eyes take during observation. (Razbadauskaitė Venskė, 2024)Face-recognition software joined with artificial intelligence systems detects emotions that processing by the human mind is beyond capability. The research demonstrates that people experience surprise and happiness simultaneously and show scepticism in their reactions. By measuring heart rate variability in combination with skin conductance (GSR) and pupil diameter neuromarketers receive additional emotional data. The technology allows neuromarketers to obtain behaviors from customers and disclose their underlying psychological motives for their actions. Brands receive comprehensive consumer profiles that merge cognitive information with emotion-based aspects through data analysis of methods that explain customer behaviors and preferences. Artificial intelligence algorithms analyze biological data to develop marketing methods which build enhanced contact with customers while developing superior market solutions. EEG records electrical activity in the brain and detects responses to stimuli in milliseconds. (Šola et al., 2024)fMRI captures blood flow changes to identify deep-brain responses to visual/auditory marketing stimuli. Galvanic Skin Response (GSR) monitors arousal levels by measuring skin conductivity. Eye-tracking pinpoints visual attention on specific screen zones or product placements. The following table 1 is a comparison of neuromarketing methods, which include their purpose, AI use, and main limitations.

Table 1 Overview of neuromarketing techniques and their AI applications

Technique	Purpose	AI Integration	Limitations
EEG	Detect brain activity	Pattern detection, real-time feedback	High cost, interpretation complexity
Eye-tracking	Identify visual attention	Heatmap analysis, gaze prediction	Limited to surface-level focus
GSR	Measure arousal	Emotional intensity mapping	Cannot determine emotional valence
fMRI	Deep brain imaging	Emotional mapping via neural patterns	Expensive, lacks portability

2.2 Role Of ML In Analyzing Emotional And Neurophysiological Data

An ML system processes multiple-dimensional neuromarketing instrument data to generate usable information through its basic operational method. A substantial amount of data emerges through the operation of EEG devices with eye trackers and facial identification sensors and biometric devices but exceeds human handling capabilities. Through deep learning machine learning algorithms, the identification of significant emotional responses and cognitive patterns and consumption behaviors of consumers becomes possible by spotting complex data patterns and unusual events. Stress detection functions in combination with satisfaction recognition become possible for ML models through extensive training which introduces them to patterns resembling excitement. After acquiring trained data ML models can calculate the consumer response to different content types and items. (Beličková, 2024)ML models create marketing content expressing the same emotional tones after acquiring understanding about distinctive negative and positive consumer reactions. Large-scale solutions enable ML technology to support businesses in segmentation through the creation of emotional personal profiles for each of their individual customers. These models become more operationally capable since they automatically enhance their ability to target customers and distribute content across development stages. (Kusá & Beličková, 2023a)

The decision system of neuromarketing applications uses customer emotions to create brand communications which generate empathy from buyers. While machine learning models enhance interpretation accuracy, ethical risks include over-personalization and intrusive behavioural manipulation. These must be mitigated with transparent data governance. The figure 4 illustrates how the consumer brain data is processed by the machine learning to develop individualized and ethical marketing policies. (Reepu, 2024) The table 2 highlights how AI-driven neuromarketing surpasses traditional methods in precision, personalization, and emotional insight.

Figure 4. ML in neuromarketing data analysis

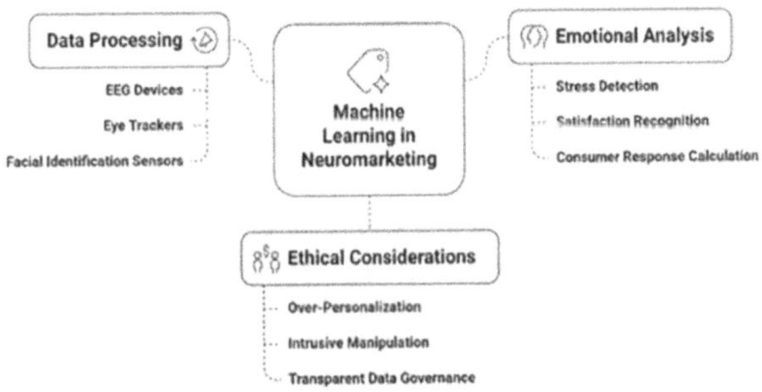

Table 2. Comparison of traditional marketing vs. AI-based neuromarketing

Aspect	Traditional Marketing	AI-Based Neuromarketing
Data Source	Surveys, focus groups, self-reports	EEG, fMRI, eye-tracking, biometric sensors
Consumer Insights	Conscious and stated preferences	Subconscious emotions and hidden triggers
Personalization	Limited, demographic-based	Real-time, individual emotion-based
Accuracy	Often subjective and biased	Objective, data-driven, higher predictive accuracy
Cost	Relatively low	Higher, but decreasing with scalable AI tools

2.3 Real-Time Behavioural Data Processing And Its Influence

The process of performing biological examinations in conjunction with psychological response analysis is the fundamental characteristic of AI-based neuromarketing. By using premium algorithms that are hosted on cloud servers, it is feasible for market-driving client input to be processed rapidly via servers that are very fast. Agent monitoring gives them the ability to provide data-based verification throughout the testing and development stages of campaigns, as well as during the building of interfaces. By using real-time platforms, clients are able to avoid losing attention by obtaining simultaneous updates of both presentation components and product information in the event that they exhibit symptoms of uncertainty when participating in online advertising sessions. (Fahim et al., 2024) The ability to adjust the content of digital signage and product displays for individual customers via the transmission of an emotion-based message is available to both physical facilities and economic centers. The generation of individualized hybrid interactions that maintain human-style communication is one of the advantageous characteristics of processing information in real time. The capacity of a company to generate experiences that replicate human relationships is critical to the success of the company in terms of maintaining customer happiness and converting customers. A/B testing observation durations are shortened as a result of this procedure, which also reduces the amount of time required for investigations. There are two key benefits that organizations get from real-time behavioural analytics, which enable them to alter their operations in response to the ever-changing requirements of their customers.

3. TRANSFORMING CONSUMER DECISION-MAKING

Neuromarketing methods are significantly amplified with AI that can help specialists to identify latent behavioral signals that drive consumer purchases. Often using traditional international preference systems and preference feedback systems that are not as effective in identifying the latent subconscious triggers that neuromarketing can generally identify using the study of human brains psychologically. (Thakur & Pasha, 2024)Firms can use EEG, facial emotion detection, and biometrics as complex technology to examine and assess customers' psychology in view of target advertisement messaging. AI systems strengthen the neuromarketing process by utilizing big data and provide opportunity to improve forecast of customer behaviors. AI neural networks typically estimate emotional reaction in relation to real-time data and this sentiment information provides companies with data to respond with content and product design. (Constantinescu et al., 2019)AI will provide a completely different, customized experience for customers by taking systematic customer paths and building a unique sequence through emotional triggers from the use of data. Consumption is increasingly more complicated, and in today's world of infinite distractions, it is now also more fragmented. The ability to create personalized experiences for customers allows brands to encourage loyalty, establish connections, and deliver value to consumers. When consumers meet their emotional needs via their shopping behavior (purchasing), they are more likely to value those products over others. Neuromarketing, made more effective through AI, enables brands to draw emotional connections to their products or services, leading to improved customer satisfaction, increased loyalty, and ultimately consumers valuing a brand's offerings against alternatives. Simply put, AI in neuromarketing helps brands create more targeted and emotional experiences. (Sevic, 2022)

3.1 How AI Unscrambles Customer Intent Through Emotional Triggers

All types of organizations across Singapore use Artificial Intelligence systems to seek out actual purchase signals within the mental unconscious domains of customer brains. Artificial Intelligence enables Neuromarketing technology to analyze instant emotions through EEG tests and image recognition technologies which operate biometric measurement devices that perform facial behavior monitoring operations. Sensory technologies use attention-oriented signals together with stress indicators to divide products for analysis. Computer algorithms evaluate user emotions to reveal hidden customer goals which exist beneath their explicit behavioral signs. The system technology examines the behavior of satisfied viewers towards content and purchasing products while they maintain their advertisement interest based on AI evaluation criteria. The deployment of human interaction depends on marketing based on emotions by processing all available customer information collected throughout time. Brand loyalty from consumers increases through marketing campaigns that enhance engagement because of emotional purchasing signal detection. (Alsharif et al., 2021)

3.2 Predictive Analytics For Personalized Marketing Campaigns

In the past, it was thought that it was impossible to boost marketing efforts with greater precision by employing predictive analytics. However, the use of machine learning technology has made it possible to consider the prospect of doing so. For the purpose of generating their predictions, the prediction engines combine information on client interactions with brain reactions derived from real-time communications. To achieve the goal that the prediction engines have set for themselves, this takes place. It is predicted that the models that have been provided will, in accordance with their predictions, deliver material that corresponds to the engagement of users and brings about advantages at the same time. Every time the user interacts with the system, the system is able to collect fresh information. (Hsu & Chen, 2020)This allows the system to maintain its prediction models up to date with various marketing solutions that are specifically customized to the requirements that are now being met. Because it is able to give one-of-a-kind material that is both cognitive and emotional to each and every consumer, mass marketing is able to attain the highest potential degree of personalization that is conceivable. via the use of predictive analytics, businesses are able to acquire the capability of engaging in conversations with clients via the utilization of approaches that seem natural, rapid, and pleasant. The figure 5 illustrates the steps of machine learning that takes consumer brain data and generates unique and ethical marketing plans.

Figure 5. Personalized marketing with predictive analytics

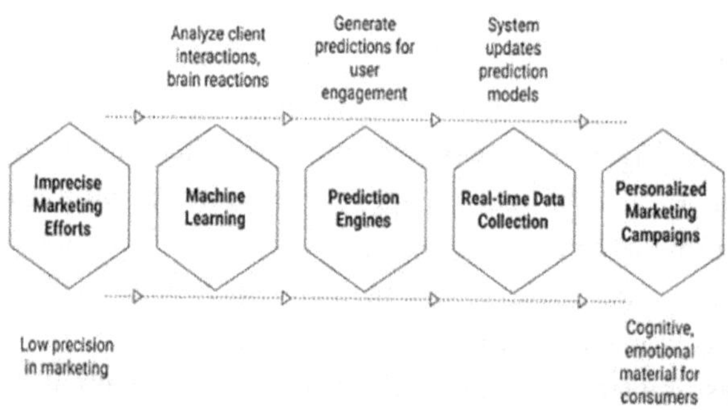

3.3 Influence Of AI Insights On Ad Placement, Content Design, And Engagement Strategies

The fundamentals of behavioural and emotional data provide AI systems the base to modernize marketing central functions including advertising selection zones and content generation systems and relational strategies. By analyzing customer responses to ads AI systems determine both time slots and locations that bring the best results. Placements operate their business through advanced mental readiness evaluations linked to situational awareness assessments in place of traditional demographic procedures. Through total perception AI acquires abilities to recognize both image-based narrative and voice-based options that create favourable emotional responses. (Aldayel et al., 2020) Through present-day market tools developers can establish emotional interactions between users by deploying various emotional decision-making principles. The feedback system within artificial intelligence enables users to receive immediately adaptive options based on artificial intelligence technology. Users trigger emotional reactions by interacting with event parts that immediately produce modifications which fit their emotional responses and mental cognitive functions. Organizations that employ artificial intelligence transform theoretical customer assumptions into quantifiable market statistics to engage customers effectively in conversations during their interactions. However, reliance on algorithmic decision-making can sometimes overlook cultural nuances or introduce bias. Hence, human oversight remains critical.

4. REAL-WORLD APPLICATIONS AND CASE STUDIES

The implementation of AI neuromarketing technologies allows different industries to boost office earnings by scaling up their customer reach. The Coca-Cola consumer goods market employs facial tracking technology combined with biometric sensors to track store-based consumer responses for enhancing store design decisions. PepsiCo reaches strategic business success by using eye tracking devices and EEG testing to boost advertising results in new product launches. Through AI and user behavior analysis Amazon and Alibaba have established personal shopping engines which suggest products that target emotional customer reactions and reveal secret user activities on their electronic commerce sites (Hakim & Levy, 2019). Quantitative and biological sensor approaches enable Hyundai automotive to build better customer experiences in every type of vehicle they produce. The examples demonstrate how neuromarketing systems with AI create and present insights about consumer decision-driving components. The development of brand loyalty relies on marketing content that presents emotions to build connections with customers through emotionally driven advertising strategies used by businesses. (Kusá & Beličková, 2023b)

4.1 Examples Of Brands Leveraging AI-Powered Neuromarketing

AI-based neuromarketing techniques enable modern corporations in different countries to understand their customer conduct in more detail. The assessment provided by AI algorithms regarding consumer emotional responses to promotional materials allows Netflix to refine its thumbnail design scheme for increased engagement rates. Nick uses biometric sensors together with facial tracking technology to achieve high-quality marketing that develops deep customer loyalty. Unilever uses artificial intelligence-based neuroscience software to monitor unconscious viewer responses in different markets across the world as part of their advertisement accountability checks. (Santy et al., 2024)Through eye tracker and EEG monitoring systems BMW improves showroom visitor engagement along with digital advertising content in the automotive market. Brand companies use Artificial Intelligence technologies to create stories that improve consumer engagement levels above standard product sales practices. The shifts in business operations use emotional data to move from traditional instinctive marketing to marketing that reflects customer feelings instead of their stated opinions.

4.2 Success Metrics: Conversion Rates, Emotional Engagement, Loyalty

Artificial intelligence applications in neuromarketing enable companies to succeed by establishing main metrics which create enduring customer relationships. The existing conversion rate measurement remains in marketer's toolbox but they now employ additional metrics consisting of biometric feedback combined with facial emotion tracking for advertising engagement assessment. (Crespo-Pereira et al., 2020) The memory retention along with branding effects for Pepsi and Coca-Cola as well as other brands can be improved through EEG and eye tracking assessments of advertising content. Visual semantics generated by AI technology enables businesses to discover their most effective combination of graphic elements through the use of visual output data. Brand loyalty reaches further than customer frequency because it requires brand attachment between customers and their preferred brands. (Heidari et al., 2024)The neuromarketing assessment generates positive emotions resulting in long-term customer value which reduces customer abandonments for businesses. Firms choose these strategies instead of shallow generic approaches to focus on emotional resonance since it drives brand success in the upcoming years.

4.3 Emotional Marketing And Its Connection To Customer Retention

When deployed for neuromarketing purposes AI systems reach exceptional performance levels producing outstanding customer retention effects. The subconscious happiness alongside nostalgia emotions that develop through brand-emotional bonds create stronger brand-consumer relationships beyond what product benefits can achieve. Customers develop into loyal lifetime market buyers during competitive situations after experiencing complete brand emotional interactions. Research organizations use technological sensors to determine emotional feedback through a combination of facial studies together with biological information collection and brain wave scanning for complete advertising content analysis. Customers develop strong brand-customer relationships through their emotional experiences at Apple and Starbucks stores. (Huang et al., 2025) AI technology gives users ongoing functionality to improve both content emotional retention and user interface qualities. Sociable relationships between clients and sellers prove more essential than customer satisfaction goals or incentive programs to develop lasting brand loyalty among customers. AI provides emotional values at every interaction to help marketing experts recognize their customer base better and create long-term binding relationships. While emotional marketing enhances retention, it may unintentionally manipulate vulnerable consumers. It is essential to balance persuasion with ethical responsibility to avoid deceptive emotional targeting.

5. ETHICAL IMPLICATIONS AND CONSUMER CONFIDENCE

Urgent attention needs to be given to AI-based neuromarketing probes because of their ethical challenges involving mental information protection and permission standards along with emotional interference risks. The combination of physical identification with brain activity data obtained through facial emotional readings and eye movements and brainwave measurement threatens personal information security and confidentiality. The actual degree of organizational information collection remains unknown to consumers because these operations occur automatically through online marketing content and store promotional tools. Every enterprise must provide complete information disclosure about available data while detailed explanations of collection strategies accompany specified purposes (Adam et al., 2021). Anonymity acquisition processes need businesses to follow ethical standards by first asking for consent from individuals and by letting them limit marketing access and refuse participation consent. When brands use neuromarketing in a correct manner they develop trust-building experiences for users that benefit consumers. AI delivers its best support to human beings through correct ethical implementations within neuromarketing procedures. The table 3 outlines the main ethical issues in neuromarketing, emphasizing risks and solutions for responsible practice.

Table 3. Ethical challenges in AI-based neuromarketing

Ethical Concern	Description	Potential Risk	Mitigation Strategy
Privacy	Collection of neural and biometric data	Data misuse and identity risks	Strong consent and anonymization
Transparency	Lack of clarity on how data is used	Erosion of consumer trust	Clear policies and disclosures
Manipulation	Exploiting subconscious emotions	Consumer vulnerability	Ethical frameworks and oversight
Accessibility	High costs limit adoption	Inequality in market use	Affordable, scalable tools

5.1 Consent, Transparency, And Responsible Data Use

In order to handle data ethically, users have to agree to impurity-free activity by using clear communication systems that adhere to ethical values and principles. With brands finding a way of capitalizing on the emotional cues and neural stimulation of the consumers (both of which are sensitive data), organizations should ensure that they have policies that articulate the channels of data collection and data utilization in a written form. The policies need to be simple and easily accessible to the users. The only way a system can be claimed to be living up to the privacy requirement is by enabling users to exercise choice by confirming the terms and conditions, which automatically do away with the identity verification procedures. Two parallel processes should be used to ensure that organizations safeguard consumer privacy restricting the gathering of essential information and also keeping users anonymous in the process of carrying out tasks on the data. The two practices lower the risk but enable the organizations to operate in line with their responsibilities. When ethically tracked and responsible approaches to neural input are used, the insights generated about product enhancements can be put into practice, yet neural signal monitoring should be accompanied by responsible design processes that do not cause consumer unease and/or feelings of exploitation. Through the implementation of underlying transparency and integrity-based privacy centric approaches, organizations can not only safeguard consumer data but, in the process, increase trust in the long-run. These tactics will assist in incorporating ethical data practices into the fundamental administrative practices and processes and, in this way, facilitate the organization to meet its commitments more effectively as a digital business entity. Marketing with ethical considerations under the banner of the rational administration and privacy is an incentive to consumer trust and leads to consumer loyalty, and the trust in question is an avenue to viable models that consider the long-term support of the brand.

5.2 Privacy Challenges Of Using Biometric And Neural Data

The biometric technology combined with neural information processes enables the detection of mind-based information that is beyond the perception of the common human beings. Information processing systems cannot control EEG readings and emotional data because password authentication methods fail while anonymization methods do not operate effectively on this information type. Inadequate existing data processing security infrastructure permits both criminal activities and tracking and profiling operations to occur. Customers were unaware of how much personal information neuromarketing experiments enabled data professionals to access because of this type of exposure to improper use and tracking. (Al-Nafjan, 2022) Novel neurotechnology receives inadequate protection through the GDPR and CCPA privacy standards despite their provided user privacy protection. General business operations need to handle this territory with caution using both secure encryption techniques and user-specific privacy guidelines and data storage constraints. The direct confrontation of these challenges enables businesses to lead as ethical leaders during the AI and emotional intelligence era through their dedicated focus on privacy protection that represents human dignity.

5.3 Building Ethical Frameworks For Neuromarketing Practices

The development of long-term successful AI based neuromarketing systems requires mandatory organization-wide ethical structures. Organizations need to develop frameworks that address both legal aspects and data ownership and the emotional manipulation of users with their psychological medical requirements (Ravikumar, Aarthi, Kurbanova, et al., 2025). Society demands the formation of inter-disciplinary ethics committees linking neuroscientists with ethicists and technologists and lawyers for determining societal consequences of neuromarketing initiatives. A robust ethical framework requires minimum four essential principles that consist of transparency and autonomy together with fairness and accountability. (Baskaran et al., 2021) The Organization conducts human rights compliance operations through periodic audits along with independent assessments and their ethical AI toolkits. Businesses need to establish user-centered organizational cultures superior to every other persuasion method for the commercial development of responsible innovation. The inclusion of ethical principles throughout product development starting from data collection through brand release operations enables companies to generate strategic plans which assure consumers about neuro and emotion-based consumer actions.

6. EMERGING INNOVATIONS IN NEUROMARKETING

The concept of neuromarketing continues to increase due to newer technologies redefining how marketers connect with the consumers. AI and neuroscience can be used to better understand the feeling and the process of making decisions under the surface, rather than relying on a shallow analytics. The new innovations are aimed at the consumer experiences and dynamic systems which dynamically change the content. The advances enhance the engagement as well as assist in the creation of brand loyalty as they create meaningful and personalized interactions. As immersive platforms and emotional AI enter businesses, neuromarketing is no longer taking a two-dimensional approach to data interpretation and is instead shifting to dynamic and experience-based systems. The shift is defined by the opportunities and by ethical aspects that should be considered in order to reach a sustainable development in the sphere, in order that innovation should be related to trust and privacy of consumers. This table 4 creates a summary of the emerging trends in neuromarketing, their benefits and major challenges in their future adoption.

Table 4. Future trends and applications of neuromarketing

Trend	Application	Benefits	Challenges
Real-Time Emotion Analysis	Adaptive ads, personalized content	Instant engagement, higher ROI	Privacy and manipulation risks
Immersive Experience (VR/AR)	Virtual shopping, product testing	Enhanced brand recall, loyalty	High cost, accessibility issues
Predictive Analytics	Forecasting consumer behavior	Accurate segmentation, tailored offers	Risk of bias in AI models
Brain-Computer Interfaces	Direct neural interaction	Next-level personalization	Ethical and legal concerns

6.1 Immersive Experience And Multi-Sensory Engagement

Neuromarketing with the help of Immersive technologies consists of Virtual Reality (VR) and Augmented Reality (AR) that offer interactive and multi-sensual experience. These tools allow the brands to produce simulative real life scenarios in which the consumers are given a chance to experience the products first hand as well as establish a greater degree of emotional and cognitive attachments. Subconscious reactions can be assessed in a more effective manner with the assistance of eye tracking, EEG, and biometric feedback and VR environments. By using sensory input in the form of images, sounds and haptics, marketers can produce campaigns that resonate with consumers. Problem of high cost (Rawnaque et al., 2020) and need to ensure that it is inclusive across multiple consumer groups is also an issue. Immersive interaction is now one of the best possible future directions of neuromarketing within the framework of which a more pronounced brand recall, emotional appeal, and sustained loyalty are attained when performed successfully.

6.2 Real-Time Emotion Analysis And Adaptive Marketing

Another innovation in neuromarketing is real-time emotion analysis, which uses AI and biometric sensors to record the immediate consumer reactions. Facial recognition, GSR and EEG technologies give real-time response on the emotional level, making marketers adjust content and messages on the fly. An example is that real time modification of adverts can be done depending on the excitement, stress or lack of interest shown by a consumer. This flexibility is better to use in campaigns and make the experiences individualized. Nevertheless, it brings up ethical issues of privacy, transparency of data, and possible control over consumer emotions. To achieve consumer trust, it is important to balance the potential of technology, and ethical responsibility. Real-time emotion analysis is therefore both an opportunity and a sensitive field that needs to be governed with utmost caution. (Sokolova et al., 2020)

7. FUTURE DIRECTIONS IN AI AND NEUROMARKETING

With the help of AI advances, the Neuromarketing will proceed with its advancement based on the three key technological areas that include personalized advertising solutions, automated live marketing programs and emotional data analysis systems. The need and expectations of the consumer market will be more accurate than ever due to technological advances in brain-computer interfaces and affective computing and generative AI. AI Technology will expand its skills to identify unconscious emotional clues in order to tailor messages automatically via various channels that include VR capabilities along with voice-assistants. Hybrid neural data in predictive behavioral models will predict marketing experiences with historical context as customers make their decisions in real time. Regulatory factors and ethical AI framework development will collaborate to ensure the resolution of data privacy concerns that would arise due to better data usage methods. Combining AI in the modern neuromarketing strategy establishes a true emotional connection that generates sales success and important ethical advances of customer-brand relationships. (Ahluwalia et al., 2023)

7.1 Future Trends In Neuromarketing: AI, Immersion & Emotion Analysis

The evolvement of AI-based neuromarketing systems will become higher when they adopt individual user interactions as a way of enhancing their functional abilities. Adjustment of messages and communication style and the methods of its delivery is the result of real-time monitoring of facial expression and artificial tracking of body signals and artificial monitoring of people with biometric measurements. Consumers have recently discovered VR and AR technology that allows marketers to design brand experiences using multi-sensory designs, based on consumer emotions. Emotional detecting systems in real time assist the marketers to adjust their marketing strategies in real time hence forming greater emotional connections with their target market. The market advancement allows marketers to develop automatic adaptable marketing solutions from basic marketing procedures. AI processing enables spaces that participate in market transformation to serve both consumer taste preferences and personal mental states and emotional conditions through which passive spectators become engaged storytellers of brands. (Kalaganis et al., 2021)

7.2 Innovations In Consumer Research

The rapid advancement of consumer research is largely attributable to the fact that neuromarketing technology driven by artificial intelligence provides instantaneous and precise information on customers. The inclusion of focus groups in conjunction with the survey methodologies that are currently in use does not disclose any subconscious behavioural factors. EEG pattern analysis, pupil dilation measures, and galvanic skin response monitoring are all components of the scientific study that are used to acquire neurodata. This data enables researchers to track genuine emotional responses from clients, as opposed to acquiring self-reported judgments. The most recent machine learning systems make use of comprehensive information analysis in order to unearth hidden data relationships. (Mashrur et al., 2022) These associations are then used to generate prediction models that are beyond the capability of human beings. Consequently, marketers are able to separate their clients into various emotional and cognitive groups by using this strategy in order to give accurate marketing tactics. Artificial intelligence technology is used by researchers in order to explore the emotional and behavioural adjustments that consumers experience over the course of numerous time periods. Marketers now have two separate opportunities to enhance their strategies by studying apparent customer behavior and examining internal decision-driving processes for comprehensive strategizing. Both of these opportunities are available to them.

7.3 The Evolving Role Of Marketers In An AI-Enhanced Ecosystem

Marketers must create operational plans for human-AI cooperation instead of managing campaigns or creating content because AI augmentation technology now exists. Marketers must master analyzing how smart systems generate data although they need to maintain their ability to understand emotional and behavioral data outcomes to achieve best performance. AI systems produce effective delivery solutions for audience targeting yet marketers need complete authentic elements and ethical bases to preserve their corporate identity. The seller must combine their practical objectives with emotional meaningful experiences which establish interpersonal human relationships. (Syvolovska et al., 2019)Marketers integrate emotion AI system with predictive analytics and content generation tools since they need continuous ethical judgment which requires marketers to work closely with neuroscientists and data scientists. Businesses should meet their targets through analytic AI integration that combines compassionate human methods with each AI implementation to guarantee truthful human engagement. The professionalization of marketing specialists through the use of AI knowledge will ensure that their brands do not lose their connection with authentic human human interaction. The figure 6 gives an insight on how AI is transforming marketing with the focus on human-AI relationships, ethical norms, and predictive analytics. It dwells on the evolving role of marketers to understand how to analyse the data, integrate emotional intelligence, and apply AI to generate content.

Figure 6. The future of marketing with AI

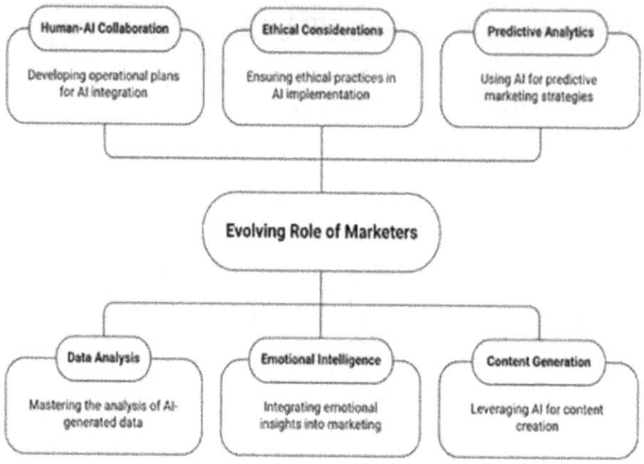

8. STRATEGIC RECOMMENDATIONS

Businesses intending to apply AI neuromarketing systems ought to start with ethical data principles and demonstrate a sense of full disclosure in asking permission to protect brain and body data. Being the first technique that small-scale marketing companies should adopt are emotion detection technologies that examine facial expressions and EEG brain signals to improve the delivery of messages and detect emotional correlations. The company needs to collaborate with data scientists and experts in the field of neuroscience and artificial intelligence to create predictive models and real-time analytics systems. A modified communication system is needed to display materials that complement present emotional states together with behavioral signals of the patient. (Atlı, 2024) The business should offer marketing staff both an understanding of AI fundamentals and moral instruction to practice ethical and imaginative research analysis. Personalized interactions based on single-voice communication will block deceptive practices in marketing activities. Neuromarketing information needs organizations to establish feedback systems which will enable trust-based emotional interactions between marketing partners. Organizations using innovative practices to establish ethical ties with human morality develop modern marketing approaches based on empathy instead of persuasion in the AI era (Ravikumar, et al., 2025). Figure 7 shows that the ethics of data drive AI-based neuromarketing on the path of empathetic practices. It identifies the main steps such as emotion identification, predictive modeling, communication adaption, staff training and feedback systems that can make marketing responsible and human-centered.

Figure 7. Ethical AI neuromarketing implementation

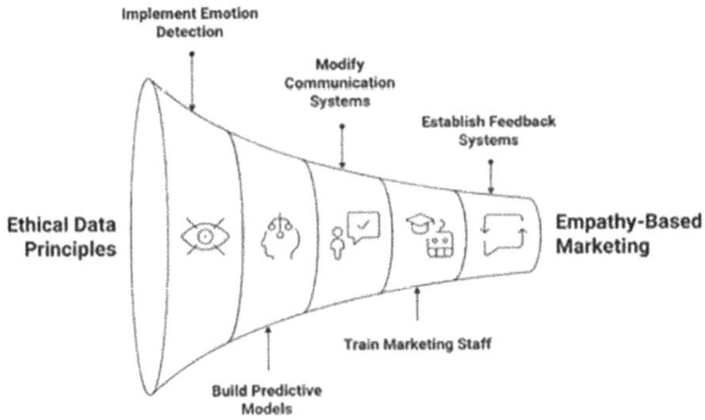

8.1 Best Practices In Integrating AI-Powered Neuromarketing

AI-powered neuromarketing systems require organizations to develop strategic plans through a particular implementation process. The initial step for organizations should involve establishing expert teams which unite marketing staff with members from neuroscience and data science departments. The order of operations requires EEG testing and face and eye observatory analysis to proceed one after the other during experiments that rely on pilot data. Systems performing real-time analytics require dashboards to present emotional tracking data which enables automatic responses through emotional metrics. The group division process performed by electronic systems using computer learning leads to behavioral consumer predictions based on the analysis of emotional patterns. (Yadav, 2024)The establishment of secure criteria together with data transparency standards should define consent-based operations that require complete regulatory oversight of data storage. Leadership groups need to create neuromarketing assessment systems based on emotional involvement measures to measure customer retention performance with emotional bond markers as main rating indicators. Organizations should fuse neuromarketing methods into their brand origins to create actual customer connections against deceptive marketing methods. Operational effectiveness of neuromarketing programs with AI functions results from quiet ethical practices and integration guidelines.

8.2 Balancing Emotional Intelligence With Ethical Responsibility

AI technology reaches its highest level of performance when companies implement basic ethical duties to their systems through emotional intelligence. Increases in trust with consumers must precede the delivery of practical value to their consumers by organizations working to stop emotional data abuse through deceptive practices. The implementation of ethical neuromarketing demands users to comprehend both types of data as well as their planned applications from the very beginning of the data collection process. Because AI programs undergo systematic training to deal with bias, they develop solutions that benefit population segments of all kinds. (Rathour et al., 2025) Applications of emotional intelligence approaches create stronger business-to-customer relationships yet business executives should refrain from concealing their methods of targeting clients. Brands need to set boundaries regarding the monitoring of subconscious signals emitted by consumers since all aggressive brand-consumer interaction methods violate legal standards. AI tools will power neuromarketing operations so the organization needs to develop internal rules for their management along with protocols for tool auditing. Marketers acquire the ability to stop unethical communication practices through their training in both emotional literacy and storytelling methods which address data ethics. Modern business success through Artificial Intelligence implementation in marketing activities requires both effective strategies and honourable treatment of customers.

8.3 Guidelines For Businesses, Marketers, And Researchers

Organizations need to create operational guidelines to keep up with Neuromarketing technology since the technology advances rapidly on its evolving path. GDPR regulations need business-specific guidelines to establish user authorization and confirm data visibility systems. Security solutions for organizations should proceed from external party assessments to strengthen their accountability framework. Organizations achieve better results by using authentic emotional content rather than manipulation through the process of turning analytical data into sincere genuine storytelling approaches. AI-based marketing campaign development needs joint work between data scientists or behavioral specialists with marketers who will execute ethical procedures. (Federal Rvacheva, 2024)These scientific and moral approvals of neuromarketing devices and procedures come from investigators who provide their endorsement following validation. Research results should be made publicly available as an educational tool for business industries. A continuous schedule of department meeting connections supported by educational training will maintain a harmonious integration of technical abilities and moral concepts and creative abilities. The business sector will gain neuromarketing success through developing trust-based operations that provide equivalent value for consumers and brands.

9. CONCLUSION

AI-based neuromarketing applications generate new commercial periods through strategies which companies use for consumer interaction and decision-making. Artificial intelligence joint ventures with neuroscience technologies enable marketers to build processing systems for studying human brain functions and emotional responses from large patient datasets. AI-powered neuromarketing systems conduct conventional user interaction testing to prove their ability in revealing concealed buying drivers. The acquisition of real-time neurophysiological and emotional information occurs through the combination of EEG systems with eye-trackers and facial expression instruments and biometric monitors used by marketing professionals. Builder program fluency enables retailers to strengthen their understanding of their audience base to achieve exact market targeting through machine learning data analysis.

The artificial intelligence system controlling neuromarketing can now identify customer intentions because it observes their emotional response patterns. The analytics models predictive analytics delivers to digital companies enable them to redesign content and advertisements so they can offer personalized services to customers. Modern neuromarketing technology also enables market segmentation in such a way that the connections to the brands that customers accept are trustworthy since they have dealt directly with acceptable material. Business operations have verified the feasible modes of implementation of these technologies. The AI-neuromarketing systems enable corporations to design enjoyable brand experiences to the customers and increase revenue efficiency through meeting emotional customer needs. The consistent customer retention occurs due to the strategic emotional marketing since the marketing establishes ethical relationships between retailers and customers.

Responsibility comes with power. Evidence of ethical principles is a functional necessity to obtain acceptance of the adoption of neuromarketing. This accumulation of neural data by companies has generated several ethical and legal issues that threaten the privacy imperatives alongside requiring consent authorization that also exhibit inadequacies in data security and transparency infrastructure. Superbly understanding data collection methods requires human beings to be trained on how to manage their personal data. Brand protection only implementable using a developed set of ethical principles as such policies prevent companies being legally exposed and preserving the trust of the people in business. The AI-based neuromarketing systems will create a unified framework of operations in all industries over the next few years. The integration of AI adaptation on the basis of real-time emotional feedback recognition and AR/VR technology enable the customers to receive better individualized promotional planning. Companies that rely on research innovation are able to offer enhanced customer services when they re-engineer their markets using innovative strategies. Leaders of today need to merge technological aptitude with ethical values in addition to emotional proficiency and creative thinking aptitude to succeed in AI-oriented business management of market-oriented companies.

The combination strategies between companies results in complete neuromarketing benefits as the firms combine their technological infrastructures to create research procedures that satisfy human needs without compromising the ethics standards. An organized business success strategy is formed as a result of the application of traditional technology acceptance frameworks and ethical systems of innovation management. The technology of the neuromarketing systems that were developed based on artificial intelligence gave birth to the modern commercial interfaces that enhanced the standard business practices. The genuine customer-algorithm exchange process preserves the business integrity through the use of human values as the data processing mechanism. In the current decision-making system artificial intelligence assists human decision-making by ensuring that human control of emotional reactions and rational decisions remains intact. The global markets must adopt new systems of understanding so as to embrace sustainable business partnerships that will propel business growth. Going forward, there is an urgent need to base neuromarketing concepts on sound ethical foundations and open consumer communications methods to build trust and long-term relationships.

REFERENCES

Adam, M., Wessel, M., & Benlian, A. (2021). AI-based chatbots in customer service and their effects on user compliance. *Electronic Markets*, *31*(2), 427–445. DOI: 10.1007/s12525-020-00414-7

Ahluwalia, G. K., Sasane, J. J., & Pathak, G. (2023). Neuromarketing in marketing 6.0: Exploring the intersection of consumer psychology and advanced technologies. *The Scientific Temper*, *15*(04), 3531–3539. DOI: 10.58414/SCIENTIFICTEMPER.2024.15.4.64

Al Fauzi, A., & Widyarini, L. A. (2023). Neuromarketing: The physiological tools for understanding consumer behaviour. [MJSSH]. *Malaysian Journal of Social Sciences and Humanities*, *8*(1), e002081. DOI: 10.47405/mjssh.v8i1.2081

Al-Nafjan, A. (2022). Feature selection of EEG signals in neuromarketing. *PeerJ. Computer Science*, *8*(e944), e944. DOI: 10.7717/peerj-cs.944

Aldayel, M., Ykhlef, M., & Al-Nafjan, A. (2020). Deep learning for EEG-based preference classification in neuromarketing. *Applied Sciences (Basel, Switzerland)*, *10*(4), 1525. DOI: 10.3390/app10041525

Alsharif, A. H., Md Salleh, N. Z., & Baharun, R. (2021). To better understand the role of emotional processes in decision-making. *International Journal of Academic Research in Economics and Management Sciences*, *10*(2). Advance online publication. DOI: 10.6007/IJAREMS/v10-i2/9883

Atlı, D. (2024). Analyzing turkey's premier e-commerce marketplaces by predictive eye tracking method. *Journal of Business in The Digital Age*. DOI: 10.46238/jobda.1490101

Bansal, S., & Gupta, M. (2022). Towards using artificial intelligence in neuromarketing. In *Promoting Consumer Engagement Through Emotional Branding and Sensory Marketing* (pp. 16–23). IGI Global., DOI: 10.4018/978-1-6684-5897-6.ch002

Baskaran, S., Mahadi, N., & Abd Rasid, S. Z. (2021). Multiple intelligence and entrepreneurial opportunity recognition – a failsafe approach of neuromarketing. *Journal of Research in Marketing and Entrepreneurship*, *23*(2), 318–338. DOI: 10.1108/JRME-05-2020-0049

Beličková, P. (2024). AI-powered insights: Strengthening nonprofit communication through neuromarketing. *Media & Marketing Identity*, 22–29. DOI: 10.34135/mmidentity-2024-02

Constantinescu, M., Orindaru, A., Pachitanu, A., Rosca, L., Caescu, S.-C., & Orzan, M. C. (2019). Attitude evaluation on using the neuromarketing approach in social media: Matching company's purposes and consumer's benefits for sustainable business growth. *Sustainability (Basel), 11*(24), 7094. DOI: 10.3390/su11247094

Crespo-Pereira, V., Legerén-Lago, B., & Arregui-McGullion, J. (2020). Implementing neuromarketing in the enterprise: Factors that impact the adoption of neuromarketing in major Spanish corporations. *Frontiers in Communication*, *5*, 576789. Advance online publication. DOI: 10.3389/fcomm.2020.576789

Fahim, I., Haramouni, L., Majdi, M. K., & Elkandoussi, F. (2024). The application of AI in neuromarketing. In *AI and Data Engineering Solutions for Effective Marketing* (pp. 48–68). IGI Global., DOI: 10.4018/979-8-3693-3172-9.ch003

Hakim, A., & Levy, D. J. (2019). A gateway to consumers' minds: Achievements, caveats, and prospects of electroencephalography-based prediction in neuromarketing. *Wiley Interdisciplinary Reviews: Cognitive Science*, *10*(2), e1485. DOI: 10.1002/wcs.1485

Heidari, M., Verderese, D., & Saviano, M. (2024). Exploring the contribution of neuroscientific approach to sustainable smart tourism. *ITM Web of Conferences, 62*, 03001. DOI: 10.1051/itmconf/20246203001

Hsu, L., & Chen, Y.-J. (2020). Neuromarketing, subliminal advertising, and hotel selection: An EEG study. [AMJ]. *Australasian Marketing Journal*, *28*(4), 200–208. DOI: 10.1016/j.ausmj.2020.04.009

Huang, F., Peng, D., & Teo, T. (2025). AI affordances and EFL learners' speaking engagement: The moderating roles of gender and learner type. *European Journal of Education*, *60*(1), e70041. Advance online publication. DOI: 10.1111/ejed.70041

Jukić, D. (2023). Time to say goodbye: A neuromarketing perspective. *Media & Marketing Identity*, 175–183. DOI: 10.34135/mmidentity-2023-18

Kalaganis, F. P., Georgiadis, K., Oikonomou, V. P., Laskaris, N. A., Nikolopoulos, S., & Kompatsiaris, I. (2021). Unlocking the subconscious consumer bias: A survey on the past, present, and future of hybrid EEG schemes in neuromarketing. *Frontiers in Neuroergonomics*, *2*, 672982. DOI: 10.3389/fnrgo.2021.672982

Khushi, K. J., & Malhan, S. (2024). NeuroLogic. In *Advances in Marketing, Customer Relationship Management, and E-Services* (pp. 105–122). IGI Global. DOI: 10.4018/979-8-3693-8222-6.ch005

Kusá, A., & Beličková, P. (2023a). The role of artificial intelligence in neuromarketing research: Insights and applications. *Media & Marketing Identity*, 269–275. DOI: 10.34135/mmidentity-2023-27

Kusá, A., & Beličková, P. (2023b). The role of artificial intelligence in neuromarketing research: Insights and applications. *Media & Marketing Identity*, 269–275. DOI: 10.34135/mmidentity-2023-27

Mashrur, F. R., Rahman, K. M., Miya, M. T. I., Vaidyanathan, R., Anwar, S. F., Sarker, F., & Mamun, K. A. (2022). BCI-based consumers' choice prediction from EEG signals: An intelligent neuromarketing framework. *Frontiers in Human Neuroscience*, *16*, 861270. DOI: 10.3389/fnhum.2022.861270

Ms. Shalini, K. C., & Sudha, D. R.Ms. Shalini K CDr. R Sudha. (2024). An investigation on neurological marketing in the chocolate company: Cadbury. *International Journal of Advanced Research in Science. Tongxin Jishu*, *15260*, 377–380. DOI: 10.48175/IJARSCT-15260

Plassmann, H., Venkatraman, V., Huettel, S., & Yoon, C. (2015). Consumer neuroscience: Applications, challenges, and possible solutions. *JMR, Journal of Marketing Research*, *52*(4), 427–435. DOI: 10.1509/jmr.14.0048

Rathour, S., Badal, P. S., Kamalvanshi, V., Kushwaha, S.Sr, Sr, D., Kemboi, E., Mannepalli, B. K., & Deep, P. (2025). From brainwaves to buying behavior: Applications of non-invasive neuromarketing approaches to food choice. *Journal of Scientific Research and Reports*, *31*(6), 195–210. DOI: 10.9734/jsrr/2025/v31i63121

Ravikumar, A. S., Saparbaevich, B. R., Kumar A., S., Jumaniyozova, M., & Toshova, S. (2025). AI-enhanced clinical decision-making through a collaborative approach. In *Advances in Computational Intelligence and Robotics* (pp. 249–280). IGI Global Scientific Publishing. DOI: 10.4018/979-8-3373-3311-3.ch010

Ravikumar, R. N., Aarthi, S., Kurbanova, S., Polvanov, S., Matchanova, B., & Sathya, K. (2025). Hybrid metaheuristic optimization for neural networks in biomedical imaging. In *Metaheuristic Algorithms and Optimizing Neural Networks for Biomedical Image Processing* (pp. 197–234). IGI Global Scientific Publishing., DOI: 10.4018/979-8-3373-0523-3.ch008

Rawnaque, F. S., Rahman, K. M., Anwar, S. F., Vaidyanathan, R., Chau, T., Sarker, F., & Mamun, K. A. A. (2020). Technological advancements and opportunities in Neuromarketing: A systematic review. *Brain Informatics*, *7*(1), 10. DOI: 10.1186/s40708-020-00109-x

Razbadauskaitė Venskė, I. (2024). Neuromarketing: A tool to understand consumer behaviour. *Regional Formation and Development Studies*, 101–109. DOI: 10.15181/RFDS.V42I1.2605

Reepu. (2024). The role of artificial intelligence in neuromarketing in understanding consumer behaviour. In *Advances in Marketing, Customer Relationship Management, and E-Services* (pp. 155–176). IGI Global. DOI: 10.4018/979-8-3693-8222-6.ch007

Santy, R. D., Hamdani, M. G. Q., & Rahma, S. J. A. (2024). Enhancing online purchase intention through artificial intelligence: Transformation to digital customer experience. In *Proceedings of the International Conference on Business, Economics, Social Sciences, and Humanities - Economics, Business and Management Track (ICOBEST-EBM 2024)* (pp. 120–135). Atlantis Press International BV. DOI: 10.2991/978-94-6463-465-5_11

Sevic, N. P. (2022). Practical implementation of neuromarketing in different business industries: Challenges and trends. *Annals of Spiru Haret University Economic Series*, *22*(2). Advance online publication. DOI: 10.26458/22213

Shaw, S. D., & Bagozzi, R. P. (2018). The neuropsychology of consumer behavior and marketing. *Consumer Psychology Review*, *1*(1), 22–40. DOI: 10.1002/arcp.1006

Sokolova, L., Veriasova, G., & Zinchenko, M. (2020). Theoretical and practical aspects of introducing innovations in the enterprise's marketing activity. *Innovative Technologies and Scientific Solutions for Industries*, *0*(2 (12)), 119–126. DOI: 10.30837/2522-9818.2020.12.119

Šola, H. M., Qureshi, F. H., & Khawaja, S. (2024). Predicting behaviour patterns in online and PDF magazines with AI eye-tracking. *Behavioral Sciences (Basel, Switzerland)*, *14*(8), 677. DOI: 10.3390/bs14080677

Sung, B., Wilson, N. J., Yun, J. H., & Lee, E. J. (2019). What can neuroscience offer marketing research? *Asia Pacific Journal of Marketing and Logistics*, *32*(5), 1089–1111. DOI: 10.1108/APJML-04-2019-0227

Syvolovska, O., Neskuba, T., Aleksandrova, O., & Mkrtychyan, O. (2019). Implementation of innovative marketing technologies for higher efficiency of the marketing communication complex. *SHS Web of Conferences*, *67*, 04013. DOI: 10.1051/shsconf/20196704013

Thakur, V., & Pasha, S. A. (2024). Neuromarketing for decision making in the digital era. In *Advances in Marketing, Customer Relationship Management, and E-Services* (pp. 255–266). IGI Global. DOI: 10.4018/979-8-3693-7673-7.ch011

Uyar, A., Fidan, U., Er, B., & Uyar, K. (2025). Evaluation of emotional content advertisements by neuromarketing methods. *Mehmet Akif Ersoy Üniversitesi İktisadi ve İdari Bilimler Fakültesi Dergisi*, *12*(2), 516–541. DOI: 10.30798/makuiibf.1529125

Yadav, T. (2024). AI in neuromarketing: Understanding consumer emotions and behavior through machinc lcarning. *International Journal For Multidisciplinary Research*, *6*(5), 28154. Advance online publication. DOI: 10.36948/ijfmr.2024.v06i05.28154

KEY TERMS AND DEFINITIONS

Artificial Intelligence (AI): Computational systems that process large datasets to find patterns, predict behaviors and personalize marketing strategies.

Electroencephalography (EEG): A technique for recording the brain's activity in order to capture immediate reactions to visual or auditory stimulation

Ethical Neuromarketing: Responsible use of neural and biometric data with a focus on consent, transparency and privacy.

Eye-Tracking: Technology which tracks gaze patterns to identify visual attention and focus.

Functional Magnetic Resonance Imaging (fMRI): Imaging method that allows us to see deep brain structures in relation to making decisions.

Galvanic Skin Response (GSR): A measure of physiological arousal that is based on changes in skin conductivity.

Immersive Technologies (VR/AR): Tools that help brand owners deliver multisensory brand experiences to consumers in an interactive way.

Neuromarketing: A branch of marketing which uses neuroscience techniques to analyse consumers subconscious response to marketing stimuli.

Predictive Analytics: Predictive analytics involves using AI and statistical techniques to forecast consumer preferences and behaviors.

Subconscious Behavior: Behavior of the consumer that takes place without conscious awareness.

Chapter 5

How AI-Powered Neuromarketing Is Revolutionizing Consumer Decision-Making

Sushil Dashrath Shende
http://orcid.org/0009-0006-0439-8118
School of Business, Indira University, Pune, India

ABSTRACT

This chapter explores impact of neuroscience & artificial intelligence (AI) on consumer behavior analysis. It presents an overview of neuromarketing tools such as EEG, fMRI, eye-tracking, facial & galvanic skin response, detailing how these technologies uncover subconscious consumer responses. Through AI integration, neuromarketing achieves precision, scale, & speed in interpreting complex neural & biometric data. It further examines how companies like Coca-Cola, Unilever, & P&G apply AI-driven neuromarketing for ad optimization, product design, & personalized engagement. Ethical considerations surrounding privacy, bias, & manipulation are analyzed, along with regulatory frameworks like GDPR. It also discusses how emotional & creative stimuli influence purchasing decisions & how AI leverages these insights for hyper-personalized marketing. Finally, it outlines emerging trends such as emotionally intelligent AI, immersive technologies like AR/VR, & brain-computer interfaces, while emphasizing the importance of ethical implementation in shaping the future of consumer engagement.

DOI: 10.4018/979-8-3373-1152-4.ch005

SECTION I:UNDERSTANDING CONSUMER BEHAVIOR: THE REVOLUTION IN NEUROSCIENCE

1.1. Introduction

The rapid advancement of digital technologies has reshaped how consumers interact with brands, products, and marketing communications. Traditional research tools—such as surveys, interviews, and focus groups—remain useful but are limited by reliance on conscious self-reporting, susceptibility to bias, and inability to access subconscious drivers of behavior.

Neuromarketing emerged to address these constraints by integrating neuroscience, psychology, and marketing to examine the neural and physiological mechanisms that underpin consumer decision-making. Techniques such as EEG, fMRI, eye-tracking, GSR, and facial expression analysis provide insight into emotional arousal, attention, reward processing, and memory formation, involving brain regions such as the prefrontal cortex, amygdala, nucleus accumbens, insula, and hippocampus.

Artificial intelligence significantly expands the capabilities of neuromarketing. AI allows rapid processing of complex neural and biometric data, increasing precision, scalability, and predictive power. Machine learning models detect subtle neural signatures of engagement and emotional response, while deep learning supports interpretation of multimodal datasets. As a result, neuromarketing has become increasingly dynamic, data-driven, and applicable to real-world marketing contexts.

The study focuses on understanding how neuroscientific tools uncover subconscious processes, how AI enhances neuromarketing analytics, and how ethical, emotional, and behavioral factors shape consumer decision-making. Its objectives include examining neural mechanisms, evaluating AI-driven neuromarketing applications, identifying ethical challenges, exploring behavioral biases, and assessing emerging technologies. The research is guided by questions related to neural responses, AI's analytical contributions, consumer engagement, ethical risks, and future technological developments.

Adopting a qualitative, exploratory design, the study synthesizes secondary data from neuroscience, psychology, marketing, and AI literature. A thematic analysis identifies core themes involving neural processes, emotional responses, AI analytics, and ethical considerations. The work is organized into five chapters covering the introduction, literature review, methodology, analysis, and conclusions.

1.2. Historical Evolution of AI Integration in Neuromarketing and Consumer Decision-Making

The integration of artificial intelligence (AI) into neuromarketing has evolved alongside advances in neuroscience and consumer behavior research. In the early 2000s, neuromarketing emerged through the use of neuroscientific tools such as functional magnetic resonance imaging (fMRI) and electroencephalography (EEG), which enabled the examination of subconscious consumer responses beyond self-reported measures (Ariely & Berns, 2010; McClure et al., 2004). Early findings highlighted the central role of emotion and unconscious neural processes in shaping consumer decision-making (Plassmann et al., 2012).

During the 2010s, developments in machine learning and big data analytics enhanced the interpretation of complex neurophysiological datasets, including EEG, eye-tracking, and biometric signals. This integration shifted neuromarketing from descriptive analysis toward predictive modeling of consumer preferences (Plassmann et al., 2015). More recently, advances in deep learning and real-time neuroanalytics have enabled personalized marketing, emotion-based segmentation, and rapid optimization of marketing stimuli. Consequently, consumer decision-making is increasingly conceptualized as a dynamic interaction between cognitive and emotional processes, examined through data-driven and ethically guided AI frameworks (Eijlers et al., 2020).

Neuroscience has transformed the way businesses understand consumer behavior by offering direct insights into the brain's responses to marketing stimuli. Techniques such as neuroimaging, EEG (electroencephalography), functional magnetic resonance imaging (fMRI), eye-tracking, and biometrics reveal deeper insights that go beyond traditional methods like surveys and focus groups (Plassmann et al., 2015). For instance, companies have used neuroimaging to predict ad effectiveness by measuring emotional and cognitive responses.

The following sections highlights these techniques and their success stories, demonstrating the advantages of a neuroscience-driven approach, explores how neuroscience revolutionizes consumer behavior analysis.

1.3. Definitions

"Consumer neuroscience combines insights and methods from neuroscience, psychology, and marketing to understand how consumers' brains respond to marketing stimuli and make decisions." — Plassmann, H., Ramsøy, T. Z., & Milosavljevic, M. (2012)

"Consumer neuroscience is the study of the brain to predict and potentially even manipulate consumer behavior and decision making." — (Ariely & Berns, 2010)

1.4. Key Concepts

- **Neural Mechanisms of Decision-Making**: Studies how different brain regions (e.g., prefrontal cortex, amygdala, and insula) influence purchasing behaviors.
- **Neuroimaging Techniques**: Methods like EEG (*E*lectro *E*ncephalo *G*raphy) and fMRI (*f*unctional *M*agnetic *R*esonance *I*maging) measure real-time neural activity to predict consumer preferences.
- **Emotional and Cognitive Engagement**: Understanding how emotions drive brand loyalty and customer experiences.
- **AI-Enhanced Neuromarketing**: Machine learning and predictive analytics help interpret brain data for targeted marketing strategies.

1.5. Intersection of Neuroscience, Psychology, and Marketing

Consumer neuroscience bridges the gap between traditional marketing psychology and cutting-edge neuroscience. It integrates:

- **Neuroscience**: Examines brain function in response to stimuli like advertisements, product packaging, and branding.
- **Psychology**: Studies cognitive biases, decision-making heuristics, and emotional influences on purchasing behavior.
- **Marketing**: Uses insights from neuroscience and psychology to create more effective advertising strategies and personalized customer experiences.

SECTION II: NEUROSCIENCE TOOLS IN CONSUMER BEHAVIOR ANALYSIS

The field of consumer neuroscience employs a range of tools to understand consumer decision-making at a neural and physiological level. These tools provide insights into *subconscious reactions, emotional engagement, and cognitive processing* when consumers interact with brands, advertisements, and products.

Four key methods:

a) *Neuroimaging Techniques* – Functional Magnetic Resonance Imaging (Fmri)
b) Electroencephalography (EEG)
c) *Biometric Measurements* - Eye-tracking Technology, Facial Expression Analysis, Galvanic Skin Response (GSR), Heart Rate Variability

Let's explore each method, along with its applications, success stories, and detailed insights.

2a. Neuroimaging Techniques – FMRI (functional Magnetic Resonance Imaging)

- FMRI measures *changes in blood flow in the brain* to determine areas of heightened neural activity.
- It captures activity in regions like the *prefrontal cortex (decision-making), amygdala (emotions), and nucleus accumbens (reward processing).*
- Uses the *Blood Oxygen Level Dependent (BOLD) signal* to detect neural responses to marketing stimuli.

Application (Neuroimaging Techniques) in Consumer Neuroscience:

- **Brand Preference Analysis**: A study by McClure et al. (2004) found that Coca-Cola branding activated the prefrontal cortex, indicating the influence of brand perception over actual taste.

Success Stories (Neuroimaging Techniques):

Super Bowl Ads & Brain Activation: A 2019 neuromarketing study used Fmri to analyze responses to Super Bowl commercials. The study found that ads with strong emotional storytelling activated the *ventromedial prefrontal cortex*, correlating with increased consumer recall and purchase intent.

Table 1. FMRI-based consumer insights

Branding Element	Brain Region Activated	Consumer Response
Strong Emotional Storytelling	Ventromedial Prefrontal Cortex	Higher brand recall, loyalty
Rewarding Products	Nucleus Accumbens	Higher purchase intent
Uncertainty in Pricing	Insula	Consumer hesitation

2b. Electroencephalography (EEG)

- EEG measures *electrical activity in the brain* via electrodes placed on the scalp.
- Tracks real-time *emotional arousal and cognitive load* with high temporal resolution.

• Useful for *tracking subconscious responses to ads, packaging, and website interfaces.*

Applications in Consumer Neuroscience:

- **Engagement Metrics**: EEG detects which moments in an advertisement *generate the most attention and emotional engagement.*

Success Story: EEG & Digital Advertising

A 2021 study analyzed EEG responses to different online ad formats. *Interactive ads* generated *higher frontal lobe activation*, indicating better engagement compared to static banner ads.

Table 2. EEG-detected engagement in advertisements

Ad Format	EEG Engagement Score (0-100)	Consumer Behavior Outcome
Static Banner	4500%	Low engagement, ignored
Video Ad	7200%	Moderate engagement
Interactive Ad	8900%	High engagement, longer viewing time

2c. Biometric Measurements

- *Eye tracking* measures *fixation points, saccades, and gaze duration* to assess attention.
- *Facial expression analysis* detects *micro expressions* using AI to infer emotional reactions to content.
- *Heart rate variability (HRV)* assesses emotional excitement during exposure to ads.
- *Galvanic Skin Response (GSR)* Skin conductance measures *sweat gland activity* as an indicator of emotional arousal.

Applications in Consumer Neuroscience:

- **Website Usability Testing**: Tracks where users look first on a webpage (e.g., call-to-action buttons, images).
- **Ad Placement Optimization**: Determines the most *visually engaging sections* of an ad or packaging.

- **Adrenaline & Excitement Measurement**: Used in *sports marketing and action-based commercials.*
- **Fear-Based Marketing**: Analyzes physiological responses to *public health and insurance ads.*

Success Story: E-Commerce Eye Tracking

A retail website tested different homepage layouts using eye tracking. *Consumers focused most on the pricing section*, leading to a redesign where key product benefits were placed near price information.

Table 3. Eye-tracking insights on ad design

Ad Element	Fixation Time (Seconds)	Consumer Focus Ranking
Brand Logo	150%	3rd
Product Image	380%	1st
Call to Action (CTA)	270%	2nd

Success Story: Horror Movie Trailers & Skin Conductance

A neuromarketing firm tested horror movie trailers using skin conductance. *Spikes in GSR correlated with higher audience recall and intent to watch the movie.*

Table 4. Physiological response to emotional ads

Ad Type	Average Heart Rate (BPM)	Skin Conductance Level
Comedy Ad	72 BPM	Low
Fear-Based Ad	85 BPM	High
Emotional Story Ad	80 BPM	Moderate

The neuroscience toolkit enhances our ability to *decode consumer decision-making processes at a subconscious level.* Each method provides unique advantages:

- *fMRI* for deep brain insights into emotional and cognitive reactions.
- *EEG* for real-time measurement of consumer engagement.
- *Eye Tracking & Facial Expression Analysis* for visual and emotional attention metrics.

Having established the core neuroscientific tools used to capture subconscious consumer responses, the discussion now shifts from methodology to meaning—examining how these neural signals translate into cognitive, emotional, and behavioral patterns that shape consumer decision-making.

SECTION III: THE ROLE OF NEUROSCIENCE IN UNDERSTANDING CONSUMER BEHAVIOR

3a. Cognitive and Emotional Triggers in Consumer Decision-Making

- **Attention & Memory:** Neuroscience reveals that emotionally engaging content leads to higher recall and brand loyalty.
- **Sensory Marketing:** Certain colours, sounds, and textures trigger subconscious associations that influence purchase behavior.
- **Decision-Making Biases:** Insights into biases like loss aversion and anchoring help brands craft persuasive messaging.

Table 5. Cases - neuromarketing application

Company	Neuromarketing Application	Results & Impact
Pepsi vs. Coca-Cola (fMRI Study)	fMRI detected stronger emotional responses for Coke branding	Confirmed brand loyalty is rooted in emotional connection, not just taste
Hyundai	Eye-tracking to optimize car dashboard design	Increased user satisfaction by 20%
Google Ads	EEG-based ad testing for consumer engagement	Improved ad recall rates by 25%
Disney	Facial recognition to measure audience reactions to movie trailers	Adjusted content for higher emotional engagement

Success Story: Google's EEG-Optimized Ads

Google used *EEG technology* to test consumer reactions to advertisements. The study measured brainwave activity to determine which ad elements *triggered the highest engagement*. Google used this data to refine ad design, leading to *a 25% increase in brand recall* (Eijlers et al., 2020).

Table 6. EEG, fMRI brain mapping based improvements

Neuromarketing Metric	Traditional Method	Neuroscience-Based Improvement
Ad Recall Rate	60%	85% with EEG insights
Consumer Engagement	Self-reported	Real-time EEG data processing
Brand Loyalty Prediction	50% (Survey-Based)	90% with fMRI Brain Mapping
Eye-Tracking Heatmap Analysis	Manual	AI-enhanced pattern recognition

These insights highlight how neuroscience deepens understanding of attention, memory, and bias in consumption contexts. Building on this foundation, the next section explores the specific neural mechanisms and brain regions that underlie consumer choices.

SECTION IV: HOW NEUROSCIENCE ENHANCES CONSUMER INSIGHTS

This section examines the neural architecture of consumer decision-making, focusing on how distinct brain regions, emotional systems, and unconscious processes interact to influence purchasing behavior.

4a) Key Brain Regions Involved in Consumer Choices

Consumer choices activate multiple brain regions responsible for *reward processing, memory, emotional response, and rational thinking*. Key regions include:

Table 7. Brain regions involved in consumer choices

Brain Region	Function	Role in Consumer Decision-Making
Prefrontal Cortex (PFC)	Rational decision-making	Evaluates product benefits, pricing, & long-term utility
Amygdala	Emotional processing	Responds to emotional stimuli in ads, fear-based marketing
Nucleus Accumbens	Reward & pleasure	Activated by discounts, exclusive offers & brand loyalty
Insula	Risk & loss aversion	Reacts to high prices, detects unfair pricing
Hippocampus	Memory encoding	Influences brand recall & product familiarity

Success Story: Luxury Branding & Brain Activation

A 2017 fMRI study found that luxury brands like Gucci and Rolex activated the *nucleus accumbens*, indicating strong reward processing. In contrast, generic brands showed weaker activation, suggesting emotional attachment and perceived exclusivity drive purchase intent (Plassmann et al., 2017).

4b) The balance between emotional vs. rational decision-making

Consumer choices often involve a *tug-of-war* between emotion-driven and logic-based decisions. Neuromarketing research categorizes these two systems as:

- **System 1 (Emotional, Fast, Automatic Thinking)**
  - Driven by the *amygdala and limbic system*
  - Influences impulse buying, hedonic consumption
  - Triggered by *storytelling, social proof, and sensory marketing*
- **System 2 (Rational, Slow, Deliberate Thinking)**
  - Controlled by the *prefrontal cortex*
  - Associated with *price comparison, product evaluation, and logical reasoning*
  - More active in *B2B purchasing and high-involvement decisions*

Success Story: Emotional Ads vs. Rational Ads A neuromarketing experiment tested consumer responses to two ad types:

1. *Emotional Ad (Storytelling-based)* – Evoked *high amygdala activity*, increased brand recall.
2. *Rational Ad (Fact-driven)* – Activated the *prefrontal cortex*, led to careful price-based decision-making.

Table 8. Neural activation in ad effectiveness

Ad Type	Brain Region Activated	Consumer Behavior
Emotional Ad	Amygdala, Nucleus Accumbens	Higher engagement, brand recall
Rational Ad	Prefrontal Cortex	Increased analytical decision-making

4c) Unconscious Influences on Consumer Behavior

Most consumer decisions are influenced by *subconscious processing*, meaning individuals are often unaware of why they prefer certain brands or products.

Neuromarketing studies have identified key unconscious factors:

i. Priming & Subliminal Messaging
ii. Loss Aversion & Scarcity Effect
iii. Social Proof & Herd Mentality

Let us now look at each of these key factors.

i) *Priming & Subliminal Messaging* - Exposure to *brand-related cues* subconsciously increases preference (e.g., Apple logos prime creativity).

Example: A study found that customers exposed to *smiley faces in product packaging* were 20% more likely to rate the product favorably.

ii) *Loss Aversion & Scarcity Effect* - The *insula* reacts negatively to potential loss, explaining why *limited-time offers* increase purchase urgency.

Example: "Only 3 left in stock" prompts immediate buying behavior.

iii) *Social Proof & Herd Mentality* - Seeing high ratings and reviews triggers *mirror neuron activity*, encouraging consumers to follow trends.

Example: Amazon product pages displaying "bestseller" tags increase conversion rates by 35%.

Table 9. Unconscious biases in consumer behavior

Influence Type	Neurological Basis	Marketing Application
Priming	Implicit memory activation	Subtle brand exposure increases recall
Scarcity	Insula (loss aversion)	"Only a few left" triggers urgency
Social Proof	Mirror Neurons	User reviews increase credibility

The brain plays a *pivotal role in consumer decision-making*, balancing *rational evaluation (prefrontal cortex) and emotional impulses (amygdala, nucleus accumbens)*. Neuromarketing techniques provide valuable insights into:

- How *brands create emotional engagement*
- The *importance of subconscious biases in purchasing*
- The *role of AI and neuroscience in optimizing marketing strategies*

As AI-driven neuromarketing advances, businesses must navigate the *ethical implications* of influencing consumer behavior at a subconscious level while ensuring *transparency and responsible marketing* .

Together, these findings demonstrate that consumer decisions emerge from a dynamic interplay between conscious evaluation and subconscious influence. The following section illustrates how these neuroscientific insights are applied in real-world marketing contexts.

SECTION V: APPLICATIONS OF NEUROSCIENCE IN MARKETING

Neuromarketing applies neuroscience principles to optimize *product design, advertising, pricing strategies, and brand perception*. AI-powered neuromarketing techniques, including *EEG, fMRI, and biometric tracking*, provide deeper insights into consumer behavior, allowing companies to create more engaging and effective marketing strategies.

5.1. Product Design and Packaging

- **Color psychology**: Bright colours (e.g., red, yellow) trigger impulse purchases, while muted tones (e.g., blue, green) build trust.
- **Texture and material**: Tactile engagement influences consumer perception of product quality.
- **Eye-tracking studies**: Consumers focus on central images and brand logos before reading labels.

Success Story: Pepsi vs. Coca-Cola Packaging

A neuromarketing study found that consumers experienced *greater emotional arousal when shown Coca-Cola's curvy bottle* than Pepsi's straight-edged design, suggesting *shape plays a role in brand recall and emotional connection* (Plassmann et al., 2012).

Table 10. Packaging elements influencing consumer engagement

Design Feature	Neuromarketing Insight	Impact on Consumers
Bright Colors	Trigger impulse purchases	Increased sales
Textured Packaging	Engages sensory memory	Higher brand recall
Minimalist Design	Reduces cognitive load	Faster decision-making

5.2. Advertising Effectiveness

Neuromarketing tools measure consumer responses to ads in real-time, revealing:

- **Emotional peaks**: Moments that capture maximum attention.
- **Cognitive load**: Whether the ad is too complex or engaging.
- **Brand association**: How strongly consumers link the ad to the brand.

Success Story: Super Bowl Ads

A 2019 neuromarketing analysis of Super Bowl commercials found that:

- *Humour-based ads* activated the amygdala (emotional response) and had high brand recall.
- *Storytelling ads* engaged the prefrontal cortex (rational thinking), improving brand trust.

Table 11. Ad formats & consumer engagement

Ad Type	Brain Region Activated	Consumer Response
Humour-Based	Amygdala, Nucleus Accumbens	High recall, viral sharing
Storytelling	Prefrontal Cortex	Increased trust, brand loyalty
Celebrity Endorsement	Mirror Neurons	Persuasive impact

5.3. Pricing Strategies

Neuromarketing has revolutionized pricing strategies by uncovering how the brain perceives price tags:

- **Charm pricing**: Prices ending in *.99* feel lower due to left-digit anchoring.

- **Decoy pricing**: A mid-tier price option makes the expensive option seem more reasonable.
- **Bundle pricing**: Reduces cognitive strain and enhances perceived value.

Success Story: Apple's Pricing Strategy

Apple's pricing model utilizes *decoy pricing* to push consumers toward premium products. When Apple introduced a mid-tier MacBook, sales of the highest-priced model *increased by 25%* due to perceived value shifts (Ariely & Berns, 2010).

Table 12. Neuromarketing-based pricing effects

Pricing Strategy	Psychological Effect	Consumer Behavior
Charm Pricing ($9.99)	Left-digit bias	Higher sales conversion
Decoy Pricing	Perceived value shift	Upselling success
Bundle Pricing	Simplifies decision-making	Higher purchase intent

5.4. Brand Perception and Loyalty

Brand perception is shaped by subconscious emotions, experiences, and associations:

- *Consistent branding* activates the hippocampus (memory storage), reinforcing brand recognition.
- *Social proof and testimonials* trigger mirror neurons, increasing trust.
- *Emotional branding* strengthens consumer loyalty.

Success Story: Nike's Emotional Branding

Nike's *"Just Do It"* campaign leverages emotional triggers (aspiration, empowerment) to create deep neural connections. A 2018 fMRI study found that Nike's ads *activated the prefrontal cortex (motivation center) more than competitors' ads* (Yoon et al., 2018).

Table 13. Factors driving brand loyalty

Branding Element	Neurological Basis	Impact on Loyalty
Consistent Logo & Colours	Hippocampus (Memory)	Increases recognition
Storytelling Campaigns	Amygdala (Emotion)	Stronger emotional bonds
User Reviews & Ratings	Mirror Neurons (Social Proof)	Higher trust levels

While these applications demonstrate the practical value of neuroscience in marketing, recent advances in artificial intelligence have significantly expanded the scale, speed, and precision with which such insights can be generated.

SECTION VI: AI INTEGRATION AND ADVANCEMENTS IN NEUROMARKETING

As neuromarketing generates increasingly complex neural and biometric datasets, artificial intelligence has emerged as a critical enabler—transforming raw neuro-data into actionable, real-time marketing intelligence.

6.1.AI: Improving Precision, Scale, and Speed

Neuromarketing – the fusion of neuroscience and marketing – explores how consumers' brains respond to advertising and branding. Artificial intelligence (AI) has emerged as a pivotal enhancer in this field, enabling marketers to probe the subconscious drivers of consumer behavior with unprecedented precision, scale, and speed. Traditional neuromarketing tools like EEG brainwave monitoring, eye-tracking, and biometric sensors yield vast and complex data on attention, emotion, and memory. AI's role is to interpret these data patterns far more accurately and rapidly than humans ever could. In essence, AI acts as a catalyst that automates and amplifies neuromarketing insights – from decoding subtle neural responses to predicting future buying behavior. This section outlines how AI dovetails with neuromarketing, fundamentally improving the accuracy of insights, scaling up data analysis, and accelerating the speed of consumer research.

6.2 AI's Contribution to Neuromarketing

AI technologies have deeply integrated with neuromarketing methods, revolutionizing how researchers analyze and apply brain data in marketing. Key AI techniques – machine learning (including deep learning), computer vision, natural language processing (NLP), and predictive analytics – collectively enhance the *precision, scale, and speed* of neuromarketing insights.

Precision: AI algorithms improve the accuracy of interpreting neural and psychological data. For example, machine learning models can sift EEG signals or fMRI brain scans to detect patterns that correlate with specific emotions or attention levels, reducing the chance of human error in interpretation. Deep learning networks excel at finding nonlinear relationships in these complex datasets, e.g. linking a combination of brain-wave patterns to a consumer's subconscious preference for a product. AI-driven image recognition software can analyze facial expressions from video to classify emotional reactions with high granularity (joy vs. surprise, etc.). These AI tools often outperform traditional statistical analyses, yielding more *precise insights* into what messaging or design elements genuinely engage the brain. As a result, marketers can pinpoint which ad elements trigger positive neural responses (like reward or trust regions of the brain) and which cause negative reactions (stress or confusion signals) with far greater confidence (Plassmann et al., 2015; Eijlers et al., 2020). For instance, a deep learning model might reveal that a particular color scheme in an ad elicits subtle anxiety in viewers – a nuance that might be missed without AI-assisted analysis (Dave, 2024). By decoding such subtle cues, AI increases the signal-to-noise ratio in neuromarketing data, honing-in on what truly matters to consumer decision-making.

Scale: AI enables neuromarketing to be conducted at a scale previously unattainable through manual methods. Traditional neuroscience experiments with small focus groups can now be expanded to much larger samples because AI can handle the *high volume of data* produced. Brain-monitoring techniques generate enormous datasets (for example, a single EEG session can produce thousands of data points per second per participant). AI systems are adept at processing these large streams in parallel. In practical terms, this means studies that once involved a dozen subjects can be scaled up to hundreds or thousands of subjects, across diverse demographics, without sacrificing analytical rigor. AI cloud computing platforms can aggregate biometric data from multiple locations in real time, making neuromarketing studies geographically scalable as well. As one industry expert noted, *"Artificial intelligence is allowing us to combine the best of neuroscience with the speed and efficiency of digital marketing, creating a new paradigm where emotional and cognitive data become central to strategic decision-making."*. In other words, AI permits neuromarketers to integrate data from many sources – brain signals, eye movements, heart rate, facial cues, even text from consumer feedback – into one holistic analysis. This *breadth of data* improves the generalizability of insights. For example, an AI may analyze millions of social media comments with NLP to gauge consumer sentiment while simultaneously examining neuroimaging data for emotional responses to marketing content, linking the two levels of data. By doing so, AI makes neuromarketing insights scalable to large populations and numerous consumer touchpoints (Pola, 2023). It also means marketing campaigns can be tailor-made for individual segments: AI can identify distinct neural response patterns in different consumer groups and help create targeted strategies for each (The Marketing Hustle, 2024).

Speed: Perhaps the most immediate benefit of AI in neuromarketing is the dramatic increase in *speed of data analysis and execution.* AI algorithms can analyze neurophysiological data in *real time*, delivering instant feedback during an experiment. This capability stands in stark contrast to traditional neuromarketing studies, which might take weeks for experts to manually interpret results post-hoc. For example, modern facial coding AI can evaluate a viewer's moment-by-moment micro-expressions as they watch a commercial and report emotional engagement scores immediately, enabling researchers to adjust stimuli on the fly. Similarly, AI-driven eye-tracking analysis can visualize within seconds which parts of a webpage or product packaging are drawing attention and for how long. The result is an agile marketing approach: companies can iterate and optimize ads or designs in near-real-time based on neural reactions. One report succinctly noted that AI's advent is "enhancing the precision, speed, and depth of consumer insights gleaned from neuromarketing tools". Speed also matters when deploying insights. AI-powered predictive analytics can rapidly crunch neuromarketing data to forecast which marketing strategy will likely perform best, allowing businesses to make quicker data-driven decisions. For instance, if a particular advertisement causes spikes in brain regions associated with positive emotion, an AI system can immediately flag that ad as a strong candidate to roll out broadly, even before a campaign ends. Case studies have shown that this quick feedback loop helps firms beat competitors to market with content that is neurologically optimized (Globant, 2025). In summary, AI transforms neuromarketing into a faster, more responsive discipline – one that keeps pace with digital-era marketing cycles.

In technical terms, the synergy of AI with neuromarketing technologies manifests in several applications.

Predictive modelling: AI can take historical neuro-response data and train models to predict future consumer choices or reactions (Yadav, 2024). For example, if brainwave patterns and heart rate variability from prior product tests are linked to purchase decisions, a machine learning model can learn those patterns. Marketers could then input new biometric data (say from a new ad test) and the AI model would predict the likelihood that the ad will succeed in the market. These predictive analytics turn neuromarketing from a descriptive tool into a *predictive tool*, allowing proactive strategy rather than reactive adjustments themarketinghustle.com.

Natural Language Processing (NLP) combined with neuromarketing – sometimes called "neuro-linguistic marketing." AI NLP algorithms can analyze voice tone and language from customer service calls or focus group discussions, correlating linguistic sentiment with neural indicators of stress or excitement. This reveals not just what consumers say, but how their subconscious feels as they say it, offering a 360-degree view of customer sentiment. All these AI capabilities contribute to making neuromarketing more powerful and practical.

In summary, AI's contributions span the entire neuromarketing process: data collection (through automation and IoT sensors), data analysis (through ML/DL models identifying hidden patterns), and data application (through predictive and prescriptive analytics that inform real-world marketing decisions).

To illustrate how these AI-driven capabilities translate into tangible business outcomes, the following cases highlight organizations that have successfully integrated AI with neuromarketing techniques.

6.3.AI-Driven Neuromarketing Cases

AI-driven neuromarketing is not just theoretical; many companies have successfully leveraged it to optimize their marketing and product strategies. This section presents documented case studies of businesses that integrated AI with neuromarketing techniques, yielding measurable improvements in marketing performance.

Unilever – Personalized Marketing via Neuro AI: Global consumer goods company Unilever applied AI-enhanced neuromarketing to personalize its advertising and boost brand loyalty. Unilever collected a rich dataset on consumers, including biometric responses, purchase histories, and social media engagement, and used AI neural networks to analyze this trove for patterns in individual preferences. By linking neuroscientific indicators (like arousal levels in response to ad imagery) with each consumer's profile, the AI could predict which marketing content would best appeal to specific segments. The company then deployed personalized digital campaigns tailored to these insights – for example, showing a consumer a product video with scenes that the model predicted would spike that person's subconscious interest. The personalized neuromarketing approach paid off substantially. Unilever reported a *25% increase in customer engagement* with the AI-tailored ads, compared to generic ads, as measured by click-through and view durations. More importantly, *conversion rates jumped 30%* for these personalized campaigns, indicating that consumers were far more likely to make a purchase when the ad appealed to their individual neuro-profile. Follow-up surveys also found a *20% increase in brand loyalty* metrics among consumers who received the AI-personalized content. This case highlights how combining AI with neuromarketing allows ultra-targeted marketing – effectively "marketing to the individual's mind" – resulting in higher engagement and sales.

Procter & Gamble (P&G) – Optimizing Product Design: Consumer products leader P&G used AI-driven neuromarketing to inform product design and in-store experiences. P&G's researchers conducted eye-tracking studies in which participants interacted with different product packaging and shelf displays, while AI software analyzed their gaze patterns and facial expressions. The AI was able to determine which design features captured attention (for example, a particular color accent that caused shoppers' pupils to dilate, a sign of interest) and which elements induced emotional positivity or frustration. By iteratively tweaking designs and immediately testing them with AI analysis, P&G arrived at optimized packaging designs that were both visually attention-grabbing and emotionally appealing. The impact in market was significant: the neuromarketing-optimized product designs led to a *35% increase in user satisfaction scores* in consumer testing. These improved designs also translated into roughly a *20% sales increase* for those products after implementation, as shoppers found the packaging more appealing and the in-store displays more intuitive to navigate (Globant, 2025). P&G's case underscores that neuromarketing with AI isn't limited to ads – it can guide product development and retail strategy by revealing how consumers nonconsciously interact with product features.

Automotive Advertising – Emotional Triggers: In the automotive industry, a car manufacturer applied AI to facial expression and galvanic skin response data collected while consumers watched its commercials. The AI analysis unveiled specific emotional "triggers" – for instance, it found that scenes emphasizing family safety elicited micro-expressions of happiness and relief, correlating with stronger purchase intent, whereas fast-cut action scenes caused signs of stress in some viewers. By re-editing the ad to focus more on the emotionally positive elements identified by AI (and toning down the stress-inducing sequences), the company was able to align the commercial more closely with viewers' true emotional drivers. Subsequent campaign performance showed improved outcomes, validating the AI's guidance (Dave, 2024). While exact figures weren't publicly disclosed in this study, it exemplifies how AI can decode viewer emotions and suggest creative optimizations that make marketing more effective on a subconscious level.

Media & Entertainment – Trailer Effectiveness: An entertainment company (studio) leveraged AI-driven neuromarketing to evaluate movie trailers. They monitored test audiences with EEG and facial coding as viewers watched different trailer versions for an upcoming film. AI algorithms then pinpointed which scenes maintained high attention (strong neural focus signals) and which moments provoked the most positive emotional spikes. Using these insights, the studio re-cut the final trailer to begin with the most attention-grabbing scene and include more of the content that elicited joy/surprise, while removing a segment that the AI indicated caused confusion. The refined trailer achieved significantly higher engagement on digital platforms (e.g., greater view-through rates) and the film's opening weekend performance exceeded projections, which the marketers partly attributed to the optimized trailer. This case illustrates AI's utility in the creative process: by objectively identifying what the brain loves (or dislikes) about a piece of content, AI-guided edits can make marketing media more compelling.

Collectively, these case studies confirm that AI-driven neuromarketing is delivering real value across industries. Companies are seeing higher engagement, conversion rates, and customer satisfaction by tapping into AI's ability to decode the brain. Whether it's tweaking an ad, personalizing a website, or designing a product package, AI provides a data-driven compass for marketers to navigate the complex terrain of consumer emotions and decisions. Importantly, the successes also highlight the variety of AI applications (from computer vision to neural networks) and neuromarketing measures (EEG, biometrics, etc.), underscoring that this interdisciplinary approach can be adapted to many business challenges.

SECTION VII: BRIDGING THE GAP: WHEN NEUROSCIENCE MEETS AI

The convergence of *Artificial Intelligence (AI)* and *neuroscience* in marketing has revolutionized how brands understand consumer decision-making. Traditional neuromarketing techniques / technologies generate vast and complex datasets that are difficult to interpret in real time. AI, particularly *Machine Learning (ML) and Deep Learning*, enhances neuromarketing by improving the precision, speed, and scalability of data analysis (Plassmann et al., 2015).

Key AI-Neuroscience Intersections

AI enables neuromarketing to go beyond surface-level analysis by identifying hidden *cognitive and emotional patterns.* The major intersections between AI and neuroscience in marketing include:

7.1. AI in Neuroimaging Analysis

- **EEG & fMRI Interpretation:** AI enhances the accuracy of *brain activity decoding* by using ML algorithms to detect subconscious consumer preferences.
- **Real-time Processing:** Traditional neuroimaging studies take weeks to analyze, but AI enables real-time evaluation of *brand recall and ad engagement* (Eijlers et al., 2020).
- **Emotion Recognition:** AI models, trained on EEG and fMRI data, predict consumer emotions and sentiment based on neural activity (Coca-Cola's neuroscience-based ad testing case study).

7.2. AI-Driven Eye-Tracking & Facial Recognition

- AI-powered *eye-tracking* identifies where consumers focus on an ad, packaging, or product display (Liao et al., 2019).
- *Facial coding algorithms* detect micro-expressions, revealing subconscious emotional responses to branding (P&G's packaging optimization case study).
- AI integration with *computer vision* enables automated sentiment analysis in *video ads and UX/UI testing*.

7.3. Predictive Consumer Behavior Modelling

- *Deep learning algorithms* analyze neuromarketing data to predict consumer engagement and conversion probabilities.
- AI personalizes content based on *biometric responses*, adapting digital experiences dynamically.
- AI-driven *neuromarketing segmentation* categorizes consumers based on their *neural and emotional triggers*.

Rather than reiterating detailed case narratives, the following table consolidates representative examples that demonstrate how AI–neuroscience integration has delivered measurable marketing impact across industries.

Table 14. Cases - AI-neuroscience application

Company	AI-Neuroscience Application	Results & Impact
Coca-Cola	EEG & AI to optimize advertisements	20% higher engagement, 10% increase in brand recall
Unilever	AI-driven facial coding for personalized ads	30% higher conversion rate
Procter & Gamble (P&G)	AI-enhanced eye-tracking for packaging design	35% improvement in user satisfaction
Netflix	AI-powered emotion recognition for content recommendations	15% increase in viewership retention
Ford	AI-based biometrics for emotional car ad optimization	12% higher emotional connection with consumers

As AI-enhanced neuromarketing grows more powerful, its capacity to influence consumer cognition raises important ethical questions. The next chapter critically examines these concerns, focusing on privacy, autonomy, bias, and responsible governance.

SECTION VIII: THE ETHICS OF NEURO-INFORMED MARKETING

AI-powered neuromarketing offers groundbreaking insights into consumer behavior but also presents significant ethical dilemmas. By combining neuroscience and artificial intelligence, marketers gain access to subconscious consumer responses, raising concerns about *privacy, autonomy, data security, bias, and manipulation* (Plassmann et al., 2015).

Key Ethical Concerns & Considerations in AI-Driven Neuromarketing

8.1. Privacy & Consumer Consent

- **Collection of Biometric Data:** AI-driven neuromarketing gathers sensitive biometric data (EEG, fMRI, facial expressions, eye movement) to predict consumer choices.
- Regulations require *transparent data collection* and use.
- **Lack of Informed Consent:** Many consumers are unaware of how their neurophysiological data is used in advertising. Consumers must provide *explicit consent* before participating in neuro-marketing studies.
- **Legal & Regulatory Issues:** Compliance with *GDPR, CCPA, and biometric data regulations* is crucial to prevent unauthorized data usage (Liao et al., 2019).
- **Respect for privacy** is both a legal and ethical mandate; failure to safeguard neural data can lead to public backlash and legal penalties, undermining the very trust that marketers seek to build.

8.2. Manipulation vs. Persuasion

- **Exploitation of Subconscious Responses:** AI models predict emotional vulnerabilities and influence decision-making at a subconscious level.
- Ethical neuromarketing should *enhance user experience* rather than exploit subconscious biases.
- AI-driven behavioral targeting *blurs the line between persuasion and manipulation.*
- **Ethical vs. Deceptive Marketing:** Brands may create highly persuasive but manipulative ads based on AI-derived neuroresponses (Murphy & Illes, 2018).

8.3. Algorithmic Bias in AI Models

- **Demographic Bias:** AI-trained models may misinterpret emotional expressions across different racial, gender, or cultural backgrounds (Eijlers et al., 2020).
- Companies should ensure *fair representation in training datasets.*
- AI models must undergo *bias audits* to prevent demographic misinterpretations in *emotional recognition.*
- **Ethical AI Practices:** Regular audits and bias correction techniques should be implemented to prevent discrimination.

8.4. Consumer Autonomy & Free Will

- AI-powered neuromarketing can limit consumer free will by influencing purchasing decisions without conscious awareness.
- AI-driven emotional targeting raises concerns about *consumer autonomy.*
- Ethical frameworks must ensure AI *enhances rather than overrides consumer choice.*

Table 15. Cases - Ethical concern

Company	Ethical Concern	Resolution & Impact
Facebook & Cambridge Analytica	Unauthorized data harvesting & consumer profiling	Led to GDPR regulations on biometric and behavioral data privacy
Amazon's AI Recruitment Tool	Gender-biased algorithm	Bias audits and transparency policies implemented
Apple Face ID	Biometric data security	Strong encryption & device-side processing to prevent misuse
Google Ads Sentiment Targeting	Emotional exploitation in advertising	Shift towards transparency and consent-based targeting
Unilever's Neuro-Personalized Ads	Ethical persuasion vs. subconscious influence	Compliance with ethical AI guidelines & data minimization

Case 1: Cambridge Analytica Scandal

- Cambridge Analytica harvested Facebook users' psychographic data to *manipulate voter behavior*, sparking global concerns on AI-driven behavioral profiling (Cadwalladr & Graham-Harrison, 2018).
- **Impact:** New data protection laws such as GDPR enforced stricter regulations on neuro-informed marketing.

Case 2: Unilever's Ethical AI in Neuromarketing

- Unilever used *facial emotion recognition AI* for ad personalization while *ensuring consumer privacy and informed consent.*
- Resulted in a *30% engagement boost* while maintaining ethical data use (Plassmann et al., 2015).

Table 16. Ethical issues

Ethical Issue	Consumer Impact	Regulatory Response
AI Bias in Neuromarketing	20% lower accuracy for minority groups	Bias audits mandated under GDPR
Privacy Violations	75% of users unaware of neuromarketing data collection	Consent-based AI models recommended
Manipulation Concerns	63% of consumers distrust neuro-targeted ads	Ethical AI transparency reports introduced
Consumer Autonomy	40% of respondents feel AI limits choice	Regulations promoting explainable AI models

8.5 A brief overview of industry standards and certification bodies

To highlight the regulation of neuromarketing on a global scale, it's important to mention certification bodies and industry standards that ensure ethical and responsible practices in the field. One of the key organizations that regulate neuromarketing practices is the Neuromarketing Science & Business Association (NMSBA). The NMSBA provides guidelines and promotes best practices for the use of neuroscience in marketing. The association emphasizes the importance of transparency, informed consent, and respect for consumer privacy in neuromarketing research and applications.

Additionally, global data protection regulations, such as the General Data Protection Regulation (GDPR) in Europe, play a crucial role in governing how neuromarketing data, especially biometric and neurophysiological data, is collected, stored, and utilized. GDPR mandates that consumers provide explicit consent before their data can be used, and it also requires companies to ensure that personal data is anonymized and secure.

By adhering to these standards and certifications, companies can ensure that their neuromarketing strategies respect consumer autonomy and privacy, promoting responsible and ethical use of neuroscience and AI in marketing.

SECTION IX: BEHAVIORAL BIASES, CONSUMER AUTONOMY, AND AI

Behavioral economics has long established that consumers do not make purely rational decisions. Instead, *cognitive biases*, *heuristics*, and *emotional influences* shape purchasing behavior. AI-powered neuromarketing leverages these insights to *predict and influence consumer choices*, but this raises concerns about consumer autonomy and ethical AI use (Plassmann et al., 2015).

9.1 Key Behavioral Biases in Consumer Decision-Making

Table 17. Behavioral biases in consumer decision-making

Bias	Description	Impact on Consumer Behavior
Anchoring Bias	Consumers rely heavily on the first piece of information they see	Price framing influences willingness to pay
Loss Aversion	People fear losses more than they value gains	Urgency marketing ("Limited-time offers") boosts sales
Confirmation Bias	Consumers seek information that aligns with pre-existing beliefs	Personalized ads reinforce existing preferences
Bandwagon Effect	Consumers follow what others are doing	Social proof and reviews influence purchases
Choice Overload	Too many options lead to decision paralysis	Simplified recommendations enhance decision-making

9.2 AI's Role in Behavioral Bias Exploitation and Consumer Influence

9.2.1. Personalized Pricing and Anchoring Bias

- *AI-powered pricing algorithms adjust prices based on user behavior and willingness to pay.*
- **Example**: *Amazon's dynamic pricing* uses historical data to present different prices based on user engagement.

9.2.2. Urgency Marketing and Loss Aversion

- *E-commerce platforms use AI to trigger urgency-driven sales.*

- **Example**: Booking.com displays "Only 2 rooms left!" based on real-time demand predictions, increasing conversions by *20%*.

9.2.3. AI-Driven Social Proof and Bandwagon Effect

- AI analyzes social media trends and *amplifies high-engagement products.*
- **Example**: TikTok's *For You Page (FYP) algorithm* promotes viral trends, leading to spikes in product sales.

9.2.4. Simplifying Choices to Overcome Choice Overload

- AI reduces cognitive effort by curating personalized recommendations.
- **Example**: Netflix's *AI recommendation system* boosts engagement by *80%.*

Table 18. Cases - Bias leveraged

Company	Bias Leveraged	AI-Driven Impact
Amazon	Anchoring Bias	Dynamic pricing increases sales by 15%
Booking.com	Loss Aversion	Urgency messaging improves conversions by 20%
Netflix	Choice Overload	AI-driven recommendations increase watch time by 80%
Instagram Ads	Confirmation Bias	Personalized ads lead to 35% higher click-through rates
TikTok Trends	Bandwagon Effect	Viral trends drive instant product demand

Case 1: Amazon's AI-Powered Anchoring and Dynamic Pricing

Amazon personalizes product prices based on browsing history, competitor pricing, and *consumer spending behavior.* By presenting an initial higher price before revealing a discount, AI *exploits anchoring bias*, leading to *a 15% increase in sales* (Lambrecht & Tucker, 2019).

Case 2: Netflix's AI Overcoming Choice Overload

Netflix's recommendation engine *uses AI to analyze viewing patterns* and suggest content tailored to individual users. This eliminates *choice paralysis*, leading to *an 80% increase in watch time* (Gomez-Uribe & Hunt, 2016).

Industry Trends in AI-Driven Behavioral Targeting

1. **AI-Powered Hyper-Personalization** – *Tailored content, pricing, and promotions* based on real-time data.
2. **Emotional AI & Sentiment Analysis** – AI detects *real-time emotions* to optimize advertising.
3. **Neuro-Targeted Ads** – Predictive AI determines *which ad will trigger the highest engagement.*
4. **Regulatory Frameworks on AI Ethics** – Increasing scrutiny on *manipulative AI-driven marketing practices.*
5. **Explainable AI (XAI) for Transparency** – Consumers demand *more control over algorithmic decision-making.*

Table 19. AI-driven impact vs traditional marketing

Metric	Traditional Marketing	AI-Driven Impact
Ad Click-Through Rate (CTR)	3%	35% (AI-personalized ads)
Conversion Rate (E-commerce)	5%	20% (with AI urgency messaging)
Recommendation Engagement	50%	80% (Netflix AI model)
Personalized Pricing Impact	Static Pricing	15% increase in revenue
Consumer Trust in AI	60% skeptical	45% prefer AI-driven suggestions

SECTION X: THE ROLE OF EMOTION AND CREATIVITY IN CONSUMER DECISION-MAKING

The Science of Emotion in Consumer Decision-Making

10.1. Emotional Triggers in Marketing

Table 20. Emotional triggers in marketing

Emotion	Consumer Response	Marketing Application
Happiness	Increases brand loyalty	Positive storytelling in ads
Sadness	Encourages empathy & action	Charity & cause-related marketing
Fear	Drives urgency	Security & insurance ads

continued on following page

Table 20. Continued

Emotion	Consumer Response	Marketing Application
Surprise	Enhances recall	Unexpected elements in ads
Anger	Provokes strong engagement	Social justice & activism campaigns

10.2. How AI Measures and Leverages Emotion

- **Facial Emotion Recognition (FER)**: AI analyzes *micro-expressions* to detect emotional responses.
- **EEG & fMRI Emotion Mapping**: Tracks *neural activity* associated with emotional engagement.
- **Sentiment Analysis in social media**: AI interprets *tone, keywords, and emojis* to assess brand sentiment.
- **Voice Emotion AI**: Detects emotional tone in customer interactions.

10.3 Creativity and Storytelling in Marketing

a. The Neuroscience of Storytelling

- *Engages the brain's mirror neurons*, making brand messages more relatable.
- *Boosts memory retention*, with stories being 22x more memorable than facts alone (Berger, 2013).
- *Emotional storytelling activates the limbic system*, increasing brand affinity.

b. AI-Powered Creativity in Advertising

- AI generates *personalized ad content* based on emotional analysis.
- Deep learning models enhance *visual aesthetics and ad placement strategies.*
- AI-driven video editing optimizes *scene selection based on emotional impact.*

Table 21. Cases - AI-driven impact of emotion used

Company	Emotion Used	AI-Driven Impact
Nike	Motivation & Inspiration	AI-optimized ad sequencing led to a 40% increase in brand engagement
Coca-Cola	Happiness	AI-driven storytelling improved recall rates by 30%
Amazon Alexa	Trust & Familiarity	Sentiment analysis improved customer retention by 25%

continued on following page

Table 21. Continued

Company	Emotion Used	AI-Driven Impact
Disney	Surprise & Joy	AI-curated movie trailers increased audience engagement by 50%
Dove	Empathy	AI-powered social impact campaigns gained 3x higher social shares

Case 1: Coca-Cola's AI-Powered Storytelling

Coca-Cola leveraged *AI and emotion recognition technology* to optimize ad sequencing. AI analyzed audience reactions and *adjusted the storytelling elements* to maximize engagement, leading to *a 30% increase in recall rates* (Plassmann et al., 2015).

Case 2: Disney's AI-Enhanced Creativity in Movie Trailers

Disney used *AI to curate emotionally compelling movie trailers* by analyzing audience *facial expressions and engagement levels*. The result was a *50% increase in trailer watch-through rates*, proving that AI-enhanced creativity enhances consumer interest (Berger, 2013).

Table 22. AI powered marketing impact

Marketing Metric	Traditional Method	AI-Enhanced Impact
Ad Engagement Rate	5%	40% (Emotion-optimized AI ads)
Brand Recall	60%	90% (AI-enhanced storytelling)
Sentiment Accuracy	70% (Manual Analysis)	95% (AI Sentiment Analysis)
Video Completion Rate	50%	80% (AI-edited trailers)
Personalized Content Engagement	30%	60% (AI-driven recommendations)

Summary

Emotions play a *pivotal role in consumer decision-making*, and AI enhances marketers' ability to *analyze and leverage these emotions effectively*. By integrating *emotion recognition, AI-powered storytelling, and creative optimization*, brands can create *more compelling and personalized experiences*. However, ethical challenges such as *emotional manipulation, AI bias, and privacy concerns* must be addressed to maintain *consumer trust and regulatory compliance*. The future of AI-driven marketing lies in *balancing emotion, creativity, and ethical responsibility* to drive meaningful consumer engagement.

SECTION XI: THE FUTURE OF NEUROMARKETING: OPPORTUNITIES, RISKS, AND CHALLENGES

Neuromarketing, the fusion of neuroscience and marketing, has transformed the way companies understand and engage consumers. With the rise of *AI, biometrics, and real-time neuroanalytics*, the future of neuromarketing presents both *exciting opportunities and significant ethical challenges* (Plassmann et al., 2015).

11.1.Emerging Opportunities/Trends in Neuromarketing

a. AI-Powered Real-Time Neuromarketing

Table 23. AI-powered real-time neuromarketing

Technology	Application	Projected Impact
EEG & AI Integration	Instant analysis of consumer emotions in live settings	Real-time ad personalization
fMRI with Machine Learning	Predicting subconscious brand preferences	Enhanced product-market fit
Biometric Sentiment Analysis	AI detecting emotional responses via facial recognition	Higher engagement in video marketing
Neuro-AI Chatbots	Customer service driven by emotional intelligence	Improved consumer experience
Brain-Computer Interfaces (BCIs)	Direct neural input for product selection	Personalized shopping experiences

Emotionally Intelligent AI Systems: Another trend is the development of AI systems that not only analyze emotions but also *respond* to them appropriately. So-called emotionally intelligent AI, often implemented in customer service chatbots or virtual shopping assistants, is being informed by neuromarketing findings. For instance, if a chatbot can detect a customer's frustration from their voice or facial expression (a capability made possible by AI emotion recognition), it can adapt its approach – perhaps by changing its tone or escalating to a human agent. The trend here is an evolution from AI simply *measuring* customer emotions to AI actively *modulating* its behavior based on those emotions. In effect, the AI becomes a real-time marketer, adjusting its strategy (messaging, offers) in response to the customer's subconscious cues.

b. Integration of AR/VR and Immersive Technologies in Future Neuromarketing

- **Virtual Reality (VR) Ad Testing**: AI analyzes neural responses in immersive VR simulations.
- **Augmented Reality (AR) Shopping**: Consumers interact with virtual products while AI tracks gaze and engagement.
- *AI-driven personalization in AR/VR spaces* enhances product recommendations based on *subconscious reactions.*

As augmented reality (AR) and virtual reality (VR) technologies mature, neuromarketing is extending into these immersive domains. One trend is the creation of *virtual reality neuromarketing labs* where consumers wear VR headsets (and sometimes EEG caps) and walk through simulated stores or test virtual products, while AI collects and interprets their neurophysiological responses. This can guide real-world store design or product development. The forthcoming AR devices like Apple's Vision Pro goggles are expected to further drive such research, as noted by marketing futurists (Future of Marketing Institute, 2023). The implication is that AI-driven neuromarketing will play a significant role in the design of the *metaverse* or any virtual commerce spaces – ensuring these new environments are neurologically optimized for user engagement and purchasing behavior.

c. Personalized Neuromarketing at Scale

- AI enables ultra-targeted campaigns based on *neuro-segmentation.*
- *Real-time dynamic content adaptation* allows marketing messages to shift based on users' brain activity.
- *AI is bridging individual neurodata with individual content delivery*, aiming to maximize relevance and engagement on a person-by-person basis.
- **Faster A/B Testing:** AI reduces campaign testing time from weeks to days by automating neuromarketing analysis.
- *AI-Powered Hyper-Personalization – Tailored content, pricing, and promotions* based on real-time data.

d. Market Growth:

The neuromarketing industry itself is experiencing robust growth, much of it attributable to AI enhancements that boost its effectiveness. Market research forecasts show the global neuromarketing market size was valued around *\$1.5–1.6 billion in 2023* and is projected to reach *\$3–3.5 billion by the early 2030s*, which represents a healthy compound annual growth rate (CAGR) of roughly 8–10% verifiedmarketresearch.com .

For example, one report estimates a growth from $1.57 billion in 2023 to $3.56 billion in 2032 (CAGR ~8.9%). Another analysis expects about $3.19 billion by 2030 at ~8.9% CAGR marketresearchfuture.com . The consistency of these figures underscores a steady upward trend. This growth is driven by increasing demand for deeper consumer insights, improvements in neurotechnology hardware (making data collection easier and cheaper), and the integration of AI which significantly improves ROI for neuromarketing initiatives. In essence, businesses are investing more in neuromarketing because AI is helping deliver actionable results, justifying the expenditure. The trend suggests neuromarketing will capture a larger share of marketing research budgets in coming years, often complementing or even replacing traditional techniques like surveys and focus groups.

e. Convergence with Data Privacy Regulations:

Industry trends show neuromarketing discussions increasingly coupled with privacy and data ethics. As AI makes neuromarketing more powerful, regulators and industry groups are paying attention. *For example*, the General Data Protection Regulation (GDPR) in the EU classifies biometric and neurological data as sensitive personal data, which means companies must handle neuromarketing data under strict consent and anonymization rules. There is a trend where companies publicly emphasize ethical practices in neuromarketing – some publish "neuromarketing codes of conduct" – to pre-empt backlash. This trend doesn't slow AI adoption, but it does shape *how* it's implemented, with a focus on transparency (e.g., informing study participants or users when their data is being collected for neuromarketing purposes).

f. Global Regulatory Perspectives, Legislation

To further broaden the perspective on neuromarketing regulations, it's vital to consider the emerging neuro-rights legislation in countries like Chile, as well as the ongoing discussions at the international level, particularly within UNESCO. Chile has been a trailblazer in advocating for neuro-rights, becoming the first country to propose a legal framework that safeguards the neurological data and rights of individuals. This legislation is designed to protect people from unauthorized neuro-data collection, manipulation, and discrimination, ensuring that citizens' cognitive and emotional data is not misused by both private and public entities. This move reflects growing concerns about the potential for neuromarketing to exploit unconscious consumer responses without adequate oversight.

In addition, UNESCO has been actively engaging in global discussions about the ethical implications of neuromarketing and the use of neurotechnology. These discussions center on creating global standards and regulations that respect human rights and dignity, aiming to strike a balance between technological advancements and individual freedoms. UNESCO's focus on neuro-rights calls for the establishment of frameworks that prevent any potential violations related to cognitive privacy and autonomy, as well as the ethical use of brain data in marketing.

These global perspectives are crucial in ensuring that neuromarketing practices evolve within a well-regulated environment that prioritizes consumer rights and autonomy.

SECTION XII: SUMMARY

The examination of neuromarketing and artificial intelligence demonstrates that the integration of neuroscientific tools with advanced computational models provides a more comprehensive understanding of consumer behavior than traditional self-report methods. Techniques such as EEG, fMRI, eye-tracking, galvanic skin response, and facial expression analysis enable researchers to access subconscious emotional and cognitive processes that strongly influence purchasing decisions, memory encoding, brand preference, and attention to advertising stimuli. Artificial intelligence further enhances this capacity by enabling the rapid processing of multimodal biometric data, improving predictive accuracy, identifying hidden neural patterns, and facilitating real-time interpretation of complex engagement signals. Together, neuromarketing and AI address the study's objectives by demonstrating how brain-behavior relationships, emotional responses, cognitive biases, and automated analytics shape consumer decisions in both experimental and real-world contexts.

The chapter also highlights the importance of ethics in neuromarketing, particularly concerning privacy, autonomy, manipulation, data sensitivity, and algorithmic bias. As shown in the reviewed material, the increasing use of AI-enhanced neurodata in industries such as advertising, entertainment, retail, and digital platforms underscores the need for rigorous ethical frameworks and transparent guidelines to prevent misuse and protect consumer rights. Furthermore, the discussion of neural mechanisms—including the functions of the amygdala, prefrontal cortex, nucleus accumbens, hippocampus, and insula— clarifies how emotional and cognitive drivers contribute to consumer preferences and decision-making, thereby directly addressing the objective of identifying the biological foundations of consumer responses.

REFERENCES

Ariely, D., & Berns, G. S. (2010). Neuromarketing: The hope and hype of neuroimaging in business. *Nature Reviews. Neuroscience, 11*(4), 284–292. DOI: 10.1038/nrn2795 PMID: 20197790

Berger, J. (2013). *Contagious: Why things catch on*. Simon & Schuster.

Cadwalladr, C., & Graham-Harrison, E. (2018). *Revealed: 50 million Facebook profiles harvested for Cambridge Analytica in major data breach*. The Guardian. https://www.theguardian.com/news/2018/mar/17/cambridge-analytica-facebook-influence-us-election

Dave, P. (2024, January 2). *AI-powered neuromarketing: Mind control or the future of consumer behavior analysis?* The Marketing Hustle. https://themarketinghustle.com/ai-marketing/ai-powered-neuromarketing/

Eijlers, E., Boksem, M. A. S., & Smidts, A. (2020). Measuring neural arousal for advertisements and its relationship with advertising success. *Frontiers in Neuroscience, 14*, 736. DOI: 10.3389/fnins.2020.00736 PMID: 32765214

Future of Marketing Institute. (2023, July 19). *It's all in your head: A look at neuromarketing [Infographic]*. https://futureofmarketinginstitute.com/its-all-in-your-head-a-look-at-neuromarketing/

Globant. (2025). *Neuro AI and neuromarketing: Transforming marketing campaigns* [Blog post]. Stay Relevant by Globant. https://stayrelevant.globant.com

Gomez-Uribe, C. A., & Hunt, N. (2016). The Netflix recommender system: Algorithms, business value, and innovation. *ACM Transactions on Management Information Systems, 6*(4), 1–19. DOI: 10.1145/2843948

Lambrecht, A., & Tucker, C. (2019). Algorithmic pricing and consumer behavior: The role of transparency. *Marketing Science, 38*(5), 773–792. DOI: 10.1287/mksc.2019.1158

Liao, C. H., Sun, Y., Yu, C., & Chan, H. C. (2019). Neuromarketing insights: The role of AI in consumer decision-making. *The Journal of Consumer Research, 46*(3), 567–582. DOI: 10.1093/jcr/ucy028

McClure, S. M., Li, J., Tomlin, D., Cypert, K. S., Montague, L. M., & Montague, P. R. (2004). Neural correlates of behavioral preference for culturally familiar drinks. *Neuron, 44*(2), 379–387. DOI: 10.1016/j.neuron.2004.09.019 PMID: 15473974

Murphy, E. R., & Illes, J. (2018). Neuroethics in marketing: Balancing persuasion and consumer autonomy. *Journal of Business Ethics*, *152*(2), 275–292. DOI: 10.1007/s10551-018-3971-3

Plassmann, H., Ramsøy, T. Z., & Milosavljevic, M. (2012). Branding the brain: A critical review and outlook. *Journal of Consumer Psychology*, *22*(1), 18–36. DOI: 10.1016/j.jcps.2011.11.010

Plassmann, H., Venkatraman, V., Huettel, S., & Yoon, C. (2015). Consumer neuroscience: Applications, challenges, and possible solutions. *JMR, Journal of Marketing Research*, *52*(4), 427–435. DOI: 10.1509/jmr.14.0048

Pola, G. (2023). *Neuromarketing: Neuroscience and AI decode consumer emotions*. Tech4Future. https://tech4future.info/en/neuromarketing-predictive-marketing-neuroscience-and-ai/

Yadav, T. (2024). AI in neuromarketing: Understanding consumer emotions and behavior through machine learning. *International Journal of Future Management Research*, *6*(5), 18–27.

Chapter 6
Role of AI-Powered Neuromarketing in Revolutionizing Consumer Decision-Making

Navyashree Gowthalli Chandregowda
http://orcid.org/0000-0003-4834-5211
Manipal Academy of Higher Education, India

Seetha Khandige
http://orcid.org/0009-0002-4797-2950
Manipal Academy of Higher Education, India

Anujeet Saha
http://orcid.org/0009-0002-6225-2329
Manipal Academy of Higher Education, India

ABSTRACT

In today's complex digital era, marketers face the challenge of understanding the subconscious factors that drive consumer decisions, which traditional self-reported research often fails to capture. Neuromarketing addresses this by combining marketing with neuroscience, using tools like fMRI, EEG, and biometrics to uncover unintentional reactions. The application of artificial intelligence (AI) to this subject is a significant advancement, boosting the accuracy, speed, and scope of consumer insights. This chapter looks at how neuromarketing is changing as a result of AI-powered methods including machine learning, deep learning, and emotional ana-

DOI: 10.4018/979-8-3373-1152-4.ch006

lytics. It draws on key neuroscientific and psychological theories to explain how AI interprets human thought and emotion. Real-world applications across industries, along with ethical considerations around privacy and autonomy, are explored as well. The chapter concludes by outlining future trends, including emotionally adaptive systems and brain-computer interfaces, offering a forward-looking view of personalized and ethical marketing.

INTRODUCTION

For centuries, people have sought to understand how decisions are made. This question sustains disciplines such as philosophy and psychology while also advancing neuroscience research (Cherubino et al., 2019). Understanding the science and decision-making process is essential for marketing success. The fast-paced growth of information technology has led to a considerable increase in the use of digital multimedia content for various purposes. Given the abundance of multimedia content, personal preferences and interests significantly influence the shaping of a customized selection. Understanding consumer preferences and decision-making, is a critical factor in achieving successful marketing outcomes (Adalarasu et al., 2025).

Referred to as the "astonishing hypothesis" by Nobel Prize winner Francis Crick, it proposes that every aspect of human experience, including emotions, thoughts, behaviors, and consciousness, stems solely from brain activity (Harrell, 2019). For marketing professionals, this idea holds the potential to minimize uncertainty and speculation, offering a more precise understanding of consumer behavior through neurobiology, leading to the field called neuromarketing.

As the name implies, neuromarketing is a cutting-edge discipline at the nexus of marketing and neuroscience that uses a variety of neuroscientific techniques and technologies to better understand how customers react to various stimuli. Understanding human behavior in a marketing context is the main objective of neuromarketing, which provides insights that are frequently unavailable through conventional marketing research methods (Aprilianty et al., 2024).

Techniques like surveys and focus groups, in traditional marketing, typically depend upon data provided by the participants themselves, which can be biased and inaccurate because consumers may not fully understand or accurately express their preferences (Ariely & Berns, 2010). Neuromarketing, by contrast, examines subconscious processes through neuroscientific techniques, offering a more extensive understanding of how individuals perceive brands, advertisements, and products on a neural basis (Plassmann, Ramsøy, & Milosavljevic, 2012). Using brain imaging technologies and biometric tools, neuromarketing allows researchers to measure consumers' emotions, attention, memory recall, and the mechanisms behind decision-making. This equips companies with the ability to craft highly effective business strategies that resonate with consumer desires, often beyond their conscious awareness (Morin, 2011). To fully grasp the scientific basis and comprehensive approach of neuromarketing, it is essential to delve into the psychological and neurological theories that underpin consumer decision-making and guide its methodologies.

THEORETICAL FOUNDATIONS OF NEUROMARKETING

Neuromarketing is rooted in psychological and neurological theories that explain consumer decision-making. One of the most relevant frameworks is Dual-Process Theory, proposed by Krämer amd Kahneman (2011), which divides human thinking into two systems:

System 1-Fast, Intuitive Thinking

This system operates automatically and subconsciously, processing information quickly and effortlessly. It is responsible for snap judgments, emotional reactions, and impulse purchases (Kramer & Kahneman, 2011). Marketers aim to trigger System 1 responses through emotionally engaging advertisements, catchy slogans, and sensory cues like colors, sounds, and scents (Zaltman, 2003).

System 2- Slow, Rational Thinking

This system is deliberate and effortful, requiring conscious thought and logical analysis. It is activated when consumers carefully evaluate product features, compare prices, or read reviews before making a purchase. While rational appeals (e.g., product benefits, quality claims) target System 2, research suggests that most purchasing decisions are influenced more by System 1 than System 2 (Ariely & Berns, 2010).

Understanding this distinction allows marketers to optimize campaigns that appeal to the subconscious mind, thereby increasing brand preference and purchase intent (Plassmann et al., 2012).

Neuromarketing and consumer decision-making

It is commonly acknowledged that neuromarketing can be used to improve pricing tactics, make more enjoyable and useful products, and launch more successful social media campaigns. This relatively young field offers a unique perspective by investigating the unconscious processes that affect consumer choice. By applying ideas from marketing, psychology, and neuroscience, neuromarketing aims to uncover the underlying motivations and desires that influence consumer choices (V.M & K.V, 2024).

Making the right decision necessitates assessing pertinent sensory inputs. This has been thoroughly examined in the context of marketing and involves several cognitive abilities, which include working memory, learning, attention, and the motor system. To explain people's behavior and decision-making processes, neuromarketing examines specific brain processes that are triggered by marketing-related inputs (Ouzir et al., 2024).

The promise of this concept for marketers is that neurobiology can lessen the ambiguity and speculation that have historically hampered attempts to comprehend consumer behavior. Consumer neuroscience, another name for neuromarketing, involves the study of the brain to predict and potentially shape the actions and choices of consumers. In recent years, ground-breaking research has supported neuromarketing, which was previously regarded as an expensive "frontier science," by showcasing its potential to benefit marketers (Harrell, 2019).

To achieve these objectives and practically investigate the brain processes triggered by marketing inputs, neuromarketing employs a range of advanced scientific methods. This section will explore the most widely used techniques that enable researchers to gain these deep insights into consumer responses.

KEY NEUROMARKETING TECHNIQUES

Neuromarketing relies on scientific methods to study consumer responses to marketing stimuli. Some of the most widely used techniques include:

Functional Magnetic Resonance Imaging (fMRI)

fMRI tracks variations in brain blood flow, enabling investigators to determine which areas of the brain are activated during particular cognitive and emotional activities (Mao, 2009). Application in Marketing- fMRI research has revealed that strong brands activate the brain's reward centers, particularly the ventromedial prefrontal cortex and the nucleus accumbens, which are linked to pleasure and decision-making (McClure et al., 2004). McClure et al. (2004) conducted a famous fMRI experiment where participants blindly compared the taste of Pepsi and Coca-Cola. When unaware of the brand, participants' brain activity showed no significant preference between the two sodas. However, when they were told which brand they were drinking, Coca-Cola activated the prefrontal cortex, a region linked to brand loyalty and emotional attachment. This demonstrates how branding influences consumer preferences at a neurological level, even when product taste is identical.

Electroencephalography (EEG)

EEG records real-time reactions to marketing stimuli by measuring the electrical activity of the brain using sensors placed on the scalp (Luck, 2014). Unlike fMRI, which provides detailed spatial information about brain activity, EEG is useful for measuring emotional engagement, attention levels, and subconscious reactions in milliseconds (Vecchiato et al., 2011). EEG is widely used to evaluate: TV commercials and digital ads (which elements generate positive or negative reactions), Website user experience (how users emotionally respond to design layouts), and Packaging and product displays (which designs capture the most attention). Ohme et al. (2009) utilized EEG to evaluate the emotional reactions of consumers to TV advertisements. The study found that ads triggering greater frontal asymmetrical activation (linked to positive emotions) correlated with higher purchase intentions. This shows that neuromarketing can quantify and evaluate effectiveness beyond self-reported surveys.

Eye-Tracking Technology

Eye-tracking devices analyze gaze patterns, measuring fixation points, saccades (eye movements), and pupil dilation to determine where a person's attention is focused (Duchowski, 2017). Its application in Marketing includes determining the parts of an advertisement or website that draw the most attention, helping to optimize product packaging for maximum shelf appeal, and identifying effective ad placement in digital marketing. Wedel & Pieters (2008) studied how eye movement patterns influence ad recall. Their research found that consumers process visual information hierarchically, first noticing bold visuals, followed by text and brand logos. Marketers can use these insights to strategically position key elements in advertisements.

Galvanic Skin Response (GSR) & Heart Rate Monitoring

GSR measures sweat gland activity, which indicates emotional arousal. Heart rate monitoring assesses changes in cardiovascular activity in response to stimuli (Boucsein, 2012). Applications in Marketing include the evaluation of the emotional intensity of advertising content, the identification of moments in a video ad that evoke strong reactions, and helping to refine sensory marketing strategies (e.g., in-store music, ambient lighting). Hazlett & Hazlett (1999) used GSR to compare emotional engagement in TV commercials. They found that emotional ads elicited stronger physiological responses than rational ads, leading to better recall and brand impact.

Neuromarketing signifies a paradigm shift in consumer research, providing a scientific understanding of decision-making processes. As AI and machine learning enhance neuromarketing, the future will see even more personalized and emotionally intelligent marketing strategies.

AI-POWERED NEUROMARKETING - TURNING A NEW LEAF IN NEUROMARKETING

From now on, it is nearly impossible to discuss any topic or situation without mentioning artificial intelligence (AI), as it is steadily evolving into an essential part of our everyday routines. Furthermore, its influence on human lifestyles is rapidly expanding and is anticipated to be instrumental in transforming civilizations in the near horizon. Additionally, AI is expected to revolutionize how marketers assess and analyze consumer behavior (Mouammine & Azdimousa, 2019). Marketers may more accurately analyze and understand one's subconscious tendencies while shopping by integrating AI with neuromarketing technologies. The combination of AI and neuromarketing allows marketers to customize their campaigns better and traverse the intricate terrain of customer decision-making (V.M & K.V, 2024). AI, with where it has reached today, can be leveraged to customize marketers' outreach strategies, to align with consumers' emotions, preferences, and behaviors, build deeper connections, enhance engagement, and foster stronger loyalty to their brand (Beličková, 2024).

Neuromarketing research heavily relies on strategies like eye tracking, emotional analysis, neuro-pricing, content optimization, and influencing public perceptions of the brand. AI has a significant impact on these strategies to improve their accuracy and provide more insight into the data that is collected. From the perspective of measuring accuracy, AI might make neuromarketing more intriguing. Research has demonstrated that an AI-driven system can be highly capable of accurately extracting and identifying all human emotions, regardless of a person's gender or ethnicity (V.M. & K.V., 2024). The integration of AI into neuromarketing marks a major advancement, enhancing the accuracy, efficiency, and scope of consumer insights gathered through neuromarketing tools. By combining AI with neuromarketing, marketers can anticipate future actions of consumers and tailor their marketing approaches as needed. This enables them to construct more targeted and impactful marketing strategies, developing campaigns and content that resonate deeply with individual customers, fostering greater engagement, and strengthening brand loyalty (Baltezarević & Baltezarević, 2024). Building on the transformative influence of AI in enhancing traditional neuromarketing strategies, it is crucial to understand the foundational theoretical frameworks that explain how artificial intelligence processes data and influences consumer behavior within this integrated discipline.

AI-Powered Neuromarketing

To comprehend and affect consumer behavior, the multidisciplinary discipline of AI-powered neuromarketing combines knowledge from marketing, psychology, neuroscience, and artificial intelligence. The application of AI in neuromarketing is grounded in various theoretical frameworks that explain how the brain analyzes data, forms decisions, and responds to marketing stimuli. This section explores the key theoretical foundations of AI-powered neuromarketing, with references to academic literature and real-world applications.

Neuroscientific Theories in AI-powered Neuromarketing

Dual-Process Theory (Krämer & Kahneman, 2011). The Dual-Process Theory, proposed by Daniel Kahneman (2011), suggests that human cognition operates through two separate systems: System 1, which operates quickly, instinctively, and is influenced by emotions, and System 2, which functions more slowly, thoughtfully, and analytically. System 1 plays a dominant role in everyday decision-making, relying on heuristics and subconscious cues, while System 2 is activated when individuals engage in complex problem-solving or rational evaluation.

AI-powered neuromarketing utilizes this theory by employing tools such as facial recognition, eye-tracking, and EEG (electroencephalography) to analyze System 1 responses to advertisements, product packaging, and online content. AI algorithms can process these physiological and behavioral signals to determine the emotional impact of marketing stimuli and optimize them for maximum engagement. Meanwhile, System 2 processes are leveraged in AI-driven A/B testing, sentiment analysis, and machine learning models that predict rational decision-making patterns based on past behaviors. For example, the recommendation mechanism of Netflix utilizes AI to assess user preferences, relying on System 1 to encourage impulse-based content consumption while also catering to System 2's logical preferences for curated viewing lists (Gomez-Uribe & Hunt, 2015).

Somatic Marker Hypothesis (Damasio, 1994). The Somatic Marker Hypothesis posits that emotions are vital in decision-making by associating past experiences with physical reactions, like fluctuations in heart rate, galvanic skin response, and neural response. When making a decision, the brain recalls these emotional markers to guide choices, often without conscious awareness.

In AI-powered neuromarketing, machine learning algorithms analyze biometric data from wearable devices, EEG headsets, and fMRI scans to understand consumers' subconscious emotional responses to branding and advertising. For example, AI-driven emotional analytics can assess how a consumer's heart rate or facial expressions change when viewing an ad, allowing brands to refine their messaging for a more positive impact. Coca-Cola has optimized advertising campaigns by determining the most emotionally engaging material through the use of AI-driven neuromarketing techniques (Venkatraman et al., 2015).

Neurological Reward Processing (Dopamine & Decision-Making). Dopamine has a key role in reward-seeking behavior and decision-making, according to neuroscientific research. Research by McClure et al. (2004) shows that pleasurable stimuli, like appealing ads, special offers, and product design, have a profound effect on the brain's reward system, especially the nucleus accumbens. AI-powered neuromarketing employs deep learning algorithms and fMRI-based predictive analytics to detect dopamine-related neural activity in response to marketing content.

AI-driven recommendation systems, such as those used by Spotify, Facebook, and TikTok, are designed to maximize dopamine release by analyzing engagement patterns, click-through rates, and content interaction. By tracking users' preferences and continuously adjusting recommendations, AI ensures that marketing stimuli remain highly rewarding, promoting sustained customer relationships and fostering brand allegiance (Huang & Rust, 2021).

Psychological Theories in AI-Powered Neuromarketing

Prospect Theory (Kahneman & Tversky, 1979). This theory, formulated by Kahneman and Tversky (1979), explains how individuals perceive gains and losses differently, often making irrational choices based on perceived value rather than actual utility. The idea emphasizes the framing effect, which is the way information is presented influencing people's decisions, and loss aversion, which is the tendency for people to fear losses more than they value comparable gains.

AI-powered neuromarketing applies this theory by using predictive analytics to test different framing strategies for product pricing, promotions, and advertising messages. For example, AI-driven dynamic pricing algorithms used by Amazon adjust prices based on consumer sentiment, past behavior, and real-time demand (Smith & Chen, 2019). Framing a price as a "limited-time offer" or "discounted bundle" significantly enhances consumer perception of value, leading to higher conversion rates.

Mere Exposure Effect (Zajonc, 1968). The theory introduced by Robert Zajonc (1968), implies that even if a person does not consciously remember viewing a stimuli, repeated exposure to it enhances their preference for it. This principle is fundamental in advertising, where frequent exposure to a brand enhances familiarity and trust.

AI-powered neuromarketing leverages this theory by optimizing ad placements, ensuring that consumers are repeatedly exposed to a brand across multiple platforms and devices. YouTube's AI-driven ad targeting, for instance, ensures that users encounter the same brand at different touchpoints, reinforcing brand recognition and preference. Machine learning algorithms also determine the optimal frequency of exposure to prevent ad fatigue, balancing engagement without overwhelming the consumer (Campbell & Grimm, 2019).

Emotional Contagion Theory (Hatfield et al., 1993). This theory, which was proposed by Hatfield et al. (1993), states that people subconsciously mimic and adopt the emotions of those around them. This phenomenon is particularly relevant in social media marketing, where user-generated content and influencer endorsements drive consumer emotions.

AI-powered neuromarketing integrates facial recognition technology and sentiment analysis to detect and amplify emotionally resonant content. Platforms like TikTok and Instagram use AI to analyze engagement patterns and prioritize emotionally engaging content in users' feeds. Studies show that advertisements featuring high-energy, positive emotions elicit stronger consumer engagement and brand recall (Pentina & Zhang, 2016).

Cialdini's Principles of Persuasion (Cialdini, 1984). Likeability, reciprocity, consistency, scarcity, social validation, and authority are the six principles of persuasion proposed by Robert Cialdini in his 1984 book "Influence: The Psychology of Persuasion." Marketers have found some of these to be quite helpful (Cialdini & Goldstein, 2002). For instance, Cialdini brought up a research done in a candy store in episode 55 of the podcast "Speaking of Psychology" (2018), which features Audrey Hamilton. Here, the manager gave a piece of chocolate as a welcome gift to half of the guests. It was shown that while not all of them purchased chocolate, they were 42% more likely to purchase candies. The increased likelihood of buying wasn't due to sampling the chocolate's quality but rather a sense of obligation to reciprocate after receiving a gift. He also mentioned another study done in a supermarket, where among all the promotions offered for various brands, the most effective one—outperforming the others by double—was the promotion that limited purchases to a specific number of items per customer, i.e., working on the principle of scarcity. Thus, these principles show great promise in the field of marketing. AI can be used here to adjust pricing and stock displays to create a sense of urgency.

Self-determination theory (Deci & Ryan, 1985). According to this theory of motivation, humans have three basic psychological needs: relatedness (the need to experience a meaningful connection to others), competence (the sensation of mastery), and autonomy (the ability to act in a way that gives one a true sense of choice and control). To increase apparent autonomy, AI is used by services like Netflix and Spotify to recommend content based on user preferences. Another illustration is Sephora's Virtual Artist, an AI chatbot that offers support without being intrusive and lets users freely consider their selections. (Khandelwal et al., 2023; Oahn, 2024).

Leveraging these neuroscientific and psychological insights, a core strength of AI in neuromarketing lies in its advanced capability to identify complex patterns and accurately predict consumer behavior, moving beyond retrospective analysis to proactive forecasting.

Identifying patterns and predicting behaviour

Predicting consumer behavior relies on various methods and tools to forecast future actions and decisions. One widely used approach is historical data analysis, where past consumer behavior is examined to uncover purchasing trends, product preferences, and patterns that can inform future predictions. Machine learning algorithms examine massive datasets, spot intricate patterns, and develop predictive models trained on historical data to anticipate future behavior based on new inputs (Juárez-Varón et al., 2024). Predicting the behavior of clients is made easier by grouping them according to common traits (Singhal, 2023). The distinct patterns and preferences that each customer segment tends to exhibit can be used to tailor marketing strategies and offerings. Surveys and customer feedback can provide valuable information by asking customers directly about their expectations and ambitions, which can assist forecast future behavior (Agag et al., 2023). By evaluating discussions and opinions on social media, online reviews, and other platforms, sentiment analysis technology (Punetha & Jain, 2023) can be utilized to enhance this approach even more. Businesses can better predict changes in consumer behavior by evaluating how the general public views a product or brand. Furthermore, recommendation models—which are extensively used in streaming services and e-commerce—analyze user interactions to forecast pertinent goods or content, increasing client happiness and personalization (Venkatraman et al., 2015).

Businesses can test different strategies and measure client reactions via experiments and A/B testing, which compares two versions of something to discover which performs better (Gallo, 2017). The results of these tests can then be used to guide future decisions. Understanding the context in which decisions are made—including current events, market trends, economic swings, and seasonal considerations—can be essential to influencing customer behavior. Notably, combining multiple methods and data sources often leads to more accurate consumer behavior predictions. By strengthening e-payment systems, elevating customer sentiment, and increasing personalized services, research has shown that AI can significantly impact consumer behavior (Adwan & Aladwan, 2022). The capacity of deep learning models, especially ensemble architectures, to accurately classify complex variations in consumer behavior has surpassed that of standard machine learning models (Hakami & Mahmoud, 2022). Additionally, with classification accuracies of over 90%, it has been shown that combining AI models with marketing data through decision-making methods like decision trees and genetic algorithms can predict consumer behavior in both online and offline retail settings (Gkikas et al., 2022). Additionally, studies show that the nature of consumer-AI relationships is significantly influenced by factors including trust, attachment, empathy, loyalty, and gender traits. According to Pop et al. (2023), this emphasizes how crucial it is to understand these dynamics in order to successfully include AI into customer interactions.

Through the analysis of visual attention patterns and cognitive processes, AI-powered eye-tracking technology is essential for forecasting consumer behavior. According to research, eye-tracking data can be used to predict decision-making processes based on visual focus and uncover customer preferences when paired with machine learning techniques like K-means clustering (Kar, 2020). To improve college magazines, make them more appealing, and make them easier to use, Šola et al. (2024) used artificial intelligence and eye-tracking technologies to precisely forecast client behaviors and preferences. The study comprised three college publications that were available online and in PDF format. User experience was assessed using neuromarketing eye-tracking AI prediction software that was trained on a sizable consumer neuroscience dataset that included eye-tracking data from 180,000 users.

The findings of this study about the modality of the magazine, the fonts, and other visuals such as the layout, are key to developing an engaging magazine. This is just one example of the many ways AI can be used to predict behaviour and revolutionize marketing.

Another example comes from the field of education, where AI primarily employs machine learning, deep learning, and advanced analytics to track a person's speed in relation to others. As AI technologies advance, they make it easier to spot teaching and learning gaps, which eventually raises educational standards (Biswas & Patra, 2023).

Another illustration comes from the medical field, where a research revealed that 25% of the 100 million Americans who have diabetes go undetected. Untrained experts and a lack of current technologies have resulted in untreated cases of diabetes in certain impoverished countries. Computer algorithms can provide dietary advice, machine learning can track blood sugar levels, and "personal health companions" can remind people to take their prescription drugs. Furthermore, risk-predictive algorithms or artificial neural networks are used by the Apple Watch, which was created in partnership with Aetna, to maximize performance (Biswas & Patra, 2023).

An example specific to marketing is given by Amazon, the largest online retailer in the USA. Here, AI provides location-specific pricing, customer-centric search and personalization (Biswas & Patra, 2023). Some beauty or cosmetic brands also allow virtual try-ons of their products using AI.

Having explored AI's broad capabilities in predicting behavior across different domains, we now turn our focus to how artificial intelligence is specifically integrated with and revolutionizes the key neuromarketing technologies and strategies discussed earlier, thereby deepening consumer insights.

Integration of AI with neuromarketing tools

The integration of AI with the previously described neuromarketing technologies and strategies is covered in the part that follows.

A noteworthy study identified functional brain networks linked to brand perception using fMRI data and machine learning techniques (Santos & Santos, 2024). In order to better understand consumer preferences, this study used explainable AI (xAI) strategies to distinguish between preferred and indifferent brands during early processing phases. Khondakar et al. (2024) conducted a comprehensive review that looked at EEG-based neuromarketing and highlighted how AI may be used to evaluate EEG data in order to understand consumer preferences and decision-making processes. The study underlined how crucial AI is for interpreting intricate EEG data and forecasting how customers would react to different marketing stimuli. In a different study, Phutela et al. (2022) suggested using EEG signal analysis to comprehend how customers respond to ads and items, both positively and negatively. They classified customer replies using machine learning techniques including Naive Bayes and Support Vector Machine, and they were able to predict customer decisions with a considerable degree of accuracy. The integration of AI and eye tracking has already been mentioned above in the study by Šola et al., on improving college magazines. Another example is a systematic review which examined the synergistic use of eye-tracking and AI in marketing communication management (Li et al., 2024). Eye-tracking helps assess visual preferences, while AI enhances personalization and campaign optimization. The paper suggested that by integrating AI and eye-tracking technologies, companies can gain a deeper understanding of consumer behavior. This would enable them to automatically generate relevant marketing messages, eliminating the need for manual intervention, and allowing for real-time adaptation of strategies to meet evolving market demands. The combination of these tools facilitates more targeted and dynamic marketing efforts.

Galvanic skin response is also an important neuromarketing technique, although it is not used as much as some of the other techniques due to lower accuracy. A study by Perez-Rosero et al. (2016) explored the correlation between autonomically-mediated changes in physiological signals, including GSR, and discrete emotional states. They developed a classification approach using AI algorithms to analyze these signals, achieving an 88.1% recognition accuracy in identifying emotional experiences. In another study, researchers developed a desktop application that detects and recognizes participants' emotions triggered by various stimuli through GSR. This application utilized AI to process GSR data, enhancing the understanding of consumer emotional responses in neuromarketing contexts.

Although not as accurate, heart rate is one of the key components in neuromarketing research, because it is easier to measure and analyze as compared to some of the other, more expensive, techniques. A systematic review examined the application of heart rate variability (HRV) in marketing research (Kakaria et al., 2022). The study highlighted HRV as a promising physiological measurement that captures psychophysiological variations in response to marketing stimuli. It emphasized the importance of distinguishing between heart rate and HRV measurements and discussed the complexities involved in analyzing HRV data, including preprocessing steps to ensure signal robustness.

Biometric technologies and facial recognition can be used to identify emotions. A limited number of Wimbledon attendees were given biometric wristbands by Jaguar in 2015, which allowed them to record "excitement" events during the competition (*Jaguar Launches #FeelWimbledon Campaign Aiming to Capture the Mood of the Championships*, 2015). These bracelets tracked the wearer's temperature and pulse rate, both of which rise in response to excitement. Biometric data can provide even more precise insights into how consumers respond to marketing messages when paired with AI-driven facial recognition. Strategies for event marketing may find this information very useful (Bansal & Gupta, 2023).

Biometric data is not used by IBM's Watson, a computer system that interprets inquiries in plain language, to determine how excited people are at an event. Rather, it creates highlight clips for the Masters golf competition using cues like fist pumps and crowd noise (Booton, 2018). This technology is easily adaptable to a wide range of uses. For example, by recognizing customer interest signals like reading a label or pausing for a longer look, Watson or a comparable AI system might track new bestsellers and successful packaging designs. These tactics are especially effective because they allow marketers to modify their messaging based on real-time data on customers' emotional reactions (Bansal & Gupta, 2023).

With consumer consent, marketers across various industries can adopt this approach for their marketing messages. Utilizing this strategy would remove the reliance on intuition when crafting effective marketing plans and eliminate the need for unreliable focus groups. Once AI is fully integrated into neuromarketing processes, marketers will be able to crowdsource their campaigns without the risk of collecting inaccurate data (Bansal & Gupta, 2023). Given the profound shifts introduced by AI in neuromarketing, it becomes imperative to evaluate these advanced methodologies against conventional marketing research practices. This comparison illuminates the significant evolution in how businesses gather insights and understand consumer behavior.

Conventional Marketing Research Methods vs. AI-driven Approaches

Bansal and Gupta (2023) outline a comparison between traditional market research methods and AI-driven approaches. According to their literature, market research is what businesses use to understand new and existing customers, competitors, and market trends. AI-driven market research examines every step of the consumer journey, from the initial contact to the feedback received after a purchase, in contrast to traditional market research. This invention has the power to completely transform the sector.

A data-driven method called market research is used to evaluate the potential of a new good or service or identify what has to be changed to make a brand more appealing. Businesses can determine their target market, acquire market intelligence, and examine customer behavior with the help of this study. The information gathered is essential for developing marketing plans that promote innovation, propel brand growth, and handle possible marketing obstacles. Forbes claims that carrying out in-depth research before introducing a new good or service gives companies the knowledge they need to make informed judgments. Pricing, branding, marketing tactics, and possible brand advancements are all influenced by this data. It also assists in finding possible target markets and gaps in the industry, as well as consumer interest in the product or service. Good market research identifies the ideal clients and identifies the most effective ways to market to them.

Market research also leads to businesses staying in contact with their consumers, through surveys and questionnaires, which are used for gathering consumer insights, offering key information about customer preferences, needs, and motivations. This makes the consumers feel valued, thus boosting consumer satisfaction and increasing sales. Market research is typically conducted in two stages:

Primary Data Collection- Both qualitative and quantitative research are used at this phase. Companies use questionnaires and surveys to communicate with consumers and collect data. The study may be targeted or exploratory. While focused research concentrates on resolving certain concerns found during the exploratory phase, exploratory research employs open-ended interview questions with a sample population.

Secondary Research- This method relies on data collected by third-party sources such as government agencies, media outlets, and research reports. Information is obtained from studies, newspapers, and various published sources.

Finding current and potential consumer markets is the first stage in primary market research. It is crucial to divide the larger market into smaller groups of consumers based on shared traits, such as requirements, hobbies, lifestyles, or demographics.

Businesses can better understand their customers and produce more accurate analysis by identifying these subgroups prior to performing social listening or CSAT surveys.

After determining the target market, three key primary research methods can be used:

Online Customer Surveys- Surveys and polls are two of the most popular methods for gauging consumer sentiment. They offer insightful information on how customers interact with a good or service.

Social Media Monitoring and Analysis- Tracking social media activity helps businesses gauge social sentiment, including customer satisfaction and brand perception, by analyzing feedback and discussions.

Focus Groups- A common method for market research, focus groups typically consist of 6–10 participants who share their opinions on new products, services, marketing ideas, and other relevant topics. By analyzing customer feedback, businesses can identify gaps in the current market and uncover unmet consumer needs.

Coming to the impact of AI on market research, it is revolutionizing market research by enhancing data collection, analysis, and decision-making. It provides deeper insights, increases efficiency, and allows businesses to make more accurate, data-driven decisions. More specifically, as summarized by Bansal and Gupta (2023), AI impacts marketing research in the following ways.

Faster delivery of research- Market research needs to be finished fast in order to remain relevant. Inaccurate sentiment analysis and out-of-date information can result from delays. Writing reports takes a lot of time and is a major part of a market researcher's job. Research delivery is frequently delayed as a result, which reduces the value of the data. AI-powered market research (Apriliantyet al., 2024) gathers data from a designated target group while continuously monitoring and evaluating keywords or themes to produce results instantaneously. AI completes this process far more quickly than a human could.

More versatile options- Data gathering techniques must be customized for the target audience in order for market research to be successful and yield insightful information. For example, poorly designed customer satisfaction surveys can result in low response rates, which affect ratings and generate erroneous data (Brace, 2018). AI technology improves surveys by incorporating real-time customer replies and making them more flexible and interactive (Chatterjee et al., 2021). Furthermore, dynamic analysis is made possible by machine learning, which enables companies to adapt their current solutions to better suit the needs of their clients (Davenport et al., 2020). *Improved quality of CX*- Research must provide extremely detailed insights for efficient budget allocation and marketing campaign planning. Human error or prejudice is one of the largest threats to the integrity of research. Leading survey questions, for example, have the potential to skew results and cause misunderstandings (Bryman, 2016). Inaccurate data analysis might result in lost revenue and inefficient marketing tactics. Traditional customer experience (CX) analysis benefits from AI's ability to produce data fast, correctly, and without human bias or error (Rust & Huang, 2021). The result is market research that is accurate, effective, and extremely detailed.

Accurate text analysis- It can be very difficult to keep track of phone records, social media comments, open-ended survey answers, and emails. Large volumes of data are processed effectively by AI-powered algorithms, which also do in-depth text analysis to uncover customer sentiments, ideas, and market wants (Cambria et al., 2020). AI can instantly evaluate hundreds of text-based reviews, comments, and survey responses by using sentiment analysis and Natural Language Processing (NLP) (Zhou et al., 2020).

Traditional market research methods have limitations, as they primarily rely on declarative data—what respondents verbally express, which may not always reflect their true thoughts. AI-driven systems, however, can analyze and identify a wide range of emotions across individuals, regardless of gender or ethnicity. Historically, the most effective way to gauge consumer interest in a product was simply to ask for their opinion. However, participants in focus groups often exaggerate or distort their responses, reducing the accuracy of the research. In recent years, AI has significantly advanced the field of neuromarketing, providing deeper and more reliable consumer insights (Mouammine & Azdimousa, 2019)..

To illustrate the tangible impact and diverse capabilities of AI integration within neuromarketing, this section presents a showcase of real-world applications across various industries, demonstrating how these advanced approaches translate into practical success.

Showcase of Applications of AI in Neuromarketing

As illustrated above, the integration of AI with neuromarketing has been and is being studied with applications spread across various domains. This section encapsulates several such examples. Merritt et al. (2023) used AI and machine learning to predict hit songs. The study "Accurately Predicting Hit Songs Using Neurophysiology and Machine Learning" explored the challenges of identifying hit songs and introduced a novel approach combining neurophysiology with machine learning to improve predictive accuracy. Traditional methods, such as analyzing lyrics, social media activity, and listener preferences, have had limited success in forecasting hit songs. The research involved measuring neurophysiological responses to a selection of songs, comparing statistical models to assess their predictive power. A basic linear statistical model using two neural measures achieved 69% accuracy in classifying hit songs, while an advanced ensemble machine learning approach significantly improved this accuracy to 97%. The study demonstrated that listeners' neural responses, particularly in the first minute of a song, can be strong indicators of its potential success. The research suggested that applying machine learning to neural data can substantially enhance predictions in the music industry and other entertainment sectors.

Çakar and Filiz (2023) applied machine learning to the field of political science to analyze voter behaviour and political leader perception. The study "Unraveling Neural Pathways of Political Engagement: Bridging Neuromarketing and Political Science for Understanding Voter Behavior and Political Leader Perception" utilized functional near-infrared spectroscopy (fNIRS) and machine learning models to examine neural activation patterns when individuals were exposed to images of political leaders. The study identified key brain regions, such as the dorsolateral prefrontal cortex (dlPFC), dorsomedial prefrontal cortex (dmPFC), and ventromedial prefrontal cortex (vmPFC), which are critical in processing political branding and voter decision-making. Among several machine learning models tested, LightGBM achieved the highest accuracy (78%), effectively predicting voter perceptions based on brain activity. The findings suggested that political branding strategies influence voter preferences at a neurophysiological level, revealing how different neural regions respond to political stimuli. Furthermore, the study emphasized the growing role of neuromarketing in political campaigns, offering insights into how candidates can optimize messaging strategies.

A success story of application of AI in neuromarketing is that of CO-RO, a multinational FMCG company, which leveraged Neurons AI to enhance its marketing strategies, improve brand awareness, and streamline internal processes (How CO-RO optimized ads & branding to win new markets with Neurons AI, n.d.). Facing intense market competition, CO-RO sought a tool to refine its packaging and advertising effectiveness beyond traditional eye-tracking methods, which had limitations in cost, geography, and iterations. With Neurons AI, the company achieved 95% accuracy in predicting visual attention, leading to a 20% boost in brand awareness in the Egyptian market. The AI-powered insights enabled rapid testing, unlimited design iterations, and cost-efficient marketing improvements. Additionally, Neurons facilitated internal decision-making by providing data-driven justifications for packaging and branding choices. CO-RO plans to further integrate AI into its operations, recognizing Neurons as a game-changer in achieving a competitive edge.

Another success story involving Neurons AI is that of Total Media, a UK-based behavioral planning agency, which integrated AI into its research and creative optimization processes to enhance consumer insights and improve marketing effectiveness (Providing Actionable Business Recommendations With Predictive AI, n.d.). Initially relying on expensive in-person biometrics labs with eye-tracking, galvanic skin response, and facial coding, the agency sought a cost-effective, scalable alternative. AI provided over 90% accuracy in predicting attention and allowed for rapid testing of visual assets, website designs, and digital creatives. By combining AI with traditional research methods, Total Media could analyze user behavior efficiently, leading to actionable insights. In one case, the agency used AI to redesign a client's website, optimizing key visual elements and calls to action, which increased engagement and conversions by 42%. The AI tool also enabled creative agencies to test short video ads and website layouts without costly participant-based studies.

According to a November, 2024 article in the Wall Street Journal, Yum Brands, the parent company of Taco Bell, Pizza Hut, and KFC, has successfully integrated AI-driven marketing strategies to enhance personalization, increase purchases, and reduce customer churn (Graham, 2024). Through AI-powered email campaigns, the company customizes offers based on factors like time of day, order frequency, and customer behavior, replacing the traditional one-size-fits-all approach. AI also automates content selection, delivery timing, and reinforcement learning for real-time campaign optimization, leading to double-digit increases in consumer engagement. Yum Brands envisions expanding AI personalization to kiosks, mobile apps, and drive-thru experiences, leveraging data on location, weather, and purchase history to tailor promotions. While traditional marketing remains essential, the company sees AI as a critical tool for enhancing creativity, efficiency, and competitive advantage, emphasizing that "humans using AI will replace humans" in the evolving marketing landscape.

The next case study of the use of AI in neuromarketing is one that we encounter all the time, artwork personalization by Netflix. According to their technology blog, Netflix continuously enhances its user experience by leveraging machine learning to personalize the artwork displayed for each title (Artwork Personalization at Netflix, 2017). Recognizing that visual elements strongly influence viewing decisions, Netflix tailors movie imagery based on individual viewing histories and preferences. For example, in promoting *Good Will Hunting*, a user inclined toward romantic films might see artwork featuring Matt Damon and Minnie Driver, while a comedy enthusiast would be shown imagery highlighting Robin Williams. Similarly, for *Pulp Fiction*, a fan of Uma Thurman would be presented artwork featuring her, whereas a John Travolta admirer would see his image. This approach ensures that every title is showcased in the most appealing way to each member. Implementing this personalization at such a large scale is highly complex. The system must handle peaks of over 20 million artwork selection requests per second with extremely low latency. Netflix does this using a contextual bandit model, which dynamically selects the best artwork from dozens of candidates based on user context. The model must adapt quickly during a title's launch phase and continue evolving as member preferences and title popularity shift over time. Performance improvements are validated through rigorous A/B testing, comparing engagement levels between control and experimental groups before full rollouts. Through personalized artwork selection, Netflix not only enhances content discovery but also strengthens member engagement, proving that even subtle personalization strategies, powered by advanced machine learning, can significantly impact the overall user experience.

While the preceding examples clearly demonstrate the immense potential and transformative power of Artificial Intelligence in reshaping marketing practices and enhancing consumer experiences, its widespread adoption concurrently introduces a range of complex ethical dilemmas that warrant careful consideration.

ETHICS OF AI IN NEUROMARKETING

As discussed previously, Artificial Intelligence has fundamentally reshaped marketing practices by offering new ways to enhance customer experiences, improve decision-making, and drive company profits. However, its adoption brings ethical dilemmas, including concerns about data privacy, consumer autonomy, fairness, and transparency. Understanding and addressing these challenges is essential for businesses seeking to leverage AI responsibly while maintaining public trust. Wang, S. (2025) outlines ethical issues faced in the integration of AI and marketing, which are briefly explained below.

Customer Experience And Ethical Challenges

While AI's promise in marketing is to create personalized, efficient customer experiences, it does not always deliver positive outcomes. Initially, customers might experience dissatisfaction, especially when AI-based classification systems are perceived as discriminatory. Studies indicate that AI algorithms, when profiling users, can inadvertently perpetuate biases based on ethnicity, social group, or economic background. In sectors like fintech (financial technology), companies use digital footprints to assess creditworthiness, leading to informational asymmetries that reinforce existing inequalities.

Moreover, the lack of emotional sensitivity in AI interactions contributes to customer dissatisfaction. AI, being data-driven, struggles to replicate the emotional engagement that human interactions naturally provide. When customers perceive recommendations as purely mechanical or feel alienated by stereotypical profiling, it diminishes trust and loyalty toward brands.

Despite these challenges, companies can address the risks associated with AI by implementing strong regulatory frameworks and maintaining transparency in their practices. Ethical AI marketing should aim to provide not only accurate personalization but also emotional resonance and fairness in customer engagement. Ensuring that AI systems avoid discriminatory outcomes and uphold clear standards of data transparency can significantly enhance the quality of customer engagement. In doing so, businesses not only deliver more meaningful, individualized experiences but also build deeper, more enduring relationships with their customers.

Balancing Personalization And Consumer Autonomy

Another ethical issue arises from AI's impact on consumer autonomy. Recommender systems and psychological targeting often nudge consumers toward specific choices, which, while convenient, can significantly limit their exposure to diverse products. Delegating decisions to AI at the information-gathering stage may result in customers feeling manipulated, particularly when the system predicts their behavior too accurately.

Loss of autonomy can lead to psychological reactance—where consumers deliberately choose less-preferred options just to assert their independence. A prolonged sense of diminished autonomy can ultimately harm a consumer's self-identity and lead to lower purchase satisfaction. However, it is also possible to view AI's role in decision-making positively. Properly designed AI systems can assist consumers in navigating overwhelming choices, thereby reducing decision fatigue. By efficiently matching products to user preferences without overtly steering them, AI can facilitate quicker, more satisfying purchasing decisions. Tools such as AI-powered digital assistants, which analyze factors like price, brand reputation, and quality, allow consumers to make informed choices without feeling restricted.

A critical factor here is customization: when AI recommendations are flexible and offer consumers the perception of control, autonomy is preserved. Research suggests that when users feel understood and respected, they tend to embrace AI recommendations more readily, resulting in greater loyalty and satisfaction. Thus, setting an appropriate level of algorithmic autonomy and fostering self-efficacy among consumers can ensure that AI supports, rather than supplants, human agency in decision-making.

Data Privacy

Among the most critical ethical concerns in AI marketing is data privacy. AI systems depend heavily on personal data to generate insights and predictions, raising legitimate fears about data security and misuse. Many customers fear that their information may be shared with third parties without their consent, fueling distrust toward AI systems.

The erosion of trust due to privacy breaches can have significant negative effects, not only on consumer experiences but also on their willingness to share data in the future. Furthermore, the problem is exacerbated by the generation of biased information by AI, which can compromise the credibility of marketing messages and compromise customer confidence.

Despite these challenges, privacy issues can be mitigated through concerted efforts by companies and policymakers. Transparent communication regarding data usage, adherence to well-structured privacy regulations, and organizational efforts to minimize information asymmetry are critical. Rebuilding confidence and promoting safe data sharing can be achieved by increasing transparency, for as by outlining the procedures for gathering, storing, and using consumer data.

Government initiatives, such as the European Commission's proposal for AI regulation, aim to ensure AI development aligns with principles of fairness, security, and accountability. Ethical frameworks like the "Ethics Guidelines for Trustworthy AI" emphasize the need for transparency and individual rights, laying the groundwork for AI applications that respect consumer privacy. With proper regulation, company accountability, and increased public awareness, AI can be implemented ethically without sacrificing innovation or consumer trust.

Over-Reliance On AI

While AI offers clear advantages in personalization and efficiency, there are concerns about its broader market implications. Some experts argue that excessive reliance on AI for product customization could erode brand differentiation. By focusing too narrowly on personalization, companies risk narrowing their product offerings, making them less innovative and reducing consumer choice.

Furthermore, an overdependence on AI might cause companies to converge toward similar business models, creating a highly competitive environment with little room for creative distinction. This could, paradoxically, weaken market positions rather than strengthen them.

Instead, AI can provide a source of long-term competitive advantage if used well. Businesses are able to quickly deploy pertinent offers and adjust to changing consumer expectations by using predictive AI systems that precisely predict customer wants. Businesses like Baidu and Toyota have made significant investments in AI to support financial services and personalized interaction, demonstrating the technology's revolutionary potential to redefine business models.

The dynamic capabilities offered by AI, such as real-time feedback, continuous learning, and adaptive marketing strategies, can deepen customer relationships and maintain competitive advantage. Organizations that strike the right balance—leveraging AI for efficiency while maintaining brand innovation—are likely to outperform their rivals in the digital economy.

Transparency In Data Use

In the realm of AI-powered neuromarketing, transparency in data use is not only morally necessary, but also crucial for building long-lasting brand loyalty, ensuring legal compliance, and gaining the trust of customers. When machine learning models utilize brain, biometric, and behavioral data to interpret subconscious preferences and predict consumer behavior, the line between manipulative persuasion and compelling marketing may become increasingly hazy (Ferrell et al., 2025). To walk this ethical tightrope, organizations must embrace honest, open, and transparent communication around the gathering, handling, and application of customer data.

Informed consent is the first step toward transparency. Customers need to understand the specific objective of the data collection and be aware of the kinds of information being collected, from eye-tracking and EEG data to facial micro-expressions and social media activity (Ferrell et al., 2025). Organizations should publish just-in-time notifications and plain-language disclosures that explain how AI models read behavioral and brain signals to customize marketing campaigns, moving away from complex legalese in privacy agreements (Acquisti, Brandimarte, & Loewenstein, 2015).

The fact that many AI systems are "black boxes" is another significant obstacle. Both customers and regulators may find it challenging to comprehend the reasoning behind algorithmic judgments when utilizing sophisticated neuromarketing techniques, especially those that use deep learning. By using explainable AI (XAI) frameworks to address this opacity, it will be easier to understand how brain-based data is used to produce outputs like product suggestions or emotional triggers (Doshi-Velez & Kim, 2017). XAI promotes consumer autonomy and more equitable marketing practices by making algorithmic logic transparent.

Accountability also depends on transparency. Users are better able to exercise their rights—such as asking for data deletion, fixing errors, or refusing to participate in AI-driven profiling—when they are fully informed about data practices. These rights are starting to be enshrined in legal frameworks that emphasize openness as a fundamental data governance principle, such as the General Data Protection Regulation (GDPR) of the European Union and the Digital Personal Data Protection Act (DPDPA) of India (European Commission, 2016; Raj, 2025).

In the end, businesses that actively embrace transparency not only lower ethical and legal risk but also gain a competitive edge in a setting where neuromarketing technologies may directly access the subconscious. Customers are becoming more discriminating and are more inclined to interact with companies that uphold cognitive privacy and use AI responsibly. Transparency continues to be the foundation of trust in the rapidly changing fields of neuroscience, data science, and marketing. It is also essential for long-term, human-centered innovation.

Ethics of AI in Neuromarketing Across Demographics

Due to differences in conventions, beliefs, and views of privacy and autonomy, the ethical use of AI in neuromarketing is particularly important in culturally varied environments. Artificial intelligence (AI) systems that are morally acceptable in one culture may be viewed as invasive or manipulative in another due to differing views on data usage, permission, and emotional targeting. Though the results are still mixed, earlier research has looked into how individual expertise affects how algorithmic recommendations and algorithmic decision-making (ADM) are perceived. According to some study, more positive attitudes regarding algorithms are typically associated with higher levels of education (Thurman et al., 2018) and more familiarity with mathematics (Logg et al., 2019). Beyond knowledge, demographics—particularly age and gender—also seem to have an impact, though the data is similarly conflicting. For example, older people are less likely than younger people to think algorithmic decisions are free from bias and have been found to favor human editors over algorithms for news distribution (Thurman et al., 2018). These patterns do not, however, apply to all studies (e.g., Logg et al., 2019). Although it is not always linked to an overall appreciation of algorithms (Logg et al., 2019; Thurman et al., 2018), gender has been found to have some bearing on how fair algorithms are perceived (Dineen et al., 2004; Pierson, 2017).

Given these complexities, it is clear that the ethical deployment of AI in neuromarketing must be sensitive not only to cultural differences but also to individual variations in knowledge, age, and perceptions of fairness. A one-size-fits-all approach risks alienating diverse audiences and undermining trust in AI-driven systems. Therefore, companies and policymakers must prioritize culturally adaptive, transparent, and inclusive AI practices to ensure that neuromarketing efforts are ethically sound and broadly accepted across different populations. Given that neuromarketing directly interacts with subconscious processes, the potential for harm or coercion is heightened if ethical considerations are overlooked. Thus, culturally aware, ethically governed AI is not just desirable but necessary for sustainable and responsible neuromarketing practices globally.

Having thoroughly examined the current applications and essential ethical considerations surrounding AI in neuromarketing, we now turn our attention to the horizon, exploring the rapidly developing future trends that are poised to further revolutionize how brands interact with and understand consumers at the deepest cognitive levels.

FUTURE TRENDS

Artificial intelligence (AI) integrated with neuromarketing, which is a discipline that combines psychology, neuroscience, and consumer behavior, is also developing quickly. A revolutionary era in which marketing becomes not only predictive but also preemptive, hyper-personalized, and emotionally resonant is being ushered in by the merging of AI and neuromarketing. In the future, a number of trends have the potential to change how consumers make decisions and impact how brands engage with people on the most personal levels of cognition. These trends highlight the ethical complexity and potential of a future where artificial intelligence (AI) will be able to understand and respond to the human brain with ever-increasing precision.

Interfaces That Are Emotionally Adaptive

The creation of emotionally adaptive interfaces—systems that react dynamically to a user's current emotional state—is a noteworthy trend that is on the horizon. Using a combination of biometric sensors (like heart rate variability, pupil dilatation, and galvanic skin response)and AI algorithms, future marketing platforms will be able to gauge a user's emotional engagement and adjust content accordingly. An emotionally adaptable system might, for instance, postpone making a sales presentation or use more reassuring language and imagery if a customer shows symptoms of stress or distraction.

These interfaces will go beyond customisation based on past behavior and explore the new area of affective computing, where virtual environments adapt in real time to users' emotional and mental states. This movement raises important ethical issues about the monetization of psychological states and emotional manipulation, even while it has the potential to greatly improve user experience and engagement (Picard, 1997).

Brain-Computer Interface Integration (BCIs)

Another area for AI-powered neuromarketing is brain-computer interfaces, or BCIs. Without depending entirely on outward behaviors or facial expressions, marketers may be able to evaluate attention, arousal, and preference by directly interacting with cerebral activity through devices like those being developed by Neuralink and OpenBCI. Non-invasive BCIs might be integrated into commonplace wearables, such as smart glasses or AR/VR headsets, to instantly transform passive neural data into useful marketing insights.

While yet hypothetical, the commercial usage of BCI data is not out of the question. When paired with AI, BCIs may allow for zero-click consumer contact, in which a user's preferences are deduced before they are consciously expressed. This presents dangers to privacy and cognitive liberty even if it could greatly improve user experiences and advertising efficiency (Ienca & Andorno, 2017).

Highly Tailored Advertising Using Generative AI

Content creation is being redefined by the emergence of generative AI, especially huge language models and image generators. These tools will make it possible for neuromarketing to automatically create customized marketing content, such as emails, product pages, videos, and ads, depending on each user's unique neural and emotional profiles. AI will be able to create personalized storylines for every customer, tailored to their values, motives, and psychological triggers, as opposed to dividing audiences into large demographic groupings.

With the help of generative AI, marketers will be able to test hundreds of different versions of creative assets in milliseconds, optimizing for long-term memory retention, emotional resonance, and click-through rates. Though it also raises worries about over-customization and identity fragmentation, this move from static information to emotionally intelligent, dynamic communications will result in deeper, more meaningful relationships between consumers and brands (Kaplan & Haenlein, 2019).

Transparent Neuromarketing and Ethical AI

As the capacity of AI-enhanced neuromarketing increases, so does the need for ethical frameworks to control its usage. Future developments are likely to concentrate on developing "responsible neuromarketing" models that include explainability, fairness, and user control at every stage of the data lifecycle. AI systems will require explainable AI (XAI) solutions, which allow consumers to understand the reasoning behind a particular piece of information or offer based on cognitive data.

Regulators and governments are starting to react. Stricter rules on AI systems that profile people are being pushed by the European Union's AI Act and revisions to international data protection legislation, particularly when those systems use sensitive information like emotions or neurological patterns. It might be necessary for future neuromarketing platforms to incorporate digital "ethics layers" that automatically check campaigns for biassed results, psychological manipulation, or informed consent violations (Floridi et al., 2018).

Digital twins of consumer behaviour

The development of digital twins—AI-powered virtual representations of distinct customers that mimic their behavior, tastes, and even cognitive reactions—is another new trend. Massive datasets, such as previous purchases, online interactions, biometric information, and possibly even neuro-signals, are used to create these digital twins. Before implementing campaigns in the real world, marketers can test them on these virtual models, anticipating not just what customers will do but also why.

With the development of digital twin technology, real-time predictive simulations of consumer decision-making may become possible, providing marketers with a low-risk setting in which to test user interfaces, messaging, and pricing. Even though it's effective, using simulated minds for marketing raises multiple ethical and legal concerns, one of which is who or what is to be held responsible for any unforeseen, undesirable occurrences (de Kerckhove, 2021).

Multisensory and Immersive Marketing Experiences

AI-powered neuromarketing is expanding into immersive and multisensory realms as the metaverse grows. Platforms for virtual and augmented reality (VR/AR) can appeal to a variety of senses, including sight, hearing, touch, and even smell, which increases the emotional and neurological effects of marketing stimuli. In this regard, artificial intelligence will be crucial in planning multimodal experiences that are customized for each customer profile.

For example, biometric feedback might be used to adjust an immersive product demo in virtual reality in real time. This could include adjusting the lighting to keep the user's attention, changing the background music to create a desired atmosphere, or changing the narrative tones to match the user's empathy levels. With the use of neuro-AI insights, this degree of sensory calibration has the potential to completely alter how customers view and interact with companies in digital spaces (Martínez-Plumed & Hernández-Orallo, 2018).

Inclusive and Cross-Cultural Neuromarketing

Making neuromarketing tools accessible and culturally adapted will be a major trend in the future as these tools proliferate around the world. Cultural differences in decision-making, emotional expression, and neural interpretation may not be taken into consideration by AI models that were mostly trained on Western cognitive and emotional data. For future AI-powered neuromarketing systems to be effective and equitable, they must be trained on a variety of datasets that represent a wider diversity of languages, races, and neurological patterns.

Data scientists, anthropologists, neuroscientists, and local stakeholders will need to work together in an interdisciplinary manner to accomplish this. In addition to expanding businesses' reach into new markets, more inclusive neuromarketing will advance moral principles that honor variations in cognitive and affective processing (Park & Huang, 2010).

CONCLUSION

In the future, additional study is required to examine how consumer individual differences impact their interactions with AI systems, how customer happiness is impacted by AI intelligibility, and how ethical considerations might be more thoroughly ingrained in AI development processes. As AI develops, businesses must place equal emphasis on technological innovation and ethical responsibility to fully reap the marketing benefits of AI while protecting consumer rights.

Businesses can guarantee that AI is a tool for improving—rather than degrading—the customer experience by taking an ethical, human-centered approach, opening the door to a more reliable and inclusive digital marketplace.

REFERENCES

Acquisti, A., Brandimarte, L., & Loewenstein, G. (2015). Privacy and human behavior in the age of information. *Science, 347*(6221), 509–514. DOI: 10.1126/science.aaa1465

Adalarasu, K., Begum, K. G., Priyan, M. V., Devendranath, C., & Sriram, G. (2025). Neuro-signaling techniques in advertisement endorsements: Unveiling consumer responses and behavioral trends. *Journal of Retailing and Consumer Services, 84*, 104175. DOI: 10.1016/j.jretconser.2024.104175

Adwan, A. A., & Aladwan, R. (2022). Use of artificial intelligence system to predict consumers' behaviors. *International Journal of Data and Network Science, 6*(4), 1223–1232. DOI: 10.5267/j.ijdns.2022.6.011

Agag, G., Durrani, B. A., Shehawy, Y. M., Alharthi, M., Alamoudi, H., El-Halaby, S., Hassanein, A., & Abdelmoety, Z. H. (2023). Understanding the link between customer feedback metrics and firm performance. *Journal of Retailing and Consumer Services, 73*, 103301. Advance online publication. DOI: 10.1016/j.jretconser.2023.103301

Aprilianty, F., Takahashi, M., & Matsuura, Y. (2024). Bridging brains and bots: The impact of AI on neuromarketing. *Procedia Computer Science, 246*, 1830–1839. DOI: 10.1016/j.procs.2024.09.687

Ariely, D., & Berns, G. S. (2010). Neuromarketing: The hope and hype of neuroimaging in business. *Nature Reviews. Neuroscience, 11*(4), 284–292. DOI: 10.1038/nrn2795

Artwork Personalization at Netflix. (2017, Dec 7). Netflix TechBlog. *Medium.* https://netflixtechblog.com/artwork-personalization-c589f074ad76

Baltezarevic, I., & Baltezarevic, R. (2024). Comprehending subconscious consumer behavior in the digital age via neuromarketing. In *Megatrend University & Institute of International Politics and Economics, ISARC.* https://www.researchgate.net/publication/384964000

Bansal, S., & Gupta, M. (2023). Towards Using Artificial Intelligence in Neuromarketing. In Gupta, M., Jindal, P., & Bansal, S. (Eds.), *Promoting Consumer Engagement Through Emotional Branding and Sensory Marketing* (pp. 16–23). IGI Global Scientific Publishing., DOI: 10.4018/978-1-6684-5897-6.ch002

Beličková, P. (2024). AI-powered insights: Strengthening nonprofit communication through neuromarketing. *Media & Marketing Identity*, 22–29. https://doi.org/DOI: 10.34135/mmidentity-2024-02

Biswas, K., & Patra, G. (2023). Role of artificial intelligence (AI) in changing consumer buying behaviour. *International Journal of Research Publication and Reviews*, *4*(2), 943–951. DOI: 10.55248/gengpi.2023.4227

Booton, J. (2018, April 5). IBM's Watson will dish out customized highlights for the Masters. *Sports Business Journal*. https://www.sportsbusinessjournal.com/Daily/Issues/2018/04/05/Technology/ibms-watson-will-dish-customized-highlights-masters/

Boucsein, W. (2012). Electrodermal activity (2nd ed.). Springer Science + Business Media. DOI: 10.1007/978-1-4614-1126-0

Brace, I. (2018). *Questionnaire design: How to plan, structure and write survey material for effective market research* (4th ed.). Kogan Page.

Bryman, A. (2016). *Social research methods* (5th ed.). Oxford University Press.

Çakar, T., & Filiz, G. (2023). Unraveling neural pathways of political engagement: Bridging neuromarketing and political science for understanding voter behavior and political leader perception. *Frontiers in Human Neuroscience*, *17*, 1293173. Advance online publication. DOI: 10.3389/fnhum.2023.1293173

Cambria, E., Schuller, B., Xia, Y., & Havasi, C. (2020). Sentiment analysis is a big suitcase. *IEEE Intelligent Systems*, *35*(5), 74–80.

Campbell, C., & Grimm, P. E. (2019). The challenges native advertising poses: Exploring potential Federal Trade Commission responses and identifying research needs. *Journal of Public Policy & Marketing*, *38*(1), 110–123. DOI: 10.1177/0743915618818576

Chatterjee, S., Rana, N. P., Tamilmani, K., & Sharma, A. (2021). The role of AI in customer engagement and experience: Evidence from the retail sector. *Journal of Business Research*, *122*, 386–400.

Cherubino, P., Martinez-Levy, A. C., Caratù, M., Cartocci, G., Di Flumeri, G., Modica, E., Rossi, D., Mancini, M., & Trettel, A. (2019). Consumer Behaviour through the Eyes of Neurophysiological Measures: State-of-the-Art and Future Trends. *Computational Intelligence and Neuroscience*, *1976847*, 1–41. Advance online publication. DOI: 10.1155/2019/1976847

Cialdini, R. (1984). *Influence. The Psychology of Persuasion*. William Morrow e Company.

Cialdini, R., & Goldstein, N. J. (2002). The science and practice of persuasion. *The Cornell Hotel and Restaurant Administration Quarterly, 43*(2), 40–50. DOI: 10.1177/001088040204300204

Damasio, A. R. (1994). *Descartes' error: Emotion, reason, and the human brain.* Putnam Publishing.

Davenport, T. H., Guha, A., Grewal, D., & Bressgott, T. (2020). How artificial intelligence will change the future of marketing. *Journal of the Academy of Marketing Science, 48*(1), 24–42. DOI: 10.1007/s11747-019-00696-0

de Kerckhove, D. (2021). The personal digital twin, ethical considerations. *Philosophical Transactions. Series A, Mathematical, Physical, and Engineering Sciences, 379*(2207), 20200367. DOI: 10.1098/rsta.2020.0367

Deci, E. L., & Ryan, R. M. (1985). *Intrinsic motivation and self-determination in human behavior*. Plenum Press., DOI: 10.1007/978-1-4899-2271-7

Dineen, B. R., Noe, R. A., & Wang, C. (2004). Perceived fairness of web-based applicant screening procedures: Weighing the rules of justice and the role of individual differences. *Human Resource Management, 43*(2–3), 127–145. DOI: 10.1002/hrm.20011

Doshi-Velez, F., & Kim, B. (2017). Towards a rigorous science of interpretable machine learning. *arXiv* preprint arXiv:1702.08608.

Duchowski, A. T. (2017). *Eye Tracking Methodology: Theory and Practice* (3rd ed.). Springer Cham., https://link.springer.com/book/10.1007/978-3-319-57883-5 DOI: 10.1007/978-3-319-57883-5

European Commission. (2016). *General Data Protection Regulation (GDPR)*. https://eur- lex.europa.eu/legal-content/EN/TXT/?uri=CELEX:32016R0679

Ferrell, M. L., Beatty, A., & Dubljevic, V. (2025). The Ethics of Neuromarketing: A Rapid Review. *Neuroethics, 18*(1), 19. DOI: 10.1007/s12152-025-09591-8

Floridi, L., Cowls, J., Beltrametti, M., Chatila, R., Chazerand, P., Dignum, V., Luetge, C., Madelin, R., Pagallo, U., Rossi, F., Schafer, B., Valcke, P., & Vayena, E. (2018). AI4People—An Ethical Framework for a Good AI Society: Opportunities, Risks, Principles, and Recommendations. *Minds and Machines, 28*(4), 689–707. DOI: 10.1007/s11023-018-9482-5

Gallo, A. (2017). A refresher on A/B testing. *Harvard Business Review*. https://hbr.org/2017/06/a-refresher-on-ab-testing

Gkikas, D. C., Theodoridis, P. K., & Beligiannis, G. N. (2022). Enhanced Marketing Decision Making for Consumer Behaviour Classification Using Binary Decision Trees and a Genetic Algorithm Wrapper. *Informatics (MDPI)*, *9*(2), 45. Advance online publication. DOI: 10.3390/informatics9020045

Gomez-Uribe, C. A., & Hunt, N. (2015). The Netflix recommender system: Algorithms, business value, and innovation. [TMIS]. *ACM Transactions on Management Information Systems*, *6*(4), 1–19. DOI: 10.1145/2843948

Graham, M. (2024, November 15). *Taco Bell and KFC's Owner Says AI-Driven Marketing Is Boosting Purchases*. The Wall Street Journal. https://www.wsj.com/articles/taco-bell-and-kfcs-owner-says-ai-driven-marketing-is-boosting-purchases-ab3a5f36?msockid=24b7fa49ae8863fc2393efafaf13628a

Gutti, D., Yadav, G. V., & Kaja, H. (2023). Influence of artificial intelligence in consumer decision-making process. In *Productivity Press eBooks* (pp. 141–155). https://doi.org/DOI: 10.4324/b23404-9

Hakami, N. A., & Mahmoud, H. A. H. (2022). Deep Learning Analysis for Reviews in Arabic E-Commerce Sites to Detect Consumer Behavior towards Sustainability. *Sustainability (Basel)*, *14*(19), 12860. DOI: 10.3390/su141912860

Harrell, E. (2019, January 23). Neuromarketing: What you need to know. *Harvard Business Review*. https://hbr.org/2019/01/neuromarketing-what-you-need-to-know

Hatfield, E., Cacioppo, J. T., & Rapson, R. L. (1993). Emotional Contagion. *Current Directions in Psychological Science*, *2*(3), 96–100. DOI: 10.1111/1467-8721.ep10770953

Hazlett, R. L., & Hazlett, S. Y. (1999). Emotional Response to Television Commercials: Facial EMG vs. Self-Report. *Journal of Advertising Research*, *39*(2), 7–23. DOI: 10.1080/00218499.1999.12466597

How CO-RO optimized ads & branding to win new markets with Neurons AI. (n.d.). Neurons. https://www.neuronsinc.com/cases/co-ro-optimize-ad-branding-retail-predict-ai DOI: 10.1007/s12115-010-9408-1

Huang, M. H., & Rust, R. T. (2021). A strategic framework for artificial intelligence in marketing. *Journal of the Academy of Marketing Science*, *49*(1), 30–50. DOI: 10.1007/s11747-020-00749-9

Ienca, M., & Andorno, R. (2017). Towards new human rights in the age of neuroscience and neurotechnology. *Life Sciences, Society and Policy*, *13*(1), 5. DOI: 10.1186/s40504-017-0050-1

Jaguar Launches #FeelWimbledon Campaign Aiming to Capture the Mood of the Championships. (2015, June 29). Jaguar Media Centre. https://media.jaguar.com/en-gb/news/2015/06/jaguar-launches-feelwimbledon-campaign-aiming-capture-mood-championships#:~:text=Jaguar%2C%20The%20Official%20Car%20of%20The%20Championships%2C%20today,associated%20with%20the%20world%27s%20number%20one%20tennis%20tournament

Juárez-Varón, D., Mengual-Recuerda, A., Zuluaga, J. C., & Corvello, V. (2024). Application of Artificial Intelligence in Neuromarketing to Predict Consumer Behaviour Towards Brand Stimuli: Case Study - Neurotechnologies vs. AI Predictive Model. [IJSSCI]. *International Journal of Software Science and Computational Intelligence*, *16*(1), 1–18. DOI: 10.4018/IJSSCI.347214

Kahneman, D., & Tversky, A. (1979). Prospect theory: An analysis of decision under risk. *Econometrica*, *47*(2), 263–291. DOI: 10.2307/1914185

Kakaria, S., Bigné, E., Catrambone, V., & Valenza, G. (2022). Heart rate variability in marketing research: A systematic review and methodological perspectives. *Psychology and Marketing*, *40*(1), 190–208. DOI: 10.1002/mar.21734

Kaplan, A., & Haenlein, M. (2019). Rulers of the world, unite! The challenges and opportunities of artificial intelligence. *Business Horizons*, *62*(1), 37–50. DOI: 10.1016/j.bushor.2019.09.003

Kar, A. (2020). MLGaze: Machine Learning-Based Analysis of Gaze Error Patterns in Consumer Eye Tracking Systems. *Vision (Basel)*, *4*(2), 25. DOI: 10.3390/vision4020025

Khandelwal, K., Patel, S., Patel, J., & Pnachal, M. (2023). A study to Know - Use of AI for personalized recommendation, streaming optimization, and original content production at Netflix. *International Journal of Scientific Research & Engineering Trends* (Vol. 9, Issue 6). https://ijsret.com/wp-content/uploads/2023/11/IJSRET_V9_issue6_435.pdf

Khondakar, M. F. K., Sarowar, M. H., Chowdhury, M. H., Majumder, S., Hossain, M. A., Dewan, M. A. A., & Hossain, Q. D. (2024). A systematic review on EEG-based neuromarketing: Recent trends and analyzing techniques. *Brain Informatics*, *11*(1), 17. DOI: 10.1186/s40708-024-00229-8

Krämer, W., & Kahneman, D. (2011): Thinking, Fast and Slow. *Stat Papers* 55, 915 (2014). https://doi.org/DOI: 10.1007/s00362-013-0533-y

Li, X., Luh, D., & Chen, Z. (2024). A Systematic Review and Meta-Analysis of Eye-Tracking studies for consumers' visual attention in online shopping. *Information Technology and Control, 53*(1), 187–205. DOI: 10.5755/j01.itc.53.1.34855

Logg, J. M., Minson, J. A., & Moore, D. A. (2019). Algorithm appreciation: People prefer algorithmic to human judgment. *Organizational Behavior and Human Decision Processes, 151*, 90–103. DOI: 10.1016/j.obhdp.2018.12.005

Luck, S. J. (2014). *An introduction to the Event-Related Potential technique* (2nd ed.). MIT Press., https://mitpress.mit.edu/9780262525855/an-introduction-to-the-event-related-potential-technique/

Mao, H. (2009). Functional magnetic resonance imaging. *Journal of Magnetic Resonance Imaging, 30*(5), 1229. DOI: 10.1002/jmri.21892

Martínez-Plumed, F., & Hernandez-Orallo, J. (2018). Dual indicators to analyse AI benchmarks: Difficulty, discrimination, ability and generality. *IEEE Transactions on Games, 12*(2), 121–131. DOI: 10.1109/TG.2018.2883773

McClure, S. M., Li, J., Tomlin, D., Cypert, K. S., Montague, L. M., & Montague, P. R. (2004). Neural correlates of behavioral preference for culturally familiar drinks. *Neuron, 44*(2), 379–387. DOI: 10.1016/j.neuron.2004.09.019

Merritt, S. H., Gaffuri, K., & Zak, P. J. (2023). Accurately predicting hit songs using neurophysiology and machine learning. *Frontiers in Artificial Intelligence, 6*, 1154663. Advance online publication. DOI: 10.3389/frai.2023.1154663

Morin, C. (2011). Neuromarketing: The Neuroscience of Consumer Behavior. *Society, 48*(2), 131–135. DOI: 10.1007/s12115-010-9408-1

Mouammine, Y., & Azdimousa, H. (2019). Using neuromarketing and AI to collect and analyse consumer's emotion: Literature review and perspectives. https://www.researchgate.net/publication/341369618_Using_Neuromarketing_and_AI_to_collect_and_analyse_consumer's_emotion_Literature_review_and_perspectives

Oahn, V. T. K. (2024). Evolving Landscape Of E-Commerce, Marketing, and Customer Service: the Impact of Ai Integration. *J. Electrical Systems* (Vols. 20–3s, pp. 1125–1137). https://pdfs.semanticscholar.org/5124/1f74c56ff1ebcc53938d9a1bde21f97f4e58.pdf

Ohme, R., Reykowska, D., Wiener, D., & Choromanska, A. (2009). Analysis of neurophysiological reactions to advertising stimuli by means of EEG and galvanic skin response measures. *Journal of Neuroscience, Psychology, and Economics, 2*(1), 21–31. DOI: 10.1037/a0015462

Ouzir, M., Lamrani, H. C., Bradley, R. L., & Moudden, I. E. (2024). Neuromarketing and decision-making: Classification of consumer preferences based on changes analysis in the EEG signal of brain regions. *Biomedical Signal Processing and Control, 87*, 105469. DOI: 10.1016/j.bspc.2023.105469

Park, D. C., & Huang, C. M. (2010). Culture Wires the Brain: A Cognitive Neuroscience Perspective. *Perspectives on psychological science: a journal of the Association for Psychological Science, 5*(4), 391–400. https://doi.org/DOI: 10.1177/1745691610374591

Pentina, I., & Zhang, L. (2016). Effects of social support and personality on emotional disclosure on Facebook and in real life. *Behaviour & Information Technology, 36*(5), 484–492. DOI: 10.1080/0144929X.2016.1258086

Perez-Rosero, M. S., Rezaei, B., Akcakaya, M., & Ostadabbas, S. (2016). *Decoding Emotional Experience through Physiological Signal Processing*. arXiv.org. https://arxiv.org/abs/1606.00370

Phutela, N. P. A., Sreevathsan, K., & Krupa, B. N. (2022) Intelligent analysis of EEG signals to assess consumer decisions: A Study on Neuromarketing. arXiv. https:// arxiv. org/ abs/ 2206. 07484

Picard, R. W. (1997). *Affective Computing*. https://doi.org/DOI: 10.7551/mitpress/1140.001.0001

Pierson, E. (2017). Demographics and discussion influence views on algorithmic fairness. *arXiv*. https://arxiv.org/abs/1712.09124v2

Plassmann, H., Ramsøy, T. Z., & Milosavljevic, M. (2012). Branding the brain: A critical review and outlook. *Journal of Consumer Psychology, 22*(1), 18–36. DOI: 10.1016/j.jcps.2011.11.010

Pop, ., Pelau, C., Ciofu, I., & Kondort, G. (2023). Factors predicting consumer-AI interactions. *New Trends in Sustainable Business and Consumption*, 592–597. https://doi.org/DOI: 10.24818/BASIQ/2023/09/068

Providing Actionable Business Recommendations With Predictive, A. I. (n.d.). Neurons. https://www.neuronsinc.com/cases/total-media-case- study?_gl=1*qvvgkm*_up*MQ.*_ga*MjExMjk5NzU3Ni4xNzQ3MTM5NzQz*_ga_X5 0CTLJMHN*czE3NTMzMDM4ODYkbzIkZzEkdDE3NTMzMDQwNTkkajQxJGwwJGgw

Punetha, N., & Jain, G. (2023). Unsupervised sentiment analysis of Hindi reviews using MCDM and game model optimization techniques. *Sadhana, 48*(4), 195. Advance online publication. DOI: 10.1007/s12046-023-02255-4

Raj, H. (2025, January 5). *The impact of the Digital Personal Data Protection Act, 2023 on data privacy and compliance in India*. The Amikus Qriae. https://theamikusqriae.com/the- impact-of-the-digital-personal-data-protection-act-2023-on-data-privacy-and-compliance- in-india/

Rust, R. T., & Huang, M. H. (2021). The AI marketing canvas: A five-stage road-map to implementing artificial intelligence in marketing. *Journal of Marketing, 85*(1), 90–108.

Singhal, V. (2023). Segmenting and Targeting Fashion Consumers Using Social Media: A Study of Consumer Behaviour. *Journal of Creative Communications, 0*(0), 09732586231203848. Advance online publication. DOI: 10.1177/09732586231203848

Smith, J., & Chen, L. (2019). AI and consumer behavior: Dynamic pricing in the digital age. *Journal of Marketing Analytics, 7*(2), 112–125. DOI: 10.1016/j.jma.2019.03.004

Šola, H. M., Qureshi, F. H., & Khawaja, S. (2024). Predicting behaviour patterns in online and PDF magazines with AI eye-Tracking. *Behavioral Sciences (Basel, Switzerland), 14*(8), 677. DOI: 10.3390/bs14080677

Thurman, N., Moeler, J., Helberger, N., & Trilling, D. (2018). My friends, editors, algorithms, and I: Examining audience attitudes to news selection. *Digital Journalism*, 7(4), pp. 447-469. DOI: 10.1080/21670811.2018.1493936

Vecchiato, G., Astolfi, L., De Vico Fallani, F., Toppi, J., Aloise, F., Bez, F., Wei, D., Kong, W., Dai, G., Cincotti, F., Mattia, D., & Babiloni, F. (2011). On the Use of EEG or MEG Brain Imaging Tools in Neuromarketing Research. *Computational Intelligence and Neuroscience, 2011*, 1–12. DOI: 10.1155/2011/643489

Venkatraman, V., Dimoka, A., Pavlou, P. A., Vo, K., Hampton, W., Bollinger, B., Hershfield, H. E., Ishihara, M., & Winer, R. S. (2015). Predicting advertising success beyond traditional measures: New insights from neurophysiological methods and market response modeling. *JMR, Journal of Marketing Research, 52*(4), 436–452. DOI: 10.1509/jmr.13.0593

V.M., J., & K.V., A. (2024). Neuromarketing with AI: A way to delve into the consumer's subconscious mind. *International Journal of Research, 15*, 76853–76857.

Wang, S. (2025). The influence of AI in marketing. *Advances in Economics Management and Political Sciences, 151*(1), 52–57. DOI: 10.54254/2754-1169/2024.19326

Wedel, M., & Pieters, R. (2008). Eye Tracking for Visual Marketing. *Foundations and Trends(R) in Marketing*, 1, issue 4, p. 231-320. https://EconPapers.repec.org/RePEc:now:fntmkt:1700000011

Zajonc, R. B. (1968). Attitudinal effects of mere exposure. *Journal of Personality and Social Psychology, 9*(2p2), 1–27. https://doi.org/DOI: 10.1037/h0025848

Zaltman, G. (2003). *How Customers Think: Essential Insights into the Mind of the Market.* Harvard University Press.

Zhou, L., Wang, T., Liu, Z., & Shi, Y. (2020). A deep learning method for sentiment classification in online reviews. *Information Processing & Management, 57*(5), 102179. DOI: 10.1016/j.ipm.2019.102179

KEY TERMS AND DEFINITIONS

A/B Testing: A method of comparing two versions of something, like a webpage or ad, to see which one performs better with users.

Algorithmic Decision-Making: The process of using computer-based rules or instructions (algorithms) to automatically make choices or solve problems based on data.

Artificial Intelligence: The development of machines or computer systems to perform tasks that typically require human intelligence: such as learning, reasoning, and decision-making.

Brand Perceptions: How consumers view and feel about a brand based on their experiences: beliefs,and interactions with it.

Machine Learning: A subset of artificial intelligence that allows machines or computer systems to learn from data and get better at tasks without being directly programmed.

Neuromarketing: An innovative discipline that combines the principles of neuroscience and marketing to study consumer responses to various stimuli, that is, it utilizes neuromarketing tools to study consumer behaviour in response to marketing stimuli, in order to enhance understanding of consumer behaviour and improve marketing strategies.

Sentiment Analysis: A method of determining the emotional tone (positive, negative, or neutral) of a piece of text.

Social Listening: The process of monitoring and analyzing online conversations about a brand, topic, or industry to gather insights and inform strategic decisions.

Chapter 7
Benefits of Combining Neuromarketing and AI

S. Ida Evangeline
http://orcid.org/0000-0003-2997-7897
Government College of Engineering, Tirunelveli, India

ABSTRACT

Neuromarketing and artificial intelligence (AI) integration is transforming the manner in which companies understand and affect consumer behaviour. Neuromarketing refers to everything that applies neuroscientific principles to marketing and helps us understand subconscious (or unintentionally) decision-making processes by examining their effect on our brain, our emotions, and our cognitive responses. The key to effective neuromarketing research is the insights of the behavioral patterns it provides, as it brings corporations to understand their consumers in a manner that is more on point than traditional methods. AI elevates these insights by allowing automation of data collection, identification of behavioral patterns, and conducting real time analysis on the data gathered, making neuromarketing research easier to scale and implement. In this chapter, we take a closer look and the perks of merging neuromarketing and AI, and their usefulness in different industries like retail, advertising, entertainment, healthcare, and customer experience.

1. INTRODUCTION

Neuroscience, marketing and artificial intelligence (AI) convergence is transforming how businesses understand and influence consumer behavior. Neuromarketing is the application of scientific principles in the field of neurosciences to achieve more insights into the subconscious ways in which we make decisions affecting our emotions, paying attention, and our cognitive response. Common but outdated

DOI: 10.4018/979-8-3373-1152-4.ch007

marketing research methods like surveys and focus groups are susceptible to bias and respondent's lack of awareness about their internal decision making processes as it often relies on self reported data. On the contrary, neuromarketing employs advanced tools like eye tracking, electroencephalography (EEG), and functional magnetic resonance imaging (fMRI) to detect physiological and neurological responses of the consumers towards marketing stimuli in order to understand better how the consumers perceive and interact with the advertisements, products, and their communication with the brand (Srivastava & Bag, 2024).

Using artificial intelligence, neuromarketing is a powerful complement to neuromarketing in that it allows us to process and analyze increasingly larger and more powerful sets of consumer data in ways that are almost unfathomably large and quick. It also helps using AI powered tools that can detect patterns, predict behaviours and help in generating personal marketing,strategicaly which will be more customised and as per the requirement (Marques dos Santos & Marques dos Santos, 2024). All those neuromarketing findings are refined using machine learning algorithms that point out which visual, auditory or textual elements are the most effective while natural language processing (NLP) measures consumer sentiment from online interactions, social media, etc. Further, AI helps scale neuromarketing research, offering businesses from diverse industry areas access to and affordability of reduced neuromarketing research. The combined usage of neuromarketing and AI offers a unique chance for developing more focused, productive, and emotionally appealing marketing campaigns (Kumar et al. 2024).

It analyzes the advantages of using neuromarketing and AI together and considers the role of both in the fields of retail and entertainment, healthcare, and public policy. In this chapter, we first talk about how companies can provide the basic service with the low service quality, then offer high service quality in the exchange for money. The chapter also covers the challenges and practical aspects of deploying these technologies, such as the requirement of AI standards and regulations. It then looks into future trends like wearable neuroimaging devices, immersive interfaces like augmented and virtual reality, and AI based emotional intelligence systems that will elevate marketing strategy again in the future. The chapter gives a complete analysis of how neuromarketing and AI can complement each other and present a viewpoint of how integrating neuromarketing in AI can reshape the marketing landscape through ethical, transparent, and consumer centric process.

2. THEORETICAL FOUNDATIONS AND RELEVANCE

The study of brain activity, thinking and decisions that are responsible for behaviour of customers is the basis of neuromarketing. Through the use of the knowledge of cognitive neuroscience and psychology, neuromarketing aims to provide insights regarding the subconscious reactions of people to marketing stimuli (Khondakar et al. 2024). Neuromarketing is different from standard market research which relies on self reported data through surveys and focus groups. Visual attention, emotional arousal and cognitive engagement can be analysed in real time through these technologies and hence they provide a more precise and objective view of the consumer preferences (Goncalves et al., 2024). For example, eye tracking technology can determine which parts of an advertisement or a website or a product packaging people look at, and EEG or fMRI can measure emotional reaction and brain areas involved in decision making. Directly measuring consumer responses provides a marketer with an additional edge as this eliminates biases and captures instinctive reactions of a consumer that he might never vocally express (Bhardwaj et al., 2024).

Artificial intelligence is very important for the expansion of the neuromarketing capabilities, for automation of data analysis, nightingale revealing and prediction of consumer behavior with high precision. In addition, they can process large amounts of neuromarketing data and discover the correlations between consumer responses to marketing elements. By allowing marketers to go through an analytical process, marketers are able to filter advertisements, product design and user experiences based on empirical evidence rather than assumptions (Ballı, 2024). The second way neuromarketing is aided by natural language processing (NLP) which further uses it to analyze textual data obtained from customer reviews, social media posts and chatbot interactions, enabling businesses to get a large scale grasp of sentiment as well as the emotional tone of their customers. Moreover, thanks to simple and AI powered, real time analytics, marketers can tweak campaigns on the fly according to the live responses of the consumers. For example, an AI system can monitor facial expressions combined with biometric feedback during a product demonstration and just as quickly, alter visuals, music, or messaging to win over the audience (Adeola et al. 2022).

In today's competitive information age where data, personalization, customer engagement, and achieving competitive differentiation, people involved in marketing will find this alignment of neuromarketing with AI especially relevant in their marketing efforts. Brands are able to leverage neuromarketing insights and use AI driven automation to build ultra-personalized marketing campaigns customised to a person's specific preferences (Bansal & Gupta, 2023). For example, AI recommended engines can leverage neuromarketing data to recommend products or content that resonates with the emotional triggers of the consumer and this ultimately increases engagement and conversion ratio. In this set up, customers are offered content that will resonate with them at a deeper psychological level that then strengthen brand loyalty among customers. Moreover, business users of both neuromarketing and AI get an edge in their understanding of choosing the best paths for executing marketing spend and campaign effectiveness with data and intelligence. With digital overload everywhere present, companies are attempting to get the attention of consumers and the ability to design marketing strategies based on subconscious consumer behavior and real time AI analysis provides meaningful opportunity to drive innovation and business growth (Varghese, 2022).

3. APPLICATIONS AND BENEFITS OF NEUROMARKETING AND AI

Integration of neuromarketing into various industries with artificial intelligence is changing the face of the market with providing deeper insights into consumer behavior and redefining the feat of marketing strategies. This has been revolutionizing business in the retail and e commerce sector for optimizing the store layout, product packages and user ux design (Attié et al. 2021). By applying eye tracking in tandem with AI analysis, retailers can learn where customers focus in a store or on a retailer's online platform, and what parts of the shopping experience are most likely to turn someone into a buyer. Analyzing consumer gaze patterns and emotional responses can help businesses optimize store layout, website interfaces, product displays and more to increase engagement and conversion. Besides, e commerce personalization through AI driven recommendation engines further elaborate by piece together consumer neuro-marketing data to propose products according to the subconscious preference thereby improving customer satisfaction and sales (Sposini, 2024).

Neuromarketing coupled with AI helps brands in recipe advertising, and content creation that create the deepest emotional reaction. Marketers then use AI in the form of these systems to analyze the emotional engagement data, using the data to explore which elements, the colors, imagery or messaging, is the most effective. The process is accelerated by Automated A/B testing powered by artificial intelligence (AI) which tests numerous ad variations in real time and drives campaigns based on neurological and behavior (i.e. virtual version) data. Thus, ads are not only visually attractive but also emotionally gripping, and therefore more effective in attracting an audience's attention and promoting brand recall (Pastukh & Yatsyshyn, 2024).

Neuromarketing and AI are very beneficial for entertainment and media industry as they provide more depth on audience engagement and its content preference. Filmmakers, streaming platforms and content creators can use AI powered brain activity and emotional responses from test screenings to refine storytelling elements, pacing, and visual effects for maximum viewer engagement (Juárez-Varón et al. 2024). AI driven predictive modeling assists media companies in predicting how audiences are likely to respond to the content, increasing the success of the film, TV show, or the digital content. Neuromarketing insights are used, for instance, by streaming platforms to optimize their content recommendation interface in order to keep the viewers engaged for longer periods (Apriliantу et al. 2024).

Aside from commercial use, neuromarketing and AI are both involved in healthcare and public policy, where health campaigns and educational materials can be more effective. AI emotion analytics promote the design of public health campaigns that are most likely to grab attention and facilitate behavior change. For example, neuromarketing study results can optimize a campaign that is aimed at promoting smoking cessation or healthy eating; based on subconscious emotional triggers. Also, the use of AI for analysis makes educational material more effective by improving content delivery in a way that reflects the current levels of cognitive engagement, therefore, the messages are more impactful and memorable (Zubareva, 2024).

This advantage, that neuromarketing has by partnering with AI, is that it helps improve customer experience and brand loyalty. In line with neuromarketing, hyper personalized marketing strategies can help brand deliver a customized content that matches the predefined choice and the emotions of the target audiences (Thakur & Pasha, 2025). Chatbots and virtual assistants powered by AI and with emotional intelligence also enable customers to communicate with the chatbots or virtual assistants with empathic and personalized communication. Because of these advancements, brands have the possibility to develop an emotional connection with their consumers and to grow a long–term loyalty and confidence (Cheredniakova et al. 2021).

The combination of the scientific understanding of who customers are and how they behave, with AI's capability to track and scale the insights on them, enables businesses across industries to develop marketing strategies that are more successful, more engaging, more relevant, and more personalized. In an ever competitive market place, this integration leads to a more satisfied customer, higher conversion rates and bettering brand-consumer relationship as well.

4. NEUROMARKETING AND AI IN CROSS-CULTURAL CONSUMER INSIGHTS

In an increasingly globalized marketplace, understanding how consumers from different cultural backgrounds respond to marketing stimuli is essential. Traditional marketing often falls short in capturing the nuanced, subconscious reactions that vary across cultural contexts. This is where the integration of neuromarketing and artificial intelligence becomes a transformative tool (Alsharif et al. 2025). By leveraging neurophysiological measurements and AI-driven analysis, marketers can decode emotional and cognitive responses across diverse populations, revealing culturally specific consumer behaviors that were previously invisible to conventional research methods.

Neuromarketing tools like eye tracking, EEG, and facial expression analysis can reveal distinct attentional patterns, emotional triggers, and decision-making cues influenced by cultural norms, values, and cognitive styles. For instance, Eastern consumers may exhibit more holistic visual attention and social cue sensitivity, while Western consumers may respond more strongly to individualistic and direct messaging (Byrne et al. 2022). AI algorithms can process and cluster these variations at scale, enabling brands to tailor content that resonates with culturally diverse audiences.

One significant advantage of AI in this domain is its capacity for multi-language natural language processing (NLP). By analyzing text, speech, and social media data in native languages, AI systems uncover culturally embedded emotional expressions and sentiment patterns. This allows marketers to craft emotionally congruent messaging that aligns with localized values and emotional norms, enhancing engagement and brand relevance (Goncalves et al., 2024).

Moreover, cross-cultural neuromarketing can aid global brands in designing region-specific user experiences, packaging, and campaign aesthetics. AI models trained on multicultural data sets can predict which visual elements (e.g., colors, symbols, facial cues) will be perceived as trustworthy, exciting, or calming in different regions. This localization strategy enhances brand trust, increases message efficacy, and prevents cultural missteps (Song et al., 2025).

As brands expand globally, the integration of neuromarketing and AI offers a powerful pathway to empathetic, ethical, and effective cross-cultural engagement. It shifts marketing from a one-size-fits-all paradigm to a more nuanced, neurocognitively attuned approach—positioning cultural sensitivity not just as a compliance metric but as a driver of consumer connection and business success.

5. ETHICAL CONCERNS AND CHALLENGES

As neuromarketing and artificial intelligence can be integrated, there exist a number of ethical and practical concerns in the area of privacy and security of data, fair use, and regulatory compliance. Another main concern is the collection and analysis of very sensitive consumer data such as brain activity, emotional responses, and subconscious reactions (Goncalves et al., 2024). Neuromarketing data, in contrast, deals with the deepest reserve of a person's internal world – the human brain, so raises sometimes sufficient ethical problems regarding informed consent and data ownership. Due to a lack of consumer understanding on how their neurological and biometric data are being used, it is business's responsibility to set rigorous data protection mechanisms and policies that grant informed consent.

In addition to these risks, the possibility of data breaches or unauthorized access heightens the risks as such personal information could be used for manipulative marketing purposes or in the worst cases for nefarious use not related to commercial interests (Minz et al. 2024).

AI bias is another major ethical challenge in the field of neuromarketing as it is necessary to guarantee fairness in the application of this technology. If AI algorithms depend on large datasets to find patterns and make predictions, then if the datasets are not inclusive and representative they can perpetuate and perpetuate existing biases (Vuković, 2024). Take for instance an AI based neuromarketing model trained on data from a particular demographic class will yield insights or suggestions in favour of that particular demographic class while neglecting or distorting the preferences of others. This inequality can lead to marketing strategies, which can actually create a sense of exclusion from some audiences and compound into the society, business and economy. Rigorous dataset validation, ongoing monitoring of AI models and the deployment of fairness enhancing techniques is done to remove bias and make neuromarketing insights a reflection of the diversity of the global consumer base (Sindhuja & Malik, 2024).

Also, the ethical dimension of neuromarketing and AI would be how close or far the distinction is between influence and manipulation. The goal of marketing is to persuade consumers, but the use of subconscious triggers make people wonder how far marketing strategies should rely on nonconscious decision making (Sposini, 2024). When you add Neuromarketing's advertising optimization scheme (based on human emotions and vulnerabilities of consumers) to the artificial intelligence's predictive capabilities, you strike gold; the hyper targeting advertising will be prepped to take advantage of unconscious consumers. It has ethical implications on autonomy and free will in consumer decision making. Consumers may be purchasing products without even realizing the psychological mechanisms at work if marketing campaigns are designed to avoid rational thought processes altogether (Hussain, 2025). To avoid exploitative practices, companies need to develop ethical guidelines that prohibit neuromarketing practices from being utilized to manipulate, but rather to improve, the consumer experience (Song et al., 2025).

Additionally, regulatory and compliance considerations are involved in the ethical landscape of integrating neuromarketing and AI. The General Data Protection Regulation (GDPR) in Europe and equivalent regulations in other areas include strict rules about collecting, saving, and employing data (Štefko et al., 2024). Neuromarketing technologies used by companies need to tread carefully when it comes to these regulations in order to avoid legal repercussions and maintain consumer trust. The success of any application utilizing neuromarketing principles and the foundation of a fair and transparent 'free market' rests on ethical AI frameworks, corporate responsibility, and industry self regulation that requires companies to provide necessary explanations and speculations about their solutions for fair market competitiveness on innovations, transparency, access, and explainability of algorithms and data. In an age where data holds high importance, businesses that have taken preemptive steps to adapt their practices to ethical standards and regulatory requirements will be in a better position to earn trust and relational continuity with consumers (Rania & Zineb, 2024).

Apart from ethical issues, there are related technical and implementation challenges to integrate neuromarketing and AI. Neuromarketing research may often be too expensive for many businesses because of the cost of the equipment, like EEG headsets and fMRI scanners (Singh et al. 2024). Furthermore, there is an expertise challenge to acquire the knowledge to analyze and interpret neurological data, and to develop AI models that are capable of extracting insights from it. However, majority of the organizations are not equipped with required infrastructure and talent to deploy these advanced marketing techniques. Furthermore, the issues of accessibility for small businesses and the emerging markets has to be raised. Thereafter emerging markets or small businesses cannot monetize the benefits of neuromarketing and AI due to certain financial and technological constraints. It will be essential to ensure that these technologies become more accessible and affordable, so that inclusivity and equal access to the cutting edge marketing tools can be promoted (Singh & Sharma, 2025).

With neuromarketing and AI on the up and up in the marketing world, it will be very important to meet these ethical and practical challenges in order to promote responsible innovation. While data driven marketing offers myriad opportunities to companies, companies that are transparent, fair and stakeholder focused will perform better in the technology ecosystems (Geetha & Hegde, 2024). For neuromarketing and AI to succeed in the long term, their success will depend not only on their ability to increase the effectiveness of marketing but also on their responsiveness to the needs of advances in ethics, rights to the consumer, and conformity with responsible business practices.

6. CASE STUDIES AND REAL-WORLD APPLICATIONS

Instead, neuromarketing and artificial intelligence is no longer just theory but an effective, widely used strategy for integration in marketing and consumer interaction in various industries. Several global companies have managed to leverage the power of AI powered neuromarketing to improve user experiences, personalize better, lead to conversion rate optimization. Analyzing subconscious consumer behavior can help businesses to tailor their marketing approach to be more effective and their engagement strategies more successful.

Netflix is one of the well known examples where AI driven neuromarketing is being used to further refine its content recommendation engine. Traditional consumer surveys and ratings offer little information in terms of viewer engagement, as users could not always express their actual preferences (Rania & Zineb, 2024). Instead, Netflix relies on AI behavior analysis that analyzes real—time interaction like watching duration, pause points, rewatch behavior and even eye tracking studies in test environment. With these patterns correlated to neuromarketing insights, Netflix takes the personalization of its interface, trailer selections and thumbnail displays…all with the aim of suggesting content that matches the subconscious of the viewers. This approach has worked for Netflix through its high retention rates and user engagement thus showing how AI and Neuromarketing combine to heighten the consumption of people's contents.

Amazon, similar to other companies, uses AI neuromarketing to ensure highly personalized shopping experience. The company relies on a combination of machine learning, eye tracking and sentiment analysis to predict buying behavior and suggest most relevant products (Balanagu & Boppisetty, 2025). Amazon's AI algorithm studies not only what users purchase but also future possible purchases by studying the browsing behavior, dwell time on product pages, and based on facial recognition studies, it has the capability to process the emotional reaction of the buyer. That also enables platform to target promoted search outcomes, product placements and promotional banners customary to subconscious triggers that force termination decisions. Amazon's "Customers Who Bought This Also Bought" is an AI based recommender system that is based on neuromarketing principles such that the product recommendations are in sync with the cognitive biases and emotional drivers of the consumers.

AI driven neuromarketing has not only transpired on the two main entertainment and e-commerce sectors, but also heavily influenced political campaigns and social networks. Currently, neuromarketing techniques are used by political strategists to read voters' minds at a subconscious level. Sentiment analysis tools powered by AI scour tens of thousands of social media conversations, consumption patterns of news, as well as biological responses to campaigners' advertisements. Political parties use this data to construct extremely targeted campaign messages to appeal to specific voter segments. For example, AI driven neuromarketing cues were used to ALTER digital ads and social media messaging IN reference to the 2016 U.S. presidential election; so political content WOULD BE framed such that it triggers the strongest emotional response, and cannot be distinguished as truly indistinguishable for different types voter demographics. As AI Neurons lead to neuromarketing that can shape narratives based on subconscious biases, it has been adaptable in political communications, in ethical terms that could have an influence on democratic processes (Hidalgo & Ramírez, 2024).

Neuromarketing insights are applied in the world of social media marketing, for instance Facebook, Instagram, and TikTok use them to optimize content engagement. Instead, AI algorithms keep tabs on users' behavior: how quickly they scroll, how long over which element of content they hover and other patterns of engagement, so as to measure which kinds of content cause the most emotional arousal. Studies on neuromarketing established that emotionally charged content such as which can be humorous, inspiring, or controversial are more likely to attract more engagement. This data is constantly analyzed by AI systems and content feeds are adjusted to get users to interact with an aim of reinforcing engagement loops that keeps users on the platform for longer periods. For instance, TikTok uses AI bauiled neuromarketing by observing which videos hold a person's attention for longer and unconsciously engages them, and use it to perfect its recommendation engine (Shahzad et al. 2024).

Another use of AI driven neuromarketing is to improve customer loyalty programs where AI enable brands to deepen the emotional connection they have with their customers. For example, Starbucks and Nike use AI to study customer emotions and behaviors in order to vary the incentives to loyalty. Starbuck's uses its AI mobile app to take past purchases, time of day and emotional triggers of certain products to personalize offers and discounts (Alsharif et al. 2025). Starbucks can predict when customers are most likely to be receptive to promotions by using the neuromarketing insights and ensure that rewards feel timely and relevant. Likewise, the loyalty program of Nike uses biometric and sentiment analysis in a way that AI driven neuromarketing gauges emotional reactions to new product launches. To make better marketing strategies, Nike analyzes how consumers are interacting with sneaker releases, thus the limited edition of dropping items to create excitement and urgency (Panighrahi & Arunima, 2024).

Real world applications of when and how AI and neuromarketing are essentially transforming the way marketing is being strategized across industries are shown below. Companies can narrow down their approaches to content recommendation, e commerce personalisation, political messaging, social media engagement and brand loyalty by tapping into unconscious consumer behaviour. But they demonstrate too the ethical obligation on business to apply AI for neuromarketing with transparency and ethics, preserving consumer privacy and autonomy while facilitating engagement in positive ways. The merger of AI and neuromarketing will only become more advanced with time, and so, while it opens new doors for innovation, it will also give marketers to walk a fine line between influence and manipulation.

7. FUTURE TRENDS AND IMPLICATIONS

Although the empirical use of neuromarketing has not yet been widely adopted, the theory of neuromarketing and its marriage to artificial intelligence is expected to proliferate exponentially in the upcoming years supported by technological innovation and consumer expectations for ethical and transparent marketing practices. The rise of wearable neuroimaging devices and edge AI is one of the most promising development, paving the runway for less expensive and scalable means of neuromarketing (Millagala & Gunasinghe, 2024). In the past, neuromarketing research has been done using expensive and complex technologies like fMRI and EEG which made it hardly accessible to most companies except for the large corporations that can afford substantial amounts of money to conduct research. However, the advent of portable EEG headsets, biometric wearables, and AI-crafted analytics in real time is going to democratize neuromarketing, allowing businesses of all sizes to gather and make sense of neurophysiological data much more effectively (Bajaj et al. (2024)). By leveraging wearable devices along with AI driven edge computing, brands will be able to capture real time consumer responses on-site, providing them with the instant insights as to how emotional engagement and decision making is taking place in natural environments, rather than in controlled laboratory settings (Singh et al. 2024).

AI ethics and transparency going to be the need of hour as more and more people adopt neuromarketing and AI. Increased concern regarding privacy and consent over how personal data is collected, analyzed, and used has led to consumers who are more aware of how their personal data is collected, analyzed, and used. Therefore, governments and regulatory bodies should introduce stricter guidelines that would ensure that neuromarketing practices comply with ethical standards and data protection laws (Šola et al., 2024). The brands that are proactive in setting transparent data policies and ethical AI frameworks will outcompete by retaining consumer trust. If companies are not addressing these points, there is the chance they could experience reputational damage as well as regulatory scrutiny, which only pushes the need for responsible AI use up the list of priorities for marketers. Fairness, explainability and consumer autonomy will most likely be at the heart of ethical AI initiatives and marketing strategies within the proxy that will be focused on ensuring that consumers are not exploited through subconscious vulnerabilities but that customer experience can also be enhanced in an ethical and respectful way (Devendran et al. 2025).

An important trend for the future of neuromarketing is the mixing with the other immersive technologies including augmented reality technology and virtual reality technology. When utilizing neuromarketing insights along with these technologies, new brand engagement frontiers are opened, building interactive and emotionally engaging experiences. In the case of AR powered shopping applications, these applications analyze the real time eye movement and emotional response of a consumer to provide more personalized product recommendations and optimize the in store navigation. In VR environments the brands can do subconscious test with virtual advertisements, product placements or branded immersive storytelling experiences that can be improve the marketing strategy most impactfully. Through the ability to detect emotional and cognitive engagement within virtual environments, brands have new possibilities to cultivate experiences which are more engaging and more memorable, in turn, bonding consumers to the brand (Awasthi et al. 2024).

Moreover, AI driven emotional assistants are expected to create ways through which customers will experience AI emotions through immersive experiences, instead of traditional text based interfaces. Thus, virtual assistants and chatbots with superior emotional intelligence that can see through consumers' emotions by their voice tonality, facial expressions, and other physiological signals will be capable of delivering very individualized and empathic responses. True AI-driven assistants will entirely change customer service by foreseeing needs, fitting discuss types supported on enthusiastic cues and convey customized suggestions continuously. With AI developing further, such assistants will be less artificial and form genuine brand – consumer relationships that are of the human variety and cannot be considered as mere transactional exchanges (Taneja et al. 2025).

Neuromarketing, AI and emerging technologies converge to overturn the marketing playing field to more accurately, interactively and ethically sound strategies. While these innovations occur businesses must balance using big consumer insights while remaining ethical. Rather, only brands that commit to being transparent, inclusive and consumer centric will not only have an advantage, but indirectly be making a significant contribution towards an intelligent, immersive and respectful of consumer autonomy future of marketing (Fahim et al. 2024). With neuromarketing and AI working hand in hand, however, there is potential for all that is exciting with evolution, but that also carries the weight of the long term success of these transformative technologies in mind.

8. ROI AND BUSINESS STRATEGY: MEASURING THE IMPACT OF NEURO-AI MARKETING

While the scientific sophistication of neuromarketing and artificial intelligence integration is evident, its business value ultimately hinges on return on investment and strategic impact. Companies adopting neuro-AI solutions must justify their implementation not only with theoretical benefits but also with tangible outcomes such as increased conversion rates, brand loyalty, customer lifetime value, and marketing efficiency (Antonissen et al. 2025).

To measure ROI, businesses can deploy a combination of quantitative metrics and neurocognitive indicators. Key performance indicators might include uplift in click-through rates, sales conversions, ad recall, emotional engagement scores, and cost per acquisition. With AI-driven tools, companies can continuously monitor these indicators and isolate which neuromarketing interventions—like emotional framing, adaptive visuals, or real-time personalization—correlate with behavioral outcomes (Anderson, 2025).

Additionally, AI facilitates real-time A/B and multivariate testing informed by neuromarketing data. By dynamically adjusting content based on users' subconscious responses, brands can achieve higher personalization efficacy and campaign agility. For instance, marketers can test ad versions tailored to different neuroprofiles (e.g., impulsive vs. analytical decision-makers) and allocate budget toward the best-performing variations, reducing wasted spend.

Strategically, the integration of neuromarketing insights into business intelligence platforms offers cross-functional benefits. Product teams can adapt features based on real-time feedback loops; UX designers can shape emotionally intuitive experiences; and C-suites can align marketing budgets with empirical data rather than intuition. This convergence supports data democratization, empowering decision-makers at all levels to act on neuro-informed insights (Cohan, 2024).

Moreover, businesses can compare ROI of neuro-AI campaigns against traditional marketing initiatives to validate cost-effectiveness. While initial implementation costs may be higher due to specialized equipment or AI infrastructure, the long-term gains—enhanced targeting precision, customer retention, and brand equity—often outweigh early investments. Companies that measure and optimize these outcomes can shift from reactive marketing to proactive value creation (Jääskeläinen et al. 2025).

In conclusion, ROI measurement is not merely about financial returns, but about strategic alignment. When neuromarketing and AI are implemented with clear goals, continuous testing, and ethical oversight, they unlock a new paradigm where marketing becomes not just persuasive, but profoundly predictive and performance-driven.

9. CONCLUSION

Neuromarketing and artificial intelligence are integrated in such a way that results in a complete go in the marketing landscape by providing amazing accuracy, efficiency and personalization. Companies that couple neuroscience's insight into how we respond subconsciously with artificial intelligence's capacity to sift and interpret big data can develop marketing strategies that are more personalized, compelling, and thrilling. This synergy enables brands to overcome common research methods and get deeper answers into emotional triggers, cognitive engagement and decision making. It automates the gathering of data, finding patterns and allows real time adaptability that drives positive results within the marketing efforts that will be tailored to the consumers on a subconscious level and be personally relevant to them. Companies and brands are realizing the potential of these technologies combined whether in the retail, advertising, entertainment, health or customer experience space, they drive innovation and build stronger connections with audiences.

As a result, ethical innovation in AI driven neuromarketing becomes more and more necessary as these capabilities are expanding. Influence of consumer behaviour by subconscious insights is the biggest advantage for the business, but on the downside, it raises some ethical issues of privacy, transparency and manipulation. Neuromarketing companies have to make sure that neuromarketing applications adhere to responsible data practice that include consumer autonomy and informed consent. Marketing must be designed in such a way that AI systems are unbiased, inclusive, and transparent, making sure that marketing is ethical and respectful in contrast to exploitative. The ethical use of these technologies relies on regulatory frameworks and corporate responsibility initiatives that businesses should proactively address in order to gain the consumer trust and long term credibility needed to be successful.

In the future, research and industry applications will relate to improving neuromarketing methodologies, enhancing AI sentiment analysis, and investigating the applications of cutting edge technologies like augmented reality, virtual reality, and wearable neuroimaging devices. This evolution will continue; the AI software will take over the customer interactions while the real time neuromarketing analytics will be affordable to all the businesses. Neuroscience and AI are about to merge into the cusp of a new era — where marketing is becoming more intuitive, impactful and personalized in brand experiences. This must be the area to process as the field makes progress, while trying to find the delicate harmony between innovation and ethicalness, so that future marketing becomes data driven yet customer focused, inclusive and transparent.

REFERENCES

Adeola, O., Evans, O., Ndubuisi Edeh, J., & Adisa, I. (2022). The future of marketing: artificial intelligence, virtual reality, and neuromarketing. *Marketing communications and brand development in emerging economies Volume I: Contemporary and future perspectives*, 253-280.

Alsharif, A. H., Wang, J., Isa, S. M., Salleh, N. Z. M., Dawas, H. A., & Alsharif, M. H. (2025). The synergy of neuromarketing and artificial intelligence: A comprehensive literature review in the last decade. *Future Business Journal*, *11*(1), 170. DOI: 10.1186/s43093-025-00591-x

Anderson, C. (2025). Industry Corner Live With Synchron CEO Tom Oxley. *IEEE Pulse*, *16*(3), 43–49. DOI: 10.1109/MPULS.2025.3572578 PMID: 40668684

Antonissen, N., Tryfonos, O., Houben, I. B., Jacobs, C., de Rooij, M., & van Leeuwen, K. G. (2025). Artificial intelligence in radiology: 173 commercially available products and their scientific evidence. *European Radiology*, *36*(1), 1–11. DOI: 10.1007/s00330-025-11830-8 PMID: 40707732

Aprilianty, F., Takahashi, M., & Matsuura, Y. (2024). Bridging Brains and Bots: The Impact of AI on Neuromarketing. *Procedia Computer Science*, *246*, 1830–1839. DOI: 10.1016/j.procs.2024.09.687

Attié, E., Le Bars, S., & Quenel, I. (2021). Towards ethical neuromarketing 2.0 based on artificial intelligence. In *Handbook of research on applied data science and artificial intelligence in business and industry* (pp. 619–638). IGI Global. DOI: 10.4018/978-1-7998-6985-6.ch029

Awasthi, A., Nneoma, N. R., Shukla, P., Kumari, S., Sahil, S., Gandhi, N. K., & Agustin, F. E. (2024). The role of emotions in consumer brand loyalty: A Neuromarketing Approach. *International Journal of Tourism and Hospitality in Asia Pasific*, *7*(1), 104–116. DOI: 10.32535/ijthap.v7i1.2901

Bajaj, R., Ali Syed, A., & Singh, S. (2024). Analysing applications of neuromarketing in efficacy of programmatic advertising. *Journal of Consumer Behaviour*, *23*(2), 939–958. DOI: 10.1002/cb.2249

Balanagu, S. S. N., & Boppisetty, J. (2025). The Brain as a Market: Understanding Neurological Consumer Responses. In *The Quantum AI Era of Neuromarketing* (pp. 61–92). IGI Global Scientific Publishing.

Ballı, A. (2024). Comparison of Studies Conducted in the Field of Neuromarketing and Artificial Intelligence Using Bibliometric Method. *Journal of Mehmet Akif Ersoy University Economics and Administrative Sciences Faculty*, *11*(3), 980–1010. DOI: 10.30798/makuiibf.1416687

Bansal, S., & Gupta, M. (2023). Towards using artificial intelligence in neuromarketing. In *Promoting consumer engagement through emotional branding and sensory marketing* (pp. 16–23). IGI Global.

Bhardwaj, S., Thapa, S. B., & Gandhi, A. (2024). Advances in neuromarketing and improved understanding of consumer behaviour: Analysing tool possibilities and research trends. *Cogent Business & Management*, *11*(1), 2376773. DOI: 10.1080/23311975.2024.2376773

Byrne, A., Bonfiglio, E., Rigby, C., & Edelstyn, N. (2022). A systematic review of the prediction of consumer preference using EEG measures and machine-learning in neuromarketing research. *Brain Informatics*, *9*(1), 27. DOI: 10.1186/s40708-022-00175-3 PMID: 36376735

Cheredniakova, A., Lobodenko, L., & Lychagina, I. (2021, April). *A study of advertising content in digital communications: the experience of applying neuromarketing and traditional techniques. In 2021 Communication Strategies in Digital Society Seminar (ComSDS)*. IEEE.

Cohan, P. (2024). Generative AI Consulting. In *Brain Rush: How to Invest and Compete in the Real World of Generative AI* (pp. 67–109). Apress. DOI: 10.1007/979-8-8688-0318-5_4

Devendran, A., Kumaran, S., Tanguturi, R. C., & Neeraja, B. (2025). Overview of Neuromarketing: Foundations and Development. In *The Quantum AI Era of Neuromarketing* (pp. 29–60). IGI Global Scientific Publishing.

Fahim, I., Khalil, M. M., & Fatima, E. (2024, April). Unlocking Consumer Minds: A Comprehensive Exploration of Neuromarketing Techniques and Consumer Decision Processes. In *The International Workshop on Big Data and Business Intelligence* (pp. 355-364). Cham: Springer Nature Switzerland. DOI: 10.1007/978-3-031-65018-5_33

Geetha, V., & Hegde, S. N. (2024). Mapping the Consumer Mind: Neuromarketing Applications in Personalization and Targeting. *Library of Progress-Library Science, Information Technology & Computer, 44*(3).

Goncalves, M., Hu, Y., Aliagas, I., & Cerdá, L. M. (2024). Neuromarketing algorithms' consumer privacy and ethical considerations: Challenges and opportunities. *Cogent Business & Management*, *11*(1), 2333063. DOI: 10.1080/23311975.2024.2333063

Hidalgo, M. S. T., & Ramírez, A. M. (2024). Political Communication, Neuroscience and Ethics: Challenges for the power of managing and predicting political consumer behaviors. *Ciencia Latina Revista Científica Multidisciplinar*, *8*(1), 12185–12195. DOI: 10.37811/cl_rcm.v8i6.14978

Hussain, S. (2025). The ethical frontier: AI-enabled neuromarketing and conscious consumerism. [DSSR]. *Dialogue Social Science Review*, *3*(1), 1040–1048.

Jääskeläinen, P., Sanchez, C., & Holzapfel, A. (2025, June). Anticipatory Technology Ethics Reflection By Eliciting Creative AI Imaginaries Through Fictional Research Abstracts. In *Proceedings of the 2025 ACM Conference on Fairness, Accountability, and Transparency* (pp. 125-136). DOI: 10.1145/3715275.3732011

Juárez-Varón, D., Mengual-Recuerda, A., Zuluaga, J. C. S., & Corvello, V. (2024). Application of Artificial Intelligence in Neuromarketing to Predict Consumer Behaviour Towards Brand Stimuli: Case Study-Neurotechnologies vs. AI Predictive Model. [IJSSCI]. *International Journal of Software Science and Computational Intelligence*, *16*(1), 1–18. DOI: 10.4018/IJSSCI.347214

Khondakar, M. F. K., Sarowar, M. H., Chowdhury, M. H., Majumder, S., Hossain, M. A., Dewan, M. A. A., & Hossain, Q. D. (2024). A systematic review on EEG-based neuromarketing: Recent trends and analyzing techniques. *Brain Informatics*, *11*(1), 17. DOI: 10.1186/s40708-024-00229-8 PMID: 38837089

Kumar, P., Chowdhury, S., & Madhavedi, S. (2024). Role of Neuromarketing and Artificial Intelligence in Futuristic Marketing Approach: An Empirical Study. *Journal of Informatics Education and Research*, *4*(2), 10–52783.

Marques dos Santos, J. P., & Marques dos Santos, J. D. (2024). Explainable artificial intelligence (xAI) in neuromarketing/consumer neuroscience: An fMRI study on brand perception. *Frontiers in Human Neuroscience*, *18*, 1305164. DOI: 10.3389/fnhum.2024.1305164 PMID: 38584851

Millagala, K., & Gunasinghe, N. (2024). Neuromarketing as a digital marketing strategy to unravel the evolution of marketing communication. In *Applying Business Intelligence and Innovation to Entrepreneurship* (pp. 81–105). IGI Global. DOI: 10.4018/979-8-3693-1846-1.ch005

Minz, N. K., Bhardwaj, I., Prakash, A., & Yadav, M. (2024). Ethics in Neuromarketing: A Systematic Literature Review. *Neuroscientific Insights and Therapeutic Approaches to Eating Disorders*, 101-125.

Panighrahi, A., & Arunima, D. (2024). Dopamine manipulation and its role in effective advertising. *Journal of Management Research and Analysis, 11*(3), 192–199. DOI: 10.18231/j.jmra.2024.033

Pastukh, O., & Yatsyshyn, V. (2024). Development of software for neuromarketing based on artificial intelligence and data science using high-performance computing and parallel programming technologies. *Вісник Тернопільського національного технічного університету, 113*(1), 143-149.

Rania, S., & Zineb, R. (2024, April). Integration of Artificial Intelligence in Neuromarketing: Ethical and Regulatory Implications. In *The International Workshop on Big Data and Business Intelligence* (pp. 278-291). Cham: Springer Nature Switzerland. DOI: 10.1007/978-3-031-65014-7_26

Shahzad, M. F., Yuan, J., Arif, F., & Waheed, A. (2024). Inside out. Social media videos and destination branding. Neuromarketing using EEG technique. *Journal of Islamic Marketing, 15*(3), 886–918. DOI: 10.1108/JIMA-08-2022-0236

Sindhuja, S., & Malik, R. (2024). Exploring the Ethical Issues and Considerations in Neuromarketing. In *Sensible Selling Through Sensory Neuromarketing* (pp. 144–163). IGI Global. DOI: 10.4018/979-8-3693-4236-7.ch008

Singh, G., & Sharma, U. (2025). Green Finance: Neuromarketing and the Ethics of Influence. In *Neuromarketing's Role in Sustainable Finance* (pp. 285-308). IGI Global.

Singh, K., Kumar, A., & Singh, G. (2024). Navigating the Neuromarketing Landscape: Valuable Insights for Businesses in a Post-Pandemic World. *Journal of Business-To-Business Marketing, 31*(3), 261–279. DOI: 10.1080/1051712X.2024.2361784

Šola, H. M., Qureshi, F. H., & Khawaja, S. (2024). Exploring the untapped potential of neuromarketing in online learning: Implications and challenges for the higher education sector in europe. *Behavioral Sciences (Basel, Switzerland), 14*(2), 80. DOI: 10.3390/bs14020080 PMID: 38392433

Song, G., Gazi, M. A. I., Waaje, A., Roshid, M. M., Karim, R., Rahaman, M. A., Min, Z., & Senathirajah, A. R. B. S. (2025). The Neuromarketing: Bridging Neuroscience and Marketing for Enhanced Consumer Engagement. *IEEE Access : Practical Innovations, Open Solutions, 13*, 40331–40353. DOI: 10.1109/ACCESS.2025.3545742

Sposini, L. (2024). Impact of New Technologies on Economic Behavior and Consumer Freedom of Choice: From Neuromarketing to Neuro-Rights. *Journal of Digital Technologies and Law, 2*(1), 74–100. DOI: 10.21202/jdtl.2024.5

Srivastava, G., & Bag, S. (2024). Modern-day marketing concepts based on face recognition and neuro-marketing: A review and future research directions. *Benchmarking*, *31*(2), 410–438. DOI: 10.1108/BIJ-09-2022-0588

Štefko, R., Ondrijová, I., & Tomková, A. (2024, September). Neuromarketing Research From the Consumers' Perspective. In *Global Business Conference 2024 Proceedings* (p. 118).

Taneja, S., Sharma, K., & Shamsuddin, Z. (2025). Overview of Neuromarketing: Principles, Methods, and Applications. In *Neuromarketing's Role in Sustainable Finance* (pp. 423–436). IGI Global.

Thakur, V., & Pasha, S. A. (2025). Neuromarketing for Decision Making in the Digital Era. *The Quantum AI Era of Neuromarketing*, 255-266.

Varghese, P. (2022). Neuromarketing and artificial intelligence for effective future business. *IUJ Journal of Management*, *1*(1), 240–254.

Vuković, D. (2024). Ethical issues in the application of neuromarketing research. *MAP social sciences, 4*, 67-81.

Zubareva, I. (2024). Possibilities of applying artificial intelligence in neuromarketing research to improve the efficiency of promoting banking products. In *Development Through Research and Innovation* (pp. 145-152).

KEY TERMS AND DEFINITIONS

A/B Testing: A method for comparing two versions of a marketing element (like an ad or webpage) to determine which performs better. AI can automate and enhance this process in neuromarketing.

Artificial Intelligence (AI): Technology that simulates human cognitive functions—such as learning and problem-solving—to analyze consumer data, detect patterns, and automate personalized marketing strategies.

Augmented Reality (AR) and Virtual Reality (VR): Immersive technologies that, when combined with neuromarketing insights, create interactive brand experiences and allow measurement of emotional and cognitive engagement.

Consumer Behavior: The study of how individuals respond psychologically, emotionally, and cognitively to marketing efforts, with an emphasis on subconscious processes.

Data-Driven Marketing: A marketing approach that relies on empirical data and analytics—rather than assumptions—to inform strategy, content, and targeting decisions.

Electroencephalography (EEG): A technique that records electrical activity of the brain to assess emotional and cognitive responses to marketing content in real time.

Emotional Engagement: The degree to which consumers emotionally react to marketing stimuli. Neuromarketing measures such responses to optimize content that resonates with feelings and improves recall.

Emotional Intelligence Systems: AI systems designed to recognize and respond empathetically to human emotions using cues like voice tone, facial expressions, and physiological signals.

Ethical AI: The responsible development and application of AI systems to ensure transparency, privacy, fairness, and bias mitigation in marketing and consumer data analysis.

Eye Tracking: A method that measures where and how long a person looks at visual content. Used in neuromarketing to identify attention and visual interest in ads, websites, and packaging.

Functional Magnetic Resonance Imaging (fMRI): A neuroimaging technique that detects brain activity by measuring changes in blood flow, used in neuromarketing to observe which brain regions respond to specific marketing stimuli.

Machine Learning: A branch of AI that uses statistical techniques to enable systems to learn from data, improving predictions over time—applied in neuromarketing to refine targeting strategies and content optimization.

Natural Language Processing (NLP): AI technology for analyzing human language, used in neuromarketing to interpret sentiment in customer reviews, social media posts, and chatbot interactions.

Neuromarketing: The application of neuroscience and psychology to marketing, focusing on understanding subconscious decision-making through tools like EEG, fMRI, and eye tracking to measure brain and emotional responses to marketing stimuli.

Personalization: Customizing marketing messages, recommendations, and user experiences based on individual preferences and behavioral insights derived from neuromarketing and AI analysis.

Predictive Modeling: The use of AI to forecast future consumer behaviors or preferences based on patterns in historical and real-time data.

Wearable Neuroimaging Devices: Portable devices like EEG headsets or biometric trackers that allow real-time, natural environment data collection for neuromarketing analysis.

Chapter 8
Unlocking Consumer Insights:
AI and Neuromarketing in Modern Marketing

Aayushi Jain
SRM University, Sonepat, India

Pawan Kumar
http://orcid.org/0000-0003-2059-9818
SRM University, Sonepat, India

Shikha Rani
SRM University, Sonepat, India

ABSTRACT

The study highlights the emerging topic of neuromarketing and AI and its impact on marketing strategies. Neuromarketing integrates neuroscience, psychology, and marketing to understand consumer buying behavior. AI is the programs, machines or systems that demonstrate the human intelligence. This chapter explores the AI tools used in marketing and focuses on combining AI and Neuromarketing to improve marketing strategies. In the current chapter, some real-life case studies are also discussed which helps in understanding neuromarketing in the era of AI. This chapter indicates ethical questions about neuromarketing and AI. It suggests that neuromarketing and AI have the potential to change the way marketers understand and influence consumer buying decisions.

DOI: 10.4018/979-8-3373-1152-4.ch008

AI (ARTIFICIAL INTELLIGENCE)

A computerized logical analysis technique that aims to build computer systems that make decisions akin to those made by humans is known as artificial intelligence *(Davenport et al., 2020)*. Complex computer algorithms and judgments that closely watch our everyday digital lives and act like intelligent humans based on data gathered about human behavior are the essence of artificial intelligence (AI). The most crucial component of artificial intelligence is expert systems. They make an effort to mimic human reasoning and optimization. It might turn into a crucial instrument for creating and carrying out a business's marketing plans *(Biswas & Patrab, 2023)*.

AI is now used in many different applications, such as virtual assistants like Siri, language translators, and facial recognition. We scarcely notice it because it is so prevalent in daily life. AI technology is being incorporated into the operations of numerous businesses across various industries *(Rajdhar & Brahme, 2020)*. In terms of productivity and creativity potential, implementing AI will assist economies and companies in several ways. But as AI advances, more occupations will become obsolete, necessitating the need for more adaptable abilities. Online searches and the dependability of the user experience as a whole have been significantly impacted by AI. AI is currently a very prominent topic *(Bhardwaj, 2025)*. As everyone is talking about, it is true that this new technology will change several sectors. AI is now utilized in a wide range of applications, including facial recognition, language translation, and virtual assistants like Siri. It is so common in day-to-day existence that we hardly realize it *(Murthy et al., 2016)*. Many companies in a variety of industries are integrating AI technology into their operations. AI implementation will help economies and businesses in many ways, including in terms of productivity and creativity potential. However, as artificial intelligence develops, more jobs will become outdated, requiring more flexible skills *(Niranjan et al., 2021)*. AI has had a big impact on online searches and the overall reliability of the user experience.

Marketing teams use AI-based tools to delve deeper into social media profiles and keyword searches *(Meshram et al., 2021)*. Many potential purchases are made by the 43% of companies that personalize the consumer experience. At the same time, 90% of brands will make use of some form of personalized marketing by 2020 (Figure 1).

USAGE OF AI TECHNIQUES IN MARKETING

Figure 1. Usage of AI technique in marketing

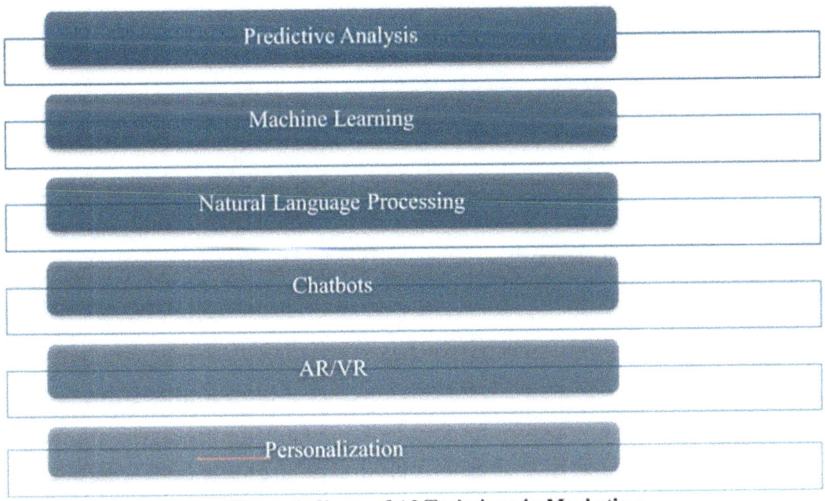

1) Predictive Analysis

Businesses may make extremely accurate predictions about trends and behaviors seconds, days, or years in the future by using both historical and current data. Regression and classification models are the two main model types used in predictive analytics (Figure 2). Data is categorized using classification models, which can also be used to forecast a customer's likelihood of responding to a marketing email *(Haleem et al., 2022)*. Regression models, on the other hand, forecast continuous outcomes, such as the potential lifetime revenue a customer may provide. These models assist companies in making data-driven, well-informed decisions *(Murthy et al., 2016)*.

Figure 2. Predictive Analysis in marketing

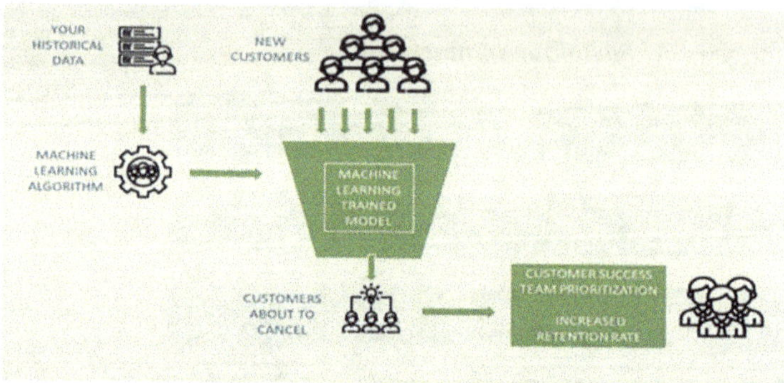

(Smolic, 2024)

Regression analysis identifies relationships between variables and is ideal for understanding how one factor influences another, like price changes affecting sales. Decision trees are intuitive models that classify data based on variables, making them useful for interpreting decision-making processes, even with incomplete data *(Anderson & Wilson, 2017)*.

Predictive analytics is widely used across industries like banking, retail, health-care, and manufacturing to streamline operations, increase revenue, and reduce risk. It enables real-time fraud detection, predicts customer conversion and purchase behavior, and supports risk assessment in areas like credit scoring and insurance *(Garcia & Rodriguez, 2019)*. Businesses also use it for operational efficiency through inventory and resource forecasting, customer segmentation for targeted marketing, and maintenance forecasting to prevent equipment failures. By leveraging big data and machine learning, predictive analytics drives smarter, forward-looking business decisions *(Nesamoney, 2015)*.

Companies using Predictive Analysis in marketing

Predictive analytics is widely used across industries to anticipate future outcomes based on historical data. Many top companies leverage this technology to gain a competitive edge and enhance customer experiences *(Kumar & Garg, 2018)*.

- **American Express:** In the financial sector, American Express uses predictive models to detect fraudulent transactions and forecast customer churn, enabling better risk management and customer retention strategies.

- **Zillow:** Real estate platform Zillow uses predictive analytics to generate property value estimates (Zestimates), aiding buyers and sellers with informed decisions.
- **Uber:** Transportation company Uber leverages predictive models to forecast ride demand and adjust pricing dynamically.

These companies showcase how predictive analytics transforms data into actionable insights, enhancing decision-making and driving business growth.

2) Machine Learning

Machine learning (Figure 3) can be applied in a variety of ways, including semi-supervised, unsupervised, and supervised learning *(Johnson & Williams, 2017)*. Supervised learning, which is best suited for applications with obvious input-output links, such as spam detection, uses labeled data to train algorithms for precise classification or prediction. Contrarily, unsupervised learning uses techniques like PCA or k-means to analyze unlabeled data and find latent patterns or groupings that are helpful for dimensionality reduction, pattern identification, and consumer segmentation *(Smith,2018)*.

Figure 3. Machine learning

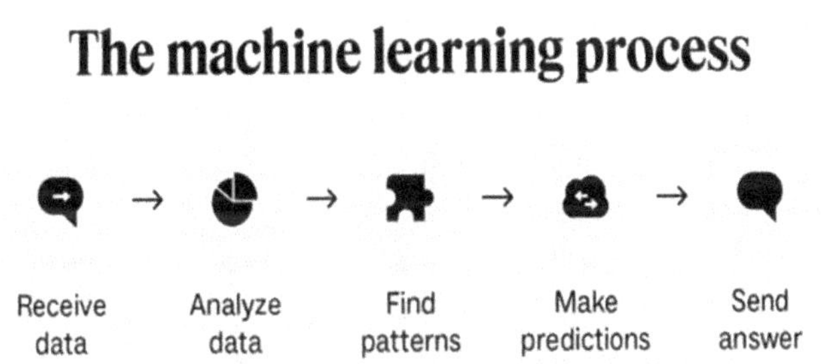

(Marshall, 2025)

In marketing, machine learning is commonly utilized to improve consumer experiences, boost return on investment, and improve decision-making. In order to forecast behavior, customize content, and improve campaigns, it assists companies in analyzing vast amounts of consumer data. For example, marketers can target the appropriate audience with customized messages by using machine learning algorithms to segment audiences based on demographics, preferences, and behavior *(Park & Kang, 2016)*. Additionally, it drives attrition prediction, pricing optimization, real-time online ad bidding, and recommendation algorithms (such as those utilized by Amazon or Netflix). All things considered; machine learning facilitates more effective, data-driven decision-making for marketers *(*Abdullah, *2025).*

Companies using Machine learning in marketing

Many leading companies today are actively leveraging *machine learning (ML)* techniques to revolutionize their marketing strategies.

- **Amazon: Amazon** is a prime example, using ML to analyze customer behavior and provide personalized product recommendations, which significantly boosts sales and user engagement.
- **Netflix: Netflix** relies on ML algorithms to study viewing patterns and offer tailored content suggestions, enhancing customer retention and satisfaction.
- **Google:** Google uses machine learning extensively in its advertising services, particularly in Google Ads, to optimize bidding strategies and improve targeting precision.
- **Coca- Cola:** Consumer brands like Coca-Cola employ ML to scan social media and customer data for emerging trends, enabling them to craft timely and effective marketing campaigns. In the beauty industry,

3) NLP

Natural Language Processing (NLP), a subset of artificial intelligence (AI) and computer science, uses machine learning to help computers understand and interact with human language (Figure 4). It integrates rule-based linguistic modeling with statistical methods, machine learning, and deep learning to enable digital systems to interpret, analyze, and generate both written and spoken language *(Johnson & Williams, 2017)*. NLP advancements have played a crucial role in the development of generative AI, powering everything from large language models' communication skills to image generation systems' understanding of user prompts *(Park & Kang, 2016)*.

Figure 4. Natural learning processing

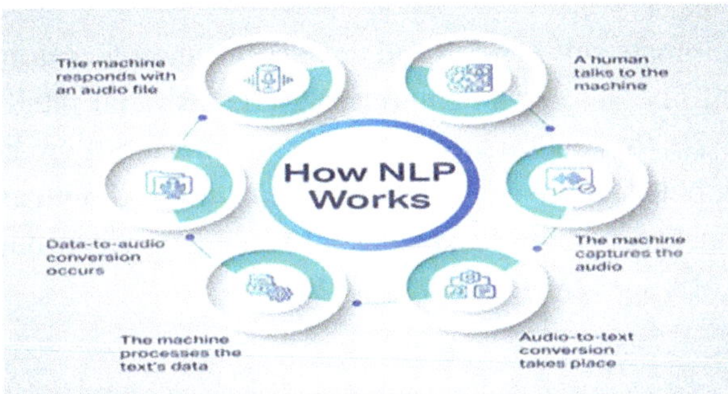

(Shaip, 2025)

Companies using NLP in marketing

Several prominent companies are leveraging Natural Language Processing (NLP) in marketing to enhance customer engagement, sentiment analysis, chatbots, and personalized content creation.

- **Meta:** Meta (Facebook) incorporates NLP in sentiment analysis and to moderate content, ensuring that ads are contextually placed and emotionally resonant. This improves the relevance and effectiveness of marketing campaigns.
- **Netflix:** Netflix applies NLP to analyze user reviews and social media chatter, helping it promote shows with the most buzz and optimize its content recommendations.
- **HubSpot**: HubSpot, a leading marketing software company, uses NLP in its tools for content creation, automated email responses, and chatbots to improve customer service and automate repetitive marketing tasks.
- **Spotify:** Spotify incorporates NLP to analyze song lyrics and user-generated content to refine music recommendations and target advertisements based on mood and theme.

These companies show how NLP is being used to understand language, extract insights, and deliver personalized and meaningful marketing experiences across platforms.

4) Chatbots

Businesses automate self-service and create outstanding customer experiences more quickly with the help of an enterprise-grade artificial intelligence solution *(Taylor & White, 2020)*. Answers to pre-programmed queries are no longer necessary for FAQ chatbots (Figure 5): Combining generative AI with an organization's knowledge base makes it simpler and quicker to automatically produce solutions to a greater variety of issues *(Kim & Park, 2019)*.

Figure 5. Chatbot

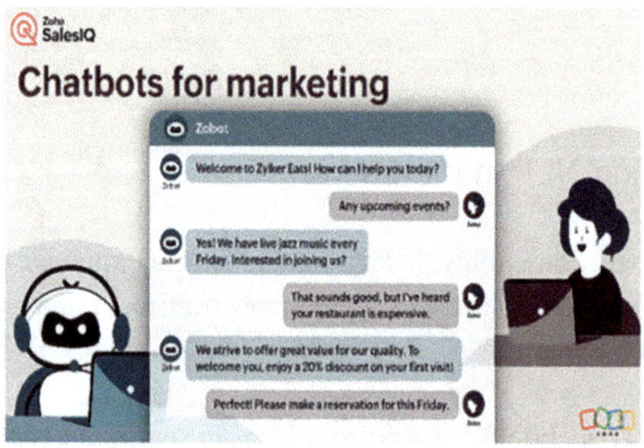

(Gupta, 2024)

Companies using Chatbots

Several top companies across industries use chatbots for marketing to enhance customer engagement, automate responses, and drive conversions. Here are some notable examples:

- **H&M** – The fashion retailer uses a chatbot on its website and mobile app to help users find outfits based on their preferences. It guides them through personalized styling and offers product suggestions, streamlining the shopping experience.
- **Domino's Pizza** – Through its chatbot "Dom," Domino's allows customers to place orders, track delivery, and even repeat past orders via platforms like Messenger and their mobile app.

- **KLM Royal Dutch Airlines** – KLM's chatbot provides booking confirmation, flight status updates, and travel tips, keeping customers engaged and informed throughout their journey.
- **L'Oréal** – L'Oréal's chatbot helps customers discover the right skincare and beauty products through quizzes and personalized advice, enhancing the digital shopping experience.
- **eBay** – eBay's ShopBot on Messenger helps customers find items, compare prices, and receive personalized suggestions, simplifying the search and purchase process.

These companies use *AI-powered chatbots* to make marketing more interactive, efficient, and personalized, ultimately driving better customer satisfaction and brand loyalty.

5) AR/VR

Augmented Reality (AR) and Virtual Reality (VR) are transforming marketing by creating immersive and interactive experiences that engage customers more deeply (Figure 6). AR allows brands to overlay digital content onto the real-world using smartphones or AR glasses—like virtual try-ons in fashion and beauty (e.g., Lenskart, L'Oréal) or previewing furniture in your home, e.g., IKEA Place app *(Anoop, 2021)*. VR creates fully immersive environments, often used for virtual tours, product demos, or storytelling experiences—common in real estate, automotive, and tourism industries *(Babatunde et al., 2024)*. Brands like Nike, Pepsi, and Marriott have used VR to offer immersive brand stories or virtual event participation. Both technologies help increase customer engagement, boost conversions, and build memorable brand interactions.

Figure 6. AR/VR

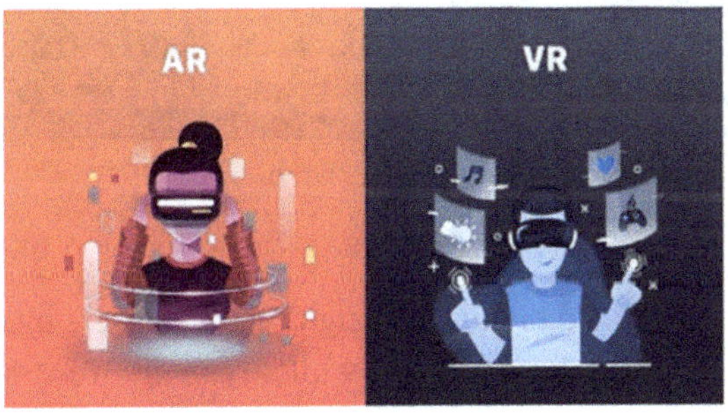

(Luminita, 2023)

Companies using AR/VR in marketing

IKEA incorporates augmented reality (AR) with its "IKEA Place" app, enabling customers to see how furniture would appear and fit within their home environments. By using smartphones, users can place life-sized 3D models of IKEA products in their spaces virtually. This helps improve purchasing decisions and minimizes the likelihood of returns.

Nykaa: Nykaa leverages AR for its virtual try-on feature in beauty products. Customers can see how different shades of lipsticks, foundations, or eyeshadows look on their face using their phone cameras. This tech boosts confidence in online purchases and personalizes the shopping experience.

Lenskart: Lenskart uses AR to let users virtually try on eyeglasses and sunglasses through its app and website. It helps customers see how frames look on their faces, increasing confidence and convenience in online eyewear shopping.

6) Personalization

Personalization in marketing involves tailoring messages, content, offers, and interactions to individual customer preferences and behavior (Figure 7). Companies use personalization to create more relevant and engaging experiences, which significantly improves customer satisfaction and loyalty *(Abdullah, 2025).*

Figure 7. AI personalization

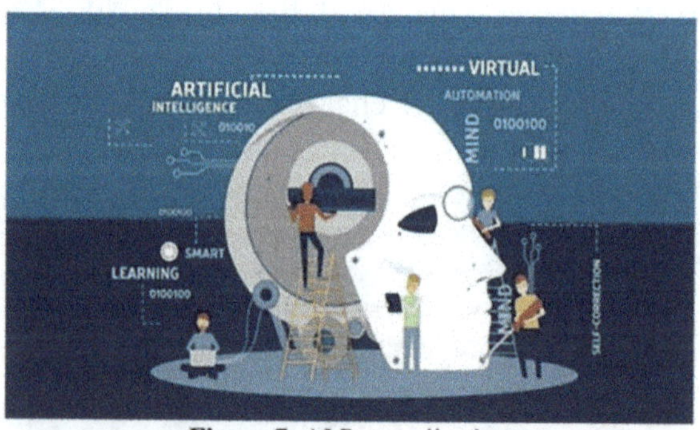

(Kumar, 2024)

For instance, personalized email campaigns address users by name and suggest products based on their purchase history, while dynamic website content changes according to a visitor's location or interests. Brands like Amazon and Netflix excel in offering customized product or content recommendations, increasing both engagement and sales *(Brown & Jones, 2019).* Personalized ads and push notifications help deliver the right message at the right time, enhancing the effectiveness of marketing efforts *(Babatunde et al., 2024)*. Additionally, chatbots and customer service platforms use customer data to provide faster and more relevant support. Overall, personalization boosts conversion rates, deepens customer relationships, and makes marketing more efficient and impactful.

Companies Using Personalization in Marketing

Many leading companies across industries use personalization in marketing to enhance customer experience and drive engagement. Here are some notable examples:

- **Netflix** – Uses sophisticated algorithms to personalize content recommendations based on viewing history, ratings, and preferences, making the platform more engaging for users.
- **Sephora** – Offers personalized product recommendations based on past purchases and quiz results, and uses AI to help users find the right shade or product for their skin tone.
- **Nike** – Provides personalized product suggestions and custom shoe options via its app and website, enhancing user engagement and loyalty.
- **Starbucks** – Uses its mobile app to offer personalized offers, rewards, and product suggestions based on customer purchase history and preferences.

Table 1 highlights companies use personalization as a key marketing strategy to build deeper relationships with customers, increase conversions, and improve brand loyalty.

Table 1. Companies using AI techniques in marketing

Company	Industry	AI Technique Used	Purpose
Amazon	E-commerce	Recommendation Engines, NLP	Personalized product suggestions, dynamic pricing
Google	Technology/Ads	Machine Learning, Predictive Analytics	Smart ad bidding, targeting, performance optimization
Netflix	Entertainment	AI-based Content Filtering & Recommendations	Personalized content delivery, user retention
Meta (Facebook)	Social media	AI for Targeted Ads, Image Recognition	Audience segmentation, relevant ad delivery
Spotify	Music Streaming	Machine Learning, Deep Learning	Personalized playlists and ad targeting

continued on following page

Table 1. Continued

Company	Industry	AI Technique Used	Purpose
Coca-Cola	FMCG	Data Analytics, Image Recognition	Consumer insights, targeted marketing campaigns
Sephora	Retail/Beauty	Virtual Try-On (AR/AI), Chatbots	Personalized shopping, customer engagement
Nike	Sportswear	AI Chatbots, Predictive Analytics	Customized product recommendations, marketing
Lenskart	Eyeglasses & lenses	AR	Helps customers see how frames look on their faces, increasing confidence and convenience in online eyewear shopping.
L'oreal	Beauty	AR/VR	Allow users to try makeup virtually.
Starbucks	Food & Beverage	Predictive Analytics, Machine Learning	Personalized promotions, loyalty management
H&M	Retail/Fashion	Customer Behaviour Analysis, Email Automation	Personalized emails, inventory optimization
Nykaa	Beauty	AR/VR	Boosts confidence in online purchases and personalizes the shopping experience.
IKEA	Furniture	AR	Helps users virtually to place true-to-scale 3D models of IKEA furniture using their smartphones

(Source: Compiled by Author)

NEUROMARKETING

Ale Smidts introduced neuromarketing in 2002 *(Boricean, 2009)*. The cutting-edge marketing discipline known as "neuromarketing" uses neuroscience to study consumer behavior. Neuromarketing is the term used to describe the use of neuroscience in marketing. The study of the structure and development of the nervous system is known as neuroscience *(Kahneman, 2011; Gakhal & Senior, 2008)*. By applying the findings of market research, neuroscience seeks to unleash the intellect and fundamentally change the way that every good or service is purchased. Modern neuroscience methods such as eye tracking, brain imaging, and facial recognition software are used in this kind of marketing to gain understanding of how people think and make decisions about what to buy. Additionally, it seeks to uncover underlying causes that can help brands establish stronger connections with their target market *(Lindstrom, 2008; Stasi et al., 2018)*.

Understanding the relationship between consumers and brands—more especially, the reasons behind consumers' preference for particular goods or services over others—is the fundamental objective of neuromarketing. Neuro marketers use a range of research methods to achieve this, including eye tracking to gauge graphic consideration, facial recognition to examine emotional reactions, and EEG to monitor electrical activity in the brain. Brands can obtain insights into their customers by using brain scanning to monitor various aspects of brain activity, including eye movement, pupil change, facial expressions, heart rate, and emotions *(Garcia and Saad, 2008)*. Neuro marketers can gain important insights into how consumers interact with organizations by collecting data from these tests and applying sophisticated algorithms to analyze it *(Lindstrom, 2008; Muñoz-Leiva et al., 2019)*.

Marketing efforts can be shaped and educated with the help of this data, increasing their impact on sales. Businesses can differentiate themselves in a competitive market by using neuromarketing to personalize their campaigns to the demands of certain clients *(Kottier, 2014; Eser et al., 2011)*. Its ultimate goal is to identify the choice variable, examine how the brain affects consumer behavior, and look into how people choose different things. This type of commercialization is not contemporary. It is an innovative approach to marketing analysis. It offers guidance for creating marketing tactics such product design, packaging, branding, and the efficacy of advertising.

Using personalization approaches like customized emails or targeted advertisements, they can also create strategies that have a higher chance of engaging clients and generating sales *(Ruanguttamanun, 2014)*. By requesting feedback from target customers at an early stage, neuromarketing can also be used for product creation, helping businesses create goods that better meet their demands *(Fisher et al., 2010; Crespo-Pereira et al., 2017; Yadava et al., 2017)*. Based on customer input gathered during testing, businesses can modify current products using neuromarketing techniques *(Kottier, 2014)*.

TOOLS AND TECHNIQUES OF NEUROMARKETING

(I) With recording brain activity (Figure 8)

Figure 8. Neuromarketing techniques with brain recording

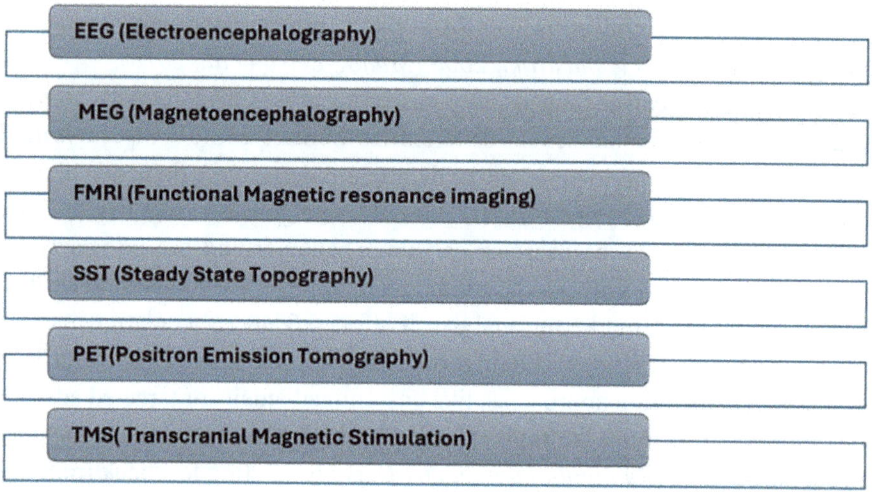

1) EEG (Electroencephalography)

Electroencephalography (EEG) is a neurological research method used to measure brain activity (Figure 9). In neuromarketing, it is frequently employed to observe mental processes—such as problem-solving or decision-making, to predict consumer behavior *(Cruz et al., 2016)*. It is used for Measuring brain activity provides objective insights into consumer responses, capturing unconscious reactions that often drive behavior more than conscious reasoning *(Costa et al., 2016)*. These measurements are highly accurate, down to the millisecond, allowing marketers to evaluate first impressions and immediate brain responses to advertisements or branding. Additionally, analyzing cognitive activities helps predict customer thought patterns and determine optimal pricing strategies for products or services *(Alvino et al., 2018)*.

EEG is used in various marketing and commercial evaluation processes. It is applied to assess and develop advertisements, evaluate new marketing initiatives, and analyze the effectiveness of film trailers. It also plays a crucial role in testing website design and usability, enhancing in-store customer experiences, and evaluating the impact of taglines *(Kumar et al., 2017)*. The average cost of conducting such evaluations typically varies depending on the scope and technology used, but it can range from a few thousand to several lakhs of rupees per project.

Figure 9. EEG scanner

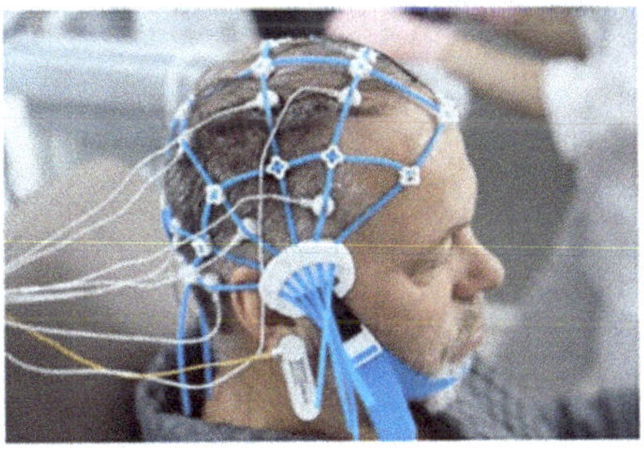

(OneWelbeck, n.d.)

2) MEG (Magnetoencephalography)

Magnetoencephalography (Figure 10) is a non-invasive medical diagnostic that detects neuromagnetic activity in the brain using a superconducting quantum interference device (SQUID) and a computer *(Costa et al., 2016)*. MEG detects, records, and analyses magnetic fields created by electrical currents in the brain. The distribution of these magnetic fields is shown against an anatomical image of the brain to aid in locating the source of activity. MEG assesses brain function and is the most advanced method for recording and evaluating the brain in action. It assesses perceptibility, attention, and memory.

This technique is primarily used to identify the functional areas of the brain by mapping centers responsible for sensory, motor, language, and memory activities *(Eser et al., 2011)*. It also plays a crucial role in precisely locating the source of epileptic seizures. By capturing magnetic potentials associated with brain activity at the scalp level, it aids in effective planning and accurate localization for medical or research purposes.

This technique is operated in various marketing and research contexts, such as evaluating new campaigns and testing advertisements to gauge consumer response. It is also used for testing packaging design to determine its appeal and effectiveness *(Fisher et al., 2010)*. Additionally, it helps in identifying consumer needs and preferences, and is applied in sensory testing to assess reactions to different product attributes like taste, smell, or texture.

Figure 10. MEG

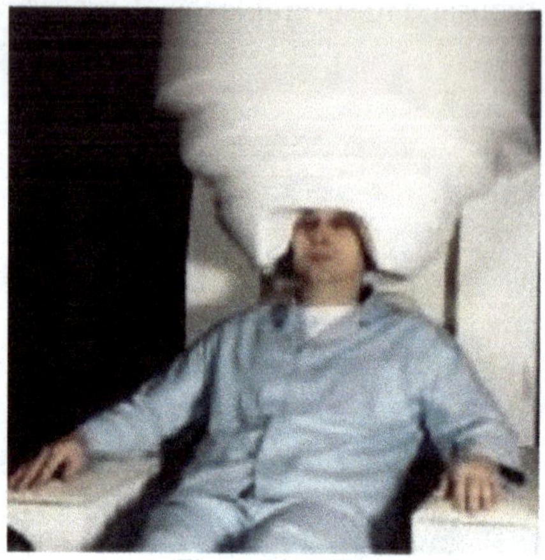

(Dooley, 2025)

3) Functional Magnetic Resonance Imaging

Neuroscience tools like fMRI are widely used in marketing through techniques such as Neuro Ad Testing (Figure 11), analyzing unconscious emotions and behaviors triggered by commercials and comparing them to benchmarks for effective advertising, helping to optimize ads and reduce spending *(Alsharif et al., 2022)*. Neuro Concept Testing uses fMRI to assess initial emotional reactions to ad concepts, allowing marketers to refine ideas before launch. In NeuroBranding, fMRI creates a unique Neuro Brand Signature by mapping neural associations linked to a brand in the consumer's brain *(Jiménez-Marín et al., 2022)*. It also helps evaluate new products by examining how marketing communications and packaging influence customer perception and purchase intent *(Plassmann et al, 2007)*.

FMRI are employed to evaluate new projects and test or develop advertisements and video content by analyzing consumers' subconscious reactions. These methods also help in testing packaging designs, evaluating optimal pricing strategies, and repositioning brands for better market alignment *(Jiménez-Marín et al., 2022)*. Additionally, neuromarketing aids in predicting consumer decisions, determining their underlying needs, and conducting sensory evaluations to enhance product appeal, ultimately leading to more effective and targeted marketing strategies *(Bakardjieva & Kimmel, 2017)*.

Figure 11. Brain image looking at print advertisement

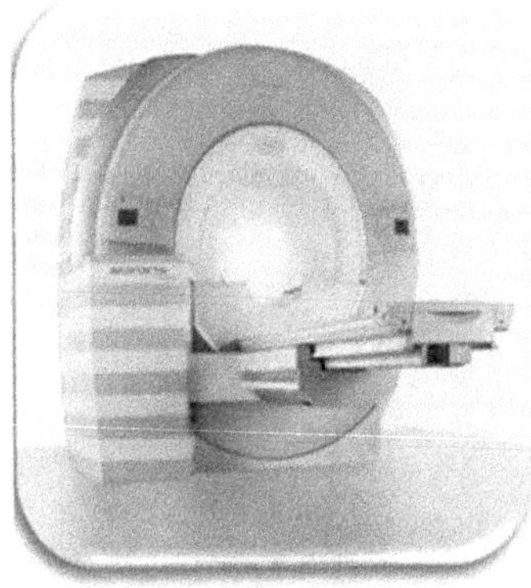

(Ruanguttamanun, 2014)

4) SST (Steady State Topography)

Steady State Topography (SST) is a tool commonly used in cognitive neuroscience and neuromarketing to track quick fluctuations in brain activity (Figure 12). It evaluates consumer reactions, emotional sensitivity, engagement levels, the effectiveness of video content, and long-term memory retention *(Alvino et al., 2018)*. SST enables researchers to monitor fast-paced brain responses, making it valuable for understanding how consumers process and respond to marketing stimuli.

SST is employed to evaluate advertisements, new trailers, and printed materials or images by measuring the audience's subconscious responses. This approach helps marketers understand emotional engagement, attention levels, and memory recall associated with visual and video content. By gaining insights into how viewers react neurologically, businesses can refine their creative elements for greater impact and effectiveness.

Figure 12. SST

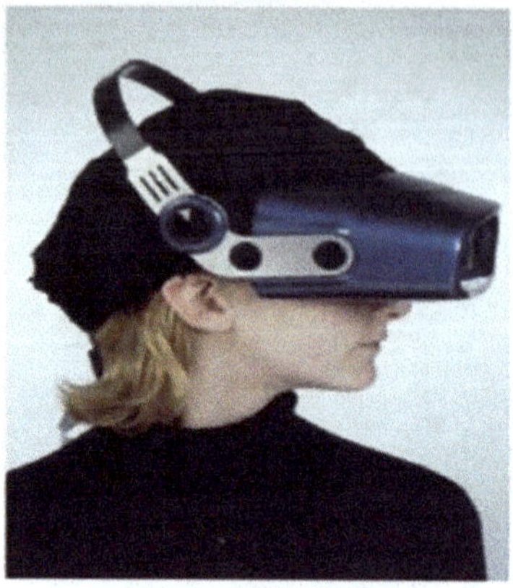

(Harris et al., 2018)

5) Positron Emission Tomography:

Positron Emission Tomography (PET) is used to evaluate physiological functions by analyzing blood flow, metabolism, neurotransmitter activity, and sensory perception, including emotional valence (Figure 13). It offers quantitative data, making it possible to track changes over time, whether due to disease progression or reactions to specific stimuli *(Eser et al., 2011)*.

PET is testing new products, advertisements, and packaging designs to understand consumer responses at a subconscious level *(Fisher et al., 2010)*. It helps in identifying emotional triggers, attention patterns, and purchase intent. This insight allows brands to refine their strategies for better engagement and effectiveness.

Figure 13. PET

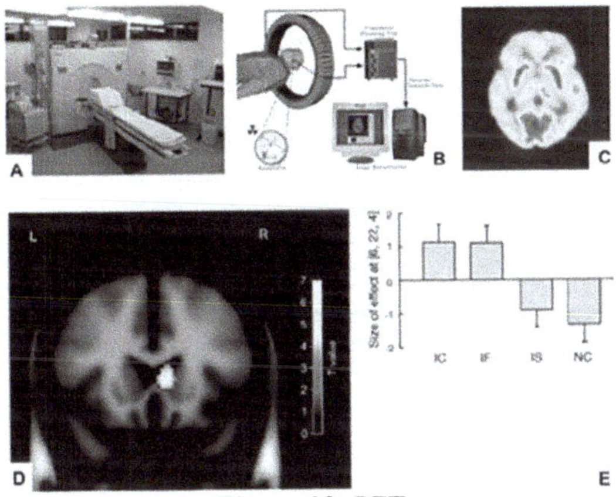

(Charron et al., 2008)

7) Transcranial Magnetic Stimulation:

TMS is a noninvasive technique that uses magnetic fields to influence brain activity, particularly in areas 1–2 cm beneath the scalp (Figure 14). It is often used when other treatments are ineffective and is helpful in assessing attention, cognition, and behavioral changes.

TMS is used to test new products, advertisements, packaging designs, and other marketing stimuli. It helps marketers understand consumers' subconscious reactions and emotional responses. This enables the creation of more impactful and persuasive marketing strategies based on real-time brain activity insights.

Figure 14. TMS

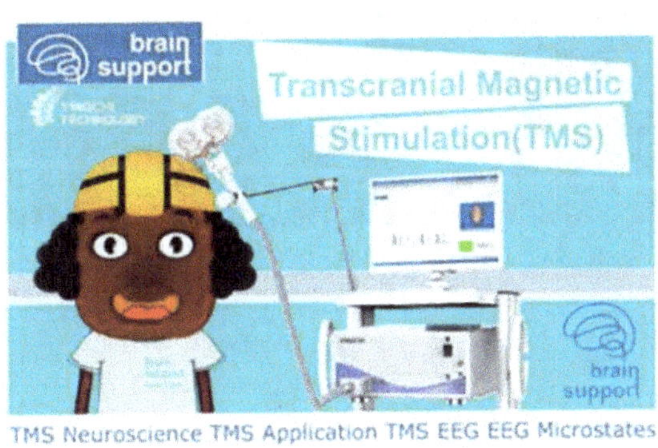

(Brain Support, 2023)

(II) Without recording brain activity (Figure 15)

Figure 15. Neuromarketing techniques deprived of recording brain activity

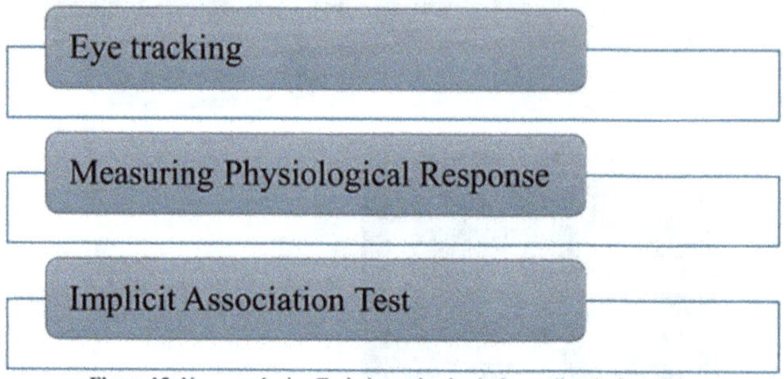

1) Eye Tracking

Eye tracking (Figure 16) occurs when a subject's pupil dilation varies while he stares at stimuli, based on where he is looking, how long he is staring, and where he is looking in space *(Boraston & Blakemore, 2007)*. Eye-tracking technology uses sensors to monitor and record the movement of your eyes *(Gheorghe et al. 2023)*. This information may be used to determine what you're looking at, how you're looking at it, and how you feel about what you're seeing. Eye tracking technology is a method of sensing and recording eye movements and gaze. It mainly tracks the eyes of one or more people *(Vehlen et al., 2021)*.

Figure 16. Eye tracking

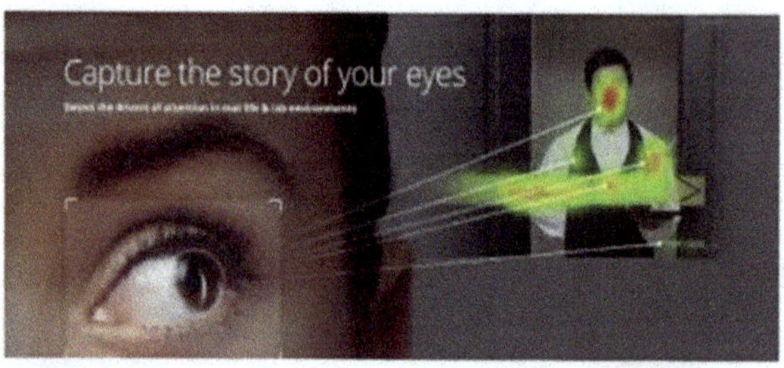

(Neurorelay, 2016)

2) Measuring Physiological Response

Physiological Responses is operated in various marketing and research scenarios, such as testing advertisements, movie trailers, and website designs to analyze user engagement and attention patterns. It is also used to identify in-store reactions and observe consumer behavior in natural environments. This technology helps marketers understand what captures consumer attention, enabling better design and strategic decisions.

3) IAT (Implicit Association Test)

Implicit Association Test (IAT) commonly used in marketing to assess consumer preferences and biases. Applications include selecting the right celebrity for brand promotion, identifying target segments through market segmentation, and distinguishing a brand from its competitors through brand differentiation.

Table 2 Shows Companies Using Neuromarketing

- Hyundai employed EEG techniques to design their automobile exteriors. Hyundai employed the EEG approach to learn about consumer preferences and what motivates customers to make purchasing decisions *(Imtiaz, 2024)*.
- PayPal's brain wave study reveals a preference for rapid services.
- PepsiCo used biometric answers to understand why women preferred baked lays, including single-serve packaging and advertising *(Imtiaz, 2024)*.
- Coca-Cola has used neuromarketing techniques to better understand how consumers react to its branding and advertising initiatives. For example, they used EEG (electroencephalography) and fMRI (functional magnetic resonance imaging) to assess brain activity in response to various container designs and commercials. This information assists them in optimizing their marketing strategy to better resonate with consumers *(Kumar et al., 2017)*.
- Frito-Lay has used neuromarketing to investigate consumer preferences and responses to product packaging, flavors, and advertising. They can learn about what features of their products and marketing materials attract consumers' attention and trigger favorable emotional responses by using techniques like eye tracking and biometric measures *(Kumar et al., 2017)*.

Table 2. Neuromarketing techniques impact on customers

Company	Industry	Neuromarketing Technique used	Purpose of Neuromarketing
Frito Lay	Food	Eye Tracking and Biometric Measurements	Study consumer preferences and responses to product packaging, flavors, and advertising.
Coco-Cola	Food	fMRI	Effective advertisement of product
Hyundai	Automotive	EEG	Study consumer's reaction when viewing the sport's car
Pepsico	Food	EEG and fMRI	Idea for single- serve packaging and corresponding ad campaign
Google	Media	EEG and Eye Tracking	Evaluate how users interact with their search engine interface, ads, and other digital platforms
Cheetos	Food	EEG and Facial Expression Analysis	Adjusted commercial, products and packaging on the basis of neuromarketing based research
Yahoo	Media	EEG	Study consumer's reaction to a television commercial

(Source: Compiled by researcher)

CONSUMER DECISION MAKING PROCESS THROUGH AI AND NEUROMARKETING

First, we will discuss about consumer decision making process. Consumer decision making process refers to the refers to the series of steps that individuals go through when choosing, purchasing, using, and evaluating products or services to satisfy their needs or desires *(Krishanan et al.,2023)*. This process helps marketers understand how consumers make buying decisions and what influences their choices.

> *"Consumer decision-making is the process by which individuals select, organize, and interpret information to make choices among alternatives" (Loudon and Della Bitta, 1993).*

Consumer Decision-Making Model (Figure 17)

Figure 17. Consumer decision-making model

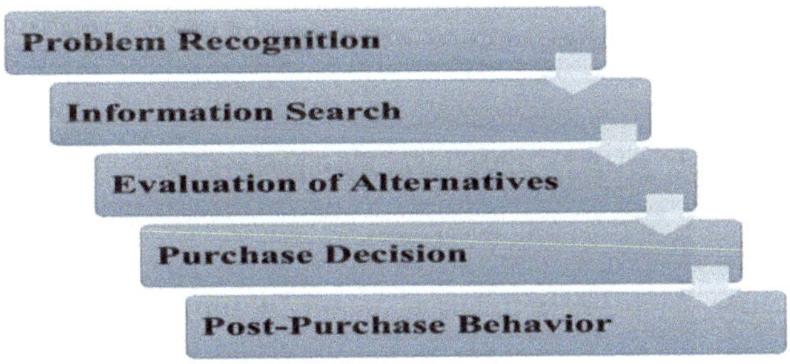

1. Problem Recognition

The process starts when a consumer realizes they have a need or a problem. This need can be triggered internally (e.g., hunger) or externally (e.g., seeing an ad).

2. Information Search

Once the need is recognized, the consumer looks for information about possible solutions. They may use internal sources (past experience) or external sources (ads, online reviews, word of mouth).

3. Evaluation of Alternatives

The consumer compares different products or brands based on features, prices, quality, or reviews to decide which one best meets their needs.

4. Purchase Decision

After evaluating the options, the consumer selects the product they want to buy. However, last-minute factors like discounts or peer suggestions can influence the final choice.

5. Post-Purchase Behavior

After buying and using the product, the consumer assesses their satisfaction. If satisfied, they may become loyal to the brand; if not, they may return the product or leave a negative review.

INTEGRATION OF AI AND NEUROMARKETING

Neuromarketing, despite its growing popularity, still faces skepticism from academicians and experts who view it as a science with limitations. These limitations often stem from the challenges of accessing complex tools like EEG (Electroencephalography) and eye-tracking systems, the subjective interpretation of emotional data, and the relatively high costs associated with conducting large-scale neuromarketing research *(Bhardwaj et al., 2023)*. However, the integration of artificial intelligence (AI) with neuromarketing is revolutionizing this field, gradually overcoming many of its traditional constraints. With the advent of AI, these tools and techniques are becoming more accessible, efficient, and accurate, paving the way for a more refined and data-driven approach to understanding consumer behavior *(Shah & Shukla, 2022)*. This synergy between neuromarketing and AI promises a future where brands can decode human emotions and cognitive processes with unmatched precision.

Neuromarketing focuses on studying the brain's response to marketing stimuli to understand subconscious consumer behavior. Techniques like EEG and eye tracking are particularly valuable because they monitor neuropulses, eye movements, pupil dilation, and attention levels in real time *(Guixeres et al., 2017)*. These tools offer insights into a consumer's emotional engagement, interest, and decision-making process. By observing how consumers respond to advertisements, packaging, websites, or product placements, companies can obtain unbiased and direct measurements of emotional reactions. However, while neuromarketing tools gather this rich data, interpreting it meaningfully and scaling it across various demographics poses challenges—this is where AI steps in. Artificial intelligence excels at processing massive datasets and finding meaningful patterns that human analysts might miss *(Kaur & Sharma, 2021)*. In the context of neuromarketing, AI acts as a bridge between raw emotional data and practical marketing strategies. It can identify subtle, non-obvious correlations between emotional responses and consumer preferences, thus enabling marketers to optimize campaigns with a higher degree of personalization. Moreover, AI employs predictive analytics to forecast future trends, helping marketers stay ahead of consumer needs and expectations.

When AI and neuromarketing converge, the results can be transformative (Figure 18). AI processes the rich emotional and cognitive data collected through neuromarketing techniques, uncovering hidden behavioral patterns that might influence purchasing decisions *(Bansal & Gupta, 2023)*. For instance, if EEG signals indicate heightened emotional arousal during a specific segment of a commercial, AI can isolate the exact elements—be it visuals, sound, or messaging—that triggered that response. It can then suggest refinements to the content to amplify its emotional appeal. Similarly, AI can analyze thousands of facial expression recordings to determine which product features or promotional messages resonate most with a specific audience segment. One significant advantage of this fusion is the ability to deliver marketing campaigns that are not only personalized but emotionally intelligent *(Ishtiaque et al., 2023)*. AI continues to evolve, it will enhance the accuracy, scalability, and accessibility of neuromarketing. This will allow businesses to make data-backed, emotionally attuned decisions that deepen customer connections and drive long-term brand loyalty *(Ndiku et al., 2022)*.

Figure 18. Consumer decision making process

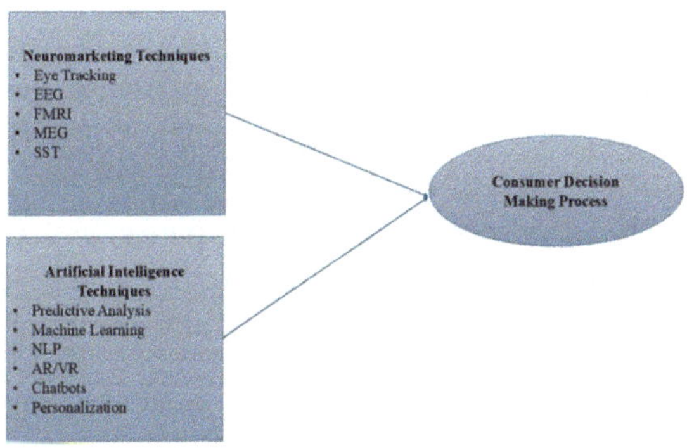

RELEVANCE OF AI IN NEUROMARKETING

Artificial intelligence (AI) has significantly transformed marketing by enabling deeper insights, enhanced personalization, and greater efficiency. One of its key benefits is data analysis, allowing marketers to process vast amounts of data from social media, email, web traffic, and search engines rapidly, leading to improved performance and higher return on investment (ROI). AI also aids in understanding customer needs and expectations by identifying patterns in consumer behavior, enabling marketers to tailor their products, services, and messaging to meet individual preferences *(Capatina et al., 2020)*. Through AI-powered tools, businesses can identify target audiences with precision and deliver personalized experiences, thereby enhancing customer engagement, loyalty, and lifetime value. Additionally, machine learning models assist marketing experts in recognizing current trends and predicting future consumer reactions, enabling them to replicate successful strategies *(Chi-Hsien & Nagasawa, 2019)*. AI platforms can analyze customer behavior with human-like understanding, interpreting emotions, intentions, and preferences swiftly and accurately. This empowers marketers to make informed decisions and design campaigns that resonate more deeply with their audience *(Huang & Rust, 2021)*.

IMPACT OF AI AND NEUROMARKETING ON CONSUMER BUYING DECISION

The integration of neuromarketing and artificial intelligence (AI) forms a transformative synergy that is reshaping how brands understand and influence consumer behavior. Neuromarketing provides insights into the subconscious emotional and psychological factors that drive purchasing decisions, while AI enables marketers to analyze vast amounts of consumer data *(Varghese, 2022)*. Together, they allow for the creation of deeply personalized marketing strategies. Neuroscience helps identify emotional triggers and motivations, and AI applies these findings to develop messaging tailored to individual psychological profiles. This enhanced understanding of consumer psychology enables marketers to connect with their audiences on a more intimate and impactful level *(Hakan, 2018)*.

One of the most significant advantages of combining neuromarketing and AI is the ability to adapt and optimize marketing strategies in real time. AI systems can continuously monitor campaign performance and apply neuromarketing insights to adjust messaging, timing, and delivery channels for maximum effectiveness *(Agrawal et al., 2019)*. Automated A/B testing allows for rapid experimentation, helping brands quickly determine which messages resonate best with their target audience. If neuromarketing studies reveal that a specific emotional cue or sensory element performs well, AI can swiftly adjust campaigns across platforms to capitalize on these insights *(Bag et al., 2021)*.

Emotional engagement is a crucial driver of consumer behavior, and this fusion allows marketers to fine-tune their emotional appeals. Neuromarketing techniques identify which visual and auditory cues elicit strong emotional responses, while AI refines these elements by tracking real-time engagement metrics *(Darázs, 2024)*. Campaigns can be developed to target specific consumer emotions such as excitement, trust, or nostalgia, enhancing their resonance. As a result, brands are able to create memorable and emotionally compelling experiences that capture attention and drive action.

Predictive capabilities are another powerful outcome of this integration. AI leverages historical and real-time data to forecast future buying behaviors, and when informed by neuromarketing insights, these predictions become more accurate and actionable. For instance, understanding why consumers make certain decisions—beyond what they buy—enables more effective targeting and communication *(Adeola et al., 2022)*. AI can also map the consumer journey, identifying crucial touchpoints where neuromarketing insights can be applied to influence decisions and improve user experience at every stage.

Finally, this combined approach greatly enhances customer experience and brand loyalty. AI-driven tools such as chatbots can offer personalized interactions that are both intuitive and emotionally engaging, thanks to underlying neuromarketing data. By continuously analyzing customer feedback and responses, brands can fine-tune their approaches to better align with consumer expectations and emotional states *(Kumar et al., 2024)*. Over time, these emotionally intelligent interactions help build stronger connections and trust, resulting in higher customer retention. AI can also monitor social media and online communities to understand broader social influences, helping brands tap into community sentiments and build brand advocacy effectively.

ENHANCING MARKETING STRATEGIES: THROUGH AI AND NEUROMARKETING

The combination of artificial intelligence (AI) and neuromarketing is revolutionizing the way brands approach marketing by enabling a deeper understanding of consumer behavior and delivering personalized, emotionally resonant campaigns (Alsharif et al., 2020*)*. Neuromarketing techniques such as EEG (electroencephalography) and fMRI (functional magnetic resonance imaging) help marketers measure the brain's emotional and cognitive responses to various marketing stimuli. When AI is applied to this data, it can process vast amounts of neurological and behavioral information to identify consumer trends and preferences with high accuracy *(Peltier et al., 2024)*. Unlike traditional marketing surveys that rely on conscious feedback, AI-powered analysis of neuromarketing data reveals unconscious reactions, providing insights that were previously difficult to uncover *(Kartajaya et al., 2019)*.

This powerful synergy also enables personalization at scale. AI algorithms can take the insights derived from neuromarketing studies and apply them to craft tailored messaging that resonates with individual consumers *(Kumar et al., 2024)*. Real-time data collection and analysis allow brands to dynamically adapt content based on emotional responses, ensuring that every touchpoint is relevant and engaging. This level of personalization enhances customer experiences and improves campaign performance by making each interaction feel uniquely meaningful to the consumer.

In addition, predictive analytics powered by AI is a major benefit of this combination. By analyzing neuromarketing data, AI models can anticipate consumer behavior even before it occurs. This predictive ability allows brands to stay ahead of consumer needs and customize their offerings accordingly *(Gajić, 2023)*. Furthermore, by understanding which emotional triggers are most likely to lead to conversions, marketing teams can optimize their campaigns around strategies that are proven to work, ultimately improving return on investment (ROI).

The fusion of AI and neuromarketing also contributes significantly to enhancing customer experience. AI can utilize neuromarketing insights to map the entire customer journey, highlighting areas that may cause friction and identifying opportunities for deeper engagement. When combined with immersive technologies like augmented reality (AR) and virtual reality (VR), brands can create rich, interactive experiences that connect with consumers on a deeper emotional level. These enhanced experiences not only captivate attention but also foster long-term loyalty *(Cenamor et al., 2019)*.

A/B testing and iterative experimentation also become more precise and effective with AI and neuromarketing. AI can conduct sophisticated A/B tests by measuring emotional responses captured through neuromarketing tools, determining which variations generate the strongest reactions *(Kaur & Sharma, 2021)*. This enables continuous improvement of marketing strategies based on real-time feedback. As campaigns evolve with consumer preferences, brands remain agile and more attuned to their audience.

Furthermore, this integration promotes ethical and responsible marketing practices. By focusing on enhancing the consumer experience rather than manipulating behavior, companies can use AI and neuromarketing to make informed, transparent decisions. Ethical use of data fosters trust, and brands that are open about how they collect and use neuromarketing insights are more likely to retain loyal customers *(Kumar et al., 2024)*. Lastly, AI enables cross-channel consistency by integrating neuromarketing insights across various platforms. This ensures that the emotional and psychological triggers identified are applied uniformly, helping to create a cohesive brand story *(Alsharif et al., 2020)*.

DISCUSSION

The integration of Artificial Intelligence (AI) and neuromarketing represents a significant advancement in modern marketing strategies, enabling brands to understand and influence consumer behavior at a deeper, more emotional level. Traditionally, neuromarketing has faced challenges such as high costs, limited access to tools like EEG and fMRI, and the subjective nature of interpreting emotional data *(Eser et al.,*

2011). However, AI helps overcome these limitations by analysing large datasets quickly and identifying patterns that are not easily detectable by human analysts. This powerful synergy enhances marketing precision by enabling real-time analysis and adaptation. For instance, if neuromarketing tools detect a specific emotional response to a campaign element, AI can immediately suggest and implement changes to maximize emotional engagement. Such dynamic adjustments make marketing more responsive and effective *(Bhardwaj et al., 2023).* Moreover, AI enhances the scalability of neuromarketing research, making it feasible for brands to apply insights across diverse consumer segments and large markets.

One of the most transformative aspects of this integration is its ability to create emotionally intelligent campaigns. AI can tailor content based on individual psychological profiles and emotional triggers, allowing for highly personalized and engaging interactions. Predictive analytics further empowers marketers to anticipate consumer behaviors and trends, giving businesses a competitive edge by staying ahead of consumer expectations *(Kaur & Sharma, 2021).* Furthermore, this convergence supports ethical marketing by emphasizing consumer-centric strategies. Rather than manipulating behavior, AI and neuromarketing aim to understand and meet consumer needs more effectively. Cross-platform consistency also ensures that emotional engagement is sustained across all brand touchpoints, fostering loyalty and trust.

CONCLUSION

The integration of neuromarketing and artificial intelligence (AI) has the potential to revolutionize the marketing industry by offering deeper insights into consumer behavior and enabling more effective, data-driven strategies. Neuromarketing delves into the subconscious processes of consumers, uncovering emotional responses, preferences, and motivations that traditional marketing methods often overlook. By tapping into brain activity and emotional triggers through techniques like EEG and fMRI, marketers gain access to invaluable data about how consumers truly react to advertisements, packaging, or branding elements. This allows for more accurate predictions of consumer behavior and the development of messages that resonate more profoundly with the target audience. Artificial intelligence complements this process by processing and analyzing vast amounts of consumer data in real time. Through AI, marketers can identify hidden patterns and behavioral trends that would otherwise go unnoticed. Moreover, the fusion of AI and neuromarketing promotes ethical marketing practices. As marketers gain a deeper understanding of the consumer psyche, they can craft campaigns that not only attract attention but also respect individual autonomy and privacy. AI algorithms can help eliminate human bias in decision-making processes, promoting fairness and inclusivity in marketing initiatives.

In conclusion, the combination of neuromarketing and artificial intelligence is shaping the future of marketing by offering enhanced behavioral understanding, enabling deep personalization, improving the user experience, and raising important ethical considerations. As these technologies continue to evolve, marketers must strike a balance between innovation and responsibility. By leveraging the strengths of both AI and neuromarketing while adhering to ethical principles, businesses can build more meaningful relationships with consumers and achieve greater long-term success. This chapter underscores the transformative potential of this fusion and highlights its crucial role in defining futuristic marketing approaches.

SCOPE AND RELEVANCE OF STUDY

The integration of Artificial Intelligence (AI) with neuromarketing has expanded the scope of consumer behavior analysis by enabling real-time, emotion-driven insights. Neuromarketing tools such as EEG, fMRI, and eye-tracking capture subconscious reactions to marketing stimuli, while AI processes this complex data to uncover patterns that inform targeted strategies. The relevance lies in AI's ability to personalize marketing content, predict consumer behavior, and optimize campaigns based on emotional engagement. This results in more accurate decision-making and increased consumer satisfaction. Technologies like AR and NLP further extend this scope by offering immersive and interactive experiences, as demonstrated by IKEA's AR app that enhances purchase decisions. The combination of AI's analytical power with neuromarketing's emotional insights allows marketers to build stronger, more meaningful connections with consumers. As AI continues to evolve, its role in neuromarketing will become increasingly vital for businesses aiming to achieve customer-centric and emotionally resonant marketing outcomes

FUTURE IMPLICATION

For Marketers

AI-enhanced neuromarketing tools allow deep insights into consumer behavior, enabling highly targeted and personalized advertisements. However, marketers must remain honest and avoid exaggeration. Building trust is crucial, and any claims influenced by AI analysis should be accompanied by disclaimers if results may differ in practice.

For Policymakers

It is essential to establish clear ethical and legal frameworks governing AI-powered neuromarketing. These regulations should align with organizational SOPs and be validated by ethics committees and neuroscience experts. Special care must be taken to safeguard vulnerable groups such as children, the elderly, and those with health issues from undue psychological influence.

For Researchers

Ethical practices are equally vital. AI tools must not compromise consumer privacy or be used without informed consent. Researchers should avoid manipulating consumer responses and ensure that all neuromarketing techniques involving AI are pre-tested for safety and accuracy.

REFERENCES

Abdullah, M. S. (2025). Examining The Effect of AI-Powered Personalization on Customer Loyalty: A Meta-Analysis of E-Commerce Studies. *Review of Applied Science and Technology, 4*(02), 309–338. DOI: 10.63125/780spe97

Adeola, O., Evans, O., Ndubuisi Edeh, J., & Adisa, I. (2022). The future of marketing: artificial intelligence, virtual reality, and neuromarketing. *Marketing communications and brand development in emerging economies Volume I: Contemporary and future perspectives*, 253-280.

Agrawal, A., Gans, J. S., & Goldfarb, A. (2019). Artificial intelligence: The ambiguous labor market impact of automating prediction. *The Journal of Economic Perspectives, 33*(2), 31–50. DOI: 10.1257/jep.33.2.31

Alsharif, A. H., Salleh, N. Z. M., Al-Zahrani, S. A., & Khraiwish, A. (2022). Consumer behaviour to be considered in advertising: A systematic analysis and future agenda. *Behavioral Sciences (Basel, Switzerland), 12*(12), 472. DOI: 10.3390/bs12120472

Alsharif, A. H., Salleh, N. Z. M., Baharun, R. B., & Safaei, M. E. H. D. I. (2020). Neuromarketing approach: An overview and future research directions. *Journal of Theoretical and Applied Information Technology, 98*(7), 991–1001.

Alvino, L., Constantinides, E., & Franco, M. (2018). Towards a better understanding of consumer behavior: Marginal utility as a parameter in neuromarketing research. *International Journal of Marketing Studies, 10*(1), 90–106. DOI: 10.5539/ijms.v10n1p90

Anderson, R., & Wilson, S. (2017). AI-powered predictive analytics in customer retention strategies. *Journal of Business Analytics, 14*(3), 112–128.

Anoop, M. R. (2021). Artificial intelligence and marketing. *Turkish Journal of Computer and Mathematics Education, 12*(4), 1247–1256.

Babatunde, S. O., Odejide, O. A., Edunjobi, T. E., & Ogundipe, D. O.Sodiq Odetunde BabatundeOpeyemi Abayomi OdejideTolulope Esther EdunjobiDamilola Oluwaseun Ogundipe. (2024). The role of AI in marketing personalization: A theoretical exploration of consumer engagement strategies. *International Journal of Management & Entrepreneurship Research, 6*(3), 936–949. DOI: 10.51594/ijmer.v6i3.964

Bag, S., Gupta, S., Kumar, A., & Sivarajah, U. (2021). An integrated artificial intelligence framework for knowledge creation and B2B marketing rational decision making for improving firm performance. *Industrial Marketing Management, 92*, 178–189. DOI: 10.1016/j.indmarman.2020.12.001

Bakardjieva. E., & Kimmel. A (2017). Neuromarketing Research Practices: Attitudes, Ethics, and Behavioral Intentions. *ethics and Behavior,* 27 (3), 179-200.

Bansal, S., & Gupta, M. (2023). Towards using artificial intelligence in neuromarketing. In *Promoting consumer engagement through emotional branding and sensory marketing* (pp. 16–23). IGI Global.

Bhardwaj, C. (2025). *Artificial intelligence – Revamping user experience in mobile banking apps*. Retrieved from: https://appinventiv.com/blog/artificial-intelligence-revamping-user-experience-in-mobile-banking-apps/

Bhardwaj, S., Rana, G. A., Behl, A., & de Caceres, S. J. G. (2023). Exploring the boundaries of Neuromarketing through systematic investigation. *Journal of Business Research, 154*, 113371. DOI: 10.1016/j.jbusres.2022.113371

Biswas, K., & Patrab, G. (2023). Role of artificial intelligence (AI) in changing consumer buying behaviour. *Int. J. Res. Publ. Rev*, *4*(02), 943–951. DOI: 10.55248/gengpi.2023.4227

Boraston, Z., & Blakemore, S. J. (2007). The application of eye-tracking technology in the study of autism. *The Journal of Physiology*, *581*(3), 893–898. DOI: 10.1113/jphysiol.2007.133587

Boricean, V. (2009, November). Brief history of neuromarketing. In *ICEA–FAA. The International Conference on Economics and Administration* (pp. 14-15).

Brain Support. (2023). Religion Brain, Overt anf Covert Attention, Consciousness, Motivation, Emotion and Craving- TMS and Neuroscience, TMS Application, TMS EEG, EEG Microstates, NIRS and behavior. Retrieved from https://brainlatam.com/blog/religion-brain-overt-and-covert-attention-consciousness-motivation-emotion-and-craving-tms-and-neuroscience-tms-application-tms-eeg-eeg-microstates-nirs-and-behavior 4629?v=KrejFfh_4Sg&list=PLthhhS9Fdxp2ZdXvBiHERTymBN-1zyhvXT on 4th January, 2023.

Brown, A., & Jones, C. (2019). AI-driven Personalization: A Comprehensive Review. *Journal of Consumer Behaviour*, *12*(4), 567–580.

Capatina, A., Kachour, M., Lichy, J., Micu, A., Micu, A. E., & Codignola, F. (2020). Matching the future capabilities of an artificial intelligence-based software for social media marketing with potential users' expectations. *Technological Forecasting and Social Change*, *151*, 119794. DOI: 10.1016/j.techfore.2019.119794

Cenamor, J., Parida, V., & Wincent, J. (2019). How entrepreneurial SMEs compete through digital platforms: The roles of digital platform capability, network capability and ambidexterity. *Journal of Business Research, 100*, 196–206. DOI: 10.1016/j.jbusres.2019.03.035

Charron, S., Fuchs, A., & Oullier, O. (2008). Exploring brain activity in neuroeconomics. *Revue d'Économie Politique, 118*(1), 97–124. DOI: 10.3917/redp.181.0097

Chi-Hsien, K., & Nagasawa, S. (2019). Applying machine learning to market analysis: Knowing your luxury consumer. *Journal of Management Analytics, 6*(4), 404–419. DOI: 10.1080/23270012.2019.1692254

Costa, J., Freitas, C., & Paiva, T. (2016). Brain imaging during advertising: A neuromarketing study of sound and pictures. *The Marketing Review, 15*(4), 405–422. DOI: 10.1362/146934715X14503490535 94

Crespo-Pereira, V., Martínez-Fernández, V. A., & Campos-Freire, F. (2017). Neuroscience for Content Innovation on European Public Service Broadcasters. *Comunicar: Media Education Research Journal, 25*(52), 9–18. DOI: 10.3916/C52-2017-01

Cruz, C. M. L., Medeiros, J. F. D., Hermes, L. C. R., Marcon, A., & Marcon, É. (2016). Neuromarketing and the advances in the consumer behaviour studies: A systematic review of the literature. *International Journal of Business and Globalisation, 17*(3), 330–351. DOI: 10.1504/IJBG.2016.078842

Darázs, T. (2024). The role of artificial intelligence in neuromarketing: A comparative analysis of AI-driven and traditional methods. *Marketing and Management Identity*, 70.

Davenport, T., Guha, A., Grewal, D., & Bressgott, T. (2020). How artificial intelligence will change the future of marketing. *Journal of the Academy of Marketing Science, 48*(1), 24–42. DOI: 10.1007/s11747-019-00696-0

Dooley, R. (2025). MEG Scanner Use Rising. Retrieved from https://www.neurosciencemarketing.com/blog/articles/meg-scanner-use-rising.html

Eser, Z., Isin, F., & Tolon, M. (2011). Perceptions of marketing academics, neurologists, and marketing professionals about Neuromarketing. Journal of Marketing Management, 27 (7- 8), 854-868.

Fisher, C. E., Chin, L., & Klitzman, R. (2010). Defining neuromarketing: Practices and professional challenges. *Harvard Review of Psychiatry, 18*(4), 230–237. DOI: 10.3109/10673229.2010.496623

Gajić, J. (2023). Advanced technologies as a framework for sustainable marketing campaigns (AI application in neuromarketing). In *Sinteza 2023-International Scientific Conference on Information Technology, Computer Science, and Data Science* (pp. 180-184). Singidunum University.

Gakhal, B., & Senior, C. (2008). Examining the influence of fame in the presence of beauty: An electrodermal 'neuromarketing' study. *Journal of Consumer Behaviour, 7*(4-5), 331–341. DOI: 10.1002/cb.255

Garcia, A., & Rodriguez, M. (2019). AI-powered Marketing Automation: A Case Study of Successful Implementation. *Journal of Interactive Marketing*, *30*(4), 301–315.

Garcia, J. R., & Saad, G. (2008). Evolutionary neuromarketing: Darwinizing the neuroimaging paradigm for consumer behavior. *Journal of Consumer Behaviour, 7*(4-5), 397–414. DOI: 10.1002/cb.259

Gheorghe, C. M., Purcărea, V. L., & Gheorghe, I. R. (2023). Using eye-tracking technology in Neuromarketing. *Romanian Journal of Ophthalmology*, *67*(1), 2.

Guixeres, J., Bigné, E., Ausin Azofra, J. M., Alcaniz Raya, M., Colomer Granero, A., Fuentes Hurtado, F., & Naranjo Ornedo, V. (2017). Consumer neuroscience-based metrics predict recall, liking and viewing rates in online advertising. *Frontiers in Psychology*, *8*, 1808. DOI: 10.3389/fpsyg.2017.01808

Gupta, Y. (2024). *Chatbot marketing: A definitive guide*. Retrieved April 30, 2025, from https://www.zoho.com/blog/salesiq/chatbot-for-marketing.html

Hakan, B. O. Z. (2018). *Emotion extraction from facial expressions by using artificial intelligence techniques*. BRAIN–Broad Research in Artificial Intelligence and Neuroscience.

Haleem, A., Javaid, M., Qadri, M. A., Singh, R. P., & Suman, R. (2022). Artificial intelligence (AI) applications for marketing: A literature-based study. *International Journal of intelligent networks, 3*, 119-132.

Harris, J. M., Ciorciari, J., & Gountas, J. (2018). Consumer neuroscience for marketing researchers. *Journal of Consumer Behaviour*, *17*(3), 239–252. DOI: 10.1002/cb.1710

Huang, M. H., & Rust, R. T. (2021). A strategic framework for artificial intelligence in marketing. *Journal of the Academy of Marketing Science*, *49*(1), 30–50. DOI: 10.1007/s11747-020-00749-9

Imtiaz, F. (2024). Neuromarketing techniques Used by Brands. Retrived from https://www.linkedin.com/pulse/neuromarketing-techniques-used-brands-farhat-imtiaz-uqwpf/ on March 18, 2024.

Ishtiaque, F., Mashrur, F. R., Miya, M. T. I., Rahman, K. M., Vaidyanathan, R., Anwar, S. F., Sarker, F., & Mamun, K. A. A. (2023). AI-based consumers' preference prediction using a research-grade BCI and a commercial-grade BCI for neuromarketing: A systematic comparison. 2023 *International Conference on Electrical, Computer and Communication Engineering (ECCE),* 1-6.

Jiménez-Marín, G., Alvarado, M. D. M. R., & González-Oñate, C. (2022). Application of sensory marketing techniques at marengo, a small sustainable men's fashion store in Spain: Based on the hulten, broweus and van Dijk model. *Sustainability (Basel), 14*(19), 12547. DOI: 10.3390/su141912547

Johnson, M., & Williams, S. (2017). Data analytics in marketing: Challenges and opportunities. *Journal of Marketing Analytics, 19*(1), 78–92.

Kahneman, D. (2011). *Thinking, Fast and Slow*. Farrar, Straus and Giroux.

Kartajaya, H., Kotler, P., & Hooi, D. H. (2019). Marketing 4.0: moving from traditional to digital. *World Scientific Book Chapters*, 99-123.

Kaur, S., & Sharma, R. (2021, July). Emotion AI: integrating emotional intelligence with artificial intelligence in the digital workplace. In *Innovations in Information and Communication Technologies (IICT-2020) Proceedings of International Conference on ICRIHE-2020, Delhi, India: IICT-2020* (pp. 337-343). Cham: Springer International Publishing. DOI: 10.1007/978-3-030-66218-9_39

Kim, S., & Park, J. (2019). Voice search optimization: Strategies for marketers. *Journal of Digital Marketing, 21*(3), 112–128.

Kottier, W. G. (2014). *The added value of neuromarketing tools in the area of marketing research* (Bachelor's thesis, University of Twente).

Krishanan, M. M., Dhinakaran, D. P., & Rajalakshmi, M. (2023). Consumer purchase behavior towards Patanjali products in Chennai. *INFOKARA Research, 12*(3), 21–27.

Kumar, A. (2024, April 15). *AI for personalized marketing: Delivering targeted experiences to customers*. Retrieved from https://www.linkedin.com/pulse/ai-personalized-marketing-delivering-targeted-customer-aditya-kumar-4cytc

Kumar, H., Mathur, N., & Jauhari, S. (2017). Consumer's perception towards neuromarketing in India with special reference to Kano model. *International Journal of Research–Granthaalayah, 5*(4), 135–142. DOI: 10.29121/granthaalayah.v5.i4.2017.1803

Kumar, P., Chowdhury, S., Madhavedi, S., & Lakshminarayana, K. (2024). Role of neuromarketing and artificial intelligence in futuristic marketing approach: An empirical study. *Journal of Informatics Education and Research, 4*(2), 560–567.

Kumar, V., & Garg, M. L. (2018). Predictive analytics: A review of trends and techniques. *International Journal of Computer Applications, 182*(1), 31–37. DOI: 10.5120/ijca2018917434

Lindstrom, M. B. (2008). *Truth and lies about why we buy*. Crown Business.

Loudon, D. L., & Della Bitta, A. J. (1993). *Consumer Behaviour: Concepts and Applications* (4th ed.). McGraw-Hill.

Luminita, D. (2023, March 27). *The role of AR and VR in marketing: How to create immersive experiences for your customers.* Retrieved from https://www.linkedin.com/pulse/role-ar-vr-marketing-how-create-immersive-experiences-lumi-done

Marshall, C. (2025). *Deep learning vs. machine learning: A complete guide*. Retrieved from https://www.zendesk.com/sg/blog/machine-learning-and-deep-learning/

Meshram, E. P., Bhambulkar, R., Pokale, P., Kharbikar, K., & Awachat, A. (2021). Automatic detection of fake profile using machine learning on instagram. *international journal of scientific research in science and technology, 8*(1), 117-127.

Muñoz-Leiva, F., Hernández-Méndez, J., & Gómez-Carmona, D. (2019). Measuring advertising effectiveness in Travel 2.0 websites through eye-tracking technology. *Physiology & Behavior, 200*, 83–95. DOI: 10.1016/j.physbeh.2018.03.002

Murthy, D., Gross, A., & McGarry, M. (2016). Visual social media and big data. Interpreting Instagram images posted on Twitter. *Digital Culture & Society, 2*(2), 113–134. DOI: 10.14361/dcs-2016-0208

Ndiku, A. C., Ghedira-Chkir, R., Khalifa, A. B., & Dogui, M. (2022, May). Electroencephalography signal classification for automatic interpretation of electroencephalogram based on Artificial Intelligence. In *2022 8th International Conference on Control, Decision and Information Technologies (CoDIT)* (Vol. 1, pp. 636-640). IEEE. DOI: 10.1109/CoDIT55151.2022.9803951

Nesamoney, D. (2015). *Personalized digital advertising: How data and technology are transforming how we market.* Pearson Education.

Neurorelay (2016). Eye Tracking in Neuromarketing Research. Retrieved from http://neurorelay.com/2016/09/11/eye-tracking-in-neuromarketing-research/ on 11th September, 2016.

Niranjan, K., Narayana, K. S., & Rao, M. N. (2021, January). Role of artifical intelligence in logistics and supply chain. In *2021 international conference on computer communication and informatics (ICCCI)* (pp. 1-3). IEEE. DOI: 10.1109/ICCCI50826.2021.9402625

OneWelbeck. (n.d.). *Private EEG (Electroencephalograms)* [Photograph]. Retrieved from https://onewelbeck.com/tests-diagnostics/eeg-electroencephalography/

Park, H., & Kang, M. (2016). AI and human collaboration: A framework for future research. *JMR, Journal of Marketing Research, 33*(1), 45–58.

Peltier, J. W., Dahl, A. J., & Schibrowsky, J. A. (2024). Artificial intelligence in interactive marketing: A conceptual framework and research agenda. *Journal of Research in Interactive Marketing, 18*(1), 54–90. DOI: 10.1108/JRIM-01-2023-0030

Plassmann, H., Ambler, T., Braeutigam, S., & Kenning, P. (2007). What can advertisers learn from neuroscience? *International Journal of Advertising, 26*(2), 151–175. DOI: 10.1080/10803548.2007.11073005

Rajdhar, M. P. S., and Brahme, M. M. (2020). Artificial Intelligence AI Influence is Changing Consumer Buying Behavior in Online Shopping. *JournalNX*, 169-172.

Ruanguttamanun, C. (2014). Neuromarketing: I put myself into a fMRI scanner and realized that I love Louis Vuitton ads. *Procedia: Social and Behavioral Sciences, 148*, 211–218. DOI: 10.1016/j.sbspro.2014.07.036

Shah, P., & Shukla, A. N. (2022). Artificial Intelligence for Natural Intelligence. In *Artificial Intelligence for Societal Development and Global Well-Being* (pp. 22–42). IGI Global Scientific Publishing. DOI: 10.4018/978-1-6684-2443-8.ch002

Shaip. (2025, March 26). *What is NLP? How it works, benefits, challenges, examples*. Retrieved from https://www.shaip.com/blog/what-is-nlp-how-it-works-benefits-challenges-examples/

Smith, J. (2018). The role of artificial intelligence in marketing strategies. *JMR, Journal of Marketing Research, 25*(3), 112–130.

Smolic, H. (2024). *What is predictive analytics in marketing and how can it help?* Retrieved from https://graphite-note.com/predictive-analytics-in-marketing/

Stasi, A., Songa, G., Mauri, M., Ciceri, A., Diotallevi, F., Nardone, G., & Russo, V. (2018). Neuromarketing empirical approaches and food choice: A systematic review. *Food Research International, 108*, 650–664. DOI: 10.1016/j.foodres.2017.11.049

Taylor, R., & White, L. (2020). Chatbots and virtual assistants: Revolutionizing customer interactions. *Harvard Business Review, 38*(2), 45–60.

Varghese, P. (2022). Neuromarketing and artificial intelligence for effective future business. *IUJ Journal of Management*, *1*(1), 240–254.

Vehlen, A., Spenthof, I., Tönsing, D., Heinrichs, M., & Domes, G. (2021). Evaluation of an eye tracking setup for studying visual attention in face-to-face conversations. *Scientific Reports*, *11*(1), 2661. DOI: 10.1038/s41598-021-81987-x

Yadava, M., Kumar, P., Saini, R., Roy, P. P., & Prosad Dogra, D. (2017). Analysis of EEG signals and its application to Neuromarketing. *Multimedia Tools and Applications*, *76*(18), 19087–19111. DOI: 10.1007/s11042-017-4580-6

Chapter 9
Neuro-Optimization and Revolutionizing Product and Ad Design Using AI

T. Venkat Narayana Rao
http://orcid.org/0000-0002-1996-1819
Sreenidhi Institute of Science and Technology, India

G. Harsha Vardhan Reddy
Sreenidhi Institute of Science and Technology, India

K. Siva Kumar Gowda
http://orcid.org/0009-0004-8957-0276
Sreenidhi Institute of Science and Technology, India

B. Sujith Kumar
Sreenidhi Institute of Science and Technology, India

ABSTRACT

Neuro-optimization is altering the approach towards product or ad design by blending neuromarketing and artificial intelligence (AI). AI is once again revolutionizing how brands communicate with consumers by enhancing ways of measuring feelings and metrics, enhancing response capture. Real-time design optimisation enables efficient advertisement, product and experience prototyping and improvement. Brands employ AI features like content split testing to influence the cognitive and emotional experiences of its audience to promote better UX. In its future, AI neuro-optimization can present a level of personalization and emotional appeal in the marketing exposure to customers which will be higher.The application of AI in relations to marketing is expected to keep advancing which means that ethical approaches to innovation will

DOI: 10.4018/979-8-3373-1152-4.ch009

be the key to sustainable client relations and trust. This chapter focus on how AI advances works when granting consumers an opportunity to be evaluated instantly and allows for changes to be made in real-time.

1. INTRODUCTION

The fast evolution of the artificial intelligence (AI) has had a massive impact on the modern marketing practices, especially with regard to product designing, advertising, and consumer interaction. Data-driven technologies are becoming more important in organizations that need to know their consumers, their feelings, decisions, etc. In this regard, neuromarketing has become a significant practice that incorporates the findings of consumer psychology and neuroscience into the study of the subconscious responses of consumers to marketing stimuli. In conjunction with AI, neuromarketing helps marketers to go beyond the conventional survey-based approaches and have real-time insights on consumer behavior in a more in-depth way. Marketing research methods based on conventional methods would tend to rely on self-reported information, which might not be a complete representation of the emotional responses, focus tendencies, and unconscious decision making. The AI-based neuromarketing overcomes these drawbacks through eye-tracking, facial expression analysis, electroencephalography (EEG), and biometric data which objectively quantifies consumer responses. Artificial intelligence improves these methods by running large amounts of behavioral and emotional data, finding patterns, and creating advertising and product design strategies to be optimized in real-time. Theoretically speaking, AI-based neuromarketing is based on known provisions of consumer psychology and neuroscience, specifically, theories of emotion, attention, memory, and perception. These bases are enhanced by AI which deciphers intricate psychological and neurological cues into practical marketing data that aids in personalised and adaptive promoting approaches. Nevertheless, ethical issues associated with privacy of data, biasing of algorithms, transparency, and consent of consumers become more relevant because of the growing application of AI-based neuromarketing.

This chapter combines theory and practice of consumer psychology and neuroscience with neuroscience as well as practical applications of AI-driven neuromarketing. It discusses the improvement of emotional intelligence, optimization of real-time design, and individual marketing plans using AI and also touches on both ethical and managerial issues. The chapter is intended to give the audience a balanced perspective on the opportunities and challenges that the use of AI-driven neuromarketing presents to contemporary advertising and consumer engagement.

1.1 Understanding Neuro-Optimization in Marketing

Neuro-optimization processes enable the evaluation of neuroscience and artificial intelligence neural interactions for building elite marketing strategies. Through Neuromarketing techniques including brain functional tracking with eye movement tracking and emotional response analysis the neuro-optimization process serves as an important detection method to guide customer behaviour during shopping (Alsharif & Mohd Isa, 2024). The application of artificial intelligence systems delivers important data which enables marketers to build targeted marketing campaigns that affect both intellectual and emotional responses of consumers.

1.2 The Role of AI in Enhancing Consumer Engagement

Behaviour analytics functions precisely because of AI algorithms operating inside computer systems. Recent processing software operatings on digital platforms conducts real-time monitoring of data collection while following patterns which bypass typical survey techniques and focus groups. Businesses gain advanced advertising capabilities by using system-based user behaviour analytics to track purchasing behaviours. Using data analytics in combination helps companies quickly make product modifications that lead to better effective marketing strategies. Large-scale personalized content delivery functions as the primary benefit AI systems offer to businesses in their marketing strategies (Sung, et al.,2021). Artificial intelligence constructs personal promotional choices and recommendation plans through processing integrated internet user data from website activities combined with social media behavior and previous network associations. Customized content distribution through technology promotes elevated consumer pleasure and higher conversion rates since the presented material specifically appeals to individual preferences.

1.3 Shaping the future of marketing

AI marketing applications will expand further because of their strategic integration. Technology that tracks customer emotional states with cognitive feedback patterns will advance the development path for improved interaction solutions. The benefits of AI technology create significant ethical concerns about data protection and AI discrimination and the development of control systems. The resolution of identified problems between ethical AI-driven neuromarketing and consumer-friendly practices remains necessary to protect their ethical conduct. Neuro-optimization technology together with AI offers marketing complete consumer insights paired with established strategies to reach potential clients. Artificial intelligence allows brands to monitor current data to design custom content platforms which improve their emotional marketing approach. Businesses must develop equitable measures so innovation harmonizes with ethical standards for developing ethical marketing practices which protect consumer transparency and trust.

2. AI IN CONSUMER BEHAVIOUR ANALYSIS

Artificial Intelligence applications provide businesses with novel approaches to interpret their customer activities. Prior research based on historical data and surveys and focus groups yielded unpredictable findings when businesses studied consumer behavior which demanded long periods of time for analyzing data. The present-day AI system speeds up data interpretation through analytical methods applied to various kinds of digital exchange signals and biological signals and purchasing data. Businesses deploy improved operational capabilities to analyze customer choices combined with emotional responses along with decision-making processes for developing targeted marketing strategies.

2.1 How AI Collects and Analyses Consumer Data

The techniques allow big data processing and machine learning to analyze platform activities that stem from system collection data. Numerous machine learning algorithms produce behavioral predictions through data analysis of surfing data with social media profiles and search logs and transaction records. Modern NLP processing technology within artificial intelligence enables systems to extract customer feedback from product reviews which provides brands with insights about public reactions to their products.

Neuromarketing tools function within artificial intelligence-enabled electronic systems that merge frontal electroencephalography devices which monitor brain activities with prefrontal cortex electroencephalography devices (Ferm, et al.,2022). Systems that recognize facial patterns and track eye activity enable detection of automatic customer reactions through their combination. Brand materials found in interactive marketing locations lead customers to exhibit emotional responses. AI assistance enables marketers to obtain verbal feedback and neurological signals for developing marketing strategies that meet cognitive and psychological customer needs.

2.2 Real-Time Feedback and Adaptive Marketing

AI provides real-time feedback as its greatest tool for consumer behavior analysis. AI Analytics delivers faster feedback than traditional marketing analytics since data reports take long periods to generate. Product adaptation occurs dynamically because this ability lets businesses hear feedback directly from users who encounter their marketing operations.

Electronic commerce platforms make use of AI components which monitor both website paths and purchasing habits of their customers. Users who repeatedly view particular items on the platform will get personalized recommendations and discount offers from AI systems through retargeted advertising to increase chances of conversion. The analysis from AI technology enables Netflix and Spotify to generate customized content recommendations that will prevent users from stopping their consumption.

AI produces valuable consumer insights by evaluating varied marketing tests that take place during A/B testing. Robotized testing processes get replaced through AI-driven methods which detect the best combinations of ad visuals and headlines and call-to actions that generate maximum outcomes for each audience subgroup. The automated optimization speed increases simultaneously with better marketing decision accuracy levels reached through automated processes.

2.3 The Impact of AI on Consumer Experience

Organizations apply AI-powered discussions about their customers to create personalized content which improves user satisfaction. The immediate assistance of artificial intelligence software allows users to get product suggestions that boost their satisfaction during their interactions (Ameen, et al.,2021). Customers build stronger brand loyalty through AI-based personalization since they receive personalized care while generating better commercial results.

The use of artificial intelligence for analysis fails to deliver marketing benefits because customer privacy and security concerns arise when processing personal information. Data processing requires absolute agency and fulfills mandatory transparency requirements as well as necessary compliance with legal data protection regulations.

3. REAL-TIME DESIGN OPTIMIZATION

Real-time design optimization emerges as a groundbreaking marketing principle that Artificial Intelligence (AI) introduced into marketing operations. The AI-based dynamic system enables brand transformation of advertising materials that include packaging and UX designs through tracking consumer trends. Real-time optimization using AI allows businesses to speed up their decision process because AI enhances design development speed through testing and revision when customers engage with their products.

3.1 How AI Facilitates Real-Time Design Optimization

AI tools evaluate design characteristics through the analysis of extensive database information that identifies what customers prefer. The tracking of emotional user behaviors in real-time uses machine learning algorithms that analyze behaviors for engagement identification purposes. The processing system integrates website data with social activity records and biometric data and eye-tracking sensor readings to modify website color schemes as well as structural components together with text elements and communication types. Different advertisement versions undergo testing through AI software which enables immediate identification of the version that creates consumer engagement. AI systems produce automatic content transformation through the winning aspects discovered in exceptional advertising materials (Gyory et al., 2022). Companies can use targeted marketing content to reduce consumer uncertainties by providing precise behaviors to their target markets.

3.2 AI in Ad and Product Design Optimization

Advertising is hugely promoted and AI driven real time optimization with small change in design will effect audience's response. The analytics system of dynamic ad optimization tools adjusts every aspect of the ad including graphics content and placement location through live user feedback. As an example of this, AI can spot emotional reactions of viewers watching an ad and change the elements of it like background colours, product placement or call to action button to make it more appealing.

Artificial Intelligence solutions perform optimization tasks for product design practices. Companies may use AI to derive knowledge from customer's interactions with prototypes, and adjust the particular features based on it (Gao et al., 2023). For instance, heat maps generated via technologies powered by AI track where the users are focusing on the website or packaging design to enable the designers to make these adjustments based on the insights, so it can be made more user-friendly and visually appealing. Through repetitive procedure companies can maintain products and advertisements that stay current so they maximize their ability to reach target audiences.

3.3 Personalization Through AI-Based Testing

Artificial intelligence in A/B and multivariate testing enables brands to create distinct experiences, catering to different segments of their consumer base, in the process. This strategy includes fielding simultaneous different design variations and measuring success for different user groups. Underneath conventional testing, it usually takes weeks for data to be fed back, but AI delivers in just a number of seconds and brands can change things on the go.

Take an online retailer, for instance. Product pages are personalized depending on the actions registered by the client immediately in an online store. If this consumer seems to return to a particular set of products, AI adjusts the display of such products on the website so as to improve the experience while shopping. In much the same way, targeted email campaigns make real-time optimization employable by AIs to customize the subject lines, images, and offers aligned with the individual's interests.

3.4 Challenges and Ethical Considerations

Real-time design optimization provides pragmatic advantages alongside growing concerns in data privacy and algorithmic bias. While AI uses consumer data for design solutions, this may lead to ethical dilemmas in the organizational structure with no regulations in place overseeing the matter at hand. To maintain consumer trust, brands must enforce transparency regarding data collection and follow ethical regulations. The over-dependence on AI-driven design would in turn, stifle human creativity in producing less-original marketing contents.

Thus, real-time design optimization will be quite important for brands to create highly engaging personalized experiences while ethically managing their ascent with the advancement in marketing. These concerns are discussed in detail in Section 6.

3.5 AI-Driven Advertising vs Traditional Advertising Design

The conventional methods of creating an advertisement include using intuition, reference to previous advertising campaigns and conducting focus groups or using surveys after the advertisement has run are time-consuming, expensive and have difficulty assessing the consumer response to the advertisement in real time.

AI-based advertisement design allows for continuous improvement through the ongoing assessment of consumer behaviour, feelings/emotions and engagement metrics, and through the adaptive nature of AI system can change the visual design or message at any given moment during the run of the advertisement based on what it learns. Unlike static advertisements produced through traditional methods, AI-based advertisement design are adaptive, personalised, dynamic, data-influenced and therefore generate a greater response from consumers.

Compared to traditional advertisements, AI offers a new means of creating advertisements. By making it possible to continue the improvement of advertising campaigns while the campaigns are being run, AI has enhanced not only the speed and the accuracy of creating advertisements, but also changed the way that advertising campaigns are created from a reactive methodology to one focused on proactive improvement.

4. AI-BASED CONTENT TESTING AND PERSONALIZATION

Personalization has evolved into a key building block in modern digital marketing ushering in a new era of Artificial Intelligence (AI) in customer interaction. AI-powered personalization gives business firms an opportunity to look through the mine of customer data, including browsing history, purchasing behaviors, and social media interactions helping them to deliver the most relevant content. AI makes use of real-time insight, automation, and machine learning for predicting the needs of customers, broadcasting personalized advertisements, fine-tuning product recommendations, and elevating user experiences. This highly targeted approach would dramatically upsurge engagement and customer satisfaction and greatly boost conversion rates as well as brand loyalty.

4.1 How AI Enhances Personalized Marketing

The pool of consumer data refers to anything, from browsing history to the actual purchasing patterns, attitude on social interactions through social media, and demographics can be analyzed with Artificial Intelligence-aided tool that's geared to create bespoke marketing strategies. Personalized marketing-enabled by AI, offers the basic premise that mass marketing is no longer a viable option compared to personalization-it's relevant to the individual.

The algorithms train on the evidence stream and learn which parts of that collaboration to focus on and build a summary of that value-added feature through the social interaction of behaviour (Iyelolu et al.,2024). The recommendation engines of Netflix and Amazon collect user preference data in order to recommend movies or products in real time, guaranteeing that the most relevant recommendations will be linked to recent consumer activity regarding the product.

With the help of Natural Language Processing, AI can provide personalized interactions with the clients through understanding customer sentiment and structure of language. NLP is the backbone of chatbots and virtual assistants that personalize the answers and in fact give those interactions a modicum of humanity and warmth. This enhances personalization and greatly augments customer experience and solidifies brand loyalty.

4.2 AI-Driven A/B Testing and Content Optimization

AI-based A/B test and content optimization tools help personalization in their own way in marketing campaigns. A/B testing traditionally involved the maneuver whereby two versions of an ad, email, or website are presented to a certain percentage of the audience to determine which of the two was more effective. While it was imagined to be a manual task, AI automates the task to instantly calculate multiple variations of content alternative options for the marketing campaign from the onset.

AI can analyse how individual emails have been opened and clicked on in real-time and create reports accordingly so that email marketing campaigns run more effectively (Iyer et al.,2020). High engagement with an email may come from a particular subject line or call to action, so the artificial intelligence can make adjustments for further emails to be sent out going forward in accordance with what yielded favorable results during the phase of testing. This offers a guarantee that marketing content remains optimized for effect. AI-run dynamic content generation allows for personalized advertisements to be created by brands. AI on various platforms, such as Google Ads and Facebook Ads, customizes the actual ad copy, visual content, and placement based on individual user conduct. This way, consumers will be seeing ads that speak to their preferences, thereby maximizing the likelihood of engagement and conversion.

4.3 Personalization in E-Commerce and Customer Experience

AI-powered personalization diverts the shopping experience into a whole new dimension. Employing the right tricks, online retailers recommend products based on previous purchases, search engine history, and shopper behavior in real-time. A personalized homepage, personalized discount messages, and soon-to-be AI-powered chat support will enable an easy and enjoyable shopping experience.

In addition, hyper-personalization of pricing strategies for brands is also being done by AI-assisted techniques based on consumer behavior and market trends such as consumer demand and competitor pricing. This gives brands the capability to offer personalized discounts or to do dynamic pricing wherein everybody is catered for separately.

4.4 Ethical Considerations in AI-Driven Personalization

Many benefits, but this in turn raises critical questions in the arena of ethicality involving consequent challenges to the data privacy and possible manipulation of consumers. AI personalization needs heaps of data from users to provide them with good usability. If data isn't handled responsibly, it can amount to disproportionate attacks on the rights of users; besides this, personalization can be very intrusive, thus endangering heavy brand reliance.

Allaying fears would require the development of transparency around data collection, giving users direct authority over their data, as well as observance of established practices for ethical AI development. The perfect amount that assures consumer trust and brand loyalty is then measured between personalization and privacy.

5. CASE STUDIES: AI IN NEUROMARKETING

AI will totally change neuromarketing; from highly compelling ads to the appeal of product packaging to lessening of overall customer experiences. Coca-Cola, Nike, and PepsiCo have all successfully championed AI-driven neuromarketing to increase consumer engagement and boost sales. AI automates marketing strategies through real-time data study, machine learning, and automation, allowing brands to personalize their marketing strategies, predict consumer behaviors, and reach consumers on an emotional level; these developments are generally designed to help businesses build better campaigns, resonating with the audience in a manner which does, in the end, improve renown and conversion rate.

5.1 Coca-Cola: AI-Powered Consumer Engagement

Coca-Cola has always been one step ahead of their marketing innovation through artificial intelligence in order to cover both consumer audiences and cope with emotionally-driven ads. To understand people's emotional feelings expressed through social media interactions, the firm conducts AI-powered sentiment analysis, thus being able to modify branding strategies on real time. This keeps Coke's marketing campaigns fresh and relevant in tune with the changing needs of customers.

Coca-Cola continues to experiment with AI and image recognition to analyse consumer-generated content (Deshmukh et al.,2025). Through analysis of the millions of images shared on social media, Coca-Cola uses this technology to track trends and themes, and determine brand sentiments. Such analyses enable Coca-Cola to create its marketing strategies along with the trends that would cater to consumer preferences.

Another important secretive project remaining to be underway by Coke under the AI wing is the inhalation into predictive analysis for product development. AI analyzes huge data sets to find flavor trends much before any products are released with regard to variations in consumer tastes. All of these elements help in ensuring the successful introduction of a drink to the target market, an exercise that proves turning to maximum brand loyalty.

5.2 Nike: AI-Driven Personalized Marketing

Nike integrated AI into its marketing and sales processes in a seamless manner, engendering a personalized marketing campaign through machine learning according to personal likes of consumers. An enormously spurred AI-based recommendation agent suggests goods for selection on the grounds of customer behavior, earlier purchases, and browsing history. Such in-depth personalization helps the client with product suggestions that probably suit their interests, thereby enhancing the shopping experience.

Nike's AI-led programs do not take a break when it gets to digital marketing. The company uses artificial intelligence augmented by augmented reality, this is the Nike Fits app that has made it very much easier for its customers to find the correct size by simply placing the foot in front of the camera of a smartphone. This greatly boosts customer satisfaction as it reduces return costs for both the company and the customer.

Nike employs AI in predictive marketing, whereby machine learning algorithms analyze the data of millions of customers. The insights generated from the analysis allow them to release the correct products at the right time so that the marketing campaigns coincide with movements in consumer demand. With an analysis of real-time consumer data, Nike has geared highly targeted interactive advertisements toward the possibility of raising engagement and sales.

Nike further goes in for AI-supported dynamic content generation of digital advertisements. Scaffolding systems for determining individual customer needs are used; AI simultaneously monitors user interactions, changing ads, images, messages, and offers in real-time in order to cater more aptly to different preferences. Such approaches allow Nike to run more effective ads and foster a stronger relationship with consumers.

5.3 PepsiCo: AI in Product Packaging and Advertisement Optimization

PepsiCo leverages neuromarketing with the help of artificial intelligence to improve its product packaging and advertising strategies. It is all about using AI-based tracking technology to measure consumers' attention and emotional responses to various packaging designs. With these data, PepsiCo can create some eye-catching packaging that could grab the consumers' attention at a glance and incite the purchase urge.

AI enables PepsiCo to employ machine-learning algorithms to amalgamate clues gleaned from social media and web views from all over, and the websites illustrating customer perceptions into their marketing strategies (Brooks et al.,2022). The data addition allows for changing directions based on influence and preference.

PepsiCo also employs AI-powered A/B testing for ad optimization. Typical A/B tests would set up single ads against each other in a one-on-one competition. A/B testing traditionally produces insight into a specific ad that performed better but only one at a time. On the other hand, AI takes A/B testing several notches higher, processing many versions of the ads in parallel. It can take the best-performing ad version with the most engagement, targeting different segments of the audience to maximize ad engagement and conversions.

5.4 Key Takeaways from AI-Driven Neuromarketing

The Coca-Cola, Nike, and PepsiCo case studies show how AI is revolutionizing the marketing world with deep consumer insights, real-time personalization, and ad optimization. AI-driven strategies allow brands to predict consumer behavior, personalize messaging, and enhance user experience, resulting in increased engagement and increased sales.

As AI technology continues to advance, more and more brands will incorporate advanced neuromarketing techniques into their marketing plans. But businesses will also need to address ethical concerns such as data privacy and algorithmic bias to make AI-driven personalization transparent, fair, and consumer-friendly. By finding the right balance between innovation and ethics, AI-driven neuromarketing will further shape the future of advertising and consumer engagement.

6. ETHICAL CONSIDERATIONS IN AI-DRIVEN NEUROMARKETING

With Artificial Intelligence (AI) leading the field of neuromarketing, ethical issues are piling up. AI enables brands to create highly customized, data-driven advertising campaigns that achieve greater consumer engagement and optimal advertising ROI. It does this at the expense of generating actual issues in the shape of privacy intrusion, data security threat, algorithmic bias, and consumer manipulation. Ethical use of AI is the key to maintaining consumer confidence, protecting user information, and preventing exploitative ads. Transparency, fairness, and responsibility are the cornerstones to maintain ethical balance between innovation and responsible use of AI in advertising.

- Data Privacy and Consumer Consent
- Algorithmic Bias and Fairness

- Consumer Manipulation and Emotional Exploitation
- Transparency and Responsible AI Governance

6.1 Privacy and Data Security Risks

One of the biggest ethical issues in AI powered neuromarketing is consumer data privacy. AI systems use vast amounts of personal data, biometric data, online behaviour, purchase history and social media activity to tailor marketing. But collection and use of this data raises questions of consent and security.

Many consumers don't know how their data is being used and that's a violation of their privacy rights (Yadav et al.,2024). Companies must have transparent data collection practices, get explicit user consent and comply with data protection laws like GDPR and CCPA. AI driven marketing should prioritize consumer data protection to prevent unauthorized access and misuse.

Also there's the risk of data breaches where sensitive consumer info may be exposed or exploited by hackers. Businesses must have strong cybersecurity measures like encryption and multi factor authentication to protect consumer data.

6.2 AI Bias and Fairness in Marketing

AI algorithms are only as unbiased as the data they are trained on. If AI models are trained on historically biased datasets, they can reinforce and amplify those biases, leading to discriminatory marketing practices. For example, an AI system trained on biased data may target ads disproportionately based on age, gender, race, or socio-economic status, potentially leading to unfair or exclusionary marketing strategies.

To combat bias in AI-driven marketing, companies must focus on:

- Diverse and representative training data: Ensuring AI models are trained on inclusive datasets that reflect diverse consumer demographics.
- Regular audits of AI systems: Conducting fairness assessments to detect and eliminate biases in algorithmic decision-making.
- Ethical AI frameworks: Implementing responsible AI principles that promote fairness, inclusivity, and equal treatment of all consumers.

6.3 Consumer Manipulation and Ethical Advertising

AI's ability to analyse emotions, predict behaviours, and personalize content raises concerns about consumer manipulation. By using neuromarketing techniques such as facial recognition and sentiment analysis, brands can craft highly persuasive advertisements that exploit human psychology (Danciu, 2014). While this can enhance user engagement, it also poses ethical risks if used to deceive or pressure consumers into making impulsive decisions.

For instance, AI-driven dynamic pricing models may adjust prices based on consumer behavior, charging different customers different prices for the same product. Similarly, overly aggressive personalization can create hyper-targeted ads that manipulate users into unnecessary purchases.

To ensure ethical AI advertising, companies should:

- Adopt transparent marketing practices that inform consumers about how AI influences their experiences.
- Avoid excessive psychological targeting that pressures consumers into making irrational purchasing decisions.
- Promote ethical advertising standards that balance personalization with consumer well-being.

6.4 Regulatory Frameworks and the Future of Ethical AI in Neuromarketing

As AI-driven marketing continues to evolve, governments and regulatory bodies are implementing stricter guidelines to ensure ethical AI use. Organizations like the European Union (EU) and the Federal Trade Commission (FTC) are developing regulations to prevent AI misuse in advertising, enforce data privacy laws, and hold companies accountable for AI-related biases.

The future of AI in neuromarketing will depend on how well businesses balance innovation with ethical responsibility. Companies that prioritize transparency, fairness, and consumer protection will build stronger customer relationships and foster long-term brand loyalty.

By integrating ethical AI principles into marketing strategies, brands can ensure that AI-driven neuromarketing enhances consumer experiences without compromising privacy, fairness, or ethical integrity.

7. AI-DRIVEN EMOTIONAL ANALYSIS IN MARKETING

The invention of Artificial Intelligence transformed brand customer interactions because it enabled advanced monitoring of complex emotional responses from clients to build new marketing systems. AI collects emotional information through listening to verbal sentiments and face expression scanning combined with biometric tests which enable marketers to obtain full behavioral data about their customers. Companies strengthen their advertising content because they use evaluated data to provide better end-user interactions and Package superior products. The personalized method of market communication both satisfies users and increases brand loyalty which strengthens marketing effectiveness.

7.1 Facial Recognition and Micro-Expressions

AI has modified facial recognition technology to allow brand operations that detect emotions in real-time by scrutinizing facial expressions as well as subtle micro-expressions. These unnoticeable facial expressions reveal naturally occurring emotional states between happy and surprised and confused emotions as well as disinterest. AI tools such as Affectiva together with Microsoft's Emotion API enable company assessment of customer advertisements response through automated monitoring of facial indicators alongside eye focus and head position (Saeed, 2021).

Companies apply facial recognition software during tests to discover which marketing combinations and product placements and color combinations generate maximum favorable reactions from customers. AI systems detect how strong and long user expressions stay that help businesses better understand what prompts awareness and emotional engagement along with audience participation.

Retail establishments implement facial recognition technology to evaluate how customers respond when they handle items within their stores. Personalized promotions along with product recommendations from AI programming will activate when consumers exhibit positive expressions for specific items thus enhancing the possibility of a purchase.

7.2 Voice Emotion Analysis

AI systems can determine emotional states by studying voice tones as well as pitching and speaking patterns. People express their emotions in voice communications by using different vocal patterns which can indicate either positive engagement or doubts or absence of strong emotions. The analytical power of artificial intelligence controls voice emotion analysis systems which operate in customer service and virtual assistants as well as chatbots to create personalized responses based on emotional states of consumers.

By using AI in call centers the technology recognizes customer distress through voice vocalization to reroute customers to representatives who handle critical matters properly. Voice tone analysis implemented by Amazon Alexa and Google Assistant enables these assistants to change their responses in ways that enhance user experience through enhanced human emotion intelligence. Voice emotion analysis serves advertising purposes for brands as a key measurement tool. Companies use consumer audio ad and voice interaction responses to improve their advertising messages and deliver stronger emotional connections with their audience.

7.3 Biometric Feedback and Neuromarketing

Neuromarketing uses neuroscience theory together with marketing practices to measure consumer behaviors by performing physical tests on advertising materials and product sense protocols. The AI-based biometric system using EEG measurement and heart rate trackers and eye movements helps marketers evaluate brand reactions which consumers have unconsciously.

I. Professionals who run EEG brainwave examinations identify active brain areas when consumers watch ads to determine the triggers of favorable engagements with advertisements.
II. Companies can measure heart rate variability patterns to identify how patient mental reactions respond to marketing content in terms of anxiety levels and mental excitement and relaxation levels.
III. The analysis performed by artificial intelligence through eye tracking helps businesses determine the exact areas where consumers direct their gaze to discover their most viewed product assets.
IV. When businesses use AI neuromarketing tools they get better control of advertisement optimization and product placement as well as branded storytelling by analyzing current emotional customer feedback.

7.4 Personalized Emotional Targeting

AI-driven emotional analysis allows brands to tailor content dynamically based on a consumer's current emotional state. By analyzing data from facial recognition, voice sentiment, and biometric feedback, AI can predict a consumer's mood and adjust advertising in real-time. For example, Spotify and Netflix use AI to suggest music and movies based on a user's emotional state. AI-powered ad platforms can also change visuals, colors, and messaging to better match a consumer's mood, making advertisements feel more relevant and engaging.

Retailers can integrate AI-powered digital displays that adjust product recommendations based on customers' emotions, creating a more immersive shopping experience. AI chatbots and virtual shopping assistants can also modify their tone and recommendations depending on a user's detected emotions, ensuring more empathetic and personalized interactions.

7.5 Ethical Considerations in AI Emotional Analysis

While the large up shoots value added by this feature of AI-driven emotional analysis are numerous, one can get unnerved when one contemplates the ethical ramifications on privacy, consent, and data security. The act of collecting biometrical and emotional data without informed consent raises ethical concerns that could end up causing damage to both as their privacy is breached. Consumers might feel uncomfortable knowing their facial expressions and emotions are being analyzed.

To solve the above issues, the brands are expected to ensure transparent data collection with users opting in to this process such that they comply with various regulations like the GDPR (General Data Protection Regulation) to safeguard the rights of those data subjects. Emotional targeting with the aid of AI must be ethical, straightforward, and consumer-oriented so that marketing remains highly attractive without being intrusive.

8. FUTURE TRENDS IN AI AND NEURO-OPTIMIZATION

The combination of Artificial Intelligence and neuro-optimization is setting forth exciting changes in the marketing landscape to enable brands to build hyper-personal, emotionally engaging, and data-driven consumer experiences. As the technology progresses, there will be a better method of measuring both emotions and predicting behaviors that will serve as a basis on how to optimize marketing. The future directions of AI and neuro-optimization are hyper-personalization, real-time adaptive marketing, brain-computer interfaces, ethical AI, and AI creative content generation. These enhancements will define the direction of brand-consumer interactions and ensure that marketing strategies become more precise and engaging.

8.1 Hyper-Personalization in Marketing

AI is revolutionizing personalization by taking a step beyond traditional demographic segmentation and tailoring very specific marketing efforts to consumers of a particular instance. Future AI systems will deploy vast swathes of behavioral and neurobiological data, such as eye-tracking, voice tonality, facial expressions, and neural responses, to drive an ultra-personalized consumer experience.

- With AI-powered dynamic advertisements, ads will change in real-time based on a viewer's detected mood and engagement level.
- AI-driven shopping assistants will examine past interactions to analyze purchase intent and provide hyper-relevant product recommendations.

- Emotionally intelligent AI algorithms will detect subtle consumer emotions and adjust content accordingly to boost engagement.

For instance, virtual AI-powered personal shoppers will be able to gauge if a consumer is feeling indecisive and get persuasive yet non-intrusive recommendations based on real-time emotional nudging.

8.2 Real-Time Adaptive Marketing

AI-driven real-time marketing adaptive systems will allow brands to tactically manage campaigns based on feedback received from a consumer. Using advanced neuro-optimization techniques, information regarding body activity captured-renotified in real-time will gauge the most apt mechanisms for delivering any given message through biometrics such as heart rate variability, EEG brain activity, and facial micro-expressions.

- AI will automatically alter images, internal texts, and audio messages that might be considered pleasing or absorbing by the current emotional state of the consumer.
- Streaming platforms will utilize AI to evaluate viewer engagement and shift live content accordingly.
- Interactive, AI-based digital billboards and smart displays will update their content based on viewer identity.

Real-time adaptability of marketing ensures that the marketing content serves up relevance and emotional engagement ripe for increasing engagements and conversions.

8.3 Brain-Computer Interfaces (BCIs) and AI in Marketing

This period of merging BCI with AI technologies will be decisive as far as how marketers gain access to consumer preferences, analyze them, and do mental feed-back collection about consumers with BCI technology that lets AI communicate fluidly and directly with consumers, allowing for in-depth insight into consumer's subconscious reactions.

- Thought-controlled, AI-enabled interfaces will let users interact with ads and products purely through the power of thought.
- The analysis of neural responses is going to replace traditional surveys and allow brands to gauge interest without involving consumers directly.

- AI will gauge real-time neural feedback for optimizing advertisement, product design, and customer experience.

For example, various BCIs might take e-commerce in the future where the platforms might completely know what the consumer needs even before the consumer enters into a search-out process, leading to a shopping experience without any disturbances.

8.4 Ethical AI and Consumer Privacy

With AI-driven neuro-optimization extending its arms, data privacy, AI bias, and manipulation of consumers would take center stage in the current arrays of challenges. Brands will have to ensure transparent AI frameworks with a focus on responsible marketing practices.

- Regulations regarding AI will mandate businesses to declare how biometric and behavior data is collected and utilized.
- Detection algorithms for biases will hinder aberrant targeting and discriminatory marketing.
- AI-powered privacy-focused personalization will empower consumers to own their data while enjoying personalized experiences.

By ensuring that AI is ethical, fair, and transparent, brands will win consumer trust and long-term engagement.

8.5 AI-Driven Creative Content Generation

In artificial intelligence lies one of the strongest connections that businesses will use to create emotionally engaging marketing actions. The most notable applications are AI-programmed ads in real time that change according to the emotion felt by the buyer, AI-developed narratives for each individual viewer, and AI-devised virtual influencers who interact with customers within augmented or virtual reality environments. As AI creativity continues to develop, the campaigns that come to life will not become emotionally more intelligent, experiential, and powerful but will allow brands to connect on deeper levels with consumers by creating engagement through personalized, adaptive content experiences within digital and interactive environments.

9. AI'S ROLE IN PREDICTIVE CONSUMER BEHAVIOUR ANALYSIS

Presently, AI is superseding traditional methods, used in particular for consumer behavior analysis, into grounds close to one's heart. It will learn and slices through big data to search for pristine patterns and offer purchase predictions for the customer. The count would include machine learning, behavior analytics, real-time data processing, and, opinion mining of web content allowing brands to leverage. These insights directly help brands increase engagement, improve retention, and drive higher conversions. With such insight, marketers can provide targeted advertising, personalization of product recommendations, and niche-specific content, leaving present-day marketing effective, biased on data, and consumer-centric.

9.1 AI-Powered Data Collection and Analysis

Software platforms applying AI analyze consumer information gathered from various backgrounds, such as:

- website interaction (i.e., clicks, time spent on the website, abandoned carts),
- social media actions (i.e., likes, shares, comments),
- purchase history and transaction record,
- biometric and emotional information (like eye tracking, facial expressions, and sentiment analysis).

This way, the AI programs can generate, analyze and use behavioral insights to predict the intent of the customer in real time based on their online behavior. For instance, a customer behavior analysis tool that is driven by AI could be capable of telling precisely when a customer is about to abandon their online shopping cart, thus permitting live communication to reach the customer with incentives- like discounts or product recommendations- that are most likely to get them to continue with their purchase arrangement.

9.2 Predictive Analytics and Consumer Insights

AI predictive analytics enable businesses to predict customer behavior based on their earlier interactions and preferences. Some distinguishing features are:

- Predicting purchase intent – AI predicts when a customer might decide to purchase based on their buying histories and browsing patterns.

- Churn prediction – AI detects signs indicating that a customer might stay with the business and preempts their departure with retention strategies, such as personalized offline offers or re-engagement emails.
- Demand forecasting – AI detects market trends, economic trends, and seasonality and ensures that companies have efficient inventory turnover and marketing promotions.

Predictive AI is further used by online retail to match product recommendations with customer preferences, hence increasing sales and customer satisfaction.

9.3 AI-Driven Personalization in Consumer Behaviour Analysis

One of the most remarkable uses of AI in predicting consumer behavior is through personalization. This is accomplished by AI in several ways: Segmenting audiences based on their behaviors, demographics, and psychographics. Providing tailored content recommendations based on previous interactions. Adjusting marketing messages in real time to align with consumer interests. For instance, Netflix and Spotify utilize AI algorithms to anticipate what users might enjoy and offer suggestions; similarly, Amazon employs algorithms to analyze browsing and purchasing patterns to recommend other relevant products, all aimed at improving the online shopping experience.

9.4 Sentiment Analysis and Emotional Intelligence

The sentiments, feelings, and opinions of consumers are gathered by brands through media conversations, customer surveys, and facial recognitions while testing ads and products. The sentiment analysis allows the business to coordinate leads generated from marketing campaigns with audience emotion, thus ensuring their effectiveness. The understanding of human emotions by AI allows marketers and branding agents to express messages to evoke positive emotional reactions, a bond of increased engagement, and ultimately brand loyalty. The growth and increasing importance of AI will significantly improve customer engagement and overall marketing effectiveness in emotional intelligence marketing.

9.5 AI in Real-Time Consumer Behaviour Adaptation

From the above, artificial intelligence aids in real-time changes of the plan based on consumer responses, which are analyzed for up-to-date modifications:

- Remote AI Dynamic Pricing whereby prices are adjusted to reflect specific real-time demand scenarios, competitor pricing information, and user behaviours
- Interactive Chatbots and Virtual Assistants that personalize conversations and tailor them down to the level of need recognition and offer recommendations based on preference
- A fully engaged recommendation engine-AI-based recommendations personalized based on customer interactions for the recommendations

A case in point is seen with travel and hospitality providing for in-near real-time price adjustment based on real-life and real-time input into the demand, actual online searching propensity that then informs the system of requisite competitive rates achieved with excessive conversions.

9.6 Ethical Considerations in AI-Driven Consumer Analysis

While AI has clearly demonstrated numerous advantages regarding its ability to predict consumer behaviour, there remain significant challenges associated with this technology. Aside from the ongoing concerns regarding consumer privacy and the potential for security breaches due to the inherent biases that exist within these AI-based tools, marketers are also faced with questionable/unethical marketing practices based on the psychological cues or subliminal messages sent to consumers' minds.

It is therefore essential that as marketers continue to embrace the use of AI responsibly and responsibly implement policies that govern how data are collected and used, that marketers develop data protection mechanisms to protect against data breaches, while at the same time enabling the marketer to achieve optimum marketing results.

While the use of AI within the context of consumer behaviour analysis continues to evolve and grow, for the time being, it has primarily been used to support and enhance the marketer's ability to develop more personalized and targeted marketing campaigns for consumers, while at the same time allowing them to create customer experiences that better match consumer needs and expectations. When implemented mindfully, AI can provide marketers with an unprecedented advantage when developing hyper-personalised, engaging marketing campaigns, using robust analytics and insights all developed for the purpose of creating long-lasting relationships with consumers.

10. MANAGERIAL AND PRACTICAL IMPLICATIONS

This chapter highlights ways for marketing professionals and other leaders of businesses to make positive changes as a result of their findings. The first opportunity available to organisations is the ability to use technology that allows real-time tracking of consumer behaviour and emotion via artificial intelligence (AI). Another opportunity for these organisations is the need for marketing managers and others involved in marketing to understand the ethical implications of using AI systems for marketing purposes and that marketing managers have a responsibility to acquire consumer permission and understanding of how these technologies will be utilised.

Finally, despite the importance of AI technology for accessing more personalised marketing data, it is essential for marketing managers to have their own internal governance systems in place to effectively identify, rectify and exclude potentially biased algorithms from consideration when making decisions about how best to market products. These strategies will also assist organisations with building a greater level of trust with their customers and comply with existing regulations regarding consumer data privacy.

11. CONCLUSION

The chapter fits in the current body of research of neuromarketing because it combines the previous theories of consumer research and neuroscience with modern AI-based marketing methods. The chapter supplemented theoretical bases and practical insights to gain a better insight into the benefits of artificial intelligence to emotional intelligence, real-time design optimization, and personalized marketing approaches in advertising and consumer engagement.

As it is revealed in the chapter, AI-based neuromarketing can allow organizations to understand subconscious consumer behavior, emotional reactions, and decision-making processes in a better way that is frequently hard to capture with the help of traditional marketing methods. The capabilities enable marketers to create adaptive advertising campaigns, product design, and more related consumer experience, which enhances engagement and brand performance.

Besides the theoretical value, this chapter is a valuable source of practical information about the responsible use of AI-driven technologies that marketers and business professionals can use. The need to focus on ethical issues associated with data privacy, algorithmic bias, transparency, and consumer consent is highlighted by the need to make sure that innovation does not negatively affect consumer trust and compliance with the regulations.

Lastly, the chapter provides research opportunities in the future, such as the long-term effectiveness of AI-personalized marketing on consumer perceptions and the changing ethical limits of neuromarketing as AI technologies keep developing.

REFERENCES

Alsharif, A. H., & Mohd Isa, S. (2024). Revolutionizing consumer insights: The impact of fMRI in neuromarketing research. *Future Business Journal*, *10*(1), 79. DOI: 10.1186/s43093-024-00371-z

Ameen, N., Tarhini, A., Reppel, A., & Anand, A. (2021). Customer experiences in the age of artificial intelligence. *Computers in Human Behavior*, *114*, 106548. DOI: 10.1016/j.chb.2020.106548 PMID: 32905175

Brooks, R., Nguyen, D., Bhatti, A., Allender, S., Johnstone, M., Lim, C. P., & Backholer, K. (2022). Use of artificial intelligence to enable dark nudges by transnational food and beverage companies: Analysis of company documents. *Public Health Nutrition*, *25*(5), 1291–1299. DOI: 10.1017/S1368980022000490 PMID: 35232511

Danciu, V. (2014). Manipulative marketing: Persuasion and manipulation of the consumer through advertising. *Theoretical and Applied Economics*, *21*(2), 591.

Deshmukh, S. B., Panchbhai, A., Gorkhe, M., Behare, N., Behare, S. N., Yeole, S. M., . . . Sharma, S. (2025). Driving Sales and Customer Engagement: AI-Powered Recommendation Systems in Personalized Marketing. In *Real-World Applications of AI Innovation* (pp. 361-388). IGI Global Scientific Publishing.

Gao, B., Wang, Y., Xie, H., Hu, Y., & Hu, Y. (2023). Artificial intelligence in advertising: Advancements, challenges, and ethical considerations in targeting, personalization, content creation, and ad optimization. *SAGE Open*, *13*(4), 21582440231210759. DOI: 10.1177/21582440231210759

Gyory, J. T., Soria Zurita, N. F., Martin, J., Balon, C., McComb, C., Kotovsky, K., & Cagan, J. (2022). Human versus artificial intelligence: A data-driven approach to real-time process management during complex engineering design. *Journal of Mechanical Design*, *144*(2), 021405. DOI: 10.1115/1.4052488

Iyelolu, T. V., Agu, E. E., Idemudia, C., & Ijomah, T. I. (2024). Leveraging artificial intelligence for personalized marketing campaigns to improve conversion rates. *International Journal of Engineering Research and Development*, *20*(8), 253–270.

Iyer, M., Reddy, A., Nair, A., & Nair, P. (2020). Enhancing Ad Targeting Optimization through AI-Driven Techniques: Utilizing Reinforcement Learning and Genetic Algorithms. *International Journal of AI Advancements*, *9*(4).

Saeed, U. (2021). Facial micro-expressions as a soft biometric for person recognition. *Pattern Recognition Letters*, *143*, 95–103. DOI: 10.1016/j.patrec.2020.12.021

Sung, E. C., Bae, S., Han, D. I. D., & Kwon, O. (2021). Consumer engagement via interactive artificial intelligence and mixed reality. *International Journal of Information Management, 60*, 102382. DOI: 10.1016/j.ijinfomgt.2021.102382

Yadav, S. J. (2024). AI Bias and Fairness: Ethical Considerations in Service Marketing Strategies. In *Integrating AI-Driven Technologies Into Service Marketing* (pp. 49-64). IGI Global.

Chapter 10
New Product Development With Neuromarketing

Michael Oyedele Oyenuga
http://orcid.org/0000-0001-9921-5711
Woxsen University, India

Thomas Heinrich Musiolik
http://orcid.org/0000-0001-7749-4721
Woxsen University, India

ABSTRACT

By understanding how the brain reacts to various stimuli, neuromarketing can offer guidelines for product design, branding, and as well as much of a marketing strategy. The purpose of this paper is to explore the new product development outcomes of neuromarketing, investigate which techniques can contribute toward understanding consumer behaviour, and determine how they can be successful for firms using neuromarketing. The approaches employed are literature review and case study.Empirical evidence and case studies suggest that neuromarketing can revolutionise the creation of new products, and it should be a compulsory element for every business in the competitive world. In addition, the chapter contributes to the literature by helping to clarify how neuromarketing tools may be organised for being used effectively in NPD by bridging consumer psychology to marketing praxis. Ultimately, the chapter advocates for a robust integration and encourages firms to shift from traditional methodologies to more adept, neuromarketing approaches in their new product development strategies.

DOI: 10.4018/979-8-3373-1152-4.ch010

INTRODUCTION

The accelerating pace of innovation and the complexity of consumer markets have made New Product Development (NPD) increasingly risky and resource-intensive. Traditional marketing research methods, surveys, interviews, and focus groups often rely on self-reported data that is subject to bias, social desirability, and limited introspection. As a result, firms face persistent challenges in accurately predicting consumer preferences, reducing launch failures, and aligning product offerings with evolving market demands. Neuromarketing, an emerging interdisciplinary field at the intersection of neuroscience, psychology, and marketing, offers a powerful complement to conventional approaches by uncovering subconscious drivers of consumer behaviour that traditional methods frequently overlook.

Neuromarketing employs neurophysiological tools such as functional magnetic resonance imaging (fMRI), electroencephalography (EEG), and eye-tracking systems to measure emotional and cognitive responses to product concepts, packaging, advertising, and brand stimuli (Singh et al., 2023; Nilashi et al., 2020). These techniques provide insights into how consumers process information, make decisions, and form attachments, enabling organisations to refine product design and marketing strategies with greater precision. For example, fMRI can reveal brain activity associated with emotional resonance when consumers view alternative packaging designs, while EEG can capture moment-to-moment engagement during advertising exposure. Such data-driven insights reduce reliance on speculation and allow firms to prototype, test, and iterate more effectively.

The integration of neuromarketing into NPD addresses several pressing challenges. First, it shortens, the iteration, cycle by enabling real-time feedback on prototypes and concepts, thereby reducing development costs and time-to-market (Bojić et al., 2021). Second, it enhances the accuracy of demand forecasting by linking subconscious emotional responses to purchase intentions (Cardoso et al., 2022). Third, it strengthens marketing communication by guiding message framing, media targeting, and campaign design to evoke desired consumer reactions ("Consumer Behaviour Through Neuromarketing Approach," 2021). Beyond product design, neuromarketing thus becomes a strategic tool for aligning innovation with consumer psychology.

However, the adoption of neuromarketing also raises ethical and managerial concerns. The use of neuroscientific data introduces questions of consumer autonomy, privacy, and manipulation, requiring organizations to balance innovation with transparency and responsible practice (Goecking et al., 2021). Moreover, the high costs of advanced tools such as fMRI and EEG necessitate careful evaluation of return on investment, particularly for small and medium-sized enterprises. These challenges underscore the need for frameworks that integrate neuromarketing insights into NPD while safeguarding ethical standards and managerial feasibility.

Therefore, neuromarketing represents both an opportunity and a responsibility for firms engaged in product innovation. By bridging the gap between consumer insights and product development, it enables organisations to design offerings that resonate emotionally and cognitively with target audiences. This chapter explores how neuromarketing can be systematically integrated into each stage of the NPD process, highlights its benefits and limitations, and examines the ethical and strategic implications of its use in the age of AI-driven marketing.

FUNDAMENTALS OF NEUROMARKETING

Neuromarketing brings together aspects of neuroscience, psychology, and marketing to help researchers understand how consumers respond to marketing stimuli across their subconscious mind. Neuromarketing aims to unravel the intricate cognitive and emotional mechanisms driving consumer behaviour by applying scientific methods. Hence, this convergence of marketing along with neuroscience provides better insights into processes which impact consumer preferences, motivations and decisions.

Neuromarketing is based on the idea that much of what motivates us as consumers is unconscious (Kajla et al., 2023). Traditional marketing research is based on self-reported data (e.g., surveys, interviews), prone to biases and social desirability (Oyenuga et al., 2023). Traditional marketing methods are also complemented by neuro-marketing, which studies the neural-cognitive processes involved in purchasing, and what factors affect these decisions using brain scanning techniques fMRI, EEG, eye-tracking, and others. The empirical study of motivation researchers in the early 1960s found that individuals were motivated by certain needs, and it facilitated a deeper understanding of why people buy things, connecting the link between what motivates people and what people do (Mansor et al., 2021).

Neuromarketing also intersects with behavioral economics, offering insights into heuristics, biases, and decision-making shortcuts. Concepts such as loss aversion, framing effects, and nudging help explain why consumers respond differently to identical stimuli depending on context. Integrating these theories with neuroscientific data enhances the predictive power of product and campaign design (Kahneman, 2011; Thaler & Sunstein, 2008).

There are many systematic uses to employ neuromarketing, from validating advertising appeal to comprehension of product innovation. For example, neuromarketing studies are also able to reveal which specific colours, shapes, or sounds generate affective reactions in the consumers, giving the marketers help for the choice of the components of the corporate brand that may appeal to the target audience (Núñez-Cansado & Domínguez, 2020). Also, through neuromarketing, organisations are capable of increasing customer experience by offering goods and services that satisfy the consumer´s needs and desires, consequently, increasing customer sense of satisfaction and loyalty (Kukharska, 2025).

While neuromarketing has useful findings, it also raises ethical questions of privacy and consumer behaviour manipulation. Since neuromarketing-based instruments can be misused, credibility must be taken into account in practice, and the instrument must be employed mindfully and responsibly (Siddique et al., 2022). Although the incorporation of neuromarketing into business is not just a piece of cake (Núñez-Cansado & Domínguez, 2020), argued that, through further cooperation between researchers and practitioners, reliable and ethically defensible methodologies will be established to support both brands and consumers.

NEW PRODUCT DEVELOPMENT PROCESS

The New Product Development (NPD) process involves multiple stages, each playing an important role in making sure that the product is not only attuned to consumer needs but also in line with the strategic goals of the business. Below is a step-by-step breakdown of the NPD process with an outline of each phase:

Idea Generation: The first step of the NPD process is to create a set of ideas for new products. And they can come from many sources, including market research, customer feedback or competitive analysis, as well as from technology advances. This phase is traditionally supported by brainstorming, focus groups, and creative workshops. An open mind and collaboration of cross-functional teams (marketing, sales and Research and Development) is key to broadening the horizon of imagination. The diversity of perspectives at this juncture may catalyse the generation of new ideas for further development (Durst et al., 2018).

Idea Screening: Second, after ideas are generated, the next stage is screening, evaluating the ideas and sifting through them. This all-important phase helps us to identify the concepts most likely to fly and consign those that aren't viable or not in line with the organisation's strategic aims. The screening factors may include the market potential, cost impact, technical feasibility, smooth compatibility with the consumer's preference, etc. Thus, companies can improve the allocation of their resources and pay attention to what counts (Situmeang et al., 2017).

Concept Development and Testing: The second process beyond idea screening is to refine the ideas to more tangible concepts. That includes product features, target audience, and benefits. At this stage, companies spend most of their time testing concepts, inviting the consumer to react to concepts. By running surveys, focus groups or interviews, they can ask questions that tell them how people are likely to respond to the story itself and its various elements. It enables the idea to be tailored to the requirements of the market, based on the feedback, and before being developed (Tang et al. 2014).

Marketing Strategy Development: The next stage is designing the marketing plan for the new product. This plan consists of target market identification, positioning, competitive analysis, pricing strategies, and promotional plans. One of the most effective ways to create a marketing strategy that promotes the success of a new product or service is for collaboration to occur between the marketing and product development teams for a marketing plan that complements the product's strengths and addresses the expectations of the target audience (Shrivarthini & V, 2022).

Business Analysis: After defining a marketing strategy, the organisation performs a business analysis, which evaluates the new product's business potential and profitability. This includes sales forecasts, production costs, pricing strategies, and profit projections. A rigorous analysis allows decision-makers to consider the financial considerations and balance those with the company's capabilities in resources. It assists in identifying whether firms should invest or drop out of the project depending on possible returns (Zahay et al. 2011).

Product Development: The product development stage takes the concept and turns it into a physical prototype of the product. In this stage, the production department works closely with multiple functions (both engineering and design) to build the product according to the specs provided in the previous phases and by using prototypes, they can avoid creating a product that does not work or one that is of poor quality. An internal test, which includes feedback, is put in place to help make further improvements (Bhuiyan, 2011).

Test Marketing: And after product development, many companies conduct a test marketing on a limited number of market segments to analyse the success of the product. The businesses can then use that stage to gather real-world data on consumer acceptance and marketing effectiveness before a full-scale launch. Test marketing allows organisations to discover problems, receive customer feedback, and adjust their marketing strategies as needed. Such an iterative approach is important to avoid risks related to the market launch of a wider offering (Boehe, 2010).

Test Marketing in New Product Development: Test marketing is a stage in the New Product Development (NPD) process, which is used by companies to determine whether a product will be successful in a full-scale launch. The product is released into a small-scale market to get real-world feedback on consumer reactions, predicted sales, and the overall effectiveness of marketing strategies. There are many advantages of test marketing, such as reducing risks, finding consumer acceptability, and modifying marketing efforts using actual consumer behaviour(Oyenuga & Labiyi, 2024).

Test marketing strategies can vary significantly between businesses and are all subject to advantages and disadvantages. A standard form of test marketing is launching the product in specific geographic areas which represent the general target market. This approach is useful to study criterion-related, concurrent, or construct validity, and allows precise or laboratory control, real-time adjustments based on actual sales, and gross and detailed feedback (Dahan & Srinivasan, 2000). On the other hand, simulated test marketing which is a virtual shopping environment where consumers interact with a product before it is launched in the marketplace can help determine whether a product is potentially helpful, helping determine the best price to produce and validate market acceptance quickly and on a budget (Fader et al., 2003).

Controlled test marketing is another way of testing, which means one select group of consumers is exposed to the product and the marketing materials, and their reaction and purchase intention are measured. It is also less expensive and time-consuming than a full-scale test of the market, but not necessarily as effective for translating the particular nuances of the market (Panigrahi et al., 2003). On the other hand, sequential test marketing involves introducing the product gradually or in multiple phases, enabling companies to gather data and adjust marketing approaches progressively before a national rollout (Oyenuga et al., 2021).

Test marketing enables companies to pinpoint problems before doing a full-scale release, thus avoiding expensive mistakes and misalignments with what consumers want. Through its real introduction, the test marketing enables firms to better tailor their positioning, message, and promotion to the needs of test-market consumers, yielding a better fit product to the market (Durmuşoğlu & Barczak, 2011). It also mitigates risk by providing an estimate of market demand, which is necessary to obtain support to allocate an inordinate amount of resources to final design and production (Jagpal et al., 2006).

Yet test marketing does come with caveats. One significant drawback is the risk of sharing testing phase new product information with competition, allowing them to respond with similar launches and potentially creating strategic disadvantages (Panigrahi et al., 2003). Besides, test marketing is expensive due to multiple test markets, and this extraneous cost puts the companies, particularly small firms with limited resources, in a fiscal bind (Laksana 2023). In addition, consumer behaviour can differ radically depending on context (Marcus et al., 2020), and the test market results may not necessarily proxy for full launch performance, leading to rather poor forecasts for eventual market success (Lees & Wright, 2004).

Product Launch: The final stage of the NPD process is the product launch, where the new product is introduced to the broader market. This stage involves implementation of the marketing plan, launch of the promotional plan and distribution through chosen channels. The latter is generally followed by watching and checking out how it will work out. Successful implementation in the First Market is critical as it forms the basis for how the product is first received and for its future action in the marketplace (Ernst et al. 2014; Guimarães et al. 2019).

INTEGRATING NEUROMARKETING INTO THE NEW PRODUCT DEVELOPMENT PROCESS

Deep neuroscientific insights are applied to all stages of product innovation, and neuromarketing's role in the New Product Development (NPD) process is enhanced. This incorporation allows the businesses to ease into aligning their products according to the consumer demand and, hence, upon their market launch, improves their success rate.

Idea Generation: During this stage, neuromarketing techniques can be used to reach into the subconscious mind of the customers to understand what resonates with them. Tools like an EEG or even an fMRI can be applied during design workshops to capture emotional reactions to different concepts, and that can help to reveal pathways into latent needs that other, more traditional feedback loops might not get through. Ideation can thereby be widened to imaginative concepts that would otherwise be missed (Singh et al. 2023).

Idea Screening: In the idea screening stage, neuromarketing can facilitate a deeper assessment of the viability and desirability of ideas. However, firms can use focus groups with biometric measurements to pinpoint which ideas reflect positive emotional participation and positive attraction (neural reactions to different concepts). This data-informed process allows for the ideas with the highest potential to be identified and then progressed (Fauzi & Riyanto, 2022).

Concept Development and Testing: As ideas have matured, neuromarketing can prove to be useful for optimal testing, offering insights into what customers are looking for in a product, its attributes and features. Using eye-tracking technology, firms can see how potential customers interact with prototypes or visuals of their products, learning which elements grab attention and generate positive reactions. Furthermore, implicit association tests can guide emotionally associating product concepts with consumers based on existing frames, allowing for changes to development before full-scale implementation that can help align the product more closely with consumer expectations (Bajaj et al., 2023).

Development of Marketing Strategy: Through basing marketing strategies on neuromarketing understanding, companies can produce messages that resonate with end-consumers emotionally, while also developing strategies and positioning. This knowledge of the brain mechanics of decision-making allows the advertising industry to produce targeted advertisements which tap into what works, deep narratives and powerful emotions. Such a match of marketing activities and appeals is more closely associated with the peaks of emotional involvement with the audience, which in turn leads to the purchase intention (Daugherty et al., 2018).

Business Analysis: By merging neuromarketing and business analytics, companies gain a more comprehensive picture of what the market may or may not do once a new product is released. With the help of neurological data linked to consumer reactions, companies can obtain a sense of likely purchase patterns, brand associations and emotional responses to potential pricing strategies. This type of analysis (Table 1) can give a better indication, compared to product assumptions, of whether a product could succeed in the marketplace based on actual consumer behaviour.

Table 1.

Tool	Approximate Cost per Study	Use Case	ROI Potential
fMRI	$10,000–$50,000	Deep emotional mapping	High for high-stakes launches
EEG	$2,000–$10,000	Real-time engagement tracking	Moderate for iterative testing
Eye-Tracking	$500–$5,000	Visual attention analysis	High for packaging and UI/UX
Implicit Association Tests	<$500	Subconscious brand associations	High for brand positioning

Managers must weigh these costs against potential reductions in launch failure, improved targeting, and enhanced consumer satisfaction.

Product Development: Several hundred real-time, early-user reactions to design changes are communicated to product teams so they can model final products around what users want. This responsiveness improves product quality and reduces the likelihood of producing a product that fails to meet market demand (Alsharif et al., 2023).

Test Marketing: The product can be tested in a controlled environment with neuromarketing techniques, and the market reaction can be analysed at once. During these test marketing sessions, companies monitor biometric measurements to gauge how engaged, satisfied, and willing to purchase they are. This empirical evidence can be used in reducing the risk of the marketing strategy and indicating which benefits to make before reaching higher volume stages (Crespo-Pereira et al., 2020).

Product Launch: Neuromarketing serves us extremely well by providing an excellent means of testing how consumers react to marketing campaigns and products, all of which will allow product launches to show evidence of emotional engagement, brand loyalty, and satisfaction, not wild speculation that influences future product iterations or marketing campaigns. This ongoing scrutiny allows organisations to adapt their strategies based on consumer feedback and hence, keep pace with consumer demands in the longer term (Rachman et al., 2024).

Figure 1. Neuromarketing-Driven NPD Toolkit is a framework showing how neuromarketing insights inform managerial decisions across the NPD process

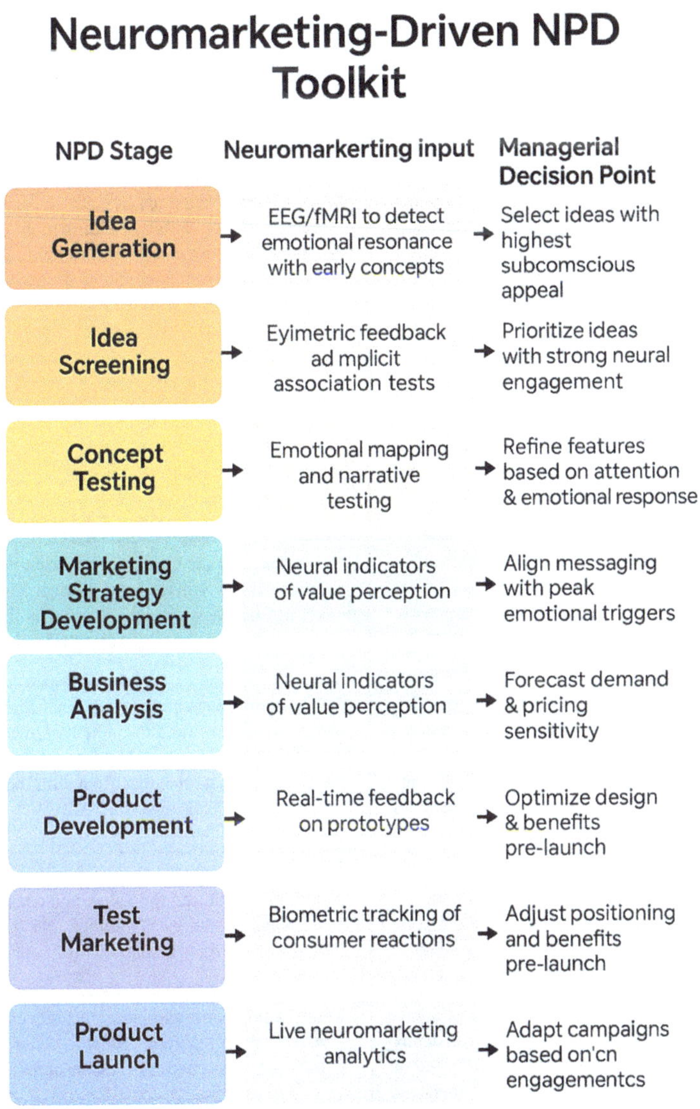

Figure 1 illustrates how neuromarketing techniques such as fMRI, EEG, eye-tracking, and biometric feedback can be strategically integrated into each stage of the NPD process. By capturing subconscious consumer responses, managers can make more informed decisions about idea selection, concept refinement, marketing strategy, and launch execution. The framework highlights the dual role of neuromarketing: reducing uncertainty in product innovation while enhancing emotional resonance with consumers

Table 2 summarises how neuromarketing can be strategically utilised in various stages of the NPD process.

Table 2.

NPD Stage	Integration of Neuromarketing	Description
1. Idea Generation	Analysis of consumer responses to various products through focus groups and brainstorming sessions using neuromarketing techniques	Neuroscience techniques can expose deeper consumer wishes and motivations, yielding more creative and appropriate product ideas. Such as Selling and retailing, fMRI can assist in detecting emotional responses to proposed concepts, leading teams toward ideas with the greatest promise in terms of appeal "Harnessing Neuromarketing Techniques to Enhance Brand Engagement"(2023).
2. Idea Screening	Use neuromarketing metrics to measure ideas across feasibility using emotional response and preferences data.	When filtering ideas through neural metrics, firms can weed out those ideas that consumers do not feel strongly about or that do not capture consumer expectations, directing resources only towards the most promising concepts (Bajaj et al., 2023).
3. Concept Development and Testing	Use neurophysiological studies (e.g., eye-tracking and EEG) to measure consumer responses to product prototypes and advertising messages.	Knowledge of the consumer experience of varying ideas allows firms to hone product features and marketing strategies pre-launch, thus minimising failure risk (Zito et al., 2021).
4. Marketing Strategy Development	Remember that emotional and cognitive neuroscience knowledge has been combined to build targeting to identify and engage with specific consumer segments.	Neuromarketing can discover what characteristics of a product or brand resonate with/mean most to consumers emotionally, which can guide branding and promotional strategies that align with those emotions (Zhu et al., 2022).
5. Business Analysis	Use neuromarketing information to determine consumer willingness to pay, and assess expected sales using neural response data as covariates.	Such subconscious assessments influence consumer feelings regarding the value, and consequently, psychologically adjusted anticipations of these items that affect their demand (Bojić et al., 2021).
6. Product Development	Test, measure, analyse and optimise your product structure to incorporate changes based on neuromarketing feedback.	In fact, using neuromarketing techniques, companies can test and adjust the product to better fit the pain points and preferences of the consumer (Varón et al., 2020).

continued on following page

Table 2. Continued

NPD Stage	Integration of Neuromarketing	Description
7. Test Marketing	Stuff neuromarketing-based pilot tests to track actual responses to products by selected demographics before scaling in the market.	Understanding the sentiment of consumers, their decisions, and behaviour would be vital to optimising the strategies for launch and marketing messages that minimise failed (Daldıran, 2023).
8. Product Launch	In the post-launch period, implement dynamic targeting of promotions and communications as customer response is observed live, based on data from neuromarketing techniques.	Having this adaptive strategy makes engagement stronger at the same time that it can optimise the starting momentum of sales due to the immediate adaptability of the product to consumer feedback that is being tracked with neuromarketing tools (Zito et al., 2021).

Thus, using neuromarketing at all stages of the NPD process not only increases responsiveness, but it also assists organisations to determine more innovative, attractive and successful products. As the neuroscience of marketing advances, it offers great insights into the psychological behaviour, principles, and theories of consumers, thus enabling organisations to fine-tune their offerings to customers.

HOW NEUROMARKETING BRIDGES THE GAP BETWEEN CONSUMER INSIGHTS AND PRODUCT INNOVATION.

Neuromarketing bridges the gap between consumer insight and product innovation, combining neuroscience and traditional marketing methodologies to gain a deeper understanding of the way consumers act. This approach makes use of cutting-edge technologies like fMRI (functional magnetic resonance imaging), electroencephalography (EEG), and other special equipment which measure physiological responses to reveal deeper subconscious motivations and emotions that direct purchasing decisions (Mada, 2024; Kumar et al., 2024). For instance, such scientific methods will help marketers to understand emotional reactions to different stimuli; thèrefore, they could develop products with a stronger impression on individuals to w-hom the product offers are to be directed (Venskė, 2024).

In addition, the combination of neuromarketing methods and traditional methods of marketing research highlights the value of mixed research design. The joining of neuromarketing and classical methods diminishes the subjective bias that often exists in marketing evaluation, and therefore enhances the captured data, and it more useful to design more accurate products according to consumers´ tastes (González et al., 2020). This hybrid model provides a richer insight into consumers' purchasing behaviour by providing an opportunity for both researchers and marketers to investigate the cognitive and affective aspects of their purchasing behaviour and ultimately directs product innovation and tailors promotional strategies (Kansra et al., 2022).

Neuromarketing even suggests some specific dos and don'ts for product and advertising design. Similarly, when consumers subconsciously react to the various marketing messages, product positioning will be better grounded on the foundation of how consumers subconsciously react (Hsu & Chen, 2020). This is particularly true in the tourism and hospitality industry, where the emotional side of the experience plays a crucial role in the customer's decision-making process (Gaafar & Al-Romeedy, 2021; Oyenuga & Akwen, 2025).

Also, there is a problem with the ethics of using neuromarketing. On the one hand, the use of neuroscience in marketing involves very promising areas and opportunities for innovation. But on the other hand, it comes with the need to observe and ensure the principles of transparency and consumer autonomy. As Goecking et al.(2021) indicate that ethical frames and guidance are needed to help manage these nuanced interactions. Therefore, to maintain consumer confidence and balance this with product evolution that is enriched with neuroscience-based informed insights, following established ethical standards is advantageous towards new product innovation from neuromarketing techniques (Rachman et al., 2024).

Neuromarketing responses are not universally consistent. Cultural norms, economic conditions, and consumer expectations shape how individuals process marketing stimuli. For instance, collectivist cultures may respond more strongly to community-oriented messaging, while individualistic cultures prioritize personal benefit.

Emerging markets such as India, Brazil, and Nigeria present unique neuromarketing opportunities due to rising digital engagement and diverse consumer segments. Case studies from Indian tech startups and African fintech firms show how neuromarketing can guide product localization, mobile UX design, and culturally resonant branding.

So, neuromarketing is a vital link between consumer behaviour and product innovation. Ultimately, equipped with this exciting new toolkit, companies will use this alongside more conventional marketing approaches to get a better idea of what they want and need from a product and a better way to position an innovative product (Oyenuga et al., 2019) for the emotional component in the market.

ROLE OF NEUROMARKETING IN NEW PRODUCT DEVELOPMENT

By employing neuroscientific techniques to study the consumer reaction to different statements, organisations are empowered to take important decisions regarding product development, advertisement and customer engagement. One of the main advantages of neuromarketing is that it helps to better understand the subconscious ways in which we customers make purchasing decisions. Conventional market research techniques depend on self-reported data, which can be subjective or biased. Through the use of neuromarketing tools (including brain imaging and biometric measures), organisations can capture responses to products, advertisements and brand communication in real time. Profound understanding of these subconscious motivators can help in catering to the demand of their function by fueling a product which can satisfy their functional needs as well as connect them emotionally, leading to a shift in their shopping habits and decision process (Kansra et al. 2022). This approach enables contributors to give better products to their audience.

With neuromarketing, brands can draw and even carve out customer segments through emotional response, rather than demographics (Lee & Broderick, 2020). This enables organisations to focus on ascertaining the likes of different communities, about a product or a certain form of messaging, to guarantee that their products address the varied needs within consumer populations. In addition, to ease this complex process, neuromarketing is used to go beyond history and to open new doors to focused and effective marketing, which can often not be accessed using the traditional marketing approaches (Singh et al., 2023). This targeted data-driven approach, especially the use of virtual reality, assists enterprises in developing more relevant products that are more likely to take off in the market (Alam et al., 2024).

Also, neuromarketing enables firms to create naming strategies that resonate with people emotionally. According to Recuerda et al.(2021) and Oyenuga et al (2019), understanding consumer emotional responses can serve to inform more accurate brand messaging and positioning. Neuromarketing is also applied to methods and techniques, and using return on investment, branding processes and identifying the key appeals materials keys in branding logos, taglines, etc., are related to areas that trigger the target audience's emotions in the market. In that way, neuromarketing perfects the sensory areas of product design, which significantly improves the complete customer experience. Bajaj et al.(2023) argue that insights into rhythm in sensory perception and consumer experience led to innovative product development behaviours that enhance sensory appeal and stimulate positive user experience. By understanding how aspects such as colour, texture and smell influence the decision-making process, businesses can design products that not only do the job but are also a pleasure to use, leading to increased brand loyalty and brand advocacy (Oyenuga & Fredrick, 2023).

However, with the never-ending advancements of neuromarketing in the 21st century, few organisations are beginning to grasp the extent of deep learning and its use in consumer development. Organisations need to use neuromarketing responsibly while respecting privacy and, wherever necessary, their consent (Lekshmi et al., 2024).

BENEFITS OF NEUROMARKETING IN NEW PRODUCT DEVELOPMENT

Neuromarketing combines insights from psychology and neuroscience, resulting in valuable insights into the way consumers interact with products and brands. Such total product knowledge can improve the design process, resulting in products that not only fulfil a market need but also have a greater affinity for the consumer. From improving customer experience to informing product design and features, neuromarketing can help design a user-focused product. Neuromarketing techniques are employed from the evaluation of neural response, and therefore help predict how a consumer will respond to marketing information, even before the product is available on the market (Alsharif et al., 2023). From analysing the consumer emotions and their cognitive responses, organisations can improve their product offerings to provide the right product, in the right form, for the right place and at the right time (Oyenuga & Labiyi, 2024). Investigating the antecedents of consumers' preferences can help organisations to potentially modulate how their products are designed to enhance desire for and use of them (Oyedele et al, 2020).

Also, neuromarketing is the cheapest way to launch a new product. With techniques like eye-tracking and biometric measurements, companies can watch how potential customers interact with products in ways that surpass the old focus groups or polls. Nilashi et al. (2020) argue, drawing on neuroscience methods, that firms can adopt a robust way of estimating consumer responses and be able to make evidence-based actions without the risk of product failure or minimal such risk. In so doing, it enables firms to plan and produce products that can position them to gain a competitive advantage (Nduji et al, 2023).

Furthermore, it leverages product creation and ideas, generating creativity through the use of the data of the so-called consumer neuroscience. For instance, understanding how sensory experiences such as taste, sight, sound, etc., affect consumer predisposition can be used to craft engaging experiences that elicit optimal emotions. García et al. (2024) stress the potential of neuromarketing to optimise the decision-making process in the local retail spaces as a new channel that can help understand consumer preferences to influence product improvements. This will help them build appealing product stories, visuals, and features that speak to consumers' emotions.

Additionally, neuromarketing's applications in analysing consumer emotional responses to packaging, branding, and advertising are also significant contributors to the new product development process. Through the means of Electroencephalography

(EEG) or functional magnetic resonance imaging (fMRI), marketers can comprehend which components incite emotions of positivity and therefore acceptance, but also which elements provoke aversion and thus rejection. As a result, brands can design the package and tell marketing stories adapted to the emotions of consumers to have a higher probability of recciving acceptance of the product when it appears in the market (Fauzi & Riyanto, 2022).

The advantages of neuromarketing are considerable, but organisations must also recognise the ethical impact of using neuromarketing. These risks include the collection and potential exploitation of consumers' data, especially their biometric data. Organisations should be ethical when implementing neuromarketing methods in product development (Chen, 2023) because when companies have clear and ethical standards for how they use data, they can earn consumer confidence while benefiting from the advantages of neuromarketing.

CASE STUDIES AND APPLICATIONS OF NEUROMARKETING IN NEW PRODUCT DEVELOPMENT

Since the advent of neuromarketing, it has become an indispensable asset for new product development (NPD), enabling marketers and product teams to gain more profound insights into sources of consumer preferences, emotional responses, and decision-making strategies. Neuroscience has the potential to help companies identify how to best market their own products and shape product design.

Coca-Cola is one company that has employed neuromarketing techniques to evaluate consumer responses to its product packaging and advertising. With the help of neuromarketing techniques, Coca-cola has been able to measure emotional responses to a variety of label designs and advertising formats, therefore this provides the firm with the solid rationale to develop brand attributes that emotionally appeals to human customers and, hence more specifically targeting marketing campaigns and product launches (Alsharif et al. 2023). This is a perfect example of neuromarketing's power to drive the perception of a product into the minds of consumers and make it more attractive in the marketplace.

Another notable example can be seen in Procter & Gamble (P&G), which uses neuromarketing to create skincare. The company, for instance, did studies that used eye tracking and biometric readings to gauge how people responded emotionally to ads for the products. Through the analyses, the patterns of emotional engagement and attention, P&G could determine precisely which features in its commercials elicited the most positive emotion. This study not only provided empirical evidence on the use of marketing messages but also facilitated the formulation of products and package presentation to satisfy the preferences of its target consumers (Crespo-

Pereira et al., 2020). The research reduces risks and opens the avenues for making informed decisions, which in turn enhances the success rates for new products through evidence-based decision making.

Moreover, neuromarketing has had its influence in the food sector, as in the case of the Campbell Soup Company, which has applied these methods to maximise their product's development (Sánchez-Núñez et al., 2021). This enabled them to inform their product formulation decisions by linking flavours collated by the consumers they valued more with their neural activity. This innovative approach provided scientific justification for marketing decisions and thus illustrated how neuromarketing can contribute to optimising NPD processes in the food and beverage industry.

Cosmetics industries have also used information from neuromarketing to develop new products according to the desires. For example, beauty and personal care companies like L'Oréal use neuromarketing to conduct tests on formulations and branding to see how consumers are likely to respond. Studies in the field of neuromarketing demonstrate the influence of fine changes in customer preferences on product development and branding of L'Oréal based on the emotional responses of customers to marketing stimuli that could lead to the optimisation of customer satisfaction (Lekshmi et al., 2024). Knowing what makes their products resonate emotionally, beauty brands can generate more effectively engaging narratives that speak to their audience.

In India, *NeuroVista Foods*, a mid-sized agribusiness start-up, adopted neuromarketing techniques to refine its product packaging and advertising strategies. With limited resources compared to multinational competitors, the firm partnered with a local university to conduct eye-tracking and EEG studies on consumer responses to packaging colors and slogans. Findings revealed that vibrant green tones and concise, trust-oriented taglines significantly increased consumer attention and emotional engagement. By integrating these insights, NeuroVista Foods improved brand recall and customer satisfaction, achieving a 25% increase in repeat purchases within one year. This case illustrates how SMEs in emerging markets can leverage affordable neuromarketing collaborations to build brand equity, even under resource constraints.

While more research has to be done into NPD in general, the application of neuromarketing at NPD stages certainly has many promising use cases, given the some of the NPD processes rely heavily on human decision making processes and could leverage the insights and techniques provided by neuromarketing techniques, leaders who intend to use neuromarketing have to take into account the ethical considerations associated with such use.

It is critical to establish solid ethical structures to ensure that data collection techniques do not violate consumer privacy and freedom of choice. Use of neuromarketing mechanisms can plausibly raise ethical concerns, and therefore, the potential for unethical manipulation or buyer discomfort needs to be avoided (Kim et al., 2016). By encouraging transparency and being the custodian of ethical marketing practices, brands can ride the wave of neuro marketing without breaking the trust of the consumers.

CHALLENGES OF USING NEUROMARKETING IN NEW PRODUCT DEVELOPMENT

Neuromarketing attracted a lot of attention because it is an efficient consumer insight tool that aids in the new product idea generation process. However, it brings a lot of challenges that organisations need to handle to effectively implement neuromarketing.

The biggest challenge of neuromarketing is the difficulty and expense of neuroimaging studies. Moya et al.(2020) demonstrate that the complexity of the experimental design itself and the increased specialisation of mortar and pestle can render neuromarketing research impractical. These are complicated challenges, and therefore, the need to think and plan, and an organisation would have difficulty justifying the investment required to undertake these studies when the return on investment is not guaranteed. This complexity causes companies to rely on traditional market research processes that do not reflect the underlying nuances of preference and response.

In addition, there are considerable limitations to how neuromarketing data can be subjectively interpreted. There is an urgent need to augment neuromarketing with variations of traditional marketing practices because studies relying exclusively on neuromarketing technology may produce misleading and shortsighted findings (González et al., 2020).

A different problem is with the ethical dilemma of using neuromarketing techniques. As researchers look at the cognitive and emotional drivers of consumer behaviour, where does the line fall between appropriate commercial practices and manipulation?

Nepotism in neuromarketing research, such as using sensitive data without informed consent, could evoke ethical concerns about consumer autonomy and the refreshing of vulnerabilities within an informed consent framework. Research emphasises the need for ethical standards in neuromarketing practices, especially as they spread to different markets and industries ("Harnessing Neuromarketing Techniques to Enhance Brand Engagement", 2023).

In addition, neuromarketing approaches usually do not fare well in measuring long-term consumer behaviour and preferences. While these mechanisms are capable of measuring real-time emotional reactions, they fall behind in their ability to predict later purchasing behaviours or future brand loyalty (Sánchez-Núñez et al., 2021). This temporal gap creates evidence that can disrupt the efficiency of product testing, product development processes. Using such a mechanism, it is very possible that a model that excels in a laboratory environment will not be translatable to market acceptance once the product is released. Thus, organisations need to understand that neuromarketing insights should help inform and not determine product development decisions.

Additionally, the field of neuromarketing can become complex due to fast-changing consumer expectations and advancements in technologies. Together with an increase in technical literacy among consumers, all these trends translate into a lot higher expectations for the features of the products, brand engagement metrics, as well as the personalisation of conversations that businesses need to have with them, fuelling an endless search for innovation in products and marketing.

Despite the idea of neuromarketing providing insight into consumer preferences, the approach must also adapt to the changing landscape in terms of its continuing relevance and efficacy (Cardoso et al., 2022). Such organisations risk being left behind in competitive markets whose strength is their agility and response to consumer feedback.

ETHICAL AND POLICY CONSIDERATIONS IN NEUROMARKETING

As neuromarketing techniques delve into subconscious consumer responses, ethical concerns surrounding autonomy, manipulation, and data privacy become increasingly significant. Organisations must prioritise transparency, informed consent, and the responsible use of biometric and neurophysiological data. Regulatory frameworks such as the General Data Protection Regulation (GDPR) in the European Union, the Health Insurance Portability and Accountability Act (HIPAA) in the United States, and India's Digital Personal Data Protection (DPDP) Act provide legal safeguards for the collection and use of consumer brain data. To uphold ethical standards, firms should disclose neuromarketing methodologies during research participation, avoid messaging strategies that exploit subconscious vulnerabilities, ensure the anonymisation and secure storage of sensitive data, and align their practices with the ethical guidelines established by the American Psychological Association (APA). These measures are essential for maintaining consumer trust and ensuring that neuromarketing is applied in a socially responsible and legally compliant manner.

Beyond regulatory compliance, the application of neuromarketing raises deeper ethical questions that warrant critical scrutiny (Isa et al., 2019; Venskė, 2024). Central to these concerns are issues of consumer autonomy, manipulation, privacy, and informed consent (Goecking et al., 2021; Ülman et al., 2014). As Bojić et al. (2021) emphasise, the development and deployment of neuromarketing devices, despite their predictive potential, require ongoing moral consideration, particularly in safeguarding consumer agency. This aligns with Javor et al. (2013), who argue that the commercialisation of neuroscientific knowledge for financial gain lies at the heart of ethical debates surrounding neuromarketing.

Yet another important ethical issue underlines fostering unconscious consumer processes, popularly known as the 'buy button' phenomenon, which has been emphasised by Fauzi and Riyanto (2022). It is the power to vend, unquestioned, that allows the manipulation of ethical marketing tactics. In addition, management of incidental findings on neuroimaging studies provides an additional array of ethical challenges that would not be considered or addressed in a standard drug trial, obligating the development of standards and guidelines to responsibly navigate incidental findings (Bradfield, 2021).

Another issue is data privacy, which could be the beginning of coercive consumption strategies. Lekshmi et al.(2024) highlight the moral concern regarding the acquisition of sensitive neurophysiological data among customers. To this already rich analysis on the aforesaid ethical issues, Pratap and Mandal (2023) add new insights, discussing the importance of transparency in the case of neuromarketing studies involving invasive procedures, such as brain wave scanning.

STRATEGIC IMPLICATIONS FOR MARKETERS AND PRODUCT TEAMS

In recent years, new product development (NPD) practitioners have begun to adopt neuromarketing as a valuable input to their processes, decoupling the more stable and fundamental aspects of large datasets from the noisy and volatile nature of NPD. Employing neuroscience to engage with customers on a deeper, data-driven level could help companies make more informed decisions, interact with customers better, and create products that closely reflect market needs.

The strategic implications of neuromarketing in NPD are that businesses will be able to pinpoint consumers' unarticulated preferences and emotional drivers. Traditional marketing research often relies on self-reported data, which can be biased or limited by people's capacity to articulate their feelings. Therefore, methods such as neuromarketing, such as electroencephalography (EEG) and functional magnetic resonance imaging (fMRI) assist in identifying subconscious responses, which can help the market participants to judge emotional interaction with a product (Nilashi et al., 2020). Such knowledge is the necessary information for organisations to innovate and produce products that people will adopt in the market.

Furthermore, neuromarketing can give valuable insights into the ideas and prototypes of a product to test their feasibility before its launch. Because of this, marketers' brand design and packaging can be tested and reiterated time and time again until they are finally rolled out into the marketplace with the confidence that the consumer will react positively (Harnessing Neuromarketing Techniques to Enhance Brand Engagement, 2023). More importantly, organisations can harness the neural responses to better launch the product in the marketplace and how best to position the company in the marketplace.

If a brand is capable of applying some neuromarketing heuristics correctly, that brand can generate a positive image, and its products are likely to be released (Nilashi et al., 2020). Moreover, this novel approach to prototyping and iteration brings the product closer to the consumer, so there is less risk of a catastrophic misalignment.

A key role of neuromarketing is to facilitate interdepartmental collaboration; hence, incorporating neuroscience into marketing practice is a great challenge that requires cross-functional synergy between domain specialists from the fields of psychology, data science and product design to explore. This perspective allows the marketing team to be more effective in evaluating multiple levers on consumer insight and how they come up against with the NPD process(Byne et al., 2022).

Also, neuromarketing strategies can guide branding methods that resonate with consumers. Marketers can create messaging that resonates authentically by addressing the three aspects that shape consumer perceptions, meaning that they will explore how emotional and cognitive factors influence consumer perceptions of brands. The vital understanding of emotional ties created through neuromarketing research will vastly improve the brand's ability to reach out to the customer (Vences et al., 2020) because when consumer feels emotionally engaged in something, their brand loyalty is higher, thus, when brands are aware of this and promote such values, those are the ones that consumers are likely to follow.

However, companies also need to recognise the ethical implications of utilising neuromarketing. Because the techniques deployed in neuromarketing delve further into the mental processes underlying decision making, they raise questions of consumer privacy and consent. For businesses, transparency is crucial to avoid reputational damage and lose consumer trust (Evanschitzky et al., 2012). Companies should inform exactly how they collect, analyse and exploit any consumer data on their platform for marketing benefits, a step that ultimately proves to be a win-win situation for both the marketers as well as consumers.

Therefore, for marketers and product teams engaged in NPD, neuromarketing provides them with strategic insights. By utilising discoveries from neuroscience research, businesses can better understand consumer behaviours on a more in-depth level, design products in a way that is more optimised, and structure marketing strategies in a way that resonates deeply with their audience. This approach also helps to reduce the risks associated with new product launch failures, leading to a more engaged and loyal customer base over time. However, with the inherent complexities of neuromarketing, it will be critical for businesses to prioritise ethical issues and transparency to guarantee sustainable and responsible use of these techniques in marketing practice.

FUTURE TRENDS IN NEUROMARKETING AND NEW PRODUCT DEVELOPMENT

Neuromarketing is progressing at a meteoric pace, and it has many exciting new applications which will radically alter the way we execute new product development (NPD). It's the job of neuromarketing to transform this process into tangible lessons to help improve product design, marketing strategy, and overall engagement, as firms realise that they need to understand more about what's leading consumers and shoppers to behave.

A second direction that neuromarketing evolves in is the increasing adoption of neural and biometric methods of capturing consumer preference and emotional responses in "real time". The collective mapping of cognitive processes and the alignment of the same to the traditional marketing data are key for the success of the new product development programmes, as it enables the organisations to develop offerings that make the right impact on the target segment (Zhu et al., 2022).

In the coming years, as neuroimaging technology continues to improve, these methods will only provide even richer and more precise insights to brands and product developers that will ensure that brands remain ahead of the curve in understanding what consumers want. Machine learning and AI in neuromarketing is another sector that is expected to be utilised more. According to Singh et al. (2023), utilising AI technologies to analyse complex datasets from different sources may deeply analyse consumer behaviour as well as the market trends, leading to decisions in NPD that were previously considered unrealistic. By combining AI with neuromarketing tools, marketers can know in advance consumer behaviour, customise product features, and create marketing strategies that better match market needs. AI's ability to analyse data on a deeper level will not only contribute to the efficiency of product development, but it will also allow for creativity to thrive as the technology will reveal insights that point to innovative directions.

Moreover, there is a growing raft of interdisciplinary work, whereby neuromarketing emerges, or even merges with, other disciplines such as behavioural economics and psychology. For instance, Bajaj et al.(2023) demonstrate the great potential of utilising consumer physiological reactions to marketing stimuli in enhancing advertising campaign effectiveness. With this intersection of knowledge, marketing strategies will encompass even more aspects of human behaviour.

The ethics of neuromarketing also determine what its future will look like. The use of such insights raises important ethical considerations, and organisations must be aware of these issues when utilising neuroscientific techniques in marketing and advertising. Laying a foundation for fair guidelines and transparency in data handling is the crux of gaining consumers, and due to the need for sensitive data in neuromarketing, organisations are encouraged to develop an ethical responsibility culture that maintains the privacy rights of consumers without hindering the efforts of neuromarketing programs.

Beyond that, as consumers become savvier about the tools used in neuromarketing, there will also be growing pressure for greater transparency and oversight in sales and marketing practices. In a landscape where consumers are growing more mindful of leveraging their data and the psychological pulls employed in their marketing, while you may have had the upper hand a few years ago, now, in terms of value, you'll need to modify your approach to cater to new expectations to win these customers. As that takes place, working towards a consumer and educated market will help mitigate possible resistance to neuromarketing practice.

Therefore, together with state-of-the-art neuroimaging, machine learning interdisciplinary collaboration, neuromarketing enables businesses to understand consumer psychology for developing novel products and advertising strategies. But along with that, evolution has come a deeper moral consideration and growing consumer awareness of how those techniques are being deployed, which demands moderation in how neuromarketing practices are implemented. With the continued development of neuromarketing, businesses must find a way to leverage these findings without forsaking ethical responsibility to foster a marketing world centred around sustainability and the consumer.

CONCLUSION

Neuromarketing has emerged as a transformative complement to traditional approaches in New Product Development (NPD), offering organisations the ability to access subconscious consumer insights that conventional surveys and focus groups often miss. By integrating neuroscientific tools such as fMRI, EEG, and eye-tracking into each stage of the NPD process, firms can reduce uncertainty, accelerate iteration cycles, and design products and campaigns that resonate more deeply with consumer emotions and cognition.

This chapter has demonstrated how neuromarketing enhances idea generation, screening, concept testing, business analysis, product development, test marketing, and product launch. The proposed *Neuromarketing-Driven NPD Toolkit* provides a structured framework for managers to translate neural data into actionable decision points, ensuring that innovation is both consumer-centric and strategically aligned.

Beyond technical applications, neuromarketing raises important ethical and managerial considerations. Issues of privacy, autonomy, and manipulation must be addressed through transparent practices and compliance with global regulations such as GDPR, HIPAA, and India's DPDP Act. Embedding ethical governance into neuromarketing strategies is essential for building trust and sustaining credibility in this emerging field.

Looking forward, the convergence of neuromarketing with AI, predictive analytics, and digital commerce opens new pathways for innovation. Real-time biometric tracking, virtual reality testing, and cross-cultural applications will expand the scope of neuromarketing beyond FMCG into sectors such as healthcare, education, and public policy. For managers, this means not only adopting neuromarketing tools but also developing organizational readiness to integrate interdisciplinary insights from behavioral economics, consumer neuroscience, and innovation management.

In summary, neuromarketing is not simply a set of tools but a strategic enabler of innovation. It bridges the gap between consumer psychology and product development, offering firms the opportunity to reduce launch failures, improve targeting, and create emotionally resonant products. For researchers, it opens new avenues for interdisciplinary inquiry; for policymakers, it raises urgent questions of regulation and consumer protection; and for managers, it provides a roadmap to harness neuroscience responsibly for competitive advantage.

REFERENCES

Alam, M. N., Turi, J. A., Bhuiyan, A. B., Kharusi, S. A., Oyenuga, M., Zulkifli, N., & Iqbal, J. (2024). Factors influencing intention for reusing virtual reality (VR) at theme parks: The mediating role of visitors' satisfaction. *Cogent Social Sciences*, *10*(1), 2298898. Advance online publication. DOI: 10.1080/23311886.2023.2298898

Alsharif, A., Salleh, N., Abdullah, M., Khraiwish, A., & Ashaari, A. (2023). Neuromarketing tools used in the marketing mix: A systematic literature and future research agenda. *SAGE Open*, *13*(1), 21582440231156563. Advance online publication. DOI: 10.1177/21582440231156563

Bajaj, R., Syed, A., & Singh, S. (2023). Analysing applications of neuromarketing in efficacy of programmatic advertising. *Journal of Consumer Behaviour*, *23*(2), 939–958. DOI: 10.1002/cb.2249

Bhuiyan, N. (2011). A framework for successful new product development. *Journal of Industrial Engineering and Management*, *4*(4). Advance online publication. DOI: 10.3926/jiem.334

Boehe, D. (2010). The influence of coordination mechanisms on new product development in MNC subsidiaries. *BAR - Brazilian Administration Review*, *7*(1), 79–97. DOI: 10.1590/S1807-76922010000100006

Bojić, L., Tucaković, L., & Nikolić, N. (2021). Neuromarketing unmasked: A review of current state in the field. *Ekonomika Preduzeca*, *69*(7-8), 403–413. DOI: 10.5937/EKOPRE2108403B

Bradfield, O. (2021). Shining a light also casts a shadow: Neuroimaging incidental findings in neuromarketing research. *Neuroethics*, *14*(3), 459–465. DOI: 10.1007/s12152-021-09463-x

Cardoso, L., Chen, M., Araújo, A., Almeida, G., Dias, F., & Moutinho, L. (2022). Accessing neuromarketing scientific performance: Research gaps and emerging topics. *Behavioral Sciences (Basel, Switzerland)*, *12*(2), 55. DOI: 10.3390/bs12020055 PMID: 35200306

Chen, Y. (2023). Comparing content marketing strategies of digital brands using machine learning. *Humanities & Social Sciences Communications*, *10*(1), 57. Advance online publication. DOI: 10.1057/s41599-023-01544-x

Crespo-Pereira, V., Lago, B., & Arregui-McGullion, J. (2020). Implementing neuromarketing in the enterprise: Factors that impact the adoption of neuromarketing in major Spanish corporations. *Frontiers in Communication, 5*, 576789. Advance online publication. DOI: 10.3389/fcomm.2020.576789

Dahan, E., & Srinivasan, V. (2000). The predictive power of internet-based product concept testing using visual depiction and animation. *Journal of Product Innovation Management, 17*(2), 99–109. DOI: 10.1111/1540-5885.1720099

Daldıran, K. (2023). Emprical neuromarketing studies: an overwiew of Turkey, 3(2), 54-72. https://doi.org/DOI: 10.61725/abj.1360469

Daugherty, T., Hoffman, E., Kennedy, K., & Nolan, M. (2018). Measuring consumer neural activation to differentiate cognitive processing of advertising. *European Journal of Marketing, 52*(1/2), 182–198. DOI: 10.1108/EJM-10-2017-0657

Durmuşoğlu, S., & Barczak, G. (2011). The use of information technology tools in new product development phases: Analysis of effects on new product innovativeness, quality, and market performance. *Industrial Marketing Management, 40*(2), 321–330. DOI: 10.1016/j.indmarman.2010.08.009

Durst, S., Hinteregger, C., Temel, S., & Yeşilay, R. (2018). Insights from the later stage of the new product development process: Findings from Turkey. *European Journal of Innovation Management, 21*(3), 456–477. DOI: 10.1108/EJIM-08-2017-0102

Ernst, H., Kahle, H., Dubiel, A., Prabhu, J., & Subramaniam, M. (2014). The antecedents and consequences of affordable value innovations for emerging markets. *Journal of Product Innovation Management, 32*(1), 65–79. DOI: 10.1111/jpim.12171

Evanschitzky, H., Eisend, M., Calantone, R., & Jiang, Y. (2012). Success factors of product innovation: An updated meta-analysis. *Journal of Product Innovation Management, 29*(S1), 21–37. DOI: 10.1111/j.1540-5885.2012.00964.x

Fader, P., Hardie, B., & Zeithammer, R. (2003). Forecasting new product trial in a controlled test market environment. *Journal of Forecasting, 22*(5), 391–410. DOI: 10.1002/for.869

Fauzi, A., & Riyanto, A. (2022). Neuromarketing: The philosophy and culture of consumerism in indonesia. *Malaysian Journal of Social Sciences and Humanities (Mjssh), 7*(1), 325–334. DOI: 10.47405/mjssh.v7i1.1237

Gaafar, H. & Al-Romeedy, B. (2021). Neuromarketing as a novel method to tourism destination marketing: evidence from Egypt. Journal of Association of Arab Universities for Tourism and Hospitality, 0(0), 0-0. https://doi.org/DOI: 10.21608/jaauth.2021.109864.1275

García, F., Ríos, B., Chamorro, S., Rojas, L., Rodríguez, M., Yarleque, A., & Arismendiz, A. (2024). The power of neuromarketing as a fuel to drive purchases in local retail (piura 2024"). *Journal of Educational and Social Research, 14*(6), 503. DOI: 10.36941/jesr-2024-0189

Goecking, O., Muÿlder, C., Martins, H., & Felisberto, J. (2021). Neuromarketing genetics: A systematic review of literature. *Journal of Contemporary Marketing Science*, *4*(1), 69–82. DOI: 10.1108/JCMARS-04-2020-0019

González, M., Baraybar-Fernández, A., & Fernández, M. (2020). The application of neuromarketing techniques in the Spanish advertising industry: Weaknesses and opportunities for development. *Frontiers in Psychology*, *11*, 2175. Advance online publication. DOI: 10.3389/fpsyg.2020.02175 PMID: 33013560

Guimãrães, T., Paranjape, K., & Walton, M. (2019). An expanded model of success factors for NPD performance. *International Journal on Management of Innovation & Technology, 16*(07), 1950054. Advance online publication. DOI: 10.1142/S0219877019500548

Harnessing Neuromarketing Techniques to Enhance Brand Engagement. (2023). *NA*, 4–37. https://doi.org/DOI: 10.57125/FS.2023.12.20.01

Hsu, L., & Chen, Y. (2020). Neuromarketing, subliminal advertising, and hotel selection: An EEG study. *Australasian Marketing Journal*, *28*(4), 200–208. DOI: 10.1016/j.ausmj.2020.04.009

Isa, S., Mansor, A., & Razali, K. (2019). *Ethics in neuromarketing and its implications on business to stay vigilant.* Kne Social Sciences., DOI: 10.18502/kss.v3i22.5082

Jagpal, S., Jedidi, K., & Jamil, M. (2006). A multibrand concept-testing methodology for new product strategy*. *Journal of Product Innovation Management*, *24*(1), 34–51. DOI: 10.1111/j.1540-5885.2006.00231.x

Javor, A., Koller, M., Lee, N., Chamberlain, L., & Ransmayr, G. (2013). Neuromarketing and consumer neuroscience: Contributions to neurology. *BMC Neurology*, *13*(1), 13. Advance online publication. DOI: 10.1186/1471-2377-13-13 PMID: 23383650

Kajla, T., Raj, S., Kansra, P., Gupta, S. L., & Singh, N. (2023). Neuromarketing and consumer behavior: A bibliometric analysis. *Journal of Consumer Behaviour*, *23*(2), 959–975. DOI: 10.1002/cb.2256

Kansra, P., Oberoi, S., Gupta, S., & Singh, N. (2022). Factors limiting the application of consumer neuroscience: A systematic review. *Journal of Consumer Behaviour*, *23*(1), 31–42. DOI: 10.1002/cb.2131

Kim, J., Kim, K., Han, C., Lim, J., & Im, C. (2016). Estimating consumers' subjective preference using functional near infrared spectroscopy: A feasibility study. *Journal of Near Infrared Spectroscopy*, *24*(5), 433–441. DOI: 10.1255/jnirs.1242

Kukharska, N. (2025). Neuromarketing: Essence, principles, methods, problems and prospects. *Economic Scope*, (196), 35–39. DOI: 10.30838/EP.196.35-39

Kumar, P., Chowdhury, S., & Head, S. (2024). Role of neuromarketing and artificial intelligence in futuristic marketing approach: an empirical study.. https://doi.org/ DOI: 10.52783/jier.v4i2.809

Laksana, M. (2023). Business management strategy on national news. *American Journal of Economic and Management Business (Ajemb)*, *2*(9), 352–358. DOI: 10.58631/ajemb.v2i9.60

Lee, N., & Broderick, A. (2020). Exploring the role of neuroscience in marketing: A review of neuromarketing research. *Journal of Advertising Research*, *60*(2), 191–203.

Lees, G., & Wright, M. (2004). The effect of concept formulation on concept test scores. *Journal of Product Innovation Management*, *21*(6), 389–400. DOI: 10.1111/j.0737-6782.2004.00093.x

Lekshmi, S., Joseph, M., Simon, B., Joseph, S., Jacob, G., & Lukose, A. (2024). A bibliometric analysis of the trends and impact of neuromarketing research: Peering into the consumer brain. *Cureus*. Advance online publication. DOI: 10.7759/cureus.69314 PMID: 39398830

Mada, Y. (2024). Role of neuromarketing in understanding consumer behaviour: a literature overview. Int. j. innov. eng. res. technol., 11(8), 48-56. https://doi.org/ DOI: 10.26662/ijiert.v11i8.pp48-56

Mansor, A., Isa, S., & Noor, S. (2021). P300 and decision-making in neuromarketing. *Neuroscience Research Notes*, *4*(3), 21–26. DOI: 10.31117/neuroscirn.v4i3.83

Marcus, G. O., Oyenuga, M. O., & Ahungwa, A. I. (2020). Effects of Sales Promotion on Consumer Buying Behaviour of Food Seasoning Among Nigerian Households: A Case Study of Nestle Maggi Naijapot. [BIRCIJournal]. *Budapest International Research and Critics InstituteJournal*, *3*(1), 134–139. DOI: 10.33258/birci.v3i1.724

Moya, I., Madariaga, J., & López, M. (2020). What can neuromarketing tell us about food packaging? *Foods*, *9*(12), 1856. DOI: 10.3390/foods9121856 PMID: 33322684

Nduji, R., Orji, M., Oyenuga, M., & Oriaku, C. (2023). Assessing e-business and organisational performance in Nigeria today: Evidence from Jumia Ltd, Lagos. *Britain International of Humanities and Social Sciences Journal*, *5*(2), 81–92. DOI: 10.33258/biohs.v5i2.897

Nilashi, M., Yadegaridehkordi, E., Samad, S., Mardani, A., Ahani, A., Aljojo, N., Razali, N. S., & Tajuddin, T. (2020). Decision to adopt neuromarketing techniques for sustainable product marketing: A fuzzy decision-making approach. *Symmetry*, *12*(2), 305. DOI: 10.3390/sym12020305

Núñez-Cansado, M., López, A. L., & Domínguez, D. C. (2020). Situation of neuromarketing consulting in Spain. *Frontiers in Psychology*, *11*, 1854. Advance online publication. DOI: 10.3389/fpsyg.2020.01854 PMID: 32982824

Oyedele, M. O., Jelili, B., & Bulugbe, K. (2020). E-banking and customer satisfaction in the banking industry. *Nigeria Journal of Business Administration.*, *18*(1), 112–132. https://api-ir.unilag.edu.ng/server/api/core/bitstreams/53eb4271-c536-4c99-8910-64622549ba98/content#page=120

Oyenuga, M. O., Ahungwa, A. I., & Onoja, E. (2021). Effect of Brand Equity on consumer behaviour among students of Veritas University, Nigeria: A Study of Apple Smartphones. *Marketing and Branding Research*, *8*, 48–64. DOI: 10.33844/mbr.2021.60329

Oyenuga, M. O., Akhaine, M. E., & Omale, S. A. (2023). We Need it: How Digital Marketing Tactics Influence the Purchasing Behaviour of Nigerian Millennials. *Konfrontasi Journal: Culture. Economy and Social Changes*, *10*(2), 91–105. DOI: 10.33258/konfrontasi2.v10i2.275

Oyenuga, M. O., & Akwen, P. I. (2025). Tourism and intercultural understanding in developing nations. *African Journal of Culture, History. Religion and Traditions*, *8*(1), 1–14. DOI: 10.52589/AJCHRT-OKUXNMSQ

Oyenuga, M. O., Andah, R. A., Marcus, G. O., & Agabi, A. U. (2019). Effects of Customer Relationship Management on Product Innovation in Nigeria. A Case Study of Xerox HS Nigeria Limited. *American Journal of Theoretical and Applied Business.*, *5*(4), 113–126. DOI: 10.11648/j.ajtab.20190504.15

Oyenuga, M. O., & Fredrick, E. (2023). Managing Product Features and Customer Satisfaction via Product Development, Product Branding, and Product Packaging: Evidence from CWAY Table Water. *Marketing and Branding Research*, *10*(1), 28–44. DOI: 10.32038/mbr.2023.10.01.03

Oyenuga, M. O., & Labiyi, O. (2024). *Using Marketing Mix Strategies to Influence Customer Patronage in an Indigenous Restaurant*. Rowter Journal., DOI: 10.33258/rowter.v3i1.1052

Panigrahi, B., Ede, F., & Calcich, S. (2003). A comparison of test marketing practices of large and small consumer goods manufacturing firms. *Management Research News*, *26*(6), 1–20. DOI: 10.1108/01409170310783493

Pratap, D., & Mandal, C. (2023). *Ethical perspectives of neuromarketing – a qualitative analysis*. JMCR., DOI: 10.7176/JMCR/91-01

Rachman, A., Diandra, P., & Simon, F. (2024). Emotional artificial intelligence and brand association: a neuro-bibliometric study. ijabo, 5(3), 1-16. https://doi.org/DOI: 10.61242/ijabo.24.393

Recuerda, A., Tur-Viñes, V., Varón, D., & Valero, F. (2021). Emotional impact of dishes versus wines on restaurant diners: From haute cuisine open innovation. *Journal of Open Innovation*, *7*(1), 96. DOI: 10.3390/joitmc7010096

Sánchez-Núñez, P., Cobo, M., Vaccaro, G., Peláez, J., & Herrera-Viedma, E. (2021). Citation classics in consumer neuroscience, neuromarketing and neuroaesthetics: Identification and conceptual analysis. *Brain Sciences*, *11*(5), 548. DOI: 10.3390/brainsci11050548 PMID: 33925436

Shrivarthini, V. and V, D. (2022). "a review: new product development, categories, importance and process involved in product development". International Journal of Research Publication and Reviews, 714-717. https://doi.org/DOI: 10.55248/gengpi.2022.3.10.33

Siddique, J., Shamim, A., Nawaz, M., & Abid, M. (2022). The hope and hype of neuromarketing: A bibliometric analysis. *Journal of Contemporary Marketing Science*, *6*(1), 1–21. DOI: 10.1108/JCMARS-07-2022-0018

Singh, P., Alhassan, I., & Khoshaim, L. (2023). What do you need to know? a systematic review and research agenda on neuromarketing discipline. *Journal of Theoretical and Applied Electronic Commerce Research*, *18*(4), 2007–2032. DOI: 10.3390/jtaer18040101

Situmeang, F., Leenders, M., & Wijnberg, N. (2017). New product performance and the benefit of periodically changing the relative influence balance between marketing and r&d. *Journal of Business and Industrial Marketing*, *32*(1), 179–190. DOI: 10.1108/JBIM-01-2015-0020

Tang, F., Mu, J., & Thomas, E. (2014). Who knows what innpdteams: Communication context, mode, and task contingencies. *Journal of Product Innovation Management, 32*(3), 404–423. DOI: 10.1111/jpim.12226

Ülman, Y., Çakar, T., & Yıldız, G. (2014). Ethical issues in neuromarketing: "i consume, therefore i am!". *Science and Engineering Ethics, 21*(5), 1271–1284. DOI: 10.1007/s11948-014-9581-5 PMID: 25150848

Varón, D., Tur-Viñes, V., & Mengual, A. (2020). Neuromarketing applied to educational toy packaging. *Frontiers in Psychology, 11*, 2077. Advance online publication. DOI: 10.3389/fpsyg.2020.02077 PMID: 32982857

Vences, N., Díaz-Campo, J., & Rosales, D. (2020). Neuromarketing as an emotional connection tool between organizations and audiences in social networks. a theoretical review. *Frontiers in Psychology, 11*, 1787. Advance online publication. DOI: 10.3389/fpsyg.2020.01787 PMID: 32849055

Venskė, I. (2024). Neuromarketing: a tool to understand consumer behaviour. Regional Formation and Development Studies, 101-109. https://doi.org/DOI: 10.15181/RFDS.V42I1.2605

Zahay, D., Griffin, A., & Fredericks, E. (2011). Information use in new product development: An initial exploratory empirical investigation in the chemical industry*. *Journal of Product Innovation Management, 28*(4), 485–502. DOI: 10.1111/j.1540-5885.2011.00821.x

Zhu, Z., Jin, Y., Su, Y., Jia, K., Lin, C., & Liu, X. (2022). Bibliometric-based evaluation of the neuromarketing research trend: 2010–2021. *Frontiers in Psychology, 13*, 872468. Advance online publication. DOI: 10.3389/fpsyg.2022.872468 PMID: 35983212

Zito, M., Fici, A., Bilucaglia, M., Ambrogetti, F., & Russo, V. (2021). Assessing the emotional response in social communication: The role of neuromarketing. *Frontiers in Psychology, 12*, 625570. Advance online publication. DOI: 10.3389/fpsyg.2021.625570 PMID: 34149513

Chapter 11
Neurogastronomy:
The Neuroscience of Taste, Perception, and Marketing

Ceyhun Uçuk
http://orcid.org/0000-0003-2809-6430
Tekirdağ Namık Kemal University, Turkey

ABSTRACT

This chapter investigates how neurogastronomy, artificial intelligence, and taste projection technologies are combining in marketing to provide multi-sensory, personalised consumer experiences. Neuroscientific insights are integrated with technologies such as AI-powered recommendation systems and virtual reality to help brands engage emotionally with customers. However, ethical concerns such as data privacy, cultural sensitivity, and manipulative behaviours necessitate the continued and responsible use of these technologies.

INTRODUCTION

Neurogastronomy is an interdisciplinary study topic that investigates how cognitive processes impact food perception. This approach seeks to understand how the brain perceives taste, smell, and touch, as well as how these sensory inputs influence consumer decisions. Neurobiology, psychology, economics, and marketing insights can be combined in a holistic framework to better understand the neurological mechanisms behind consumer behaviour. One of the basic assumptions in this field is that taste perception is intrinsically multimodal. According to Spence (2015), flavour is not confined to taste receptors on the tongue, but rather develops from the integration of several modalities such as vision, smell, hearing, and touch. This viewpoint is backed by the findings of Stead et al. (2022), who emphasise how

DOI: 10.4018/979-8-3373-1152-4.ch011

simultaneous management of sensory experiences in food consumption can improve the consumer experience. The integration of these senses in the brain demonstrates that taste perception is influenced not only by what is consumed, but also by presentation style and contextual cues.

Neurogastronomy considers psychological factors as well as the senses. Pribić and Azpiroz's (2018) study found that factors like satiety, past experiences, and preferences influence individuals' eating habits. As a result, food presentation, expectation creation, and marketing methods elicit favourable emotional responses from consumers, making them predictors of preference and satisfaction levels. Indeed, Herz (2015) demonstrated these linkages during the International Neurogastronomy Association's opening conference, emphasising the importance of culinary techniques and neurological reactions on consumer behaviour.

Yoon et al. (2012) investigated the neurophysiological foundation of psychological structures that influence consumer decisions, such as hunger, emotional state, and social setting. They showed how neuroscience can supplement classic behavioural theories by modelling these structures. Not only what the consumer sees or tastes, but also the cognitive schemas they hold from previous experiences, influence decision-making processes.

The impact of this research on marketing strategies is becoming more obvious because to the subfield of neuromarketing. Consumers' cognitive and emotional responses to marketing stimuli can be measured using techniques such as eye tracking, facial expression analysis, and EEGs. Zhu et al. (2022) demonstrate how these technologies can be used to methods such as advertisement design and product placement, allowing for more effective decision-making. In this scenario, effective control of "sensory cues" is particularly important for directing consumer attention.

Labban et al. (2021) discovered that different demographic groups respond differently to marketing cues, and that emotional responses are especially important in good and unhealthy food preferences. These findings are congruent with the findings of Covino et al. (2021), who emphasised that decision-making processes are influenced not only by rational calculations but also by fundamental neurological and emotional processes.

Kim et al. (2019) found that taste judgements differ based on an individual's physiological and psychological status. Taste is influenced not just by the stimulus's physical qualities, but also by the individual's prior experiences, emotional context, and cultural heritage. In this context, Jayasinghe and colleagues (2017) investigated the effect of sweetness perception on individual food choices, concluding that the taste experience is far more complicated and contextual. This knowledge not only provides a theoretical foundation but also has practical economic repercussions. According to Amran et al. (2021), neuroscientific data and methodologies drive marketing tactics and demonstrate the importance of the emotional connection that businesses have with consumers in terms of sales success.

Similarly, researchers are increasingly looking into the impact of visual presentation, container design, and ambient sounds on the food experience. Campo et al. (2021) shown that background music utilised during wine tasting increases consumer pleasure and purchase intention, whereas Spence et al. (2022) demonstrated that the visual presentation of food directly influences taste perception and preference. This shows that marketing techniques that deliberately use sensory signals have the potential to influence consumer behaviour.

In terms of regional and cultural marketing, Savelli et al. (2022) investigated the impact of local food product representations on gastronomic tourism and discovered that local aspects that resonate with consumers on sensory and emotional levels boost product desirability. This study demonstrates that marketing strategies that emphasise cultural identity can be rebuilt using neurogastronomy. Neurogastronomy provides a multifaceted framework in which sensory, cognitive, and emotional processes influence consumer behaviour and marketing methods. This approach, which goes beyond traditional economic models and focusses on the unconscious triggers of consumer decisions, serves as the foundation for both effective marketing strategies and long-term consumption patterns. Future study is expected to yield more precise insights in this area, taking into consideration elements such as cultural background, age groupings, and psychophysiological differences..

NEUROGASTRONOMY: GETTING DOWN TO BASICS

The fundamental assumption underlying neurogastronomy is that the taste sensation is fundamentally multimodal. Spence's research emphasises that taste perception encompasses not just taste (gustation) and smell (olfaction), but also visual features, aural cues, and tactile interactions (Spence, 2015). The brain combines these various sensory inputs to generate a more complete taste experience, which enriches the eating experience. Krishna and Elder's findings lend credence to this approach, revealing how cognitive and sensory inputs impact taste perception and consuming behaviours (Krishna & Elder, 2020). In the context of food consumption, context and environmental factors have a significant impact on taste perception. Colour, for example, can have a direct impact on consumers' flavour expectations; because people identify certain colours with specific tastes, these associations have the potential to steer perception (Spence & Levitan, 2022).

The basic mechanics of taste perception are highly complex, involving neuronal pathways that connect taste receptor cells to the brain and are activated by specific chemical interactions. Li and colleagues discovered that taste perception is processed through five basic qualities: sweet, salty, sour, bitter, and umami, and that brain regions such as the insula and cortex play a role in this process (Li et al., 2022). Nandorfy and colleagues claim that the combination of smell, taste, and touch is critical to a comprehensive comprehension of flavour. This multimodal fusion influences not just the immediate taste experience, but also customer preferences and future decisions.

Understanding the neurological foundation of taste perception is also useful in designing efficient marketing tactics for the food and beverage business. Neuromarketing employs neuroscientific technologies like EEG and fMRI to analyse customer preferences and decision-making processes in real time (Vela & Varga, 2022). These techniques expose customers' unconscious responses to marketing stimuli, enabling strategic reorganisation of product sensory qualities. According to research, the sensation of taste is more than just a biological process; visual design, smell marketing, and even aural manipulations can all influence taste perception. Such approaches fall under the category of sensory communication and are based on the creation of cues that target specific emotional reactions.

Environmental elements that influence customers' sense of flavour are also essential. As SEO (2020) demonstrated, a space's atmosphere - light, design, and music - can have a direct impact on consumers' perceptions of taste and the enjoyment they derive from their eating experiences. In this setting, marketers can significantly improve customer happiness and brand loyalty by designing environments that impact consumers' sensory experiences. A rising number of research suggest that gender influences flavour perception and consumption behaviour. For example, Koubaa and Eleuch (2020) shown that men and women respond differently to odour stimuli, which is reflected in taste perceptions and eating habits. These findings pave the way for the creation of gender-specific marketing models for product development and advertising tactics.

Another important topic in neurogastronomy is the interaction of the senses. Cross-modal connections, defined as one sense impacting the perception of another, allow eating experiences to grow more complex. Reinoso-Carvalho et al. (2017) discovered that when particular sounds are combined with specific foods, flavour perception changes. Brietzke and Meyer's concept of temporal self-compression demonstrates that past taste experiences conceptually simplify over time, thereby shaping consumer expectations. In this scenario, marketers can strengthen the emotional tie built with the product by employing storytelling strategies that draw on consumers' prior experiences.

Taste perception is directly tied to both biological and psychological processes, as well as the cultural background. Caneppele et al. (2022) highlight the possibilities provided by neuroscientific methods for explaining the impact of cultural variables on sensory perception. Seasonal and cultural narratives about food contain powerful emotional and sensory representations that influence consumer behaviour. The association that traditional dishes have with cultural identity might promote the creation of content in marketing tactics that emphasises nostalgia and a sense of belonging.

As sensory sciences and culinary arts collaborate more, the future of neurogastronomy will grow into applicable fields. Chefs, marketers, and academics collaborate to discover new insights into the functioning of the human senses and translate this knowledge into unique product experiences. Future study, particularly on sensory adaptation processes, could aid in our understanding of long-term preferences and avoidance behaviours by describing how responses to repeated stimuli alter with time.

In the context of sustainable food marketing, neurogastronomy has the ability to change consumers' perceptions of locally sourced, ethically sourced, and nutritious products. Sustainability statements accompanied by sensory cues can raise consumer behavioural awareness and environmentally friendly product preferences. As a result, a meaningful connection can be made between sensory enjoyment and ethical consuming behaviours. The neurogastronomy method focusses not only on the senses, but also on consumer decision-making processes, allowing for novel solutions that combine sensory richness with strategic marketing in the food industry. This multidisciplinary discipline, which combines taste experiences and marketing methods, is transforming the future of food experience through scientific discoveries and practical applications.

TASTE AND SENSORY PERCEPTION IN THE MARKETING STRATEGIES

Taste and sensory perception play an important role in shaping consumer behaviour and decision-making. As the food industry becomes more competitive, knowing how these sensory experiences work has become critical to devising effective marketing techniques. Businesses can create and sell products and experiences that engage with customers on a deeper level using methodologies informed by sensory psychology, neuroscience, and consumer behaviour literature. This detailed research looks at the impact of taste and sensory perception on marketing tactics from multiple perspectives, shedding light on the implications for both brands and consumers. Consumer behaviour is so dependent on sensory inputs that logical decision-making processes alone cannot explain it; these impressions have a direct impact on an individual's attitudes, perceptions, and preferences. Lintong et al. (2023) found that the flavour factor has a substantial impact on purchasing decisions, particularly in food-related products, and is a predictor of consumer happiness and loyalty. The study emphasises that the taste variable has a beneficial effect on purchasing decisions and that, in this context, taste perception should be considered a fundamental component in marketing strategies (Lintong et al., 2023).

According to Elimelech et al. (2024), the human brain interprets taste and flavour sensations in a multimodal environment, therefore marketing tactics should target not only the sense of taste but also the visual, aural, olfactory, and tactile senses. This multisensory method allows for the holistic construction of consumer perception, which enriches the taste experience. Wang and Chang (2022) and Ares et al. (2022) demonstrate that sensory cues like restaurant atmosphere and product packaging can directly influence consumer preference by eliciting significant emotional responses.

Understanding the nuances of taste perception gives firms a huge advantage in terms of product creation and marketing communication. According to Duarte et al. (2021), taste is a subjective experience that is influenced by genetics, cultural traditions, and personal preferences. In this context, it is important to consider the role of these individual and cultural elements while creating marketing strategies. Su et al.'s (2024) study on consumer purchasing decisions for plant-based milk replacements found that familiarity with product attributes and advertising exposure positively influenced customer willingness to pay. This case demonstrates that when new items are brought to the market, consumers who are well-informed and familiar with the product's sensory qualities are more likely to purchase it.

External components such as packaging, promotion, and brand identification have a strong influence on taste perception in marketing. Hermienti and Wardi's (2019) research shows that packaging design and labelling can raise hedonic expectations, which can influence customer decisions. Wang and Chang (2022) demonstrated that packaging design is more than just an aesthetic feature; it is also a perceptual guide, as container colour has a major impact on taste expectations.

Culture influences the relationship between taste perception and marketing methods. Ares et al. (2022) discovered that culturally appropriate packaging not only attracts attention, but also improves communication with the target audience and influences purchasing decisions. Gundala and Singh's (2021) study, on the other hand, emphasised the sensitivity of young and educated consumers to natural aromas and healthy product preferences; it demonstrated that the preference for organic products is increasingly associated with the pursuit of emotional and sensory satisfaction. These findings demonstrate that customised marketing strategies based on demographic factors can be tailored to sensory preferences.

Seo's (2020) research demonstrates how background music employed in restaurants influences consumer perception and enjoyment of the dining experience. This shows that auditory branding might boost customer happiness by matching the surroundings to the brand identity.

Taste is both a physical and emotional experience. Duarte et al. (2021) demonstrate that emotional attachments with food have a significant impact on purchase intention, particularly when combined with health-related marketing messages. According to Çil and Pangburn (2017), experiential narratives that evoke emotions like nostalgia, warmth, and familiarity increase brand loyalty and deepen consumers' emotional connection to the product. Seo's (2020) research demonstrates how background music employed in restaurants influences consumer perception and enjoyment of the dining experience. This shows that auditory branding might boost customer happiness by matching the surroundings to the brand identity.

Digital marketing alters the interaction between the consumer and the brand, shaping the impression of taste accordingly. Mishra et al. (2024) discovered that digital advertising had a beneficial impact on brand awareness and purchasing decisions, with presentations that stress the flavour aspects of items having a particularly strong impact on the consumer. Salem (2018) claimed that effective user contact in digital settings is critical for establishing trust and reinforcing the idea of quality. It is apparent that study into taste and sensory perception will be critical in guiding future marketing efforts. Segmentation models based on thorough analyses of taste preferences, sensory experiences, and demographic data will allow for more focused and effective advertisements.

In this setting, combining data-driven marketing methods with sensory-appealing strategies is crucial for raising conversion rates and retaining customers. Taste and sensory perception are important aspects that influence consumer behaviour and determine the success of marketing efforts. A marketing strategy that incorporates sensory experiences, emotional connections, and cultural distinctions will not only help to strengthen consumer bonds, but will also allow for the long-term increase in brand value. In today's changing market environment, comprehensive tactics based on sensory science, digital marketing, and consumer psychology will be critical to gaining a competitive advantage in the food industry.

THE ROLE OF COLOR AND PACKAGING

Colour and packaging design are among the most significant visual aspects that influence consumer perception, expectations, and thus product preference, particularly in food and beverage items. Several studies have revealed that colours have a direct impact on taste perception. Warm colours, such as yellow and orange, are connected with sweetness, but dark colours can elicit more complex emotional reactions and perceptions of quality. However, advancements in artificial intelligence technology enable marketers and manufacturers to optimise packaging tactics based on sensory perceptions and customer preferences.

Several studies have found that colours influence customer emotions and purchasing decisions. Warm tones (red, orange) evoke enthusiasm and excitation, while cool tones promote confidence, tranquilly, and professionalism (Piqueras-Fiszman & Spence, 2012). According to Piqueras-Fiszman and Spence's study, changing the colour of the cup used to serve a drink affects taste perception. This is interesting because it demonstrates how simple visual details can alter taste expectations.

Even before the food is tasted, the colour of the packaging can set sensory expectations. Wang and Chang (2022) discovered that red packaging improved the sense of sweetness, even before the taste test. This research demonstrates how important visual colour cues are in creating the product experience. Consumers frequently link certain colours with specific flavours. Yellow and green colours represent sweetness and freshness, while dark tones represent bitterness or intensity (Żukowska et al., 2025). The visual signals offered by the packaging can lead to biases regarding the product by directing taste expectations. According to Akpinar-Bayizit et al. (2017), appealing packaging factors like colour have a direct impact on consumer purchasing decisions. As a result, selecting colours in container design that correspond to sensory expectations is critical to consumer pleasure.

Artificial intelligence (AI) has been a significant tool in packaging design in recent years. By analysing enormous data sets on colour, taste, and design preferences, AI algorithms aid in the development of consumer-friendly packaging. Peng et al.'s (2022) study demonstrates that machine learning is effective in predicting the attractiveness of colour combinations, allowing brands to make better educated judgements. Coca-Cola's red colour is an excellent example of how colour strategy influences consumer perception. According to He and Lv (2021), Coca-Cola's famous red colour not only adds visual distinction, but it also enhances brand loyalty by being connected with feelings like enthusiasm and energy. Similarly, green tones are typically picked by healthy food businesses since they are associated with a sense of health. Theben et al. (2020) demonstrated that green reinforces health messages and is particularly effective in products connected with healthy life.

The strategic use of colour combinations can also influence consumer perception. According to Huang et al. (2020), combining warm and cool colours improves the visual attractiveness of packaging and has a beneficial impact on product evaluation. This emphasises the need for marketers to properly plan colour harmonies. Colour preferences can vary depending on cultural setting, thus these distinctions should be considered during the design process. Kwon et al. (2024) emphasised that different cultures can have distinct emotional and cognitive responses to colours, therefore cultural sensitivity should be included in marketing efforts.

Colour choices should also be consistent with the brand's overall positioning. Colour inconsistency can confuse the buyer. Xiao et al. (2021) said that technical aspects, particularly colour saturation, might influence consumer perception and that a consistent colour strategy should be implemented over the entire product line. Packaging and colour choices should be assessed not only for aesthetic reasons, but also as a prerequisite for sensory experiences. Colour preferences have a direct impact on how consumers perceive the product's taste, health advantages, and overall quality. Brands can build packaging strategies that are attentive to consumer expectations while also taking aesthetic and sensory harmony into account thanks to data analysis powered by AI. Understanding the psychological effects of colours and their function in taste perception can give marketers a competitive advantage in terms of brand loyalty, consumer happiness, and purchase behaviour.

SENSORY STRATEGIES

Sensory marketing is gaining popularity in the marketing industry as a strategy for improving consumer experience and brand loyalty by utilising a variety of sensory inputs. Brands that appeal to the senses of taste, smell, and touch, particularly in the food and beverage industry, can generate memorable experiences by developing an emotional connection with customers.

One of the most visible examples of sensory branding is the use of fragrance in establishments such as coffee shops. The distinct aroma of freshly brewed coffee not only draws customers, but also boosts product appreciation and brand loyalty. The multi-sensory strategy involves generating complete brand experiences that appeal to more than one sense. Sensory experiences, according to scholars such as Hultén and Hepola, are an important component of brand management because they influence consumer perceptions, preferences, and behaviours (Shahid et al., 2022; Hepola et al., 2017). The use of numerous sensory stimuli results in a richer and more engaging consumer experience, increasing emotional attachment to the brand.

Taste is one of the most important senses, particularly in the food and beverage business. According to research, visual and olfactory cues can influence taste characteristics. The product's look and fragrance influence expectations about its flavour, affecting total consumer satisfaction (Moreira et al., 2017). The coffee fragrance experienced when visiting coffee shops enhances the enjoyment of the product's flavour and reinforces brand loyalty.

Coffee brands frequently engage the senses of taste and smell with free samples, scent diffusers, and in-store brewing experiences. This method not only seeks quick delight, but it also fosters long-term brand preferences and loyalty. According to Shahid and colleagues, sensory marketing stimuli improve the brand experience, increasing emotional attachment and brand loyalty (Shahid et al., 2022). When customers correlate pleasant sensory experiences with coffee companies with positive emotional states, their loyalty to the brand grows.

Scent is more than just a background element; it interacts with people, influencing their perceptions and behaviours. This method, often known as "scent marketing," can elicit emotional responses and brand associations (Errajaa et al., 2021). Because the sense of smell has a profound influence on memory and emotions, it is a valuable tool in branding efforts. The fragrance of fresh coffee in coffee shops might trigger childhood memories or calming experiences, resulting in a deep emotional bond with the customer. According to Upadhyaya, sensory branding, which includes aroma, is crucial for differentiating from competitors and building a unique brand identity. Empirical study has also shown that smell marketing is effective. For example, Errajaa and colleagues demonstrated that smells that are consistent with the brand image have a good impact on customer emotions and boost the success of marketing efforts (Errajaa et al., 2021). Furthermore, Muli et al. (2023) claim that sensory brand experiences influence consumer behaviour and that well-planned sensory features drive repeat purchases.

In addition to taste and smell, the sense of touch plays an essential role in sensory branding. Touch has been linked to emotional experiences, which influence decision-making processes and customer satisfaction. According to research, tactile interactions help to develop a relationship with the product and increase perceptions of quality. In coffee shops, the texture of the packaging, the temperature of the cup, and the weight of the product all add considerably to the whole sensory experience. Several research have indicated that tactile sensations have psychological impacts and can influence brand perception (Moreira et al., 2017).

Neuroscientific investigations provide new insights into how sensory experiences influence consumer behaviour. These studies look at how sensory inputs are processed in the brain, which reveals how businesses may communicate with customers on a neurological level. According to Caneppele et al. (2022), neuroscientific methods can help study the effects of sensory marketing on customer decisions and brand loyalty. According to Gao and Lan's research on sensory brand experience, the emotional involvement elicited by these sensory sensations is closely related to brand authenticity and loyalty.

NEUROGASTRONOMY TOOLS POWERED BY ARTIFICIAL INTELLIGENCE

Technological advancements, particularly in artificial intelligence (AI), have considerably expanded the subject of neurogastronomy by providing sophisticated tools for analysing sensory perception and customer preferences. Neurogastronomy integrates scientific study on how the brain perceives and processes flavours while broadening the traditional bounds of gastronomy. In this way, it enriches our comprehension of gastronomic experiences. According to Gordon M. Shepherd, a pioneer in the discipline, neurogastronomy investigates the impact of sensory experiences on taste, scent, and our thoughts about food (Havermans & Hendriks-Hartensveld, 2019). Using neuroscience data, researchers and chefs may develop experiences that appeal not only to taste but also to the emotional and psychological aspects of eating behaviour.

AI is ushering in a new age for neurogastronomy. AI solutions based on machine learning algorithms may analyse massive datasets of sensory perceptions, preferences, and consumer behaviour. This data-driven method allows us to forecast how people will react to various food stimuli based on their previous behaviours and preferences. AI can be used to analyse sensory data from taste testing, consumer surveys, and even social media sentiment analysis (Varshney et al., 2019). AI provides novel approaches to evaluating consumer preferences for scent, taste, and overall gastronomic experiences. AI can use sentiment analysis to assess how consumers experience specific cuisines in real time by analysing feedback on social media and internet platforms. Emotional responses to flavours or dishes might help firms better customise their products to client expectations (Spence, 2016).

In a recent study, researchers employed AI algorithms to examine the correlations between many sensory components, including taste, texture, scent, and visual presentation. This research predicts how customers will perceive specific pairings, allowing chefs and producers to create novel recipes that maximise sensory satisfaction (Varshney et al., 2019). Recent breakthroughs in neurobiology have demonstrated that taste and smell are inextricably linked in flavour perception. AI-powered research methodologies can model these intricate connections, allowing us to better grasp how specific flavour components influence overall sensory impressions. Certain flavours have been demonstrated in studies to either improve or impair taste perception (Li et al., 2022). AI models may also replicate the impact of texture and temperature on taste, studying how different combinations enhance or diminish flavour profiles. For example, intentionally blending different textures, such as crunchy, creamy, or chewy, can considerably improve the entire flavour experience (Nandorfy et al., 2022).

Neurogastronomy investigates the intricacies of taste perception using both AI and neuroscientific methods. These technologies include neuroimaging, electrophysiological tests, and computer modelling. Neuroimaging techniques like Functional Magnetic Resonance Imaging (fMRI) and Electroencephalography (EEG) enable researchers to see which parts of the brain are active when people encounter distinct tastes, textures, or scents. For example, research demonstrating that bittersweet chocolate activates specific parts of the brain have highlighted the complicated interplay between taste modalities and emotional reactions (Robertson et al., 2021). By processing and analysing this imaging data, AI can find patterns between brain activity and sensory experience, expanding our knowledge of why some flavours are more enjoyable.

AI integration with neurogastronomy technologies has the potential to bring practical benefits to restaurants, food makers, and gastronomy experts. These technologies enable brands to create personalised eating experiences that consumers will connect with emotionally. Restaurants can employ AI to analyse client preferences and tailor menus to regional taste trends. AI analytics, combined with taste test data, enables restaurants to optimise menus for maximum appeal and satisfaction (Spence, 2016). For example, customer reviews, meal ratings, and tasting feedback can all be used to determine the most popular meals and rebuild the menu accordingly.

Food makers can use neurogastronomy principles and artificial intelligence to create new goods that are tailored to consumer tastes. Companies can increase product innovation and reduce risk by modelling alternative flavour combinations and anticipating consumer responses. Using AI for sensory product testing can accelerate development by decreasing expenses and time (Зинченко et al., 2024). Sensor-based AI algorithms created by IBM's "Chef Watson" analyse hundreds of component combinations and sensory qualities to recommend new recipes that maximise flavour (Varshney et al., 2019). These tools enable chefs and food innovators to push creative boundaries.

AI-powered sensory analysis can assist businesses in providing immersive consumer experiences by optimising the environment in which food is served or consumed. According to research, ambient fragrances and background music have a considerable impact on taste perception. Restaurants can utilise AI analysis to change the lighting, aroma, and sound to create unique sensory environments, thereby improving the entire eating experience. Despite these promising uses, using AI to neurogastronomy presents certain hurdles. One of the most significant issues is the massive amount of data needed to adequately train AI algorithms. This data must include a wide range of customer sensory preferences and experiences in order for predictive models to effectively represent distinct consumer groups (Spence, 2016). Furthermore, ethical concerns such as data privacy and consumer consent must be properly addressed while gathering sensory experience data. Transparency in data use and a commitment to consumer privacy are crucial for establishing trust between businesses and customers.

Neurogastronomy enabled by AI has the potential to alter our understanding and improvement of culinary experiences. Restaurants and food manufacturers may create personalised experiences that engage customers on both an emotional and sensory level by combining neuroscientific insights with advanced AI analytics. As the gastronomic world evolves, incorporating AI into neurogastronomy will enable new flavour breakthroughs and consumer engagement opportunities. As these tools and methodologies are developed further, the potential for creating remarkable dining experiences where science and art intersect in the culinary arena will grow.

HOW NEUROGASTRONOMY COULD AFFECT MARKETING CAMPAIGNS?

Marketers can use neuroscience findings to more successfully impact consumer behaviour by creating advertisements that not only catch attention but also elicit emotional responses and improve decision-making processes. One of neurogastronomy's marketing benefits is its capacity to comprehend consumer preferences and behaviours using sensory analysis methodologies. Sensory qualities including taste, fragrance, and visual appeal can be carefully adjusted to boost the perceived value of food products. According to research, visual marketing messages have a considerable impact on consumers' brain responses, which affects perceptions of product palatability and attractiveness (Spence et al., 2022). Using fragrance marketing and visual techniques can create a multisensory dining experience that resonates deeply with consumers (Girona-Ruíz et al., 2021).

Neurogastronomy emphasises the importance of emotions in consumer decision-making processes. Several studies have found that emotional impact is important in consumer evaluations of food, and that specific sensory presentations elicit higher levels of attention and engagement (Recuerda et al., 2021). Marketers may use this knowledge to create ads that not only showcase the sensory features of the product, but also seek to elicit an emotional connection with the brand. According to current research, sensory signals have a substantial impact on consumer emotions. This emphasises the importance of marketing tactics that consider the interaction of numerous sensory modalities in order to obtain effective results.

In addition to emotional and sensory aspects, knowing the neurological mechanisms that drive consumer decisions enables the development of more tailored marketing techniques. Neuroscientific methods such as EEG and fMRI have demonstrated that sensory qualities and unconscious biases about food technologies frequently impact customer preferences and choices (Amran et al., 2021; Medina et al., 2020). This means that marketers must create messages that appeal not only to apparent customer preferences, but also to the implicit neurological processes that influence how consumers interact with food goods.

Furthermore, as the competitive landscape in the food market becomes more complex, the necessity for marketing strategies with solid scientific underpinnings grows. Neuromarketing research goes beyond traditional methodologies and provides important insights into customer behaviour, allowing for more effective evidence-based initiatives (Spence, 2016; Zhu et al., 2022). The use of neuroscientific insights to improve decision-making processes in marketing is consistent with broader trends in strategic management (Caneppele et al., 2022). Neurogastronomy has the ability to transform food marketing efforts by taking a holistic, multisensory approach that includes emotional engagement, sensory experience, and neuroscientific insights.

By deliberately integrating these characteristics, marketers can improve consumers' attachment to their food goods, boost brand loyalty, and ultimately achieve commercial success.

Experiential Marketing: Experiential marketing strives to generate lasting experiences between businesses and consumers, and it offers substantial benefits in terms of improving the taste experience through the use of multimodal stimuli. Integrating multisensory aspects such as music, images, and tactile factors, particularly in restaurants, can improve perceived flavour (Velasco et al., 2013; Stead et al., 2022). According to research, visual, aural, taste, smell, and touch cues have a greater impact on consumer behaviour when combined. For example, the sound of a spilt drink might elicit a sense of warmth in the consumer, influencing flavour perception (Velasco et al., 2013). Sensory stimuli provide emotional reinforcement, which is useful for enhancing consumer happiness and brand loyalty. Visually appealing, fragrant, and tactile items foster stronger interactions with customers (Cornil & Chandon, 2016; Schifferstein, 2021). Furthermore, digital experiences improved by technology such as augmented reality (AR) and virtual reality (VR) allow for multimodal marketing outside physical venues (Petit et al., 2019).

Customized Products: Machine learning contributes to brand loyalty by allowing the creation of personalised products based on consumer preferences. Recommendation systems make product recommendations based on previous encounters (Mustafa et al., 2024; Nelaturi & Devi, 2019). These technologies offer product personalisation through techniques like as deep learning and collaborative filtering (Portugal et al., 2018; Kong et al., 2024). These recommendations can be revised over time based on user input, improving their relevancy (Cui, 2024). Furthermore, this data can be utilised to build consumer-specific products; on e-commerce platforms, this method can improve conversion rates and client loyalty (Li et al., 2023). Predictive analytics also improves operational efficiency in areas like inventory management and consumer demand forecasting (Alom et al., 2019). Personalised marketing gives experiences that align with consumers' identities and values, making it more effective (Mustafa et al., 2024).

Methods of Promotion: Disruptive technology-based promotional strategies allow firms to communicate with consumers digitally via sensory ways. Virtual reality commercials boost interaction by mimicking product-related taste, auditory, and visual experiences. By fostering strong emotional ties, sensory marketing strategies boost the possibility of repeat purchases and favourable word-of-mouth communication (Rajaobelina et al., 2019; Wörfel et al., 2022). Proper sound and visual pairings can enhance flavour perception and impact consumer quality rating (Nghiêm-Phú, 2017; Rybowska & Dawidowska, 2024). Restaurant surroundings or virtual shelves can be reproduced using VR, allowing customers to "try without tasting" (Fatmawati et al., 2017). AI and machine learning enable personalised digital experiences, tailoring material to consumer preferences (Navrátilová & Milichovský, 2015). This method builds brand loyalty by connecting with consumers on an emotional and sensory level.

ETHICAL DIMENSIONS

The application of neurogastronomy in marketing provides crucial insights into consumer behaviour, particularly in terms of taste preferences. However, this method presents a variety of ethical concerns. Marketers must employ neurogastronomy ethically and honestly. In this context, transparency in data use, avoidance of manipulative methods, and cultural sensitivity are among the ethical problems raised in marketing strategies. Neurogastronomic approaches primarily use sensitive data to analyse consumers' taste preferences and behavioural patterns. This poses ethical issues regarding data privacy and individual confidentiality. According to Kumar and Suthar (2024), businesses should present their data collection and usage policies in a clear and understandable manner; they emphasise the importance of informing consumers about why their data is collected, how it is processed, and with whom it is shared. Transparency underpins both legal and ethical responsibilities.

Neurogastronomy evaluations have the potential to steer customer behaviour, which could lead to deceptive marketing techniques. It is unethical for firms to abuse consumer weaknesses for financial advantage. Munoz and Mallin (2019) find that sales professionals occasionally justify unethical behaviours by claiming that they "do no harm," which creates risky ground. Such techniques, which have the potential to disrupt the consumer's emotional and cognitive processes, must be founded on good ethical standards; otherwise, consumer trust and brand reputation may suffer. Adherence to ethical standards is a must for firms looking to include neurogastronomy into their marketing strategies. In this case, solutions based on "good practice examples" should be implemented. According to Mittelstadt et al. (2016), incorporating human interaction into AI-based decision-making processes is crucial for generating fair outcomes. Compliance by marketers with both legal requirements and ethical conventions will boost consumer trust while also creating long-term brand value.

The cultural context should be considered when evaluating the ethical implications of neurogastronomy-based marketing methods. Ethical perspectives may differ between cultures, and this is directly reflected in marketing strategies. According to Arli and Pekerti (2016), according to cultural ethical standards in foreign marketing activities improves customer trust and relationships with brands. As a result, cultural diversity must be considered while developing marketing strategy.

In summary, neurogastronomy presents remarkable opportunities in the field of marketing due to its ability to provide consumer-specific sensory experiences, but it also imposes fundamental ethical obligations such as data security, manipulation risk, adherence to ethical principles, and cultural sensitivity. Adopting these concepts holistically would help to increase consumer confidence while also boosting brand value in the long run.

THE FUTURE OF NEUROGASTRONOMY AND ARTIFICIAL INTELLIGENCE

The future of neurogastronomy, particularly when combined with artificial intelligence (AI) and flavour projection technologies, has the potential to fundamentally alter customers' food and taste experiences. At the heart of this advancement is the capacity to use data analytics and human-machine interactions to generate immersive sensory experiences. By incorporating multimodal data, these technologies can boost customer engagement and provide significant insights on preferences and behaviours. Taste projection and immersive technologies allow people to experience food through several senses at the same time, including visual, hearing, touch, taste, and smell, using techniques such as virtual reality (VR) and augmented reality. Donga et al. (2024) highlight how interactive gadgets are employed in immersive environments to facilitate sensory exploration, which enhances the gourmet experience. The combination of tastes, visual and audio stimuli allows consumers to interact with gourmet goods on a deeper level.

Studies highlighting the impact of understanding emotional components in culinary tourism on enhancing customer satisfaction back up the role of AI technologies in developing unique gastronomic experiences (Hsu et al., 2022). By analysing consumer input and preferences, AI may be used to build ideal sensory experiences, hence increasing brand loyalty and customer involvement in the food industry. Immersive technology, such as VR, can enhance experiences by linking sensory information to consumer emotions. Bogicevic et al. (2024) show how VR can alter marketing applications, particularly in the hospitality sector, and improve the quality of experience by affecting potential customers on an emotional level. Such immersive previews enable marketers to create memorable and emotionally resonant experiences, hence positively influencing purchasing decisions. Zhang and Song (2022) found that sensory signals can impact customer behaviour by providing immersive experiences, hence supporting technology-supported sustainable practices.

Sensory signals are critical in establishing emotional attachment, particularly in food-focused marketing efforts, and they reinforce positive behavioural intentions.

The Internet of Senses (IoS) is gaining popularity as a method for improving human-computer interaction by combining AI and sensory technology. This technique has the potential to profoundly alter how food brands interact with customers. Personalised and immersive multi-sensory experiences boost consumer engagement, creating new marketing opportunities (Gambera et al., 2022). The incorporation of technology in sensory experiences is a significant aspect in increasing user engagement. Flavián et al. (2021) highlight how the incorporation of VR devices improves consumers' perceptions of sensory richness, which boosts consumer engagement. These findings imply that marketers must truly grasp the interaction between technology and sensory perception in order to provide more effective experiences.

Despite all of these technological possibilities, ethical concerns should be central to the use of AI and immersive technology in neurogastronomy. Transparency and accountability are critical in the collecting and utilisation of customer preference data. The balance between personalisation and privacy should be safeguarded by ethical standards that prevent potential manipulations. The application of these technologies in marketing should be governed not just by technological capabilities, but also by ethical values. The future of neurogastronomy, aided by artificial intelligence and taste projection technologies, has the potential to fundamentally alter consumer experiences. Immersive and multi-sensory spaces can boost consumer connection while also providing valuable data to guide future gastronomic advances. However, it is critical that this advancement be carried out with an ethical framework that respects consumer rights and preferences.

CONCLUSION

The content of this book chapter demonstrates how the integration of neurogastronomy, artificial intelligence, and flavour projection technologies can alter food experiences for both consumers and brands. Understanding consumers' sensory impressions and behavioural tendencies using scientific approaches enables multidimensional interactions, particularly in marketing efforts. While neuroscientific data provides a solid foundation for understanding how consumers react to taste, smell, texture, and visual elements, AI-powered analyses enable the creation of novel applications such as personalised product recommendations, targeted campaigns, and real-time user experience improvements. Tools such as taste projection technologies and virtual reality (VR) enhance the consumer's emotional connection to the product by providing multi-sensory experiences even in non-physical surroundings, hence improving brand loyalty. While experiential marketing, in particular, stands out for techniques that increase taste perception through multi-sensory stimuli, AI-based personalisation apps enable the offering of items that are tailored to the consumer's individual tastes. In this context, the digitalisation of culinary experiences is altering not only consumption habits, but also the presentation and portrayal of food culture. However, this transition must occur within ethical constraints. Data privacy, manipulation risk, and cultural sensitivity are particularly important considerations for the long-term viability of neurogastronomic marketing. Transparent management of consumer data, respect for different communities' cultural standards, and prudence in areas vulnerable to emotional manipulation will be critical for the long-term acceptability of these technologies.

REFERENCES

Akpinar-Bayizit, A., Yilmaz-Ersan, L., Ozcan, T., Delikanli-Kiyak, B., Yıldız, E., & Vural, H. (2017). *Consumers' behavior towards table olives.* Etp International Journal of Food Engineering., DOI: 10.18178/ijfe.3.1.83-88

Alom, M., Carminati, B., & Ferrari, E. (2019). Adapting users' privacy preferences in smart environments., 165-172. DOI: 10.1109/ICIOT.2019.00036

Amran, A., Ibrahim, S., Malim, N., Hamzah, N., Sumari, P., Lufti, S., & Abdullah, J. (2021). Data acquisition and data processing using electroencephalogram in neuromarketing: A review. *Pertanika Journal of Science & Technology, 30*(1), 19–33. DOI: 10.47836/pjst.30.1.02

Ares, G., Velázquez, A., Vidal, L., Curutchet, M., & Varela, P. (2022). The role of food packaging on children's diet: Insights for the design of comprehensive regulations to encourage healthier eating habits in childhood and beyond. *Food Quality and Preference, 95*, 104366. DOI: 10.1016/j.foodqual.2021.104366

Arli, D., & Pekerti, A. (2016). Who is more ethical? cross-cultural comparison of consumer ethics between religious and non-religious consumers. *Journal of Consumer Behaviour, 16*(1), 82–98. DOI: 10.1002/cb.1607

Bogicevic, V., Liu, S., Kandampully, J., Seo, S., & Rudd, N. (2024). Experiential marketing to gen z: Fine-tuning brand experience through virtual reality. *Journal of Hospitality & Tourism Research (Washington, D.C.), 48*(8), 1424–1438. DOI: 10.1177/10963480241256564

Brietzke, S., & Meyer, M. (2021). Temporal self-compression: behavioral and neural evidence that past and future selves are compressed as they move away from the present. https://doi.org/DOI: 10.1101/2021.01.22.427831

Campo, R., Rosato, P., & Battisti, E. (2021). Multisensory analysis and wine marketing: Systematic review and perspectives. *British Food Journal, 124*(10), 3274–3292. DOI: 10.1108/BFJ-03-2021-0222

Caneppele, N., Serra, F., Pinochet, L., & Ribeiro, I. (2022). Potential and challenges for using neuroscientific tools in strategic management studies. *RAUSP Management Journal, 57*(3), 235–263. DOI: 10.1108/RAUSP-01-2021-0014

Çil, E., & Pangburn, M. (2017). Mass customization and guardrails: "you can not be all things to all people". *Production and Operations Management, 26*(9), 1728–1745. DOI: 10.1111/poms.12716

Covino, D., Viola, I., Paientko, T., & Boccia, F. (2021). Neuromarketing: Some remarks by an economic experiment on food consumer perception and ethic sustainability. *Rivista di Studi sulla Sostenibilità*, (1), 187–199. DOI: 10.3280/RISS2021-001011

Cui, C. (2024). Career interest assessment: college students career planning based on machine leaning. jes, 20(6s), 1633-1644. DOI: 10.52783/jes.3083

Donga, J., Gomes, P., Sá, V., Marques, A., & Pereira, J. (2024). Interaction devices for multi-sensory exploration in immersive environments., 357-364. DOI: 10.17979/spudc.9788497498913.50

Duarte, P., Teixeira, M., & Silva, S. (2021). Healthy eating as a trend: Consumers' perceptions towards products with nutrition and health claims. *Revista Brasileira de Gestão de Negócios*, *23*(3), 405–421. DOI: 10.7819/rbgn.v23i3.4113

Elimelech, E., Ert, E., Parag, Y., & Hochman, G. (2024). Exploring the impact of visual perception and taste experience on consumers' acceptance of suboptimal fresh produce. *Sustainability (Basel)*, *16*(7), 2698. DOI: 10.3390/su16072698

Errajaa, K., Legohérel, P., Daucé, B., & Bilgihan, A. (2021). Scent marketing: Linking the scent congruence with brand image. *International Journal of Contemporary Hospitality Management*, *33*(2), 402–427. DOI: 10.1108/IJCHM-06-2020-0637

Flavián, C., Ibáñez-Sánchez, S., & Orús, C. (2021). Integrating virtual reality devices into the body: effects of technological embodiment on customer engagement and behavioral intentions toward the destination., 79-94. DOI: 10.4324/9781003176039-8

Gambera, D., Duarte, E., & Riccò, D. (2022). Internet of senses (ios) and internet of sensory health (iosh): a new technology epiphany.. DOI: 10.54941/ahfe1001403

Gao, F., & Lan, X. (2020). Sensory brand experience: Development and validation in the chinese context. *Frontiers in Psychology*, *11*, 1436. Advance online publication. DOI: 10.3389/fpsyg.2020.01436 PMID: 32793024

Girona-Ruíz, D., Cano-Lamadrid, M., Carbonell-Barrachina, Á., López-Lluch, D., & Sendra, E. (2021). Aromachology related to foods, scientific lines of evidence: A review. *Applied Sciences (Basel, Switzerland)*, *11*(13), 6095. DOI: 10.3390/app11136095

Gundala, R., & Singh, A. (2021). What motivates consumers to buy organic foods? results of an empirical study in the united states. *PLoS One*, *16*(9), e0257288. DOI: 10.1371/journal.pone.0257288 PMID: 34506582

Havermans, R., & Hendriks-Hartensveld, A. (2019). Does mri acoustic noise affect chemosensory perception? *Chemosensory Perception*, *13*(1), 11–18. DOI: 10.1007/s12078-019-09257-9

He, X., & Lv, X. (2021). From the color composition to the color psychology: Soft drink packaging in warm colors, and spirits packaging in dark colors. *Color Research and Application*, *47*(3), 758–770. DOI: 10.1002/col.22748

Hepola, J., Karjaluoto, H., & Hintikka, A. (2017). The effect of sensory brand experience and involvement on brand equity directly and indirectly through consumer brand engagement. *Journal of Product and Brand Management*, *26*(3), 282–293. DOI: 10.1108/JPBM-10-2016-1348

Herz, R. (2015). Birth of a neurogastronomy nation: The inaugural symposium of the international society of neurogastronomy. *Chemical Senses*, •••, bjv073. Advance online publication. DOI: 10.1093/chemse/bjv073 PMID: 26657144

Hsu, F., Liu, J., & Lin, H. (2022). Affective components of gastronomy tourism: Measurement scale development and validation. *International Journal of Contemporary Hospitality Management*, *34*(9), 3278–3299. DOI: 10.1108/IJCHM-09-2021-1112

Huang, J., Wang, Z., Liu, H., & Yu, L. (2020). Similar or contrastive? impact of product–background color combination on consumers' product evaluations. *Psychology and Marketing*, *37*(7), 961–979. DOI: 10.1002/mar.21361

Jayasinghe, S., Kruger, R., Walsh, D., Cao, G., Rivers, S., Richter, M., & Breier, B. (2017). Is sweet taste perception associated with sweet food liking and intake? *Nutrients*, *9*(7), 750. DOI: 10.3390/nu9070750 PMID: 28708085

Kim, S., Byun, J., Jung, J., & Choi, J. (2019). Clinical characteristics and gustatory profiles in patients with subjective taste complaints. *Journal of Oral Medicine and Pain*, *44*(3), 103–111. DOI: 10.14476/jomp.2019.44.3.103

Kong, W., Tai, T., Naveen, P., & Santoso, H. (2024). Performance evaluation on e-commerce recommender system based on knn, svd, coclustering and ensemble approaches. *Journal of Informatics and Web Engineering*, *3*(3), 63–76. DOI: 10.33093/jiwe.2024.3.3.4

Koubaa, Y., & Eleuch, A. (2020). Gender effects on odor-induced taste enhancement and subsequent food consumption. *Journal of Consumer Marketing*, *37*(5), 511–519. DOI: 10.1108/JCM-02-2019-3091

Krishna, A., & Elder, R. (2020). A review of the cognitive and sensory cues impacting taste perceptions and consumption. *Consumer Psychology Review*, *4*(1), 121–134. DOI: 10.1002/arcp.1069

Kumar, D., & Suthar, N. (2024). Ethical and legal challenges of ai in marketing: An exploration of solutions. *Journal of Information Communication and Ethics in Society*, *22*(1), 124–144. DOI: 10.1108/JICES-05-2023-0068

Kwon, M., Jeon, E., & Han, Y. (2024). The social side of color: How social exclusion influences preferences for color combination. *Psychology and Marketing*, *41*(7), 1649–1667. DOI: 10.1002/mar.22002

Labban, A., Ma, Y., & Dubé, L. (2021). A neurobehavioral account of differential consumer responses to price and in-store display between un/healthy food. *European Journal of Marketing*, *55*(11), 2988–3009. DOI: 10.1108/EJM-07-2020-0565

Li, J., Fu, J., Gao, J., Zhou, R., Wang, K., & Zhou, K. (2023). Effects of the spatial patterns of urban parks on public satisfaction: Evidence from shanghai, china. *Landscape Ecology*, *38*(5), 1265–1277. DOI: 10.1007/s10980-023-01615-z PMID: 37051135

Li, Y., Tan, Z., Wang, J., Cai, Y., Wang, M., Zhou, W., & Wang, L. (2022). Responses of chemosensory perception to stimulation of the human brain. *Annals of Neurology*, *93*(1), 175–183. DOI: 10.1002/ana.26532 PMID: 36218015

Lintong, E., Hardini, R., & Digdowiseiso, K. (2023). The influence of taste, word of mouth and consumer satisfaction on panada dapur mayank south jakarta purchasing decisions. *Jurnal Syntax Admiration*, *4*(1), 419–429. DOI: 10.46799/jsa.v4i1.856

Medina, C., Martínez-Fiestas, M., Viedma-del-Jesús, M., & Casado-Aranda, L. (2020). The processing of price during purchase decision making: Are there neural differences among prosocial and non-prosocial consumers? *Journal of Cleaner Production*, *271*, 122648. DOI: 10.1016/j.jclepro.2020.122648

Mishra, A., Sah, K., & Bhatta, S. (2024). Effectiveness of digital advertising in kathmandu valley. *Nep. J. Mgt.*, *11*(2), 172–188. DOI: 10.3126/njm.v11i2.68865

Mittelstadt, B., Allo, P., Taddeo, M., Wachter, S., & Floridi, L. (2016). The ethics of algorithms: Mapping the debate. *Big Data & Society*, *3*(2), 2053951716679679. Advance online publication. DOI: 10.1177/2053951716679679

Moreira, A., Fortes, N., & Ramiro, S. (2017). Influence of sensory stimuli on brand experience, brand equity and purchase intention. *Journal of Business Economics and Management*, *18*(1), 68–83. DOI: 10.3846/16111699.2016.1252793

Muli, J., Mugambi, R., & Bitok, J. (2023). Sensory brand experience and post-purchase behavior among millennial guests of classified hotels in nairobi city county, kenya. *Journal of Hospitality and Tourism Management*, *6*(5). Advance online publication. DOI: 10.53819/81018102t2290

Munoz, L., & Mallin, M. (2019). Unethical sales behavior neutralization: The impact of salesperson role variables and moderating effects of role relationship orientation. *Journal of Business and Industrial Marketing*, *34*(1), 62–79. DOI: 10.1108/JBIM-10-2017-0243

Mustafa, G., Jhamat, N., Arshad, Z., Yousaf, N., Abdal, M., Maray, M., Alqahtani, D., Merhabi, M. A., Aziz, M. A., & Ahmad, T. (2024). Ontocommerce: Incorporating ontology and sequential pattern mining for personalized e-commerce recommendations. *IEEE Access : Practical Innovations, Open Solutions*, *12*, 42329–42342. DOI: 10.1109/ACCESS.2024.3377120

Nandorfy, D., Watson, F., Likos, D., Siebert, T., Bindon, K., Kassara, S., & Francis, I. (2022). Influence of amino acids, and their interaction with volatiles and polyphenols, on the sensory properties of red wine. *Australian Journal of Grape and Wine Research*, *28*(4), 621–637. DOI: 10.1111/ajgw.12564

Navrátilová, L., & Milichovský, F. (2015). Ways of using guerrilla marketing in SMEs. *Procedia: Social and Behavioral Sciences*, *175*, 268–274. DOI: 10.1016/j.sbspro.2015.01.1200

Nelaturi, N., & Devi, G. (2019). A product recommendation model based on recurrent neural network. *Journal Européen des Systèmes Automatisés*, *52*(5), 501–507. DOI: 10.18280/jesa.520509

Nghiêm-Phú, B. (2017). Sensory marketing in an outdoor out-store shopping environment–an exploratory study in Japan. *Asia Pacific Journal of Marketing and Logistics*, *29*(5), 994–1016. DOI: 10.1108/APJML-09-2016-0178

Peng, M., Tong, Y., Xu, Z., Jiang, L., & Huang, H. (2022). How does the use of simultaneous contrast illusion on product-background color combination nudge consumer behavior? a behavioral and event-related potential study. *Frontiers in Neuroscience*, *16*, 942901. Advance online publication. DOI: 10.3389/fnins.2022.942901 PMID: 35968366

Piqueras-Fiszman, B., & Spence, C. (2012). The influence of the color of the cup on consumers' perception of a hot beverage. *Journal of Sensory Studies*, *27*(5), 324–331. DOI: 10.1111/j.1745-459X.2012.00397.x

Portugal, I., Alencar, P., & Cowan, D. (2018). The use of machine learning algorithms in recommender systems: A systematic review. *Expert Systems with Applications*, *97*, 205–227. DOI: 10.1016/j.eswa.2017.12.020

Pribić, T., & Azpiroz, F. (2018). Biogastronomy: Factors that determine the biological response to meal ingestion. *Neurogastroenterology and Motility*, *30*(7), e13309. Advance online publication. DOI: 10.1111/nmo.13309 PMID: 29392797

Rajaobelina, L., Lacroix, C., & St-Onge, A. (2019). Does experiential advertising impact credibility? *International Journal of Bank Marketing*, *37*(1), 171–191. DOI: 10.1108/IJBM-01-2017-0021

Recuerda, A., Tur-Viñes, V., Varón, D., & Valero, F. (2021). Emotional impact of dishes versus wines on restaurant diners: From haute cuisine open innovation. *Journal of Open Innovation*, *7*(1), 96. DOI: 10.3390/joitmc7010096

Reinoso-Carvalho, F., Touhafi, A., Steenhaut, K., Ee, R., & Velasco, C. (2017). Using sound to enhance taste experiences: an overview., 316-330. DOI: 10.1007/978-3-319-67738-5_19

Robertson, J., Ferreira, C., Reyneke, M., & Rosenstein, D. (2021). I think i like this: Assessing conscious versus subconscious wine taste responses using neuroscientific techniques. *International Journal of Wine Business Research*, *34*(1), 37–51. DOI: 10.1108/IJWBR-09-2020-0047

Rybowska, A., & Dawidowska, K. (2024). Sensory Marketing According To Shopping Centre Customers. *Scientific Journal of Gdynia Maritime University, 129 (129): 46, 61.*

Salem, M. (2018). Effects of perfume packaging on basque female consumers purchase decision in spain. *Management Decision*, *56*(8), 1748–1768. DOI: 10.1108/MD-04-2017-0363

Savelli, E., Gregory-Smith, D., Murmura, F., & Pencarelli, T. (2022). How to communicate typical–local foods to improve food tourism attractiveness. *Psychology and Marketing*, *39*(7), 1350–1369. DOI: 10.1002/mar.21668

Seo, H. (2020). Sensory nudges: The influences of environmental contexts on consumers' sensory perception, emotional responses, and behaviors toward foods and beverages. *Foods*, *9*(4), 509. DOI: 10.3390/foods9040509 PMID: 32316596

Shahid, S., Paul, J., Gilal, F., & Ansari, S. (2022). The role of sensory marketing and brand experience in building emotional attachment and brand loyalty in luxury retail stores. *Psychology and Marketing*, *39*(7), 1398–1412. DOI: 10.1002/mar.21661

Spence, C. (2015). Multisensory flavor perception. *Cell*, *161*(1), 24–35. DOI: 10.1016/j.cell.2015.03.007 PMID: 25815982

Spence, C. (2016). Neuroscience-inspired design: From academic neuromarketing to commercially relevant research. *Organizational Research Methods*, *22*(1), 275–298. DOI: 10.1177/1094428116672003

Spence, C., & Levitan, C. (2022). Exploring the links between colours and tastes/flavours. *Journal of Perceptual Imaging*, *5*(0), 000408-1, 000408–000416. DOI: 10.2352/J.Percept.Imaging.2022.5.000408

Spence, C., Motoki, K., & Petit, O. (2022). Factors influencing the visual deliciousness / eye-appeal of food. *Food Quality and Preference*, *102*, 104672. DOI: 10.1016/j.foodqual.2022.104672

Stead, S., Wetzels, R., Wetzels, M., Odekerken-Schröder, G., & Mahr, D. (2022). Toward multisensory customer experiences: A cross-disciplinary bibliometric review and future research directions. *Journal of Service Research*, *25*(3), 440–459. DOI: 10.1177/10946705221079941

Su, W., Gao, Z., Li, S., & Sheng, J. (2024). Determinants of consumer purchase decisions of plant-based milk alternatives: The role of preferences for product attributes. *China Agricultural Economic Review*, *17*(1), 191–211. DOI: 10.1108/CAER-08-2023-0225

Theben, A., Gerards, M., & Folkvord, F. (2020). The effect of packaging color and health claims on product attitude and buying intention. *International Journal of Environmental Research and Public Health*, *17*(6), 1991. DOI: 10.3390/ijerph17061991 PMID: 32197334

Upadhyaya, M. (2017). Emotional connect between brand and consumer through sensory branding. *American Journal of Industrial and Business Management*, *07*(04), 352–359. DOI: 10.4236/ajibm.2017.74025

Varshney, L., Pinel, F., Varshney, K., Bhattacharjya, D., Schörgendorfer, A., & Chee, Y. (2019). A big data approach to computational creativity: the curious case of chef watson. Ibm Journal of Research and Development, 63(1), 7:1-7:18. DOI: 10.1147/JRD.2019.2893905

Vela, M., & Varga, Á. (2022). Unveiling neuromarketing and its research methodology. *Encyclopedia*, *2*(2), 729–751. DOI: 10.3390/encyclopedia2020051

Wang, C., & Chang, F. (2022). The influence of packaging color on taste expectations and perceptions. *Color Research and Application*, *47*(6), 1426–1441. DOI: 10.1002/col.22812

Wörfel, P., Frentz, F., & Tautu, C. (2022). Marketing comes to its senses: A bibliometric review and integrated framework of sensory experience in marketing. *European Journal of Marketing*, *56*(3), 704–737. DOI: 10.1108/EJM-07-2020-0510

Xiao, C., Zhu, H., Wang, X., & Wu, L. (2021). Vividly warm: The color saturation of logos on brands' customer sensitivity judgment. *Color Research and Application*, *46*(6), 1347–1359. DOI: 10.1002/col.22682

Yoon, C., Gonzalez, R., Bechara, A., Berns, G., Dagher, A., Dubé, L., Huettel, S. A., Kable, J. W., Liberzon, I., Plassmann, H., Smidts, A., & Spence, C. (2012). Decision neuroscience and consumer decision making. *Marketing Letters*, *23*(2), 473–485. DOI: 10.1007/s11002-012-9188-z

Zhang, Y., & Song, Y. (2022). The effects of sensory cues on immersive experiences for fostering technology-assisted sustainable behavior: A systematic review. *Behavioral Sciences (Basel, Switzerland)*, *12*(10), 361. DOI: 10.3390/bs12100361 PMID: 36285930

Zhu, Z., Jin, Y., Su, Y., Jia, K., Lin, C., & Liu, X. (2022). Bibliometric-based evaluation of the neuromarketing research trend: 2010–2021. *Frontiers in Psychology*, *13*, 872468. Advance online publication. DOI: 10.3389/fpsyg.2022.872468 PMID: 35983212

Żukowska, P., Raj, D., Luccas, V., Ross, C., Kardas, M., & Bolini, H. (2025). Sensory-emotion relationships in white chocolate of modified color and sweetener among polish and brazilian consumers. *Journal of Food Science*, *90*(2), e70006. Advance online publication. DOI: 10.1111/1750-3841.70006 PMID: 39915283

Chapter 12
Mind Games:
Decoding the Subconscious Triggers of Manipulation Using Consumer Neuroscience and AI

Ana Iorga
http://orcid.org/0009-0003-4741-0824
Buyer Brain, UK

Denisa Cristina Alina Berceanu
http://orcid.org/0009-0008-0229-0095
University of Bucharest, Romania

Ana Maria Lepar
http://orcid.org/0009-0004-0763-5436
Balkan History Association, Romania

ABSTRACT

The rapid proliferation of artificial intelligence (AI) in online communication is reshaping how information is created, disseminated, and consumed. From personalized chatbots to AI-generated content and deepfake videos, these technologies are not only transforming engagement but also challenging our ability to discern truth from fabrication. This chapter explores the intersection of AI and consumer neuroscience in the context of manipulation, examining how AI leverages subconscious human processes to influence perceptions and decisions. The chapter delves into the psychological mechanisms that make individuals susceptible to manipulative messages, such as trust, fear, and cognitive biases. By integrating insights from neuroscience, it uncovers the subconscious drivers of behavior, providing a deeper understanding of how AI technologies can either empower or exploit individuals.

DOI: 10.4018/979-8-3373-1152-4.ch012

The chapter also highlights the ethical challenges posed by AI-driven manipulation, advocating for accountability and safeguards in AI development to minimize harm and ensure transparency.

In recent years, artificial intelligence has become a transformative force in online communication, reshaping how individuals, businesses, and organizations interact with one another. AI-generated content now dominates digital spaces, with tools like ChatGPT enabling users to refine their messages and enhance engagement, while companies leverage sophisticated bots to drive interactions. Platforms like Facebook have even launched AI-generated accounts, purportedly to boost engagement, signaling how integral AI has become in shaping the conversations we encounter online. This growing prevalence of AI in communication extends beyond text, with advancements in generative AI leading to the creation of AI-produced movies and deepfake videos that convincingly depict events that never occurred. Such content blurs the line between reality and fabrication, leaving viewers uncertain about what to trust in the digital world.

While these developments present exciting opportunities for innovation, they also bring significant ethical and societal challenges. The power of AI to influence perceptions and decisions is immense, and when wielded irresponsibly, it can result in manipulation on an unprecedented scale.

This chapter aims to delve into the intersection of AI, neuroscience, and manipulation, exploring how these technologies shape perceptions and behaviors, and what makes individuals susceptible to certain messages. By combining insights from consumer neuroscience and behavioral science, the chapter seeks to uncover the psychological triggers and mechanisms at play, offering a deeper understanding of both the risks and opportunities posed by AI in communication. Through this exploration, it will provide a critical foundation for addressing the ethical dilemmas surrounding AI-enabled persuasion and for fostering greater accountability in the use of these powerful tools.

To fully understand the disruptive impact of AI-generated communication, it is essential to first situate these developments within the broader historical trajectory of advertising and persuasive messaging. The evolution of advertising has always been closely tied to the dominant media technologies of the time – from print and radio to television and the internet – each shift introducing new opportunities for influence and redefining the relationship between message creators and audiences (Manovich, 2013). Recent studies reaffirm the long-standing pattern that advertising adapts in response to shifts in media technology. As new platforms emerge, they not only introduce novel formats but also reshape how brands engage with audiences. For instance, Hu (2025) illustrates how the rise of short-form, affordance-rich platforms like TikTok has transformed brand–audience interaction, emphasizing immediacy and user participation. Building on this, Athaide et al. (2025) show how digital technologies are restructuring the traditional marketing funnel, enabling more targeted and data-driven engagement. This transformation continues with the integration of artificial intelligence. Martin (2024) traces the shift from traditional advertising to AI-driven campaigns, illustrating how companies like Coca-Cola have used tools such as reinforcement learning and large language models to personalize content, enhance consumer insights, and boost engagement and brand perception. Leveraging AI-driven insights, Coca-Cola experienced increased engagement rates and significant improvements in brand perception. Complementing these insights, Yang et al. (2023) highlight the critical need for explainable AI, as advertising systems increasingly rely on opaque algorithms that influence user experience and decision-making.

Today, AI represents not just the next step in this progression but a fundamental transformation in scale, personalization, and the simulation of human authenticity (Kaplan & Haenlein, 2019). By tracing the historical evolution of advertising strategies and communication channels, we gain critical insight into how AI disrupts longstanding traditions of influence, setting the stage for an unprecedented level of psychological and behavioral impact.

This historical perspective also provides a framework for examining the mechanisms that make AI-generated messages uniquely potent. Persuasive communication has always depended on an interplay between media format, message design, and audience receptivity and emotional reactions (Heath et al., 2006). Recent empirical work continues to validate Heath et al. (2006) model. For example, Voorveld et al. (2024) demonstrate that voice prosody and communication modality significantly influence perceived personalization and brand attitudes. Carrasco-Farré (2024) shows that messages generated by large language models can achieve persuasive effects by employing lexical complexity and moral framing. A 2025 meta-analysis further confirms that characteristics such as synchronicity and haptic feedback in media formats affect both cognitive and emotional engagement (Orazi et al, 2025). What differentiates today's AI-driven content is its ability to operate below the level of conscious awareness, often leveraging user data to craft messages that align with implicit preferences and emotional triggers (Pangarkar et al., 2023). Understanding the trajectory of persuasive techniques across time is thus vital to assessing both the promises and the perils of AI-powered communication and to ensuring that ethical boundaries evolve in tandem with technological capabilities.

FROM PRINT TO PIXELS: THE EVOLUTION OF ADVERTISING TOWARD THE AGE OF AI

There is a saying that "advertising is the soul of commerce" and to a large extent, this holds true. Since the 16th century, when Jan Haller, often credited as the first printer of advertisements, began circulating printed commercial messages, the advertising industry has evolved dramatically, continually adapting to technological advancements.

For centuries, newspapers were the dominant medium for advertising. However, the past hundred years have seen a rapid expansion in communication channels. The 20th century introduced radio and television, fundamentally transforming how brands reached their audiences. With the rise of personal computers, followed by the mass adoption of smartphones and tablets, a new era began. The Internet revolutionized the advertising landscape, enabling companies to publish and personalize content like never before. Over the past two decades, digital platforms, including social media, online publications, and websites, have become the primary channels for advertising.

Online advertising operates through algorithms that respond to users' digital behavior: the news they consume, the search queries they input and the content they share on social media. In this context, the primary goal for advertisers is to efficiently reach the most relevant audience. In the early 21st century, this was achieved through big data and graph algorithms that mapped relationships and shared interests among users. Since the 2020s, however, the industry has increasingly integrated artificial intelligence, opening a new phase of precision and personalization in advertising strategies.

A 2023 study indicates that over 75% of consumers are already engaging with AI-powered services or devices (Argan et al., 2023), a significant figure that is projected to grow steadily in the coming years. Given AI's ability to generate content based on vast volumes of data, one of the most prominent areas of application is advertising. These advancements are largely driven by technologies such as Natural Language Processing (NLP), Image Recognition, Speech Recognition, Machine Learning, Natural Language Generation (NLG), and generative tools for both image and speech (Ford et al., 2023).

A major milestone in the development and public adoption of AI tools was marked by the release of ChatGPT in November 2022, which, as noted by Huh et al. (2023), generated "unprecedented attention and interest in AI." ChatGPT quickly became a widely used virtual assistant, supporting a diverse range of tasks. One of the defining features of conversational AI tools consists in their ability to draw on a continuously updated body of knowledge, shaped by the content they process and, in some cases, refined by user feedback. This dynamic foundation enables these tools to offer responses that oftentimes surpass the breadth and speed of traditional human-led research.

Given that AI systems require large volumes of data to produce relevant and personalized content, companies bear significant legal and ethical responsibilities. They must ensure that users are informed about how their online behavior is being tracked and utilized to train these algorithms. Furthermore, there is a growing imperative for transparency: organizations should clearly communicate how user data is collected, the mechanisms used to process it, where and how it is stored, and for how long this information is retained (Gao et al., 2023).

Another important dimension of AI usage in marketing relates to its limited ability to accurately interpret human emotions. As noted by Başev (2024), AI systems still struggle to fully understand the emotional nuances of consumers, which limits their capacity to assess the emotional impact of content on audiences.

A key area of interest in the context of AI-driven personalization is the role of user-generated content on social media platforms. This includes posts that individuals create, share, or like, the links they distribute among their networks, the photos and videos they upload, and the comments they leave on various posts. These actions constitute valuable behavioral data that AI systems analyze to infer user preferences and deliver algorithmically curated content. Such algorithms are designed to maximize user engagement by reinforcing familiar patterns of interest, often resulting in the repeated exposure to similar content. Over time, this process contributes to the formation of "echo chambers," digital environments where users are predominantly exposed to information that aligns with their pre-existing beliefs and attitudes. These environments, commonly referred to as "filter bubbles," limit ideological diversity and can reinforce cognitive biases (Gupta & Bansal, 2024). Moreover, the homogenization of online content driven by algorithmic bias further reduces exposure to opposing viewpoints, amplifying polarization and narrowing users' informational horizons (Putri et al., 2024). Thus, the interplay between user behavior and AI personalization has far-reaching implications for digital discourse and the reliability of online information.

Echo chambers have proven to be highly effective environments for targeted advertising, significantly influencing consumer behavior and ideological alignment. Gupta and Bansal (2024) highlight that "echo chamber-endorsed items or businesses may improve consumer loyalty and purchasing intent," as individuals are more receptive to messages that resonate with their pre-existing beliefs. However, the same mechanisms that make echo chambers effective for marketing also render them susceptible to the spread of misinformation. During the COVID-19 pandemic and various election cycles, these environments were exploited to disseminate false information, polarize public opinion, and manipulate voter sentiment. For instance,

Keller et al. (2020) found that political astroturfing on Twitter coordinated disinformation campaigns, exacerbating the echo chamber effect.

A critical concern within echo chambers is the absence of robust mechanisms for validating the information shared. This lack of verification leaves individuals responsible for discerning the accuracy or authenticity of the content they encounter. As Chou et al. (2018) assert, addressing health-related misinformation on social media requires proactive strategies, yet the onus often falls on users to navigate the veracity of information. The self-reinforcing nature of echo chambers, combined with algorithm-driven content curation, underscores the need for enhanced media literacy and critical thinking skills among users to mitigate the risks associated with misinformation.

While current research in the field has primarily focused on the evolution of algorithms, specifically, how systems generate content such as advertisements, news, academic updates, or social events, and how they ingest and process data to produce new outputs, this perspective alone is insufficient for fully understanding the impact of AI on marketing practices. Mariani et al. (2022) note that while AI technologies have been extensively studied for their capabilities in data processing and content generation, there is a significant gap in integrating these technical aspects with psychological and neuroscientific insights into consumer behavior. Understanding how individuals respond to AI-generated content requires not only technical analysis but also a deeper examination of cognitive and emotional factors. Pentina et al. (2023) emphasize the importance of exploring the "nomological networks" of key constructs such as agency, autonomy, authenticity, reciprocity, and empathy in the context of human–AI interactions.

Furthermore, the application of AI in neuromarketing has shown promise in providing more accurate and precise analyses of consumer behavior and decision-making processes. Fahim et al. (2024) conducted a systematic literature review and found that integrating AI with neuromarketing techniques allows for a better understanding of the subconscious factors influencing consumer choices. They state that "the application of AI in neuromarketing allows for more accurate and precise analysis of consumer behavior and decision-making processes." However, they also acknowledge the ongoing ethical debates surrounding the use of such technologies, indicating a need for further research in this area

There is a pressing need for interdisciplinary research that bridges the gap between AI-driven sentiment analysis and the psychological and ideological profiles of consumers. While sentiment analysis has been extensively utilized to gauge public opinion on political matters, its application in understanding the interplay between consumer behavior and political ideology remains underexplored. Bhatia (2018) proposes that "ideological leanings of an individual can often be gauged by the sentiment one expresses about different issues", suggesting that analyzing sentiments towards specific topics can help identify political ideologies.

CODING THE CONSUMER: AI, PSYCHOLOGY, AND THE SCIENCE OF CHOICE

Advances in generative AI are rapidly changing how consumers perceive and process advertisements and content. AI systems can tailor messages to individuals' psychological profiles in real time, creating highly persuasive personalized appeals. Across several experiments, AI-generated messages matched to recipients' personalities "exhibit significantly more influence than non-personalized messages" (Matz et al., 2024). In other words, leveraging personal data to customize ad language can enhance advertising effectiveness. For marketers, this means that AI enables personalized persuasion at scale, far beyond what human copywriters could achieve alone.

However, consumer reactions to AI-generated content are nuanced. NielsenIQ neuroscience research indicates that many consumers intuitively recognize AI-generated ads and often judge them more harshly than human-made ones (NielsenIQ, 2024). Unfavorable descriptors such as "annoying," "boring," or "confusing" were more commonly applied to AI-generated marketing images. The study found a negative brand halo effect: AI ads elicited weaker memory activation and dampened brand perceptions relative to traditional ads. Additionally, low quality AI images required greater cognitive effort to process. This suggests that while AI offers efficiency, careless use can backfire. High creative quality and relevance remain essential, otherwise consumers may disengage or form negative associations with the brand.

Consumers' perceived accuracy also influences their willingness to accept AI-generated advertisements. Gu et al. (2024) found that when consumers judged AI-generated ads to be highly accurate or lifelike, they were more willing to accept and engage with those ads. Conversely, ads that seemed unnatural triggered avoidance. In marketing terms, an AI ad must both align with existing brand imagery and feel "smart" or human-like enough to satisfy consumers' expectations. Otherwise, its persuasive potential is undermined.

As AI and consumer neuroscience extend into global markets, it is increasingly important to recognize that subconscious persuasion triggers such as emotional resonance, fluency, and trust cues, can vary significantly across cultural and demographic groups. Recent studies highlight that intercultural empathy with AI varies significantly. Americans responded positively to deliberative AI engagement, while Latin American participants perceived such interactions as culturally inaccurate (Villanueva et al., 2025). Similarly, cross-cultural comparisons between Germany and South Korea found that AI trust and perceived explainability are deeply influenced by both cultural norms and topic sensitivity (Kang et al., 2025). Furthermore, emerging frameworks like Affective-CARA suggest that AI systems should adapt emotionally and contextually based on a user's cultural background, conceptually reinforcing that one-size-fits-all marketing may fail to resonate globally (Pussadeniya et al., 2025). This underscores the need for culturally adaptive communication strategies. For example, imagine a global wellness brand using AI personalization to tailor its messaging across markets. In collectivist cultures, the campaign might highlight communal wellness and ancestral practices, while in individualist cultures, it may emphasize personal achievement or self-care journeys. Such tailored approaches demonstrate how implicit trust drivers are shaped not only by platform and format, but also by the cultural values that frame emotional and cognitive processing.

At a macro level, the integration of AI into marketing is subtly reshaping how consumers make decisions. Through cognitive offloading and the strategic use of heuristics, AI can guide choices in ways that feel effortless but also bypass deeper analytical reasoning. This dual-edge capacity, to empower and to exploit, makes the ethical and psychological scrutiny of AI in advertising more important than ever.

While AI tools offer unprecedented opportunities for personalization and persuasion, their effectiveness hinges on an understanding of human cognition, emotion, and perception. For marketers and designers, this means not just optimizing algorithms, but also aligning AI outputs with the psychological needs, cognitive styles, and trust dynamics of their audiences.

THE TRUST PARADOX AND THE CENTRAL ROLE OF PERSONALITY

In the evolving ecosystem of digital marketing, trust has become a pivotal variable influencing how consumers interact with content, particularly when that content is generated by artificial intelligence. As previously discussed, the widespread adoption of AI in advertising has introduced new forms of personalization and decision-making assistance, often streamlining consumer choices through cognitive offloading. Yet, this very efficiency can bypass deeper analytic scrutiny, leaving consumers more susceptible to influence, but also more vulnerable to manipulation or misinformation. At the heart of this trade-off lies the issue of trust.

Trust in AI-generated content operates differently from trust in human sources. Recent work by Montag et al. (2023) found that individuals' trust in AI systems was essentially uncorrelated with their trust in other people. In their neuroimaging study, self-reported trust in humans and trust in AI products were dissociable constructs with minimal overlap. In practical terms, a consumer's disposition to trust their peers or leaders does not straightforwardly predict their willingness to trust algorithmic information. Some people may be naturally skeptical of strangers yet willing to follow an AI recommendation, or vice versa.

This dissociation means marketing strategies must consider trust differently for AI channels. For instance, Buchanan (2021) found that trust in a source did not significantly determine whether individuals would share false political news. Even when participants encountered disinformation, whether they trusted its originator (for example, a known news outlet) had little effect on their willingness to propagate it. Instead, personality traits like low conscientiousness and the degree to which one personally believed the content were stronger predictors of sharing. This suggests that consumers often rely more on content congruence than source reputation, especially on social media.

Personality and cognitive style modulate these attitudes. For example, highly agreeable individuals tend to trust automated systems more (Riedl, 2022), but an agreeable person may nevertheless distrust a news media outlet they perceive as partisan. The interplay between personality traits and susceptibility to persuasive messaging (especially when delivered through AI) has become a critical area of investigation in consumer psychology.

As AI-generated content grows more sophisticated and increasingly personalized, understanding how individual psychological profiles influence engagement becomes essential. For example, personality factors such as narcissism do not merely affect how people present themselves or relate to others; they also shape how individuals interpret information, respond to perceived threats, and process persuasive messages, including those embedded in advertisements and conspiracy narratives. In particular, traits associated with self-enhancement and overconfidence can make some individuals more receptive to narratives that affirm their worldview or position them as uniquely informed. This perspective is especially relevant when considering how certain consumer segments might engage with sensational or manipulative content in AI-mediated environments.

Narcissism, a cluster of traits involving self-superiority, entitlement, and the desire to stand out has emerged as a robust predictor of conspiracy belief. For example, Cichocka et al (2022) note that narcissistic individuals' need for dominance, control, and uniqueness predisposes them to endorse conspiracy theories. In other words, conspiracy narratives allow narcissists to feel special compared to others (Imhoff & Lamberty, 2020). Empirical studies confirm this link. Cosgrove and Murphy (2023) found that higher levels of both grandiose and vulnerable narcissism significantly predicted stronger conspiracy endorsement. Similarly, narcissistic traits have been consistently associated with greater conspiracy belief in large international surveys (Cichocka et al., 2016; Gundersen et al., 2024). In practical terms, narcissistic consumers may be drawn to sensational or contrarian messages (for example, fringe political ads or provocative brand narratives) because these messages appeal to their sense of superiority and uniqueness.

Psychologically, narcissism relates to a lack of intellectual humility (Bak & Kutnik, 2021). While prior research suggests that acknowledging the limits of one's knowledge is generally perceived positively, recent findings indicate that individual differences in trait narcissism and intellectual humility significantly moderate these perceptions. Specifically, individuals high in narcissism are less likely to perceive such admissions as intellectually humble and are less inclined to view those who express humility as warm or competent. Conversely, individuals high in trait intellectual humility tend to interpret such statements more favorably, amplifying the perceived warmth and competence of the speaker (Huynh & Romero Gonzalez, 2023). Narcissists often exhibit overconfidence in their own reasoning and a dismissive attitude toward evidence that contradicts their views. This low humility may amplify conspiratorial thinking. Narcissistic individuals frequently adopt conspiracy theories as a way of standing out from the crowd and feeling superior or intelligent relative to others. In contrast, those higher in humility are more willing to revise beliefs in light of new information, making them less prone to conspiratorial fixations. Education and cognitive factors can moderate this tendency. Narcissism predicts conspiratorial beliefs, but higher cognitive reflection (a measure of analytic thinking) reduces this effect. Specifically, people with stronger cognitive reflection skills were less likely to let narcissistic impulses drive them toward misinformation (Cosgrove & Murphy, 2023).

CRITICAL THINKING AND MISINFORMATION IN AI ADVERTISING

A complementary strand of research examines cognitive style, especially the ability to think analytically or critically, as a defense against misinformation. In general, individuals with higher cognitive reflection and analytic thinking skills are better at discerning truth from falsehood. In their study of social media users during the COVID-19 pandemic, Ali and Qazi (2022) found that higher cognitive reflection was associated with significantly greater accuracy in distinguishing true versus false headlines. Those with higher CRT (Cognitive Reflection Test) scores were more likely to use and trust formal expert sources (for example, WHO, official news outlets) and even showed more prudent real behavior (willingness to pay for protective masks). Conversely, people with lower analytic thinking tended to rate misinformation as more plausible. Cognitive reflection acted as a protective factor against misinformation. Participants with higher CRT scores showed greater truth discernment and were less susceptible to fake news.

This finding generalizes to conspiracy endorsement as well. Analytic thinkers, who engage in slow, effortful processing, are significantly less likely to endorse conspiracy theories (Gjoneska, 2021). In contrast, intuitive, impulsive thinking styles correlate with conspiracy belief. For example, another study found that critical thinking ability in the context of argumentation is negatively associated with belief in conspiracy theories (Lantian et al., 2021). In practical terms, consumers who rely on gut feelings or heuristics over deliberation are more vulnerable to conspiracy-laden misinformation and sensationalist advertising.

In the context of AI-generated advertising, these cognitive factors play a similar role. AI ads can exploit heuristic cues, like novelty or emotional appeals (Alessandro et al., 2024) that resonate particularly with less analytical consumers. However, individuals who habitually question information and seek evidence will scrutinize even personalized AI content. When people actively engage their analytic system, they are better able to resist persuasion by false or misleading messages. Thus, promoting critical media literacy and encouraging deliberation can help consumers evaluate AI-generated ads and news more effectively.

This imperative becomes even more pressing in light of findings by Gerlich (2025), which reveal that frequent use of AI tools is negatively correlated with critical thinking abilities, primarily due to increased cognitive offloading. Younger users, who are typically more dependent on AI technologies, exhibited notably lower critical thinking scores, while higher education emerged as a protective factor supporting analytic reasoning regardless of AI use. Together, these insights suggest that while AI-generated content may strategically target cognitive shortcuts, an overdependence on AI tools could further erode individuals' capacity for critical evaluation. This underscores the urgent need for educational strategies that not only foster critical thinking but also promote mindful engagement with AI technologies, especially in media and advertising contexts.

EXPOSING IMPLICIT SUSCEPTIBILITY TO AI MISINFORMATION WITH THE IAT

As AI-generated content becomes more persuasive and harder to detect, researchers are turning to implicit methods to understand how it shapes attitudes and beliefs, often below conscious awareness. One powerful tool in this effort is the Implicit Association Test (IAT), a computer-based psychological test that measures the strength of automatic associations in a person's mind. In simple terms, people tend to perform sorting tasks faster and more accurately when the pairing of items aligns with strong mental associations, and slower when pairings conflict with those associations. The IAT leverages this effect by having participants quickly sort words or images into categories that are combined in ways that can be either "congruent" or "incongruent" with their mental associations.

Originally developed by Greenwald, McGhee, and Schwartz in 1998, the IAT was designed to tap into "implicit attitudes" – that is, evaluative biases or associations that people may not be consciously aware of (Greenwald et al., 1998). It was inspired by earlier work on implicit memory showing that prior exposure can unconsciously influence responses (Greenwald & Banaji, 1995). In the paper they proposed that just as we have implicit memory, we also have implicit attitudes that can influence our behavior without conscious intent. The IAT was born as a method to capture these elusive mental associations. Its theoretical underpinnings draw on cognitive psychology and neuroscience: the idea that strongly associated concepts in the mind will facilitate faster cognitive processing when paired together (a principle related to semantic priming and spreading activation in memory), whereas loosely associated or contradictory concepts will interfere with each other, slowing down processing.

Many consumer decisions are driven by quick, emotional reactions rather than slow, rational deliberation. The IAT, by its nature, measures the speed of an automatic reaction, making it well-suited to study the kinds of snap judgments that often occur in a store aisle or when seeing an advertisement. Understanding what drives consumers has long fascinated psychologists, and over time, one insight has remained consistent: much of our decision-making happens beneath the surface. Research in consumer psychology emphasizes that automatic processes (like intuitions and feelings) play a large role in attitudes and purchase decisions (Maison et al., 2004). This idea has only gained strength in recent research. Gregory & Banks (2025), for instance, show that when people rely on intuitive, "System 1" thinking, they not only make decisions more quickly and effortlessly but also report feeling more satisfied with their choices. At the same time, biometric studies using eye-tracking reveal how emotional reactions guide attention and shape responses in real time (Escandon-Barbosa et al., 2025). Eye Tracking is a technique whereby an individual's eye movements are measured so that the researcher knows where a person is looking at any given time, and how their eyes are moving from one location to another (Poole & Ball, 2006). These studies paint a clear picture. Consumers are not just thinkers but feelers, and it is often their immediate, emotion-driven impulses that tip the scales in purchase decisions.

The IAT shines in situations where self-report might be suspect. For example, consider a new product that targets an identity-related preference (say, an eco-friendly product that appeals to environmental values). Consumers might all explicitly say they care about the environment, but an IAT could measure if they implicitly associate that product or brand with positive concepts like "responsible" and "effective," or if perhaps they harbor skepticism (e.g., implicitly linking it to "ineffective" or "overpriced"). Those subconscious associations could predict whether their environmental concern actually translates into purchasing the product (Steiner et al., 2018).

In summary, the IAT brings to marketing research the ability to measure true underlying attitudes that consumers might not say out loud. It helps marketers design campaigns that resonate with the implicit mind, not just the explicit opinions. This can be the difference between a campaign that *seems* like it should work (because people said they liked it in a poll) and one that *actually* works (because it connects with consumers' automatic positive associations). The next section will illustrate how the IAT's ability to probe subconscious reactions has been leveraged in a very different but critical context: understanding how people respond to AI-generated misinformation and manipulative messages.

WHEN FALSE FEELS TRUE. IMPLICIT RESPONSES TO AI-GENERATED MISINFORMATION

One of the emerging applications of the IAT is in the study of misinformation and disinformation, especially as artificial intelligence enables the creation of increasingly believable but false content. In the digital age, AI tools can generate realistic fake news articles, images, or videos (so-called "deepfakes"). These manipulative messages pose a challenge: people might be influenced by them without realizing it, or even if they consciously recognize a piece of information as false, it might still affect their implicit attitudes and future susceptibility. The IAT offers a methodology to investigate these subtle effects.

Traditional research on misinformation often relies on explicit outcomes: e.g., asking people "Do you believe this headline?" or testing if they can recall which stories were false. However, misinformation can have subconscious effects on individuals' beliefs and behavior. For instance, simply being exposed to false claims can plant a "memory trace" or familiarity that later on feels like truth, a phenomenon known as the illusory truth effect, where repeated exposure increases perceived accuracy (Udry & Barber, 2023; Pennycook et al., 2020). People might vehemently deny believing a false story, yet still be influenced by it in their actions or implicit judgments. The IAT is a fitting tool to capture these under-the-surface changes because it can detect shifts in association that the person might not self-report.

In the realm of AI-generated fake videos or images, suppose AI produces a very convincing fake video of a politician engaging in corrupt behavior. Viewers might later take an IAT that pairs images of that politician with words like "ethical" or "corrupt." If the deepfake was effective, viewers (even those who suspect or know the video was fake) might show slower reactions when the politician's face is paired with "ethical" (and faster when paired with "corrupt"), compared to a control group who never saw the fake video. This would reveal an implicit dent in the politician's reputation caused by the AI falsehood. Such an approach can quantify the stealth impact of disinformation on public figures' images or on public trust (Dan, 2025).

IATs are also being used to identify who is most susceptible to misinformation by examining personality traits and cognitive styles at an implicit level. A study by Menicocci et al. (2024), done as part of research on "cognitive warfare", combined eye-tracking with IATs to see how people who fall for fake news differ from those who do not. The implicit measure can sometimes be a better predictor of behavior in these contexts. Indeed, by analyzing participants' implicit attitudes and behaviors together, the study aimed to "characterize individuals with tendencies to misidentify fake and real news."

The link between IAT results and misinformation susceptibility is thus becoming clearer through such studies. We see that misinformation can implant or strengthen implicit associations, whether about brands, policies, social groups, or factual beliefs, that drive behavior and judgments in subtle ways (Bastick, 2021; Traberg et al., 2024). Likewise, individuals' pre-existing implicit biases can make them targets for specific false messages. For instance, someone with an implicit bias against a certain group might be quick to accept a fake news story vilifying that group because it "feels" true at a gut level. Conversely, someone with a strong implicit trust in mainstream institutions might be more resistant to conspiracy theories. By measuring these biases, researchers can predict and understand patterns of who falls for what kind of fake content (Sultan et al., 2024).

From an AI and communications perspective, the IAT serves as a kind of early detection system for the effects of new forms of propaganda or disinformation. AI-generated content can be so lifelike that it persuades people before they have time to critically reflect (Dan, 2025). Using implicit measures, we can detect that persuasion in progress. For example, after exposure to a deepfake video, an IAT might reveal that viewers implicitly associate the fake video's claim with reality, signaling that the fake has begun to shape perceptions. Such implicit shifts might occur even when explicit beliefs haven't yet changed or are in flux. In a sense, the implicit attitude might be a leading indicator – a canary in the coal mine – showing that a manipulation is taking hold (Cone et al., 2021). This is fundamental for designing countermeasures. If we find that certain misinformation consistently alters implicit associations, we might develop "inoculation" strategies (analogous to a vaccine) to prevent those changes, or "debiasing" strategies to reverse them (Cook et al., 2017; Roozenbeek et al., 2022).

The IAT has become an indispensable methodology in studying the power of AI-driven misinformation. In a world where AI can fabricate highly realistic but false messages, traditional defenses (like simply asking people "do you believe it?") might fall short of capturing the full impact. The IAT steps in to measure the implicit imprint that such messages leave on our minds – the subtle shifts in what feels true or how we emotionally evaluate a topic. By doing so, it not only uncovers the hidden effectiveness of manipulative content but also helps identify who might be most vulnerable and why. The use of IATs in this domain reinforces a key insight: our cognition has multiple layers (explicit and implicit), and even when the explicit layer rejects a lie, the implicit layer might quietly absorb it (Bastick, 2021; Vinay et al., 2025).

LITERATURE GAPS. FILLING IN THE MISSING PIECES

Despite the growing body of research on trust in media, most studies rely heavily on self-reported measures, which are prone to social desirability and conscious biases (King, 2024; Metzger & Flanagin, 2015). Few investigations employ implicit techniques such as the IAT to explore subconscious associations with different sources of information. Yet, studies in social cognition have long demonstrated that implicit attitudes can diverge significantly from explicit responses, especially in value-laden domains like media trust (Greenwald et al., 2009). To bridge this gap and gain deeper insight into the automatic, often unacknowledged dimensions of media trust, this study moves beyond conventional self-report methods by employing the Implicit Association Test (IAT). Since self-reported responses are often shaped by social desirability and conscious bias, they may not fully capture underlying attitudes. To overcome this limitation, we used a dual-IAT design aimed at uncovering subconscious associations with both traditional and AI-generated information sources. This approach allows for a more comprehensive and nuanced understanding of media trust, revealing implicit biases that remain hidden in explicit measures and offering a valuable contribution to the evolving literature on trust in media.

Moreover, most of the previous research has typically focused on trust in either traditional media (for example, television, newspapers) or social media (for example, Facebook, Twitter), without including alternative sources such as influencers, family, or government institutions in the same framework (Tsfati & Ariely, 2014). For instance, in a large COVID-19 survey the most-trusted sources were government communications and personal doctors, even more so than social media (Figueiras et al., 2021). Similarly, Wasikc (2025) found that U.S. users who follow social-media influencers (SMIs) actually reported higher trust in news media than non-followers, with trust in influencer content improving media trust across the board. Such findings suggest that so-called alternative sources can bolster or reshape trust in mainstream media. Yet, to the best of our knowledge, no study has systematically compared trust in traditional outlets, social platforms, influencers, and institutions together. The research presented in this chapter addresses this multidimensional gap by comparing implicit attitudes toward a diverse set of sources and by doing so via automatic, non-deliberative processes.

As already discussed above, critical thinking is widely accepted as a protective factor against misinformation and false beliefs (Orosz et al., 2024; Pennycook & Rand, 2019; Stanovich & West, 2007). However, existing literature tends to treat critical thinking as a static trait, often measured through generic logic or reasoning tasks. Contextual, situational assessments of critical thinking, especially in digital environments filled with persuasive content, remain scarce (Facione, 2011). Furthermore, while AI-generated content such as advertisements, deepfakes or synthetic news articles is rapidly advancing in realism and prevalence, little is known about how people critically evaluate such content. Research in media literacy is still catching up with the challenges posed by synthetic media, and few studies include applied decision-making scenarios where participants must assess credibility in real-world-like settings (Floridi & Chiriatti, 2020). The authors' research fills this gap by using realistic situational questionnaires to gauge how people respond to AI-generated persuasive messages, such as too-good-to-be-true weight-loss ads.

The link between narcissism and conspiracy beliefs has been explored in personality psychology, with some studies suggesting that narcissistic individuals are more prone to adopting conspiratorial thinking as it reinforces their sense of uniqueness or superiority (Cichocka et al., 2016; March & Springer, 2019). In online contexts, narcissistic individuals have been shown to actively spread misinformation. For example, a simulated Twitter task found grandiose narcissism was one of the only traits positively associated with retweeting false information (Haupt et al., 2024). These studies underscore narcissists' role in propagating falsehoods. Yet the question of media trust (for example, whether narcissistic people preferentially trust certain channels) has not been directly examined. In other words, we lack research on how narcissistic worldviews interact with trust in various media or in emerging technologies. Our work aims to address this by relating narcissism to both implicit trust and responses to AI-driven content.

CONNECTING THE DOTS BETWEEN NEUROSCIENCE AND AI

The authors embarked on a research to investigate how individuals trust (or distrust) traditional media and AI-generated content by employing a multi-method approach that includes IAT, self-report questionnaires, and in-depth interviews. The objective was to assess critical thinking and to capture both subconscious biases and consciously held beliefs related to conspiracy thinking, narcissistic traits, and patterns of media consumption.

A key goal was to examine how implicit trust, as measured by the IAT, correlates with explicit susceptibility to misinformation and conspiracy beliefs. Interest was particularly high in understanding how personality traits like narcissism and cognitive styles such as critical thinking shape both automatic and deliberate attitudes toward information sources.

Demographic factors were included to understand their influence on trust. In particular, special attention was given to whether critical thinkers were more skeptical of AI misinformation and whether narcissistic traits increased conspiracy endorsement. This multi-method approach helped reveal the psychological patterns behind trust in today's digital world.

Key Data

A total of 105 participants from Romania were recruited for the study. Of these, 75 completed both the IAT assessments and the declarative questionnaires, while 30 took part in in-depth interviews.

Within the group that completed the online study, most of them (around 71%) identified as women, while about 26% identified as men. Participants ranged in age from 19 to 80 years, with an average age of about 40 years, showing a mix of both younger and older adults. Most participants were from urban areas. In terms of education, the group was quite diverse. Many had completed a university degree (40%) or held a Master's degree (37%). Participants were recruited through social networks using a snowball sampling method. Data collection took place between March and April 2025.

The study was divided into three modules: module 1 consisted of two IAT assessments, designed to measure their subconscious trust in information sources and AI. Module 2 consisted of self-report questionnaires that explored respondents' beliefs in conspiracy theories, critical thinking skills, narcissism, perceptions of AI-generated content, and media consumption habits. Module 3 consisted of in-depth interviews with 30 selected participants to gain deeper insights into the results.

Probing the Subconscious: The Methods Behind the Metrics

Implicit Association Tests (IAT)

To assess biases and attitudes regarding trust in both traditional information sources and AI-generated content, two IAT assessments were designed that focused on:

(1) Trust in information sources – evaluated how participants implicitly associated trust or distrust with various information sources, such as government, mainstream media, traditional mass media, alternative blogs, specialized/scientific websites, influencers, television, social media, family, friends, and colleagues.
(2) Level of naivete – measured implicit trust or distrust in AI-generated ads. Participants were asked to categorize images as either *credible* or *doubtful*. The tested images were AI-generated ads related to health products, alternative energy devices, consumer rights, celebrity rumors, or historical discoveries.

Self-reported Assessment

Belief in conspiracy theories was assessed using an adapted version of the General Scale of Conspiratorial Beliefs (Ariely, 2023). The original instrument comprised 23 items addressing various conspiracy theories prevalent in the United States. To ensure relevance to the Romanian context, some items were replaced with conspiracy theories specific to Romania, while others were retained from the original scale. The retained items were translated into Romanian. The final questionnaire consisted of 24 items assessing belief in conspiracy theories. Responses were recorded on a six-point Likert scale, measuring the degree of conviction for each statement, ranging from 1 (definitely false) to 6 (definitely true). Examples of items included: "Covid-19 was created as a bioweapon in a Chinese or US laboratory" and "The US moon landing was staged by NASA in a film studio".

Narcissism was assessed using the Narcissism (Dominance) Scale from the California Psychological Inventory (CPI) - Romanian version (Goldberg et al., 2006; Iliescu et al., 2019). The scale consists of 11 items measuring narcissistic personality traits. Responses were recorded on a six-point Likert scale, ranging from 1 (strongly disagree) to 6 (strongly agree). Example items include: "Am quick to correct others" and "Challenge others' points of view".

Critical thinking was assessed using a revised version of the Critical Thinking about Conspiracies (CTAC) Test (O'Mahony et al., 2024). The original questionnaire evaluates individuals' susceptibility to implausible beliefs and conspiracy theories by measuring their ability to critically analyze controversial claims. It consists of single-choice questions, each presenting a scenario related to a specific situation (e.g. government actions, scientific discoveries, or societal events), with response options ranging from rational skepticism to conspiracy-driven interpretations. The original test includes eight scenarios (five implausible and three plausible). The original instrument was modified by selecting five scenarios from the original version and incorporating additional items relevant to the Romanian context, resulting in a total of 11 scenarios with distinct response options. The retained items were translated into Romanian. Responses were coded as 1 for correct answers and 0 for incorrect answers.

Individuals' *responses to AI-crafted promotional messages* served as a proxy for assessing respondent's critical thinking abilities and their vulnerability to pseudoscientific claims, misinformation, and algorithmically generated content. This section included 11 scenarios, each paired with an AI-generated image illustrating the context. The scenarios covered a range of topics, including health products, alternative energy devices, celebrity rumors, claims and consumer rights and historical discoveries. Each scenario presented a claim (often exaggerated, implausible, misleading or plausible) followed by a question designed to measure the participant's likelihood of believing, sharing, or purchasing based on the provided information. Responses were structured on a 4-answers spectrum, ranging from high acceptance (e.g., immediate belief or purchase) to strong skepticism (e.g., outright rejection due to a lack of scientific evidence). Before administering the questionnaire, the scenarios were evaluated with a panel of 10 individuals to ensure clarity, content validity, and appropriate difficulty levels. The pre-testing phase allowed for refining ambiguous items and confirming that the scenarios effectively captured the intended constructs. Cronbach's alpha was calculated at .68, demonstrating an acceptable internal consistency.

To assess participants' ability to discern AI-generated content, they were tasked with identifying which images, if any, they believed were created by artificial intelligence, with the option to select multiple images.

The assessment contained several questions that evaluated the participants' trust in different sources when confronted with conflicting reports about a political crisis, their trust in political reforms and institutions, social media usage, and their confidence in news outlets. Each topic was evaluated with a single factual or situational question, using either single or multiple choice options. These questions were used to better understand the context of the participants and provide a solid foundation for the statistical analysis of the data.

In-depth Interviews

To gain deeper insights into the psychological dynamics behind trust and skepticism toward traditional and AI-generated information, in-depth interviews were conducted with 30 selected participants. These interviews aimed to complement the quantitative data by exploring participants' personal experiences, feelings, and reflections on encountering misinformation and AI-produced content. During the interviews, participants were asked about their awareness of AI-generated media, how they distinguished between accurate and fake information, and their emotional responses to conspiracy theories and manipulative messages. Their media consumption habits, trust in various information sources, and perceptions of their own critical thinking abilities were also discussed. The qualitative approach was added in order to understand the nuances behind implicit and explicit attitudes, revealing how individuals process, accept, or reject information in a complex media landscape shaped increasingly by artificial intelligence.

Inside the Mind's Mirror: Key Outcomes of the Research

The data reveal several key psychological patterns among participants, shedding light on how individuals process information in a media-saturated environment. Overall, the sample showed a moderate tendency to believe in conspiracy theories, though with significant individual variation. Some participants were highly skeptical, while others readily endorsed conspiratorial narratives. Similarly, narcissistic or dominance traits such as grandiosity and heightened self-focus were present, but not at extreme levels.

Evaluating Fake vs. Realistic Content

Participants showed a moderate level of critical thinking when evaluating fake content. The greater variability in these scores suggests that while some participants are quite discerning and skeptical of fake information, others are more likely to accept it, indicating differences in critical thinking skills across the group. In contrast, participants demonstrated more consistent and somewhat lower scores when assessing realistic content, indicating a more uniform ability to recognize believable information. The smaller variability here implies that most participants similarly perceive plausible content as credible, reflecting a shared baseline of critical evaluation. Psychologically, this pattern suggests that while people generally apply critical thinking effectively to realistic information, their critical thinking varies more widely when faced with fake or questionable content. This may be due to individual differences in skepticism, cognitive biases, or familiarity with the subject matter.

This pattern was echoed in interviews. For instance, one participant said, *"If something sounds too weird to be true, I usually just scroll past it, but if it's shared by someone I know, I might look into it more."* Others admitted that the *style* or *visual quality* of content played a big role in how believable it felt. One person commented, *"Even if the ad seemed a bit exaggerated, the fact that it looked professional made me trust it more."* These remarks highlight how subjective cues and context influence judgment. Critical thinking doesn't always kick in when it should.

The Influence of AI on Credibility Judgments

One particularly intriguing aspect of the study involves how participants responded to AI-generated advertisements. Participants showed a tendency to trust AI content when it appeared realistic and plausible. Even when presented with implausible AI-generated ads, many participants still rated them with a moderate level of credibility. This might indicate a cognitive bias toward trusting polished, professional-looking content, or perhaps a lack of familiarity with the subtle ways AI can create misleading media. Consider, for instance, a hypothetical startup that launches an AI-generated ad campaign for a brain-enhancement supplement. The ads, crafted entirely through generative AI, display photorealistic doctors, stylized efficacy graphs, and glowing testimonials, all designed to evoke scientific authority and emotional reassurance. Despite the absence of actual clinical evidence, the ads spread widely across social media and wellness blogs. The plausibility of the design, combined with emotionally resonant cues, makes them feel trustworthy to many viewers. This highlights the subtle but potent ways AI can manipulate perceived credibility. As such content becomes more prevalent, it raises urgent ethical and cognitive questions: How can consumers be empowered to recognize synthetic persuasion? To what extent do visual polish and emotional tone override factual accuracy in the formation of trust? Addressing these concerns requires not only improved media literacy but also stricter standards for transparency in AI-generated communication.

Cognitive Links. Conspiracy thinking and critical evaluation

A deeper analysis reveals several important relationships between cognitive and psychological traits. Most notably, conspiratorial thinking is strongly negatively correlated with critical thinking performance. This suggests that individuals who more readily endorse conspiracy theories tend to perform worse on tasks requiring critical evaluation of information, particularly when discerning false or misleading content. Interview responses support this pattern. When asked how they respond to information that contradicts their beliefs, participants with conspiratorial thinking often say things like, *"I just know it cannot be right."* This response highlights a common psychological mechanism (confirmation bias) where individuals tend to reject evidence that challenges their existing worldview. Such behavior can hinder critical thinking and the ability to objectively evaluate information, reinforcing conspiratorial thinking and making it harder for these individuals to critically engage with alternative viewpoints.

Trust in AI and Susceptibility to Misinformation

Additionally, conspiracy beliefs show a moderate positive correlation with the perceived credibility of fake AI-generated content, indicating that those who are more prone to conspiratorial thinking are also more likely to find even obviously implausible AI content believable. Similarly, belief in conspiracy theories is associated with greater overall trust in AI-generated material, regardless of plausibility. This pattern was reflected during the interviews when participants were shown various images created by AI. Many of them did not recognize most of the images were AI-generated. This suggests that their trust in AI content extends broadly, regardless of how realistic or believable the material actually is. In fact, belief in conspiracy theories was linked to a higher overall trust in AI-generated content, which may reflect a broader susceptibility to accepting information that aligns with their worldview, even when it comes from artificial sources.

The study also evaluated participants' ability to correctly identify whether certain images were generated using artificial intelligence. All the visuals included in this task were, in fact, AI-generated, yet participants were not informed of this beforehand. The goal was to assess their perceptual accuracy and susceptibility to synthetic content. Despite the fact that all images were in fact generated by AI, some of the respondents identified many of them as realistic or natural, considering them to be human-made. This tendency highlights a key cognitive bias: people are often guided by visual fluency. If an image is easy to process, emotionally resonant, or consistent with familiar visual cues, they tend to accept it as real. Such findings suggest a general psychological vulnerability toward trusting well-crafted digital content, especially when individuals lack prior experience or training in recognizing synthetic media.

Age Differences in Belief Systems

Imagine a Facebook community tailored specifically for older adults seeking "uncensored news" and "alternative health advice." The group frequently shares videos questioning mainstream science, reposts long-form narratives about government overreach, and offers tips for "detoxing from misinformation." While its content avoids overtly aggressive tones, the themes consistently reinforce suspicion toward institutions and valorize "independent thinking." For members in their 50s and 60s, many of whom have witnessed decades of shifting political climates, technological revolutions, and cultural upheaval, this community provides not just information, but a sense of agency and belonging.

This scenario reflects broader psychological patterns uncovered in the current analysis. The analysis reveals distinct psychological patterns emerging across different age groups, particularly in relation to belief in conspiracy theories. Among all the variables examined, conspiratorial thinking shows the most pronounced variation across age categories, indicating that age is meaningfully linked to how individuals process and interpret socially charged or suspicious narratives. Individuals in their 50s and early 60s tend to endorse conspiratorial beliefs more strongly than any other group. This heightened inclination may reflect a combination of cognitive, emotional, and social factors unique to this life stage (such as increased skepticism, social marginalization, or exposure to media narratives) that reinforce mistrust. In contrast, younger adults, especially those in their 20s and 30s, exhibit significantly lower levels of conspiratorial thinking, possibly due to greater digital literacy or more adaptive coping strategies in the face of complex information.

This trend was echoed in the interviews. Older participants often spoke with a tone of caution or even cynicism toward mainstream sources. One participant in their 60s told us, *"You just can't trust the news anymore. They always have some agenda. After all these years, I've learned to read between the lines."* This kind of thinking reflects how accumulated experiences can lead to more guarded beliefs and a tendency to question official narratives. Younger participants, on the other hand, often seemed more confident navigating today's complex information landscape. For example, a 26-year-old said, *"If something sounds weird, I usually Google it. There's just so much misinformation especially on Social Media and it's important to double-check."* Their approach suggests that growing up with digital tools may help them think more critically and avoid falling for questionable content.

Mediation Effects. Critical Thinking as a Protective Factor

The psychological profile that emerges from the mediation analysis suggests a complex cognitive and perceptual dynamic underlying conspiratorial thinking. At the core of this dynamic lies the critical thinking ability, particularly the skill involved in identifying and rejecting implausible or deceptive information. Individuals who perform poorly on tasks requiring such discernment tend to exhibit a significantly stronger inclination toward conspiracy beliefs.

However, this relationship is not entirely direct. A notable mediating factor in this pathway is the individual's perception of fake AI-generated content, which accounts for 11% of the effect. People who struggle with critical evaluation are more likely to attribute unwarranted credibility to obviously artificial or unrealistic AI-generated media. This inflated trust in implausible digital content, in turn, contributes to their increased susceptibility to conspiracy theories.

This mediational pattern reveals an important psychological vulnerability: individuals with lower critical thinking skills do not merely fail to detect falsehoods, they may also overestimate the authenticity of content that should be easily dismissed.

This perceptual bias appears to act as a bridge, linking cognitive deficits with broader belief systems characterized by suspicion, mistrust, and a tendency to adopt alternative, non-mainstream explanations. The interviews offered clear examples of how this plays out in real life. Some participants admitted they couldn't always tell what was real or fake online. One person said, *"If the ad looks good and the message fits what I already believe, I just assume it's true."* Others shared that they were impressed by how polished the AI-generated content looked, even when they knew it was fake. As one participant put it, *"It's scary how real it seems. I wouldn't be surprised if many people fall for it."*

This profile reflects a cognitive-perceptual loop in which deficient analytic reasoning and misplaced trust in deceptive digital content reinforce each other, culminating in a worldview prone to conspiracy beliefs. Interventions aiming to enhance media literacy and critical reflection may be crucial in disrupting this cycle. Improving individuals' ability to evaluate the plausibility of emerging media formats (especially those generated by AI) may help mitigate the psychological mechanisms that foster conspiratorial ideation.

Trust And Bias – Results That Challenge Assumptions

Trust in Media Channels

The results of the IAT assessments reveal a notable divergence between participants' subconscious attitudes and their overt, self-reported preferences regarding the sources of information. For example, several media channels that are frequently criticized or distrusted at an explicit level, such as social media and alternative blogs, were found to elicit high levels of implicit trust. Conversely, sources typically viewed as credible in public discourse, including scientific websites and governmental platforms, were associated with lower levels of subconscious trust. These discrepancies underscore the importance of distinguishing between what people say they trust and what their cognitive-affective systems actually associate with credibility, particularly in contexts where emotional resonance and habitual exposure can subconsciously shape belief formation.

For example, when asked, most respondents say that they prefer established online press and official government sources, when faced with a major political crisis involving conflicting narratives. In contrast, only 9% admit that they trust social media as a means for accurate information during moments of political uncertainty. In terms of social media usage, Facebook dominates as the most used platform, with Instagram trailing behind. Other platforms like TikTok, Twitter (X), or Snapchat are barely used, and very few participants report not using social media at all. This usage pattern suggests that older platforms with more established user bases continue to play a key role in media consumption, while newer ones have yet to gain serious traction in this sample.

One surprising finding was related to the high implicit trust in TV, social media, and alternative blogs. The elevated levels of implicit trust observed for these channels can be understood through the lens of affective conditioning, repetition, and perceived immediacy. Television remains a powerful medium due to its multisensory nature – visual, auditory, and narrative elements combine to enhance emotional engagement (Lang, 2006; Bettiga & Noci, 2024), which is a key driver of implicit associations. Social media, while often viewed critically in explicit measures, fosters implicit trust through habitual use, peer validation, and emotionally charged content that is frequently encountered and easily processed (Yadav et al., 2015; Hatamleh et al, 2023). Alternative blogs, though lacking institutional credibility, often present information in a highly confident, direct tone and appeal to personal narratives or conspiratorial framing – forms of communication that bypass analytical scrutiny and instead foster intuitive acceptance (Pennycook & Rand, 2019). These sources are effective in creating strong affective responses and therefore become cognitively "fluent," reinforcing trust on an implicit level.

In contrast, government websites, scientific sources, and even familial advice elicited lower levels of implicit trust, which may appear paradoxical but is consistent with dual-process theories of cognition. These sources are often associated with deliberative, System 2 processing (Kahneman, 2011), requiring more cognitive effort and presenting information in abstract or complex formats. For example, scientific websites frequently employ technical jargon and probabilistic language that reduce reader engagement and emotional resonance – two factors essential for implicit belief formation (Green & Brock, 2000; Li et al., 2025). Government communication is often perceived as bureaucratic, impersonal, or even manipulative, particularly in political climates where trust in institutions is low (Hetherington & Rudolph, 2015). Family, while emotionally intimate, may not be seen as credible from a knowledge-based perspective, and thus does not elicit strong implicit associations with trustworthiness in informational contexts. These sources may be explicitly endorsed but fail to engage the rapid, affective systems that underlie implicit judgment.

The findings also align closely with cognitive principles of familiarity, processing fluency, and exposure frequency, all of which significantly shape implicit attitudes. The mere exposure effect (Zajonc, 1968; Van Dessel et al., 2019) posits that repeated exposure to a stimulus enhances affective evaluations, even in the absence of conscious recognition. Media that is encountered daily, such as social networks and television, benefit from this psychological bias. Additionally, processing fluency, or the ease with which information is mentally processed, is associated with truth judgments; people are more likely to implicitly trust information that is linguistically simple and visually coherent (Reber & Schwarz, 1999; Winkielman & Nowak,

2022). Alternative blogs and social content often present in a high-fluency format, using simple narratives, bold headlines, and emotionally salient visuals. These features allow them to bypass skepticism and generate automatic trust responses, regardless of factual accuracy. In contrast, scientific texts or governmental updates often demand effortful comprehension, which can reduce perceived reliability at a subconscious level, despite being factually rigorous.

Another explanatory mechanism for the distribution of trust scores lies in the affect heuristic – a mental shortcut in which emotional responses guide judgments about credibility and risk (Slovic et al., 2007; Lu & Xiao, 2023). Media channels that evoke strong emotional reactions, such as fear, outrage, empathy, or awe, are more likely to be implicitly trusted because the affective response is misattributed to the credibility of the message. Social media platforms and alternative blogs are particularly adept at leveraging emotional content, often at the expense of informational accuracy. Their content architectures are optimized for virality, not verification, leading to a prevalence of emotionally charged content that activates implicit acceptance (Vosoughi et al., 2018). Meanwhile, institutional sources, like scientific blogs or government sites, tend to present emotionally neutral or dispassionate information. While this enhances their objective validity, it diminishes their capacity to trigger the affective responses necessary for implicit trust formation. This dynamic illustrates why emotionally manipulative messages can become believable, even if their factual basis is weak or entirely fabricated.

Taken together, these IAT findings reveal a critical disjunction between explicit and implicit trust in media environments. Imagine that a global wellness brand launches an AI-generated advertising campaign for a product called "Wellness Water", a mineral-rich beverage claimed to enhance energy, sleep, and immune function. The campaign runs across platforms like Instagram and TikTok, featuring soothing music, glowing testimonials from influencers, and AI-generated infographics referencing vague 'scientific studies.' Although no independent evidence supports the product's claims, the campaign rapidly goes viral. Taken together, these IAT findings reveal a critical disjunction between explicit and implicit trust in media environments. The media sources that are most successful in generating intuitive belief responses are not necessarily those grounded in truth, but rather those that leverage emotion, fluency, familiarity, and frequency to engage subconscious trust mechanisms. This creates a cognitive vulnerability: messages from emotionally resonant yet intellectually unreliable sources can be accepted as truth simply because they "feel" credible. In the context of AI-generated persuasive content, particularly content that mimics legitimate formats while spreading misinformation, these findings are deeply relevant. They suggest that manipulative messages can achieve believability not by appealing to logic, but by triggering implicit trust pathways that have been reinforced through habitual media exposure and emotional design.

As such, understanding and measuring implicit trust is not only methodologically valuable, but essential to navigating an age of computational persuasion and information ambiguity.

The IAT results suggest that implicit trust is shaped less by accuracy and more by emotional resonance, exposure frequency, and accessibility. Media channels like TV and social media – which are immersive, emotionally engaging, and omnipresent – benefit from these subconscious trust mechanisms. Conversely, government and scientific content, despite their credibility, often fail to establish strong implicit trust because they lack emotional salience or are perceived as less relatable.

Implicit Trust in Conspiracy Theories

The IAT results assessing belief in various conspiracy theories revealed that, on average, participants maintained a neutral stance, suggesting a general cognitive distancing or ambivalence toward conspiratorial narratives at the subconscious level. This neutrality may reflect increased public skepticism, informational fatigue, or a lack of affective salience associated with many such narratives (Imhoff & Lamberty, 2020). However, a striking exception emerged in the case of *angel therapy*, a belief system rooted in spiritual and metaphysical frameworks rather than political or scientific deception. Now, imagine that an AI-powered mobile app called "Celestial Healing" is launched, claiming to deliver personalized angel therapy through guided meditations, energy forecasts, and spiritual affirmations. Marketed as a tool for emotional resilience and mental health, the app features soft visual aesthetics, calming music, and testimonials from influencers describing transformative experiences. While it avoids overt conspiracy rhetoric, the underlying premise promotes metaphysical beliefs about angelic interventions and divine energies influencing daily life. The app quickly garners a devoted user base, especially among individuals experiencing stress, grief, or uncertainty. This hypothetical yet plausible case underscores a deeper psychological phenomenon. This narrative elicited the highest levels of implicit trust among all conspiracy types tested. Unlike more politically charged or institution-focused conspiracies, angel therapy operates within a domain that evokes comfort, transcendence, and personal empowerment. These emotionally resonant qualities may enhance affective fluency and tap into underlying existential needs, which have been shown to increase susceptibility to belief, particularly under conditions of uncertainty or perceived lack of control (Whitson & Galinsky, 2008). The high IAT score suggests that while participants may not explicitly endorse such ideas, they nonetheless associate them with positive emotional valence and implicit credibility – demonstrating how conspiracies framed in spiritually affirming or therapeutic language can bypass rational scrutiny and generate subconscious belief (Lindeman & Aarnio, 2007).

ETHICAL CONSIDERATIONS

As AI technologies become increasingly integrated into persuasive communication, particularly through marketing, media, and behavioral targeting, their capacity to manipulate consumer attitudes and behaviors raises ethical concerns. Unlike traditional advertising, AI-generated content can be hyper-personalized, emotionally resonant, and indistinguishable from human-authored messages, amplifying its persuasive power while bypassing users' conscious scrutiny (Floridi et al., 2018). This convergence of automation and affective influence risks eroding individual autonomy, as decisions may be shaped more by algorithmic design than by rational agency. When used in environments of implicit trust (e.g., social networks), such AI-driven persuasion can subtly reinforce biases, misinformation, or consumption habits, all without the user's explicit awareness or consent (Miller et al., 2017).

These dynamics demand robust accountability frameworks to ensure that developers and deploying organizations are held responsible for the outcomes of AI-driven messaging. The opacity of many AI systems (especially deep learning models) makes it difficult to trace decision-making pathways or assess intent, thereby complicating issues of legal and moral responsibility (Mittelstadt et al., 2016). Moreover, manipulative content often emerges from feedback loops within data-driven recommendation systems, where maximizing engagement is prioritized over ethical communication. To mitigate these harms, accountability mechanisms must extend beyond technical performance metrics and incorporate social, psychological, and normative considerations in system design and deployment (Raji et al., 2020).

To uphold transparency and minimize manipulation, AI governance must adopt principles that include explainability, data provenance, and user agency. This includes implementing explainable AI (XAI) systems that allow users and regulators to understand how persuasive content is generated and why it is targeted (Doshi-Velez & Kim, 2017). Further, regulatory safeguards should promote consent-based personalization and include options for users to opt out of algorithmically manipulated content streams. Ethical AI design must therefore shift from a reactive model (responding to manipulation after harm is done) to a proactive paradigm that anticipates and designs against psychological vulnerabilities (Morley et al., 2020). Such safeguards are especially urgent as AI becomes capable not only of mimicking human communication but of exploiting implicit trust heuristics with increasing precision.

Industry and Regulatory Efforts to Ensure Safety and Transparent AI

Amid increasing concern about the influence of artificial intelligence (AI) on critical thinking, user autonomy, and information integrity, both private-sector actors and regulatory bodies have taken significant steps to embed ethical safeguards into AI systems. Central among these efforts are initiatives to promote transparency, user safety, and accountability.

Leading technology companies are integrating transparency mechanisms directly into system design. Microsoft's Responsible AI Transparency Report (2024) outlines how its Copilot Studio team enhanced system safety by adopting iterative testing, content filtering, and automatic citation features. These interventions led to a measurable improvement in in-domain model accuracy, rising from 88.6% to 95.7%. Similarly, Meta has extended transparency initiatives into the advertising space, mandating disclosure labels for generative AI-created or modified ads (Meta, 2025). These appear both alongside sponsored content and within metadata menus. From early 2024, advertisers in sensitive domains (e.g., health, housing, and finance) must explicitly declare any AI-generated elements. Furthermore, Meta prohibits the use of its generative tools in political or social issue advertising (Meta, 2024; Daily AI, 2023).

These examples reflect a broader industry shift. Rather than obscuring AI's role, companies are actively developing tools to disclose it (such as context indicators, labeling protocols, and user interface adaptations) to reduce risks of manipulation or misinformation. Microsoft's broader governance model, described as "map, measure, and manage," supports this aim by refining model grounding, improving citation accuracy, and enhancing contextual relevance. GitHub Copilot, for instance, has partnered with designated Responsible AI leads to address domain-specific risks, including potentially harmful code suggestions (Microsoft, 2024).

These initiatives illustrate a growing consensus: transparency is a requirement for responsible AI. Companies are institutionalizing oversight frameworks, conducting human rights impact assessments, and aligning development practices with formal AI principles. Red-teaming, documentation protocols, user control mechanisms, and audit trails are increasingly standard elements of AI lifecycle management.

Regulatory and Ethical Frameworks

In parallel, governments and international organizations are codifying transparency requirements into law. The European Union's AI Act defines transparency as traceability and explainability and mandates that high-risk systems (e.g., credit scoring, employment screening, infrastructure) include documentation, usage instructions, and user disclosures. Developers of general-purpose AI must disclose training data summaries and provide integration guidance (EU AI Act, n.d.).

The United States has taken a similar stance. The Federal Trade Commission (FTC) has clarified that AI technologies are not exempt from consumer protection laws. In a notable case, the FTC sued Rite Aid for deploying a facial recognition system that disproportionately misidentified women and people of color as shoplifters. The Commission emphasized that companies must anticipate and monitor harm at all stages of AI deployment (Federal Trade Commission, 2025).

International guidelines reinforce these regulatory developments. The OECD's AI Principles, adopted by over 40 countries, stress the need for trustworthy and human-centered AI (OECD, n.d.). UNESCO's Recommendation on the Ethics of AI calls for explainability, transparency, and the principle of "do no harm." Meanwhile, standard-setting bodies such as ISO and NIST are contributing risk-based frameworks to guide implementation (United Nations, 2020).

Organizational Insights and Risk Management Trends

Recent industry surveys corroborate the centrality of these issues in practice. Deloitte's 2024 State of Generative AI report found that regulation and risk are now among the top concerns for enterprises, prompting organizational restructuring and the appointment of executive-level AI governance roles (Deloitte, n.d.). McKinsey's global AI survey reports that nearly half of companies have experienced negative impacts from generative AI (a rise from 44% the previous year) leading to intensified risk mitigation practices, especially in relation to misinformation, cybersecurity, and intellectual property (McKinsey & Company, n.d.).

Public trust remains a critical driver of these shifts. A 2025 PwC report found that 85% of consumers are more inclined to trust companies that use AI ethically, while 74% of employees report higher job satisfaction under ethical AI policies (Soon, 2025). These findings underscore both reputational risk and business value tied to transparency.

Finally, concerns about future risks, including those associated with artificial general intelligence (AGI), have pushed the global policy agenda further. At the 2023 AI Safety Summit at Bletchley Park, 28 countries, including the United States and China, signed a joint declaration emphasizing the need for responsible AI development and warning of potential catastrophic consequences from unchecked advanced systems (Judge, Nitzberg, & Russell, 2025).

CONCLUSIONS & DISCUSSIONS

The findings presented in this chapter carry significant implications for marketing and advertising, particularly in an environment increasingly shaped by artificial intelligence (AI) and algorithmically generated content. As synthetic messages grow more linguistically, visually, and contextually convincing, often indistinguishable from human-created communication, consumers' ability to critically evaluate message authenticity is increasingly undermined (Kreps & Kriner, 2020; Westerlund, 2019).

Implicit trust in media sources such as television, social media, and alternative blogs, despite their often contested credibility, highlights the power of affective and habitual exposure in shaping consumer belief systems. This suggests that marketing strategies grounded in emotional resonance, narrative fluency, and repeated exposure are more likely to succeed than those reliant solely on rational or factual messaging (Petty & Cacioppo, 1986). In practice, this means that campaigns delivered through emotionally engaging and frequently accessed platforms can embed brand messages more deeply in consumers' associative networks, even if the content is not consciously remembered or endorsed.

AI-enhanced marketing systems, such as generative language models and predictive personalization engines, are increasingly adept at crafting messages that exploit the heuristics underlying implicit trust: repetition, emotional salience, fluency, and familiarity (Reber & Schwarz, 1999). When such content is delivered through channels already associated with high subconscious trust (e.g., influencers or visually rich social media platforms), it gains a powerful advantage in persuasion, regardless of factual accuracy. This is consistent with affective theories of belief formation, which posit that people are more likely to believe information that "feels" true, even in the absence of evidence (Slovic et al., 2007; Pennycook & Rand, 2019). Marketers must be aware that message design no longer operates in a neutral cognitive space. Instead, persuasion is increasingly rooted in implicit processes, where trust is triggered not by logic or accuracy, but by affective cues and contextual familiarity.

Moreover, the results indicate that consumers may implicitly trust emotionally charged or spiritually framed narratives more than institutionally verified ones. This holds particular relevance for marketers leveraging wellness, lifestyle, or personal transformation themes. The unexpected high implicit trust in angel therapy points to a broader consumer openness to metaphysical or emotionally comforting narratives, especially when presented in visually fluent and emotionally salient formats. In the marketing context, this suggests that consumers are not only vulnerable to false information but may actively gravitate toward narratives that fulfill psychological needs for meaning, agency, or control, especially during periods of uncertainty (Whitson & Galinsky, 2008). AI-generated messages designed to align with these latent emotional drivers could therefore foster brand attachment or behavioral compliance without conscious deliberation. While this enhances the efficiency of commercial communication, it also raises critical ethical concerns regarding consent, manipulation, and the erosion of informed decision-making.

Despite its contributions, this study presents several limitations that should be acknowledged. First, the research was conducted with a relatively small sample size, which limits the generalizability of the findings. While the combination of Implicit

Association Tests (IAT), quantitative questionnaires, and qualitative interviews offers a rich, multi-method approach, the small number of participants constrains statistical power and may not adequately capture the diversity of attitudes across broader populations. Future research should aim to replicate these findings using larger and more demographically representative samples to strengthen external validity.

Second, the categorization of information sources (such as mainstream media, influencers, family, or government institutions) remains relatively broad. While the mixed-method design enables the identification of patterns across these categories, it does not account for important distinctions within them (for example, trust in public broadcasting vs. partisan news, or health experts vs. lifestyle influencers). Future studies should disaggregate these categories further to uncover more precise patterns of trust and bias.

Finally, the AI-generated content used in the study, while designed to closely mimic authentic online ads, was presented in a controlled research setting. Participants' reactions to such content may differ in natural media environments, where distractions, emotional states, and social context can shape interpretation. Experimental designs that simulate real-world media conditions or employ field experiments could improve validity.

IMPLICATIONS FOR MARKETING AND ADVERTISING

In light of these insights, marketers must adopt a more reflective and ethically grounded approach to content development and channel strategy. Implicit methodologies such as the IAT should be more widely integrated into campaign testing, not only to measure subconscious associations but also to safeguard against unintended or unethical psychological effects. The emotional resonance and visual fluency of AI-generated content, especially when paired with trusted influencers or familiar platforms, can powerfully shape consumer perceptions without conscious awareness. As such, marketing strategies should consider not just what messages are being delivered, but how and through whom they are conveyed, recognizing that implicit trust may be built on cues unrelated to message accuracy or credibility.

Moreover, regulatory frameworks may need to evolve to address the psychological dimensions of AI-driven persuasion, particularly as synthetic content becomes more pervasive and indistinguishable from reality. This includes reassessing disclosure standards, algorithmic transparency, and the psychological safety of digital advertising environments. Just as data privacy became a regulatory priority in the wake of digital surveillance concerns, implicit persuasion (especially when tied to personal vulnerabilities) should be treated as a matter of public concern.

The convergence of emotionally manipulative AI and subconscious trust heuristics demands a new marketing paradigm, one that balances efficacy with responsibility, and performance with transparency (Floridi et al., 2018). Practically, this means that designers of persuasive technologies, such as recommender systems and chatbot-based marketing tools, should be trained in behavioral ethics and user-centered design principles. Ethical design should include friction points that allow users to pause, reflect, or verify sources before acting on persuasive messages, especially in high-stakes domains like health, finance, or politics.

These findings also have implications for consumer education. Media literacy programs must expand their focus beyond critical thinking and fact-checking to include emotional literacy and awareness of implicit cognitive biases. Understanding how fluency, familiarity, and emotional tone influence believability is essential for navigating persuasive digital environments.

Finally, researchers and institutions studying digital communication should continue developing interdisciplinary methodologies that combine behavioral science, AI ethics, and marketing analytics. Only by bridging these domains can we fully understand and responsibly shape the evolving dynamics of trust in a synthetic media ecosystem.

REFERENCES

Act, E. U. A. I. (n.d.). *Key issue. Transparency Obligations.* https://www.euaiact.com/key-issue/5

Alessandro, G., Dimitri, O., Cristina, B., & Anna, M. (2024). The emotional impact of generative AI: Negative emotions and perception of threat. *Behaviour & Information Technology, 44*(4), 676–693. DOI: 10.1080/0144929X.2024.2333933

Ali, A., & Qazi, I. A. (2022). *Cognitive reflection is associated with greater truth discernment for COVID-19 headlines, less trust but greater use of formal information sources, and greater willingness to pay for masks among social media users in Pakistan. Harvard Kennedy School (HKS).* Misinformation Review., DOI: 10.37016/mr-2020-101

Argan, M., Dinç, H., Kaya, S., & Tokay Argan, M. (2023). Artificial Intelligence (AI) in Advertising: Understanding and Schematizing the Behaviors of Social Media Users. *ADCAIJ: Advances in Distributed Computing and Artificial Intelligence Journal, 11*(3), 331–348. DOI: 10.14201/adcaij.28331

Ariely, D. (2023). *Misbelief: What makes rational people believe irrational things.* Heligo Books.

Athaide, G. A., Jeon, J., Raj, S. P., Sivakumar, K., & Xiong, G. (2025). Marketing innovations and digital technologies: A systematic review, proposed framework, and future research agenda. *Journal of Product Innovation Management, 42*(1), 144–165. DOI: 10.1111/jpim.12741

Bak, W., & Kutnik, J. (2021). Domains of intellectual humility: Self-esteem and narcissism as independent predictors. *Personality and Individual Differences, 177*, 110815. DOI: 10.1016/j.paid.2021.110815

Başev, S. E. (2024). The role of artificial intelligence (AI) in the future of the advertising industry: Applications and examples of AI in advertising. *International Journal of Education Technology and Scientific Researches, 9*(26), 167–183. DOI: 10.35826/ijetsar.729

Bastick, Z. (2021). Would you notice if fake news changed your behavior? An experiment on the unconscious effects of disinformation. *Computers in Human Behavior, 116*, 106633. DOI: 10.1016/j.chb.2020.106633

Bettiga, D., & Noci, G. (2024). The influence of television content on advertisement: A neurophysiological study. *Frontiers in Psychology, 15*, 1266906. DOI: 10.3389/fpsyg.2024.1266906 PMID: 38371708

Bhatia, S. (2018). Topic-specific sentiment analysis can help identify political ideology. *arXiv preprint arXiv:1810.12897*. DOI: 10.18653/v1/W18-6212

Buchanan, T. (2021). Trust, personality, and belief as determinants of the organic reach of political disinformation on social media. *The Social Science Journal*, •••, 1–12. DOI: 10.1080/03623319.2021.1975085

Carrasco-Farre, C. (2024). Large language models are as persuasive as humans, but how? About the cognitive effort and moral-emotional language of LLM arguments. *arXiv preprint arXiv:2404.09329*. https://doi.org//arXiv.2404.09329DOI: 10.48550

Chou, W. Y. S., Oh, A., & Klein, W. M. (2018). Addressing health-related misinformation on social media. *Journal of the American Medical Association*, *320*(23), 2417–2418. DOI: 10.1001/jama.2018.16865 PMID: 30428002

Cichocka, A., Marchlewska, M., & Biddlestone, M. (2022). Why do narcissists find conspiracy theories so appealing? *Current Opinion in Psychology*, *47*, 101386. DOI: 10.1016/j.copsyc.2022.101386 PMID: 35816915

Cichocka, A., Marchlewska, M., & De Zavala, A. G. (2016). Does self-love or self-hate predict conspiracy beliefs? Narcissism, self-esteem, and the endorsement of conspiracy theories. *Social Psychological & Personality Science*, *7*(2), 157–166. DOI: 10.1177/1948550615616170

Cone, J., Flaharty, K., & Ferguson, M. J. (2021). The long-term effects of new evidence on implicit impressions of other people. *Psychological Science*, *32*(2), 173–188. DOI: 10.1177/0956797620963559 PMID: 33428852

Cook, J., Lewandowsky, S., & Ecker, U. K. (2017). Neutralizing misinformation through inoculation: Exposing misleading argumentation techniques reduces their influence. *PLoS One*, *12*(5), e0175799. DOI: 10.1371/journal.pone.0175799 PMID: 28475576

Cosgrove, T. J., & Murphy, C. P. (2023). Narcissistic susceptibility to conspiracy beliefs exaggerated by education, reduced by cognitive reflection. *Frontiers in Psychology*, *14*, 1164725. DOI: 10.3389/fpsyg.2023.1164725 PMID: 37484083

Daily, A. I. (2023, November). *Meta has updated policies to require labeling of AI-generated ads*. https://dailyai.com/2023/11/meta-has-updated-policies-to-require-labeling-of-ai-generated-ads/

Dan, V. (2025). Deepfakes as a Democratic Threat: Experimental Evidence Shows Noxious Effects That Are Reducible Through Journalistic Fact Checks. *The International Journal of Press/Politics*, *19401612251317766*, 19401612251317766. Advance online publication. DOI: 10.1177/19401612251317766

Deloitte. (n.d.). *State of generative AI in the enterprise*. https://www.deloitte.com/us/en/what-we-do/capabilities/applied-artificial-intelligence/content/state-of-generative-ai-in-enterprise.html

Doshi-Velez, F., & Kim, B. (2017). Towards a rigorous science of interpretable machine learning. *arXiv preprint arXiv:1702.08608*. https://doi.org//arXiv.1702.08608DOI: 10.48550

Escandon-Barbosa, D., Salas-Paramo, J., López-Ramírez, M. P., & Pava-Cárdenas, A. (2025). The role of cognitive processes in healthy consumption food products: An eye-tracking technology study. *Journal of Marketing Analytics*, *13*(1), 96–110. DOI: 10.1057/s41270-023-00261-3

Facione, P. A. (2011). Critical thinking: What it is and why it counts. *Insight assessment, 1*(1), 1-23.

Fahim, I., Haramouni, L., Majdi, M. K., & Elkandoussi, F. (2024). The Application of AI in Neuromarketing: A Systematic Literature Review. *AI and Data Engineering Solutions for Effective Marketing*, 48-68. DOI: DOI: 10.4018/979-8-3693-3172-9.ch003

Federal Trade Commission. (2025, January). *AI risk and consumer harm*. https://www.ftc.gov/policy/advocacy-research/tech-at-ftc/2025/01/ai-risk-consumer-harm

Figueiras, M. J., Ghorayeb, J., Coutinho, M. V. C., Marôco, J., & Thomas, J. (2021). Levels of Trust in Information Sources as a Predictor of Protective Health Behaviors During COVID-19 Pandemic: A UAE Cross-Sectional Study. *Frontiers in Psychology, 12*, 633550. DOI: 10.3389/fpsyg.2021.633550 PMID: 34366960

Floridi, L., & Chiriatti, M. (2020). M. GPT-3: Its Nature, Scope, Limits, and Consequences. *Minds and Machines*, *30*(4), 681–694. DOI: 10.1007/s11023-020-09548-1

Floridi, L., Cowls, J., Beltrametti, M., Chatila, R., Chazerand, P., Dignum, V., Luetge, C., Madelin, R., Pagallo, U., Rossi, F., Schafer, B., Valcke, P., & Vayena, E. (2018). AI4People—An ethical framework for a good AI society: Opportunities, risks, principles, and recommendations. *Minds and Machines*, *28*(4), 689–707. DOI: 10.1007/s11023-018-9482-5 PMID: 30930541

Ford, J., Jain, V., Wadhwani, K., & Gupta, D. G. (2023). AI advertising: An overview and guidelines. *Journal of Business Research, 166*, 114124. DOI: 10.1016/j.jbusres.2023.114124

Gao, B., Wang, Y., Xie, H., Hu, Y., & Hu, Y. (2023). Artificial intelligence in advertising: Advancements, challenges, and ethical considerations in targeting, personalization, content creation, and ad optimization. *SAGE Open*, *13*(4), 21582440231210759. DOI: 10.1177/21582440231210759

Gerlich, M. (2025). AI Tools in Society: Impacts on Cognitive Offloading and the Future of Critical Thinking. *Societies (Basel, Switzerland)*, *15*(1), 6. DOI: 10.3390/soc15010006

Gjoneska, B. (2021). Conspiratorial beliefs and cognitive styles: An integrated look on analytic thinking, critical thinking, and scientific reasoning in relation to (dis) trust in conspiracy theories. *Frontiers in Psychology*, *12*, 736838. DOI: 10.3389/fpsyg.2021.736838 PMID: 34712182

Goldberg, L. R., Johnson, J. A., Eber, H. W., Hogan, R., Ashton, M. C., Cloninger, C. R., & Gough, H. C. (2006). The International Personality Item Pool and the future of public-domain personality measures. *Journal of Research in Personality*, *40*(1), 84–96. DOI: 10.1016/j.jrp.2005.08.007

Green, M. C., & Brock, T. C. (2000). The role of transportation in the persuasiveness of public narratives. *Journal of Personality and Social Psychology*, *79*(5), 701–721. DOI: 10.1037/0022-3514.79.5.701 PMID: 11079236

Greenwald, A. G., & Banaji, M. R. (1995). Implicit social cognition: Attitudes, self-esteem, and stereotypes. *Psychological Review*, *102*(1), 4–27. DOI: 10.1037/0033-295X.102.1.4 PMID: 7878162

Greenwald, A. G., McGhee, D. E., & Schwartz, J. L. K. (1998). Measuring individual differences in implicit cognition: The implicit association test. *Journal of Personality and Social Psychology*, *74*(6), 1464–1480. DOI: 10.1037/0022-3514.74.6.1464 PMID: 9654756

Greenwald, A. G., Poehlman, T. A., Uhlmann, E. L., & Banaji, M. R. (2009). Understanding and using the Implicit Association Test: III. Meta-analysis of predictive validity. *Journal of Personality and Social Psychology*, *97*(1), 17–41. DOI: 10.1037/a0015575 PMID: 19586237

Gregory, C., & Banks, A. P. (2025). Netflix and chill: Intuitive decision making predicts satisfaction and happiness with real-world choices. *Current Psychology (New Brunswick, N.J.)*, *44*(12), 1–13. DOI: 10.1007/s12144-025-07999-2

Gu, C., Jia, S., Lai, J., Chen, R., & Chang, X. (2024). Exploring Consumer Acceptance of AI-Generated Advertisements: From the Perspectives of Perceived Eeriness and Perceived Intelligence. *Journal of Theoretical and Applied Electronic Commerce Research, 19*(3), 2218–2238. DOI: 10.3390/jtaer19030108

Gundersen, A. B., van der Linden, S., Piasecki, J., Ryguła, R., Noworyta, K., & Kunst, J. R. (2024). Predicting Misinformation Beliefs Across Four Countries: The Role of Narcissism, Conspiracy Mentality, Social Trust, and Perceptions of Unsafe Neighborhoods. *Journal of Social and Political Psychology, 12*(2), 265–283. DOI: 10.5964/jspp.13385

Gupta, T., & Bansal, S. (2024). Beyond echo chambers: Unraveling the impact of social media algorithms on consumer behavior and exploring pathways to a diverse digital discourse. *Journal of Marketing Studies, 7*(1), 15–37. DOI: 10.47941/jms.1799

Hatamleh, I. H. M., Safori, A. O., Habes, M., Tahat, O., Ahmad, A. K., Abdallah, R. A. Q., & Aissani, R. (2023). Trust in social media: Enhancing social relationships. *Social Sciences (Basel, Switzerland), 12*(7), 416. DOI: 10.3390/socsci12070416

Haupt, M. R., Cuomo, R., Mackey, T. K., & Coulson, S. (2024). The role of narcissism and motivated reasoning on misinformation propagation. *Frontiers in Communication, 9*, 1472631. DOI: 10.3389/fcomm.2024.1472631

Heath, R., Brandt, D., & Nairn, A. (2006). Brand Relationships: Strengthened by Emotion, Weakened by Attention. *Journal of Advertising Research, 46*(4), 410–419. DOI: 10.2501/S002184990606048X

Hetherington, M. J., & Rudolph, T. J. (2015). *Why Washington won't work: Polarization, political trust, and the governing crisis.* University of Chicago Press., DOI: 10.7208/chicago/9780226299358.001.0001

Hu, R. (2025). The Evolution of Social Media Affordances and the Changing Landscape of Digital Marketing. Advances in Economics. *Management and Political Sciences, 189*(1), 136–141. DOI: 10.54254/2754-1169/2025.BL23889

Huh, J., Nelson, M. R., & Russell, C. A. (2023). ChatGPT, AI Advertising, and Advertising Research and Education. *Journal of Advertising, 52*(4), 477–482. DOI: 10.1080/00913367.2023.2227013

Huynh, A. C., & Romero Gonzalez, R. A. (2023). The fine line between intellectual humility and arrogance: Perceiving humility among the intellectually humble and narcissistic. *The Journal of Positive Psychology, 19*(4), 599–610. DOI: 10.1080/17439760.2023.2230455

Iliescu, D., Popa, M., & Dimache, R. (2019). Adaptarea românească a Setului Internaţional de Itemi de Personalitate: IPIP-Ro. *Psihologia Resurselor Umane, 13*(1), 83–112. https://hrp-journal.com/index.php/pru/article/view/148

Imhoff, R., & Lamberty, P. (2020). A bioweapon or a hoax? The link between distinct conspiracy beliefs about the coronavirus disease (COVID-19) outbreak and pandemic behavior. *Social Psychological & Personality Science, 11*(8), 1110–1118. DOI: 10.1177/1948550620934692 PMID: 38602949

Judge, B., Nitzberg, M., & Russell, S. (2025). When code isn't law: Rethinking regulation for artificial intelligence. *Policy and Society, 44*(1), 85–97. DOI: 10.1093/polsoc/puae020

Kahneman, D. (2011). *Fast and slow thinking*. Allen Lane and Penguin Books.

Kang, S., Potinteu, A. E., & Said, N. (2025, April). ExplainitAI: When do we trust artificial intelligence? The influence of content and explainability in a cross-cultural comparison. In *Proceedings of the Extended Abstracts of the CHI Conference on Human Factors in Computing Systems* (pp. 1-7). https://doi.org/DOI: 10.1145/3706599.3720222

Kaplan, A., & Haenlein, M. (2019). Siri, Siri, in my hand: Who's the fairest in the land? On the interpretations, illustrations, and implications of artificial intelligence. *Business Horizons, 62*(1), 15–25. DOI: 10.1016/j.bushor.2018.08.004

Keller, F. B., Schoch, D., Stier, S., & Yang, J. (2020). Political astroturfing on twitter: How to coordinate a disinformation campaign. *Political Communication, 37*(2), 256–280. DOI: 10.1080/10584609.2019.1661888

King, B. M. (2024). Social Desirability Biased Responding: Are Researchers Listening? *Psychol Behav Sci Int J., 21*(5), 556075. DOI: 10.19080/PBSIJ.2024.21.556075

Kreps, S. E., & Kriner, D. L. (2020). Model uncertainty, political contestation, and public trust in science: Evidence from the COVID-19 pandemic. *Science Advances, 6*(43), eabd4563. Advance online publication. DOI: 10.1126/sciadv.abd4563 PMID: 32978142

Lang, A. (2006). Using the limited capacity model of motivated mediated message processing to design effective cancer communication messages. *Journal of Communication, 56*(suppl_1), S57–S80. DOI: 10.1111/j.1460-2466.2006.00283.x

Lantian, A., Bagneux, V., Delouvée, S., & Gauvrit, N. (2021). Maybe a free thinker but not a critical one: High conspiracy belief is associated with low critical thinking ability. *Applied Cognitive Psychology, 35*(3), 674–684. DOI: 10.1002/acp.3790

Li, G., Teng, Y., Kawai-Yue, J., Ahmed, U., Tantiwongse, A. S., Liang, J. Y., . . . Chilton, L. B. (2025). Audience Impressions of Narrative Structures and Personal Language Style in Science Communication on Social Media. *arXiv preprint arXiv:2502.05287*. https://doi.org//arXiv.2502.05287DOI: 10.48550

Lindeman, M., & Aarnio, K. (2007). Superstitious, magical, and paranormal beliefs: An integrative model. *Journal of Research in Personality*, *41*(4), 731–744. DOI: 10.1016/j.jrp.2006.06.009

Lu, J., & Xiao, Y. (2023). Heuristic Information Processing as a Mediating Factor in the Process of Exposure to COVID-19 Vaccine Information and Misinformation Sharing on Social Media. *Health Communication*, *39*(12), 2779–2792. DOI: 10.1080/10410236.2023.2288373 PMID: 38016931

Maison, D., Greenwald, A. G., & Bruin, R. H. (2004). Predictive validity of the Implicit Association Test in studies of brands, consumer attitudes, and behavior. *Journal of Consumer Psychology*, *14*(4), 405–415. DOI: 10.1207/s15327663jcp1404_9

Manovich, L. (2013). *Software takes command*. Bloomsbury Academic. DOI: 10.5040/9781472544988

March, E., & Springer, J. (2019). Belief in conspiracy theories: The predictive role of schizotypy, Machiavellianism, and primary psychopathy. *PLoS One*, *14*(12), e0225964. DOI: 10.1371/journal.pone.0225964 PMID: 31794581

Mariani, M. M., Perez-Vega, R., & Wirtz, J. (2022). AI in marketing, consumer research and psychology: A systematic literature review and research agenda. *Psychology and Marketing*, *39*(4), 755–776. DOI: 10.1002/mar.21619

Martin, A. (2024). Artificial Intelligence Transformations in Digital Advertising: Historical Progression, Emerging Trends, and Strategic Outlook. *Preprints*. https://doi.org/DOI: 10.20944/preprints202411.0569.v2

Matz, S. C., Teeny, J. D., Vaid, S. S., Peters, H., Harari, G. M., & Cerf, M. (2024). The potential of generative AI for personalized persuasion at scale. *Scientific Reports*, *14*(1), 4692. DOI: 10.1038/s41598-024-53755-0 PMID: 38409168

McKinsey & Company. (n.d.). *The state of AI*. https://www.mckinsey.com/capabilities/quantumblack/our-insights/the-state-of-ai

Menicocci, S., Lupo, V., Ferrara, S., Giorgi, A., Serra, E., Babiloni, F., & Borghini, G. (2024). Fake-News Attitude Evaluation in Terms of Visual Attention and Personality Traits: A Preliminary Study for Mitigating the Cognitive Warfare. *Behavioral Sciences (Basel, Switzerland)*, *14*(11), 1026. DOI: 10.3390/bs14111026 PMID: 39594326

Meta. (2024, April). *Meta's approach to labeling AI-generated content and manipulated media.* https://about.fb.com/news/2024/04/metas-approach-to-labeling-ai-generated-content-and-manipulated-media/

Meta. (2025, February). *Gen AI transparency: How Meta is building transparency into ads and products.* https://about.fb.com/news/2025/02/gen-ai-transparency-metas-ads-products/

Metzger, M. J., & Flanagin, A. J. (2015). Psychological approaches to credibility assessment online. *The handbook of the psychology of communication technology*, 445-466. https://doi.org/DOI: 10.1002/9781118426456.ch20

Microsoft. (2024). *Responsible AI transparency report 2024.* https://cdn-dynmedia-1.microsoft.com/is/content/microsoftcorp/microsoft/msc/documents/presentations/CSR/Responsible-AI-Transparency-Report-2024.pdf

Miller, T., Howe, P., & Sonenberg, L. (2017). Explainable AI: Beware of inmates running the asylum or: How I learnt to stop worrying and love the social and behavioural sciences. *arXiv preprint arXiv:1712.00547.*

Mittelstadt, B. D., Allo, P., Taddeo, M., Wachter, S., & Floridi, L. (2016). The ethics of algorithms: Mapping the debate. *Big Data & Society*, *3*(2), 2053951716679679. Advance online publication. DOI: 10.1177/2053951716679679

Montag, C., Klugah-Brown, B., Zhou, X., Wernicke, J., Liu, C., Kou, J., Chen, Y., Haas, B. W., & Becker, B. (2023). Trust toward humans and trust toward artificial intelligence are not associated: Initial insights from self-report and neurostructural brain imaging. *Personality Neuroscience*, *6*, e3. DOI: 10.1017/pen.2022.5 PMID: 38107776

Morley, J., Floridi, L., Kinsey, L., & Elhalal, A. (2020). From what to how: An initial review of publicly available AI ethics tools, methods and research to translate principles into practices. *Science and Engineering Ethics*, *26*(4), 2141–2168. DOI: 10.1007/s11948-019-00165-5 PMID: 31828533

Nielsen, I. Q. (2024, April 17). *NIQ research uncovers hidden consumer attitudes toward AI-generated ads.* https://nielseniq.com/global/en/news-center/2024/niq-research-uncovers-hidden-consumer-attitudes-toward-ai-generated-ads/

O'Mahony, C., Linehan, C., & Murphy, G. (2024, May). The Critical Thinking about Conspiracies (CTAC) Test: Development and Validation.

Orazi, D. C., Hamby, A., Herhausen, D., Van Laer, T., Ludwig, S., Gonsalves, C., & Grewal, D. (2025). Verbal persuasion in marketing: A multimethod meta-analysis of analytical and narrative processing. *Journal of the Academy of Marketing Science, 53*(6), 1–24. DOI: 10.1007/s11747-025-01095-4

Organisation for Economic Co-operation and Development. (n.d.). *AI principles.* https://www.oecd.org/en/topics/sub-issues/ai-principles.html

Orosz, G., Faragó, L., Paskuj, B., & Krekó, P. (2024). Strategies to combat misinformation: Enduring effects of a 15-minute online intervention on critical-thinking adolescents. *Computers in Human Behavior, 159*, 108338. DOI: 10.1016/j.chb.2024.108338

Pangarkar, A., Mishra, N., & Aithal, P. S. (2023). Subconscious Branding: The Role of Artificial Intelligence in Marketing. *Future trends in Information, Communication and Computing Technology-TechHorizon: Navigating Tomorrow's Digital Frontiers. Srinivas Publication, India*, 01-14. https://dx.doi.org/DOI: 10.2139/ssrn.4674839

Pennycook, G., Bear, A., Collins, E. T., & Rand, D. G. (2020). The implied truth effect: Attaching warnings to a subset of fake news headlines increases perceived accuracy of headlines without warnings. *Management Science, 66*(11), 4944–4957. DOI: 10.1287/mnsc.2019.3478

Pennycook, G., & Rand, D. G. (2019). Lazy, not biased: Susceptibility to partisan fake news is better explained by lack of reasoning than by motivated reasoning. *Cognition, 188*, 39–50. DOI: 10.1016/j.cognition.2018.06.011 PMID: 29935897

Pentina, I., Xie, T., Hancock, T., & Bailey, A. (2023). Consumer–machine relationships in the age of artificial intelligence: Systematic literature review and research directions. *Psychology and Marketing, 40*(8), 1593–1614. DOI: 10.1002/mar.21853

Petty, R. E., & Cacioppo, J. T. (1986). The Elaboration Likelihood Model of Persuasion. In *Communication and Persuasion. Springer Series in Social Psychology.* Springer., DOI: 10.1007/978-1-4612-4964-1_1

Poole, A., & Ball, L. (2006). Eye tracking in human-computer interaction and usability. *Encyclopedia of Human Computer Interaction. Editorial Idea Group Reference, 211*, 219.

Pussadeniya, N., Nakisa, B., & Rastgoo, M. N. (2025). Affective-CARA: A Knowledge Graph Driven Framework for Culturally Adaptive Emotional Intelligence in HCI. *arXiv preprint arXiv:2506.14166.* https://doi.org//arXiv.2506.14166DOI: 10.48550

Putri, S. D. G., Purnomo, E. P., & Khairunissa, T. (2024). Echo Chambers and Algorithmic Bias: The Homogenization of Online Culture in a Smart Society. In *SHS Web of Conferences* (Vol. 202, p. 05001). EDP Sciences. https://doi.org/DOI: 10.1051/shsconf/202420205001

Raji, I. D., Smart, A., White, R. N., Mitchell, M., Gebru, T., Hutchinson, B., & Barnes, P. (2020, January). Closing the AI accountability gap: Defining an end-to-end framework for internal algorithmic auditing. In *Proceedings of the 2020 conference on fairness, accountability, and transparency* (pp. 33-44). https://doi.org/DOI: 10.1145/3351095.3372873

Reber, R., & Schwarz, N. (1999). Effects of perceptual fluency on judgments of truth. *Consciousness and Cognition*, *8*(3), 338–342. DOI: 10.1006/ccog.1999.0386 PMID: 10487787

Riedl, R. (2022). Is trust in artificial intelligence systems related to user personality? Review of empirical evidence and future research directions. *Electronic Markets*, *32*(4), 2021–2051. DOI: 10.1007/s12525-022-00594-4

Roozenbeek, J., Traberg, C. S., & van der Linden, S. (2022). Technique-based inoculation against real-world misinformation. *Royal Society Open Science*, *9*(5), 211719. DOI: 10.1098/rsos.211719 PMID: 35600423

Slovic, P., Finucane, M. L., Peters, E., & MacGregor, D. G. (2007). The affect heuristic. *European Journal of Operational Research*, *177*(3), 1333–1352. DOI: 10.1016/j.ejor.2005.04.006

Soon, L. (2025, February 28). *AI transparency and ethics: Building customer trust in AI systems*. CMSWire. https://www.cmswire.com/ai-technology/ai-transparency-and-ethics-building-customer-trust-in-ai-systems/

Stanovich, K. E., & West, R. F. (2007). Natural myside bias is independent of cognitive ability. *Thinking & Reasoning*, *13*(3), 225–247. DOI: 10.1080/13546780600780796

Steiner, G., Geissler, B., Schreder, G., & Zenk, L. (2018). Living sustainability, or merely pretending? From explicit self-report measures to implicit cognition. *Sustainability Science*, *13*(4), 1001–1015. DOI: 10.1007/s11625-018-0561-6 PMID: 30147793

Sultan, M., Tump, A. N., Ehmann, N., Lorenz-Spreen, P., Hertwig, R., Gollwitzer, A., & Kurvers, R. H. (2024). Susceptibility to online misinformation: A systematic meta-analysis of demographic and psychological factors. *Proceedings of the National Academy of Sciences of the United States of America*, *121*(47), e2409329121. DOI: 10.1073/pnas.2409329121 PMID: 39531500

Traberg, C. S., Harjani, T., Roozenbeek, J., & Van Der Linden, S. (2024). The persuasive effects of social cues and source effects on misinformation susceptibility. *Scientific Reports, 14*(1), 4205. DOI: 10.1038/s41598-024-54030-y PMID: 38378750

Tsfati, Y., & Ariely, G. (2014). Individual and contextual correlates of trust in media across 44 countries. *Communication Research, 41*(6), 760–782. DOI: 10.1177/0093650213485972

Udry, J., & Barber, S. J. (2023). The illusory truth effect requires semantic coherence across repetitions. *Cognition, 241*, 105607. DOI: 10.1016/j.cognition.2023.105607 PMID: 37742428

United Nations. (2020, December 11). *Draft resource guide on artificial intelligence (AI) strategies*. https://sdgs.un.org/sites/default/files/2020-12/Draft%20Resource%20Guide%20on%20AI%20Strategies%20Dec%2011.pdf

Van Dessel, P., Mertens, G., Smith, C. T., & De Houwer, J. (2019). Mere exposure effects on implicit stimulus evaluation: The moderating role of evaluation task, number of stimulus presentations, and memory for presentation frequency. *Personality and Social Psychology Bulletin, 45*(3), 447–460. DOI: 10.1177/0146167218789065 PMID: 30117368

Villanueva, I., Bobinac, T., Yao, B., Hu, J., & Chen, K. (2025). AI as a deliberative partner fosters intercultural empathy for Americans but fails for Latin American participants. *arXiv preprint arXiv:2504.13887*. https://doi.org//arXiv.2504.13887DOI: 10.48550

Vinay, R., Spitale, G., Biller-Andorno, N., & Germani, F. (2025). Emotional prompting amplifies disinformation generation in AI large language models. *Frontiers in Artificial Intelligence, 8*, 1543603. DOI: 10.3389/frai.2025.1543603 PMID: 40260413

Voorveld, H., Panteli, A., Schirris, Y., Ischen, C., Kanoulas, E., & Lentz, T. (2024). Examining the persuasiveness of text and voice agents: Prosody aligned with information structure increases human-likeness, perceived personalisation and brand attitude. *Behaviour & Information Technology*, •••, 1–16. DOI: 10.1080/0144929X.2024.2420871

Vosoughi, S., Roy, D., & Aral, S. (2018). The spread of true and false news online. *science, 359*(6380), 1146-1151. DOI: DOI: 10.1126/science.aap9559

Wasike, B. (2025). Influencing the news: How social media influencers affect news media trust. *Information Communication and Society*, •••, 1–18. DOI: 10.1080/1369118X.2025.2496907

Westerlund, M. (2019). The Emergence of Deepfake Technology: A Review. *Technology Innovation Management Review*, *9*(11), 40–53. DOI: 10.22215/timreview/1282

Whitson, J. A., & Galinsky, A. D. (2008). Lacking control increases illusory pattern perception. *science, 322*(5898), 115-117. DOI: DOI: 10.1126/science.1159845

Winkielman, P., & Nowak, A. (2022). Beyond the features: The role of consistency in impressions of trust. *Social Psychological Bulletin, 17*, 1–20. DOI: 10.32872/spb.9233

Yadav, A., Chakraverty, S., & Sibal, R. (2015, October). A survey of implicit trust on social networks. In *2015 International Conference on Green Computing and Internet of Things (ICGCIoT)* (pp. 1511-1515). IEEE. DOI: 10.1109/ICGCIoT.2015.7380706

Yang, Q., Ongpin, M., Nikolenko, S., Huang, A., & Farseev, A. (2023, October). Against opacity: Explainable ai and large language models for effective digital advertising. In *Proceedings of the 31st ACM International Conference on Multimedia* (pp. 9299-9305). https://doi.org/DOI: 10.1145/3581783.3612817

Zajonc, R. B. (1968). Attitudinal effects of mere exposure. *Journal of Personality and Social Psychology*, *9*(2, Pt.2), 1–27. DOI: 10.1037/h0025848

Chapter 13
Neuromarketing and AI Application to Consumer Behavior Research:
Opportunities and Challenges

Sławomir Smyczek
http://orcid.org/0000-0002-4459-2736
University of Economics in Katowice, Poland

Przemysław Kotowski
http://orcid.org/0009-0006-8123-5849
Neon Growth Inc., Canada

ABSTRACT

Traditional marketing research methods have many limitations, including high time and cost requirements and a limited ability to draw conclusions about actual consumer behavior as opposed to declared intentions. These challenges have prompted growing interest in neuromarketing, which investigates biological and neurological responses to marketing stimuli. The value of such methods depends on researchers' ability to interpret diagnostic results in a meaningful marketing context (Kenning & Linzmajer, 2011; Morin, 2011). More recently, artificial intelligence (AI) has emerged as a promising enhancement to neuromarketing techniques. This chapter aims to identify and evaluate neuromarketing methods used to study consumer behavior and to assess the potential of AI to enhance these techniques. In particular, the chapter focuses on how AI can enable real-time reaction analysis, personalize emotional engagement, and predict future consumer behavior.

DOI: 10.4018/979-8-3373-1152-4.ch013

INTRODUCTION

In today's highly dynamic market environment, understanding consumer behavior is both a theoretical and practical imperative. The significance of this field continues to grow in response to globalization, economic shifts, and cultural changes that influence consumer choices and consumption patterns. Companies seeking a competitive edge must strive to understand not just what consumers do, but why they do it, including their preferences, motivations, and emotional triggers.

Traditional marketing research methods, including both quantitative and qualitative approaches, face well-documented limitations. These include the time and cost associated with conducting research, as well as the difficulty of capturing actual consumer behavior rather than self-reported behavior. Consequently, researchers and practitioners alike are searching for more advanced methods that offer fast, reliable, and nuanced insights into consumer decision-making processes.

Approximately two decades ago, neuromarketing emerged as a promising solution. It examines biological responses, such as brain activity and physiological changes, that occur in reaction to marketing stimuli. However, the effective use of these methods depends on interpreting diagnostic data skills within a marketing context that yields actionable insights for marketers (Kenning & Linzmajer, 2011; Morin, 2011). This is one of the main, but not the only, limitations in the use of neuromarketing in consumer behavior research. Considering limitations of neuromarketing, recent years have seen growing interest in the potential use of artificial intelligence (AI) in consumer behavior research.

Taking in consideration above, this chapter aims to:

1. assess the potential for using neuromarketing methods in consumer behavior research
2. identify the new values that AI has introduced to neuromarketing, particularly in area of real-time reaction analysis, emotional personalization and predictive modeling,
3. assess opportunities and challenges of AI-driven neuromarketing implications in consumer behavior research.

Basing on identified goal research will focus on following research questions:

Q1. To what extent neuromarketing methods can be used in consumer behavior research?

Q2. How and what new values can artificial intelligence introduce to neuromarketing?

Q3. What are the possibilities of using artificial intelligence-based neuromarketing in consumer behavior research, and what are the limitations in this area?

Thus, in this chapter therefore were discuss the different medical diagnostic methods used in neuromarketing to identify various aspects of consumer behavior. Next, limitations of each neuromarketing method in given application were presented. Than the in detail possibilities of AI-driven neuromarketing in terms of opportunities and challenges were analyzed. The section on real-time reaction analysis explores how AI captures instantaneous consumer responses and how marketers can utilize this feedback to dynamically refine their strategies. The section on amplification of emotional engagement examines how AI personalizes brand experiences based on real-time emotional data, enhancing the emotional resonance and authenticity of marketing communications. The third is the section on predictive modeling investigates how AI forecasts future consumer behavior and emotional states, enabling brands to design proactive, consumer-centered marketing strategies that align with evolving needs and values. Finally, main challenges and limitation of using AI-driven neuromarketing tool were presented.

It is wort to add that, real-time reaction analysis, represents one of the most significant breakthroughs in modern neuromarketing. AI systems can now analyze facial expressions, eye movements, galvanic skin responses, and other physiological markers at the moment they occur, providing immediate feedback on consumer engagement, emotional resonance, and cognitive processing (Venkatraman et al., 2015). Real-time analysis shifts neuromarketing from a retrospective to a contemporaneous discipline, enabling dynamic optimization of advertising content, user experiences, and brand interactions. Marketers are no longer bound to post-campaign evaluations; they can refine strategies on the fly, based on instantaneous emotional and cognitive feedback (Haleem et al., 2022).

The second area, amplification of emotional engagement, capitalizes on AI's ability to personalize marketing experiences at an emotional level. Through the real-time interpretation of biometric and behavioral signals, AI-driven systems craft individualized experiences that resonate deeply with consumers' current emotional states (Plassmann et al., 2015). Whether through personalized product recommendations, emotionally attuned advertising narratives, or adaptive user interfaces, emotional personalization enhances engagement, loyalty, and brand affinity. This new capability elevates personalization beyond demographic or transactional parameters into the realm of emotional intelligence, transforming consumer-brand relationships into empathetic, responsive, and evolving dialogues (Karmarkar & Plassmann, 2019).

The third area, predictive modeling, extends AI's contribution from the present into the future. By analyzing historical emotional responses, behavioral patterns, and contextual variables, AI systems can predict not only what consumers will do but also how they will feel in response to future brand interactions (Bzdok et al., 2019). Predictive models empower marketers to anticipate consumer needs, preferences, and emotional trajectories, allowing them to design proactive strategies that meet consumers at the right time, in the right place, and with the right message. This foresight transforms marketing from a reactive, campaign-based activity into a continuous, anticipatory process (Venkatraman et al., 2015).

Together, these three areas illustrate a fundamental evolution in neuromarketing's potential and practice. They reveal a shift from isolated experimental studies to integrated, real-time systems that can sense, adapt to, and even predict consumer needs with remarkable precision. Yet, this evolution also raises profound methodological, ethical, and strategic questions. The collection and interpretation of emotional and cognitive data introduce new challenges related to privacy, consent, and the potential for emotional manipulation (Morin, 2011). As AI-driven neuromarketing becomes more powerful, it becomes imperative for brands, researchers, and policymakers to develop frameworks that safeguard consumer autonomy, promote transparency, and ensure that emotional insights are used to enhance rather than exploit the human experience.

In order to examine implications of AI in neuromarketing to identify different aspects of consumer behavior, this study adopts a theoretical approach, including academic literature, to construct a comprehensive framework for understanding the opportunities and challenges presented by AI technologies in neuromarketing. The methodology involves also synthesizing previous research on neuromarketing, AI technologies, and consumer behavior, drawing on key theoretical frameworks to build a comprehensive understanding of the subject. The research builds on the insights of prior studies to offer a conceptual analysis. The research also used real-world case studies to support and develop theoretical analyses. This approach allows for a broader discussion of the implications of AI-driven neuromarketing into consumer behavior research.

APPLICATION OF NEUROMARKETING IN CONSUMER BEHAVIOR RESEARCH

Many physiological and pathophysiological processes in the human body can be interpreted as valuable sources of insight into consumer behavior—both in the marketplace and at home, including during consumption. Human responses to environmental stimuli often involve measurable changes in physical parameters such as elevated blood pressure, increased heart rate, sweating, and altered breathing patterns (Ganong, 2007). Marketing stimuli can provoke similar physiological reactions. Signals generated by tissues and organs (Hamzehei et al., 2011; Vecchiato et al., 2011), as well as structural images of these tissues (McClure et al., 2004), have become valuable tools in consumer research. These measurements help researchers explore how individuals subconsciously react to brands, advertisements, and products. Furthermore, biological material collected from consumers can provide a wealth of marketing relevant information (Devor et al., 1999). The ability to capture and interpret such data allows marketers to move beyond self-reported attitudes, offering a more direct and nuanced understanding of how consumers experience and respond to marketing stimuli.

The medical diagnostic methods used and proposed to date in consumer behavior research are largely based on analyzing the active electrical properties of tissues. For brain activity, electroencephalography (EEG) is employed (Vecchiato et al., 2009; Vecchiato et al., 2010a; Vecchiato et al., 2010b; Babiloni et al., 2006), while electrocardiography (ECG) is used to monitor heart muscle function (Hamzehei et al., 2011). Passive electrical properties of tissues also play a significant role. However, their assessment requires the application of a specific physical factor, such as an electromagnetic field in magnetic resonance imaging (McClure et al., 2004).

Undoubtedly, in consumer behavior research that incorporates medical diagnostics, the human body should be viewed as a system of integrated tissues and organs, with the nervous system serving as the primary and coordinating component of overall functionality. The central nervous system has become the principal focus of consumer behavior research (McClure et al., 2004; Vecchiato et al., 2011), along with the reactions it elicits in other tissues and organs (Walla et al., 2011; Simola et al., 2011). Accordingly, consumer behavior studies may also utilize electromyography (Walla et al., 2011), measurements of skin conductance responses (Golin & Lyerly, 1950), or eye-tracking methods (Simola et al., 2011). It is important to emphasize that the central nervous system is fundamentally responsible for shaping consumer behavior. As a result, research into consumer responses to market stimuli—such as advertising, pricing, branding, or product packaging—as well as investigations into the internal processes occurring during market-related decision-making, primarily centers on the nervous system's role in perceiving, processing, and responding to such stimuli.

To define the scope of this study, it is important to understand that the human nervous system can be classified according to both topography and function. The first classification concerns the location of the tissue, distinguishing between the central nervous system and the peripheral nervous system. The second classification includes the somatic and autonomic nervous systems. The somatic system is responsible for interactions with the external environment and largely operates under conscious control. It innervates skeletal muscles and is responsible for the functioning of skin glands and pigment cells. The autonomic nervous system, by contrast, innervates internal organs and functions independently of conscious will (Smyczek & Turek,

2011). The nervous system, in its entirety, represents a significant source of data for marketing research. Its physiological signals can be captured and interpreted to reveal insights into consumer behavior. As such, it has already become, and continues to develop as, an important tool in the field of consumer behavior research.

A distinct area of interest is human behavior from a physiological perspective. The limbic system, a component of the brain and part of the central nervous system, serves as the physiological foundation for the subjective experience of emotions and the associated autonomic nervous system responses (Traczyk & Trzebski, 2003). From a marketing standpoint, the functions of the limbic system are particularly significant. It regulates behaviors and emotional states such as pleasure, satisfaction, and fear. In vertebrates, it is also responsible for behaviors related to food acquisition, the maintenance of homeostasis, and the processing of emotional experiences (Smyczek & Turek, 2011).

At this point, it is important to highlight the mechanisms of avoidance and acquisition, along with the reward and punishment systems. These mechanisms are integral components of the limbic system (Ganong, 2007). Stimulation of the limbic system triggers responses from the autonomic nervous system, such as changes in blood pressure and respiratory rate. These physiological changes are generated by various structures within the limbic system, although accurately attributing specific reactions to specific structures remains challenging due to the system's complexity (Ganong, 2007).

Information is transmitted within the nervous system through the interaction of neurotransmitters (modulating substances) with their corresponding receptors. From a marketing perspective, the influence of neurotransmitters on behavior is highly relevant. Among the most important neurotransmitters are serotonin, noradrenaline, adrenaline, dopamine, histamine, and acetylcholine. Dopamine is commonly associated with the brain's reward system, while acetylcholine plays a key role in the regulation of punishment-related responses (Ganong, 2007).

The widespread use of medical measurement and diagnostic equipment in consumer behavior research has led to the emergence of neuromarketing. The main practical effect of this research is the optimization of marketing stimuli for their effective application.These research includes the direct observation of behaviors such as purchasing patterns, seasonality, habits, terms of purchase and payment, locations of purchase, and product usage. It also investigates the internal mechanisms that shape consumer preferences, the processing of market information, emotional responses, and the motives behind purchasing decisions. Neuromarketing is especially useful in this second domain, as it enables the evaluation of processes occurring within the consumer's body.

One key concept in neuromarketing is the "meme," which refers to a unit of information stored in the brain (Dawkins, 2006). Neuromarketing focuses on this type of information and the methods used to measure it. These techniques are primarily applied in consumer opinion research related to advertisements, brands, products, and pricing. A review of neuromarketing literature highlights examples of consumer behavior research conducted in these areas (McClure et al., 2004; Vecchiato et al., 2011).

Local brain activity can be assessed using electroencephalography (EEG) and functional magnetic resonance imaging (fMRI). These methods make it possible to identify specific brain structures that are activated by targeted marketing stimuli (McClure et al., 2004).

In consumer behavior research, data from other bodily systems can also be valuable. For instance, electrocardiography (ECG) and voice tension analysis can complement studies of psychophysical responses. Additional techniques, such as electrogastrography or laboratory-based biochemical tests, may also be considered.

A comprehensive analysis of signals obtained from independently innervated tissues is essential to fully understanding consumer behavior. Therefore, it is worth exploring the simultaneous use of multiple diagnostic parameters, including data from ECG, EEG, skin conductance, eye tracking, and electromyography.

Studies that analyze the concentration of specific substances in the blood, which may reflect emotional states, also show significant potential. In simplified terms, one could say that the human body does not need shopping; it needs dopamine (Celebanska et al., 2011). However, directly linking dopamine levels to specific emotions remains a complex challenge.

Considering genetic analysis for consumer behavior research could also be valuable. The human genotype contains a wealth of information that may help in understanding consumer behavior. After all, a single drop of blood can reveal a great deal.

Neuromarketing offers various applications in consumer behavior research, but it comes with both advantages and disadvantages. One major advantage of using neuromarketing is the ability to obtain tangible, empirical evidence in the form of measurable parameters, rather than relying on subjective assessments. Additionally, the use of neuroimaging techniques can help eliminate irrational factors in consumer behavior. Neuromarketing methods provide real-time insights into the processes occurring in the consumer's body, offering an objective perspective on the mechanisms behind consumer behavior (Smyczek & Turek, 2011).

While minimally invasive from a medical standpoint, neuromarketing methods involve limitations from an organizational perspective. The data obtained from these methods also require extensive processing. Moreover, any research involving human subjects must adhere to bioethical guidelines, necessitating consent from the relevant ethics committee.

Another limitation is the high cost. Neuromarketing methods, especially those involving tools such as fMRI or EEG, are significantly more expensive and time-consuming compared to traditional methods such as surveys, interviews, or even direct observation.

The selection of research participants is crucial in neuromarketing studies. In addition to considering factors such as demographic profile, it is important to account for medical aspects, including physiological and pathophysiological characteristics and any medications taken by participants. These studies also require more sophisticated procedures and preparation compared to traditional research methods. In neuromarketing, preparing the consumer for research is similar to preparing a patient for diagnostic procedures.

Ethically, neuromarketing has raised concerns. While the techniques are non-invasive medically, they allow for detailed insights into the brain, which some may view as an invasion of privacy (Lee et al., 2007). Furthermore, there are fears of manipulation, as some researchers suggest that neuromarketing could be used to influence consumer behavior by locating the so-called buy button in the brain (Gazzaniga, 2005). These concerns raise important ethical questions about the potential for controlling consumer decisions through emotional reactions (Senior & Lee, 2008).

Figure 1. Limitation of using neuromarketing in consumer behavior research

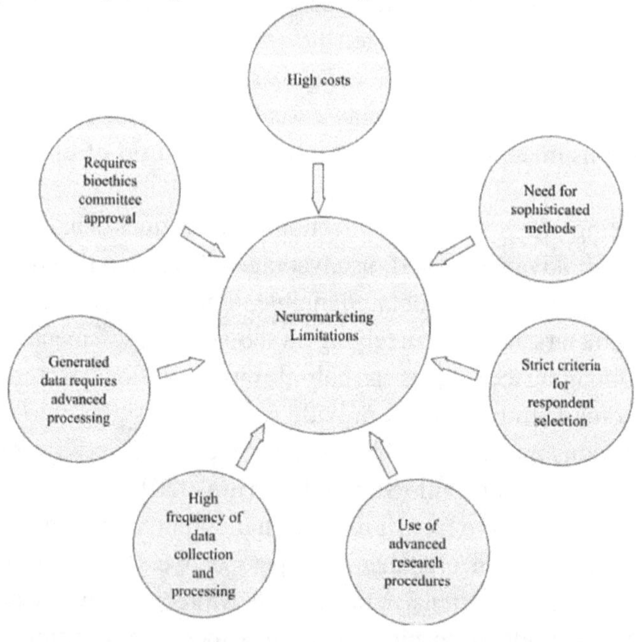

Nonetheless, neuromarketing methods have proven useful in various areas of marketing, such as product design and advertising campaigns (Vecchiato et al., 2011). However, the existing limitations of the use of particular neuromarketing methods mean that there is a constant search for their elimination and improvement in order to better and more accurately study consumer behavior.

AI-DRIVEN NEUROMARKETING APPLICATION TO CONSUMER BEHAVIOR RESEARCH

Neuromarketing, the interdisciplinary field combining neuroscience, psychology, and marketing, has traditionally relied on sophisticated yet cumbersome technologies to uncover the hidden processes underlying consumer decision-making. Neuromarketing tools have been instrumental in revealing the neural correlates of brand perception, advertising effectiveness, and purchase intent. These methods offered unprecedented glimpses into the subconscious influences on behavior, providing insights unattainable through conventional surveys or focus groups. However, despite their scientific value, traditional neuromarketing techniques have been limited by significant practical constraints. The high cost of equipment, the need for controlled laboratory settings, and the inherently time-consuming nature of data collection and analysis rendered these approaches largely inaccessible outside academic and elite corporate research environments (Plassmann et al., 2015; Smidts et al., 2014).

Moreover, these methodologies suffered from a critical shortcoming: the inability to capture real-time consumer reactions in dynamic, naturalistic settings. Neural and biometric responses had to be extracted, processed, and interpreted after the fact, often detached from the fast-moving contexts in which consumer behavior actually unfolds. As a result, marketers faced a considerable lag between stimulus exposure and actionable insight, limiting the operational utility of neuromarketing in contemporary marketing campaigns.

Recent advancements in artificial intelligence (AI) offer a transformative solution to these longstanding limitations. Machine learning, deep learning, natural language processing, and advanced data analytics have converged to produce AI systems capable of processing vast volumes of neuromarketing-relevant data in real time. Emotional expressions, eye movements, vocal inflections, biometric signals, and even subtle behavioral cues can now be analyzed instantaneously, yielding insights with a speed, precision, and scalability that were previously unimaginable (Haleem et al., 2022; Koelstra et al., 2012). This democratization of neuromarketing, fueled by accessible technologies and powerful AI-driven analytical engines, represents not just a technical improvement but a paradigm shift in how brands can understand, engage with, and anticipate the needs of consumers.

Artificial intelligence enables marketers to bridge the gap between subconscious consumer processes and actionable marketing strategies without the prohibitive costs and logistical burdens of traditional laboratory methods. AI does not merely replicate what fMRI and EEG could achieve more affordably; it expands the analytical horizon, allowing for the integration of behavioral, emotional, and contextual data into dynamic, predictive, and highly personalized marketing interventions (Karmarkar & Plassmann, 2019). While traditional neuromarketing offered snapshots of consumer brains under isolated conditions, AI-driven neuromarketing constructs a living and evolving model of consumer cognition and emotion across time and context.

There are many opportunities to use artificial intelligence in neuromarketing, but in consumer behavior research it is important to focus on three interconnected dimensions where AI's impact is most profound. First, it investigates how AI enables real-time reaction analysis, capturing and interpreting emotional and cognitive responses as they occur, allowing marketers to adapt strategies dynamically and responsively. Second, it explores the amplification of emotional engagement through personalization, demonstrating how AI customizes content to align with individual emotional states, thereby fostering deeper and more authentic connections between brands and consumers. Third, it examines the predictive modeling of consumer behavior, detailing how AI anticipates future preferences, decisions, and emotional patterns, which enables marketing strategies that are proactive rather than reactive.

Figure 2. AI-driven neuromarketing application to consumer behavior research

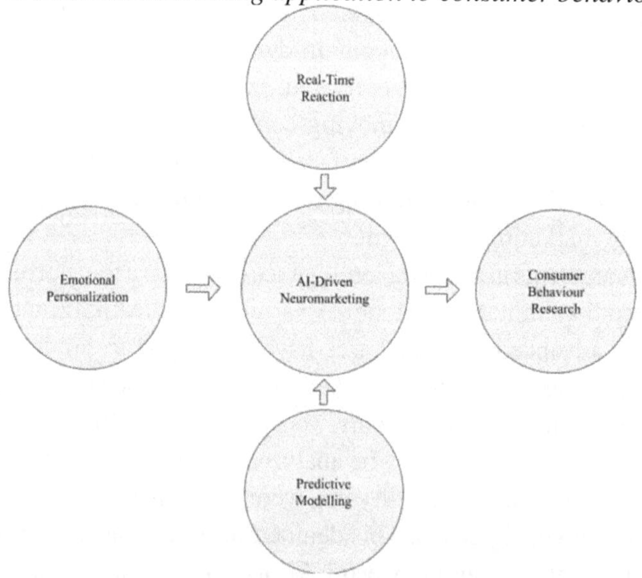

REAL-TIME REACTION ANALYSIS

The ability to analyze consumer responses in real time is one of the most significant advancements artificial intelligence brings to neuromarketing. AI's capacity to process information instantaneously allows marketers to observe how a consumer's brain reacts to a product, brand experience, or advertising campaign at the precise moment of interaction. This immediate feedback is invaluable for the development, testing, and refinement of marketing strategies, eliminating the lengthy delays associated with traditional neuromarketing techniques and providing brands with a significant competitive advantage (Rabby & Chimhundu, 2021).

Real-time reaction analysis marks a radical departure from the post-exposure evaluations that characterized earlier neuromarketing efforts. Whereas traditional approaches relied on retrospective surveys or laboratory-based brain imaging, AI empowers marketers to capture and interpret biometric and behavioral responses the moment they occur. Through advancements in machine learning and signal processing, researchers can now access instantaneous data from facial expressions, eye movements, voice tone fluctuations, galvanic skin responses, and even portable EEG readings. These technologies, when integrated with sophisticated AI algorithms, can detect micro-expressions, subtle emotional shifts, and cognitive load variations within milliseconds of exposure to marketing stimuli (Haleem et al., 2022; Smidts et al., 2014).

The capacity to register these instantaneous changes in neural and emotional states transforms the marketing development process. Facial recognition systems powered by AI, for instance, can discern complex emotional reactions such as fleeting expressions of joy, confusion, disgust, or surprise—signals that are often missed or misinterpreted through traditional survey-based feedback. Similarly, eye-tracking technologies can illuminate which specific elements of an advertisement draw consumer attention, how long that attention is sustained, and the sequence in which visual content is processed. Such granular insights offer marketers a scientifically validated method to refine messaging, optimize design elements, and ultimately increase engagement and conversion rates.

Beyond passive observation, real-time reaction analysis enables the creation of adaptive marketing experiences that respond dynamically to consumer emotions. In digital advertising, interactive web content, and immersive environments like virtual reality, AI can modify messages, visuals, or offers on-the-fly based on immediate emotional or cognitive responses. By adjusting the user experience in real time, brands can significantly heighten emotional resonance, making marketing communications feel more natural, empathetic, and personalized. This capacity for dynamic adaptation represents a monumental shift toward more responsive and consumer-centered marketing ecosystems (Plassmann et al., 2015).

Importantly, AI-driven real-time analysis drastically reduces the logistical and financial barriers that once made neuromarketing the exclusive domain of large corporations. Rather than requiring expensive fMRI machines or cumbersome EEG setups confined to research laboratories, today's neuromarketing studies can be conducted remotely using webcams, smartphones, and other widely accessible consumer technologies. This democratization of neuromarketing tools allows businesses of all sizes to gain immediate, scientifically robust insights into consumer behavior, thus leveling the competitive playing field (Karmarkar & Plassmann, 2019).

Real-time reaction analysis is not limited to emotional responses; it also extends to cognitive and physiological indicators that shed light on the complexity of consumer decision-making. Pupil dilation, for example, has been linked to emotional arousal and cognitive effort, while blink rate can reveal variations in attention and mental workload. Subtle changes in skin conductance levels reflect subconscious emotional intensity, and vocal pitch modulation can indicate excitement, hesitation, or stress. Even patterns in EEG data, collected through increasingly compact and affordable devices, can reveal markers of attention, engagement, and memory encoding (Vecchiato et al., 2011).

The integration of multiple biometric modalities further enhances the reliability of real-time analysis. By triangulating data from facial expressions, eye movements, and physiological signals, AI systems can cross-validate emotional interpretations and reduce the margin of error. This fusion of data sources not only bolsters confidence in findings but also enables a more holistic understanding of the consumer experience, capturing the interplay between affective and cognitive responses in ways that singular measures could not.

In practical applications, real-time neuromarketing is transforming how advertisements and products are tested before launch. Companies can now conduct sophisticated A/B testing that incorporates live biometric feedback, selecting creative assets that demonstrably generate stronger positive neural and emotional reactions. Brand recall studies benefit as well, with memory encoding patterns serving as predictive markers for future consumer behavior. Even subtle shifts in brand perception can be identified during the earliest stages of exposure, enabling timely refinements that can make the difference between success and failure in highly competitive markets.

Furthermore, real-time analysis empowers marketers to identify negative or unintended consumer reactions at an early stage. Signs of confusion, boredom, frustration, or disengagement can be captured instantaneously, allowing for rapid intervention. This proactive approach not only enhances the effectiveness of marketing communications but also protects brand equity by minimizing the risk of alienating consumers through poorly optimized content (Venkatraman et al., 2015).

Despite these substantial advantages, the use of real-time biometric analysis raises important ethical considerations. Capturing and interpretating emotional and physiological data, particularly without explicit and informed consent, can be perceived as both intrusive and manipulative. Researchers and practitioners must prioritize transparency, ensuring that participants understand what data is being collected, how it will be used, and the safeguards in place to protect their privacy. Data should be anonymized whenever possible, and AI models must be trained to avoid reinforcing existing biases, particularly those that could marginalize or misrepresent responses from diverse demographic groups (Haleem et al., 2022).

Another technical and interpretive challenge stems from the complexity of human emotion itself. Emotions are not always easily categorized into discrete labels such as "happy," "sad," or "angry." They often involve blends of feelings and are heavily influenced by personal context, cultural norms, and situational factors. AI models, while increasingly sophisticated, may still misinterpret or oversimplify these complex emotional states. This inherent ambiguity underscores the importance of human oversight and the need for cautious, contextually aware interpretation of real-time data.

The application of deep learning models, particularly convolutional and recurrent neural networks, has significantly enhanced the capacity of AI systems to recognize and interpret emotional patterns. These models can learn from vast amounts of unstructured data, continuously improving their predictive accuracy over time. Importantly, deep learning allows for contextualized interpretation, where an emotional reaction is not viewed in isolation but understood relative to environmental factors such as lighting conditions, device type, and prior exposure to similar stimuli (Smidts et al., 2014).

Emerging technologies exemplify how real-time reaction analysis is being deployed in the field. Platforms like Realeyes and iMotions integrate facial coding, eye-tracking, and physiological monitoring into cohesive systems that provide marketers with instant feedback on emotional and cognitive engagement. Companies like Neurons Inc. have developed predictive eye-tracking models that allow advertisers to estimate visual attention without the need for traditional hardware setups, democratizing access to neuromarketing insights.

These tools reflect a broader trend toward agile, iterative marketing processes where creative content can be tested, refined, and optimized within days rather than months. Brands can experiment with multiple variations of a campaign, gathering real-time consumer responses and using AI-driven insights to hone their messaging before committing to large-scale rollouts. This increased agility not only improves the efficiency of marketing operations but also fosters more consumer-centric and emotionally resonant brand experiences.

Nevertheless, the proliferation of real-time reaction analysis does not eliminate the value of traditional market research methods. Qualitative insights obtained through interviews, focus groups, and ethnographic studies remain crucial for understanding the deeper motivations, values, and social contexts that shape consumer behavior. The future of marketing research likely lies in the integration of real-time biometric analysis with traditional qualitative approaches, creating a hybrid methodology that leverages the strengths of both. Such integration will enable marketers to capture both the visceral, immediate emotional reactions and the reflective, narrative-driven insights that together constitute a complete picture of consumer psychology.

Looking ahead, the convergence of real-time reaction analysis with advances in wearable technology, edge computing, and affective computing will further revolutionize neuromarketing. Smartwatches, AR glasses, and biosensor-embedded textiles will provide continuous streams of emotional and cognitive data, enabling truly adaptive, personalized marketing experiences across both digital and physical environments. Virtual assistants and chatbots, equipped with emotional intelligence, will engage consumers in increasingly natural and empathetic dialogues, strengthening relational bonds and enhancing brand loyalty.

As AI systems become more transparent and interpretable, marketers will gain a clearer understanding of how and why certain emotional reactions are classified, enabling greater accountability and ethical responsibility. In this emerging landscape, real-time reaction analysis will not merely enhance marketing effectiveness; it will redefine the very nature of how brands and consumers interact, creating more human-centered, emotionally attuned ecosystems that reflect the complexity and richness of real human experiences.

Case Study: MARS Uses Real-Time Emotion AI to Optimize Ad Performance

MARS Inc., a global leader in consumer-packaged goods, faced a common challenge: how to predict which video ads would resonate with audiences before committing to full-scale campaigns. Traditional testing methods such as surveys often failed to capture in-the-moment emotional reactions that drive consumer behavior. MARS needed a faster, more accurate way to evaluate content performance across diverse markets.

To solve this, the company implemented Realeyes' PreView platform, an AI-powered tool that uses webcam-based facial coding and attention tracking to assess emotional and cognitive responses in real time. As viewers watched video ads, the platform measured attention levels, emotional engagement, and valence on a frame-by-frame basis. This allowed MARS to understand which segments of their ads sparked interest or caused disengagement, offering granular feedback within minutes rather than weeks (Realeyes, 2022).

The results were significant. By identifying high-performing creative elements and optimizing messaging prior to launch, MARS achieved a 29 percent improvement in return on investment. The company also reduced production and testing costs by avoiding investment in low-performing content. Insights were gathered remotely and rapidly, making it possible to run multiple iterations and refine campaigns with agility (Realeyes, 2023).

MARS' adoption of real-time reaction analysis illustrates how AI can move campaign validation from retrospective analysis to proactive, data-driven optimization. By measuring emotional response and attention as they happen, the company gained a competitive advantage through faster decision-making and deeper insight into consumer engagement.

This case highlights the shift from intuition-based marketing to scientifically grounded strategies made possible by Emotion AI. Real-time analysis enabled MARS to create more emotionally resonant and effective content while shortening time-to-launch and increasing overall efficiency.

AMPLIFICATION OF EMOTIONAL ENGAGEMENT THROUGH PERSONALIZATION

Marketing has long been considered an intricate fusion of art and science. The rise of artificial intelligence has further solidified this view, acting as a transformative bridge that connects creative intuition with empirical rigor. In the realm of neuromarketing, AI offers marketers an unprecedented capacity to decode and respond to the emotional architecture underlying consumer behavior. By leveraging real-time data from neural responses, biometric indicators, and behavioral patterns, AI enables the development of personalized marketing strategies that forge meaningful emotional bonds with consumers. Bonds that are deeper, more durable, and more predictive of loyalty and advocacy than those achieved through traditional methods (Mokhtari et al., 2021).

Emotions drive consumer behavior to a far greater extent than conscious deliberation. Classical marketing has long recognized the potency of emotional appeals, but such strategies historically operated at a generalized level, relying on broad demographic segmentation or gut-level creativity. Today, AI facilitates a dramatic shift toward individualized emotional personalization. By capturing and interpreting emotional responses at the personal level, AI-powered marketing strategies align with consumers' moment-to-moment emotional states, offering communications that feel more relevant, empathetic, and human.

The process of emotional personalization begins with the capture of diverse emotional signals across multiple consumer touchpoints. AI models analyze sentiment expressed in social media activity, facial expressions captured via device cameras, vocal tones interpreted through voice-enabled technologies, and biometric indicators such as heart rate variability and galvanic skin response. Deep learning architectures, particularly convolutional neural networks (CNNs) and recurrent neural networks (RNNs), have proven adept at parsing these complex, multimodal datasets to discern subtle patterns of emotional response that would elude traditional marketing research methodologies (Haleem et al., 2022; Koelstra et al., 2012).

These emotional insights do not merely sit in data repositories. AI systems dynamically adapt marketing content based on the detected emotional profile of the individual consumer. For example, when a consumer exhibits indicators of cognitive fatigue or emotional stress, the marketing system might respond by simplifying the interface, offering calming imagery, or adjusting the tone of messaging to soothe rather than stimulate. Conversely, signs of heightened excitement or curiosity might trigger the presentation of dynamic offers, vibrant visuals, or interactive experiences designed to capitalize on the consumer's heightened arousal state (Plassmann et al., 2015). Over time, these adaptive mechanisms fine-tune their understanding of each individual's emotional landscape, producing marketing experiences that evolve and become increasingly resonant through repeated interactions.

This approach is already shaping marketing strategies across diverse industries. Streaming platforms like Netflix personalize content feeds not merely by genre preference or viewing history, but also by predicting mood and emotional preferences based on interaction patterns. Luxury brands such as Gucci are investing in experiential retail environments where ambient lighting, music, and even scents adjust in response to real-time emotional sensing, creating bespoke experiences that evoke specific emotional journeys. In e-commerce, platforms like Amazon integrate emotional insights to subtly adjust product recommendations, promotional banners, and checkout experiences to align with consumers' emotional states in ways that maximize engagement and satisfaction (Karmarkar & Plassmann, 2019).

Yet, with great power comes significant ethical responsibility. The ability to detect, analyze, and act upon consumers' emotional vulnerabilities introduces profound risks of manipulation. If a consumer experiencing loneliness or sadness is targeted with emotionally charged advertising designed to amplify their vulnerability, the result may be not just higher sales, but also ethical violations of autonomy and dignity (Mokhtari et al., 2021; Morin, 2011). Transparency, informed consent, and consumer empowerment must therefore become pillars of emotional personalization strategies. Consumers must understand when and how their emotional data is being collected, and they must be provided with meaningful choices regarding how it is used. Emotional data, given its sensitivity, demands even stricter standards of data protection and anonymization than other forms of behavioral data.

Another challenge inherent to emotional personalization lies in the complexity and contextuality of human emotions themselves. Emotional expressions are not universal; they are filtered through cultural norms, individual histories, and situational variables. An AI system trained primarily on Western emotional datasets may misinterpret the facial expressions or emotional cues of consumers from other cultures, leading to personalization efforts that feel alienating or inaccurate (Smidts et al., 2014). Moreover, emotions are often mixed or ambivalent, defying neat categorization into positive or negative states. AI-driven personalization systems must therefore operate with humility and caution, recognizing the provisional nature of their interpretations.

Beyond these challenges, there is the additional concern of emotional fatigue. When marketing personalization becomes too persistent or aggressive, consumers may feel surveilled, manipulated, or emotionally exhausted. Emotional saturation can lead to defensive psychological responses, eroding trust and diminishing the effectiveness of future marketing efforts. Brands must learn to personalize not only for emotional engagement but also for emotional pacing, respecting consumers' psychological bandwidth and offering spaces for rest and autonomy within the marketing relationship (Venkatraman et al., 2015).

Despite these complexities, the future of emotional personalization holds remarkable promise. Emerging technologies such as affective computing, the development of systems that can recognize, interpret, and even simulate human emotions, will deepen the emotional intelligence of marketing systems. Virtual assistants and chatbots will engage consumers not only with scripted replies but with adaptive emotional interactions that mirror human empathy. Wearable technologies, from smartwatches to augmented reality glasses, will enable real-time, continuous emotional sensing, providing marketers with a richer and more nuanced emotional map of the consumer journey.

However, success in this future landscape will depend not merely on technological prowess but on the cultivation of ethical marketing practices. Brands that prioritize emotional transparency, respect consumer autonomy, and design experiences that genuinely seek to enhance consumer well-being will distinguish themselves in an increasingly emotionally saturated marketplace. Personalization must evolve from a manipulative tactic into a form of authentic, empathetic engagement, forging not just transactions but relationships grounded in mutual respect and emotional resonance (Karmarkar & Plassmann, 2019; Plassmann et al., 2015).

In conclusion, the amplification of emotional engagement through personalization marks one of the most exciting and transformative frontiers in the evolving field of neuromarketing. Artificial intelligence offers brands the tools to move beyond superficial demographic targeting and into the deep emotional architectures that shape consumer behavior. Yet, with this new power comes a profound ethical obligation: to wield emotional insights with wisdom, empathy, and a genuine commitment to enhancing, not exploiting, the human experience. Brands that meet this challenge will not only achieve greater marketing success; they will earn the most valuable currency of the future marketplace: authentic, enduring emotional trust.

Case Study: Netflix Leverages AI-Driven Emotional Personalization to Boost Engagement

Netflix, a leading global streaming service, sought to deepen viewer engagement beyond traditional recommendation algorithms based on genre or viewing history. The company faced the challenge of delivering content that resonated emotionally with users in real time, improving satisfaction and retention in a crowded market.

To tackle this, Netflix developed AI-powered systems that analyze user interaction data, such as watch time, pauses, skips, and browsing patterns, to infer emotional states like curiosity, excitement, or relaxation. These insights feed into deep learning models that dynamically personalize content feeds and user interfaces to align with viewers' moment-to-moment emotional needs (Gomez-Uribe & Hunt, 2016; Haleem et al., 2022).

Netflix also employs emotion-driven A/B testing for creative assets like thumbnails and trailers. By collecting real-time biometric and engagement data from select user groups, the platform rapidly identifies which emotional cues drive higher interest and retention, refining creative elements accordingly (Karmarkar & Plassmann, 2019).

The results have been significant. Personalized, emotionally aligned recommendations have increased session lengths and viewer retention, reducing content discovery fatigue and improving overall user satisfaction. This dynamic emotional personalization has helped Netflix build stronger emotional bonds with users, fostering loyalty amid fierce competition.

Netflix's approach exemplifies how AI enables brands to move beyond generic demographic targeting toward nuanced, real-time emotional engagement. It demonstrates the power of combining behavioral data with emotional insights to create personalized experiences that feel empathetic and relevant.

However, Netflix also highlights the need for ethical stewardship of emotional data, ensuring transparency and user consent to avoid manipulation or privacy violations.

PREDICTIVE MODELING OF CONSUMER BEHAVIOR

In addition to analyzing current emotional and cognitive responses, artificial intelligence is redefining the landscape of neuromarketing through its unparalleled predictive capabilities. Predictive modeling of consumer behavior, empowered by machine learning and advanced data analytics, allows marketers to move beyond reactive strategies and into the realm of proactive engagement. Rather than simply responding to consumer actions after they occur, brands can design products, messages, and experiences aligned with likely future preferences, thus fundamentally transforming the strategic planning process (Dagar & Smoudy, 2019).

The notion of predictive modeling is not entirely new to marketing. Traditional approaches utilized demographic data, historical purchasing patterns, and broad consumer trends to anticipate future actions. However, the predictive power of these methods was often limited by their reliance on static variables and linear assumptions. Artificial intelligence, by contrast, brings a new level of precision and adaptability. By integrating real-time neuromarketing data, capturing emotional responses, cognitive patterns, and biometric signals, AI systems can identify subtle, latent patterns that would be invisible to human analysts. These sophisticated models enable marketers to move beyond generalized assumptions and forecast behavior with remarkable nuance and specificity (Bzdok et al., 2019).

Machine learning algorithms, particularly support vector machines, decision trees, ensemble models such as random forests, and deep neural networks, are central to this transformation. These systems are capable of ingesting vast volumes of structured and unstructured data, detecting non-linear, multi-dimensional relationships between emotional states, cognitive processes, contextual variables, and subsequent consumer decisions. For example, a seemingly trivial combination of eye fixation durations, galvanic skin conductance, and brief facial micro-expressions recorded during exposure to an advertisement can, when properly modeled, become a highly reliable predictor of purchase intent (Plassmann et al., 2015; Huettel et al., 2015).

Predictive modeling based on neuromarketing insights also allows for a revolutionary shift in how audiences are segmented. Traditional segmentation models based on observable demographics, such as age, gender, and location, are increasingly being supplemented or replaced by psychographic and emotional segmentation. Artificial intelligence enables the clustering of consumers based on their neural and emotional response patterns, creating emotional archetypes that predict future behaviors with greater accuracy than external characteristics ever could. This affective segmentation allows brands to tailor experiences that resonate more profoundly with the underlying drivers of consumer choice (Karmarkar & Plassmann, 2019).

The applications of predictive neuromarketing are far-reaching. In product development, brands can use predictive models to forecast likely consumer reactions to prototypes before mass production, reducing financial risk and aligning product features more closely with latent consumer needs. In advertising, marketers can anticipate which creative executions will elicit the desired emotional engagement and behavioral outcomes among target segments. Even dynamic pricing models can be informed by predictive insights derived from consumers' inferred willingness-to-pay, as signaled through subconscious biometric and emotional responses (Venkatraman et al., 2015).

Real-world applications already demonstrate the power of predictive modeling. For example, Spotify employs predictive algorithms not only to recommend music based on listening history but also to infer future mood states and suggest playlists that align with or gently shape emotional trajectories. Similarly, Amazon utilizes predictive analytics to anticipate what products a consumer is likely to purchase next, dynamically adjusting its marketing communications and logistical operations to meet anticipated demand. These platforms illustrate how real-time predictive models enhance personalization while simultaneously optimizing operational efficiency (Bzdok et al., 2019).

However, predictive modeling is not without its limitations. Human behavior is fundamentally probabilistic rather than deterministic. Even the most sophisticated models can only assign probabilities, never certainties, to future actions. External shocks, such as economic downturns, social movements, personal crises, can unpredictably alter consumer behavior, undermining even the most robust forecasts. Moreover, emotional and cognitive states are inherently fluid; a prediction based on one emotional snapshot may not hold true as an individual's context or mood evolves (Smidts et al., 2014).

Another challenge lies in the complexity of emotional data itself. Emotions are highly contextual, influenced by cultural background, personal history, and situational variables. Predictive models trained on narrow or culturally homogenous datasets risk failing to generalize across diverse populations. Without careful attention to dataset diversity and algorithmic fairness, predictive systems may perpetuate biases, misinterpret emotional signals, or inadvertently exclude important consumer groups from accurate targeting (Koelstra et al., 2012).

Ethical considerations become even more pressing when predictive neuromarketing is deployed at scale. If brands can predict consumer choices before they are consciously made, they acquire a form of influence that, if misused, could erode consumer autonomy. When does prediction cross the line into manipulation? How much pre-emptive personalization is too much? Ethical frameworks must be established to ensure that predictive insights are used to enhance consumer well-being rather than exploit vulnerabilities. Transparency regarding the presence of predictive systems, meaningful consumer consent, and limits on how predictions are operationalized should be central to responsible neuromarketing practices (Morin, 2011).

The emotional dimension of predictive modeling further complicates ethical considerations. If marketers can anticipate not only what consumers will do but also how they will feel, there is a risk of weaponizing emotional forecasting for purely commercial ends. For example, triggering impulse purchases during moments of predicted emotional vulnerability may yield short-term gains but carry long-term reputational and ethical costs. As such, the use of emotional prediction should be framed not merely as a tool for increasing efficiency but as a means of building deeper, more respectful consumer relationships (Plassmann et al., 2015).

From a technical perspective, predictive modeling requires constant recalibration and validation. Consumer behaviors and emotional responses evolve over time, influenced by broader cultural, economic, and technological shifts. Models must be updated with fresh data, re-trained to account for emerging patterns, and rigorously tested against changing conditions. Advances in online learning algorithms and real-time adaptive modeling are making this ongoing refinement increasingly feasible, but they also demand that marketers invest in continuous model stewardship and avoid complacency (Bzdok et al., 2019).

Looking forward, the future of predictive modeling in neuromarketing points toward greater integration with real-time adaptive systems. Rather than generating static forecasts, predictive engines will operate continuously, updating their inferences moment-to-moment as new biometric and behavioral data streams in. Smart environments, wearable devices, and IoT-enabled platforms will provide a constant flow of emotional and cognitive signals, enabling marketing systems to predict and adapt to consumer states with ever-increasing fluidity (Venkatraman et al., 2015).

Moreover, affective computing technologies are pushing predictive modeling into new frontiers. Systems capable of not only recognizing but also simulating and adapting to human emotions will allow brands to test hypothetical marketing scenarios virtually, forecasting emotional responses to future campaigns without the need for extensive field testing. This will not only enhance agility and innovation but also reduce the risk of large-scale campaign failures (Plassmann et al., 2015).

Ultimately, predictive modeling represents a paradigm shift in neuromarketing. It transforms marketing from a reactive discipline to a predictive and collaborative one, enabling brands to co-create consumer journeys based on authentic emotional understanding rather than retrospective analysis. Yet the power of prediction demands a parallel commitment to ethics, transparency, and human-centered design. Brands that wield predictive neuromarketing responsibly by enhancing rather than exploiting the human experience, will not only achieve superior market outcomes but will also contribute to building a more empathetic, respectful, and emotionally intelligent digital economy.

In sum, artificial intelligence is fundamentally transforming the field of neuromarketing by addressing longstanding limitations of traditional methods and unlocking new dimensions of consumer insight. The integration of AI technologies enables a shift from retrospective, lab-based studies to dynamic, real-time engagement with consumer behavior. This transformation is evident in three key, interrelated areas: real-time reaction analysis, emotional personalization, and predictive modeling.

AI-driven real-time reaction analysis allows marketers to capture and interpret consumer responses the moment they occur. Unlike traditional neuromarketing approaches that rely on post-exposure surveys or lab-bound neuroimaging tools, AI can process facial expressions, eye movements, vocal patterns, and biometric data instantaneously. This immediacy facilitates dynamic optimization of marketing content and enables brands to respond empathetically and adaptively to consumers' cognitive and emotional states as they unfold. Such responsiveness enhances the effectiveness of campaigns while reducing costs and expanding access to smaller enterprises. However, this technological capability raises ethical concerns, particularly regarding privacy, consent, and the potential misuse of intimate emotional data.

Building upon real-time insights, AI also empowers emotional personalization by adapting marketing content to the emotional state of individual consumers. By decoding nuanced affective signals across digital touchpoints, AI enables brands to move beyond generic demographic targeting. Marketing experiences become deeply resonant as they adjust in tone, imagery, or interface depending on whether a consumer exhibits signs of excitement, stress, or fatigue. This capability fosters authentic and emotionally intelligent brand-consumer relationships that evolve over time. Examples range from mood-aware content curation in streaming services to immersive retail environments that respond to real-time biometric feedback. Yet, the ability to tailor communications so precisely introduces ethical dilemmas. Misuse of emotional data may lead to manipulation, emotional fatigue, or exclusion of consumers from culturally diverse backgrounds if models are not carefully trained on representative datasets.

Finally, predictive modeling represents the culmination of AI's neuromarketing potential and enables marketers to anticipate future consumer behaviors and emotional trajectories. By analyzing past and present data streams, including biometric responses, neural indicators, and contextual variables, AI systems can forecast with remarkable specificity what consumers are likely to do and feel next. This foresight transforms marketing into a proactive discipline and allows brands to develop offerings and messages that preemptively align with emerging needs and moods. Such capabilities redefine segmentation strategies by moving from surface-level demographics to deep emotional archetypes. However, this power must be wielded responsibly. Predictions are inherently probabilistic and can be skewed by cultural bias or evolving consumer contexts. Without robust ethical safeguards, predictive modeling risks crossing the line from persuasive influence to coercion.

AI is not merely enhancing neuromarketing; it is reshaping it into a fluid, real-time, emotionally intelligent system of consumer engagement. While the potential for deeper connection and marketing efficacy is vast, it must be matched by a commitment to transparency, cultural sensitivity, and respect for consumer autonomy. As brands increasingly operate in emotionally attuned digital ecosystems, their long-term success will depend not only on technological innovation but also on the ethical wisdom with which these tools are deployed.

Case Study: Spotify's Predictive Modeling Elevates Personalized Music Experiences

Spotify, a global leader in music streaming, transformed its personalization strategy by adopting AI-driven predictive modeling to anticipate users' future emotional states and listening preferences. Facing intense competition and the challenge of retaining subscribers, Spotify aimed to deliver a more intuitive, emotionally resonant music experience.

Using machine learning algorithms, Spotify analyzes large-scale behavioral data—including listening history, skip rates, session times, and playlist interactions—to forecast users' evolving moods and preferences (Gomez-Uribe & Hunt, 2016). Where available, real-time biometric and interaction signals enhance these predictions, allowing dynamic adaptation of playlists and recommendations to align with listeners' moment-to-moment emotional states (Huang & Rust, 2021).

Key features like *Discover Weekly* and *Daily Mix* are continuously updated through AI systems that detect subtle shifts in user taste and mood. Mood-based playlists, such as "Chill Vibes" and "Workout Boost," further leverage predictive insights to match users' emotional needs, driving deeper engagement and satisfaction.

Spotify's predictive models also facilitate emotional and behavioral segmentation, moving beyond traditional demographics to cluster users into nuanced archetypes that better reflect underlying motivations (Ricci et al., 2015). This refined segmentation enables more effective targeting and content curation, enhancing user retention and reducing churn.

The business impact is substantial. Spotify reports increased average listening times and improved subscription renewal rates linked to predictive personalization. By anticipating user desires before explicit signals, the platform fosters a seamless, emotionally attuned experience that strengthens customer loyalty.

Spotify also acknowledges ethical responsibilities by maintaining transparency about data usage and providing users control over personalization settings. This commitment balances innovative AI application with respect for consumer autonomy.

CHALLENGES OF APPLYING AI-DRIVEN NEUROMARKETING TO CONSUMER BEHAVIOR RESEARCH

The application of artificial intelligence in neuromarketing introduces profound opportunities for understanding consumer behavior, but it also presents several critical challenges. These challenges fall into three interrelated areas: ethical and legal concerns, cultural and demographic variability, and technical and methodological limitations.

First, ethical and legal considerations are becoming increasingly urgent. AI-driven neuromarketing often relies on sensitive biometric and emotional data, including facial expressions, eye movements, and galvanic skin response. While these signals can improve marketing precision, they also raise serious concerns about emotional manipulation, consent, and data privacy. The use of personal, subconscious signals to influence purchasing decisions walks a fine ethical line. Regulations such as the General Data Protection Regulation (GDPR) demand strict compliance, particularly around transparency and user consent. However, as emotional data is more intimate than traditional behavioral data, existing legal frameworks may be insufficient for the scope of AI-enhanced personalization (Mokhtari et al., 2021). A deeper, dedicated discussion of these issues would benefit from separate treatment beyond this chapter.

Second, AI systems often struggle with cultural and demographic nuance. Emotional expressions and their interpretations vary significantly across populations. An algorithm trained on Western facial data, for instance, may misread the emotional cues of consumers from other cultural backgrounds. These misclassifications can undermine personalization efforts and inadvertently exclude or misrepresent key segments. Creating diverse, inclusive datasets and culturally adaptive models remains a major challenge in ensuring fairness and effectiveness in global applications of neuromarketing (Haleem et al., 2022).

Third, technical and methodological limitations persist. AI systems used in neuromarketing must process multimodal data, combining neurophysiological signals, behavior, and environmental context, and identify subtle emotional patterns. This requires sophisticated model architectures, substantial training data, and ongoing recalibration. While tools such as deep learning and real-time adaptive systems offer exciting possibilities, they also carry risks of overfitting, reduced interpretability, and difficulty in validating outcomes. Researchers must remain cautious about inferring too much from probabilistic emotional models and ensure rigorous testing protocols are in place (Javaid et al., 2022).

Together, these three challenge areas: ethical/legal, cultural/demographic, and technical/methodological define the key constraints facing AI-driven neuromarketing today. Addressing them will require interdisciplinary cooperation, inclusive design, and an evolving ethical framework that protects consumers while enabling innovation. Future research should continue to refine AI's role in neuromarketing while centering human dignity, cultural diversity, and transparency.

CONCLUSION

Conducting consumer behavior research using traditional methods is a valuable cognitive tool and forms the foundation for both operational and strategic marketing decisions within an enterprise. However, obtaining comprehensive information that enables decision-making regarding the selection and implementation of market strategy is best achieved through research incorporating modern technologies in the field of neuromarketing. Consumer behavior research based on neuromarketing methods must rest on a solid theoretical framework. These methods cannot rely solely on empirical observation. The use of neuromarketing in consumer behavior research creates a synergy effect. Integrating traditional research methods with neuromarketing allows researchers not only to capture consumers' declared opinions but also to access information at the subconscious level.

Medical diagnostics used in neuromarketing enable researchers to examine the brain's internal structures. However, it would be an overstatement to suggest that such tools provide direct insight into the human mind. Neuromarketing allows researchers to move closer to identifying the real mechanisms behind consumer decision-making processes, offering more accurate insights into what consumers truly need and how they make market choices.

The integration of artificial intelligence into neuromarketing represents one of the most significant transformations the field has undergone since its inception. Traditional neuromarketing, grounded in laboratory-based techniques such as functional magnetic resonance imaging (fMRI) and electroencephalography (EEG), provided a means of exploring the subconscious drivers of consumer behavior. Yet its high costs, logistical challenges, and delayed data interpretation limited its practical applications. Today, artificial intelligence delivers more than an incremental improvement. It represents a fundamental shift that enables real-time analysis, scalability, predictive capabilities, and highly personalized consumer engagement strategies (Plassmann et al., 2015; Smidts et al., 2014).

This chapter has explored three interrelated dimensions through which artificial intelligence is revolutionizing neuromarketing: real-time reaction analysis, amplification of emotional engagement through personalization, and predictive modeling of consumer behavior. Together, these advancements mark the evolution of neuromarketing from a discipline focused on observation to one centered on dynamic interaction, continuous learning, and emotional intelligence.

Real-time reaction analysis represents a foundational breakthrough, addressing one of the most significant limitations of traditional neuromarketing methods. By utilizing artificial intelligence to process facial expressions, eye-tracking data, galvanic skin responses, and other biometric signals instantly, marketers can now obtain immediate feedback on consumer engagement and emotional resonance (Haleem et al., 2022; Koelstra et al., 2012). This capability allows for agile and adaptive refinement of marketing strategies in real time, rather than relying on delayed, post-event analysis. Real-time neuromarketing does more than accelerate feedback cycles; it redefines the temporal relationship between brands and consumers, fostering more responsive, flexible, and empathetic forms of interaction.

The amplification of emotional engagement through AI-powered personalization extends this transformation even further. Emotional personalization allows brands to tailor content, messaging, and experiences not only to consumer preferences but also to the emotional states that precede, accompany, and follow consumer interactions. By adapting to real-time emotional signals, brands can create more resonant, authentic, and enduring relationships with consumers (Karmarkar & Plassmann, 2019; Venkatraman et al., 2015). Emotional engagement moves beyond attention-capture strategies and into the deeper, more human realm of meaning-making and relational bonding. In a saturated marketplace where consumers are inundated with information, the ability to connect emotionally and personally becomes a vital differentiator.

Predictive modeling, the third transformative dimension explored, shifts the focus of neuromarketing from reactive to proactive. AI systems trained on historical emotional, cognitive, and behavioral data can forecast likely future consumer behaviors, preferences, and even emotional trajectories. These predictive capabilities allow brands not only to anticipate consumer needs but also to design experiences that meet those needs in advance, often before the consumer is consciously aware of them (Bzdok et al., 2019; Morin, 2011). When implemented ethically and transparently, this anticipatory marketing approach can produce experiences that feel intuitive, personalized, and supportive, thereby strengthening consumer trust and loyalty.

Taken together, real-time analysis, emotional personalization, and predictive modeling form an integrated and evolving ecosystem of consumer engagement. This system mirrors, and in some cases enhances, the social and emotional intelligence typically associated with human interaction. AI-driven neuromarketing enables brands to sense, interpret, and respond to consumer states with a fluidity and sensitivity that were once limited to human-to-human relationships.

Yet, alongside these profound opportunities lie equally profound challenges. The ethical landscape of AI-driven neuromarketing is complex and still largely uncharted. The collection, analysis, and application of emotional and cognitive data raise significant concerns regarding privacy, autonomy, and manipulation. When brands possess the ability to detect and influence emotional states at scale, the line between persuasion and coercion becomes dangerously thin (Morin, 2011; Plassmann et al., 2015). Consumers may find themselves guided or nudged toward decisions without full awareness of the emotional mechanisms involved. If left unregulated, such practices could erode consumer trust, invite regulatory scrutiny, and ultimately undermine the very relationships that brands aim to build.

Furthermore, technical limitations persist. Human emotions are inherently complex, fluid, and context-specific, often resisting straightforward classification. Even the most advanced AI systems may misinterpret or oversimplify emotional signals, particularly when applied across culturally diverse populations (Smidts et al., 2014). Without careful attention to training data, validation methods, and cross-cultural sensitivity, predictive systems risk reinforcing biases, excluding marginalized groups, or producing interactions that feel uncanny, inappropriate, or even manipulative.

The future success of AI-driven neuromarketing will depend not only on technological innovation but also on the establishment of ethical, human-centered practices. Transparency must be treated as a core principle, with brands clearly disclosing when and how emotional and cognitive data are collected and used. Informed consent should be substantive and meaningful, rather than reduced to a routine checkbox. Most importantly, predictive insights should be used to enhance consumer experience and well-being, not to exploit emotional vulnerabilities for short-term commercial advantage.

Moreover, interdisciplinary collaboration will be essential. Insights from neuroscience, psychology, ethics, sociology, and cultural studies must guide the design, implementation, and oversight of AI-driven neuromarketing systems. A narrow, technologically deterministic approach will be insufficient. Only through a holistic, multidisciplinary perspective can the full potential of neuromarketing be realized in a responsible and sustainable manner.

Looking ahead, the integration of artificial intelligence into neuromarketing points toward a future in which consumer-brand relationships are not merely transactional but also experiential, emotional, and co-created. Brands that succeed will be those that view consumers not as targets to be optimized but as partners in an evolving and emotionally intelligent dialogue. When treated with care and respect, emotional data can serve as a catalyst for deeper understanding, mutual value creation, and authentic human connection.

As this chapter has illustrated, the convergence of artificial intelligence and neuromarketing presents extraordinary possibilities. Real-time analysis supports dynamic responsiveness. Emotional personalization strengthens engagement. Predictive modeling allows for anticipatory care. However, these powerful capabilities also demand equally strong ethical responsibility. As brands navigate this new terrain, they face a crucial choice: to use emotional intelligence as a means of manipulation or as a foundation for marketing practices that are more authentic, respectful, and human-centered.

The path forward will not be easy. It will require not only technological advancement but also intellectual humility, constant vigilance, interdisciplinary collaboration, and a firm commitment to ethical principles. As artificial intelligence becomes more deeply embedded in neuromarketing practices, the imperative to balance innovation with accountability grows more urgent. While AI enables new levels of real-time interaction, emotional alignment, and behavioral prediction, it also introduces risks of surveillance and influence that must be addressed with caution, transparency, and care.

The collection and analysis of emotional and cognitive data pose complex ethical challenges that extend beyond traditional privacy concerns. Emotional states, unlike transactional or demographic data, are deeply personal and highly context-dependent. Misinterpreting or exploiting such data can lead to unintended consequences, including emotional manipulation, exclusion, or psychological distress. For this reason, organizations must adopt transparent practices that clearly communicate what data is being collected, how it is being interpreted, and for what purposes it is being used. Informed consent must be both meaningful and empowering, giving consumers the ability to make conscious decisions about their participation in emotionally intelligent marketing systems.

Furthermore, the deployment of artificial intelligence tools must be guided by cultural and psychological sensitivity. Emotions are not universal in their expression or meaning; they are shaped by sociocultural frameworks, individual experiences, and situational factors. Predictive models that are not rigorously tested for bias and contextual nuance may reinforce stereotypes or marginalize underrepresented groups. It is therefore essential to diversify training datasets, involve interdisciplinary stakeholders in the design of systems, and establish ongoing oversight mechanisms to ensure fairness and inclusivity.

Looking ahead, the field of neuromarketing must transition from a model based on consumer control to one centered on consumer collaboration. Artificial intelligence should be used not to manipulate decisions but to co-create value by anticipating needs in ways that honor autonomy and build trust. Brands that succeed will be those that use emotional data not solely to increase sales, but to cultivate understanding, enhance consumer experiences, and promote well-being.

Ultimately, the most meaningful reward lies not only in commercial success but also in helping to shape a digital economy that respects and reflects the emotional richness, complexity, and dignity of the human experience. This is the central promise and lasting responsibility of AI-driven neuromarketing in the years ahead.

REFERENCES

Babiloni, F., Cincotti, F., Mattia, D., Mattiocco, M., Bufalari, S., De Vico Fallani, F., Tocci, A., Bianchi, L., Marciani, M. G., Meroni, V., & Astolfi, L. (2006). *Neural basis for the brain responses to the marketing messages: A high resolution EEG study. Proceedings of the Annual International Conference of The IEEE Engineering in Medicine and Biology Society*, 3676–3679. DOI: 10.1109/IEMBS.2006.260485

Bzdok, D., Altman, N., & Krzywinski, M. (2019). Statistics versus machine learning. *Nature Methods*, *15*(4), 233–234. DOI: 10.1038/nmeth.4642 PMID: 30100822

Celebanska, A., Tomaszewska, D., Lesniewski, A., & Opallo, M. (2011). Film electrode prepared from oppositely charged silicate submicroparticles and carbon nanoparticles for selective dopamine sensing. *Biosensors & Bioelectronics*, *26*(11), 4417–4422. DOI: 10.1016/j.bios.2011.04.054 PMID: 21641787

Dagar, M. A. A., & Smoudy, A. K. (2019). The role of artificial intelligence on enhancing customer experience. *International Review of Management and Marketing*, *9*(4), 22–31. DOI: 10.32479/irmm.8166

Dawkins, R. (2006). *The Selfish Gene*. Oxford University Press.

Devor, E. J., Magee, H. J., Dill-Devor, R. M., Gabel, J., & Black, D. W. (1999). Serotonin transporter gene (5-HTT) polymorphisms and compulsive buying. *American Journal of Medical Genetics*, *88*(2), 123–125. DOI: 10.1002/(SICI)1096-8628(19990416)88:2<123::AID-AJMG5>3.0.CO;2-S PMID: 10206229

Ganong, W. F. (2007). *Physiology (Fizjologia)*. Wydawnictwo Lekarskie PZWL.

Gazzaniga, M. S. (2005). The brain as boondoggle. *Harvard Business Review*, *84*, 66.

Golin, E., & Lyerly, S. B. (1950). The galvanic skin response as a test of advertising impact. *The Journal of Applied Psychology*, *34*(6), 440–443. DOI: 10.1037/h0055197 PMID: 14803411

Gomez-Uribe, C. A., & Hunt, N. (2016). The Netflix recommender system: Algorithms, business value, and innovation. *ACM Transactions on Management Information Systems*, *6*(4), 1–19. DOI: 10.1145/2843948

Haleem, A., Javaid, M., Asim Qadri, M., Pratap Singh, R., & Suman, R. (2022). Artificial intelligence (AI) applications for marketing: A literature-based study. *International Journal of Intelligent Networks*, *3*, 119–132. DOI: 10.1016/j.ijin.2022.08.005

Hamzehei, A., Fathiana, M., Farvaresh, H., & Gholamian, M. R. (2011). A new methodology to study customer electrocardiogram using RFM analysis and clustering. *Management Science Letters, 1*(2), 139–148. DOI: 10.5267/j.msl.2010.03.009

Huang, M.-H., & Rust, R. T. (2021). Engaged to a robot? The role of AI in service. *Journal of Service Research, 24*(1), 1–20. DOI: 10.1177/1094670520902266

Huettel, S. A., Song, A. W., & McCarthy, G. (2015). *Functional magnetic resonance imaging*. Sinauer Associates.

Javaid, M., Haleem, A., & Singh, R. P. (2022). Neuromarketing and its applications in Industry 5.0: A state-of-the-art review. *Sensors International, 3*, 100162.

Karmarkar, U., & Plassmann, H. (2019). Personalized marketing and the ethical use of emotional data. *JMR, Journal of Marketing Research, 56*(4), 567–584.

Kenning, P., & Linzmajer, M. (2011). Consumer neuroscience: An overview of an emerging discipline with implications for consumer policy. *Journal für Verbraucherschutz und Lebensmittelsicherheit, 6*(1), 111–125. DOI: 10.1007/s00003-010-0652-5

Koelstra, S., Muhl, C., Soleymani, M., Lee, J. S., Yazdani, A., Ebrahimi, T., & Patras, I. (2012). DEAP: A Database for Emotion Analysis Using Physiological Signals. *IEEE Transactions on Affective Computing, 3*(1), 18–31. DOI: 10.1109/T-AFFC.2011.15

Lee, N., Broderick, A. J., & Chamberlain, L. (2007). What is "neuromarketing"? A discussion and agenda for future research. *International Journal of Psychophysiology, 63*(2), 199–204. DOI: 10.1016/j.ijpsycho.2006.03.007 PMID: 16769143

McClure, S. M., Li, J., Tomlin, D., Cypert, K. S., Montague, L. M., & Montague, P. R. (2004). Neural correlates of behavioral preference for culturally familiar drinks. *Neuron, 44*(2), 379–387. DOI: 10.1016/j.neuron.2004.09.019 PMID: 15473974

Mokhtari, S., Ashtari, A., & Taherikia, F. (2021). The future of neuromarketing in the age of AI. *Journal of Consumer Behaviour, 20*(4), 954–965.

Mokhtari, S., Yen, K. K., & Liu, J. (2021). Effectiveness of artificial intelligence in stock market prediction based on machine learning. *International Journal of Computer Applications, 183*(7), 1–8. DOI: 10.5120/ijca2021921347

Morin, C. (2011). Neuromarketing: The New Science of Consumer Behavior. *Society, 48*(2), 131–135. DOI: 10.1007/s12115-010-9408-1

Plassmann, H., Ramsøy, T. Z., & Milosavljevic, M. (2015). Branding the brain: A critical review and outlook. *Journal of Consumer Psychology*, *22*(1), 18–36. DOI: 10.1016/j.jcps.2011.11.010

Rabby, F., & Chimhundu, D. R. (2021). Artificial Intelligence in Digital Marketing Influences Consumer Behavior: A Review and Theoretical Foundation for Future Research. *Journal Name*, *25*(5).

Realeyes. (2022). *Realeyes PreView: Creative Effectiveness Testing with Emotion AI*. Retrieved from https://www.realeyesit.com

Realeyes. (2023). *Case Study: MARS Achieves 29% ROI Improvement Using Emotion and Attention AI*. Retrieved from https://www.realeyesit.com/resources/case-studies

Ricci, F., Rokach, L., & Shapira, B. (2015). Recommender systems: Introduction and challenges. In *Recommender Systems Handbook* (pp. 1–34). Springer. DOI: 10.1007/978-1-4899-7637-6_1

Senior, C., & Lee, N. (2008). A manifesto for neuromarketing science. *Journal of Consumer Behaviour*, *7*(4-5), 263–271. DOI: 10.1002/cb.250

Simola, J., Kuisma, J., Oörni, A., Uusitalo, L., & Hyönä, J. (2011). The impact of salient advertisements on reading and attention on web pages. *Journal of Experimental Psychology*, *17*, 174–190. PMID: 21604909

Smidts, A., Hsu, M., Sanfey, A. G., Boksem, M. A. S., Ebstein, R. B., Huettel, S. A., Kable, J. W., Karmarkar, U. R., Kitayama, S., Knutson, B., Liberzon, I., Lohrenz, T., Stallen, M., & Yoon, C. (2014). Advancing consumer neuroscience. *Marketing Letters*, *25*(3), 257–267. DOI: 10.1007/s11002-014-9306-1

Smyczek, S., & Turek, A. (2011). Applicability of medical diagnostics in consumer behavior research (Możliwość zastosowania diagnostyki medycznej w badaniach zachowań konsumentów). *Research Papers of Wrocław University of Economics*, *237*, 65–74.

Traczyk, W. Z., & Trzebski, A. (Eds.). (2003). *Human physiology with elements of applied and clinical physiology (Fizjologia człowieka z elementami fizjologii stosowanej i klinicznej)*. Wydawnictwo Lekarskie PZWL.

Vecchiato, G., Astolfi, L., De Vico Fallani, F., Cincotti, F., Mattia, D., Salinari, S., Soranzo, R., & Babiloni, F. (2010a). Changes in brain activity during the observation of TV commercials by using EEG, GSR and HR measurements. *Brain Topography*, *23*(2), 165–179. DOI: 10.1007/s10548-009-0127-0 PMID: 20033272

Vecchiato, G., Astolfi, L., De Vico Fallani, F., Salinari, S., Cincotti, F., Aloise, F., Mattia, D., Marciani, M. G., Bianchi, L., Soranzo, R., & Babiloni, F. (2009). *The study of brain activity during the observation of commercial advertising by using high resolution EEG techniques. Proceedings of the Annual International Conference of The IEEE Engineering in Medicine and Biology Society*, 57–60.

Vecchiato, G., Astolfi, L., De Vico Fallani, F., Toppi, J., Aloise, F., Bez, F., Wei, D., Kong, W., Dai, J., Cincotti, F., Mattia, D., & Babiloni, F. (2011). On the use of EEG or MEG brain imaging tools in neuromarketing research. *Computational Intelligence and Neuroscience*, *2011*, 643489b. DOI: 10.1155/2011/643489 PMID: 21960996

Vecchiato, G., De Vico Fallani, F., Astolfi, L., Toppi, J., Cincotti, F., Mattia, D., Salinari, S., & Babiloni, F. (2010b). The issue of multiple univariate comparisons in the context of neuroelectric brain mapping: An application in a neuromarketing experiment. *Journal of Neuroscience Methods*, *191*(2), 283–289. DOI: 10.1016/j.jneumeth.2010.07.009 PMID: 20637802

Venkatraman, V., Dimoka, A., Pavlou, P. A., Vo, K., Hampton, W., Bollinger, B., & Winer, R. S. (2015). Predicting advertising success beyond traditional measures: New insights from neurophysiological methods and market response modeling. *JMR, Journal of Marketing Research*, *52*(4), 436–452. DOI: 10.1509/jmr.13.0593

Walla, P., Brenner, G., & Koller, M. (2011). Objective measures of emotion related to brand attitude: A new way to quantify emotion-related aspects relevant to marketing. *Public Library of Science One*, 6.

Chapter 14
Neuromarketing Applications and Ethical Implications in Consumer Behavior Analysis

Shalini Tripathi
Symbiosis institute of Digital and Telecom Management, Symbiosis International University, India

Saikat Gochhait
http://orcid.org/0000-0003-4583-9208
Symbiosis institute of Digital and Telecom Management, Symbiosis International University, India

Prabakaran Raghavendran
http://orcid.org/0009-0001-7333-6555
Department of Mathematics, Easwari Engineering College, Chennai, India & Department of Mathematics and Science Education, Faculty of Education, Harran University, Sanliurfa, Turkey

ABSTRACT

Neuromarketing, an interdisciplinary field merging neuroscience and marketing, aims to understand consumer behavior by examining the neural processes behind decision-making and preferences. This paper explores the potential and challenges of neuromarketing, which, by using tools like fMRI and EEG, uncovers subconscious responses to marketing stimuli that traditional research methods often miss. Neuromarketing offers businesses the chance to make data-driven decisions in product design, advertising, and brand management, enabling more tailored and effective marketing strategies. However, the field faces ethical issues related to consumer

DOI: 10.4018/979-8-3373-1152-4.ch014

privacy, the manipulation of subconscious preferences, and substantial financial and technical barriers, which hinder widespread adoption. Despite these concerns, neuromarketing holds the promise of enhancing consumer insight and fostering ethically responsible advertising when used thoughtfully. Recognizing both the opportunities and limitations of this field is crucial for businesses in today's market.

1. INTRODUCTION

Consumer behavior in this very competitive business environment has become a key issue to understand. The conventional method of market research applies typically the questionnaire-type techniques, and highly depends on self-reports, which does not shed much light on more intricate elements of consumer preference, which are more likely subconscious. In order to bridge this gap, neuromarketing combines neuroscience and marketing. This sheds light on what exactly goes into consumer decision-making and provides a first-hand insight into the inner mechanisms of the human brain when it comes to marketing stimuli exposure by means of such tools as fMRI, EEG, etc.

It discusses the theoretical basis, practice, and ethics when applying neuromarketing. This emerging topic is what we will present in this book to suggest that it not only can but is more likely to transform the current state of thinking of how businesses can tap and know consumers in the modern market that has become so fast moving. The understanding of what makes consumers act is commonly referred to as the Holy Grail in terms of gaining an edge, thus it may be why individuals act the way they do, why they get stimulated into their tastes, and how they may respond to some marketing operations.

The conventional tools like questionnaires and self-reporting have the following advantages: they are informative, at least to that extent that the consumer is aware of and capable of describing it. Neuromarketing, on the other hand, examines the unconscious neuromarketing that influences thoughts and emotions and thus investigate more deeply how consumers form judgment and react to wants and needs.

Neuromarketing is not a continuation of the techniques employed in the current but is a new concept in the conceptualisation of consumer behaviour. Neuromarketing can only deliver valuable inputs which might be used as a strategic guide to businesses only when the consumer sophistication and market complexity increase and as a result the businesses come up with a powerful strategy which will leave an impact at both the conscious and unconscious frontiers.

In this chapter, we will address the promises and challenges of neuromarketing and analyze the ethical dilemmas that it introduces. Such exploration will provide information about the potential re-invention of business propositions through neuromarketing, and it will prove to be a game-changer within research about consumers. This chapter examines the concept of neuromarketing and the possibility of merging an interdisciplinary field that involves the application of neuroscience principles in collaboration with marketing research to learn the consumer behavior on a deeper level.

Traditional marketing such as self-reporting and conscious choice-making often resort to data from the subjects, while subconscious and emotional processes influencing the consumers' choices have also been examined for their impact by neuromarketing which thus offers a complementary viewpoint. The chapter starts with laying down the conceptual underpinnings and explaining the basic terms that are crucial for understanding the neuromarketing research. It then goes on to discuss the main neuroscientific methods and equipment used in marketing which are responsible for monitoring and measuring the brain's reactions to marketing stimuli. After that, usage of neuromarketing in different sectors is portrayed in terms of their alliance with the strategic value aspect for businesses. Ethical issues and difficulties of the application of neuromarketing are afterwards subjected to scrutiny and controversy. The chapter draws to a close, at last, by restating main points, mapping future avenues for research and practicing implications for marketers and researchers.

Neuromarketing is basically the merging of neuroscience and marketing. The neuroscientific theories and measurement techniques are used for the decoding, examining, and forecasting of the consumer's behavior. The whole idea is to open up the black box of the brain and see what neural mechanisms are responsible for the consumers buying the product or not, in the first place, to get a complete picture of the flow of attention, emotion, memory, and finally, decision-making. The most prevalent techniques that have been used in the neuromarketing studies are functional magnetic resonance imaging (fMRI) which detects the blood-oxygen-level changes caused by brain activity and electroencephalography (EEG) which measures the electrical impulses in the brain to determine the levels of attention and emotional involvement with the brand or product. Others like the tracking of eye movements and measuring of the skin's conductivity (which can show the degree of emotional response) are additional methods that help to clarify the neural data by presenting the body's physiological reactions to the marketing stimuli. When all these tools are used in unison, they do provide a more thorough and objective understanding of consumer reactions than just relying on the conventional survey-based techniques.

2. LITERATURE REVIEW

Neuromarketing is the emerging paradigm that involves neuroscience with the principles of marketing to comprehend the way consumers make decisions. Consumer preference is little or not at all captured using survey method or behavioural data within traditional marketing. Neuromarketing fills this control with neurophysiological tools that tap into the real-time experience of the brain by the information they sense, according to the marketers.

Initial studies have illustrated neuromarketing utility shaping consumer mind. (Devaru, 2018) present their findings with early evidence on emotional and cognitive millions which direct consumer buying decision credits to the subconscious reactions of the consumers. The above explorations have led to a shift in the mindset of an organization considering maximizing spending on neuromarketing tools for developing and innovating strategic branding and advertising activities.

Neuromarketing research mainly studies EEG technology, which records brainwave activity to perceive consumer responses. (Amin et al., 2020) have illustrated that EEG-based studies give researchers the insight needed to interpret various parameters like engagement, attention, and emotional arousal during product exposure. This method has proven to be especially effective for substance testing, advertisements, websites, and packaging before they are put on the market. Moving forward, (Shah et al., 2022) have been able to develop an ensemble model to classify emotions from EEG signals, thereby increasing the accuracy of real-time consumers' sentiments classification.

With a thorough analysis of the theoretical framework and methodology of neuromarketing research, (Royo-Vela and Varga, 2022) presented a general view of current practices. They stressed the importance of multidisciplinary teamwork so that psychology, neuroscience, computer science, and marketing knowledge combine in useful ways to yield valid and reliable outcomes. Contrasting this, (Robaina-Calderín and Martín-Santana, 2021) by carrying out a mega content analysis, stressed the need to solve some ethical considerations and methodological inconsistencies, which usually impede the ability to generalize findings in neuromarketing.

Marketers have always attempted to understand the psychological triggers for consumer actions, and neuromarketing offers the same motivation but from a more scientific approach. (Arora and Jain, 2020) and (Mishra and Shukla, 2020) placed emphasis on how neuromarketing is useful for decoding how consumers process visual cues, branding elements and emotions so companies may effectively tailor their communication strategies. From this collective work, it is established that consumer behaviour is therefore not just the outcome of logical evaluation but is much more accompanied by instinctive and emotional accounts.

There (Solomon, 2018) deeply analyzed where neuromarketing could be used in product design, brand perception, and loyalty building. He also cited formidable challenges: the construction of high cost, ethical issues around consumer manipulation, and absence of widely accepted research protocols. (Gill and Singh, 2020) build upon this by reviewing various neuromarketing techniques and classifier algorithms for emotion analysis while focusing on the potentials of visual-emotion mining in impacting real business digital advertising and e-commerce environments.

Among further technological advancements have come innovative applications in neuromarketing. Through an EEG-based BCI (Brain-Computer Interface), (Mashrur et al., 2022) sought to develop an intelligent neuromarketing framework that predicts consumer-choice behaviour from EEG data. This system holds promise to personalize shopping experiences in situations of real time. After analyzing the biological basis of consumer behaviour, (Barbasso et al., 2018) further elaborated that electric activity in the midbrain and diencephalon influence such behaviours as impulse buying and habitual responses, thus offering a neuroanatomical basis for consumer psychology.

Meanwhile, in a bibliometric analysis, (Alsharif et al., 2021) the attraction of interest in the field of neuromarketing has been increasing and global in the past five years. The discussion has observed an upward trend in the interdisciplinary partnerships and a paradigm shift into AI integration in neuromarketing tools with reference to the growing maturity in the field. In this respect, (Cuns et al., 2019) suggested that emotional experiences are one of the primary factors in product design and assumed that neuromarketing metrics would be beneficial during the initial stages of designing a product to boost consumer satisfaction, along with brand differentiation.

In the continuum of design, new studies perpetuate the discourse of convergence between neuromarketing and other computational procedures. Indicative of the centrality of their research to cryptographic security, (Gunasekar and Raghavendran, 2024) further contended how radically transformative algorithms like the R Transform would enhance the security of data in critical deliberations when working with the sensitive consumer neural information during neuromarketing solutions to problems. Notably, (Paliwal and Gochhait, 2023) described machine-learning in human activity recognition classification methods that overlap with neuromarketing in the meaning of signal processing, behavior modeling, and real-time prediction, which shows that more and more technologies merge in the functions of users.

Altogether, everything this literature review brings up suffices to claim that neuromarketing has already outgrown the status of an area of theoretical or even experimental research and become a strategic tool with direct implications on numerous contemporary business activities. Due to cross-disciplinary innovation and integration, the field of horizon expansion is presented, encompassing emotion-based branding, personalized marketing, neuro-driven product design, and ethics.

The studies in recent times emphasize the growing application of neuromarketing in business environments that are not just imaginary but also actual. It could be done by simply having the global companies that specialize in consumer goods employing EEG and eye-tracking techniques with the sole purpose of making their packaging more attractive and achieving higher awareness of their brands. The same applies to the advert business where the neuromarketing has been used to gauge the emotional reaction to the TV and online advertisements, which are yet to be aired and therefore enable companies to gauge customer response more efficiently. Over the last five years, the research showed that campaigns employing neuromarketing concepts easily beat the traditional ones in terms of recall and emotional impact. These examples not only provide evidence for the practical importance of neuromarketing but also highlight its usefulness outside controlled laboratory settings.

The increase in the use of neuromarketing to understand consumer motivations has also given rise to lots of studies about the neural basis of consumer behavior. The focus of the earlier studies was mainly on the shortcomings of the conventional self-reporting techniques and the emphasis of the participation of the subconscious in the decision-making process. It has come to pass that emotional and neural reaction often occur before conscious recognition and hence, the consumers still cannot fully articulate the influences that affect their purchasing behavior. The recent neurological literature has communicated the viability feature of new tools from the field of neuromarketing, such as fMRI, EEG, eye-tracking, and biometric measures. The studies show not only the ability of brain indicators of, for example, attention, emotion, and memory to predict consumer preferences but also their greater accuracy of forecasting than the traditional surveys in consumer research. Besides that, literature pays special attention to industry-related studies in which the role of neuromarketing in areas such as advertising effectiveness, product design, and brand positioning is illustrated across various sectors. On the other hand, the advancements made in this area are at the same time pointed out in the literature as gaps that need to be filled. The limited standardization of methods, the very high costs of implementation, and the never-ending ethical debates are the main factors that keep neuromarketing in a non-widespread adoption mode. The gaping holes in the lit make it very clear that more empirical studies need to be done. However, they should be the ones that will combine technological advancement with ethical responsibility. The current research is a part of this large group of studies as it under takes in-depth analysis of both the opportunities and the ethical dilemmas which neuromarketing provides in studying consumer behavior.

3. THEORETICAL BACKGROUNDS OF NEUROMARKETING

One such term is neuromarketing that makes an effort to merge neuroscience and marketing in an effort to crack the complicated functioning of the human brain that may possibly affect consumer behavior. Advanced forms of neuroimaging are leveraging the way the brain actually reacts to the impact of marketing, and thereby gives researchers a better and often subconscious insight into the choices of a consumer than more traditional methods could ever capture.

3.1 Neuroimaging Methods in Neuromarketing

Neuromarketing has some more advanced neuroimaging devices as compared to the others; in fact, Neuromarketing is based on utilizing Functional Magnetic Resonance Imaging and Electroencephalography to analyze the neural response of consumers to marketing stimuli. It becomes possible to look inside the brain through these tools and observe the activity such that the findings of emotional and cognitive reactions are far greater than could be gathered with purely traditional self-report methods. By using these technologies, neuromarketing is able to measure the real consumer response towards an advertisement, packaging of the product or the brand in a subconscious level thus giving the marketers very powerful tools in understanding the hidden drivers of behavior. Neuroimaging technology may appear to be complicated but its use in neuromarketing is very clear and simple. fMRI and EEG are the main methods that are employed to track consumer brain reactions to marketing stimuli and to collect non-conscious reactions. Instead of dealing with very complex brain mechanisms, marketers apply these techniques to spot the trends concerning the consumers' cognitive state, their emotional involvement, and memory creation. This way of interpreting neural signals enables the marketers to easily identify consumer preference and thus neuromarketing serves the purpose of reconciling between scientific measurement and marketing practices.

3.2 Understanding Consumer Decision-Making

Consumer decision-making forms the crux of neuromarketing. Unlike traditional market research which often relies on self-reported data prone to biases and conscious filters, neuromarketing goes directly to the unconscious, where many decisions take their roots. Due to the subconscious basis of many decisional verdicts mainly by emotions and instincts rather than bare facts, neuromarketing unveils the unconscious dictates which generally govern consumer choice. Consequently, from the investigation into the more subtle factors, marketers will have deeper insight as to how consumers are choosing at an emotional and instinctive level.

3.3 Subconscious Level of Consumer Preferences

Neuromarketing examines the subconscious world in the discovery of the bases of consumer preferences. While traditional research is only capable of surface-level understanding, neuromarketing has the ability to reveal deeper, unconscious preferences drivers. This can be as simple as instincts of safety and social bonding, or a much more subtle need of self-actualization, as the goal of neuromarketing is to understand neural substrates behind these drives. By matching marketing strategies and tapping into natural motivations, businesses can create a deeper connection between consumers and their products as well as their messages and the brand.

4. CHALLENGES AND ETHICAL CONCERNS

Based on the theoretical foundation of neuromarketing, techniques of neuroscientific approach are the primary source of the observation and measurement of consumer reactions made by the researchers. With these techniques, marketers can see in the brain how the rewards, feelings, and choices of the consumer gets activated by particular stimuli such as ads, package designs, or logos. The methods capture neural and physiological responses in real-time, thus, giving empirical proof of the consumer's engagement and the formation of his/her preference. This methodological approach enables the researchers to go beyond mental self-reporting to get to know the subconscious activities that influence the consumer buying behavior.

It's not without cost and ethical hurdles, primarily as far as both points are concerned. Modern apparatus used in Neuroimaging are from fMRI to EEG machines where the price tag reaches exorbitant levels. Thus, the majority of small businesses will find the apparatus practically inaccessible. Specialized expertise is also a problem, in addition to technical problems concerning neuroimaging data. Beyond that, important ethical considerations also involve the areas of privacy and informed consent in neuromarketing as well as manipulation possibilities.

Regulatory frameworks are extremely important in directing the ethical usage of neuromarketing. Among them, the General Data Protection Regulation (GDPR) as one of the data protection laws stipulates the strictest requirements for personal and biometric data including neural information processing, collection and storage. The rules have laid down the requirements of obtaining the subject's consent, cutting down the amount of data collected to the least possible and allow subjects to exercise their right to privacy. Along with the laws, professional ethical standards created by research and marketing associations advocate for transparency, accountability, and respect for consumer autonomy. The right observance of both the law and the ethics makes the neuromarketing a socially responsible and ethical practice. In neuromarketing, the acceptance of privacy issues is conditional on the use of transparent research practices, coupled with a robust data security. The organizations, to a great extent, can create a picture of transparency by properly informing the subjects about the data collection's purpose, the ways of doing so, and the methods of data analysis and storage. Along with the use of data security measures like anonymization, encryption, and access control policies, the sensitive neural data is additionally safeguarded against misappropriation or unauthorized access. Thus, companies can risk less ethically while still keeping customers' goodwill and reliance on neuromarketing research.

Figure 1. Architecture of a neuromarketing research framework

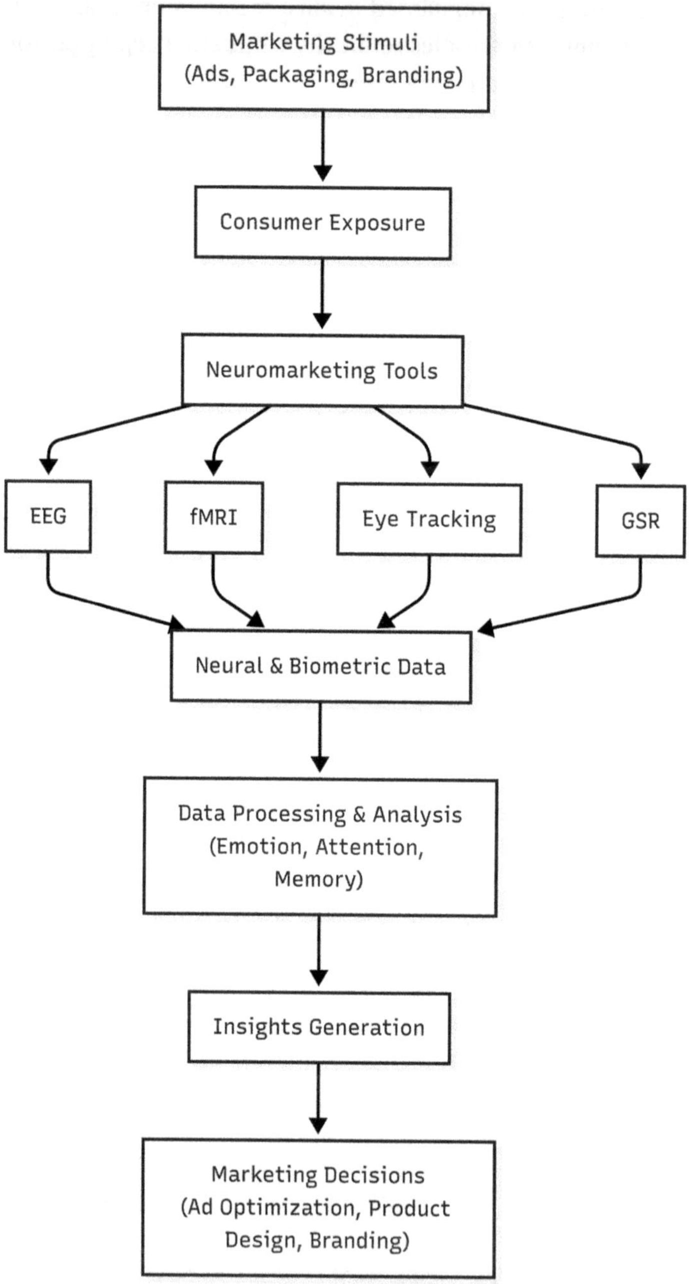

Figure 1 illustrates the architecture of a neuromarketing research framework, highlighting the sequential process through which marketing stimuli are transformed into actionable insights using neuroscientific and analytical tools.

4.1 Privacy and Data Protection

The most important ethical problem with neuromarketing is privacy. Most consumers would be opposed to knowing the fact that their brain activities for marketing are being surveilled. Therefore, maintaining data integrity and anonymity is utmost important for the neuromarketer. Participants can be made aware of the nature of study and as to what use is being made of neural data by the neuromarketers and they can withdraw from the study whenever they want. The only way that these concerns could be addressed is for neuromarketing to develop strict protocols regarding data protection that would meet regulatory standards and public expectations for privacy and confidentiality.

4.2 Ethical Limitations of Neuromarketing

Subconscious influence gives rise to many ethical issues about the marketer's power to influence consumer choice. Neuromarketers are always on the knife-edge of persuasion and manipulation because subconscious influence can subtly alter choice without people being fully conscious of it. Ethical practices and transparency are the need of the hour in these matters to avoid any kind of manipulative behavior on the neuro marker's side. Clear guidelines and always keeping issues transparent is what is needed for neuromarketers to ensure that vulnerable ends are not used for manipulative purposes.

Manipulation vs. Informed Choice Another of the most important challenges is to ensure that neuromarketing strategies are engaged in informed choices by the consumer and not in the covert manipulation of the consumer. The neuromarketer should not try to enhance the choice-making capability of consumers, but rather to promote ways of consumer manipulation that violate autonomy.

Transparency and Informed Consent. Neuromarketing should be upfront in its practice. Participants should be giving their informed consent, which means having realized the reason why their data is being collected, what it will be used for and why the study needs to be conducted. Such an openness keeps the consumers trustful and ethically viable.

Respect towards Vulnerabilities: Neuromarketers should have sensitivity to the vulnerabilities of the consumers. Neuroimaging may lead to insensitive insights such as fears or insecurities that are never a way to gain business. Instead, these are used in a responsible manner by the neuromarketers to make consumers better and happier.

Accountability and Industry Standards: Neuromarketing calls for high ethical standards and industry standards. Operators should work within boundaries which are defined by codes of practice. Checks and balances of accountability should be in third-party audits and ethical review boards, which would then make sure the standards were adhered to with the welfare of the consumer in mind.

4.3 Ethical Framework for Neuromarketing

The ethical framework for neuromarketing should have the basic areas of privacy, transparency and protection of consumers through responsible and fair use of neuroimaging technologies.

4.3.1 Privacy Controls

Informed Consent Neuromarketing research should always require explicit informed consent of participants. Forms that are provided for participants to sign should state clearly what the goals of the study are, what kind of information will be gathered and how it will be used. The participants also have to be informed that they can withdraw their participation from the research at any time.

De-identification of Data Neuroimaging data should be de-identified to ensure the privacy of the participants. This is done by removing personal identifiers from such a way that no neural data can be traced back to any participant.

Data Security: Standard data security measures must be put into place at the neuromarketing research centers, using secure storage, encryption, and audits. With such checks,Unauthorized access and hence sensitive data could be avoided.

Clear Communication: Neuromarketers should be transparent with participants as well as consumers about their approach. For example, they need to make correct communication about information that is extracted from neural levels as how it is being collected and analyzed along with its utilization to prevent misinterpretation and gain their trust.

Consumer Education: Neuromarketing professionals need to educate consumers of the benefits and limitation of neuromarketing so that they are well-informed in making a decision as to whether to interact with neuro-marketed products or services.

4.4 Practical Applications in Marketing

One important place where the neuromarketing plays its role is in designing and packaging of the products. What Neuromarketing does is place more beyond normal market research studies by exploring the neurological responses of consumers. This helps business to gain insight into which features and attributes become processed in such ways which would draw nice brain responses. Companies, therefore, are able to optimize the aesthetics and ergonomics of packaging in a way that will resonate with consumers at a deep subconscious level. This the approach is significant not just in that the products become functional to the need but the approach also develops an extensive emotional attachment, and enhances consumer appeal, with eventually brand loyalty. Neuromarketing has its impact in the fields of advertisements and brand management perhaps most of all.

Advertisements are created with neuroscientific results. It makes it precise or accurate advertising campaigns by getting the knowledge of nervous system which underlies decisions of the consumer while making choice. Thus, it creates message and visuals that generate particular emotional responses in the targeted consumers. Neuromarketing makes advertisements get stuck at the subconscious levels of the consumers so that they become more appealing and memorable. This also applies to brand management, through which a business can apply neuro insights in forming and strengthening brand identities that are supported by deep desires and values of the targeted audiences (Barbasso et al., 2018).

As the world today becomes more data-driven, businesses depend on neuromarketing as a foundation of data-driven decision-making. This neuroscience-marketing wedding is potentially a boon for companies in evolving their marketing strategy from the soundest empirical evidence which is backed by neuroscience discovery. Instead of wholly relying on the normal market research, the business houses can get into the insidious neural response of the customers for streamlining their campaign. Data-driven decisions in this respect, not only helps realign marketing campaigns in a better way, but also gives birth to an atmosphere of responsiveness and adaptability in an ever-changing marketplace. Finally, neuromarketing works well to change the business field of marketing through offering of workable applications that range from product design and packaging, advertising and brand management, and data-driven decision-making. Through understanding the neural processes that underlie consumer behavior, businesses are better placed to create products and campaigns that touch the consumers at the very core, settling the issues of brand loyalty and success in the market. Neuromarketing has a long-term impact on the marketing ever-changing, and it goes beyond the information brought in through neuroimaging in application phases of products design and packaging the aesthesis of a product. As they dig deep into the essence of why is it beautiful, they can see the neural level reaction of customers to different product features. Thus companies don't only make products that make their customers go 'wow,' but make subconscious wants and needs of consumers. Therefore this holistic method of product development will shake up the industries seriously and establish the new standards for the consumer experience (Mashrur et al., 2022).

Neuromarketing has also set up new avenues to advertisement and brand management. It is capitalizing on the emotional and cognitive functionality of the brain to develop campaigns that go under the rational filters on a consumer level and deep into their psyche. In addition, Neuromarketing has opened up the possibility of more targeted advertising; messages are targeted at those most likely to respond to the messages; thus optimizing marketing budgets and minimizing waste. Neuromarketing is an emerging science, although in its developing stages, it's gaining more and more significance. Companies need it, in order to make data-driven decisions. Companies are receiving lots of neural data but they still need to know how to use the information in their favour. With advanced analytics and machine learning, it's now easier than ever to find actionable insights in complex neuroscientific data. It will be beneficial for marketing strategies and even product design, market position and customer experience.

Neuromarketing has to be suitably ethical as well. Consumer rights and privacy should be respected, and companies must guarantee transparency, informed consent, and compliance with industry standards.

4.5 Optimizing Ad Effectiveness

The ad world is a very competitive one. The aim here, not only to get the attention of consumers once, but hold on to it. Neuromarketing has been the game changer in increasing the efficiency of advertisements to provide a sophisticated view into how the consumers have perceived the advertisements and provide the ability to formulate more effective campaigns (Royo-Vela and Varga, 2022).

- Unravelling Consumer Responses towards Advertisements - Neuromarketing develops the science behind advertisement analysis by explaining the way the brains of consumers respond to various forms of stimuli for advertisements. Traditional market research is conducted based on self-reported information that may not be an efficient way to convey the intricacies in consumer responses. Neuromarketing, on the other side, it is the subconscious, exposing the real emotional and intellectual response of the audience to ads. The ads are very well designed in order to provoke particular emotional responses and the public marketing supports the advertisers in order to perfect the messages and the visuals to maximize the effects. Decoding such neural responses helps the advertisers to know what really attracts more in their target audience; therefore, they can build more attractive and memorable adverts.

Emotional Engagement and Brand Loyalty - At the heart of effective advertising is emotion. Excels at Engaging - In a similar way, ads that appeal to the emotional centers of the brain, e.g. showing natural feelings of happiness, empathy, or thrill, can generate much more deeply-felt and long lasting emotional attachment with consumers. Emotional connections build brand loyalty as a result of consumers having a chance to retain in the memory and choose brands that made good impressions on them emotionally. Neuromarketing helps advertisers to build campaigns which appeal at an emotional level, more than just for sales that come as a result of the short term but also long term brand loyalty.

Effective Advertising Campaigns: Neuromarketing enables the advertisers to optimize different aspects of their advertising campaign including the advertisement placement and duration and the content of advertisements. Using neuroscientific information, advertisers make cleverly target their advertisements at a specific point where the viewer will be more likely to take notice of their message. Additionally, neuromarketing is used to find out the right duration for an advertisement that does not over impose on and hold the audience. Content optimization is also another great benefit of the neuro insights is to guide the advertisers in the creation of the content and images that appeals to the unconscious need and even preferences of the viewer. As a result, a better advertisement campaign that would be more effective and have a better connection with the target audience but would also provide better returns on investments (Gill and Singh, 2020).

The potential of Neuromarketing Neuromarketing has the potential to open many avenues Neuromarketing is at the junction between neuroscience and Marketing, offers vast landscapes of opportunities for businesses looking to gain an edge in understanding and influencing consumer behavior. Here, we examine the wide open field of opportunity in neuromarketing using the medium of the story as well as bullet points:

1) Unconscious Understanding: Neuromarketing offers the capability to explore the unconscious mind of consumers, uncovering hidden motivations, preferences and decision-making processes that may not be consciously expressed (Mishra and Shukla, 2020).
2) Better Product Design: With access to neural response, now businesses can design products and even the packaging so that they resonate in the subconscious of the consumers, hence making them, not just functional objects, but also emotionally relevant.
3) Targeted Advertisement: Neuromarketing provides the opportunity to design an advertisement which provokes a desired emotional response. The advertising that results from this is much more powerful and remembered.
4) Data-Driven Decisions: With the development of neuromarketing and its growth, there is a lot of data available regarding the neural responses of the consumers.

Such data can be used for data-driven decisions so that businesses can refine their marketing approaches better on the basis of empirical neuroscientific data.

5) Better Customer Experience - Knowledge of how customers react to the various elements of the customer experience from website design to in-store interaction enables businesses to design their customer journeys better so as to maximise satisfaction.
6) Ethical and Responsible Practice: There are opportunities in neuromarketing in terms of ethical standards, respect for privacy, and manipulation. It is this ethical context on which the discipline of trust and credibility is founded.
7) Sector Growth: This growth of the neuromarketing sector is an invitation to the professionals, researchers and technology developers to participate in this new growing sector.
8) Personalized marketing: Neuromarketing offers the chance for personalized marketing on the scale, where products and services, even can be tailor to one's neural response and preferences.

4.6 Results and Discussion

The application of the techniques from the field of neuroscience to the study of marketing has already yielded some valuable results and as such, they will play an important role in the field of marketing in the future. Consumer decisions as revealed through studies conducted with neuro-imaging machines are, more often than not, first and primarily processed through emotional and subconscious processes and only then are they rationally analyzed if at all. It has been revealed by fMRI, EEG and other related techniques that the brain's responsiveness to marketing stimuli is closely linked with the activation of the neural pathways related to the above processes of reward anticipation, emotional resonance and retention of memory. All this leads up to the end where we can conclude that, albeit sometimes unconsciously, consumers would still want to buy a certain product or brand above another one. Marketers through the interpretation of these neural responses could indeed further develop their strategies in such a way that they would be in a much closer alignment with the real consumer motivations and behavioral traits through the insights they derived from the different methods used.

Combining the knowledge of aspects of the neuroscience to the findings results of the marketing research gives tremendous results and discussions transformed into the field from the Neuromarketing research. The core of neuromarketing is neuroimaging research which unloads valuable insight into consumer behavior in explaining how the brain reacts to different marketing stimuli. Methods such as fMRI and EEG give a glimpse of the consumer's mind and what type of marketing strategies and stimuli will cause the positive responses from the brain. Not only do these results help validate certain marketing approaches, they also challenge prevailing wisdom, revealing the subtleties of consumer preference that conventional research methods are prone to overlook. It is the ability of neuromarketing to go beyond the conscious understanding of consumers' behavior. Traditional market research relies usually on self-reported data that does not really reflect the subtleties of consumer decision-making. Neuromarketing opens the subconscious mind and reveals unconscious drivers for consumers. Consumers behave instinctively or emotionally; the driving factors are usually invisible. Neuromarketing reveals these unconscious drivers that explain why consumers choose one product over another or why they are positively prompted to respond to certain advertisements. These findings become treasured possessions for business when interpreted and used to shape marketing campaigns to consumers' real needs and want them.

Neuromarketing applications have shown measurable impact in different sectors and industries. In the fast-moving consumer goods (FMCG) industry, companies have applied eye-tracking and EEG techniques to test packaging design and thus, have found out which visual elements are the most attractive and most easily recognized as belonging to the brand. The same thing is done for the advertisement industry, where neuromarketing is used to test commercials before their release by gauging the viewers' emotional involvement and memory of the message, resulting in higher effectiveness of the campaign and better recall of the message. In the same way, the digital and entertainment industries have also employed neuromarketing tools to analyze how involved users are with online content, trailers, and interfaces, thus, enabling companies to improve content according to real consumer responses. These examples underscore the strategic importance and the practical challenges involved in the use of neuromarketing for real-world business applications.

The implications of the findings of neuromarketing are deep and the strategies in marketing has to be revamped and updated within each industry. Companies that have this knowledge of the neural underpinnings of consumer behavior at their disposal can fine tune their marketing strategies to pinpoint perfection. Optimization will include how to place the advertisements, creating content and even time of campaigns. A marketer with neuroscience knowledge can do much better at framing the right message and images at a deep, emotive level. The end result is the creation of campaigns of greater potency than not effective only at drawing in eyeballs but ones that persist long after they have been viewed. Most times data-driven decision-making drives the input of neuromarketing adds yet another empirical study that ought be factored with consumer response that businesses will subsequently input shaping their ways 3. Neuromarketing, while in the process of development presents several ethical dilemmas and the input into consumer psychology is no small matter a good balance between influence and manipulation. It is at this point that an ethical framework needs to be drawn. Steps to Privacy Measures lead off center stage, with rules for informed consent as well as protection of the participant's privacy being significant on the ethical pinnacle and at the law. Transparency regarding the neuromarketing practices with customers as a fundamental step so that consumers are aware of what is being collected and analyzed and, thereby, trust can be built and informed choices can be made about participation. In addition, industry wide ethical standards need to be developed as it pertains to what would be considered ethical and unethical as it relates to the use of neuromarketing knowledge. Such standards are key to responsible practice in the neuromarketing field and hence, maintain its integrity and viability (Alsharif et al., 2021).

Neuromarketing has been a great asset to a lot of different industries, showing that it is adaptable and has significant strategic importance. In retail, for example, techniques such as eye-tracking and EEG from the neuromarketing tool kit can help to optimise store layouts, shelf arrangements, and even product design by identifying the visual aspects of products that consumers pay most attention to and therefore remember readily. Moreover, in advertising, neural metrics not only helps in measuring the emotional impact of commercials and taglines, but the visual imagery too. This in turn enables the marketing people to come up with more audience-engaging marketing campaigns. The same thing happens in the case of digital and entertainment sectors, which use neuromarketing to gauge the engagement of users with the content, previews, and interfaces. These are just a few examples to the benefit that neuromarketing brings to the marketing departments by way of accurate, data-driven decisions and also enhanced marketing performance.

Even though the potential benefits are there, the use of neuromarketing still brings the issue of ethics to the forefront which has to be discussed very carefully. One of the consumer autonomy, privacy, and informed consent issues is the major concern. Since the technologies used in neuromarketing get hold of subconscious responses, the detractors are claiming that such practices may go beyond the limit of persuasion and become manipulation. The evaluation of the ethics of the neuromarketing practices can be undertaken on the basis of the principles laid down including transparency, respect for personal autonomy, and responsible handling of consumers' data. To illustrate, the use of neuromarketing in political or extremely persuasive advertising contexts has already engendered controversies about the possibility of such techniques to excessively sway public opinion. These difficulties reveal the demand for unambiguous ethical benchmarks, governmental regulation, and universal standards across the industry in order to make sure that the neuromarketing practice is done in a fashion that is both responsible and ethical.

The results are in support of the basic concept of neuromarketing that consumer choices are primarily based on the subconscious and emotional factors. Neuromarketing not only provides the marketers with the empirical evidence to characterize consumer engagement and preference in more accurate way but also opens up the new modern way of measuring such factors through the insight obtained that are beyond the reach of traditional research methodology. The factors obtained through the research mean that marketing campaigns cannot only be more effective but also less ephemeral if they are in the right emotional direction.

From a tactical standpoint the results suggest that neural data-driven marketing decisions may be able to increase the level of advertising, product design and brand positioning through strength of their marketing. Still, these pros and cons of marketing have to be considered from the ethical perspective and especially issues of consumer's right to know and privacy concern. Access to the very core of the mind of the consumers, brings up the question of manipulation in the sphere of marketing and it underlines the need for ruling out such instances through transparency and adherence to the moral codes.

The adoption of neuromarketing to marketing strategy implies a radical transformation in the mode of interpretation of the consumer's behaviour. The area of neuromarketing is not to replace but to supplement the traditional research methods, on the condition of being used in a responsible manner, thus providing greater insights while remaining ethically sound.

5. CONCLUSION

In the face of dynamic changing consumer behavior analysis and marketing strategies, neuromarketing is one of the new frontiers of the brain between neuroscience and marketing.

In this research paper we tried to take a look into the world of neuromarketing, the theoretical foundation of Neuromarketing, applied use-cases, ethical implications and the opportunity and challenges of Neuromarketing. However despite all this, with all of neuromarketing comes the hurdles. Ethical aspect features large in prominence mainly due to its ability to subliminally manipulate the decisions of consumers and hence blurring the line between persuasion and manipulation. Ensuring privacy to the consumer and even more importantly ensuring that ethical standards are clearly defined across industries will be important. Further, neuroimaging technology entails huge capital investments and considerable amount of technical expertise; hence, it will only be available to some business houses. Still, despite all these limitations, there are numerous neuromarketing opportunities that are promising. Businesses are now better equipped with understanding the unconscious force guiding the behaviour of the consumers to help tailor their marketing according to that end competitive edge strategies. Furthermore, the booming neuromarketing industry offers an opportunity for practitioners and researchers to make a major contribution to this emerging discipline. To sum up, neuromarketing increased the consumer behavior analysis greatly by showing the processes behind the decision making that are non-conscious. With the combination of neuroscience and marketing research, companies can make stronger and more emotionally connecting, as well as consumer-focused plans. But the future of the neuromarketing is attached to the ethical issues, the consumer's privacy protection and the determination of the ethical practice by establishing the guidelines. As for the future research, it should include the study of the cross-cultural applications, the long-term neural impacts of the marketing exposure, the interface of the latest technologies like AI and ML with the neuromarketing data. If the implementation is done in a well-balanced and ethical way, neuromarketing will have the potential to be the core area of modern marketing research.

In a nutshell, Neuromarketing is a paradigm change that companies see and control consumers. This field is quite interreacting one, demanding deep knowledge of ethics, high cost as well as social responsibility. The understanding and embracing of these challenges and opportunities may help the businesses that are searching for firm footing in this complicated domain of consumer conduct and to exploit the potential of neuromarketing. Neuromarketing is becoming a corner stone in the modern marketing landscape and is changing the way businesses engage with and understand their audience, in unprecedented ways in the past.

The period that will follow for neuromarketing will be greatly dependent on the technology, analytics, and primary governance on the use of data. The launch of various technologies like Artificial Intelligence and Machine Learning, among others, is viewed as smashing the neural data prediction barrier thus; more insightful, and scalable directions would be provided. With the declining rates of these technologies, neuromarketing may soon be one of the services to go on the majority of the companies. Furthermore, cutting edge research will move deeply into character studies of consumers in different cultures, the neuro imprint of repeated exposure to marketing and the syntax of neuromarketing coupled with digital marketing platforms. The setting of moral guidelines that are uniform and nature that is regulatory will be very important in ensuring that the upwards trend of neuromarketing does not sway off the path of being socially responsible and customer-oriented.

REFERENCES

Alsharif, A. H., Md Salleh, N. Z., Baharun, R., & Rami Hashem, E. (2021). Neuromarketing research in the last five years: A bibliometric analysis. *Cogent Business & Management*, *8*(1), 1978620. DOI: 10.1080/23311975.2021.1978620

Amin, C. R., Hasin, M. F., Leon, T. S., Aurko, A. B., Tamanna, T., Rahman, M. A., & Parvez, M. Z. (2020, December). Consumer behavior analysis using EEG signals for neuromarketing application. In *2020 IEEE Symposium Series on Computational Intelligence (SSCI)* (pp. 2061-2066). IEEE. DOI: 10.1109/SSCI47803.2020.9308358

Arora, H., & Jain, P. (2020). Neuromarketing: A tool to understand consumer psychology. *Psychology and Education*, *57*(9), 3754–3762.

Barbasso, L., Tardivo, G., Viassone, M., & Serravalle, F. (2018). Neuromarketing in customer behaviour—customers' diencephalic and Mid-Brain implications in purchase dynamics. In *Innovation and Capacity Building: Cross-disciplinary Management Theories for Practical Applications* (pp. 11–29). Springer International Publishing. DOI: 10.1007/978-3-319-90945-5_2

Cuns, M. C., Pollán, M. E. M., & Amboage, E. S. (2019, June). The generation of experiences as a differentiating strategic factor in the design of products: An approach from Neuromarketing. In *2019 14th Iberian Conference on Information Systems and Technologies (CISTI)* (pp. 1-5). IEEE.

Devaru, S. D. B. (2018). Significance of neuromarketing on consumer buying behavior. *International Journal of Technical Research & Science*, *3*(03), 114–121. DOI: 10.30780/IJTRS.V3.I3.2018.015

Gill, R., & Singh, J. (2020, December). A review of neuromarketing techniques and emotion analysis classifiers for visual-emotion mining. In *2020 9th International Conference System Modeling and Advancement in Research Trends (SMART)* (pp. 103-108). IEEE. DOI: 10.1109/SMART50582.2020.9337074

Gunasekar, T., & Raghavendran, P. (2024). Applications of the R Transform for advancing cryptographic security. In *Driving transformative technology trends with cloud computing* (pp. 208–223). IGI Global. DOI: 10.4018/979-8-3693-2869-9.ch011

Mashrur, F. R., Rahman, K. M., Miya, M. T. I., Vaidyanathan, R., Anwar, S. F., Sarker, F., & Mamun, K. A. (2022). BCI-based Consumers' choice prediction from EEG signals: An intelligent Neuromarketing framework. *Frontiers in Human Neuroscience*, *16*, 861270. DOI: 10.3389/fnhum.2022.861270 PMID: 35693537

Mishra, G., & Shukla, M. (2020). Neuro marketing: A tool to understand consumer psychology. *International Journal of Technical Research & Science*, *5*(6), 8–10. DOI: 10.30780/IJTRS.V05.I06.002

Paliwal, I., & Gochhait, S. (2023). Classification of machine learning and power requirements for HAI (Human Activity Identification). In *Proceedings of the 2023 International Conference on Inventive Computation Technologies (ICICT)* (pp. 199-204). DOI: 10.1109/ICICT57646.2023.10134470

Robaina-Calderín, L., & Martín-Santana, J. D. (2021). A review of research on neuromarketing using content analysis: Key approaches and new avenues. *Cognitive Neurodynamics*, *15*(6), 923–938. DOI: 10.1007/s11571-021-09693-y PMID: 34790262

Royo-Vela, M., & Varga, A. (2022). Unveiling neuromarketing and its research methodology. *Encyclopedia*, *2*(2), 729–751. DOI: 10.3390/encyclopedia2020051

Shah, S. M. A., Usman, S. M., Khalid, S., Rehman, I. U., Anwar, A., Hussain, S., Ullah, S. S., Elmannai, H., Algarni, A. D., & Manzoor, W. (2022). An ensemble model for consumer emotion prediction using EEG signals for neuromarketing applications. *Sensors (Basel)*, *22*(24), 9744. DOI: 10.3390/s22249744 PMID: 36560113

Solomon, P. R. (2018). Neuromarketing: Applications, challenges and promises. *Biomedical Journal of Scientific & Technical Research*, *12*(2), 9136–9146. DOI: 10.26717/BJSTR.2018.12.002230

Chapter 15
Ethical Implications of AI in Neuromarketing in the Context of Consumer Privacy

Sławomir Smyczek
http://orcid.org/0000-0002-4459-2736
University of Economics in Katowice, Poland

Samir Semaan
http://orcid.org/0009-0006-8089-309X
Ginovi UG, Germany

ABSTRACT

The integration of artificial intelligence into neuromarketing has redefined how businesses analyse consumer behaviour and tailor their marketing strategies. Traditional neuromarketing have provided valuable insights into subconscious decision-making processes. However, with neuromarketing AI's possibilities has become more precise, scalable, and personalized than ever before. While these advancements offer businesses powerful tools to enhance consumer engagement, they also introduce significant ethical concerns. AI-driven neuromarketing raises pressing questions about consumer privacy, informed consent, and data security. Chapter purpose is to explore the ethical implications of AI-powered neuromarketing by identifying key challenges, including risks of consumer manipulation, potential misuse of sensitive biometric data, and regulatory gaps. Additionally, the study proposes solutions to mitigate ethical concerns, offering recommendations for businesses and policymakers to strike a balance between leveraging AI's potential and protecting consumer rights.

DOI: 10.4018/979-8-3373-1152-4.ch015

INTRODUCTION

Neuromarketing, at its core, combines neuroscience and marketing to better understand consumer behaviour by analysing subconscious emotional and cognitive responses. Unlike traditional marketing methods, which rely on self-reported data that can be biased or inaccurate, neuromarketing employs advanced technologies like EEG, fMRI, and eye-tracking to measure involuntary physiological reactions, providing objective insights into consumer preferences (Lee et al., 2017).

The incorporation of AI into neuromarketing has further revolutionized the field, enabling companies to process and analyse vast datasets with unprecedented accuracy. AI-driven models can detect intricate behavioural patterns, predict purchasing decisions, and create highly personalized marketing campaigns in real-time (Ramsoy, 2019). While this enhances marketing efficiency and consumer engagement, it also raises critical ethical concerns. Unlike conventional consumer data—such as browsing history or past purchases—neuromarketing techniques capture deeply personal neural and biometric information, offering unprecedented access to an individual's subconscious thoughts and emotions.

This raises several ethical and regulatory questions:

- Should companies have unrestricted access to consumers' neural and biometric data?
- Are consumers fully aware of how their subconscious responses are being analysed and used?
- How can AI's decision-making processes be made more transparent and accountable?

Beyond privacy concerns, AI-powered neuromarketing also challenges consumer autonomy. The ability to influence purchasing decisions at a subconscious level blurs the line between ethical persuasion and manipulative marketing. Additionally, the opaque nature of AI's decision-making processes—the so-called "black box" problem—makes it difficult for regulators and consumers to scrutinize how marketing strategies are developed and whether they operate fairly (Pasquale, 2015).

Given these challenges, this chapter aims to:

1. Examine the new values AI has introduced to neuromarketing, particularly in enhancing predictive accuracy, hyper-personalization, and the potential to influence consumer behaviour at a subconscious level
2. Identify and analyse the ethical implications of AI-driven neuromarketing, focusing on privacy, transparency, potential consumer manipulation and algorithm bias.

3. Propose solutions to mitigate ethical concerns while maintaining the benefits of AI-driven neuromarketing.
4. Assess existing regulations such as GDPR and CCPA, highlighting gaps and offering recommendations for more AI-specific governance.

By addressing these issues, this chapter seeks to provide businesses, policymakers, and industry leaders with a comprehensive framework for implementing ethical AI-powered neuromarketing. The purpose is to ensure that innovation in marketing remains responsible, transparent, and aligned with consumer rights.

In order to explore the ethical implications and opportunities of AI in neuromarketing, this chapter adopts a theoretical approach, grounded in an extensive review of the existing literature and law regulations. The methodology involves also synthesizing previous research on neuromarketing, AI technologies, and ethical concerns, drawing on key theoretical frameworks and regulatory perspectives to build a comprehensive understanding of the subject. Literature reviews, theoretical models, and existing legal frameworks helps to identify the key ethical challenges, such as consumer privacy, transparency, and potential manipulation, while also exploring the opportunities that AI introduces in terms of predictive accuracy and personalized marketing strategies.

The content of this chapter is structured as follows. The first section provides a literature review of neuromarketing and the role of AI in transforming consumer behaviour analysis. This is followed by an exploration of the ethical implications AI presents in neuromarketing, specifically focusing on privacy concerns, the "black box" problem, and consumer manipulation. The third section shifts to the empirical analysis, which examines the new opportunities AI offers in neuromarketing, such as hyper-personalization and subconscious influence. The final section discusses the current regulatory landscape, offering recommendations for developing AI-specific policies that can balance innovation with consumer protection. Throughout, the paper emphasizes the need for clear guidelines and ethical practices in implementing AI in neuromarketing, aiming to provide a roadmap for businesses, policymakers, and researchers to ensure a responsible and transparent approach.

By integrating both theoretical insights and empirical analysis, this chapter seeks to offer a nuanced perspective on how AI can shape the future of neuromarketing while navigating its ethical challenges.

LITERATURE REVIEW

Neuromarketing - Overview and Tools

Neuromarketing is an interdisciplinary field that combines neuroscience, psychology, and marketing to better understand consumer behaviour. Traditional marketing techniques, which often rely on self-reported data such as surveys, interviews or focus groups, are limited by biases and inaccuracies. Neuromarketing, however, offers a more direct method for studying consumer preferences by observing subconscious emotional and cognitive responses using technologies like EEG, fMRI, and eye-tracking.

Neuromarketing employs a range of advanced tools that help businesses understand consumer behaviour at a deeper level, particularly focusing on emotional and subconscious responses. These tools provide valuable insights that traditional marketing methods, which rely on self-reported data, cannot offer (Smyczek & Turek, 2011). By measuring physiological and neural reactions to stimuli, neuromarketing tools allow researchers to uncover how consumers truly feel about a product or advertisement, even when they cannot articulate it themselves.

One of the most widely used tool in neuromarketing is electroencephalography (EEG). EEG works by measuring electrical activity in the brain through electrodes placed on the scalp. The computer records the brain's electrical activity on the screen or on paper as waves. Nowadays usually specially designed software analyses the EEG data collected. It detects different brainwave patterns, such as those associated with attention, emotion, or decision-making, in response to marketing stimuli. EEG is particularly useful for identifying emotional engagement with content, allowing marketers to gauge the emotional intensity of a consumer's response (Ariely & Berns, 2010). For instance, it can reveal whether a consumer is actively engaged or bored while watching an advertisement, providing real-time insights into how compelling or emotionally engaging the content is. By understanding the emotional engagement level, businesses can optimize their ads to ensure they capture consumer attention and resonate emotionally. Although the technique of EEG is a relatively old method, it is still considered to be an appropriate way to measure changes in the electrical field in certain brain regions (Ariely & Berns, 2010; Morin, 2011).

Currently is using more and more often in connection with above HD-EEG (High Density Electroencephalography), which is an advanced research technique that allows for very detailed and precise measurement of the brain's electrical activity, using a larger number of electrodes compared to standard EEG. HD EEG can gather very accurate brain activity information while the consumer is exposed to a particular stimulus. Additionally the data gathered will allow to produce highly accurate heat map images of the brain processes which will be included in the report produced (Kumar & Singh, 2015).

Another powerful tool in the neuromarketing toolbox is functional magnetic resonance imaging (fMRI). An fMRI scanner is used to measure the blood oxygen level, which can give an indication of increased brain activity in certain regions (Ariely, & Berns, 2010). The magnetic field is able to recognize the blood oxygen content in the brain. Therefore, if neural activity in a certain brain area is increasing, the oxygen-rich blood increases too because oxygen is required by the brain to work. FMRI is a form of non-invasive neuroimaging technology that is primarily used for marketing purposes. The interest in it has increased enormously during the past decades since it makes it possible to isolate certain systems of neurons that are connected with specific functions of the brain (Wilson, Gaines, & Hill, 2008). This isolation of the neural system is a highly complex task and is only facilitated by todays advanced technology (Kumlehn, 2011).

FMRI is especially useful for exploring deep emotional responses, such as those related to brand loyalty or subconscious preferences (Lee et al., 2017). For example, studies have shown that emotional reactions often play a greater role in purchase decisions than logical reasoning, and fMRI helps marketers understand the underlying brain activity driving these decisions. The ability to pinpoint which parts of the brain are engaged during an ad or product experience helps companies design marketing strategies that trigger the right emotional responses, ultimately influencing purchasing behavior. By tracking the movement of a consumer's eyes, marketers can determine where a person focuses their attention when viewing an advertisement or product. Eye-tracking can reveal which aspects of an ad (such as the product itself, the brand logo, or a call to action) draw the most attention and for how long (Morin, 2011). These insights are particularly useful for optimizing ad designs, website layouts, and product packaging. For instance, if consumers consistently focus on the product but ignore the brand logo, companies might consider repositioning the logo to ensure it gets noticed. By understanding visual attention, companies can make informed decisions about the placement of key elements in their marketing materials, increasing their chances of making a lasting impression on the consumer.

Another method used in neuromarketing is Galvanic Skin Response or skin conductance. This method is used to measure the temperature of the skin and its electrical conductance, which varies depending on the skin moisture level. Skin conductance is used to identify and measure psychological and physiological arousal. It's most common use is in lie detecting technology. The pulse rate is also measured through galvanic skin response. The fluctuations in the pulse reveal the level of excitement or stress that the person experiences as a response to certain triggers (Kumar & Singh, 2015; Leonard, & Rayport, 1997).

The integration of these tools—EEG, fMRI, eye-tracking, and facial coding, as well other methods —into neuromarketing has allowed businesses to gain a deeper understanding of how consumers think, feel, and react on a subconscious level. These tools provide a more accurate and detailed picture of consumer behaviour than traditional marketing methods, allowing companies to tailor their marketing strategies more effectively. However, as the use of these technologies expands, it's crucial to address the ethical concerns related to privacy, consent, and the potential for manipulation. Companies must ensure they use these powerful tools responsibly, respecting consumer autonomy while leveraging the insights they provide to create more effective and engaging marketing experiences.

Neuromarketing aims to uncover the subconscious processes behind decision-making. As such, it focuses on studying emotional responses to stimuli, including advertisements, brand logos, and even product packaging. Studies have shown that consumers' emotional reactions play a significant role in their purchasing decisions. For example, research using fMRI scans has demonstrated that emotional reactions often outperform rational decision-making when predicting purchasing behaviour (Hubert & Kenning, 2008). This suggests that traditional marketing's reliance on cognitive assessments of a product's attributes may overlook the more powerful role of emotions in consumer choices.

Recent research is showing that AI's role in neuromarketing has completely changed. It's not just a helpful tool anymore it's the main driving force behind everything automated. Now, technologies like deep learning, including convolutional neural networks (CNNs) and transformer models, are being used to dig into neural signals with a level of precision that's almost scary, allowing companies to predict how engaged a consumer will be with almost crazy accuracy (Martínez-Navarro et al., 2023). But that's not all there are also new emotion recognition systems popping up that, when combined with behavioral models, can create super-personalized content on the spot, as if the brand is reading your mind (Serrano-Guerrero et al., 2023). These systems are becoming a must-have for big digital marketing campaigns, especially in e-commerce, where everything needs to be tailored almost in real-time if it's going to catch the consumer's attention.

One of the key advantages of neuromarketing is its ability to provide objective data about consumer preferences, free from the distortions of self-reported data. Traditional methods rely on participants' ability to accurately express their thoughts and feelings, but neuromarketing bypasses this limitation by directly measuring physiological responses. Technologies like EEG and fMRI capture neural activity and brain responses, while eye-tracking monitors where and how long a consumer focuses on specific visual stimuli (Ariely & Berns, 2010). These insights help marketers better understand the emotional triggers that drive brand loyalty, purchase intentions, and attitudes toward products (Lee et al., 2017).

Moreover, neuromarketing has shown its ability to segment consumers based on subconscious emotional responses, allowing businesses to tailor their marketing strategies to target specific emotional states. For instance, some studies have demonstrated that individuals who respond positively to emotionally charged advertisements are more likely to exhibit brand loyalty and repeat purchasing behaviour (Morin, 2011). This personalized approach is more effective than broad demographic targeting, which may fail to account for the emotional underpinnings of consumer behaviour.

Role of AI in Enhancing Neuromarketing

The integration of artificial intelligence (AI) into neuromarketing has dramatically expanded the potential of this field. Recent research is showing that AI's role in neuromarketing has completely changed. It's not just a helpful tool anymore it's the main driving force behind everything automated. Now, technologies like deep learning, including convolutional neural networks (CNNs) and transformer models, are being used to dig into neural signals with a level of precision that's almost scary, allowing companies to predict how engaged a consumer will be with almost crazy accuracy (Martínez-Navarro et al., 2023). But that's not all there are also new emotion recognition systems popping up that, when combined with behavioural models, can create super-personalized content on the spot, as if the brand is reading your mind (Serrano-Guerrero et al., 2023). These systems are becoming a must-have for big digital marketing campaigns, especially in e-commerce, where everything needs to be tailored almost in real-time if it's going to catch the consumer's attention. While traditional neuromarketing techniques provide valuable insights into subconscious decision-making, AI introduces a new dimension by enabling the processing and analysis of vast amounts of data in real time. AI-driven algorithms can analyse complex datasets, including biometric, neural, and behavioural signals, to detect patterns and trends that human analysts might miss. This enhanced capability allows marketers to gain deeper, more accurate insights into consumer behaviour and predict purchasing decisions with greater precision (Ramsoy, 2019; Lee et al., 2017).

AI enables marketers to analyse not just the emotional responses of consumers but also their physiological states, preferences, and future behaviour. With AI-powered analytics, businesses can create predictive models that go beyond observing current reactions, helping to forecast future trends and consumer behaviour. For instance, AI can aggregate data from multiple consumer touchpoints (e.g., social media activity, past purchases, biometric reactions) to create a holistic profile of the consumer. This is far more precise than traditional segmentation methods, which often rely on demographic data alone (Grewal et al., 2021). By predicting future preferences, AI allows businesses to tailor their marketing strategies more effectively and in real-time.

One of the most profound contributions of AI to neuromarketing is the ability to create hyper-personalized marketing experiences. Traditional personalization involved offering consumers products based on their past behaviour or demographic profiles. However, AI goes further by analysing deeper, more individualized signals, such as emotional responses and subconscious preferences. Through machine learning algorithms, AI can dynamically adjust marketing messages based on a consumer's current emotional state, providing a personalized experience that resonates at a subconscious level (Chaffey, 2023). For example, AI-powered tools can adjust advertising content in real time based on facial recognition software or physiological data, ensuring that consumers are exposed to marketing stimuli that will elicit the most favourable emotional response.

Furthermore, AI's ability to predict emotional reactions has made it a powerful tool in real-time adaptive marketing strategies. By constantly analysing biometric data, AI can detect subtle changes in consumer emotions as they interact with products or advertisements. This allows businesses to fine-tune their marketing materials for optimal impact, delivering the right message at the right time. This adaptability is crucial in today's fast-paced digital environment, where consumer preferences can change rapidly.

Ethical Considerations of AI-Driven Neuromarketing

The integration of artificial intelligence (AI) into neuromarketing brings with it significant advantages, particularly in enhancing predictive accuracy and personalizing consumer experiences. However, it also raises complex ethical concerns that must be carefully addressed. One of the most pressing issues is the potential for AI to manipulate consumer behaviour at a subconscious level, which makes it harder for consumers to retain control over their purchasing decisions. This form of subconscious manipulation is concerning because it exploits consumers' emotional responses without their full awareness or consent (Lee et al., 2017). Unlike traditional marketing, where consumers are more conscious of their decision-making, AI systems can subtly influence behaviour, making it difficult for individuals to recognize the extent to which their choices are shaped.

At the heart of these concerns is the "black box" problem associated with AI algorithms. Many AI systems, particularly those used in neuromarketing, operate in ways that are not easily understood, even by the developers who create them. This opacity in decision-making processes is a major challenge, especially when the algorithms are designed to predict or influence subconscious emotional responses. When consumers cannot easily access or understand how decisions are being made, it becomes impossible to ensure that these processes are ethical and transparent (Pasquale, 2015). As AI continues to evolve, the need for clear ethical guidelines and transparent AI systems grows more urgent. For AI-driven neuromarketing to be trusted by consumers, the systems must be explainable, allowing both consumers and marketers to understand how their data is processed and how marketing decisions are made. This transparency is crucial for maintaining consumer trust and preventing the misuse of AI technologies.

Recent studies are starting to show that AI-driven neuromarketing might create something called cognitive vulnerability profiles basically, these profiles sort consumers based on how easily they can be influenced emotionally (Barredo-Arrieta & Badiola, 2022). And these profiles could be used to target people when they're emotionally vulnerable, which raises a lot of questions about fairness and manipulation. Some scholars are also pointing out that the huge amounts of biometric data gathered for marketing could accidentally spill the beans on someone's mental health or psychological state, making privacy risks even worse (Naeem, 2024). All these findings really highlight the need for stronger rules and protections, going way beyond the usual data protection laws we have today.

Another major ethical dilemma centres around consumer privacy. AI-driven neuromarketing often involves the collection of deeply personal data—such as neural signals and biometric responses—that provide unprecedented access to an individual's subconscious thoughts and emotions. This raises serious questions about how much data should be collected, who has access to it, and how it is used, without infringing on consumer rights. While regulations like the General Data Protection Regulation (GDPR) and the California Consumer Privacy Act (CCPA) offer some level of protection, they were not designed with the unique challenges of AI-driven neuromarketing in mind. These regulations largely focus on traditional forms of personal data, but AI systems often work with more complex, sensitive data, such as biometric readings and neural signals, which fall outside the scope of current privacy definitions (Ramsoy, 2019). This gap in existing privacy protections emphasizes the urgent need for updated regulations that account for the complexities and risks associated with AI technologies.

The ethical challenges in AI-driven neuromarketing extend beyond privacy concerns. One of the most critical issues is the potential for manipulation. AI's ability to detect and predict emotional responses allows marketers to craft highly personalized campaigns that target consumers at a deeper, subconscious level. While this can lead to more engaging and effective marketing strategies, it also opens the door to exploitation. Consumers may be targeted in ways they are unaware of, or even manipulated into making decisions without their explicit consent. Theoretical discussions surrounding the ethics of persuasion highlight the fine line between influencing consumer choices and taking advantage of subconscious biases (Pasquale, 2015). As AI becomes more adept at predicting and shaping consumer behaviour, businesses must be cautious not to cross this ethical line, ensuring that their practices remain fair and transparent.

In addition to these concerns, algorithmic bias presents a significant ethical challenge. If AI systems are trained on biased data, the outcomes they produce can perpetuate or even amplify existing societal prejudices. This could lead to discriminatory practices, where certain groups are unfairly targeted or excluded. Ethical guidelines stress the importance of ensuring that AI algorithms are carefully monitored and audited for fairness, with mechanisms in place to prevent any unintended bias in marketing campaigns. AI should be designed to promote equality and inclusivity, not to reinforce harmful stereotypes or deepen societal inequalities. Regular audits and oversight are necessary to ensure that AI systems are fair and unbiased in their decision-making processes (Pasquale, 2015).

Ultimately, while AI offers remarkable potential for improving neuromarketing, it is clear that its use comes with significant ethical responsibilities. Businesses, regulators, and technology developers must work together to create transparent, fair, and accountable AI systems (Pasquale, 2015). This involves not only implementing robust data privacy measures but also ensuring that AI is used in ways that respect consumer autonomy, protect their rights, and maintain their trust (Zuboff, 2019). As the use of AI in neuromarketing continues to grow, it is essential that ethical considerations remain at the forefront of technological advancements (Ramsoy, 2019; Lee et al., 2017).

The ethical considerations surrounding AI in neuromarketing are vast, particularly when addressing algorithmic bias. AI systems rely on vast datasets to learn patterns and make predictions about consumer behaviour, but if these datasets are flawed, the results will be skewed (Angwin et al., 2016). One of the critical ethical concerns is the risk of perpetuating existing societal biases through AI algorithms. For instance, if an AI system is primarily trained on data from one demographic group, it may fail to represent the preferences, behaviours, or needs of underrepresented groups, resulting in discriminatory marketing practices. This could manifest in advertising content being unfairly targeted or excluded based on race, gender, or socioeconomic background, ultimately undermining consumer autonomy (Binns, 2018; Holstein et al., 2019).

Moreover, algorithmic bias in neuromarketing risks eroding trust in AI-powered systems. When consumers recognize that AI systems make decisions based on biased datasets, they may feel that their autonomy is compromised or that they are being unfairly manipulated. Therefore, it is crucial for businesses to prioritize data diversity in AI training, ensuring that their algorithms are designed to be inclusive and equitable. AI systems should be regularly audited to identify any inherent biases, and corrective actions should be taken to mitigate these biases (Binns, 2018; Holstein et al., 2019). Furthermore, transparency in AI decision-making is essential to build consumer trust. By making algorithms explainable, businesses can demonstrate their commitment to fairness, showing that AI-driven marketing strategies are developed and implemented in an ethical manner (Pasquale, 2015; Zhang & Chen, 2019).

One of the most significant ethical concerns in AI-powered neuromarketing is the potential for algorithmic bias. AI systems learn patterns from the data they are trained on, and if this data is inherently biased, the resulting AI model will perpetuate those biases. In neuromarketing, this could mean certain demographic groups are unfairly targeted or excluded from marketing strategies based on gender, race, or socioeconomic status. For example, if an AI model is primarily trained on data from one consumer demographic, it may fail to recognize the preferences of another, leading to a form of discrimination where marketing strategies are either too generalized or too narrowly targeted (Binns, 2018; Holstein et al., 2019).

The solution to this challenge lies in the diversification of data. To ensure that AI systems are fair and inclusive, data used for training must reflect the diversity of consumers. Additionally, AI models should undergo regular audits to identify and correct any biases that may develop over time (Angwin et al., 2016). Bias detection tools can be integrated into the AI development process, helping businesses track and adjust algorithms that show signs of unfair targeting or stereotyping. Moreover, businesses must adopt transparent practices that make the algorithms explainable, ensuring that consumers and regulators can scrutinize how decisions are made. This will help build trust and accountability in AI-driven marketing practices (Dastin, 2018).

Legal Considerations of AI in Neuromarketing

While the ethical concerns surrounding AI in neuromarketing are crucial, it is also important to consider the legal frameworks that govern these practices. Current regulations, such as the General Data Protection Regulation (GDPR) in the European Union and the California Consumer Privacy Act (CCPA), aim to protect consumer data and ensure transparency in data collection. However, these regulations were not specifically designed to address the challenges posed by AI, especially in the context of neuromarketing. For example, GDPR provides guidelines on personal data protection, but it does not fully address how AI systems that analyse biometric and neural data should be regulated. The use of such sensitive data challenges the definition of personal data under these regulations and complicates the process of obtaining informed consent. As AI technologies evolve, there is a growing need for updated regulations that specifically address the complexities of AI in neuromarketing (Pasquale, 2015).

In addition to existing regulations such as the GDPR and CCPA, the European Union's AI Act (2021) has emerged as a significant attempt to regulate AI technologies. While the Act introduces important measures for transparency, accountability, and data governance, it falls short in addressing the unique challenges posed by AI in neuromarketing. The regulation primarily targets high-risk AI systems, yet many AI applications in marketing—particularly those analysing subconscious consumer behaviour through biometric and neural data—may not be sufficiently regulated. Furthermore, the lack of clarity on how AI-driven neuromarketing should be governed, particularly with respect to the 'black box' nature of AI decision-making, highlights the need for more comprehensive, AI-specific regulations to ensure consumer protection in this field. (Pasquale, 2015; Gorwa et al., 2020; Zengler & Rosenbaum, 2019).

A few recent regulatory studies are saying that new laws, like the EU AI Act (which is set to be enforced between 2024 and 2026), will label AI-powered emotional recognition and biometric profiling in marketing as "high-risk" stuff (European Parliament, 2023). What this means is that companies will have to be way more transparent they'll need to explain how their models work, show their logic, and assess risks properly. On top of that, the OECD's 2022 and 2023 recommendations on AI also stress that neuromarketing, in particular, will need clear and explicit consent from consumers. They've also pointed out that AI systems that manipulate emotions might face restrictions as new international rules are put in place (OECD, 2023). All of this suggests that, in the near future, neuromarketing is going to be under much tighter regulations and governance.

Given the growing complexity of AI technologies, particularly in neuromarketing, current data protection regulations like the GDPR and CCPA are increasingly inadequate to address the unique challenges posed by AI-driven marketing. These regulations primarily focus on personal data and consumer privacy, but they do not account for the more complex and sensitive biometric data that AI systems collect, such as neural data and subconscious emotional responses. In light of these gaps, there is an urgent need for AI-specific regulatory frameworks that can provide clearer guidance on how businesses should handle these new types of personal data (Gorwa et al., 2020; Binns, 2018).

AI-specific regulations should include clear definitions of what constitutes sensitive data in the context of AI in marketing. These laws should establish guidelines for consumer consent, ensuring that consumers fully understand what data is being collected and how it will be used. Additionally, transparency must be a cornerstone of these regulations. AI systems must be explainable, so that consumers and regulators alike can understand how decisions are being made (Zengler & Rosenbaum, 2019). Businesses should be required to disclose not only how data is used but also how algorithms work and how consumer data is analysed. Furthermore, these regulations should emphasize consumer rights, including the ability to opt-out of data collection and access to how their data is processed (European Commission, 2021; Pasquale, 2015).

Despite the existence of frameworks like the General Data Protection Regulation (GDPR) and the California Consumer Privacy Act (CCPA), significant regulatory gaps remain in addressing the unique challenges posed by AI in neuromarketing. These laws were primarily designed to govern traditional data privacy concerns, focusing on personally identifiable information (PII), but they do not fully account for the sophisticated ways in which AI systems process neural, biometric, and emotional data (Pasquale, 2015; Goodman & Flaxman, 2017). As AI continues to evolve, these regulatory frameworks are increasingly inadequate to address the complexities of modern marketing techniques that involve deeply personal data, such as consumers' subconscious responses to advertisements and emotional triggers (Gorwa et al., 2020; Lee et al., 2017).

One of the major gaps is the lack of clear guidelines on how to handle new types of personal data, such as biometric readings or neural signals, which are becoming integral to AI-powered neuromarketing. Furthermore, the "black box" nature of AI decision-making creates a transparency issue that current regulations fail to address effectively. AI algorithms often operate in ways that are not fully understood, even by their developers, making it difficult to assess whether these systems are being used fairly and transparently. This lack of clarity creates challenges for consumers who may not fully comprehend how their data is being used or manipulated.

In response to these gaps, there is a growing need for AI-specific regulations that not only define new forms of sensitive data but also set standards for transparency, accountability, and fairness in AI systems. These regulations should mandate that businesses disclose how AI algorithm's function, ensure consumers are fully informed about how their data is used, and establish clear protocols for consumer consent. By creating more robust regulatory frameworks, policymakers can address the ethical risks of AI in neuromarketing, protect consumer rights, and foster greater trust in AI-powered marketing technologies.

METHODOLOGY

This study adopts a theoretical approach, drawing extensively on previous research, scholarly articles, and policy documents. The analysis is grounded in a comprehensive review of academic literature on neuromarketing, AI and ethics. The methodology involves synthesizing findings from seminal works, theoretical models, and regulatory analyses (such as those concerning GDPR and CCPA) to construct a robust theoretical framework. This framework is used to examine the ethical challenges and opportunities that arise from the integration of AI into neuromarketing practices.

In order to examine the ethical implications and opportunities of AI in neuromarketing, this study adopts a theoretical approach, utilizing literature reviews, theoretical models, and existing legal frameworks, including academic literature, to construct a comprehensive framework for understanding the challenges and possibilities presented by AI technologies in neuromarketing.

The methodology involves also synthesizing previous research on neuromarketing, AI technologies, and ethical concerns, drawing on key theoretical frameworks and regulatory perspectives to build a comprehensive understanding of the subject.

The research does not rely on empirical primary data through interviews or case studies; rather, it builds on the insights of prior studies to offer a conceptual analysis. This approach allows for a broader discussion of ethical theories, regulatory gaps, and the implications of AI-driven neuromarketing without the variability introduced by individual company practices.

RESULTS AND DISCUSSION

Opportunities of AI in Neuromarketing

The advent of artificial intelligence (AI) has transformed the landscape of neuromarketing, offering businesses unprecedented capabilities to understand and influence consumer behaviour. AI's integration into neuromarketing has created significant opportunities, particularly in enhancing predictive accuracy, enabling hyper-personalization, and influencing consumer decisions at a subconscious level.

AI's ability to predict consumer behaviour with a high degree of accuracy is one of its most exciting prospects in neuromarketing. By analysing vast datasets from multiple touchpoints, including biometric data, neural signals, and consumer behaviours, AI can predict future purchasing decisions before the consumer even articulates them (Lee et al., 2017; Ramsoy, 2019). For instance, by studying facial expressions and eye-tracking data, AI systems can infer a consumer's emotional reactions to a product and, based on this, predict whether the consumer is likely to purchase that product. This enables hyper-personalization in marketing, where every interaction a consumer has with a brand is uniquely tailored to their preferences (Chaffey, 2023).

What makes AI even more powerful is its ability to analyse patterns over time. It doesn't just look at immediate reactions but can predict long-term consumer behaviour by observing trends in how emotions correlate with past decisions. This allows brands to build predictive models that go beyond demographics, instead focusing on emotional and subconscious signals to tailor product recommendations. For example, AI can predict the emotional triggers that drive brand loyalty, suggesting not just products the consumer has looked at, but products they're likely to love based on their emotional history. This is much more effective than traditional marketing methods that only rely on purchase history or demographic profiles (Ariely & Berns, 2010; Grewal et al., 2021).

Predictive Accuracy

One of the most remarkable contributions of AI to neuromarketing is its ability to predict consumer behaviour with an unprecedented level of accuracy. Traditionally, marketing strategies were based on broad demographics and historical purchasing data, which provided limited insights into the underlying psychological drivers of consumer decisions. With AI, however, businesses can analyse vast amounts of neural, biometric, and behavioural data in real-time to detect patterns and trends that were previously undetectable (Lee et al., 2017).

For example, AI algorithms can analyse facial expressions, eye movement, and even physiological responses to advertisements, giving marketers a much deeper understanding of how consumers truly feel about a product. This data can be used to create models that predict future purchasing behaviour with remarkable precision. Studies show that AI can predict consumer choices better than traditional methods, as it factors in emotional responses and subconscious cues that heavily influence decision-making (Chaffey, 2023). The predictive power of AI enables businesses to not only tailor their marketing strategies but also anticipate consumer needs before they even articulate them.

Netflix Case Study

Netflix are getting really clever with how they use AI to understand what makes viewers tick. In 2022 and 2023, they partnered up with some neuromarketing experts to dive into how people feel when they watch trailers. Instead of just guessing, they used fancy tech like facial coding and EEG to actually see what emotions were sparking in viewers while they watched. With all that data, Netflix fed it into AI models that were way more spot on than the usual A/B tests they were doing (Southgate & Zhao, 2023). As a result, they started tweaking trailer sequences and even those small, almost invisible moments in a show's preview like micro-expressions on actors' faces to match what viewers were responding to emotionally. This wasn't just for fun, either. It led to a noticeable bump in click through rates, helping Netflix show the right content at the right emotional moment, making everything feel much more personal and engaging.

Hyper-Personalization

AI's ability to deliver hyper-personalized experiences is another major opportunity in neuromarketing. Personalization has been a key marketing tool for years, but AI takes it a step further by delivering individualized experiences at scale. Through the analysis of neural and biometric data, AI can understand consumers' subconscious emotional states and preferences (Ramsoy, 2019). This allows businesses to create marketing campaigns that speak directly to the unique emotional triggers of each consumer, enhancing engagement and increasing the likelihood of conversion.

For instance, AI-driven algorithms can tailor advertisements based on an individual's emotional response to past content, adjusting the tone, style, and message of future campaigns to maximize emotional resonance. This level of personalization goes beyond the static personalization seen in traditional marketing (e.g., recommending products based on past purchases). It creates dynamic, responsive experiences that adapt in real-time to a consumer's changing emotional state, making the marketing message far more effective (Grewal et al., 2021).

AI's role in hyper-personalization is also evident in the development of personalized product recommendations. By analysing consumer behaviour patterns, AI can suggest products that are not just relevant but specifically aligned with an individual's subconscious desires. This creates a more intimate connection between the brand and the consumer, as the marketing feels tailored to their personal identity rather than a generic offering (Chaffey, 2023).

Coca-Cola Case Study

In 2023, Coca-Cola's "Real Magic" campaign got seriously smart with how they used AI to connect with people on a deeper emotional level. They took things beyond the usual marketing tactics by using AI-supported neuromarketing to tailor visual content to the subconscious emotions of their audience. Instead of just guessing what would resonate, Coca-Cola tapped into EEG data to measure how engaged people were with specific visuals. They then fed that info into AI systems to create and test hundreds of visual variations everything from colors to facial expressions to background ensuring that each piece of content was in sync with the emotional needs of different consumer groups (Coca-Cola Company Report, 2023). What made it even cooler was that they didn't just test for engagement, but for emotional connection. This led to A solid 18% bump in emotional connection scores, with Gen Z leading the charge. This group, known for its heightened sensitivity to authenticity and visual identity, responded exceptionally well, proving that understanding the emotional undercurrents of a brand's visuals is key to grabbing attention and loyalty.

Subconscious Influence

Perhaps the most profound impact of AI in neuromarketing is its ability to influence consumer behaviour at a subconscious level. Traditional marketing techniques often appeal to consumers' rational decision-making processes, but AI can tap into a deeper, emotional layer of decision-making that operates largely outside of conscious awareness. By analysing biometric signals such as heart rate, skin conductivity, and facial expressions, AI can gauge emotional responses to stimuli in real-time, allowing marketers to craft highly targeted messages that trigger specific emotional reactions (Pasquale, 2015).

This subconscious influence can be used to enhance brand loyalty, influence purchase decisions, and even affect attitudes toward a product without the consumer being fully aware of the manipulation. For example, AI can detect when a consumer is feeling particularly stressed or anxious and, in response, show content that is calming or reassuring. This type of emotional manipulation can significantly increase the effectiveness of advertising campaigns, but it also raises ethical concerns regarding consumer autonomy and consent (Morin, 2011; Noble, 2018).

Moreover, AI's ability to detect and influence subconscious emotions is not limited to advertisements alone. It extends to product design, website navigation, and pricing strategies. AI can optimize these elements based on how consumers emotionally respond to various features, creating a seamless experience that subtly nudges them toward making decisions without feeling coerced (Ramsoy, 2019).

Amazon Go Case Study

Amazon Go's cashier-less stores do more than just simplify the shopping process they're a showcase of how AI and subtle neuromarketing tactics shape consumer behavior without you even noticing. Between 2021 and 2023, studies revealed that Amazon uses shelf-level cameras to track not just what you pick up, but also your eye movements and micro-gestures, allowing the store's AI to rearrange products in real time to optimize subconscious purchasing decisions (Majumdar & Bose, 2023). For example, snacks are placed in the exact line of sight that the AI knows will trigger impulse buys based on biometric data. This AI-powered strategy doesn't just increase those I'll just grab this purchases it also reduces decision-making time, making the entire shopping experience faster and more efficient. By combining neuromarketing with AI, Amazon Go stores have created a shopping environment where decisions happen almost automatically, boosting sales in ways that feel completely seamless.

Ethical Challenges in AI-Driven Neuromarketing

While these advancements offer businesses powerful tools to enhance consumer engagement and drive sales, they also bring significant ethical challenges. The ability of AI to influence consumers' subconscious emotions and behaviour raises questions about autonomy and privacy. How much control should consumers have over their data, and to what extent should companies be allowed to use this data to shape consumer decisions?

The "black box" problem, where AI systems make decisions without clear explanations of how those decisions are reached, further complicates the issue. Consumers may not fully understand how their emotional responses are being used to influence their behaviour, which could erode trust in the marketing system (Goodman & Flaxman, 2017). This is particularly concerning given that AI's power to manipulate subconscious reactions may not be immediately apparent to consumers, making it difficult for them to give truly informed consent (Binns, 2018; Dastin, 2018).

In response to these challenges, scholars argue for the development of clearer regulatory frameworks that specifically address the nuances of AI in neuromarketing. Current regulations such as the GDPR and CCPA were not designed with AI's capabilities in mind and are ill-equipped to handle the complexities of biometric and neural data collection. There is a growing consensus that AI-specific regulations are needed to ensure that businesses use AI ethically while protecting consumers' rights and privacy (Pasquale, 2015).

According to the paper *Ethical AI in Retail: Consumer Privacy and Fairness* (2024), recent research on AI in retail shows that consumers are becoming increasingly concerned about how much personal data is being collected and how fairly AI systems operate. The evidence reveals that shoppers are worried not just about privacy breaches, but also whether AI is making decisions in their best interest, especially when it comes to product recommendations or pricing. The paper highlights that these growing concerns point to a clear need for businesses to ensure transparency in their data collection practices, implement stronger data protection safeguards, and conduct regular audits of their algorithms. Without these steps, retailers risk losing consumer trust, which could ultimately affect their long-term success.

AI-Driven Neuromarketing and Data Privacy

One central concern is the issue of data privacy. The advanced capabilities of AI allow for the collection and analysis of neural and biometric data at a depth that traditional marketing methods could not reach. Theoretical analyses have demonstrated that such sensitive data, when gathered without explicit, informed consent, poses significant risks to individual privacy and autonomy. Academic research (Ariely

& Berns, 2010; Morin, 2011) has shown that privacy violations in this context can lead to a loss of consumer trust and potentially harmful societal consequences.

While data privacy remains a pressing issue, it is important to understand that consumer trust is increasingly tied to transparency in data usage. Businesses now operate in an environment where consumers are more informed and concerned about how their personal data is used. The implementation of transparent privacy policies is no longer enough; businesses must be proactive in educating consumers on how their data is being utilized and give them real control over it. With AI-powered neuromarketing, the use of deep learning algorithms that analyse neural patterns and physiological responses requires a robust framework for informed consent, which goes beyond simply asking for approval to collect data. It must include clear communication about the specific types of data being collected, how they will be processed, and why it is necessary for the business to gather such data. Without this transparency, even well-intentioned companies risk undermining trust and jeopardizing consumer relationships (Binns, 2018; Goodman & Flaxman, 2017; Nissenbaum, 2011).

AI-Driven Neuromarketing and Transparency

Transparency represents another major challenge. The literature reveals that many AI systems function as 'black boxes,' where the decision-making process is obscured. This lack of transparency not only hinders accountability but also prevents consumers from fully understanding how their personal data is used. The theoretical work of scholars such as Pasquale (2015) underscores that this opacity is problematic in contexts where decisions have profound implications for individual rights.

The challenge of AI transparency extends beyond the consumer-business relationship. From a regulatory standpoint, there is an urgent need for legislation that mandates explainability of AI systems. Regulators must recognize that the current lack of accountability in AI-driven decision-making is not just an ethical issue but also a legal concern. As AI systems make decisions based on patterns in data, the lack of clarity on how these decisions are made could inadvertently lead to discriminatory outcomes. For instance, if an AI system used for marketing makes decisions based on biased training data, it could unfairly target certain groups while excluding others. To address this, regulators may need to introduce standards for explainability, ensuring that AI models can not only be audited but also interpreted by consumers and independent reviewers alike. For businesses, adopting explainable AI models will not only improve trust but also reduce the risks of legal challenges related to algorithmic bias or unfair marketing practices (Goodman & Flaxman, 2017).

AI-Driven Neuromarketing and Consumer Manipulation

Manipulative practices form a further ethical dilemma. The predictive power of AI in neuromarketing may be employed in ways that exploit consumers' subconscious biases. Theoretical frameworks in ethics draw a fine line between persuasive communication and manipulation. Research indicates that when consumers are not fully aware of how their data is being exploited, there is a risk of undermining their autonomy and making them vulnerable to coercive marketing practices.

The issue of manipulation in AI-driven neuromarketing is not just about ethical boundaries—it is also about consumer autonomy. By influencing purchasing decisions at a subconscious level, AI may violate a consumer's ability to make fully informed decisions. The increasing ability of AI to predict and even shape consumer preferences based on neural and physiological responses poses a threat to the fundamental principles of autonomy and freedom of choice. In an ethical sense, the question arises: to what extent should businesses use these tools to influence behaviour? Companies must be cautious in their use of subconscious marketing tactics, ensuring they do not exploit vulnerable consumers, especially in cases where consumers are unaware of how deeply their preferences are being shaped. This may involve creating clear boundaries for the use of AI in consumer decision-making, ensuring that AI-driven neuromarketing is used responsibly and ethically (Zuboff, 2019).

The collection and analysis of neural and biometric data in neuromarketing raises profound privacy concerns that go beyond the traditional collection of personal data. These technologies allow businesses to track subconscious emotional responses, facial expressions, and even brain activity. Such data can provide an intimate understanding of consumers' desires, fears, and preferences. However, this level of access to personal, subconscious data raises the question of how much privacy consumers are willing to give up in exchange for more personalized marketing. The ethical dilemma is compounded when this data is collected without the explicit, informed consent of the consumer, making it difficult for them to fully comprehend how their most personal responses are being used (Morin, 2011; Ariely & Berns, 2010).

For instance, consider how facial recognition software can be employed not just to identify a consumer but to assess their emotional state, making it possible to customize advertisements in real-time based on a consumer's mood. In some cases, this level of influence might cross ethical lines, especially when it involves manipulating a consumer's decision-making process without their full understanding or consent. Data breaches, where sensitive consumer information is exposed, only further heighten these concerns, and have resulted in loss of trust in companies handling personal data. Regulations like the General Data Protection Regulation (GDPR) in Europe attempt to address these issues, but they primarily focus on data protection rather than the nuances of subconscious data collection (Goodman & Flaxman, 2017; Morin, 2011).

AI-Driven Neuromarketing and Algorithmic Bias

Lastly, the issue of algorithmic bias emerges from previous studies that have highlighted how biased data inputs can lead to discriminatory outcomes. The academic literature shows that if the training data for AI systems is inherently biased, the resulting outputs may perpetuate or even exacerbate existing societal inequalities.

Algorithmic bias is particularly concerning in the context of neuromarketing, as it can perpetuate existing societal stereotypes or even deepen inequalities. For instance, an AI model trained on data that lacks diversity may fail to represent the preferences and behaviours of certain groups, leading to inaccurate targeting or exclusion. This kind of bias could unfairly disadvantage minority groups or reinforce harmful stereotypes. To mitigate these risks, data diversity should be prioritized during AI training, ensuring that a wide range of perspectives and behaviours are considered. Businesses must adopt strategies that not only focus on the quality of their AI models but also on the ethical considerations of data sourcing and model transparency. Researchers and businesses alike should invest in developing methods to detect and correct biases in AI systems, as part of their ethical obligation to ensure fairness in neuromarketing practices (Binns, 2018).

SOLUTIONS AND RECOMMENDATIONS

Despite these challenges, the theoretical analysis suggests that it is possible to leverage AI's potential while upholding ethical standards. A balance can be struck by integrating robust consent mechanisms and employing advanced data anonymization techniques. Scholars argue that clear, transparent policies and the development of explainable AI models are crucial for restoring consumer trust (Pasquale, 2015; Ramsoy, 2019). The literature emphasizes that when consumers understand the rationale behind AI-driven decisions, they are more likely to accept and support the technology (Lee et al., 2017; Grewal et al., 2021).

Moreover, the ethical use of AI in neuromarketing requires a solid regulatory foundation. Although existing frameworks like GDPR and CCPA offer some protection, academic critiques point out that these regulations may not fully capture the nuances of AI's capabilities. The theoretical discussion calls for updated regulatory measures that address the unique challenges of AI-driven practices while maintaining a balance between innovation and consumer rights.

Developing Ethical Guidelines and Best Practices

Drawing on previous research, this paper proposes a set of ethical guidelines for AI-powered neuromarketing. First, it is essential to prioritize informed consent. Consumers must be fully aware of what data is being collected, how it is used, and the potential risks involved. Academic research recommends the implementation of clear consent frameworks that leave little room for ambiguity.

Data anonymization is another key component. Techniques such as differential privacy can ensure that personal data remains protected even when analysed at scale. The theoretical literature supports the notion that anonymization not only safeguards privacy but also allows for meaningful data analysis without compromising individual rights.

Furthermore, the development of explainable AI models is critical. Research indicates that transparency in AI decision-making fosters greater accountability and trust. Organizations should strive to make their algorithms interpretable, thus enabling both regulatory oversight and consumer understanding.

Finally, regular audits and a commitment to continuous improvement are essential. The theoretical models discussed in the literature highlight the need for ongoing monitoring of AI systems to identify and rectify any biases or ethical shortcomings. Self-regulation, supplemented by independent oversight, is recommended as a means to maintain high ethical standards in the rapidly evolving field of neuromarketing.

An equally important aspect of ethical AI-powered neuromarketing is consumer education. Such educational initiatives could be delivered through various platforms—ranging from online resources and webinars to collaborations with academic institutions and industry associations. By empowering consumers with knowledge, businesses will not only meet ethical obligations but will also help mitigate the risks of consumer manipulation. Moreover, when consumers are informed, they are more likely to engage with AI-driven marketing tools voluntarily and consciously, which improves the ethical implementation of these technologies (Ramsoy, 2019).

Additionally, fostering awareness about data privacy rights and providing consumers with the tools to control their data can create a more inclusive digital environment. Businesses should be proactive in creating easily accessible methods for consumers to opt-out, review data usage, and understand their rights under current data protection regulations such as the GDPR and CCPA.

A crucial element in ensuring the ethical use of AI-driven neuromarketing is the education of consumers. Many consumers are unaware of how their data is being collected and used, particularly when it involves subconscious data like biometric responses. Businesses should not only inform consumers about their data rights but also educate them on AI technologies and their impact on decision-making. A more educated consumer is likely to make more informed decisions regarding the products they engage with and understand how their data is being used in personalized marketing.

One potential strategy is the development of consumer education programs that explain how neuromarketing tools work, what kinds of data are being collected, and how it influences their choices. These programs could be delivered through online platforms, webinars, and even interactive tools that allow consumers to see how their emotions and behaviours are being analysed in real-time. By proactively providing clear, accessible information, businesses can empower consumers to take control of their data, making the marketing process more transparent and less manipulative.

Developing Regulations for Consumer Rights Protection

Regulatory measures and ethical guidelines are essential to ensure that businesses comply with privacy standards and protect consumer rights. However, businesses must also take an active role in educating and engaging consumers about the implications of AI-driven neuromarketing. By fostering a more aware consumer base, companies can build stronger relationships, enhance brand loyalty, and demonstrate their commitment to corporate responsibility. This proactive approach ensures that the benefits of AI in neuromarketing are realized without compromising consumer trust. When companies inform and empower consumers, they not only comply with legal frameworks but also contribute to a more transparent and ethical marketing environment.

While regulations like the General Data Protection Regulation (GDPR) and the California Consumer Privacy Act (CCPA) provide a solid foundation for protecting consumer data, they were not specifically designed to address the unique challenges posed by AI-driven neuromarketing. Recent EU directives on AI have made strides in regulating emerging technologies, but there are still gaps, particularly when applied to the nuanced and complex nature of neuromarketing. Scholars argue that a more tailored regulatory framework is needed—one that goes beyond basic data protection and addresses the ethical concerns of manipulating subconscious consumer behaviour. Such a framework should safeguard privacy while ensuring AI systems in marketing are used responsibly, respecting consumer autonomy and preventing any unethical manipulation of their emotions or decisions.

The theoretical discussion emphasizes the need for collaborative policy-making, involving regulators, academics, and industry stakeholders. This integrated approach is crucial for developing standards that are both practical and ethically sound. Updated regulations should focus on enhancing transparency, ensuring accountability, and safeguarding consumer rights, while still promoting technological innovation. By involving all relevant parties, we can create a framework that balances consumer protection with the rapid advancements in AI technology, ensuring the future of AI-driven neuromarketing remains both responsible and sustainable.

Although the current regulatory frameworks, such as GDPR, offer essential protections for personal data, their applicability to AI-driven neuromarketing is limited. GDPR primarily addresses personally identifiable data, but AI-driven neuromarketing often involves more complex datasets, such as biometric and neural data, that are harder to categorize under traditional privacy laws. These data types—such as facial recognition and biometric signals—reveal insights into consumers' subconscious emotions and preferences, far beyond the scope of conventional data protection measures.

As AI algorithms evolve, concerns about the sufficiency of GDPR's provisions on informed consent and data anonymization intensify. Neuromarketing's ability to process subconscious thoughts means that consumers may not even be aware of what data is being collected or its implications. This raises the ethical question of whether implicit consent is sufficient when AI processes such deeply personal, often invisible data (Pasquale, 2015).

Similarly, while the CCPA gives consumers control over their personal data, it also does not account for AI's advanced capabilities in neuromarketing. The law focuses primarily on traditional forms of personal data, such as browsing history or purchasing behavior. However, AI-powered neuromarketing can provide deeper insights into emotional states and preferences, like changes in facial expressions or physiological reactions. This means the CCPA, like GDPR, may need to be updated to address these new types of personal data that AI systems are now capable of processing.

The EU's recent AI regulations aim to provide a more comprehensive framework for AI, though they are still in the early stages and leave several questions unanswered. While these regulations emphasize the importance of transparency and accountability in AI systems, they often fail to provide clear guidance on subconscious data analysis or AI's use in marketing. The rapid evolution of AI requires continuous updates to legislation to remain effective.

Another critical issue is algorithmic transparency. The "black box" problem, where AI systems make decisions without clear explanations of how those decisions are reached, poses a significant challenge for accountability. Consumers may not fully understand how their data is being processed, making it difficult to ensure fairness in marketing practices. Scholars argue that regulatory frameworks should require AI systems used in neuromarketing to be explainable. Businesses must be able to provide clear, accessible explanations for how AI models make predictions or decisions, which is essential for consumer trust and ensuring fairness in AI-driven processes.

Furthermore, there is a growing call for the creation of AI-specific laws that focus not just on data protection but also on the ethical deployment of AI systems in consumer contexts. Some experts have proposed the creation of a regulatory body dedicated to overseeing AI technologies, focusing on the ethical challenges in neuromarketing and addressing gaps in current regulations. For instance, AI regulations could enforce strict guidelines on using subconscious data—requiring businesses to disclose how this data is collected, how long it is stored, and how it will be used (Pasquale, 2015).

Finally, international cooperation will be vital for shaping effective AI regulation. The global nature of AI technology necessitates aligning regulatory frameworks across borders. While national regulations like the GDPR and CCPA are crucial steps, they may not be enough to keep pace with global AI advancements. Cross-border collaboration could lead to the development of global standards for AI in marketing, ensuring consistency and fairness across international markets. Scholars have argued that global AI ethics standards can help prevent data exploitation and consumer manipulation, protecting individual rights while encouraging technological advancement (Ramsoy, 2019).

Taking in consideration above, the following recommendations are proposed:

1. Enhance Transparency: Organizations should invest in the development of explainable AI models and communicate clearly how consumer data is used.
2. Strengthen Consent Mechanisms: Robust informed consent frameworks must be implemented to ensure consumers are fully aware of the data collection process.
3. Adopt Data Anonymization Techniques: Techniques like differential privacy should be standard practice to protect individual identities.
4. Implement Regular Audits: Independent audits should be conducted to monitor AI systems for biases and ethical compliance.
5. Update Regulatory Frameworks: Policymakers should work towards developing AI-specific regulations that address the unique challenges of neuromarketing.
6. Foster Continuous Ethical Training: Organizations must ensure that employees are regularly trained on the ethical implications of AI and data privacy.
7. Increase consumer awareness: the education system at every level should include educating consumers about data protection options and recognizing the non-ethical use of AI by businesses.

LIMITATIONS AND SCOPE FOR FURTHER RESEARCH

In this chapter, the integration of AI into neuromarketing has been examined through a theoretical lens, focusing on its ethical implications, regulatory challenges, and potential for consumer manipulation. The key findings indicate that AI-powered neuromarketing significantly enhances predictive accuracy, enabling highly personalized consumer experiences and influencing decisions at a subconscious level. While these advancements bring unprecedented opportunities for businesses to optimize marketing strategies, they also raise profound ethical concerns, primarily centered around consumer privacy, data transparency, and autonomy. Additionally, the analysis highlights the existing regulatory gaps that leave room for misuse of AI technologies in neuromarketing, calling for the development of AI-specific regulations.

However, there are several limitations to this study. First, the analysis is based entirely literature reviews, theoretical models, and existing legal frameworks, which restricts the depth of empirical insights that could be obtained through primary data sources such as consumer surveys or case studies. This limitation means that the practical implications of AI in neuromarketing—such as real-world consumer reactions or corporate applications—are not fully explored. Additionally, the chapter does not consider the technological and implementation barriers that businesses might face when trying to adopt responsible AI practices. Future research could include direct industry case studies or empirical studies to gather more concrete data on the real-world application of AI in neuromarketing and its ethical challenges.

To further enrich our understanding of AI's role in neuromarketing, future research should include direct studies involving industry experts in AI and neuromarketing, as well as consumers and legal professionals. Engaging with professionals on the frontlines of this field would provide invaluable insights into the practical applications of AI technologies and their ethical considerations. Additionally, it would be beneficial to conduct consumer-focused research to explore their awareness, perceptions, and concerns regarding AI-driven neuromarketing techniques. Legal experts should also be consulted to analyse the evolving regulatory landscape and propose frameworks that ensure consumer rights are effectively safeguarded in the face of rapidly advancing AI capabilities. This comprehensive approach will contribute to a more balanced and informed perspective on AI's ethical implications in marketing.

CONCLUSION

In this chapter, we explored the integration of artificial intelligence (AI) into neuromarketing, examining both the incredible opportunities and the significant ethical challenges it brings. The use of AI in neuromarketing is transforming how businesses understand consumer behaviour, offering unparalleled insights into subconscious decision-making processes. With the ability to analyse vast amounts of neural, biometric, and behavioural data, AI allows for highly personalized and predictive marketing strategies, enhancing consumer engagement in ways that were previously unimaginable. Through hyper-personalization and real-time data analysis, businesses can now tailor their marketing efforts more precisely to individual consumer preferences, ultimately driving higher conversion rates and brand loyalty.

However, the rise of AI in neuromarketing also raises critical ethical concerns that cannot be overlooked. While AI offers powerful tools for businesses, it also introduces risks related to consumer privacy, autonomy, and informed consent. The use of sensitive data, such as neural and biometric information, raises significant questions about the extent to which consumers are aware of, and in control of, how their personal data is being used. Moreover, the "black box" problem, where AI systems operate in ways that are not fully understood, complicates efforts to ensure transparency and accountability. These challenges demand that businesses act with responsibility and transparency to maintain consumer trust and uphold ethical standards.

Throughout this chapter, the authors also discussed the current legal landscape surrounding AI in neuromarketing, notably the limitations of existing frameworks like the General Data Protection Regulation (GDPR) and the California Consumer Privacy Act (CCPA). While these regulations have made significant strides in protecting consumer data, they were not specifically designed to address the complexities of AI technologies. As AI continues to evolve and become more integrated into marketing practices, there is an urgent need for updated, AI-specific regulations that can adequately address the unique ethical and privacy challenges posed by these technologies.

To address these issues, the authors proposed several recommendations for businesses and policymakers. First, it is essential to implement robust consent mechanisms and ensure that consumers are fully informed about what data is being collected, how it will be used, and the potential risks involved. This includes adopting data anonymization techniques to protect personal identities, as well as developing explainable AI models that provide transparency about how AI-driven decisions are made. Additionally, businesses must prioritize consumer education, helping individuals understand the risks and benefits of AI-driven marketing and empowering them to make informed choices.

Lastly, this chapter emphasized the need for continuous ethical training and independent oversight to ensure that AI-driven neuromarketing practices remain fair, transparent, and aligned with consumer rights. By creating a culture of ethical awareness and fostering collaboration between businesses, regulators, and consumers, the potential of AI in neuromarketing can be harnessed responsibly.

To summarise, while AI in neuromarketing holds tremendous promise for enhancing marketing strategies and consumer engagement, its ethical implications must be carefully considered. By implementing responsible practices, transparent policies, and ethical guidelines, businesses can harness the power of AI while ensuring that consumer rights are respected and protected. The future of neuromarketing lies in striking a balance between innovation and ethics, where technology is used not just for profit, but to build long-term trust with consumers and contribute to a more transparent, accountable, and sustainable marketing landscape.

This chapter also brings some practical takeaways. AI in neuromarketing gives businesses a great way to boost engagement and personalize marketing, but with that power comes a big responsibility. Companies need to make sure they're transparent about data use, get clear consent, and check their AI systems regularly to avoid manipulation. Doing this will help keep consumers' trust and loyalty.

Policymakers also need to step up by creating stronger rules that tackle the ethical concerns of AI, like privacy and emotional manipulation. By setting clear laws and pushing for transparency, we can make sure AI in marketing works for both innovation and consumer protection.

REFERENCES

Angwin, J., Larson, J., Mattu, S., & Kirchner, L. (2016). *Machine Bias*. ProPublica.

Ariely, D., & Berns, G. S. (2010). Neuromarketing: The hope and hype of neuroimaging in business. *Nature Reviews. Neuroscience, 11*(4), 284–292. DOI: 10.1038/nrn2795 PMID: 20197790

Barredo-Arrieta, A., & Badiola, Á. (2022). Cognitive vulnerability profiling in AI-driven marketing systems. *Journal of Business Ethics, 178*(3), 621–638.

Binns, R. (2018). Fairness in Machine Learning: Lessons from Political Philosophy. *Proceedings of the 2018 CHI Conference on Human Factors in Computing Systems*.

Chaffey, D. (2023). Trends in using AI for marketing: 2023–2024. *Smart Insights*. Retrieved from https://www.smartinsights.com/digital-marketing-strategy/trends-in-using-ai-for-marketing-2023-2024/

Coca-Cola Company. (2023). *Real Magic Campaign Neuromarketing Performance Report*. Coca-Cola Insights Division.

Dastin, J. (2018). Amazon Scraps Secret AI Recruiting Tool That Showed Bias Against Women. *Reuters*. Retrieved from https://www.reuters.com/article/us-amazon-com-jobs-automation-idUSKCN1MK08G

European Commission. (2021). *Proposal for a Regulation on Artificial Intelligence*. EU AI Act.

European Parliament. (2023). *EU Artificial Intelligence Act: Final Draft for Trilogue Negotiations*. https://artificialintelligenceact.eu/the-act/

Goodman, B., & Flaxman, S. (2017). European Union regulations on algorithmic decision-making and a "right to explanation". *AI Magazine, 38*(3), 50–57. DOI: 10.1609/aimag.v38i3.2741

Gorwa, R., Binns, R., & Katzenbach, C. (2020). Algorithmic accountability: A primer. *Data & Society*. Retrieved from https://datasociety.net/pubs/ia_datasociety_2020_algorithmic_accountability_primer.pdf

Grewal, D., Roggeveen, A. L., & Nordfält, J. (2021). *The Future of Retailing*. Springer.

Holstein, K., Wortman Vaughan, J., Wallach, H., Daumé, H.III, & Wallach, D. (2019). Improving fairness in machine learning systems: What do industry practitioners need to know? *Proceedings of the 2019 CHI Conference on Human Factors in Computing Systems*. DOI: 10.1145/3290605.3300830

Hubert, M., & Kenning, P. (2008). *A neuroscientific perspective on marketing*. Wiley-Blackwell.

Kumar, H., & Singh, P. (2015). Neuromarketing: An Emerging Tool of Market Research. *International Journal of Engineering and Management Research*, *5*, 530–535.

Kumlehn, R. (2011). Rice of Neurocinema: How Hollywood studios harness your brainwaves to win Oscars. *Fastcompany*. Retrieved from https://www.fastcompany.com/1731055/rise-neurocinema-how-hollywood-studios-harness-yourbrainwaves - win-oscars.

Lee, N., Broderick, A. J., & Chamberlain, L. (2017). What is 'neuromarketing'? A discussion and agenda for future research. *International Journal of Psychophysiology*, *63*(2), 199–204. DOI: 10.1016/j.ijpsycho.2006.03.007 PMID: 16769143

Leonard, D. A., & Rayport, J. F. (1997). Spark Innovation Through Empathic Design. *Harvard Business Review*, *75*(6), 102–113. PMID: 10174792

Martínez-Navarro, M. E., Kaparakou, E. H., Kanakis, C. D., Cebrián-Tarancón, C., Alonso, G. L., Salinas, M. R., & Tarantilis, P. A. (2023). Quantitative determination of the main phenolic compounds, antioxidant activity, and toxicity of aqueous extracts of olive leaves of Greek and Spanish genotypes. *Horticulturae*, *9*(1), 55. DOI: 10.3390/horticulturae9010055

Morin, C. (2011). Neuromarketing: The new science of consumer behavior. *Society*, *48*(2), 131–135. DOI: 10.1007/s12115-010-9408-1

Nissenbaum, H. (2011). A contextual approach to privacy online. *Daedalus*, *140*(4), 32–48. DOI: 10.1162/DAED_a_00113

Noble, S. U. (2018). *Algorithms of Oppression: How Search Engines Reinforce Racism*. New York University Press. DOI: 10.18574/nyu/9781479833641.001.0001

Pasquale, F. (2015). *The Black Box Society: The Secret Algorithms That Control Money and Information*. Harvard University Press. DOI: 10.4159/harvard.9780674736061

Ramsoy, T. Z. (2019). *Introduction to Neuromarketing & Consumer Neuroscience*. Neurons Inc.

Serrano-Guerrero, J., Arco, A., & Herrera, F. (2023). Affective computing in marketing: Real-time emotional targeting. *Information Fusion*, *96*, 52–67.

Smyczek, S., & Turek, A. (2011). Applicability of medical diagnostics in consumer behavior research (Możliwość zastosowania diagnostyki medycznej w badaniach zachowań konsumentów). *Research Papers of Wrocław University of Economics*, *237*, 65–74.

Southgate, D., & Zhao, H. (2023). Predictive neuroanalytics in streaming media marketing. *Journal of Advertising Research, 63*(1), 89–102.

Wilson, M. R., Gaines, J., & Hill, P. R. (2008). Neuromarketing and Consumer Free Will. *The Journal of Consumer Affairs, 42*(3), 389–410. DOI: 10.1111/j.1745-6606.2008.00114.x

Zengler, T., & Rosenbaum, E. (2019). The 'black box' problem in AI decision-making. *Journal of Business Ethics, 161*(4), 915–927.

Zhang, B. Y., & Chen, H. (2019). Algorithmic Transparency in AI Systems: A Case Study of AI in Consumer Markets. *Journal of Business Ethics, 162*(1), 35–47.

Zuboff, S. (2019). *The Age of Surveillance Capitalism: The Fight for a Human Future at the New Frontier of Power*. PublicAffairs.

Chapter 16

Deepfake Advertising, Cognitive Dissonance, and the Future of Consumer Trust

Meenakshi Devi
http://orcid.org/0009-0005-7086-5549
Lovely Professional University, Phagwara, India

Veer P. Gangwar
Lovely Professional University, Phagwara, India

Amandeep Kaur
http://orcid.org/0009-0004-5716-7298
Chandigarh Group of Colleges, Jhanjeri, India

ABSTRACT

This study investigates the space of advertising using the lens of deepfake technology, cognitive dissonance, and consumer trust as they help companies create hyper-authentic yet potentially deceitful content with deepfakes, traditional notions of authenticity in marketing are being tested. One significant problem is cognitive dissonance, which occurs when users feel uneasy about the possibility that the information they received was fabricated or deceptive. This behavior can undermine consumer trust, raise suspicion, and damage brand reputation. This paper explores how consumers mentally process deepfake ads and how the cognitive dissonance generated by perceiving manipulation will affect trust in the long run. We discuss strategies that can be used to implement ethical practices in a deepfake-influenced advertising space, to protect the consumer relationship and brand integrity.

DOI: 10.4018/979-8-3373-1152-4.ch016

Keywords: Deepfake Advertising, Consumer Trust, Cognitive Dissonance, Ethical Marketing, Digital Manipulation, Brand Authenticity

INTRODUCTION

In recent years, online shopping has surged in popularity, largely due to the widespread use of smartphones and the affordability of internet access. In addition to being advantageous to online companies, this tendency has increased competition in the online retail market. Consequently, businesses spend a lot of money on marketing initiatives to draw clients to their websites. (Dheepalakshmi & Geetha, 2024). The researcher found that cognitive dissonance was intricately linked to the visual representation of the advertisement projected through celebrities (Ertugan & Mupindu, 2019). This connection highlighted how the presence of a well-known figure can influence consumers' perceptions and feelings, creating a complex interplay between their beliefs and the enticing portrayal designed by the ad (Bolia et al., 2016; (GUSTI et al., 2024). Businesses create products that are comfortable to use and consume by offering hedonic pleasure (Hazari et al., 2017), understanding, and a variety of other inclinations in addition to taste and aesthetic appeal (Tavares et al., 2020). The way customers perceive Internet retailers is largely shaped by two key factors: the allure of competitive pricing and the quality of customer service they receive. Prices can draw in eager shoppers with their enticing deals, while exceptional customer service creates a lasting impression, fostering trust and loyalty in a digital marketplace brimming with choices. When people learn about new product launches, sales, and services they are more inclined to make purchases digitally (Rakesh & Khare, 2012). Customer feedback/ reviews online impact customers' online retail buying choices. When assessing products before making a buy, they look for reviews. According to earlier research, internet reviews have an impact on the legitimacy and trustworthiness of online vendors and the goods they offer (Ahn & Lee, 2024; Fernandes et al., 2022; Palací et al., 2019). To make better decisions, online shoppers often participate in relationship activities. When making decisions, this method promotes greater cognitive consistency and lowers the actual risk of future decisions (Imaniya & Agus, 2019). Due to the advancements in artificial intelligence deepfakes have become increasingly common on social media, allowing for the production of highly believable fake audio and video (Nas & de Kleijn, 2024; Vizoso et al., 2021; Whittaker et al., 2023). These altered media pieces replace a person's voice or face with another's, posing a significant challenge for the media industry, as they are often shared as genuine content (Arachchi & Samarasinghe, 2024).

A deepfake is a striking manifestation of artificial intelligence (AI) technology that generates synthetic media, intricately weaving together various elements to create a seamless illusion that challenges our perceptions of reality. By artfully combining, replacing, or layering diverse materials, deepfakes blur the boundaries of authenticity, compelling us to question what is real in an increasingly digital world.(Whittaker et al., 2021). Deepfake Advertising is producing more accurate and compelling depictions of the real world i.e. digital manipulation. Consequently, it is becoming more and more difficult for the typical customer to discern between authentic information and compelling fake stuff (Chen, 2024; Mahmud & Sharmin, 2021). Customers may think that the individual in the advertisement is using or recommending the brand, but in reality, they may have never seen or used it. Customers may be misled into believing that the good is more credible or valuable than it is, which could affect their choice to buy. To assist customers in making wise selections, deepfakes must be disclosed in ads (Karpinska-Krakowiak & Eisend, 2024). These situations cause psychological discomfort in the minds of customers which is called "cognitive dissonance", because of this they feel that it will be risky if they shop via Internet. Even though online shopping is easy and comfortable, many customers struggle to fully understand the products they are purchasing, as they cannot physically interact with them. When shoppers rush their decisions, they often face cognitive dissonance due to the disparity between their predictions and the end outcome experience (Chen et al., 2021; Ling et al., 2010; Wang et al., 2018) further questioning the company's brand authenticity. Festinger first proposed the idea of cognitive dissonance in 1957, which later evolved into "Cognitive Dissonance Theory." This theory posits that when an individual holds two conflicting beliefs, they may feel a sense of discomfort. To alleviate this unease, a person can take one of three approaches: eliminate the conflicting belief, incorporate new supporting beliefs, or diminish the importance of the dissonant thoughts (Festinger, 1957; Telci et al., 2011).

The use of the Internet has surged dramatically, leading to widespread access and significant growth in online commerce (Bucko et al., 2017). Shopping online and conducting product research have become immensely popular activities. In addition to providing a wide variety of products, convenient payment methods, and delivery options, online stores also enable shoppers to save both time and money. Although purchasing through a website shares many similarities with traditional retail experiences (Sonwaney & Chincholkar, 2019), online shopping offers a unique and efficient alternative (Helmi et al., 2023; Palací et al., 2019). When used ethically, deepfake technology offers significant benefits for marketers. Its prevalence on social media allows for innovative advertising approaches. Marketers can leverage consumer tracking to create targeted commercials that resonate with various audiences and personalize content for each stage of the customer journey. Deepfakes can improve marketing communications' credibility and efficacy by incorporating human-like features like faces and voices (Arachchi & Samarasinghe, 2024). Online advertisements are increasingly focused on "synthetic advertising," which combines digital and analog methods to create and alter content. This sophisticated form of modified advertising uses automated systems and artificial intelligence (AI) to generate data. Techniques like deepfakes are often employed, resulting in convincing but fake representations of reality (Campbell et.al., 2022; Qadir et al., 2024).

In the realm of deepfakes, distinguishing between authentic and fraudulent products can be challenging. To maintain the trust of its customers, the company should follow ethical marketing for positive positioning of the brands so that their dissonance level is reduced, and they can shop online without any risk or fear. However, deepfakes offer marketing opportunities through enhanced cross-cultural connections, personalized messaging, and customer co-creation. Ultimately, there is hope that deepfakes will benefit both consumers and businesses (Whittaker et al., 2021). One of the most significant issues in the field of tech-driven advertisements is deepfake technology, fundamentally altering the way online videos are perceived and experienced (Sivathanu et al., 2023). This innovative approach harnesses the power of artificial intelligence and deep learning techniques to seamlessly blend and manipulate existing images, audio, and video clips. As a result, it creates highly realistic alternative representations of individuals, allowing for the fabrication of content that appears authentic (Kietzmann et al., 2020; Kietzmann et al., 2021). The capabilities of deepfakes not only facilitate the convincing integration or replacement of people within various media formats but also produce misleading material that closely resembles genuine reality (Sivathanu et al., 2023). With such advancements, the potential for deception is alarmingly high, raising important ethical questions about the integrity of visual content in the digital age. This paper demonstrates existing research that indicates many previous empirical and theoretical studies and offers insightful information into the meanings of deepfake technology and its influence on trust and dissonance among consumers.

The following queries are intended to be addressed in this paper:

1. In what ways does deep fake technology influence dissonance among consumers?
2. How does cognitive dissonance caused by deepfakes impact consumer trust?

The study is designed to accomplish several key objectives that will offer marketers insightful perspectives on the evolving dynamics of their industry. By investigating potential future challenges, the research enables professionals to anticipate and proactively tackle these issues before they arise. In addition, the study delves into the wider ramifications of these shifts, fostering a holistic understanding of the current marketing landscape. Moreover, it meticulously details future research goals, serving as a roadmap to steer ongoing inquiries in a productive and meaningful manner.

THEORETICAL BACKGROUND

Festinger's Theory of Cognitive Dissonance (CDT)

The concept of "cognitive dissonance was first introduced by Leon Festinger in his book following an observational study of a group referred to as "Seekers," who believed that a cataclysmic flood would wipe out the earth on December 21, 1955. Anticipating how these members might react if the predicted flood did not occur, Festinger and his colleagues closely monitored their responses. While some individuals felt deceived and viewed the situation as an unfortunate experience, the more devoted members found ways to reinterpret the circumstances, convincing themselves that they had been right all along and that their efforts had ultimately saved the world. This shift in perception seemed to serve as a defense mechanism for their beliefs and actions (Cooper, 2007; Cooper, 1998). Since that time, the ideas outlined in this work have come to be known as "Cognitive Dissonance Theory" (Festinger, 1957). The disciplines of social psychology and marketing research have both thoroughly examined Leon Festinger's Theory of Dissonance (Kağıtçıbaşı and Cemalcılar, 2014). The concept of cognitive dissonance states that it is a psychological phenomenon that arises when an individual's beliefs and the evidence that supports them contradict (Festinger, 1957). When a cognitive conflict arises, shoppers rely on a variety of elements, including beliefs, opinions, emotions, and intentions (Nordvall, 2014). As a result, that individual tries harder to lessen or eradicate the condition of conflict to achieve a state of balance between his views, patterns, viewpoints, and his traits, conduct, and circumstances. We must have a deeper comprehension of the circumstances that lead to cognitive dissonance to comprehend it as a motivating situation. Perhaps the simplest way to define dissonance is in terms of what one expects. All of us have developed a great deal of standards about what goes well and what doesn't throughout our lives. There is discomfort when such a standard is not met (Festinger, 1962).

According to Festinger (1957), dissonance between concepts is a state in which beliefs, attitudes, and actions conflict and cause discomfort. This makes a person want to change one of these things to bring the other aspects back into balance. Numerous studies have explored cognitive dissonance theory through various experimental designs. (Kretchmar, 2008) suggests that in free-choice situations, coercion can eliminate dissonance if a person is forced to act against their beliefs. In contrast,

(Festinger and Carlsmith,1959) found that dissonance arises in forced compliance situations when individuals behave contrary to their attitudes. People may express beliefs differently in private versus public settings. Additionally, in effort justification scenarios, dissonance increases when individuals engage in an unpleasant task to achieve desirable outcomes. To reduce this dissonance, they may exaggerate the quality of the results associated with the task.

As per the literature, since the development of the theory of cognitive dissonance, there has been an ample amount of studies conducted and published, (Aronson, 1992; Brehm & Cohen, 1962; Cummings & Venkatesan, 1976; Egan et al., 2007; Harmon-Jones & Mills, 2019; Hunt, 1970; Kim, 2011; O'Neill & Palmer, 2004; Oshikawa, 1968; Powers & Jack, 2013; Soutar & Sweeney, 2003; Sweeney &, Hausknecht, 2000; Telci et al., 2011). Numerous scholars have sought to challenge the cognitive dissonance theory through various avenues. Some aimed to disprove it (Chapanis & Chapanis, 1964; Elms & Janis, 1965; Rosenberg, 1965), while others proposed revisions to the original theory (Linder, Cooper, & Jones, 1967). Critics introduced alternative concepts such as individual actions and self-esteem (Aronson & Carlsmith, 1968), the distinction between attitude and behavior (Bem, 1967), unintended consequences (Cooper & Fazio, 1984), self-awareness (Duval & Wicklund, 1972), and moral integrity (Steele, 1988). Despite these efforts, Leon Festinger and his colleagues gradually established a theory that garnered substantial empirical support, preventing any of the alternative proposals from overshadowing it. Over time, cognitive dissonance theory has found a significant application in marketing, as it helps analyze the discomfort customers experience during their purchasing decisions.

Technology Acceptance Model (TAM)

TAM is widely recognized as one of the most effective frameworks for predicting and understanding why customers choose to adopt and use new technologies. Originally proposed by Davis in 1989, this model has since been extensively referenced in research to examine the elements that affect user acceptance of innovative technological solutions (Davis, 1989; Davis et al., 1989). By examining key concepts such as "perceived ease of use" and "perceived usefulness", TAM provides valuable insights into consumer behavior in the context of technological advancements. Although TAM is a very effective tool for forecasting customers' technology adoption, its structures have certain limits. To address the issue, the model must be modified to fit the particular circumstances, for example, by integrating TAM with different frameworks (Song et al., 2022). This model builds upon Ajzen and Fishbein's Theory of Reasoned Action (TRA), originally proposed in 1975. TAM replaces the attitude measurements used in TRA with specific factors influencing technology adoption, namely "Perceived Usefulness" (PU) and "Perceived Ease of Use" (PEU) (Fishbein and Ajzen, 1975). According to Davis et al. (1989), PEU is understood as the level to which someone feels that utilizing a specific system demands little effort. In contrast, perceived usefulness (PU) refers to the extent to which an individual believes that using the system can enhance their job performance.

The acceptability of Information Technology (IT) systems, particularly within the realm of e-commerce, is often evaluated from the perspective of the TAM, with further contributions from researchers (Davis, 1989; Zaineldeen et al., 2020). This model serves as a fundamental framework for understanding consumer behavior in online shopping, where individuals engage with various digital platforms to acquire goods and services. In pursuit of fostering more effective IT systems for online shopping, researchers have delved into the intricacies of user interaction and experience, culminating in a theoretical framework informed by contemporary studies on the use of online shopping technologies, (Klopping and McKinney, 2004). As digital marketing continues to evolve, it provides businesses with innovative channels to communicate not only with consumers but also with crucial stakeholders, including suppliers and employers. This transformation in the marketing landscape has led millions of individuals to explore a multitude of websites, seeking knowledge and engagement in the world of digital marketing, as evidenced by the works of Ahamed et al. (2020), Akhlaq and Ahmed (2016), Y. Chen and Barnes (2007), and even as far back as Hassan et al. (1970). This vast interest underscores the significant impact of technology on consumer experiences in the online marketplace (Jiang et al., 2009).

Theory of Planned Behaviour (TPB)

The two prominent frameworks frequently employed in research to comprehend the facts that influence individuals' intent when it comes to online purchasing behavior are the theory of planned behavior (TPB) and the technology acceptance model (TAM). Among these established theories, the TAM has proven to be particularly effective in serving as a theoretical framework for predicting both the intentions and actual behaviors of online shoppers. By examining how users perceive and accept technology, TAM provides valuable insights into the motivations driving online buying decisions, thus serving a deeper understanding of consumer behavior in the digital marketplace (Gefen et al., 2003a; Gefen et al., 2003b; Pavlou, 2003; Shim & Lee, 2011).

The Theory of Planned Behavior (TPB) was introduced by Ajzen (1991) as an extension of the earlier Theory of Reasoned Action (TRA) (Fishbein & Ajzen, 1975). The key advancement of TPB lies in the incorporation of a new element known as "Perceived Behavioral Control." This addition acknowledges that people's opinions about their capacity to carry out an activity can significantly influence their intentions and actions.

According to the TPB framework, a consumer's "Behavioral Intention," which is an indicator of how likely they are to participate in a particular activity, is shaped by three primary factors:

1. Attitude: This indicates how favorably or unfavorably the person views the action in question. A favorable attitude is likely to enhance the intention to perform that behavior.
2. Subjective Norms: This factor encompasses the perceived social pressures that influence an individual's decision-making. If important others (e.g., friends, family, or society at large) are supportive of a behavior, the likelihood of someone intending to engage in that conduct is higher.
3. Perceived Behavioral Control: This element relates to how simple or complex the conduct is seen to be by the individual. It is akin to self-efficacy beliefs, where higher assurance in one's capacity to act leads to a stronger intention to do so.

TPB has gained widespread acceptance in academic research, primarily due to its robust capability to predict behavioral intentions in various contexts, particularly in consumer behavior research. In the realm of online shopping, for instance, empirical studies have demonstrated the model's effectiveness in capturing the nuances of consumer attitudes and motivations. Research conducted by (George, 2004) and (Hansen et al., 2004) has evidenced the model's compatibility with online consumer behavior. Specifically, the work by (Hansen et al., 2004) involved a comparative analysis of both the TRA and TPB models. Their findings revealed that the TPB provides a more accurate and comprehensive explanation of consumer behavior than its predecessor, TRA. This suggests that the additional consideration of Perceived Behavioral Control is crucial for understanding and predicting the complexities of consumer intentions and actions in various contexts, including digital platforms. The concept of intention, along with its various theoretical interpretations, was initially articulated in the development of the theory of planned behavior (Ajzen, 1985) without a direct link to actual behavior. Instead, it focused on the effort to engage in a specific action. Subsequent research by (Schifter & Ajzen, 1985; Ajzen & Madden, 1986) discovered that inquiries regarding the intent to perform a behavior had a significant correlation with measures of actual behavior performance. As a result, these later measures have been widely adopted in subsequent studies due to their simplicity, now allowing researchers to describe variables more straightforwardly in terms of behavioral performance. For further insights into the notion of striving to achieve a behavioral goal, the work of Bagozzi and Warshaw (1990) also contributed a lot.

LITERATURE REVIEW

Internet shopping has emerged as one of the most popular and extensively utilized ways for people to shop in the past few decades (Morganti & Minelli, 2021). When consumers find themselves faced with decisions about what products to purchase, they increasingly rely on the vast resources of the Internet for guidance and information. A crucial initial phase in this process is the search for consumer insights and reviews (Awajan et al., 2021), which can significantly influence their choices. For businesses aiming to boost both their online and offline sales, it is essential to gain a deep understanding of the way customers navigate this landscape of information. Typically, the journey begins with the identification of a problem or need, prompting consumers to embark on a search for relevant information. Following this stage, consumers engage in evaluating alternative options (Martins et al., 2015), and formulation of a purchase decision. Companies that grasp these distinct steps in consumer behavior can tailor their strategies to enhance their clients' overall buying journey by better meeting their demands (Etco et al., 2017). Online buying refers to purchasing goods and services directly from sellers without intermediaries. It offers buyers a wide selection of products and the ability to compare prices for the best deals (Aziz and Wahid, 2018).

Additional research revealed that the main factors influencing purchasing online are quality of service, availability, low prices, offers, comparisons, convenience of use (L. Jiang et al., 2011), time, and variety of possibilities (Al-Debei et al., 2015). Furthermore, the design and features of a site may encourage shoppers to make purchases online (Buhalis et al., 2020). The actions done by online retailers to offer a range of incentives have significantly increased visitor numbers. Many consumers are enticed to shop on the websites of online giants on social media like Facebook, Instagram, Whats app, etc, and e-commerce sites such as Flipkart, Walmart, Amazon, and others by their constant advertisements of high discounts and exclusive offers. With enticing advertisements, companies like Myntra, Nykaa, Meesho, MakeMyTrip, Trivago, and others are attracting customers (Limbu et al., 2011). Despite all the advantages, internet shopping may be risky and untrustworthy to some customers. Despite having various factors, the level of consonance or dissonance experienced at the moment of purchase is also a crucial factor influencing repeat purchases. During the pre-decision or post-purchase stages of the decision-making process, consumers may experience cognitive dissonance—a concept that originates from social psychology—when there is a discrepancy between their expectations and their actual experiences. Festinger's Theory of Cognitive Dissonance (1957) suggests that this psychological discomfort prompts individuals to seek out solutions in various ways, such as reassessing their evaluation of the options, gathering new information, or altering their attitudes (Rina et al., 2024).

One more reason for dissonance among consumers is the rise of deepfake advertising of products and services, which further hampers the trust of consumers (Whittaker et al., 2021). The process of creating advertisements traditionally starts with commercials, but as technology continues to evolve, digital ads have taken the lead. Artificial intelligence (AI) and machine learning are two recent technological advancements that are challenging the traditional concepts of advertising and its content (Campbell et al., 2020; Li, 2019; Qin and Jiang, 2019). The rise of "synthetic" advertising is replacing content that was previously created and modified solely through analog and digital means (Campbell et al., 2022). Nowadays, AI-powered advertising is making significant inroads, often referred to as "synthetic advertising." This innovative approach marks a new frontier in the world of advertising, enabling the modification and tailoring of data across multiple ad versions. In synthetic advertising, we utilize advanced AI algorithms like deepfake and generative adversarial networks (GANs) to craft and adjust our advertisements (Kamble & Chaudhari, 2025). In today's interconnected world, the integration of artificial intelligence (André et al., 2018) into digital communication processes brings forth new challenges. One of the most pressing threats that undermines the reliability and quality of information is the rise of deepfakes, which are created using AI technology (Vizoso et al., 2021).

Benefits and Challenges of Deepfakes in the Field of Marketing

Although synthetic technology has many potential uses, most of the time it is employed maliciously. Long-term or short-term negative effects on our society are caused by the unethical usage of Deepfake technology. Those who use social media or other shopping sites frequently run a danger of falling for fake information. Nonetheless, there are a lot of advantages to using this technology properly (Mahmud & Sharmin, 2021). Deepfake technology has positive applications across various industries, including movies, education, digital communications, gaming, social media, healthcare, and fashion. In e-commerce and advertising, brands can use deepfake tech to showcase clothing on diverse models, transforming targeted fashion ads based on factors like time and viewer demographics. This enables consumers to see how an outfit would look on them without trying it on physically. Additionally, the technology could allow users to create digital avatars for online shopping and try on items like bridal gowns or suits virtually. AI-generated voices can further enhance branding for companies and products (Westerlund, 2019).

On the other hand, deepfakes pose significant dangers to our political structure, culture, and economy by making it harder to distinguish between true and false information, eroding public confidence in government and consumer trust, and raising cybersecurity concerns (Aggarwal et al., 2020). They create more trust issues for the broadcasting sector compared to traditional fake news (Appel et al., 2020), as they are harder to identify. While access to real video can enhance credibility, deepfakes increase the risk of fraud. Additionally, they can mislead consumers, heightening market volatility and leading to psychological discomfort and distrust toward companies (Butt et al., 2018). This discomfort may result in negative feelings toward advertisements, influencing consumer behavior (Westerlund, 2019; Chen, 2024). The overall perception of advertising may be significantly impacted by misinformation and fake news, leading to increased skepticism and a potential post-truth society (Nyilasy 2019). People struggle to recognize fake content, creating a clash between rationality and irrationality (Moravec et al., 2018). For instance, exposing content as fake can sometimes reinforce belief in that content. Additionally, even when consumers are aware that they encountered misleading ads, the persuasive impact of those ads can still linger, making them more influential over time, despite any cynicism toward AI-generated materials (Kietzmann et al., 2021).

Deepfake Advertising and Cognitive Dissonance

The term "deepfake" combines "deep learning" with "fake," highlighting how we harness deep learning techniques to generate content that looks real yet is entirely fabricated (Kamble & Chaudhari, 2025). Creating deepfakes involves employing a deep neural network to replace various elements of one creative work with those from another. This can include modifications to aspects like the face, voice, skin tone, gender, and fashion design (Kietzmann et al., 2020). Deepfakes have the potential to revolutionize advertisements since they are convincing, approachable, and innovative. The phrase "seeing is believing," which encourages individuals to believe what they see and hear, is successfully used by them (Granot et al. 2018; Porter and Kennedy 2012; Brucato 2015). Despite the fact that people are getting better at identifying fake news (Plangger and Pitt 2020), it is still tricky to challenge video "evidence". Deepfakes increase faith in media content that mimics the real world by making use of our believability criterion (Sundar, 2008). This presents a serious risk to advertisers because it is now simpler than ever to modify an advertisement by having a speaker say or perform anything they never did in a way that seems believable. This process utilizes advanced algorithms to blend and manipulate these features, resulting in realistic yet artificial representations. Intentionally manipulating content to implant false beliefs in the heads of others (i.e., misleading parties) is what it is, and deepfakes may worsen this and harm companies as well as consumers. The market is filled with dishonesty, which damages and erodes confidence in businesses and customers at large and creates psychological discomfort (Rahman et al., 2023). As consumers encounter more diverse and frequently unsettling information, they have to accept and integrate these conflicting ideas into their mental framework (Séré de Lanauze & Siadou-Martin, 2019). Uncomfortable feelings serve as a significant mediator between a person's attitudes and behaviors, driving the need to change how they act. When individuals experience a conflict between their established behavior and conflicting attitudes, they often seek to resolve this discomfort. They can address it by either adjusting their behaviors or by downplaying the importance of the new attitude. This adjustment process helps them alleviate the psychological tension created by the dissonance (Beatty and Kahle, 1988). The fabricated images or videos of products shown in advertisements mislead customers and when they become aware of this online fraud it often creates a psychological war in the mind of the individual on whether they should trust online shopping or choose the traditional method again.

Cognitive Dissonance and Consumer Trust

Customers may experience growing discomfort or conflict as they continue with the next stage of the purchasing process. According to some academics (Festinger, 1957; (Sweeney et al., 2000), there are two different kinds of dissonance: cognitive dissonance, which primarily concerns people's understanding and beliefs about themselves, and emotional dissonance, which is the unpleasant part of the decision-making process. Sweeney et al. (2000) also noted that there are two aspects of cognitive dissonance in purchasing decisions: "wisdom of purchase" and "concern over the deal." The duality known as cognitive dissonance occurs when the opinions of individuals diverge from actuality, which further erodes their trust in online businesses when the promised goods or services do not exist. The quality of the goods positively impacts customers' trust and inclination to buy. Furthermore, retailers who sell inferior items risk losing the trust of their customers (Jarvenpaa et al., 2000). The level of comfort that comes from knowing that an individual will act in a certain way is commonly referred to as trust (Mayer et al., 1995, Drake & Furner, 2020). It has been demonstrated that trust and intent to buy are impacted by various attributes including positive or negative arguments, and argument quality (Racherla et al., 2012) (Cheung et al., 2009). (Swan and Nolan, 1985), demonstrated how salespeople may gain their clients' trust by using their product skills and expertise, which may then have an appealing effect on their beliefs. Trust refers to the extent to which one party believes they can rely on the promises made by another, and it hinges on the perception of what the other side wants out of the partnership. Since relationships tend to be more enduring when trust levels are high, it is often seen as the cornerstone of various other dimensions (Yau et al., 2000; Berry, 2002).

DISCUSSION

In this paper, we discuss various existing research on deepfakes, deepfake advertising, and the positive and negative purposes of using deepfakes in marketing. This research helped in understanding the impact of deepfakes on cognitive dissonance and consumer trust. As technology is rapidly advancing, and new dimensions are emerging every day. Our study shows that deepfake technology is contributing to a decline in trust in online content. Although having lots of negativities, we have also discussed several positive uses of deepfake technology such as in e-commerce and advertising, brands can use deepfake tech to showcase clothing on diverse models, transforming targeted fashion ads based on factors like time and viewer demographics. This enables consumers to see how an outfit would look on them without trying it on physically. Additionally, the technology could allow users to create digital avatars for online shopping and try on items like bridal gowns or suits virtually. AI-generated voices can further enhance branding for companies and products (Westerlund, 2019). Our study also tried to understand cognitive dissonance among consumers when they encounter problems related to counterfeit products, fabricated information, fake celebrity endorsements, and many other issues. These factors influence customer's trust in online retailers and create a negative positioning of the company's brand. The profit generated from driving traffic to fake news websites through online platforms is growing at an alarming rate. This surge calls for a concerted effort to raise awareness among the public about the dangers of Deepfake technology and its potential for malicious applications. By educating people about the characteristics and implications of Deepfakes, we can help mitigate the spread of misinformation and the harmful consequences that accompany it. It is crucial for governments and various organizations to launch campaigns aimed at informing the public about these threats, emphasizing both digital literacy and critical thinking. Such initiatives can play a vital role in curbing the misuse of advanced technologies that can undermine trust and integrity in information sharing. The rise of AI-generated synthetic media is transforming marketing through deepfake advertising, allowing for the creation of digital influencers, tailored campaigns, and strikingly realistic celebrity endorsements (Chen, 2024; Dimuthu Maduranga Arachchi & Samarasinghe, 2024; Voramontri & Klieb, 2019). However, this innovation brings forth a host of ethical concerns, particularly regarding consumer trust and cognitive dissonance. When faced with deepfake content, consumers often experience psychological discomfort, caught between realizing the advertisement is fabricated (Cromer, 2015) and their emotional connection to it (Feng et al., 2023). Deepfake advertising has the potential to significantly enhance brand visibility and foster increased consumer engagement by creating highly personalized and innovative experiences. However, this technology also poses a considerable risk to consumer trust if audiences perceive that they are being misled or manipulated. As regulatory scrutiny around the use of artificial intelligence in marketing continues to intensify, brands find themselves in a complex position where they must skilfully navigate the intricate balance between ethical transparency and the creative possibilities offered by AI.

To sustain consumer trust in the long run, it is essential for brands to prioritize full disclosure regarding the use of deepfake content. This means informing audiences when they are viewing manipulated media and ensuring that such content is created and distributed responsibly. By embracing ethical practices and engaging in transparent communication, companies can not only mitigate the risks associated with deepfake technology but also foster a deeper connection with their audience, allowing for a more sustainable relationship built on trust.

MANAGERIAL IMPLICATIONS

Deepfake advertising brings both opportunities and risks for managers that must be strategically managed. On the one side, deepfake technology can improve personalization, lower production costs, and generate highly engaging content that resonates with customers. Managers, on the other hand, must be mindful of the ethical and legal ramifications of using synthetic media. Consumer cognitive dissonance—when people struggle to reconcile their idea of authenticity with AI-generated content—can lead to mistrust and decreased brand confidence if transparency is not maintained. To counteract these concerns, businesses should establish explicit ethical norms for disclosing deepfake content to customers. Regulatory compliance is also critical, as governments worldwide are increasingly examining AI-generated media to prevent misinformation and fraudulent advertising practices. Managers should prioritize investing in comprehensive consumer education initiatives aimed at enhancing digital literacy among viewers. These efforts should focus on equipping people who can differentiate between genuine material and that which is generated by artificial intelligence. In addition to educational programs, companies can explore innovative technological solutions such as blockchain verification or watermarking to assure content authenticity.

To effectively combat the challenges posed by deepfake advertising in the long term, organizations must adopt a strategy that emphasizes the delicate balance between innovation and social responsibility. This approach should harness the power of AI to foster increased customer engagement while firmly safeguarding trust. Furthermore, the importance of strategic brand positioning cannot be overstated. Open and transparent communication with consumers, combined with a commitment to abiding by evolving regulations, will serve as essential pillars for businesses aiming to utilize deepfake technology. By focusing on these critical elements, companies can successfully navigate the digital landscape, maintaining credibility and nurturing consumer loyalty in an increasingly sophisticated marketplace.

ETHICAL PRACTICES IN A DEEPFAKE-INFLUENCED ADVERTISING

- There should be no production or distribution of fake advertisement videos or content.
- There should be no invasion of people's privacy without their consent, which may result in stress, harassment, and other negative consequences.
- Concerns about ethics also arise from the lack of consent and transparency in the use of deep-fake advertisements.
- Marketers should ensure that their businesses are not promising any false claims that might mislead their customers, impacting their trust in the brand.
- Brands must use deep-fake technology to enhance creativity, not to mislead or share misinformation.

The technique known as deepfake has become a potent instrument with a range of beneficial applications, but it simultaneously harbors serious risks that warrant scrutiny. The potential for misuse of this advanced technology is alarming; it can be exploited to spread misinformation, infringe upon individual privacy rights, and inflict personal harm on unsuspecting victims. These significant concerns highlight the urgent need for systematic regulation and oversight to mitigate its negative impacts. As this technology advances at a rapid pace, governments across the globe are diligently engaged in the formulation of new legislative measures. These efforts aim to establish safeguards that safeguard both people and society at large from the malicious uses of deepfake technology, ensuring that its benefits can be harnessed without compromising safety or integrity (Kamble & Chaudhari, 2025).

CONCLUSION

The advancements in information and communication technology (ICT), shopping, and various maintenance tasks can now be easily managed from the comfort of the home. The rise of teleshopping in the late 20th century paved the way for the online shopping phenomenon we see today. One of the earliest studies on how attitudes influence the choice of shopping methods, whether in-store or via teleshopping, utilizing expressed preference data (Koppelman et al.,1991). The marketers use various AI-enabled technologies because they want to allure and retain them for a longer period. But in this greed, they often use synthetic or fake advertising (deepfakes) to attract customers which sometimes backfires them resulting in customers losing interest in their products or offerings. In today's competitive market, marketers are engaged in a relentless battle for every dollar in the consumer's wallet. They strive to enhance consumer satisfaction and evoke feelings of delight, yet the amount of information that is available to customers is overwhelming. about a myriad of products. This influx of choices often leads to confusion, resulting in cognitive dissonance—a psychological state where a person experiences discomfort due to holding conflicting beliefs or attitudes about a purchase. Given this complex landscape, it becomes increasingly essential for organizations to manage the post-purchase experience and the subsequent feelings of their customers. There is a profound necessity for businesses to focus on the actions and behaviors of their employees, particularly during interactions with buyers. Employee assurance and the cultivation of consumer confidence can significantly mitigate the intensity of cognitive dissonance following a purchase. Furthermore, more in-depth research is warranted to comprehend consumer behavior after impulsive buying decisions—especially when their engagement in the purchasing process is heightened, but the information available about the product is relatively scarce. It's crucial to understand how factors such as brand personality and various elements of the marketing mix influence the degree of cognitive dissonance experienced by consumers. Such insights will empower marketers to carefully select their marketing strategies and promotional techniques. The repercussions of ignoring these post-purchase dynamics can be severe, manifesting in the form of dissatisfied customers, the erosion of brand loyalty, and detrimental word-of-mouth communication that can lead to declining sales. These issues are intricately linked to the marketing actions taken by organizations and highlight the vital role of employees, particularly sales personnel, in reassuring and bolstering consumer confidence during and after the purchasing process. One more important thing is to effectively combat the challenges posed by deepfake advertising in the long term, organizations must adopt a strategy that emphasizes the delicate balance between innovation and social responsibility

By investigating the psychological effects of "deepfake technology" on consumer attitudes and trust, our research has effectively answered both the research questions raised at the initial phase of the paper. By obfuscating the distinction between truth and deceit, deepfake content causes mental confusion, leaving users unsure of what to trust. This lack of clarity feeds mistrust, which causes feelings of anxiety and a hesitancy to interact with potentially manipulative information. Furthermore, our research shows that fake news creates cognitive dissonance that severely damages consumer trust by making people more careful and less inclined to believe influencers, media outlets, or companies that may be linked to misleading information.

FUTURE RESEARCH DIRECTIONS

Nowadays, customers may explore and explore a wide range of resources for knowledge about products and services online. The opinions, advice, and information of other customers accelerate the inclination to make a purchase online (Ceyhan, 2019). The Internet gives people the ability to freely interact, share, and access information (Chan et al., 2019). The "ease of use" feature of the internet and the overload of information available on online websites sometimes makes an individual overwhelmed and confused by the mixed online review and such a situation of conflict is termed as "cognitive dissonance". Although the idea of cognitive dissonance has been extensively researched in the past, there aren't many integrated investigations that show how deepfake advertising is related. It was noted that while the reasons of cognitive dissonance resulting from individual circumstances and their consequences on businesses have been extensively studied, little research has been done on how synthetic media affects mental discomfort and trust among online buyers. In today's scenario where technology has become an important part of our lives, it becomes the utmost duty of the customer to be aware of every fraudulent activity or the fake ads being flashed on social media or other shopping sites. On the other hand, like customers, it also becomes an utmost duty of e-retailers to use the technology ethically to advertise their brands and not to mislead the customers and make profits.

REFERENCES

Aggarwal, N., Albert, L. J., Hill, T. R., & Rodan, S. A. (2020). Risk knowledge and concern as influences of purchase intention for internet of things devices. *Technology in Society*, *62*, 101311. Advance online publication. DOI: 10.1016/j.techsoc.2020.101311

Ahamed, A. F. M. J., Limbu, Y., Pham, L., & Van Nguyen, H. (2020). Understanding Vietnamese consumer intention to use online retailer websites. International Journal ofE-Adop- tion, 12(2), 1–15. DOI: 10.4018/IJEA.2020070101

Ajzen, I. (1985). From intentions to actions: A theory of planned behavior. In Kuhi, J., & Beckmann, J. (Eds.), *Action—control: From cognition to behavior* (pp. 11–39). Springer. DOI: 10.1007/978-3-642-69746-3_2

Ajzen, I. (1991). The theory of planned behavior. *Organizational Behavior and Human Decision Processes*, *50*(2), 179–211. DOI: 10.1016/0749-5978(91)90020-T

Ajzen, I., & Madden, T. J. (1986). Prediction of goal-directed behavior: Attitudes, intentions, and perceived behavioral control. *Journal of Experimental Social Psychology*, *22*(5), 45374. DOI: 10.1016/0022-1031(86)90045-4

Akhlaq, A., & Ahmed, E. (2016). Gender differences among online shopping factors in Pakistan. *Organizations and Markets in Emerging Economies*, *7*(1), 74–86. DOI: 10.15388/omee.2016.7.1.14216

Al-Debei, M. M., Akroush, M. N., & Ashouri, M. I. (2015). Consumer attitudes towards online shopping: The effects of trust, perceived benefits, and perceived web quality. *Internet Research*, *25*(5), 707–733. DOI: 10.1108/IntR-05-2014-0146

André, Q., Carmon, Z., Wertenbroch, K., Crum, A., Frank, D., Goldstein, W., Huber, J., van Boven, L., Weber, B., & Yang, H. (2018). Consumer choice and autonomy in the age of artificial intelligence and big data. *Customer Needs and Solutions*, *5*(1-2), 28–37. DOI: 10.1007/s40547-017-0085-8

Appel, G., Grewal, L., Hadi, R., & Stephen, A. T. (2020). The future of social media in marketing. *Journal of the Academy of Marketing Science*, *48*(1), 79–95. DOI: 10.1007/s11747-019-00695-1 PMID: 32431463

Aronson, E. (1992). The return of the repressed: Dissonance theory makes a come-back. *Psychological Inquiry*, *3*(4), 303–311. https://www.jstor.org/stable/1448979. DOI: 10.1207/s15327965pli0304_1

Aronson, E., & Carlsmith, J. M. (1968). Experimentation in social psychology. The handbook of Social psychology, 2(2), 1-79.

Awajan, I., Mohamad, M., & Al-Quran, A. (2021). Sentiment Analysis Technique and Neutrosophic Set Theory for Mining and Ranking Big Data from Online Reviews. *IEEE Access : Practical Innovations, Open Solutions*, *9*, 47338–47353. DOI: 10.1109/ACCESS.2021.3067844

Aziz, N. N. A., & Wahid, N. A. (2018). Factors influencing online purchase intention among university students. *International Journal of Academic Research in Business & Social Sciences*, *8*(7), 702–717. DOI: 10.6007/IJARBSS/v8-i7/4413

Bagozzi, R. P., & Warshaw, P. R. (1990). An examination of the etiology of the attitude–behavior relation for goal-directed and mindless behaviors. Unpublished manuscript, School of Business Administration, University of Michigan at Ann Arbor. Bagozzi. R. P., & Warshaw, P. R. (1990b). Trying to consume. Journal of Consumer Research, 17, 127—140.DOI: 10.1207/s15327906mbr2704_6

Beatty, S. E., & Kahle, L. R. (1988). Alternative hierarchies of the attitude-behavior relationship: The impact of brand commitment and habit. *Journal of the Academy of Marketing Science*, *16*(2), 1–10. DOI: 10.1007/BF02723310

Bem, D. J. (1967). Self-Perception: An Alternative Interpretation of Cognitive Dissonance Phenomena. *Psychological Review*, *74*(3), 183–200. https://psycnet.apa .org/doi/10.1037/h0024835. DOI: 10.1037/h0024835 PMID: 5342882

Berry, L. L. (2002). Commentary on relationship marketing. *Journal of Relationship Marketing*, *1*(1), 71–77.

Bolia, B., Jha, S., & Jha, M. K. (2016). Cognitive dissonance: A review of causes and marketing implications. *Researchers World: Journal of Arts, Science and Commerce*, *7*(2), 63–76. DOI: 10.18843/rwjasc/v7i2/06

Brehm, J. W., & Cohen, A. R. (1962). Explorations in Cognitive Dissonance. New York: Wiley. , J., Kakalejčík, L., & Ferencová, M. (2017). Internet i jego wykorzystanie w fazie przedzakupowej w Europie i Azji – Zarządzanie działaniami marketingowymi. *Polish Journal of Management Studies, 15*(2), 16–26. https://doi .org/DOI: 10.1037/11622-000

Brucato, B. (2015). Policing made visible: Mobile technologies and the importance of point of view. *Surveillance & Society*, *13*(3/4), 455–473. DOI: 10.24908/ ss.v13i3/4.5421

Buhalis, D., Parra López, E., & Martinez-Gonzalez, J. A. (2020). Influence of young consumers' external and internal variables on their e-loyalty to tourism sites. *Journal of Destination Marketing & Management, 15*, 100409. Advance online publication. DOI: 10.1016/j.jdmm.2020.100409

Butt, M. M., Yingchen, Y., Mohd-Any, A. A., Mutum, D. S., Ting, H., & Wei, K. K. (2018). Antecedents of consumer-based electronic retail brand equity: An integrated model. *Asian Academy of Management Journal, 23*(2), 69–99. DOI: 10.21315/aamj2018.23.2.4

Campbell, C., Plangger, K., Sands, S., & Kietzmann, J. (2022). Preparing for an Era of Deepfakes and AI-Generated Ads: A Framework for Understanding Responses to Manipulated Advertising. *Journal of Advertising, 51*(1), 22–38. DOI: 10.1080/00913367.2021.1909515

Campbell, C., Sands, S., Ferraro, C., Tsao, H.-Y. J., & Mavrommatis, A. (2020). From data to action: How marketers can leverage AI. *Business Horizons, 63*(2), 227–243. DOI: 10.1016/j.bushor.2019.12.002

Ceyhan, A. (2019). The impact of perception related social media marketing applications on consumers' brand loyalty and purchase intention. *EMAJ: Emerging Markets Journal, 9*(1), 88–100. DOI: 10.5195/emaj.2019.173

Chan, D. W., Olawumi, T. O., & Ho, A. M. (2019). Perceived benefits of and barriers to building information modelling (BIM) implementation in construction: The case of Hong Kong. *Journal of Building Engineering, 25*(1), 100764. DOI: 10.1016/j.jobe.2019.100764

Chapanis, N. P., & Chapanis, A. (1964). Cognitive Dissonance. *Psychological Bulletin, 61*(1), 1–22. DOI: 10.1037/h0043457 PMID: 14104612

Chen, W. K., Chen, C. K., & Silalahi, A. D. K. (2021). Understanding Consumers' Post-purchase Behavior by Cognitive Dissonance and Emotions in the Online Impulse Buying Context. *Proceedings - 2021 IEEE 22nd International Conference on Information Reuse and Integration for Data Science, IRI 2021*, 390–394. DOI: 10.1109/IRI51335.2021.00061

Chen, Y. (2024.). *Exploring the Effect of Deepfake-Based Advertising on Consumers ' Attitudes and Behaviors.*

Chen, Y., & Barnes, S. (2007). Initial trust and online buyer behaviour. *Industrial Management & Data Systems, 107*(1), 21–36. DOI: 10.1108/02635570710719034

Cheung, M., Luo, C., Sia, C., & Chen, H. (2009). Credibility of electronic word-of-mouth: Information and normative determinants of online consumer recommendations. *International Journal of Electronic Commerce, 13*(4), 9–38. https://www.jstor.org/stable/27751305. DOI: 10.2753/JEC1086-4415130402

Cooper, J. (1998). Unlearning Cognitive Dissonance: Toward an Understanding of the development of Dissonance. *Journal of Experimental Social Psychology, 34*(6), 562–575. DOI: 10.1006/jesp.1998.1365

Cooper, J. (2007). *Cognitive Dissonance-50 years of a classic theory*. Sage Publications. DOI: 10.4135/9781446214282

Cooper, J., & Fazio, R. H. (1984). A new look at dissonance. *Advances in Experimental Social Psychology, 17*, 229–268. DOI: 10.1016/S0065-2601(08)60121-5

Cromer, C. T. (2015). Consumer E-Commerce Dissonance: Innovating without Alienating Before Information Overload. *Developments in Marketing Science: Proceedings of the Academy of Marketing Science, 5*(4), 262. DOI: 10.1007/978-3-319-11797-3_149

Cummings, W. H., & Venkatesan, M. (1976). Cognitive Dissonance and Consumer Behaviour: A review of the evidence. [JMR]. *JMR, Journal of Marketing Research, 13*(8), 303–308. https://www.jstor.org/stable/3150746. DOI: 10.1177/002224377601300313

Davis, F. D. (1989). Perceived usefulness, perceived ease of use, and user acceptance of information technology. *Management Information Systems Quarterly, 13*(3), 319–340. DOI: 10.2307/249008

Davis, F. D., Bagozzi, R. P., & Warshaw, P. R. (1989). User acceptance of computer technology: A comparison of two theoretical models. *Management Science, 35*(8), 982–1003. DOI: 10.1287/mnsc.35.8.982

Dheepalakshmi, S., & Geetha, R. (2024). Exploring the Effect of Marketing Factors on Customers' Online Purchase Intention Using the Stimulus Organism Response (SOR) Framework. *International Research Journal of Multidisciplinary Scope, 5*(2), 334–344. DOI: 10.47857/irjms.2024.v05i02.0481

Dimuthu Maduranga Arachchi, H. A., & Samarasinghe, G. D. (2024). Impact of Deepfake Advertising Attributes on Consumers' Hedonic & Utilitarian Values and Brand Credibility. *Proceedings - International Research Conference on Smart Computing and Systems Engineering, SCSE 2024, April.* DOI: 10.1109/SCSE61872.2024.10550666

Drake, J. R., & Furner, C. P. (2020). Screening Job Candidates With Social Media: A Manipulation of Disclosure Requests. [JOEUC]. *Journal of Organizational and End User Computing*, *32*(4), 63–84. DOI: 10.4018/JOEUC.2020100104

Duval, S., & Wicklund, R. A. (1972). *A theory of objective self-awareness*. Academic Press.

Egan, L. C., Santos, L. R., & Bloom, P. (2007). The origins of cognitive dissonance evidence from children and monkeys. *Psychological Science*, *18*(11), 978–983. https://www.jstor.org/stable/40064856. DOI: 10.1111/j.1467-9280.2007.02012.x PMID: 17958712

Elms, A. C., & Janis, I. L. (1965). Counter-norm attitudes induced by consonant vs. dissonant conditions of role-playing. *Journal of Experimental Research in Personality*, *1*(1), 50–60.

Ertugan, A., & Mupindu, P. (2019). Understanding the relationship between celebrity endorsement on social media and consumer purchasing intention. *International Journal of Advanced and Applied Sciences*, *6*(5), 59–66. DOI: 10.21833/ijaas.2019.05.010

Etco, M., Sénécal, S., Léger, P. M., & Fredette, M. (2017). The influence of online search behavior on consumers' decision-making heuristics. *Journal of Computer Information Systems*, *57*(4), 344–352. DOI: 10.1080/08874417.2016.1232987

Feng, Z., Al Mamun, A., Masukujjaman, M., & Yang, Q. (2023). Modeling the significance of advertising values on online impulse buying behavior. *Humanities & Social Sciences Communications*, *10*(1), 728. Advance online publication. DOI: 10.1057/s41599-023-02231-7

Fernandes, S., Panda, R., Venkatesh, V. G., Swar, B. N., & Shi, Y. (2022). Measuring the impact of online reviews on consumer purchase decisions – A scale development study. *Journal of Retailing and Consumer Services*, *68*, 103066. Advance online publication. DOI: 10.1016/j.jretconser.2022.103066

Festinger, L. (1962). *Cognitive Dissonance*. Stanford University Press. DOI: 10.1038/scientificamerican1062-93

Festinger, L., & Carlsmith, J. (1959). Cognitive consequences of forced compliance. *Journal of Abnormal and Social Psychology*, *58*(2), 203–211. DOI: 10.1037/h0041593 PMID: 13640824

Fishbein, M., & Ajzen, I. (1975). *Belief, Attitude, Intention, and Behavior: An Introduction to Theory and Research. Reading, Mass.; Don Mills*. Addison-Wesley Pub. Co.

Gefen, D., Karahanna, E., & Straub, D. W. (2003a). Trust and TAM in online shopping: An integrated model. *Management Information Systems Quarterly*, *27*(1), 51–90. DOI: 10.2307/30036519

Gefen, D., Karahanna, E., & Straub, D. W. (2003b). Inexperience and experience with online stores: the importance of TAM and trust. Engineering Management, IEEE Transactions on, 50(3), 307-321. DOI: 10.1109/TEM.2003.817277

George, J. F. (2004). The theory of planned behavior and Internet purchasing. *Internet Research*, *14*(3), 198–212. DOI: 10.1108/10662240410542634

Granot, Y., Balcetis, E., Feigenson, N., & Tyler, T. (2018). In the eyes of the law: Perception versus reality in appraisals of video evidence. *Psychology, Public Policy, and Law*, *24*(1), 93–104. DOI: 10.1037/law0000137

GUSTI, N. A., FITRIANSYAH, F., DADANG, L., & RIZKY, Y. (2024). The Impact of Social Media on Online Shopping Behavior of Gen Z Consumers In Time of Covid-19 Pandemic; The Moderating Role of Celebrity Endorsements. *WSEAS Transactions on Business and Economics, 21*, 266 – 279. DOI: 10.37394/23207.2024.21.24

Hansen, T., Møller Jensen, J., & Stubbe Solgaard, H. (2004). Predicting online grocery buying intention: A comparison of the theory of reasoned action and the theory of planned behavior. *International Journal of Information Management*, *24*(6), 539–550. DOI: 10.1016/j.ijinfomgt.2004.08.004

Harmon-Jones, E., & Mills, J. (2019). An introduction to cognitive dissonance theory and an overview of current perspectives on the theory. In Harmon-Jones, E. (Ed.), *Cognitive dissonance: Re-examining a pivotal theory in psychology* (2nd ed., pp. 3–24). American Psychological Association., DOI: 10.1037/0000135-001

Hassan, M. K., Momen, M. A., & Sultana, S. (1970). Online marketing in Bangladesh: A descriptive study in the context of some selected click and mortar businesses. *Journal of Business and Technology (Dhaka)*, *5*(2), 150–165. DOI: 10.3329/jbt.v5i2.9986

Hazari, S., Bergiel, B. J., & Sethna, B. N. (2017). Hedonic and utilitarian use of user-generated content on online shopping websites. *Journal of Marketing Communications*, *23*(6), 572–591. DOI: 10.1080/13527266.2016.1143383

Helmi, A., Komaladewi, R., Sarasi, V., & Yolanda, L. (2023). Characterizing Young Consumer Online Shopping Style: Indonesian Evidence. *Sustainability (Basel)*, *15*(5), 3988. Advance online publication. DOI: 10.3390/su15053988

Hunt, S. D. (1970). Post-transaction communications and dissonance reduction. *Journal of Marketing, 34*(3), 46–51. https://www.jstor.org/stable/1249819. DOI: 10.1177/002224297003400309

Imaniya, T., & Agus, A. A. (2019). The Influence of Consumer's Decision Making Process to Online Purchase Behavior Analysis. *Proceedings - 2019 2nd International Conference of Computer and Informatics Engineering: Artificial Intelligence Roles in Industrial Revolution 4.0, IC2IE 2019*, 116–121. DOI: 10.1109/IC2IE47452.2019.8940898

Jarvenpaa, S. L., Tractinsky, N., & Vitale, M. (2000). Consumer trust in an Internet store. *Information Technology and Management, 1*(1), 45–71. DOI: 10.1023/A:1019104520776

Jiang, L., Jiang, N., & Liu, S. (2011). Consumer perceptions of e-service convenience: An exploratory study. *Procedia Environmental Sciences, 11*(PART A), 406 – 410. DOI: 10.1016/j.proenv.2011.12.065

Jiang, Q., Huang, X., & Chen, Z. (2009). Antecedents and consequences of consumers' trust in electronic intermediaries: An empirical study of hotel booking websites. *Frontiers of Business Research in China, 3*(4), 647–666. DOI: 10.1007/s11782-009-0031-1

Kağıtçıbaşı, Ç., & Cemalcılar, Z. (2014). Dünden Bugüne İnsan ve İnsanlar. (From Yesterday to Today Person and People) Evrim Publications İstanbul,168.

Kamble, A., & Chaudhari, C. (2025). Beyond Faces : A Conceptual Framework for Responsible use of Deepfake Algorithm in. *2024 International Conference on Intelligent Systems and Advanced Applications (ICISAA), January*, 1–6. DOI: 10.1109/ICISAA62385.2024.10829340

Karpinska-Krakowiak, M., & Eisend, M. (2024). Realistic Portrayals of Untrue Information: The Effects of Deepfaked Ads and Different Types of Disclosures. *Journal of Advertising, 0*(0), 1–11. DOI: 10.1080/00913367.2024.2306415

Kietzmann, J., Lee, L. W., McCarthy, I. P., & Kietzmann, T. C. (2020). Deepfakes: Trick or treat? *Business Horizons, 63*(2), 135–146. DOI: 10.1016/j.bushor.2019.11.006

Kietzmann, J., Mills, A. J., & Plangger, K. (2021). Deepfakes: Perspectives on the future "reality" of advertising and branding. *International Journal of Advertising, 40*(3), 473–485. DOI: 10.1080/02650487.2020.1834211

Kim, Y. S. (2011). Application of the cognitive dissonance theory to the service industry. *Services Marketing Quarterly, 32*(2), 96–112. DOI: 10.1080/15332969.2011.557602

Klopping, I. M., & McKinney, E. (2004). Extending the tech- nology acceptance model and the task-technology fit model to consumer e-commerce. Learning and Performance Jour- nal, 22(1), 35–48.

Koppelman, F., Salomon, I., & Proussaloglou, K. (1991). Teleshopping or store shopping? A choice model for forecasting the use of new telecommunications-based services. *Environment and Planning. B, Planning & Design*, *18*(4), 473–489. DOI: 10.1068/b180473

Kretchmar, J. (2008). Academic topic overviews: Cognitive theories. *Research Starters Education*, *1*(1), 1–5.

Li, H. (2019). Special section introduction: Artificial intelligence and advertising. *Journal of Advertising*, *48*(4), 333–337. DOI: 10.1080/00913367.2019.1654947

Limbu, Y.B., Wolf, M. and Lunsford, D.L.(2011). Consumers' perceptions of online ethics its effects on satisfaction and loyalty. Journal of Research in Interactive Marketing, Vol.5No.1, pp.71- 89. DOI: 10.1108/17505931111121534

Linder, D. E., Cooper, J., & Jones, E. E. (1967). Decision freedom as a determinant of the role of incentive magnitude in attitude change. *Journal of Personality and Social Psychology*, *6*(3), 245–254. https://psycnet.apa.org/doi/10.1037/h0021220. DOI: 10.1037/h0021220

Ling, K. C., Chai, L. T., & Piew, T. H. (2010, June 11). The Effects of Shopping Orientations, Online Trust and Prior Online Purchase Experience toward Customers' Online Purchase Intention. *International Business Research*, *3*(3), 63. DOI: 10.5539/ibr.v3n3p63

Mahmud, B. U., & Sharmin, A. (2021). Deep Insights of Deepfake Technology. *RE:view*, *5*, 13–23. https://arxiv.org/abs/2105.00192

Martins, C., Salazar, A., & Inversini, A. (2015). The internet impact on travel purchases: Insights from Portugal. *Tourism Analysis*, *20*(2), 251–258. DOI: 10.3727/108354215X14265319207632

Mayer, R. C., Davis, J. H., & Schoorman, F. D. (1995). An integrative model of organizational trust. *Academy of Management Review*, *20*(3), 709–734. https://www.jstor.org/stable/258792. DOI: 10.2307/258792

Moravec, P., Minas, R., & Dennis, A. R. (2018). Fake News on Social Media: People Believe What They Want to Believe When it Makes No Sense at All. SSRN *Electronic Journal*. DOI: 10.2139/ssrn.3269541

Morganti, F., & Minelli, E. (2021, September 16). Grocery Shopping Has Become Complicated. Managing Dual-tasks in a Supermarket for Patients with Alzheimer's Disease. *PROOF, 1*, 66–70. DOI: 10.37394/232020.2021.1.10

Nas, E., & de Kleijn, R. (2024). Conspiracy thinking and social media use are associated with ability to detect deepfakes. *Telematics and Informatics, 87*(November 2023), 102093. DOI: 10.1016/j.tele.2023.102093

Nordvall, A.-C. (2014). Consumer Cognitive Dissonance Behavior in Grocery Shopping. *International Journal of Psychology and Behavioral Sciences, 2014*(4), 128–135. DOI: 10.5923/j.ijpbs.20140404.03

Nyilasy, G. (2019). Fake news: When the dark side of persuasion takes over. *International Journal of Advertising, 38*(2), 336–342. DOI: 10.1080/02650487.2019.1586210

O'Neill, M., & Palmer, A. (2004). Cognitive dissonance and the stability of service quality perceptions. *Journal of Services Marketing, 18*(6), 433–449. DOI: 10.1108/08876040410557221

Oshikawa, S. (1968). The theory of cognitive dissonance and experimental research. *JMR, Journal of Marketing Research, 5*(4), 429–430. DOI: 10.1177/002224376800500412

Palací, F., Salcedo, A., & Topa, G. (2019). Cognitive and affective antecedents of consumers' satisfaction: A systematic review of two research approaches. *Sustainability (Basel), 11*(2), 431. Advance online publication. DOI: 10.3390/su11020431

Pavlou, P. A. (2003). Consumer acceptance of electronic commerce: Integrating trust and risk with the technology acceptance model. *International Journal of Electronic Commerce, 7*(3), 69–103. DOI: 10.1080/10864415.2003.11044275

Plangger, K., & Pitt, L. F. (2020). Brands and brand management under threat in an age of fake news. *Journal of Product and Brand Management, 29*(2), 141–143. https://www.emerald.com/insight/content/doi/10.1108/JPBM-03-2020-008/full/html. DOI: 10.1108/JPBM-03-2020-008

Porter, G., & Kennedy, M. (2012). Photographic truth and evidence. *The Australian Journal of Forensic Sciences, 44*(2), 183–192. DOI: 10.1080/00450618.2011.634835

Powers, T. L., & Jack, E. P. (2013). The influence of cognitive dissonance on retail product returns. *Psychology and Marketing, 30*(8), 724–735. DOI: 10.1002/mar.20640

Qadir, A., Mahum, R., El-Meligy, M. A., Ragab, A. E., AlSalman, A., & Awais, M. (2024). An efficient deepfake video detection using robust deep learning. *Heliyon, 10*(5), e25757. DOI: 10.1016/j.heliyon.2024.e25757 PMID: 38434385

Qin, X., and Z. Jiang. (2019). The impact of AI on the advertising process: The Chinese experience. Journal of Advertising 48 (4):338–46. doi:. 1652122DOI: 10.1080/00913367.2019

Rachcrla, P., Mandviwalla, M., & Connolly, D. J. (2012). Factors affecting consumers' trust in online product reviews. *Journal of Consumer Behaviour*, *11*(2), 94–104. DOI: 10.1002/cb.385

Rahman, A., Mustak, M., Salminen, J., & Matti, M. (2023). *Deepfakes : Deceptions, mitigations, and opportunities ¨ntym a. 154*(September 2022).

Rakesh, S., & Khare, A. (2012). Impact of promotions and value consciousness in online shopping behaviour in India. *Journal of Database Marketing and Customer Strategy Management*, *19*(4), 311–320. DOI: 10.1057/dbm.2012.30

Rina, D. R. I., Leena, D. R. P., Saranya, M., & Sreeprabha, M. R. (2024). Unraveling The Impact Of Cognitive Dissonance On Online Shopping Behavior And Post-Purchase Behavior: A Study Among Young Consumers. *Educational Administration: Theory and Practice*, *30*(4), 6768–6775. DOI: 10.53555/kuey.v30i4.2474

Rosenberg, M. (1965). *Society and the adolescent self-image*. Princeton University Press., https://www.jstor.org/stable/j.ctt183pjjh DOI: 10.1515/9781400876136

Schifter, D. B., & Ajzen, I. (1985). Intention, perceived control, and weight loss: An application of the theory of planned behavior. *Journal of Personality and Social Psychology*, *49*(3), 843–851. DOI: 10.1037/0022-3514.49.3.843 PMID: 4045706

Séré de Lanauze, G., & Siadou-Martin, B. (2019). Dissonant cognitions: From psychological discomfort to motivation to change. *Journal of Consumer Marketing*, *36*(5), 565–581. DOI: 10.1108/JCM-07-2017-2279

Shim, S. I., & Lee, Y. (2011). Consumer's perceived risk reduction by 3D virtual model. *International Journal of Retail & Distribution Management*, *39*(12), 945–959. DOI: 10.1108/09590551111183326

Sivathanu, B., Pillai, R., & Metri, B. (2023). Customers' online shopping intention by watching AI-based deepfake advertisements. *International Journal of Retail & Distribution Management*, *51*(1), 124–145. DOI: 10.1108/IJRDM-12-2021-0583

Song, Y., Yang, Y., & Chang, P. (2022). The investigation of adoption of voice-user interface (VUI) in smart home systems among Chinese older adults. *Sensors (Basel)*, *22*(4), 1614. DOI: 10.3390/s22041614 PMID: 35214513

Sonwaney, V., & Chincholkar, S. (2019). Identifying the factors impacting online consumer buying behaviour. *International Journal of Scientific and Technology Research*, *8*(8), 445–456.

Soutar, G. N., & Sweeney, J. C. (2003). Are there cognitive dissonance segments? *Australian Journal of Management*, *28*(3), 227–249. DOI: 10.1177/031289620302800301

Steele, C. M. (1988). The psychology of self-affirmation: Sustaining the integrity of the self. *Advances in Experimental Social Psychology*, *21*, 261–302. DOI: 10.1016/S0065-2601(08)60229-4

Sundar, S. S. 2008. The MAIN model: A heuristic approach to understanding technology effects on credibility. In Digital Media, Youth, and Credibility, edited by Miriam J. Metzger and Andrew J. Flanagin. The John D. and Catherine T. MacArthur Foundation Series on Digital Media and Learning. Cambridge, MA: The MIT Press, 73–100.

Swan, J., & Nolan, J. (1985). Gaining customer trust: A conceptual guide for the salesperson. *Journal of Personal Selling & Sales Management*, *52*, 39–48. https://www.jstor.org/stable/20832402

Sweeney, J. C., Hausknecht, D., & Soutar, G. N. (2000). Cognitive dissonance after purchase: A multidimensional scale. *Psychology and Marketing*, *17*(5), 369–385. DOI: 10.1002/(SICI)1520-6793(200005)17:5<369::AID-MAR1>3.0.CO;2-G

Tavares, D. R., Canciglieri, O.Junior, & Guimarães, L. B. (2020). A Systematic Literature Review of Consumers' Cognitive-Affective Needs in Product Design From 1999 to 2019. *Frontiers in Neuroergonomics*, *1*(February), 617799. Advance online publication. DOI: 10.3389/fnrgo.2020.617799 PMID: 38234307

Telci, E. E., Maden, C., & Kantur, D. (2011). The theory of cognitive dissonance: A marketing and management perspective. *Procedia: Social and Behavioral Sciences*, *24*, 378–386. DOI: 10.1016/j.sbspro.2011.09.120

Vizoso, Á., Vaz-álvarez, M., & López-García, X. (2021). Fighting deepfakes: Media and internet giants' converging and diverging strategies against hi-tech misinformation. *Media and Communication*, *9*(1), 291–300. DOI: 10.17645/mac.v9i1.3494

Voramontri, D., & Klieb, L. (2019). Impact of social media on consumer behaviour. *International Journal of Information and Decision Sciences*, *11*(3), 209–233. DOI: 10.1504/IJIDS.2019.101994

Wang, J., Yang, Z., & Brocato, E. D. (2018). An investigation into the antecedents of prepurchase online search. *Information & Management*, *55*(3), 285–293. DOI: 10.1016/j.im.2017.08.001

Westerlund, M. (2019). The emergence of deepfake technology: A review. *Technology Innovation Management Review*, *9*(11), 39–52. DOI: 10.22215/timreview/1282

Whittaker, L., Letheren, K., & Mulcahy, R. (2021). The Rise of Deepfakes: A Conceptual Framework and Research Agenda for Marketing. *Australasian Marketing Journal*, *29*(3), 204–214. DOI: 10.1177/1839334921999479

Whittaker, L., Mulcahy, R., Letheren, K., Kietzmann, J., & Russell-Bennett, R. (2023). Mapping the deepfake landscape for innovation: A multidisciplinary systematic review and future research agenda. *Technovation*, *125*(November), 102784. Advance online publication. DOI: 10.1016/j.technovation.2023.102784

Yau, O. H. M., McFetridge, P. R., Chow, R. P. M., Lee, J. S. Y., Sin, L. Y. M., & Tse, A. C. B. (2000). Is relationship marketing for everyone? *European Journal of Marketing*, *34*(9), 1111–1127. DOI: 10.1108/03090560010342494

Zaineldeen, S., Hongbo, L., Koffi, A. L., & Hassan, B. M. A. (2020). Technology acceptance model' concepts, contribution, limitation, and adoption in education. *Universal Journal of Educational Research*, *8*(11), 5061–5071. DOI: 10.13189/ujer.2020.081106

Chapter 17
Neuromarketing and the Future of AI-Driven Behavioural Design

Roshan Kumar Shiva
SR University, India

Geetha Manoharan
http://orcid.org/0000-0002-8644-8871
SR University, India

ABSTRACT

AI-powered neural marketing has transformed how organisations view and influence consumers. Emotion identification, real-time tracking, and prediction models assist AI-based neuromarketing in explaining subconscious decision-making. Traditional marketing leverages superficial data. The moral and ethical impacts of AI-based neuromarketing on client behaviour have not been substantially studied, despite progress. To close this gap, we study new technologies, their effects on marketing, and AI-neuromarketing synergy. Writing, case studies, and AI-enhanced data analysis employing wearable neurotechnology, emotion AI, and behavioural prediction models review AI-driven technologies. AI enhances personalisation, real-time engagement, and customer targeting but raises privacy and manipulation problems. Researchers, policymakers, and marketers may use the study's results to produce ethical and effective AI-driven marketing. This study's novel approach to AI and neuromarketing focuses on ethical responsibility and technical development.

DOI: 10.4018/979-8-3373-1152-4.ch017

1. INTRODUCTION

Neuromarketing and artificial intelligence (AI) have greatly transformed the way companies deal with their customers and are at the nucleus of how change in marketing is being experienced. According to Aprilianty et al. (2024), it becomes difficult to see how people work because the business environment continues to transform as people grow into their digital age. Through access to subconscious minds and leading-edge technology, businesses can align their plans with what the customer wants, feels, and makes decisions.

1.1 Understanding Neuromarketing

Neuromarketing is a very interesting field that studies how people react to marketing by integrating brain science and marketing principles (Srivastava & Bag, 2024). Neuromarketing is more profound than the standard methods of focus groups and polls, which usually reach only the surface level of what people think (Dey et al., 2024). It looks into the way our brains process advertisements, branding, packaging, and more, and thus gives clues as to what happens mentally and emotionally that goes on in a consumer's head in order to affect their decision-making. Suppose that you walk into a store and there is this really bright package. You might feel your choice was rational, driven by something like cost or usefulness.

1.2 Emergence of AI in Marketing

The whole mechanism of organizations on analyzing and processing customer data has been completely altered by artificial intelligence. As explained by Mittal et al. (2025), artificial intelligence is systems or technologies that can learn, analyze data, and even make decisions in tasks that typically require human intelligence. The power of AI in handling huge amounts of data and doing it so quickly and precisely is changing the marketing world. For example, AI can predict what a customer could buy next, depending on their past browsing patterns and purchases, even their engagement with social networks. Businesses would be able to offer personalized suggestions because of this capability, such as the "you may also like" section found on an online shopping website.

1.3 Why Neuromarketing and AI Matter Together

It is pure magic when neuromarketing and AI are combined. Although AI offers the scale through which such a finding can be acted upon, neuromarketing delivers insight into the "why" of customer actions (Umashankar & Charitra, 2024). When combined together, they afford marketers the opportunity to create experiences that are simultaneously highly compatible with human psychology yet personalized to each individual's tastes (Behl et al., 2024). Neuromarketing might find, for example, that a particular shade of blue creates the feeling of trust (Thapa et al., 2024). Based on consumer information, AI can understand which audience group responds best to that shade and adjust the ad or website design, respectively.

1.4 Purpose and Scope of This Chapter

Therefore, the aim of this chapter is to talk about the relationship between neuromarketing and AI and how they merge in an intriguing way to understand their effect on the future of behavior design. Exploring the principles of neuromarketing methodology and how it can be applied to consumer research and advertising will be the topic of the article. We will also discuss how AI is transforming the field of marketing through data analysis and customization, as well as automation (Khaneja & Arora, 2024) . The integration of these fields gives very deep opportunities in innovation. Businesses have the ability to create customized experiences to strengthen connections with their clients (Rachman et al., 2024).

1.5 A Glimpse into the Future

As AI continues to change and adapt, the use of AI in neuromarketing will only grow. Some of the emerging technologies are voice analysis, augmented reality, and emotion detection software, which are leading to the adoption of understanding and influencing customer behavior (Prakash et al., 2024). Consider a system powered by AI that is able to essentially track your mood and make your experience from online shopping more thrilling (if you are feeling adventurous) or comfortingly messaging you if you are nervous (Kajla et al., 2024). But with such great power comes great responsibility.

2. FOUNDATIONS OF NEUROMARKETING

Neuromarketing is an interdisciplinary field between marketing, psychology and neuroscience, which unearths unconscious mechanisms that guide consumer behavior, through a study of the human brain response to marketing stimuli (Rania & Zineb, 2024). With such improved understanding, businesses are now capable of formulating marketing strategies that truly resonate with consumers at a subconscious and emotive level. Traditional marketing practices, including focus groups, interviews, and questionnaires, base their decision-making on the conscious opinion of consumers. However, people fail to explain why they are doing what they are doing, thus limiting these tools (Alipour et al., 2024). The human brain processes a lot of information without the individual's conscious awareness, and most purchasing decisions are based on emotions, instincts, and gut feelings rather than logical thinking (Bernal et al., 2024). Neuromarketing offers a way to overcome this limitation by measuring brain responses to branding, advertisements, product designs, and other marketing elements (Kailash et al., 2024).

2.1 Definition and Historical Development

The formalization of neuromarketing occurred in the early 2000s. The term was coined by Ale Smidts in 2002, though it resulted from earlier studies on neuroscience, psychology, and consumer behavior. Experts have been studying for decades how the brain perceives information and emotions as a basis for the development of neuromarketing. Marketers used surveys and interviews to discover what buyers want. These methods provided valuable information, but often caught conscious reactions at the surface-level (Singh et al., 2025).

2.2 Key Neuroscientific Techniques in Marketing Research

Neuromarketing employs a range of neuroscientific and biometric tools to capture subconscious consumer responses to marketing stimuli (Sposini, 2024) . Rather than relying on lengthy technical explanations, the core tools, their applications, and practical constraints are summarized in Table 1.

Table 1. Summary of key neuromarketing tools, applications, and limitations

Neuromarketing Tool	What It Measures	Key Marketing Applications	Main Strength	Key Limitation
fMRI (Functional Magnetic Resonance Imaging)	Changes in blood oxygen levels indicating brain activation	Brand preference testing, reward evaluation, emotional branding	High spatial accuracy for deep-brain analysis	Very high cost, laboratory setting only, low real-world realism
EEG (Electroencephalography)	Electrical brainwave activity in real time	Measurement of attention, memory encoding, and emotional arousal	High time precision, portable, cost-effective	Sensitive to noise, weak spatial accuracy
Eye-Tracking	Gaze direction, fixation, pupil dilation	Website usability, packaging design, ad placement optimization	Direct measurement of visual attention	Cannot directly measure emotion
Facial Coding / Emotion AI	Facial micro-expressions indicating emotions	Feature testing, emotional engagement analysis	Scalable real-time emotion detection	Cultural and Demographic Bias Ridiculous Risk
Biometrics (Heart rate, GSR, pupil response)	Physiological arousal and stress levels	Measurement of excitement, anxiety, and engagement	Objective and automatic response capture	Cannot distinguish positive vs. negative emotions precisely

continued on following page

Table 1. Continued

Neuromarketing Tool	What It Measures	Key Marketing Applications	Main Strength	Key Limitation
Voice & Speech Analysis (AI-based)	Tone, pitch, and emotional cues in speech	Call-center analytics, voice-based emotional detection	Non-intrusive emotion monitoring	Sensitivity to accent and language
Virtual Reality (VR) + AI	Immersive behavioral and emotional interaction	Store layout simulation, product testing	High ecological validity	Expensive infrastructure
Multisensory Sensors (Smell, sound, touch)	Sensory-triggered emotional response	Experiential branding, retail design	Captures full sensory influence	Complex data interpretation

2.3 Insights into Consumer Behavior

Neuromarketing equips the business with the strong ability to understand the actual determinants that influence customers, which cannot be achieved only through surveys and focus groups (Paro et al., 2024). This knowledge empowers companies to craft an approach that resonates very strongly with customers, thus increasing the level of engagement, satisfaction, and loyalty (Khawaja et al., 2024). Let us look at the main findings that neuromarketing has unveiled regarding customer behavior.

1. Emotions Drive Decision-Making

One of the most important discoveries in neuromarketing is that emotions play a much greater role in decisions than reasoning. Although many people believe they are exercising critical thinking when deciding what to buy, in reality, emotions often play a role in the decision-making process (Devi et al., 2024). Advertising by Coca-Cola Company has always revolved around emotions such as pleasure, togetherness, and happiness over the past decades. While Coca-Cola shows the power of emotional branding, modern AI-based neuromarketing offers measurable results. When Audi tested its 60-second Quattro "Ahab" ad, the audience"s reactions were mixed and the brand connection was weak. Using facial-coding and emotion analysis, marketers identified a 30-second version that created stronger positive emotions. After launching the optimized advertisement, Audi achieved a clear business impact, including a 18.5% increase in annual sales, showing how emotional optimization can directly improve marketing performance.

2. The Subconscious Mind Matters

Most of our purchasing decisions are made unconsciously. Although we desire control over our choices, it is an automated brain process that dictates much of our behavior (Fahim et al., 2024). According to neuromarketing, for example, the color of products, sounds, scents, and even the way a store is designed will dictate our choice unconsciously. These unconscious triggers work by evoking instinctive and emotional responses rather than using the rational section of the brain. For example, sales signs and fast-food branding, such as McDonald's or KFC, frequently utilize red due to its association with energy, excitement, and urgency. Similarly, the music played in a business can also have an impact on how quickly customers browse.

3. Attention Is Scarce

Today, the rapidly moving digital environment weighs customers down with dozens of marketing messages every day. It traverses from TV commercials and billboards to emails and advertisements on social media. The boisterous presence of such information can drown a person, making attention a priceless resource, but one that is limited. In the midst of such clutter, neuromarketing helps marketers determine what captures and sustains the attention of their customers (Goncalves et al., 2024). The marketer can use technology such as eye tracking to pinpoint which areas on the website, posters, or film are getting the most of the attention.

4. Positive Experiences Build Loyalty

Deep emotional relationships are vital to building brand loyalty. A brand is likely to be associated with repeat patronage and even brand advocacy if customers connect a brand with joy, comfort, excitement, or trust (Giannakopoulos et al., 2024). Businesses can use neuromarketing to determine ingredients, such as interesting stories, personalized interaction, or an easy experience that can induce these positive emotions. For example, brands that would have provided such a smooth customer service experience would leave a remarkable mark. Brands giving such beautiful designs for a product or emotional advertisement can make way for the improvement of trust that enhances customer bonds and builds such loyal customers base which fuels long-term success.

3. ARTIFICIAL INTELLIGENCE IN MARKETING

Artificial intelligence is changing the marketing industry by empowering companies to develop more intelligent, individualized, and expedient plans. Artificial intelligence refers to computer systems that can analyze data, learn, and make decisions without human help. AI is a strong tool in the marketing world which can analyze large amounts of data, find patterns, predict how customers will act, and automate tasks that would take hours or days to complete (Bansal et al., 2024). The way marketers interact with audiences has changed with AI.

3.1 AI Technologies that transform marketing

New opportunities are to be met because of artificial intelligence technology, which is described by the following points. These technologies make it possible for enterprises to target marketing promotions, reduce operational drudgery, and process large information sets with remarkable accuracy (Alhassan et al., 2023). The key powerful AI technologies that are changing marketing are presented below.

1. Machine Learning Algorithms

A subfield of artificial intelligence known as machine learning (ML) enables computers to learn from data and improve their performance without being explicitly programmed. Marketing applies machine learning algorithms to analyze customer behavior patterns and predict future behavior (Tirandazi et al., 2023). Websites like Amazon and Netflix apply machine learning to recommend goods, films, or television series based on your previous usage. If you recently searched for kitchen appliances, perhaps you may see suggestions for products such as blenders or cookware. AI powered algorithms for billions of data, including past transactions, browsing records, and related behavior of other buyers, are going to drive up these recommendations for businesses.

2. Natural Language Processing (NLP)

The other major breakthrough in AI that is completely changing the marketing landscape has been natural language processing, or NLP. NLP is the ability of robots to understand, code and produce human language. It is the technology behind those kinds of sentiment analysis tools, voice assistants, and chatbots. Take, for example, a website's customer service chatbot; it allows you to understand your questions so as to give related responses

3. Predictive Analytics

According to Makori, R. (2023), predictive analytics is a system powered by AI that anticipates future trends and behavior based on machine learning, algorithms, and historical data. Marketing is the use of predictive analytics by companies to foretell their clients' probable next actions. For example, in e-commerce companies, predictive analytics can be applied to send a reminder or targeted offer at a specific time that a consumer might buy an item again.

3.2 Applications of artificial intelligence in Consumer Behavior Analysis

AI goes far beyond the traditional means of surveys and focus groups when it comes to depth, precision, and scalability in the analysis and understanding of customer behavior (Sengur & Goncalves, 2023). Instant analysis of gigantic volumes of data helps AI discover hidden patterns that would otherwise have gone unnoticed. For example, AI looks through browser history to determine what things or pages the user visited and how long they spent on those items. It also studies consumer behavior to know patterns like a busy season when people purchase things or a similar type of product that is purchased repeatedly.

3.3 Enhancing Customer Engagement through Artificial Intelligence

Client engagement is one of the greatest gifts of artificial intelligence to the field of marketing. While engaging in business-customer relationships in a dynamic trio of speed, rivalry, and relevancy brought about by efforts in the digital world, consumers demand personal, instant, and purposeful communication from firms. Artificial intelligence allows companies to do this through automated responses and data-driven decision-making. (Aoujil et al. (2023), we break down four key ways AI is enhancing client engagement below.

1. Personalization

Thanks to AI, customization has turned into a hyper-targeted experience with each business able to provide personalized offers, suggestions, and content to its customers' interests. What each user is likely to like can be forecast by analyzing vast quantities of user data by AI, all of which include prior interactions, browsing patterns, and purchase history. Netflix utilizes AI to suggest series and films according to customers' past watching habits, thus ensuring that there will always be something interesting and relevant for the customers.

2. Chatbots and Virtual Assistants

Chatbots and virtual assistant have also become a key driver of customer service provision by supplying instantaneous and twenty-four-hour service. They can respond to queries, assist the relevant clients to make an order, and even respond to accusations; this means that every question asked by a consumer has an answer. It means that through the communication with the consumer, a chatbot can independently and correctly answer the questions moaning the availability of goods or the regulations on shipments. It saves time and energy and customer/guest satisfaction as well as minimizing the annoyance level of consumers.

3. Real-Time Engagement

Machine Intelligence's power to process data in real-time is revolutionizing how firms interact with clients at thoughtful times. AI technologies may find ways to initiate new activities that would help sustain users' interest by analyzing their behaviour including, Web traffic, click-through and time spent per site (Rana et al., 2023). AI could automatically send a discount coupon to an abandoned basket of an e-commerce website to try to complete the transaction with the user by automatically sending a customized email or message. Such prompt action would raise the possibility of converting a consumer.

4. Predictive Recommendations

AI-driven predictive recommendation systems are changing the face of how businesses predict client demands and offer customized recommendations. Through past data analysis, including search activity, purchase history, and user interactions, AI can predict what a client would want next in terms of goods, services, or information (Adeola et al., 2022). Such websites as Amazon perform well in making recommendations based on past purchases, commonly purchased products, or patterns among similar users. These predictive suggestions can keep the customer interested with the site and improve their experience and save time.

4. INTEGRATION OF AI AND NEUROMARKETING

Neuromarketing and AI have disrupted the way in which businesses view and influence the actions of their customers. Neuromarketing, by using techniques such as eye tracking, EEG analysis and emotion detection, aims to reveal the mysterious influences behind decisions by the consumer. Through the combination of these tactics with the powers of AI to manage large volumes of information, businesses could claim a much better, richer understanding of consumer tastes and preferences (González-Mena et al., 2022). With AI integrated in neuromarketing, marketers can create advertisement that would be capable of pulling maximum engagement from the consumers with a high response rate, high conversion rates and loyal.

4.1 Synergies Between AI and Neuromarketing

The merge of usage of AI and neuromarketing leads to much better comprehension of the human mind. Utilizing neuromarketing, that now makes possible the comprehension of the emotions, of subconscious reaction, and other triggers effects of decision with senses (Gill & Singh, 2022). They all provide companies with something they have never had before, a level of accuracy in terms of forecasting, measuring, and optimizing marketing strategies.

4.2 AI-Enhanced Neuromarketing Tools

Artificial intelligence is propelling neuromarketing by improving the accuracy and the speed of analysis of emotions and behaviour. AI algorithms can analyze complex multimodal pieces of information (such as facial expressions, gaze patterns, brainwave data, and other sensory reactions) in real time. These enhancements enable marketers to have a better understanding of the response of the consumer.

4.3 Problem–Impact–Solution Chains in AI-Driven Neuromarketing

AI-powered neuromarketing carries with it several interrelated risks that need to be addressed if consistent and ethical consumer insights are to be detected. Emotional and physiological signals may be misconstrued, as an increase in arousal is not necessarily a signal of positive engagement and intent to buy and could translate into weak segmentation and misguided campaign strategies. Combining the information from a multimodal measurement with the insight of experienced humans minimizes the risk of coming to false conclusions. A problem of algorithmic bias is also at the forefront, e.g., models that are only trained on certain demographics of people, which may throw out cultural groups when making decisions or misclassify emotional responses. Hence the constant effort of auditing bias is required and more diverse training data sets. Use of biometric and neural measures throw up major issues of privacy and regulations with the need for transparent governance and consents. Finally, too much locking in automated forecasts will undermine managerial judgment AI tools should be used as strategic support systems rather than autonomous decision-makers.

4.4 Advanced Data Analytics

In neuromarketing, analyzing large volumes of data to helps reveal how people respond to marketing. This is revolutionary, as traditional neuromarketing methods always provide large, complex data sets that take enormous amounts of time and cannot be analyzed manually.

1. Predictive Analytics

AI-based predictive analytics makes predictions of future customer behavior using past information. For instance, AI could predict the nature of customer reaction to a launch of a new product or advertisement through neuromarketing history. This consequently gives room for success because the company can smoothen its plan in advance. Predictive analytics is very efficient in fine-tuning consumer experiences.

2. Sentiment Analysis

Sentiment analysis is the use of artificial intelligence to analyze the tone and emotional content of textual information, such as social media posts, reviews, and customer feedback. When combined with neuromarketing data, sentiment analysis provides a complete view of what customers think about a brand or product.

3. Customer Segmentation

These features would enable this technique to select and dissect the audiences into smaller and more specific groups. Using the insights that have been gained from Neuromarketing, AI is used to classify customers according to their emotional responses to ads. With the help of this classification, marketers can prepare and produce marketing techniques for each of these categories.

4. Real-Time Emotional Response Tracking

Another very innovative use of AI in neuromarketing is to track the responses to emotions in real-time. This means that companies can keep tabs on what customers are feeling and they can respond to it in real time with their emotions. The real-time feedback in campaigns or events using speech tone identification, facial expression analysis, feeling in social media, among others, can be supplied by the application of AI (Quenel et al., 2021). For example, companies could alter their message in real-time based on data that indicated the launch of a new product was getting fewer reactions and negative emotions from the audience.

4.5 Real- World Examples in AI- Driven Neuromarketing

The following case studies were selected to illustrate the application of AI enhanced neuromarketing in a variety of marketing contexts from advertising effectiveness and content personalization to retail experience optimization. Coca-Cola, Netflix, and IKEA cover three different industries and show how varying neuromarketing tools - from emotion AI to eye-tracking, EEG, and VR, generate quantifiable information to enable data-driven strategic decision-making.

1. Example 1: Coca-Cola — EEG & Facial Coding for Ad Optimization

Coca-Cola is a leading brand using neuromarketing and AI to improve its advertising . The company regularly conducts EEG-based studies to measure consumers' subconscious responses, focusing on key neural indicators such as attention, emotional valence, and cognitive load. These physiological signals point to specific scenes in an advertisement that evoke positive emotional responses and which parts of an advertisement cause the viewer to become confused or disengaged. In parallel, Coca-Cola employs AI-based facial-coding machines to test micro-expressions, i.e. tiny movements of facial muscles, which are signs of feeling happy, shocked or irritated. Machine-learning algorithms are then used to assess thousands of data points across different demographic groups in order for the brand to uncover universal triggers of emotion and culturally specific response models.

2. Example 2: Netflix – Emotion AI for Personalized Content

Netflix uses sophisticated emotion recognition technologies to take the personalization of their platform to a whole new level, well beyond recommendation algorithms. The company runs tests of trailers, opening sequences and thumbnail images through AI systems that track micro-deflections, the track of a person's eyes and the way in which they feel moment by moment. For instance, Netflix discovered that photographs with images of faces communicating emotion are registering higher engagement than abstract and non-communication digital content. Using these insights, its AI models automatically create multiple variations of each title's image in the form of thumbnails and assign the most effective image to each viewer based on their emotional profile and past interaction patterns. This approach helps in significantly boosting the click-through rates, viewing time and user satisfaction.

3. Example 3: IKEA - Store Layouts using VR+ Behavioral Tracking

In order to improve the effectiveness of their in-store layouts and product presentation strategies, IKEA combines virtual reality (VR) and AI-driven behavioral tracking. In controlled VR-simulations, customers "walk" through realistic digital versions of IKEA stores with their gaze, patterns of movement and emotional responses tracked throughout the simulation. AI-equipped eye tracking tools determine where the visual real estate is a point of interest, products that are left behind, and confusion or weariness when it comes to decisions. Motion-tracking data also identifies areas of navigation slowdowns or inefficiency or bottlenecks at areas of heavy usage. Facial-expression analytics mines for instances of frustration or delight and helps IKEA figure out how signage, color theme and height of a shelf make their customers feel.

4. Example 4: Luxury E-commerce – Hyper-Personalization for High-Value Sales

Luxury brands often struggled to demonstrate clear, short-term Return on Investment (ROI) with traditional marketing as they were only relying on the abstract brand equity and had long consideration cycles. AI-based neuromarketing addresses this issue by monitoring and analyzing customer emotional investment and subconscious buying intention in each and every digital touchpoint. Sophisticated AI algorithms are used to monitor micro-behaviors - time spent lingering on detailed product imagery, patterns of mouse movements and biometric capture through explicit digital consent - detecting subconscious value perception and desire. The highly-personalized online experience alters the structure and visuals of the website, along with product recommendations, in accordance with a person's emotional profile, which results in tremendous sales growth. Luxury brands that are taking advantage of this precise approach have seen up to a 30% rise in sales and reduction in corresponding cart abandonment rates. This is a measurable success and demonstrates that engaging with the emotions of customers in ways that are enhanced and tailored through AI is important to increase sales in higher profit areas and transform marketing beyond the awareness-raising process to behavior-changing processes.

Table 2. Real-world applications and measurable outcomes of AI-driven neuro-marketing

Case Study	Industry	Neuromarketing Tool	AI/ML Application	Measurable Outcome / Impact
Audi Quattro	Automotive	Facial Coding, Biometrics	Machine learning analysis of emotional engagement profiles	**18.5% increase** in annual sales attributed to optimized ad cut
Luxury E-commerce	Retail/Luxury	Biometrics, Transaction Data	Hyper-personalization algorithms	Up to **30% increase** in sales; **30% reduction** in cart abandonment rates
Netflix	Streaming/ Media	Emotion AI, Eye-Tracking	Personalized thumbnail image assignment (A/B testing)	Increased click-through rates and viewing time
IKEA	Retail/ Physical**	VR + Behavioral Tracking	Motion analytics, visual attention heatmaps	Optimization of in-store layouts, reduction of customer navigation friction

4.6 Behavioral Science Foundations Relevant to Neuromarketing and AI

1. Dual-Process Theory

This theory suggested by Daniel Kahneman and Amos Tversky talks about how people use two cognitive systems to make decisions. System 1 is fast, automatic and easy. It is emotional and more or less unconscious. It is this system that is the cause of most spontaneous consumer reactions. System 2 is slower and it requires effort. It is analytical and well considered. System 2 is used when people weigh complex information or attempt to override intuitive response to control. Neuromarketing techniques, like EEG and facial coding, are made trying to get this System 1 activity. They psychic and assess the immediate emotional and intuitive reactions before conscious reasoning takes place. AI effectively and widely applies this knowledge. It predicts what people are attracted to and provides customized content that addresses their subconscious.

2. Prospect Theory

Prospect Theory as it was discovered by Kahneman and Tversky is a theory of decisions people make. Individuals compare potential gains and losses to a personal point of comparison. They do not just rely on objective economic value alone. A key concept is loss aversion. This means people experience losses more strongly than equal gains. Neuromarketing research supports this idea. Studies show that loss-related messages activate brain areas linked to fear and urgency. AI-driven marketing applies this insight in practice. Machine-learning systems identify consumers who are sensitive to loss.

3. The Habit Loop

The Habit Loop refers to the way we are able to make any behavior automatic using a loop of cue, routine and reward. In the digital world, Artificial Intelligence works to reinforce this process by providing personalized cues, in the form of notifications, reminders or even personalized suggestions for users to re-engage. The routine may be to do browsing products, to watch content, or to interact with an app. The reward comes in the form of discounts, recommendations or other satisfying content to reinforce the behavior.

5. AI-DRIVEN BEHAVIOR DESIGN

AI-driven behavior design is a cutting-edge strategy, in which artificial intelligence can help predict, influence, and eventually improve customer behavior. AI uses data and behavioral insights to help companies craft strategies that drive customer action. From personalized experiences to predictive models, AI empowers companies to deliver of timely, relevant and context-aware interactions to drive consumer behavior, which leads to customer happiness and loyalty.

5.1 Concept and Principles of Behavior Design

The technique for structuring the way people think, make decisions, and act using the principles of design, technology, and psychology is called behavior design. It involves an understanding of the motivators, rewards and stimuli that can influence behavior and then using this to encourage behaviors such as a purchase, signing up for a newsletter or engagement with content. Three fundamental ideas form the foundation of behavior design:

1. Trigger

A trigger is usually a cause that makes someone perform an action. In behavior design, one actively places the trigger so that focus is attained and a response is provoked. For example, the shopping app may send push message containing the message informing about the flash sale in order to invite the users open the app and browse merchandise. This kind of prompt can be internal with respect to some need or wish or external as an alert or ad.

2. Motivation

Incentive is the way of a who when gets to an action. It emanates from incentives, passion or impulse and sentiment of interest or attraction that creates engagements. To lure the customers, what one gets to see is rebates, points if you want to visit the store again, or such offers for a limited period only. An example of this is a banner created out of a promotional phrase such as '20% off today only' will elicit the need to purchase and it will create the need to save. This is also the case with self-interest motivation being made by appeals to something like pleasure or an appeal to something like being special.

3. Ability

Ability is how easily someone can complete an activity. If the process appears to be complex or time-consuming, even the most motivated customers could do nothing at all. One-click buying, efficient user experiences, and intuitive website navigation ensure that customers complete actions without difficulty. E-commerce websites, for instance, Amazon.com renders checkout processes less complicated by offering the ability to have one-click payment options.

5.2 Role of AI in Shaping Consumer Behaviors

Because it enables organizations to analyze significant amounts of data, understand consumer behaviour, and predict future trends, artificial intelligence is a key tool in behavior design. Because of AI's capabilities to process real-time data, marketers can influence the customers at any point during the decision-making stage. For example, e-commerce websites employ AI to nudge consumer behavior through product recommendations generated from past search history and purchase transactions (ALSHARIF et al., 2021).

5.3 Behavioral Prediction Models

Behavioral prediction models refer to AI systems that use both historical and real-time data for future customer behavior predictions. They allow businesses to remain ahead of their audience as the behavior pattern analysis predicts such activities as clicks, sales, or content consumption.

1. Purchase Prediction

Artificial intelligence algorithms examine a variety of data points such as browsing history, cart abandonment, and demographic information to decide when a customer is most likely to make a purchase. An online store may determine, for example, that a customer purchases skincare products every three months. The shop gives the customer reminders, discounts, or product bundles in time through the information that they have obtained, anticipating when the next purchase date will occur.

2. Churn Prediction

With artificial intelligence, one can identify the clients that may unstick from or leave a platform. Most subscription services provided by Netflix and Spotify monitor the activities of their subscribers. Once artificial intelligence detects consumer's decreased engagement, the system can begin to activate re-engagement processes such as recommended specific offers or free products which help keep the client on board.

3. Content Consumption Prediction

These two, for example, uses behavioral models on the kinds of programs that a consumer is likely to continue watching in the near future through YouTube and Netflix among others. This makes use of artificial intelligence, which analyses the watching habits of the users and, on their preference, recommends related videos that interest them for longer hours. This allows for a direct boost to the overall user experience as well as harnesses the maximum amount of potential of the platform.

4. Sentiment and Response Prediction

Furthermore, AI algorithms can be used to anticipate the likely reactions of consumers to specific advertisements. The firm can even change its message to get the desired emotional response by reaching demographics, mood, and previous experiences. For example, companies introducing new products can have multiple versions of the ad and determine which would be most attractive to their target clients. Proactive marketing is comprised of the behavioral prediction models (Ioanid & Scarlat, 2021).

6. ETHICAL CONSIDERATIONS

Ethical issues of use for Artificial intelligence (AI) and neuromarketing are coming into focus as these areas develop. While these technologies provide certain useful methods to model and control customer behavior, these techniques throw several critical moral issues regarding privacy, opaqueness and the borderline between persuasion and deception. This means that businesses, regulators and academics should adequately discharge these issues for the general ethical and welfare of these instruments.

6.1 Privacy Concerns in AI and Neuromarketing

The defining ethical issue that comes with AI and neuromarketing is privacy. These technologies gather and analyse massive amounts of personal data including, internet, purchasing history, emotions, facial expressions, and brain waves. While this information is important to gain insights into customer tastes and preferences, in the wrong hands, the information can be the cause of some of the most heinous violations of privacy. For instance, neuromarketing technologies, including emotion sensing AI or faces recognition tools, may clearly monitor the customers' responses without their direct consent (Morton, 2022).

6.2 Manipulation vs. Influence: Ethical Boundaries

The line between influence and manipulation poses a critical ethical question in Neuromarketing defined as AI driven neuromarketing. Indeed, marketing always tries to influence behavior but AI and the capabilities of neuromarketing to tap into the subconscious emotional responses and psychological triggers, opens up the space for exploitation. Influence is found when brands use strategies of marketing towards consumers to drive them to act upon actions that correspond to their needs and preferences (Shenderivska et al., 2021). A clear example of the boundary between ethical influence and psychological manipulation is the 2012 Facebook Emotional Contagion Experiment. This particular study involved altering in an algorithmic manner the emotional content of newsfeeds for almost 700,000 users without explicit informed consent. The researchers have shown how they can consciously affect emotions expressed by the users on the subconscious level and decrease positive or negative content. The controversy that arose around this experiment emphasized serious ethical issues concerning autonomy, transparency and emotional misuse of data. It showed how emotional manipulation may occur when AI systems are platform-driven without user awareness or control of a system.

This example underscores the importance of AI-based neuromarketing agencies to ensure user agency and consent, and adhere to clear and ethical standards.

6.3 Methodological and Practical Limitations

Despite analytical possibilities with AI driven neuromarketing, some serious limitations of methodology and use restrict the reliability and generalisability of neuro-data. A key issue is the 'buy button' notion - the idea that certain brain activity such as in the ventral striatum is directly indicative of buying intention. Due to the multifunctional nature of neural regions, also, increased activity may not signify enthusiasm but rather anxiety or heavy thinking. In addition, despite the high resolution of fMRI, ecological validity is low because of artificial laboratory conditions and small, non-representative samples. Portable instruments such as EEG and eye-tracking are also limited because of technical issues, such as signal noise and limited interpretation of emotions. Addressing these issues requires multimodal approaches to data integration, AI-assisted pattern recognition, and an expert human to ensure valid, ethical, and context-sensitive interpretation issues, particularly when used in large-scale marketing decision-making.

6.4 Cross-Cultural and Demographic Bias in AI-Driven Neuromarketing

Algorithmic bias is a serious ethical and operational hazard in AI-based neuromarketing, and largely results from training data which do not represent global demographic and cultural diversity. Emotion-recognition systems, especially those based on facial coding are susceptible to racial and gender bias. Studies from the Mit Media Lab have shown that the commercial facial recognition models have much higher error rates for darker-skinned women (up to 35%) than for lighter-skinned men (below 1%). When used in neuromarketing situations such biases may lead to misinterpretation of consumer emotions, discriminatory targeting, and exclusion of various audience segments. Cultural differences also impact the interpretation of emotions, because culturally specific display rules govern the expression of emotions. Research suggests an in-group advantage for people's ability to recognize emotions: people's accuracy is ~9% higher if evaluators share the same cultural background. AI models trained primarily on Western datasets risk misclassifying emotional responses in global markets. To ensure fairness and analytical validity, AI-driven neuromarketing systems must employ culturally diverse training data, demographic calibration, and continuous validation across population groups.

6.5 Regulatory Frameworks and Guidelines

It is therefore imperative that there is special legislation in place to control the usage of AI and neuromarketing. Regulations across the world are coming into play the influence of consumer protection as well as technological development.

1. Data Protection Laws

Important actions towards ensuring privacy of personal information are California Consumer Privacy Act in the US and General Data Protection Regulation in EU. These rules require companies to obtain the express permission of users before they collect any of their personal information, they must provide a way for users to opt out of that collection, and they must provide transparency to the user on where and how data is being stored, shared and used. Such rules would demand caution from companies while collecting sensitive information such as biometric or emotional information for neuromarketing purposes. The consequences of violating the rules of data privacy are too serious to make the upholding of moral and legal principles an unimportant thing.

2. AI-Specific Guidelines

The newly arising ethical norms also relate to AI applications and, in particular, by the European Commission or IEEE. They guarantee the construction of AI systems operating morally on such values as justice, responsibility, transparency, and human monitoring of their activities. Thus, we should build our AI algorithms under principles of fairness and without prejudice. If the behavioral targeting AI model impacts specific groups in an unfair manner, then social inequity and ethical issues can surface. With transparent AI, the businesses using these approaches are held accountable for the decisions and the consequences of their systems.

3. Ethical Guidelines for Neuromarketing

Misuse of neuromarketing techniques has been prevented by developing ethical codes to which several professional organizations have laid down. It's one of them such as Neuromarketing Science & Business Association which referred to as NMSBA. In relation to criteria mentioned above the subject persons should be provided with complete information about the collection, usage and storage of their personal data, in order to give their informed consent for such processes. To prevent such problems, they also highlight what they call non manipulation which is also the topic of the next section.

7. FUTURE TRENDS AND IMPLICATIONS

The fast-changing pace of technology is certainly going to transform the relationship between artificial intelligence and neuromarketing. Long-term effects from developing technologies as well as more efficient artificial intelligence may shift how the consumer behavior and marketing strategies alter the involvement as well as interaction of a firm with its audiences (Ahirwar & Singh, 2025).

7.1 Emerging Technologies in Neuromarketing

Neuromarketing over the coming years will be brought by advances in technological tools which will allow it to capture consumers' behavior in real and more enhanced manner. Some of the most promising developments include:

1. Wearable Neurotechnology

Examples of wearables include EEG headsets and even the internally tracking emotion-detection eyewear which are growing increasingly sophisticated and available. The above-said technologies in differentiation to the controlled lab conditions are able to access the emotional responses and even brain activities in natural situations. Smart EEG headsets, for example, can capture the extent of engagement of a customer while shopping and provide insights on the impact designs, signs and placements of products and stores have on decision-making to purchase.

2. Emotion AI

Emotion AI, including face recognition, speech analysis, and even body language detection, is accelerating hugely. Such a system can provide companies with immediate clues regarding the feelings customers may harbor toward an advertisement, product, or service (Subramani & Manoharan, 2024). Future evolutions may permit customers to enjoy seamless fusion of emotion AI with augmented and virtual reality, that is, AR/VR, to provide immersive, emotionally responsive experiences.

3. Biometrics and Multisensory Neuromarketing

New technologies such as activity, heart, and skin conductance, and eye scanners will even more, elaborate the concealed sentiments of the consumers. AI may use those technologies for acquiring different modalities in order to determine how a combination of vision, sound and olfactory sensations impacts ones' feelings and actions (Ashtikkar et al., 2024). Brands can use this information in order to generate integrated marketing communications strategies that appeal to several senses at the same time. Moreover, as these technologies develop, they will tend to present marketers wider and more accurate information, which will enable more possibilities of innovative, local, and emotional-charged marketing tools and techniques.

7.2 Evolution of AI Capabilities

Several key trends in AI development are particularly relevant to marketing:

1. Enhanced Predictive Analytics

Organizations will be in a position to predict the customer needs with striking efficiency due to the growth of AI predictive analytical models which will be progressively sophisticated and defined. For instance, using data specific to the level of minute behavioral detail like scrolling speed or hesitance, AP proficiency might be able to predict about a customer's interest in a certain product. This in turn boosts rate of conversion through enabling marketers to offer suiting invitation at the right time.

2. Natural Language Understanding (NLU)

As the part of NLP which is oriented towards recognizing the human language aims and issues, Natural Language Understanding or NLU is a broader approach to the Artificial Intelligence. With the help of further NLU developments, such as the multi-lingual vector L, companies will be able to create chatbots and virtual assistants that produce customer sympathy and work in a contextually manner.

3. Adaptive Learning Models

Due to the incorporation of learning mechanisms, especially through batch updating means that AI systems acquire the flexibility to learn in a similar manner and adapt to new input. This means that marketing plans may be adjusted occasionally to fit customer preferences or cultural variation or even periods of time and so on. For instance, where people are not involved, the adaptive AI can, for instance, adjust an advertising theme due to regional or global trends.

4. AI-Powered Creativity

These creative marketing possibilities open with the introduction of generative AI technologies capable of producing text, pictures, and videos. It may compose interesting advertisements or text, but also develop unique video material for every customer (Durai et al., 2024). When the power of generative AI improves, the same creative endeavors is scalable in companies while the quality and originality remain on the highest possible levels. As AI continues to advance, businesses will be able to interact with their consumers in intuitive, tailored, and emotionally compelling ways.

7.3 Long-Term Impact on Consumer Behavior and Marketing Strategies

Neuromarketing and AI, when implemented into business systems, will produce long-term changes in consumer trends and in the approaches to marketing.

1. Greater Personalization and Emotional Resonance

Customers will over time develop of expectations of highly personalized messages that meet their sentiments, preferences, and beliefs(Mishra et al., 2024). Marketing is going to be more on consumers as opposed to products, consumer seeing value created through direct personal experiences giving a custom-made feel (Dangwal et al., 2023).

2. New Standards for Ethical Marketing

Because customers are slowly learning about how their data is collected and used, the practice of marketing needs to be transparent and ethical. In terms of the likelihood of success in their AI-driven neuromarketing projects, it is likely that brands placing trust, consent, and fairness as their top priorities will do better than those that don't (Bhardwaj & Chauhan, 2021). Ethical business conduct which used to be in the realm of the socially responsible will shift gears towards consumer loyalty and the reputation of the brand.

3. Increased Consumer Empowerment

Interestingly, through the use of AI and other related technologies, the consumers will gain more authority over their own decisions, while corporations obtain further tools to manipulate consumer actions in their Favor (Manoharan et al., 2024). For this reason, customers may employ personal AI assistants to scan and evaluate marketing communications with a view of receiving only that which is of interest to them. This change will force marketers to focus on quality and relevance rather than, quantity.

4. Redefining Marketing Roles and Strategies

Marketing as a job will also be transformed by AI driven neuromarketing, where marketers will no longer have to perform data-intensive tasks. AI integration will ensure that marketers spend more time crafting appropriate narratives instead of sifting through heaps of information or supervising technological use with its added advantage ensuring marketers spend more time in creating suitable narratives instead of wading through piles of data or minimizing technology misuse (Shukla et al., 2024). Marketing strategies will become less rigid, as marketing campaigns will be adapted as fast as it takes to accumulate real-time data and the change will be quicker and more efficient(Selvaraj et al., 2024).

7.4 AI–Enhanced Neuromarketing Implementation Framework

The success of adoption of neuromarketing systems using artificial intelligence needs streamlined and phased approaches involving a path connecting behavioral aims, multi-modal data gathering, sophisticated artificial intelligence analyses as well as effective ethical governance. For marketing managers, this integration means not only an upgrade in terms of technology but also a strategic change process. The framework outlined here provides a foundation to ensure that initiatives in applying neuromarketing will scale in a responsible way which delivers a return on investment and that consumers can keep trusting the organizations that implement neuromarketing.

Figure 1. AI-enhanced neuromarketing implementation framework

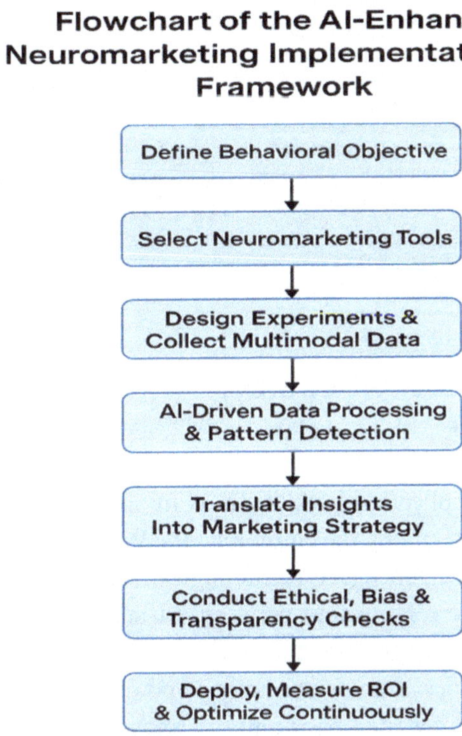

Table 3. AI-enhanced neuromarketing implementation framework for practitioners

Phase	Actionable Step (Marketing Manager Focus)	Ethical / Data Prerequisite
1. Define Objective	Align specific behavioral objectives (e.g., increase ad attention, reduce churn by X%) with overall business strategy.	Secure explicit, granular informed consent for all biometric and neural data; apply strict data minimization policies.
2. Data Readiness & Tool Selection	Select optimal multimodal tools (e.g., eye-tracking and facial coding) and assess data quality and diversity for AI training.	Conduct mandatory bias audits across demographic dimensions to prevent algorithmic discrimination.
3. Analysis & Insight Generation	Apply machine learning and predictive analytics to detect System 1 emotional patterns and segment audiences.	Ensure model transparency and continuous human oversight to avoid misinterpretation of non-causal arousal signals.

continued on following page

Table 3. Continued

Phase	Actionable Step (Marketing Manager Focus)	Ethical / Data Prerequisite
4. Optimization & Deployment	Translate insights into optimized creative design, personalized UX, and context-aware behavioral triggers.	Avoid manipulative practices and monitor emotional fatigue or exploitation risks.
5. Continuous Governance	Track ROI, engagement, and conversion metrics alongside ethical performance indicators.	Establish a cross-functional AI ethics committee and ensure compliance with global data protection regulations (e.g., GDPR, CCPA).

8. DISCUSSION AND CONCLUSION

In general, the understanding of the behavior of the customers and the possibilities to control it due to the application both artificial Intelligence and neuromarketing have evolved considerably among the entrepreneurs. We discussed about the developments of Artificial Intelligence (AI) technologies, which are the second purpose of the discussion and the relationship between AI and neuromarketing. Popular AI tools such as emotion recognition, data analysis, and prediction modeling have made it possible for businesses to create unique and engaging marketing messages. These developments offer the opportunity to transact business with customers at high and improved customer touchpoints resulting to customers being offered memorable experiences. As new technologies are made available such as wearable neurotechnology and emotion AI, these will increase neuromarketing, and even assist marketers to have a better grasp on what are the hidden factors that can influence the choices the people are making. The introduction of natural language understanding and adaptive learning models will be an important step in making marketing more accurate, scalable and innovative. The future of AI in neuromarketing is bright and has to be regulated. When used responsibly possibly these technologies can help businesses form stronger and more sustainable connections with their consumers and revolutionize the marketing discourse to be more towards meaningful interaction. Over time AI will advance so will be the ability for marketer to deliver ad products to customer that will meet their need and even enhance the standard of their living. For the positive force behind positive progress of good, transparent and consumer-oriented technologies in digitization that are neuro-marketing driven by AI, it is of the utmost importance to apply the application in conjunction with the set ethical norms, and to set technical norms.

8.1 Theoretical Implications

The findings of this chapter contribute to the theoretical advancement of neuromarketing and consumer psychology. They show how AI-based emotional and cognitive analytics improve traditional decision-making models. The use of multimodal neural, behavioral, and biometric data strengthens Dual-Process Theory. It provides real-time evidence of System 1 responses to marketing stimuli. Such insights are rarely captured through self-report methods. The chapter also extends Behavioral Design Theory. Algorithmic personalization influences the habit loop of cue, routine, and reward with greater precision.

8.2 Managerial / Practical Implications

The insights we discuss in this chapter demonstrate how organizations can shift from being observers in a reactive manner to behavior designers in a proactive and predictive manner. Managers can get more refined in customer segmentation and content development. This conclusion is backed up by quantifiable ROI results from the automotive and luxury retail sectors. However, for effective adoption there needs to be investments in ethical governance and skilled professionals. AI is ideal for use as a decision aid, rather than as an alternative for human insight. This type of approach is particularly important when interpreting emotional probabilistic data. Continuous bias audits are also required to prevent misinterpretation or the exclusion of groups of consumers. By guiding the organization as per Section 7.4, it can securely build trust and increase the market reactively and effectively using AI-driven marketing.

8.3 Final Conclusion

AI-driven Neuromarketing is transforming the world in which organizations can comprehend, forecast, and influence consumer behaviour by securing neural, emotional, and conduct data with advanced investigation models. This chapter demonstrated the convergence of AI and neuromarketing tools, which has a greater degree of precision and how they can give insights in real time, as well as how to better design behaviors. At the same time, methodological, ethical and practical limitations suggest the need for thoughtful governance and balanced managerial judgment. As AI continues to evolve, tying in AI responsibly, including being transparent in our use of data, being culturally sensitive and most importantly the broad relationship and development of AI bias with multiple teams and disciplines will be important in developing the most out of the potential that AI will provide in

REFERENCES

. Adeola, O., Evans, O., Ndubuisi Edeh, J., & Adisa, I. (2022). The future of marketing: artificial intelligence, virtual reality, and neuromarketing. *Marketing communications and brand development in emerging economies Volume I: Contemporary and future perspectives*, 253-280.

. Ahirwar, S., & Singh, M. (2025). Neurofinance Revolution: Emerging Technologies and Future Trends at the Intersection of Neuromarketing and Sustainable Finance. *Neuromarketing's Role in Sustainable Finance*, 205-230.

Alipour, P., Gallegos, E. E., & Sridhar, S. (2024). Ai-driven marketing personalization: Deploying convolutional neural networks to decode consumer behavior. *International Journal of Human-Computer Interaction*, •••, 1–19.

ALSHARIF, A. H., SALLEH, N. Z. M., Baharun, R. O. H. A. I. Z. A. T., & YUSOFF, M. E. (2021). Consumer behaviour through neuromarketing approach. *Journal of Contemporary Issues in Business and Government*, *27*(3), 344–354.

Aoujil, Z., Hanine, M., Flores, E. S., Samad, M. A., & Ashraf, I. (2023). Artificial intelligence and behavioral economics: A bibliographic analysis of research field. *IEEE Access : Practical Innovations, Open Solutions*, *11*, 139367–139394. DOI: 10.1109/ACCESS.2023.3339778

Apriliantу, F., Takahashi, M., & Matsuura, Y. (2024). Bridging Brains and Bots: The Impact of AI on Neuromarketing. *Procedia Computer Science*, *246*, 1830–1839. DOI: 10.1016/j.procs.2024.09.687

Bansal, A., Agarwal, S., & Arora, N. (2024). Market Grooming: How Neuromarketing Influences Consumers' Purchase Decisions? In *Market Grooming: The Dark Side of AI Marketing* (pp. 275-292). Emerald Publishing Limited.

Behl, A., Jayawardena, N., Shankar, A., Gupta, M., & Lang, L. D. (2024). Gamification and neuromarketing: A unified approach for improving user experience. *Journal of Consumer Behaviour*, *23*(1), 218–228. DOI: 10.1002/cb.2178

Bhardwaj, V., & Chauhan, R. (2021). Neuromarketing impact on buying behavior of customers. *Neuroscience*, 26.

Dangwal, A., Bathla, D., Kukreti, M., Mehta, M., Chauhan, P., & Sarangal, R. (2023). Neuromarketing science: A road to a commercial start-up. In *Applications of Neuromarketing in the Metaverse* (pp. 223–232). IGI Global. DOI: 10.4018/978-1-6684-8150-9.ch017

Devi, R., Bhopal, R., & Sharma, V. (2024). Decoding Neuromarketing Strategies: Unveiling Its Role on Brand Equity. In *Sensible Selling Through Sensory Neuromarketing* (pp. 184-209). IGI Global.

Dey, A. K., Das, S., Raman, A. M., & Khan, J. A. (2024). Exploring contemporary advances, infrastructure, and significance of neuromarketing in consumer behavior research. In *Artificial Intelligence and Information Technologies* (pp. 467–476). CRC Press. DOI: 10.1201/9781032700502-74

Fahim, I., Khalil, M. M., & Fatima, E. (2024, April). Unlocking Consumer Minds: A Comprehensive Exploration of Neuromarketing Techniques and Consumer Decision Processes. In *The International Workshop on Big Data and Business Intelligence* (pp. 355-364). Cham: Springer Nature Switzerland. DOI: 10.1007/978-3-031-65018-5_33

Giannakopoulos, N. T., Sakas, D. P., & Migkos, S. P. (2024). Neuromarketing and Big Data Analysis of Banking Firms' Website Interfaces and Performance. *Electronics (Basel), 13*(16), 3256. DOI: 10.3390/electronics13163256

Gill, R., & Singh, J. (2022). A study of neuromarketing techniques for proposing cost effective information driven framework for decision making. *Materials Today: Proceedings, 49*, 2969–2981. DOI: 10.1016/j.matpr.2020.08.730

Goncalves, M., Hu, Y., Aliagas, I., & Cerdá, L. M. (2024). Neuromarketing algorithms' consumer privacy and ethical considerations: Challenges and opportunities. *Cogent Business & Management, 11*(1), 2333063. DOI: 10.1080/23311975.2024.2333063

González-Mena, G., Del-Valle-Soto, C., Corona, V., & Rodríguez, J. (2022). Neuromarketing in the digital age: The direct relation between facial expressions and website design. *Applied Sciences (Basel, Switzerland), 12*(16), 8186. DOI: 10.3390/app12168186

Ioanid, A., & Scarlat, C. (2021, October). Neuromarketing tools in industry 4.0 context: A study on the Romanian market. In *International Conference Interdisciplinarity in Engineering* (pp. 370-381). Cham: Springer International Publishing.

Kailash, M. S. R., & Gautam Donga, C. S. K., NVL, C. J. F., & Sruthi, S. (2024). Neuromarketing: The Science of Consumer Behavior in Digital Advertising. *Library Progress International, 44*(3), 20211–20221.

Kajla, T., Raj, S., Kansra, P., Gupta, S. L., & Singh, N. (2024). Neuromarketing and consumer behavior: A bibliometric analysis. *Journal of Consumer Behaviour, 23*(2), 959–975. DOI: 10.1002/cb.2256

Khaneja, S., & Arora, T. (2024). The potential of neuroscience in transforming business: A meta-analysis. *Future Business Journal, 10*(1), 77. DOI: 10.1186/s43093-024-00369-7

Makori, R. (2023). The Influence of Neuro-Marketing Techniques on Consumer Decision-Making in Strategic Marketing Campaigns. *Journal of Strategic Marketing Practice*, *1*(1), 21–29.

Manoharan, G., Durai, S., Ashtikar, S. P., & Kumari, N. (2024). Artificial Intelligence in Marketing Applications. In *Artificial Intelligence for Business* (pp. 40–70). Productivity Press.

Manoharan, G., Mishra, A. B., Adusumilli, S. B. K., Chavva, M., Damancharla, H., & Lenin, D. S. (2024, May). Supervised Learning for Personalized Marketing Strategies. In *2024 International Conference on Advances in Computing, Communication and Applied Informatics (ACCAI)* (pp. 1-6). IEEE.

Manoharan, G., Preetha, P. N., Santhanalakshmi, K., Balaji, K. D., & Raja, V. (2024, March). Management of Business Using Machine Learning for Decision Making. In *2024 International Conference on Trends in Quantum Computing and Emerging Business Technologies* (pp. 1-5). IEEE. DOI: 10.1109/TQCEBT59414.2024.10545116

Mittal, S., Pandey, A., Chandel, A., & Hung, T. H. (2025). Leveraging Neuromarketing Technologies to Enhance Agile Marketing Strategies: A Study on Consumer Behavior Insights and Real-Time Adaptation. In *Digital Transformation Initiatives for Agile Marketing* (pp. 275-302). IGI Global.

Morton, F. (2022). Neuromarketing for design thinking: The use of neuroscientific tools in the innovation process. In *Organizational innovation in the digital age* (pp. 39–61). Springer International Publishing. DOI: 10.1007/978-3-030-98183-9_2

Prakash, N., Jindal, P., & Jindal, A. (2024). Neuro Marketing: Harnessing the Power of Cognitive Analysis. In *Sensible Selling Through Sensory Neuromarketing* (pp. 26-42). IGI Global.

Rachman, A., Diandra, P. K., & Simon, F. (2024). Emotional Artificial Intelligence and Brand Association: A Neuro-Bibliometric Study. *International Journal Administration. Business & Organization*, *5*(3), 1–16.

Rania, S., & Zineb, R. (2024, April). Integration of Artificial Intelligence in Neuromarketing: Ethical and Regulatory Implications. In *The International Workshop on Big Data and Business Intelligence* (pp. 278-291). Cham: Springer Nature Switzerland. DOI: 10.1007/978-3-031-65014-7_26

Selvaraj, F. J., Sheeja, R., Manoharan, G., Razak, A., Kukreja, J., & Ashtikar, S. P. (2024, June). Evaluation of Customer Loyalty and Customer Relationship Management in Mobile Communication Lesson from New Normal. In *2024 3rd International Conference on Computational Modelling, Simulation and Optimization (ICCMSO)* (pp. 216-221). IEEE. DOI: 10.1109/ICCMSO61761.2024.00052

Sengur, F. K., & Goncalves, M. V. (2023). Neuromanagement and neuromarketing: Neuroscience in organisations. In *The Routledge Companion to the Future of Management Research* (pp. 151–171). Routledge. DOI: 10.4324/9781003225508-12

Shenderivska, L., Krystopchuk, M., Nykonchuk, V., Kniazevych, A., & Shketa, V. (2021, September). Prospects of Neuromarketing Application in Communication Activities of Logistics Enterprises. In *International Conference TRANSBALTICA: Transportation Science and Technology* (pp. 682-693). Cham: Springer International Publishing.

Shukla, S. S., Rajput, K., Tripathi, S., Gambhir, V., Manoharan, G., Bukhari, S. N. H., & Younis, D. (2024). Artificial Intelligence as a Contributing Factor for Economic Growth and Sustainable Development among Emerging Economies. In *Recent Advances in Management and Engineering* (pp. 39–44). CRC Press. DOI: 10.1201/9781003532026-7

Singh, A., Singh, A., & Hooda, R. C. (2025). Neuromarketing Unveiled: Decoding the Science Behind Consumer Choices. In *Neuromarketing's Role in Sustainable Finance* (pp. 147-168). IGI Global.

Sposini, L. (2024). Neuromarketing and Eye-Tracking Technologies Under the European Framework: Towards the GDPR and Beyond. *Journal of Consumer Policy*, *47*(3), 1–24. DOI: 10.1007/s10603-023-09559-2

Srivastava, G., & Bag, S. (2024). Modern-day marketing concepts based on face recognition and neuro-marketing: A review and future research directions. *Benchmarking*, *31*(2), 410–438. DOI: 10.1108/BIJ-09-2022-0588

Subramani, K., & Manoharan, G. (2024, June). Humanizing The Role of Artificial Intelligence in Revolutionizing Emotional Intelligence. In *2024 3rd International Conference on Computational Modelling, Simulation and Optimization (ICCMSO)* (pp. 237-242). IEEE. DOI: 10.1109/ICCMSO61761.2024.00056

Tirandazi, P., Bamakan, S. M. H., & Toghroljerdi, A. (2023). A review of studies on internet of everything as an enabler of neuromarketing methods and techniques. *The Journal of Supercomputing*, *79*(7), 7835–7876. DOI: 10.1007/s11227-022-04988-1

Umashankar, K., & Charitra, H. G. (2024). A Study on the Influence of Artificial Intelligence on Brain Plasticity with Reference to Consumer Behaviour and Workplace Dynamics. In *Advances in Data Analytics for Influencer Marketing: An Interdisciplinary Approach* (pp. 323–339). Springer Nature Switzerland. DOI: 10.1007/978-3-031-65727-6_19

About the Contributors

Thomas Heinrich Musiolik is Chair Professor of Marketing & Technology at Woxsen University (Hyderabad, India), Visiting Professor at Europa University of Applied Sciences, Potsdam (Germany) and Visiting Professor at i-University (iU), Tokyo (Japan). Musiolik is holding an M.A. Management (Marketing & Communication) from FOM University of Applied Sciences for Economics and Management (Germany), BBA from Avans University of Applied Sciences (Netherlands), Diploma in Business Administration as well as Marketing and Sales Economist at the Academy of Management and Economics (Berlin). He is an expert for the European Commission and Editor-in-Chief of the Journal of Future Robot Life. Musiolik is also a scientific ambassador for Brain City Berlin. As a professor of marketing and technology, he's been researching the functions of the brain and the influence of digital media since 2011. His main research interest is in the variables that influence our experiences, regardless of the medium or technology used, and help create unique and memorable experiences. The aim of his work is to understand the creation of unique (brand) experiences and to continuously develop research methods to better understand consumer behavior. Musiolik is also researching the social changes that are emerging in the context of digitalization. In this context, he is addressing consumer behavior problems in the use of digital media such as a website or other information systems (e-learning, knowledge management, e-commerce platforms), and investigating how the interface can change consumer behavior. The overall goal of his work is to better understand digitization and its impact on the human brain and to harness it as a benefit to society. His research interests focus on consumer behavior, consumer experience, experience design, digital media, digital marketing, digital communication an artificial intelligence.

Adrian David Cheok AM FIET FIEAust FRSA is Full Professor at Nanjing University of Information Science and Technology, Director of the Imagineering Institute, Malaysia, Visiting Professor at Raffles University, Malaysia, Visiting

Professor at University of Novi Sad-Serbia, on Technical faculty "Mihailo Pupin", Serbia, Faculty of Ducere Business School, and CEO of Nikola Tesla Technologies Corporation. In 2024, Professor Adrian David Cheok was honored with induction as a Full Member into Sigma Xi USA, The Scientific Research Honor Society, a recognition that not only signifies his dedication to scientific excellence but also aligns his contributions with those of groundbreaking researchers. Sigma Xi is a beacon of distinction within the global scientific community, boasting over 200 Nobel Laureates among its members, including luminaries such as Albert Einstein. This prestigious society is renowned for its commitment to the advancement of science and engineering and includes among its distinguished members other eminent personalities like Linus Pauling and Guglielmo Marconi, whose pioneering work has indelibly shaped the landscape of modern science and innovation. Professor Cheok's association with Sigma Xi marks a pinnacle in his career, affirming his commitment to the ethos of rigorous and impactful scientific inquiry. He is a Fellow of the Institution of Engineering and Technology (IET), United Kingdom (FIET). He is Fellow of the Engineers Australia (FIEAust). He is a Fellow of the Royal Society for the encouragement of Arts, Manufactures and Commerce (RSA) (United Kingdom). He is a Fellow of the Royal Society of Statistics (United Kingdom). He is a Fellow of the Royal Asiatic Society of Great Britain and Ireland. The Governor General of Australia, Representative of Her Majesty the Queen Elizabeth II, has awarded Australia's highest honour the Order of Australia to Adrian David Cheok for his contribution to international education and research. He is Chief Scientist at Frost Digi https://www.frostdigi.ai/. He is Senior Member of the IEEE. He is Founder and Director of the Mixed Reality Lab, Singapore. He was formerly Professor of Pervasive Computing, University of London, Full Professor and Executive Dean at Keio University, Graduate School of Media Design and Associate Professor in the National University of Singapore. He has previously worked in real-time systems, soft computing, and embedded computing in Mitsubishi Electric Research Labs, Japan. He has been working on research covering mixed reality, human-computer interfaces, wearable computers and ubiquitous computing, fuzzy systems, embedded systems, power electronics. He has successfully obtained approximately $130 million dollars in funding for externally funded projects in the area of wearable computers and mixed reality from Daiwa Foundation, Khazanah National (Malaysian Government), Media Development Authority, Nike, National Oilwell Varco, Defence Science Technology Agency, Ministry of Defence, Ministry of Communications and Arts, National Arts Council, Singapore Science Center, and Hougang Primary School. The research output has included many high quality academic journal papers, research awards, keynote speeches, international exhibitions, numerous government demonstrations including to government President and Prime Ministers, broadcast television worldwide broadcasts on his research (such as CNN/ CNBC/

ABC/ Discovery/ National Geographic etc.), and hundreds of international press media articles. He has been a keynote and invited speaker at numerous international conferences and events. He was invited to exhibit for two years in the Ars Electronica Museum of the Future, launching in the Ars Electronica Festival 2003 and 2017. His works "Human Pacman", "Magic Land", and "Metazoa Ludens", were each selected as one of the world's top inventions by Wired and invited to be exhibited in Wired NextFest 2005 and 2007. He was awarded the Hitachi Fellowship, the A-STAR Young Scientist of the Year Award, and the SCS Singapore Young Professional of the Year Award. He was invited to be the Singapore representative of the United Nations body IFIP SG 16 on Entertainment Computing and the founding Chairman of the Singapore Computer Society Special Interest Group on Entertainment Computing. He was awarded an Associate of the Arts award by the Minister for Information, Communications and the Arts, Singapore. He was awarded as Fellow in Education, World Technology Network. He was awarded a Microsoft Research Award for Gaming and Graphics. He received the C4C Children Competition Prize for best interaction media for children, the Integrated Art Competition Prize by the Singapore Land Transport Authority, Creativity in Action Award, and a First Prize Nokia Mindtrek Award. He received a First Prize in the Milan International InventiON competition. He received the Gold award for best Creative Showcase ACE, He is winner of Keio University Gijyuju-sho award, awarded for the best research of the year in Keio University, Japan's oldest university. He received an SIP Distinguished Fellow Award which honours legendary leaders whose illustrious lives have positively influenced lives across generations and communities around the globe. He was awarded Young Global Leader by the World Economic Forum. This honour is bestowed each year by the World Economic Forum to recognize and acknowledge the top young leaders from around the world for the professional accomplishments, commitment to society and potential to contribute to shaping the future of the world. He was awarded "Honorary Expert" by Telefonica and El Bulli, the number one restaurant in the world. He is a Fellow of the Royal Society for the encouragement of Arts, Manufactures and Commerce (RSA), an organisation which is committed to finding innovative practical solutions to today's social challenges. His research on smell interfaces was selected by NESTA as Top 10 Technologies of 2015. In 2016, he was awarded the Distinguished Alumni Awards by University of Adelaide, in recognition of his achievements and contribution in the field of Computing, Engineering and Multisensory communication. In 2017, he entered the elite list of The h-Index for Computer Science, a list that contains only the top 0.06\% of all computer scientists in the world. In 2018, he was awarded Albert Nelson Marquis Lifetime Achievement Award. Remote kissing gadget 'Kissenger' was selected to the Top 100 Science Spinoffs and has entered the top 2% out of 5,000 global science spin-offs according to the following criteria: uniqueness of the technology/product, high commercial potential and positive impact to the humanity's well-being by Spinoff.com. He is/was Editor in Chief of the academic journals: Journal of Future Robot Life, Advances in Robotics and Automation, Transactions on Edutainment, ACM Computers in Entertainment, Lovotics: Academic Studies of Love and Friendship with Robots, and Multimodal Technologies and Interaction. He is/was Associate Editor of Advances in Human Computer Interaction, International Journal of Virtual Reality, Virtual Reality, and The Journal of Ambient Intelligence and Humanized Computing (AIHC). He is on the Editorial Board of International Journal of Arts and Technology (IJART), Journal of Recent Patents on Computer Science, The Open Electrical and Electronic Engineering Journal, International Journal of Entertainment Technology and Management (IJEntTM), The Journal of Virtual Reality and Broadcasting, and Interacting with Computers Adrian David Cheok, who was born and raised in Adelaide, Australia, graduated from the University of Adelaide with a Bachelor of Engineering (Electrical and Electronic) with First Class Honours in 1992 and an Engineering Ph.D in 1998.

Denisa Berceanu is a doctor in Psychology and a professor assistant at the Faculty of Psychology and Educational Sciences, University of Bucharest where she teaches Learning Psychology and Managerial Psychology for BA level. Denisa attributes her long-standing interest in psychology, human mind, and behavior. Her main research interests are mental health, neuroscience and consumer psychology. She is also a Senior Researcher in Consumer Neuroscience at Buyer Brain, a Neuromarketing and Consumer Neuroscience company, headquartered in London, UK.

Navyashree Gowthalli Chandregowda received her PhD degree in Psychology from Mangalore University in 2021. She has 14 years of teaching, training, and research experience in psychology and mental health. She writes about mental health-promoting habits. As a keen researcher, she has successfully completed two funded projects, presented research findings in various national and international platforms, and published articles in various national and international journals. Currently, she is working as an Assistant Professor in the Department of Clinical Psychology, Manipal College of Health Professions, Manipal Academy of Higher Education, Manipal.

Nihar Suresh Dahake is currently serving as an Assistant Professor in the Department of MBA at G H Raisoni College of Engineering, Nagpur. He holds a B.Com, M.Com, and MBA from Rashtrasant Tukdoji Maharaj Nagpur University and earned his Ph.D. from Sant Gadge Baba Amravati University, Amravati. In addition to his academic qualifications, Dr. Dahake has successfully qualified the

State Eligibility Test (SET) in both Commerce and Management, demonstrating his strong foundation in these disciplines. With a rich academic background, he brings 14 years of teaching experience and 8 years of dedicated research experience to his role. Throughout his career, he has consistently contributed to academic excellence and research development. Dr. Dahake's areas of expertise include Financial Accounting, Consumer Behavior, Marketing Management, and Financial Management. His multidisciplinary knowledge allows him to effectively engage with a wide range of topics in business and management studies. Passionate about both teaching and research, he strives to inspire students while also contributing meaningfully to the academic community through his scholarly work. His professional journey reflects a deep commitment to education, research, and the advancement of management studies in higher education institutions.

Parihar Suresh Dahake is an accomplished academician and researcher with over 15 years of experience in teaching and research in the fields of Commerce and Management. Currently serving as an Assistant Professor at the School of Management, Ramdeobaba University, Nagpur, he holds a diverse educational background, including B.Tech (Applied Electronics), MBA (Marketing & Financial Management), M.Com, PGDIBO, M.A. (Psychology), and a Ph.D. in Business Management. His doctoral work focused on the impact of marketing strategies of DTH services on consumer behavior in Nagpur. Dr. Dahake's research interests span Business Analytics, Consumer Behavior, Predictive Analytics, and Marketing Communication. A recognized Ph.D. supervisor, he guides multiple doctoral candidates under the faculty of Commerce. He has published extensively in peer-reviewed, Scopus, and ABDC-indexed journals and authored books on Marketing Management and Consumer Behavior. He also holds a patent in wage sheet automation and actively contributes as a reviewer for prestigious journals. A recipient of multiple accolades, including the Young Researcher and Research Excellence Awards, Dr. Dahake is also a sought-after speaker and trainer. His commitment to academic excellence and innovative pedagogy has made significant contributions to management education, research, and institutional development in Central India.

Meenakshi Devi is a Doctoral Candidate of Commerce at Mittal School of Business, Lovely Professional University, Phagwara, Punjab, India. Her research areas include consumer behaviour, cognitive dissonance, and Buyer's decision-making. She has a master's degree in commerce. She has attended various national- and international-level conferences and workshops

Rahela Farooqui has more than 25 years of teaching experience at the postgraduate level in the area of Marketing. Guided more than 20 PhD scholars.

Research papers published in reputed journals like Emerald, Sage etc. Delivered lectures and presented papers at International conferences in Denmark, Germany, Malaysia and Thailand. A passionate teacher, a keen learner and a sensitive person. Eager to make a difference to the lives of students by guiding and motivating them.

Praveenkumar G. D. is an Assistant Professor in the Department of Computer Technology (UG) at Kongu Engineering College, Perundurai, Erode. He is actively involved in undergraduate teaching and academic mentoring, contributing to the development of strong foundational and applied skills among students in computer science and technology. His academic interests include emerging areas of computing and technology-enabled problem solving, with a focus on aligning theoretical concepts with practical applications. Dr. Praveenkumar is committed to academic excellence, curriculum enrichment, and continuous professional development, and he actively supports institutional initiatives related to teaching innovation, student projects, and quality education.

Veer P. Gangwar, PhD in Marketing Area, UGC-NET in management and PG Diploma in Research Methodology has blended experience of around 26 years is presently associated with Lovely Professional University, Phagwara (Punjab) as Professor in Marketing, General Management, Research Methodology etc. and has served as resource person/trainer at Research Methodology Course in HRDC, and workshop on Research Methodology for projects and theses nationally and internationally. Further, he has presented research papers in many national and international conferences and attended sundry workshops and FDPs on research methodology, SPSS, Smart PLS and has to his credit many research papers in SCOPUS indexed, ABDC, UGC care listed and peer reviewed journals. Additionally, Dr Gangwar has authored and co- authored 4 books from national and international publishers.

Saikat Gochhait teaches at Symbiosis Institute of Digital & Telecom Management, Symbiosis International Deemed University Pune, India. He is Ph.D and Post-Doctoral Fellow from the UEx, Spain. He was Awarded DITA and MOFA Fellowship in 2017 and 2018. His research publication with foreign authors indexed in Scopus, ABDC, and Web of Science. He is an IEEE member.

S.Ida Evangeline, presently working as an Assistant Professor in the Department of Electrical and Electronics Engineering at the Government College of Engineering, Tirunelveli, Tamilnadu, India. She obtained her Bachelor's in Electrical and Electronics Engineering from Manonmaniam Sundaranar University in 2003, and Master's in Power Systems Engineering from Anna University, Chennai, Tamilnadu, India in 2005. She completed her PhD degree in 2023 at Anna University, Chennai,

Tamilnadu, India. She has published six research papers in international journals. Her current research interests include optimal power flow, renewable energy, soft computing, machine learning, and deep learning.

Ana Iorga is a consumer neuroscience and behavioral sciences expert with a deep abiding passion for understanding human behavior. Having spent almost two decades in working with businesses as well as academia, Ana has deep expertise in the world of design, communication and branding across diverse industries such as Finance and Insurance, Consumer Goods, Retail and Automotive. Given her unique academic background, Ana founded Buyer Brain, a consumer neuroscience company that uses neuroscience and behavioral sciences to improve CX and drive deeper customer engagement. Dr. Iorga holds a CCXP Certification and, as the Chair of CXPA's European Council, she is actively involved in expanding the CX profession across Europe. She has received several awards for her contribution to the CX and communication professions: she ranked in Top 10 in the 2023-2021 CX Stars Awards by Customer Experience Magazine, she was nominated by Advertising Week as one of the most influential women in marketing in 2020 and in 2019 she was the recipient of the GRIT Future List Award for her contribution to the insights industry. Dr. Iorga is a Medical Doctor that holds a PhD in Consumer Neuroscience and a double MBA degree in Marketing and Finance. She serves on the editorial board of NMSBA's Insights Magazine and is co-editor of Ethics in Neuromarketing, a path breaking book exploring the ethical challenges in Neuromarketing.

Seetha Khandige is currently a final-year undergraduate student of Psychology based in Karnataka, India. Deeply passionate about neuroscience, she aspires to pursue higher studies in the field. Seetha is particularly drawn to academic research and writing, and aims to build a career in academia, where she can contribute to the scientific understanding of the human brain and cognition. In addition to her academic pursuits, she is also serving as a volunteer Grants Coordinator at a non-profit organization dedicated to advancing youth mental health across India.

Przemyslaw Kotowski is a marketing strategist and former academic with over 13 years of experience leading brand, retail, and digital marketing campaigns for clients such as McDonald's, Volkswagen, Samsung, and Visa. He holds a Master's degree in Business Management from the University of Economics in Katowice, where he also lectured in Marketing, Economics, and Business Ethics from 2007 to 2011. During this time, he led research projects in corporate management and authored ten peer-reviewed publications. Kotowski later held senior roles at leading agencies including Publicis, Saatchi&Saatchi, DDB, and Camp Pacific. His work has been recognized by the Canadian Public Relations Society. He is currently a

Strategic Account Manager at Neon Growth, a marketing performance agency based in Los Angeles, California.

Pawan Kumar is a Marketing graduate with and Doctorate in Business Management from Haryana School of Business, GJUS&T, Hisar, Dr Pawan Kumar, has a strong inclination towards academics and research. He has about 4 years of teaching experience to his credit. He has published more than 15 research articles in various International and National journals of repute. He has participated in and presented research papers at more than 25 international and national conferences at IIM, IIT, and Internationally, etc. His areas of interest include Marketing Management, Rural Marketing, Computer Applications in Business, and Business Research Methods.

Ana-Maria Lepar brings over 16 years of hands-on experience in software development and academic research. She holds degrees in both Computer Science and History, and earned a PhD in History with a thesis that explores the intersection between historical scholarship and computational methodologies. She has published research articles in both computer science and historical studies, reflecting her unique interdisciplinary expertise. Her professional background includes roles as a software developer at Enghouse and Deutsche Bank, and as a lecturer at the Faculty of History. She is also a member of the Balkan History Association, contributing to cross-disciplinary research initiatives. Since 2021, Ana-Maria has been leading the Non-Financial Risk Management (NFRM) division for Deutsche Bank Romania.

Geetha Manoharan is currently working in Telangana as an assistant professor at SR University. She is the university-level PhD program coordinator and has also been given the additional responsibility of In Charge Director of Publications and Patents under the Research Division at SR University.

Shireen Naaz is a research scholar at Jamia Millia Islamia, having completed her Master's in Business Administration with a specialization in International Business from JMI, New Delhi. She is UGC-NET qualified and deeply passionate about research. Her primary areas of interest lie in neuromarketing and consumer behavior.She has been awarded the prestigious doctoral fellowship by ICSSR.

Michael Oyedele Oyenuga has a PhD in Marketing and Communication and over 25 years of scholarly and practitioner experience in education policy, digital transformation, and inclusive learning. His research interests cut across marketing, branding, consumer behaviour, education and sustainability. He is currently an Associate Professor and Assistant Dean at the School of Business, Woxsen University, Hyderabad, India.

Ravikumar R. Natarajan is an experienced academician with over 12+ years of teaching and research expertise across institutions in India, the UAE, and the Maldives. He currently serves as an Assistant Professor at Marwadi University, Rajkot, specializing in Machine Learning, Recommender Systems, and AI-driven applications in healthcare and security. He holds a Ph.D. in Machine Learning and Recommender Systems from Amity University, Jaipur, a Master of Engineering in CSE from VMRF University, Salem, and a Bachelor of Engineering in CSE from Anna University. He also has a MiniMBA from the Swiss eLearning Institute. Dr. Ravikumar has authored more than 8+ multiple SCIE/Scopus-indexed journal articles, 25+ IEEE/Springer conference papers, and co-authored a book on Artificial Intelligence. He has also published 9 patents and contributed 10+ book chapters in emerging domains such as Federated Learning, Blockchain, and Digital Twins for IGI Global, Wiley and Springer publisher. He actively mentors students through initiatives like the Research Activities Club (RAC) and Student Research Internship Training (SRIT), promoting innovation and research culture.

Shikha Rani is working as a research scholar in Faculty of Management and Commerce, SRM University Delhi NCR Sonepat Haryana.

Aarthi S is a dedicated Assistant Professor in Computer Science with over six years of teaching experience. She is currently pursuing her Ph.D. at Marwadi University, Gujarat, and holds an M.Phil. and MCA from Bharathiar University, Tamil Nadu. Throughout her academic career, Aarthi has specialized in programming languages such as C++, Java, and C, and contributed to research in recommender systems and AI-related data privacy. She has published journal articles, contributed to book chapters, and actively participated in technical workshops. Known for her student mentorship and engagement in academic events, Aarthi remains committed to fostering innovation and excellence in computer science education.

Anujeet Saha is a final-year Bachelor of Science (BSc) student in Psychology, with a strong academic foundation and a deep interest in Clinical and Neuropsychology. He is currently working as a research intern on a project focused on secondary trauma, where he is involved in examining the psychological effects of indirect exposure to traumatic experiences. His academic pursuits are guided by a curiosity about the interplay between brain function and behavior. Anujeet aspires to become a practicing clinical psychologist while actively engaging in research, with the goal of integrating clinical insight and empirical evidence to inform mental health practice.

Jeganathan Gomathi Sankar, a dedicated educator, specializes in marketing and currently teaches at the BSSS Institute of Advanced Studies. With a rich academic background, he served as a research scholar at Pondicherry University, focusing on information diffusion, ICT, Marketing technology, AI, and Data Science. Dr. Sankar's impactful research is published in reputable journals indexed in Scopus and ABDC. Formerly a faculty member at Saveetha School of Management, he contributed significantly to marketing education. Dr. Sankar's pedagogy integrates theoretical insights with practical applications, offering students a holistic understanding of contemporary marketing. Beyond teaching, he is proficient in analytical tools such as SPSS, AMOS, STATA, PowerBI, and Python, enhancing the sophistication of his research. Known for his engaging teaching style, Dr. Sankar fosters an environment encouraging critical thinking. As a member of BSSS Institute of Advanced Studies, he continues shaping future marketing professionals. His commitment to academic excellence, research, and proficiency in modern tools exemplifies his dedication to advancing knowledge in marketing and technology.

Samir Semaan is a Senior Program Manager and Managing Director at Ginovi UG. He earned his Master's degree in Engineering in 2012 and has since built an impressive career, with over 14 years of experience leading international projects across multiple countries. He has a deep interest in consumer behavior, a passion that aligns closely with his work and drives the progress of his company. He co-authored a paper on "Consumer Behavior in the Banking Sector During Economic Crises," showcasing his expertise in this area. As a certified Project Manager, He continues to leverage his extensive experience to manage complex projects while staying at the forefront of industry trends.

Jakhongir Shaturaev is an Associate Professor working in the Department of International Cooperation at Termez University of Economics and Service, Termez, Uzbekistan.

Sushil Shende is a distinguished academician and industry professional with over 26 years of combined experience in academia and industry. He holds a Ph.D. in Management Sciences, an MBA in Marketing and Finance, and a BE in Mechanical Engineering. Dr. Shende's expertise spans Marketing, Sales, Operations and General Management, with a focus on both theoretical concepts and practical applications. His teaching methodology emphasizes student engagement, and he has been recognized with the Best Faculty (Marketing) award at the World Skill Development Congress & Awards in 2025. He also holds significant responsibilities in academic administration, having served on the Academic Council and Board of Studies, and in various institutional roles such as mentoring and examination auditing. In addition to his academic accomplishments, Dr. Shende has substantial industry experience, having worked in senior roles at Multinational & National organisations. He is certified in Dale Carnegie Training Excellence and Mercuri Goldmann Key Account Management and has presented papers in international journals and conferences. His dedication to academic excellence, professional development, and institutional growth makes him a valuable asset to both his students and the broader academic community.

Surabhi Singh holds a PhD in Digital Marketing and Consumer Behaviour from Aligarh Muslim University, India. She has a strong academic background with two master's degrees and two postgraduate diplomas. In addition, she has acquired international certifications in Digital Marketing, Neuromarketing, and Marketing Analytics. With a total of 24.7 years of experience in academic and industry administration, she currently holds the position of Professor and Dean-MBA, College of Engineering, IIMT Group of Colleges, Greater Noida. Dr. Singh's academic interests span various aspects of Marketing, analytics, emerging technologies, and Strategy. She held the position of Associate Editor for two special issues, the Journal of Consumer Behaviour and the International Journal of Business Analytics. In addition, she serves on the Editorial Boards of esteemed journals, including the Emerald Journal of Emerging Market Case Studies and the International Journal of E Adoption, among others. Furthermore, she has served as a reviewer for prestigious journals. Dr. Singh has a decent publication record with over 100 papers published in reputable national and international journals, including Emerald, Inderscience, IGI Global, Sage, Springer, and Taylor & Francis. Furthermore, she has authored 3 books on Digital Marketing, Research Methodology, and Neuromarketing. She has edited 10 books on topics such as Artificial Intelligence, Affiliate Marketing, Sustainability, Cases, Skill Development, Service Innovations, NEP etc. Two of her books on Affiliate Marketing and Service Innovations in Tourism with IGI Global, USA have been indexed in Scopus. She has also been a global speaker at renowned platforms such as TEDx, Delhi University, Rama University, TMU, AIMA, ISTD, NIESBUD, NCHMCT, AICTE-funded workshop, Krirk University, and Urban Infra Summit. In addition to her academic contributions, Dr. Singh has served as a PhD guide and examiner in both private and government universities. She has successfully handled several sponsored research and consultancy projects throughout her career. In addition to her professional achievements, from August 2020 to August 2021, she served as the President of the Ghaziabad City Council in the Women's Indian Chamber of Commerce and Industry (WICCI). She has been a Senior Advisor in the Digital Education and Skills Council and a member of the advisory board of Urban Infra Group. She received the 'Most Influential Professor' award in 2024.

Sławomir Smyczek is Full Professor and Head of Consumer Research Department at the University of Economics in Katowice where he earned his

Ph.D in 2000. In 2009, the Polish Prime Minister awarded his habilitation thesis as the best in the field of economy and business. Prof. Smyczek has written over 200 publications on the subject of consumer behavior, consumer rights protection and marketing, and is also author and co-author of several monographies such as: International Services Management in the Context of Sustainable Development (2023), Consumer Exclusion. Causes, Areas and Forms of Contemporary Market Exclusion (2022), and Consumer Rights Protection. Threats and Opportunities for Enhancing Consumer Awareness (2020).

Ceyhun Uçuk is an academic specializing in gastronomy and culinary arts. He completed his PhD at Nevşehir Hacı Bektaş Veli University, focusing on neurogastronomy, gastrophysics, and food presentation. Currently, he serves as an Assistant Professor at Tekirdağ Namık Kemal University and has previously held faculty positions at various universities. Throughout his academic career, he has contributed to numerous national and international articles, book chapters, and projects, while also engaging in various educational and consultancy activities. His research is centered on neurogastronomy, synesthesia, and gastrophysics, exploring the impact of food presentation on human perception and developing innovative approaches in these fields.

Index

A

B

C

D

E

F

N

O

P

R

S

T

U

www.ingramcontent.com/pod-product-compliance
Lightning Source LLC
LaVergne TN
LVHW081248011026
849162LV00004BA/774